GREAT ATHLETES

GREAT ATHLETES

Volume 2
Capriati–Fangio
Indexes

Edited by
The Editors of Salem Press

Special Consultant
Rafer Johnson

SALEM PRESS, INC.

Pasadena, California   Hackensack, New Jersey

Editor in Chief: Dawn P. Dawson

Managing Editor: R. Kent Rasmussen	*Research Supervisor:* Jeffry Jensen
Manuscript Editor: Lauren Mitchell	*Acquisitions Editor:* Mark Rehn
Production Editor: Cynthia Beres	*Page Design and Layout:* James Hutson
Photograph Editor: Philip Bader	*Additional Layout:* William Zimmerman
Assistant Editors: Andrea Miller	Eddie Murillo
Elizabeth Slocum	

Cover Design: Moritz Design, Los Angeles, Calif.

Library of Congress Cataloging-in-Publication Data

Great athletes / edited by the editors of Salem Press ; Rafer Johnson, special consultant.—Rev.
    p. cm.
  Includes bibliographical references and index.
    ISBN 1-58765-007-X (set : alk. paper) — ISBN 1-58765-008-8 (v. 1 : alk. paper) —
ISBN 1-58765-009-6 (v. 2 : alk. paper) — ISBN 1-58765-010-X (v. 3 : alk. paper) —
ISBN 1-58765-011-8 (v. 4 : alk. paper) — ISBN 1-58765-012-6 (v. 5 : alk. paper) —
ISBN 1-58765-013-4 (v. 6 : alk. paper) — ISBN 1-58765-014-2 (v. 7 : alk. paper) —
ISBN 1-58765-015-0 (v. 8 : alk. paper)
    1. Athletes—Biography—Dictionaries. I. Johnson, Rafer, 1935-   . II. Salem Press

GV697.A1 G68 2001
796′.092′2—dc21

                                                                              2001042644

First Printing

Contents

page

Indexes

GREAT ATHLETES

JENNIFER CAPRIATI

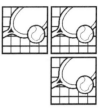

Sport: Tennis

Born: March 29, 1976
New York, New York

Early Life

Jennifer Maria Capriati was born on March 29, 1976, on New York's Long Island to Stefano Capriati, a professional tennis instructor and former motion-picture stunt-man, and Denise Capriati, an airline flight attendant. The Capriatis were a true tennis family; Denise was taking tennis lessons from Stefano on the courts in New York only seventeen hours before Jennifer was born.

Jennifer picked up a tennis racket for the first time when she was three years old. At four, she began hitting tennis balls on a regular basis. The family then moved to Lauderhill, Florida, to be in a year-round tennis environment. Stefano asked Jimmy Evert, the father of tennis star Chris Evert, to begin coaching her. Jimmy Evert agreed and coached Jennifer for five years. Jennifer became friends with Chris and practiced with her often. In 1987, the tennis star gave her a bracelet inscribed, "Jennifer, Love, Chris"; Jennifer would wear the bracelet during all of her tennis matches.

Tennis, however, was only part of Jennifer's life. She attended the Palmer Academy and consistently earned A's; she also attended the Saddlebrook International Tennis Center in Wesley Chapel, Florida.

The Road to Excellence

At the age of twelve, Jennifer began winning many amateur tournaments, and she often beat girls who were much older than she was. In 1988, she won both the national eighteen-and-under clay-court and hard-court championships as well as the junior championships at the French Open

Jennifer Capriati plays in the 2001 Australian Open. She won the title.

and the U.S. Open. The International Tennis Federation ranked her second among eighteen-and-under players.

Jennifer's obvious ability at so young an age excited tennis fans, who expected great things from her as a professional. In 1990, the Women's International Tennis Federation ruled that the earliest a young player could become a professional was in the month the player turned fourteen. The rule was made to protect players from injuring themselves physically at a young age.

In preparation for Jennifer's professional career, her parents took her to a sports-medicine clinic in Virginia to evaluate her physical development in order to prevent injuries. In November of 1989, she played an exhibition match against twenty-five-year-old Laura Gildemeister, who was ranked in the top twenty-five professionals. Thirteen-year-old Jennifer won the match by the score of 6-4, 6-1, confirming her professional-level ability. Jennifer then got a chance to hit with the legendary tennis player Martina Navratilova. Although they did not keep score, Jennifer experienced the power of Navratilova's ground strokes and serve.

The Emerging Champion

On March 6, 1990, in the month of her fourteenth birthday, Jennifer made her debut as a professional in the Virginia Slims Tournament in Boca Raton, Florida. She beat four seeded players before losing to Gabriela Sabatini in the finals. The media was calling her the "eighth-grade wonder" and the "next Chris Evert." She also played doubles in the same tournament with the great Billie Jean King, but they lost in the second round of doubles competition.

Like Evert, Jennifer developed a two-handed backhand and learned to rally endlessly from the baseline, but she hit her ground strokes with more power and came to the net more often than her idol did. Her serve was clocked at an average of 94 miles per hour, and she showed her cool nerves in pressure situations.

In 1990, Jennifer lost to Monica Seles in the finals of the French Open, becoming the youngest Grand Slam semifinalist in history. She also lost to Martina Navratilova in the Family Circle Cup finals that year. In October, she won her first professional tournament, the Puerto Rican Open,

and was ranked eighth in the world. *Tennis* magazine named her the 1990 Rookie of the Year.

Continuing the Story

Before the 1991 season, Jennifer began to work with weights in order to develop a more powerful serve and quicker footwork. Tom Gullikson of the United States Tennis Association (USTA), a former professional player, became her coach. In the past, she had trouble beating the game's top players such as Gabriela Sabatini and Monica Seles. Before the 1991 season, however, she told reporters that she had changed by becoming meaner, saying, "I like fighting."

In the 1991 quarterfinals at Wimbledon, Jennifer beat Martina Navratilova in two sets, 6-4, 7-5, to advance to the semifinals against Sabatini. Even though she lost, 6-4, 6-4, she became the youngest player ever to reach the Wimbledon semifinals.

In August, she won the Mazda Classic, beating Monica Seles in the finals. A week later, she won the Player's Challenge over Katrina Maleeva. In 1991, Jennifer was gaining confidence. She won more than $600,000 in prize money, and her

HONORS AND AWARDS	
1989	*Tennis* magazine Junior Player of the Year U.S. Olympic Committee Tennis Athlete of the Year *World Tennis* Junior Player of the Year
1990	*Tennis* magazine/Rolex Watch Female Rookie of the Year WTA Most Impressive Newcomer

NOTABLE VICTORIES	
1988	U.S. Clay Court 18s U.S. Hard Court 18s
1989	French Open Junior U.S. Open Junior
1990	Puerto Rican Open
1991	Players' Challenge
1991-92	Mazda Tennis Classic
1992	Gold Medal, Olympic women's tennis
1993	New South Wales Open
1999	Strausbourg Bell Challenge
2001	Australian Open

MILESTONES

At age fourteen became youngest Grand Slam semifinalist
Youngest competitor in Wightman Cup history

ranking rose to sixth in the world.

Jennifer continued to make her life as normal as possible. She visited friends, went to the malls to shop, used her money in practical ways, and continued to make the honor roll at school. In fact, the older players on the tour helped her with her homework. She would fax her homework to school when she was on tour.

The highlight of Jennifer's young career came in 1992, when she won the gold medal for the United States in women's tennis at the Barcelona Olympics. She defeated Steffi Graf in the final match, 3-6, 6-3, 6-4, by constantly pounding her ground strokes to Graf's backhand. Jennifer's proudest moment was to be able to represent the United States in the medal ceremony at the Olympics.

After losing in the first round of the U.S. Open in 1993, Jennifer stopped playing on the women's tour. She would not return to the tour until November, 1994. In May of that year, she had been arrested for possession of marijuana. Whether stardom had come to Jennifer too soon or not, she definitely was troubled and unable to compete at her best. In 1996, she returned to competitive tennis with more focus and inner resolve. Jennifer won her first singles titles since 1993 at Strasbourg and Quebec City in 1999. She won the Seat Open in 2000. She surprised everyone, even herself, by winning the 2001 Australian Open. After never reaching the semifinals in five appearances, she won her first grand slam title by beating Martina Hingis.

Summary

Even in a sport dominated by young players, Jennifer Capriati stood out. Her natural skills were augmented by ceaseless training and fierce determination to make her the youngest Olympic tennis champion and youngest professional ever.

Kathy Davis

Additional Sources:

Goldstein, Margaret J. *Jennifer Capriati: Tennis Sensation.* Minneapolis: Lerner Publishing, 1993.

Green, Carl R, and Roxanne Ford. *Jennifer Capriati.* New York: Crestwood House, 1994.

Lakin, Pat. *Jennifer Capriati: Rising Star.* Vero Beach, Fla.: Rourke, 1993.

Morrissette, Mikki. *Jennifer Capriati.* Boston: Little, Brown, 1991.

White, Ellen Emerson. *Jennifer Capriati.* New York: Scholastic, 1991.

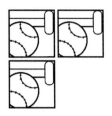

ROD CAREW

Sport: Baseball

Born: October 1, 1945
Gatun, Panama

Early Life

Rodney Cline Scott Carew was born on October 1, 1945, en route (by train) from Gatun, Panama, to Ancon, Panama. His mother, Olga, was being transported to Ancon, which had a clinic. Dr. Rodney Cline, an American physician, was on board and helped deliver Rod. For Dr. Cline's part in the delivery, Rod was given the middle name of Cline.

Gatun was a rural area. Growing up in a poor family, Rod had some obstacles to overcome. He rarely had shoes or clothes to wear to church

National Baseball Library, Cooperstown, New York

and, because of that, appeared to be rather shy. Despite the Carews' lack of wealth, Rod was provided with a bat, ball, and glove in order to occupy his time. When Rod was fifteen, the family moved to New York City. Rod had never been out of Panama, and the new life in the city was a challenge.

Rod was the second of five children of Olga and Eric Carew. Rod, his older brother, and three sisters all shared the same bedroom. His father was a painter on the Panama Canal. After they moved to New York City, his mother became a hospital therapist. Rod got plenty of encouragement in baseball from his uncle, Joseph French, a physical educator.

The Road to Excellence

Rod's baseball playing in high school was confined to sandlot ball. He maintained a job after school at a local grocery store. The sandlot he played on was next to Yankee Stadium, and that is where an unpaid Minnesota Twins scout spotted him. He was given a tryout, offered a contract, and spent the next three years in the minors.

The 1967 season found Rod as the starting second baseman for the Twins. He ended up hitting .292 and was named Rookie of the Year.

The next few years were tough on Rod because his parents separated. He was never close to his father so this made it difficult. The Twins' manager at the time, Billy Martin, took Rod under his wing, becoming like a father to him.

Rod's early years in Minnesota were not enjoyable. He had temper tantrums on the field, which the fans did not support. In 1970, he tore his knee and underwent surgery. In October of 1970, he was criticized for marrying Marilyn Levy, a white woman. In the early years of their marriage they struggled, the biggest factor being the time Rod was required to be away from home playing baseball.

STATISTICS

Season	GP	AB	Hits	2B	3B	HR	Runs	RBI	BA	SA
1967	137	514	150	22	7	8	66	51	.292	.409
1968	127	461	126	27	2	1	46	42	.273	.347
1969	123	458	152	30	4	8	79	56	**.332**	.467
1970	51	191	70	12	3	4	27	28	.366	.524
1971	147	577	177	16	10	2	88	48	.307	.380
1972	142	535	170	21	6	0	61	51	**.318**	.379
1973	149	580	**203**	30	**11**	6	98	62	**.350**	.471
1974	153	599	**218**	30	5	3	86	55	**.364**	.446
1975	143	535	192	24	4	14	89	80	**.359**	.497
1976	156	605	200	29	12	9	97	90	.331	.463
1977	155	616	**239**	38	**16**	14	**128**	100	**.388**	.570
1978	152	564	188	26	10	5	85	70	**.333**	.441
1979	110	409	130	15	3	3	78	44	.318	.391
1980	144	540	179	34	7	3	74	59	.331	.437
1981	93	364	111	17	1	2	57	21	.305	.374
1982	138	523	167	25	5	3	88	44	.319	.403
1983	129	472	160	24	2	2	66	44	.339	.411
1984	93	329	97	8	1	3	42	31	.295	.353
1985	127	443	124	17	3	2	69	39	.280	.345
Totals	2,469	9,315	3,053	445	112	92	1,424	1,015	.328	.429

Notes: Boldface indicates statistical leader. GP = games played; AB = at bats; 2B = doubles; 3B = triples; HR = home runs; RBI = runs batted in; BA = batting average; SA = slugging average

Soon things began to change for Rod. He won batting titles in 1969, 1972, 1973, 1974, 1975, 1977, and in 1978. His fan club was growing. In 1976, the Twins moved him from second base to first base, a position much more suitable for his injured knee.

The Emerging Champion

In 1977, Rod had a banner year. He received the most votes by the fans in the All-Star balloting. He finished the season with a .388 batting average (league title), 239 hits, 128 runs, 16 triples, and 38 doubles. He was named the American League's most valuable player as well as the *Sporting News* American League Player of the Year and the Major League Player of the Year.

Up to 1978, Rod and the Twins' owner, Calvin Griffith, had a good relationship, but Griffith made some careless remarks and Rod took offense at them. Eventually they talked and cleared the air of their differences, but, because of Rod's recent success, he wanted more money and knew Griffith could not deliver. In 1979, the Twins traded Rod to the California Angels. In his seven years with the Angels, he batted over .300 in all but two seasons. His nineteen-year career average ended up at the .328 mark.

A major highlight of Rod's career was when he reached 3,000 hits. It was against Tom Seaver, who was vying for his 300th pitching victory. In early August of 1985, on a Sunday afternoon, Rod Carew hit a single to reach the milestone. It was fitting that it was a single because Rod had often lined, chopped, or bunted his way to first base.

Continuing the Story

The boy born on a train in Panama had become a big leaguer in the United States. He had overcome poverty, survived rheumatic fever at age eleven, worked his way through high school instead of playing interscholastic baseball, and then was given the opportunity of a lifetime.

Even with that opportunity, he had to overcome injuries, ridicule by fans, racial bias, and language difficulty. Rod Carew survived and will go down in history as one of the all-time great hitters.

Rod's family always provided emotional support. His wife Marilyn and daughters Stephanie and Charryse have all been a source of help and strength, particularly during his oldest daughter Michelle's battle with cancer and her death in 1996. Many of his accomplishments have been

401

HONORS AND AWARDS

1967	American League Rookie of the Year
1967-81, 1983-84	American League All-Star Team
1975	Joe Cronin Award
1977	American League most valuable player
	Sporting News Major League Player of the Year
	Sporting News American League Player of the Year
	Seagram's Seven Crowns of Sports Award
	Uniform number 29 retired by Minnesota Twins
	Uniform number 29 retired by California Angels
1991	Inducted into National Baseball Hall of Fame

overlooked or overshadowed by other big names in baseball. His apparent composure and relaxed posture have often been misunderstood. He possessed great hand-eye coordination, and his fluid movement was very deceptive. He worked hard at the game and took extra batting practice throughout his career to aid his game. Rod always felt timing to be important and thus devoted himself to practice.

Rod joined the California Angels' staff as the hitting coach in 1992, and by 1995 the team's improved offense became the most productive in baseball, leading the Angels to a first-place tie with the Texas Rangers at the All-Star break. In 2000, Rod became the Milwaukee Brewers' hitting coach, where he continued to teach the skills that earned him seven American League batting titles in his nineteen years as a player.

Summary

Rod Carew will be remembered as a player who had peace of mind and as a professional who was devoted to the game of baseball. As fans recall the all-time best hitters in major league baseball, Rod Carew will stand out as one of the best.

Michael J. Fratzke

Additional Sources:

Carew, Rod, with Ira Berkow. *Carew.* New York: Simon & Schuster, 1979.

Haudricourt, Tom. "Batting Professor." *Baseball Digest* 59, no. 7 (2000).

Libby, Bill. *Rod Carew: Master Hitter.* New York: Putnam, 1976.

Verducci, Tom. "Carew's Crew." *Sports Illustrated* 83, no. 3 (1995).

STEVE CARLTON

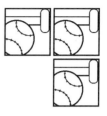

Sport: Baseball

Born: December 22, 1944
　　　Miami, Florida

Early Life

Steven Norman Carlton was born in Miami, Florida, on December 22, 1944. His father, an airline maintenance worker, had been a track athlete in high school. Steve's own interest in sports developed slowly.

He was tall and skinny as a boy with a tendency to awkwardness and shyness. Although not particularly interested in baseball, he was encouraged to join a local Little League by friends. He could not throw very hard, but he decided to try pitching.

He discovered that, even at the age of twelve, he could break off a curve ball. Because Little League batters seldom see left-handed curve balls, this pitch proved quite effective for him.

The Road to Excellence

When Steve entered high school in Miami, he continued pitching, but he was not a star. Although he was approaching his adult height of 6 feet 5 inches by the time he graduated, he had not filled out, and his fastball did not have the pop on it that major league scouts like to see. Nevertheless, his coach in American Legion baseball, John Buik, believed in him and encouraged him.

Steve entered Dade Junior College but left after one semester. He attended a tryout at Busch Stadium in St. Louis and impressed Cardinals pitching coach Howard Pollet, himself a former star left-hander.

Cardinals scout George Silvey signed Steve to a modest $5,000 contract, and in 1964, at the age of nineteen, Steve began pitching in the Western Carolinas League. His sharp curve completely baffled hitters there, and after a 10-1 start with an earned run average of 1.03, he was moved to Win-

nipeg, Canada, in the Northern League, where he went 4-4 and was again promoted, to Tulsa in the Texas League, at the end of the season.

Clyde King, then the Cardinals' minor league pitching coach, helped Steve smooth out his delivery. He was now approaching his mature weight of 220 pounds and throwing the ball much harder. Despite his youth, the Cardinals' management decided to put him on the major league roster in 1965.

The Emerging Champion

Steve saw very limited service as a twenty-year-old Cardinals pitcher. He started two games in 1965 and appeared in thirteen others for a total

of only 25 innings with no wins or losses. The next year, he was sent back to Tulsa for more experience, but after posting a 9-5 record there, was brought back and put into the starting rotation. He finished the year with a 3-3 record.

In the spring of 1967, Steve Carlton arrived as a bona fide major league pitcher. Joining a staff anchored by the great Bob Gibson, Steve won fourteen games and helped the Cardinals win the National League pennant. He had the thrill of his young life when manager Red Schoendienst called on him to start the fifth game of the World Series against the Boston Red Sox.

With the Cardinals leading the series three games to one, Steve had a chance to win the deciding game. He pitched 6 innings and gave the Red Sox only 3 hits, but an infield error led to an unearned Sox run, and Steve left the game trailing 1-0.

He lost that first Series start, but he had become a Cardinals mainstay. He won thirteen in 1968, seventeen in 1969, and, after a disappointing 10-19 in 1970, became a twenty-game winner for the first time the following year. His best pitch was a devastating slider that broke sharply down and in on right-handed batters. When he got it around the knees, which he usually could, few hitters could do much with it.

Continuing the Story

Steve was unhappy with the contract he was offered for 1972, and when he would not agree to terms, the Cardinals traded him to the Philadelphia Phillies for a good pitcher, Rick Wise.

What the Cardinals did not realize was that they had given up a great pitcher. Steve had won 77 games with the Cardinals; he would go on to win 237 more with the Phillies. In his first year in Philadelphia, he won twenty-seven games, struck out 310 batters, and finished with an earned run average of 1.97—good enough to win the National League Triple Crown for 1972. He also pitched an amazing 346 innings.

Steve's durability was unusual. He almost never missed a pitching turn. He went on to win twenty or more games four more times between

STATISTICS

Season	GP	GS	CG	IP	HA	BB	SO	W	L	S	ShO	ERA
1965	15	2	0	25.0	27	8	21	0	0	0	0	2.52
1966	9	9	2	52.0	56	18	25	3	3	0	1	3.12
1967	30	28	11	193.0	173	62	168	14	9	1	2	2.98
1968	34	33	10	232.0	214	61	162	13	11	0	5	2.99
1969	31	31	12	236.0	185	93	210	17	11	0	2	2.17
1970	34	33	13	254.0	239	109	193	10	**19**	0	2	3.72
1971	37	36	18	273.0	275	98	172	20	9	0	4	3.56
1972	41	**41**	**30**	**346.1**	**257**	87	**310**	**27**	10	0	**8**	1.97
1973	40	**40**	18	**293.1**	**293**	113	223	13	**20**	0	3	3.90
1974	39	39	17	291.0	249	**136**	**240**	16	13	0	1	3.22
1975	37	37	14	255.0	217	104	192	15	14	0	3	3.56
1976	35	35	13	252.2	224	72	195	20	7	0	2	3.13
1977	36	36	17	283.0	229	89	198	**23**	10	0	2	2.64
1978	34	34	12	247.0	228	63	161	16	13	0	3	2.84
1979	35	35	13	251.0	202	89	213	18	11	0	4	3.62
1980	38	**38**	13	**304.0**	243	90	**286**	**24**	9	0	3	2.34
1981	24	24	10	190.0	152	62	179	13	4	0	1	2.42
1982	38	**38**	19	**295.2**	**253**	86	**286**	**23**	11	0	**6**	3.10
1983	37	37	8	**283.2**	**277**	84	**275**	15	16	0	3	3.11
1984	33	33	1	229.0	214	79	163	13	7	0	0	3.58
1985	16	16	0	92.0	84	53	48	1	8	0	0	3.33
1986	32	32	0	176.1	196	86	120	9	14	0	0	5.10
1987	32	21	3	152.0	165	86	91	6	14	1	0	5.74
1988	4	1	0	9.2	20	5	5	0	1	0	0	16.76
Totals	741	709	254	5,214.1	4,672	1,833	4,136	329	244	2	55	3.22

Notes: Boldface indicates statistical leader. GP = games played; GS = games started; CG = complete games; IP = innings pitched; HA = hits allowed; BB = bases on balls (walks); SO = strikeouts; W = wins; L = losses; S = saves; ShO = shutouts; ERA = earned run average

1976 and 1982. Five times he led the National League in strikeouts; four times he won the coveted Cy Young Award as the league's best pitcher.

Until 1980, a World Series victory had eluded him, and the Phillies had not been in the fall classic since 1950, but Steve and third baseman Mike Schmidt led their team to the pennant in 1980. Steve, after winning twenty-four in the regular season and another game in the National League Championship Series, defeated the Kansas City Royals twice, including a 4-1 victory in the deciding game.

On September 23, 1983, Steve beat his old teammates, the Cardinals, 6-2 to become only the sixteenth pitcher in major league history to win three hundred games. As late as 1984, the year he turned forty, he won thirteen.

When Steve finally retired in 1988, after pitching twenty-four years in the major leagues, he had won 329 games and amassed 4,136 strikeouts, credentials guaranteed to earn him induction in baseball's Hall of Fame in 1994.

Summary

Steve Carlton never got over his shyness and went for years without granting interviews to sports journalists, but on the pitching mound, he was always an intimidating figure. He took tremendous pride in always being in shape and ready to pitch. Until the twilight of his career, he missed his turn only a few times.

He possessed a good fastball and change of pace, but it was the slider, and his control of it, that made him great. He ranks as the premier left-handed pitcher of the 1970's and one of the greatest of all time.

Robert P. Ellis

Additional Sources:

Aaseng, Nathan. *Steve Carlton: Baseball's Silent Strongman.* Minneapolis, Minn.: Lerner Publishing, 1984.

Kuenster, Bob. "Here Are the Ten Greatest Left-Handed Pitchers Ever." *Baseball Digest* 54, no. 4 (1995).

Ward, Martha Eads. *Steve Carlton: Star Southpaw.* New York: Putnam, 1975.

Wulf, Steve. "Steve Carlton." *Sports Illustrated* 80, no. 3 (1994).

HONORS AND AWARDS

1968-69, 1971-72, 1974, 1977, 1979-82	National League All-Star Team
1972	Hickok Belt
1972, 1977, 1980, 1982	National League Cy Young Award
1981	National League Gold Glove Award Uniform number 32 retired by Philadelphia Phillies
1994	Inducted into National Baseball Hall of Fame

JoANNE CARNER

Sport: Golf

Born: March 4, 1939
Kirkland, Washington

Early Life

One of the finest players in the history of women's golf was born on March 4, 1939, in Kirkland, Washington. JoAnne Gunderson (later known by her married name, Carner) was a strawberry blonde child with a strong physique. Her build, which gave her an effortless power in sports, and her innate athletic talent proved to be assets for her. At an early age, she became accustomed to winning at sports. While she was in high school, for example, she played successfully on her school's undefeated tennis team, having picked up a tennis racket for the first time ever only two weeks before the opening match.

JoAnne, who never played with dolls, began playing golf at age ten. One day her older brother, Bill, teased her, saying she would never make a good golfer because she held irons with a baseball grip and because she stepped into the ball. Before too long, however, JoAnne was outdriving Bill; consequently, he gave up the sport.

Even as a youngster, JoAnne displayed exceptionally good sportmanship. She competed for the fun of the game, never minding the outcome and never complaining or blaming others. She was also extremely friendly and unaffected toward her opponents. All of these qualities would eventually benefit JoAnne; when she became famous, it was easy to keep success in perspective.

The Road to Excellence

When JoAnne went off to college at Arizona State University, she naturally chose to earn her B.A. degree in physical education.

While a student at Arizona State, she enjoyed her first substantial win, the National Collegiate title. Then, in 1956, she reached the finals of the

JoAnne Carner tees off in a 1994 tournament.

United States Women's Amateur, but she lost. She won the United States Junior Girls title instead. The following year, she did win the United States Women's Amateur, the second youngest at the time to do so. Then, she went on to win it a total of five times: in 1960, 1962, 1966, and 1968. Fans began calling her "The Great Gundy."

JoAnne enjoyed a brilliant amateur career that lasted twelve years before she turned profes-

AP/Wide World Photos

sional. She played in Curtis Cup competition from 1958 to 1964. She also won nearly every other important amateur championship at least once, including the Western Amateur, the Intercollegiate, the Pacific Northwest, the Eastern, and the Trans-Mississippi.

Basically a left-hander, JoAnne played right-handed golf. She was equally good at match and stroke play, and was becoming known as one of the longest hitters of all time among women golfers.

In 1963, JoAnne married Donald Carner, who became her best and constant friend and strongest critic. Don bought a golf course in Seekonk, Massachusetts, and the two of them ran it together, with JoAnne managing the snack bar and winning tournaments during her vacations. For years, JoAnne had preferred to compete in amateur tournaments while beating the professionals in selected professional competitions. Don believed she ought to turn professional to prove herself as the best at the game. After she suffered a brain hemorrhage in late 1969, JoAnne became bored with amateur golf, so the couple hired a manager to run their golf course and headed off on the professional circuit in their trailer.

The Emerging Champion

Few women players have ever compiled the kind of amateur record that JoAnne Carner brought to the professionals. In her first professional seasons, however, her playing was not quite the same. She did not play as seriously as before, and somehow, she lost her swing. Her career suffered. Although she was named Rookie of the Year in 1970, still her winnings did not cover her expenses. In 1970, she won only one tournament; in 1971, only two. Meanwhile, JoAnne worked hard at her swing. Sam Snead, her mentor and friend, counseled her on her swing technique. When she recovered it, her swing was a manly swing, with no sway or lurch, as is common among women's swings. When she hit the ball, the ground shook. From then on, The Great Gundy became known as "Big Mamma."

From that time on, JoAnne excelled. She went on to finish in the top six moneywinners eight times. She won the United States Women's Open twice (1971 and 1976), to become the only

woman to have claimed victory in all three United States Golf Association (USGA) events: the Junior, Amateur, and Open. In 1982, she was the United States Ladies Professional Golf Association (LPGA) Player of the Year for the third time, and won the Vare Trophy as well. The following year, she won the World Championship of Women's Golf.

JoAnne once played Arnold Palmer in an exhibition game. After the two of them teed off, Palmer walked up to the farthest ball, assuming it was his. Big Mamma had outdriven him by 20 yards. Along with Mickey Wright, JoAnne is believed to be the only woman who has ever been able to hit long irons as well as the best men golfers.

Eventually, JoAnne climbed to rank among

MAJOR CHAMPIONSHIP VICTORIES	
1956	U.S. Junior Girls
1957, 1960, 1962, 1966, 1968	U.S. Women's Amateur
1971, 1976	U.S. Women's Open
1975, 1978	Du Maurier Classic

OTHER NOTABLE VICTORIES	
1958, 1960, 1962, 1964	Curtis Cup Team
1958-59	Pacific Northwest
1959	Western Amateur
1960	Intercollegiate
1961	Trans-Mississippi
1968	Eastern
1969	Burdine's Invitational
1970	Wendell West Open
1971, 1974	Bluegrass Invitational
1974	Desert Inn Classic
1974, 1976	Hoosier Classic
1975	All-American Classic
1977-78	Borden Classic
1980-81	Lady Keystone Open
1982	Henderon Classic McDonald's LPGA Kids' Classic Rail Charity Golf Classic
1982-83	Chevrolet World Championship of Women's Golf
1982, 1985	Elizabeth Arden Classic

the LPGA's all-time money winners, with more than $2 million. With her forty-two LPGA wins (through mid-1987), she was inducted into the LPGA Hall of Fame in 1982, and into the Women's Sports Foundation Hall of Fame five years later.

Continuing the Story

As a player, Carner proved herself consistent and durable. Possibly, her remarkable record derives from her stable home life. An extremely devoted wife, she is also the family breadwinner and career woman. Yet her marriage has endured the kind of challenges that so often destroy other marriages. JoAnne has no children or pets. Her plants survive only a month because she is on the road so much. Don accompanies her everywhere; the two of them have never been apart more than ten days total in eighteen years. They

say that the secret to their marriage is that they do not make life hard on themselves. If a difficult situation comes up that looks like it could be a problem, they have nothing to do with it.

JoAnne and Don like to fish whenever they are not on the fairways. They have a mobile home hideaway in the Smoky Mountains of Tennessee, perched above the white waters of the Tellico River. At the fishing camp where they live, they spend Saturday nights around a bonfire, listening to bluegrass music.

In 1981, the USGA honored JoAnne with the coveted Bobby Jones Award for distinguished sportsmanship. Known for her unfailing sense of humor, her response was that she thought players had to be dead to win it. She more than deserved the honor, however, with her ever-courteous attitude, her sense of humor, and her graciousness in defeat as well as victory. These qualities and more combined to make her an example of how the game of golf should be played.

In 1994, JoAnne captained the U.S. team to victory in the Solheim Cup Tournament and was named one of the LPGA's top fifty players in 2000. The Palm Beach National Golf and Country Club announced in 2001 the opening of the JoAnne Carner Golf Academy for Ladies.

Summary

One of the longest hitters of all time, JoAnne Carner became the leading money winner in LPGA history, with more than two million dollars in winnings. In addition to becoming one of golf's all-time greats, she is known for her exemplary sportsmanship, for which she received the Bobby Jones Award.

Nan White

RECORDS AND MILESTONES

First woman to have won the USGA Junior Girls, U.S. Women's Amateur, and U.S. Women's Open titles

In 1981, became the second player to cross the $1 million mark in career earnings

In 1986, became the second player in LPGA history to cross the $2 million mark

HONORS AND AWARDS

1970	LPGA Rookie of the Year Gatorade Rookie of the Year *Golf Digest* Rookie of the Year
1974	*Golf Digest* Most Improved Golfer *Golf Digest* Mickey Wright Award for Tournament Victories
1974-75, 1981-83	LPGA Vare Trophy
1974, 1981-82	LPGA Player of the Year Rolex Player of the Year
1974, 1981-83	GWAA Player of the Year
1976	Seagram's Seven Crowns of Sports Award
1981	Bobby Jones Award
1982	Inducted into LPGA Hall of Fame
1985	Inducted into PGA/World Golf Hall of Fame
1987	Inducted into Sudafed International Women's Sports Hall of Fame
1988	Honored among *Golf* magazine's 100 Heroes of Golf
2000	Honored as one of LPGA's top-fifty players

Additional Sources:

Allis, Peter. *The Who's Who of Golf.* Englewood Cliffs, N.J.: Prentice-Hall, 1983.

"Carner Feels Her Age." *Golf Digest* 53, no. 48 (2000).

Dodson, James. "Slow Walk to Immortality." *Golf Magazine* 36, no. 11 (1994).

Editors of *Golf Magazine. Golf Magazine's Encyclopedia of Golf: The Complete Reference.* New York: HarperCollins, 1993.

"Three Eras, Aces." *Golf Digest* 51, no. 12 (2000).

CONNIE CARPENTER

Sport: Cycling

Born: February 26, 1957
Madison, Wisconsin

Early Life

Raised in a cold region of the United States, Connie Carpenter was a prodigy in speed skating. In Wisconsin, first she learned to walk; then she learned to skate. The only daughter in a family that included three sons, Connie developed her competitive edge early in life. She learned that doing well was important to her. Though her brothers were also competitive, her parents were not. They created a home that was supportive and comfortable.

The Road to Excellence

Beginning in kindergarten, Connie participated in skating championships in her city of Madison. She won in her age group every year. By the seventh grade, she became serious and began training more intensely by running and biking. In 1972, she went to Norway to train with Finn Halvorsen, a Norwegian speed-skating coach. After training daily for eight months by running, sprinting, lifting weights, and taking vitamins, Connie qualified for the United States Olympic speed-skating team when she was fourteen years old. Competing in the Winter Games in Sapporo, Japan, Connie earned a seventh-place finish in the 1,500-meter speed-skating race.

After the Olympics, Connie continued to compete, but she suffered from anemia, a back problem, and finally a stress fracture in her foot. In 1976, she won the overall title at the U.S. Speed Skating Championships. However, because of an ankle injury exacerbated by the stress fracture, she could not compete at the 1976 Winter Olympics. As part of her rehabilitation, Connie cross-trained by cycling. She had turned to this sport in the past during the nonwinter months and once again used cycling to strengthen her legs.

The Emerging Champion

As a speed skater, Connie had developed strong upper-leg muscles, which are also needed to excel in cycling. As she trained in cycling, she found that her passion for it surpassed her interest in speed skating. She began competing in regional races and in 1976, 1977, and 1979 won the U.S. Road and Pursuit Championship.

She moved to Northern California to live in a climate more conducive to biking, then entered the University of California, Berkeley, and looked to compete in a new sport, rowing, because her brother had rowed on his college team. After six months of rowing, she qualified for the crew team. In 1980, Connie was part of the team that won the National Collegiate Amateur Association (NCAA) championship four-oared shell with coxswain event. Connie was an expert rower as well as an accomplished speed skater and cyclist.

Once again, however, Connie switched sports. An announcement was made that the 1984 Los Angeles Summer Olympic Games would include the women's individual road race. In 1981, she went back to cycling and won the National Road Championship. She continued to compete and was the 1982 and 1983 National Criterium champion. Also in 1983, Connie set a world record in the World Pursuit Championship.

After marrying cyclist Dave Phinney, Connie returned to the Olympics in 1984, this time on the U.S. cycling team during the Summer Games. Pacing herself on a hot race day on a difficult course, she knew she had to give a final push to win. In the final moments of the women's road race, Connie inched ahead of her U.S. teammate, Rebecca Twigg, by throwing her bike forward and crossing the finish line less than a half wheel ahead of her. The two teammates' finishing times were identical: two hours, eleven minutes, and fourteen seconds. However, Connie won the Olympic gold medal, the first Ameri-

MAJOR CHAMPIONSHIPS		
Year	Competition	Place
1976	U.S. Outdoor Speed Skating Championships	Overall Title
1976, 1977, 1979	U.S. Road & Pursuit Championships (Cycling)	1st
1980	NCAA Crew Championship	1st
1981	National Road Race (Cycling)	1st
1982, 1983	National Criterium (Cycling)	1st
1983	World Pursuit Cycling	1st
1984	Olympic Games, Road Race	Gold

Phinney, finished in fifth place in the men's road race.

Continuing the Story

After her Olympic victory, Connie continued to receive honors. She was inducted into the International Women's Sports Hall of Fame in 1990 and the U.S. Olympics Hall of Fame in 1992. In June, 2000, *Bicycling* magazine named the 1984 U.S. Olympic team's accomplishments, in which they won more medals than any other cycling team in history, as one of the

can in seventy-two years to win an Olympic medal in the sport of cycling. The U.S. cycling team earned four medals; Connie's husband, Dave

AP/Wide World Photos

Connie Carpenter after winning the first U.S. gold medal of the 1984 Olympics.

"Fifteen Greatest Moments in U.S. Cycling."

Connie and her husband compete together as a team. They settled in Copper Mountain, Colorado, to run a cycling camp. Their brochure states it is "a camp filled with experts in some of the most beautiful and mountainous territory the U. S. has to offer."

Summary

Connie Carpenter is a natural athlete who has excelled in several sports—speed skating, crew, and cycling. She has won awards and honors for all of these sports. Despite injuries, Connie's continuous participation in sports, and in particular, competitions, has made her one of the most honored female athletes in U.S. history.

Betsy L. Nichols

Additional Sources:

Layden, Joe. *Women in Sports: The Complete Book on the World's Greatest Female Athletes.* Los Angeles: General Publishing Group, 1997.

Leccese, Michael, and Arlene Pleving. *The Bicyclist's Sourcebook: The Ultimate Directory of Cycling Information.* Rockville, Md.: Woodbine House, 1991.

"Lifestyles of the Fast and Famous." *Bicycling* 29 (September, 1988): 59-61.

Martin, Scott. "The Heroes of 1984: U.S. Olympic Cyclists." *Bicycling* 37 (January, 1996): 36-41.

Phinney, David, and Connie Carpenter. *Training for Cycling: The Ultimate Guide to Improved Performance.* New York: Putnam, 1992.

HONORS AND AWARDS	
1990	Inducted into International Women's Sports Hall of Fame
1992	Inducted into U.S. Olympic Hall of Fame

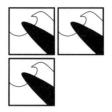

CORKY CARROLL

Sport: Surfing

Born: September 29, 1947
Surfside Colony, California

Early Life

Charles Curtis (Corky) Carroll was born on September 29, 1947. He grew up in Surfside Colony, California, about nine miles north of Huntington Beach. Corky was the only child born to a father who worked as an electrician and a mother who was a homemaker, although she had formerly worked as a radio singer in the era when radio was performed live. Against the objections of his mother, Corky spent all of his spare time in the ocean, surfing and paddle-boarding from sunrise until sunset as often as he could.

The home in which Corky was raised was located on the beach, so the ocean has always played a major role in Corky's life. He learned to swim at about the same age most children learn to walk, and it was not long before Corky and his friends began searching for anything that would float on which to ride the waves. It was at five or six years of age that Corky, for the first time, managed to stand upright on a borrowed surfboard and ride his first wave like a surfer.

The Road to Excellence

Early in the decade, "long boards," made of wood and standing nine to ten feet in length, were the standard, making surfing a sport that required not only the coordination and stamina necessary to maneuver in the surf, but sheer strength as well. Corky, an athlete dedicated to his sport, kept in top physical condition by paddleboarding and surfing daily. Because of his intensely competitive nature, Corky has always found, and often met, the challenge to be the best. This goes beyond competitive surfing into all aspects of his life. When Corky was about sixteen years of age, he was known as one of the world's fastest paddleboarders, a further example of his need to excel.

Excellence, however, does have its price. Daily exposure to the sun caused Corky to develop an eye disease called pterygium, diagnosed in 1960. It caused a natural growth to form over the eye to protect it from the harsh glare of the sun's reflection on the water. He underwent surgery, but only two weeks later, the determined young man was once again where he felt most at home, in the surf. The only visible difference in his appearance after surgery was that he acceded to wearing sunglasses.

Corky's determination and his strong, brash, humorous personality emerged at an early age. A surfer who did more than merely ride waves, Corky made eight-millimeter films, one of which was entitled *Surf Savages*, and showed them to local surfers at club meetings. He would later form musical groups that would release four albums and two singles. His reputation as a personality, as well as a "hotdogger" performance surfer, was established early in the close-knit Southern California surfing community.

The Emerging Champion

Surfing in the 1960's enjoyed enormous popularity as a sport and as a life-style. Surfing in Southern California centered in Huntington Beach, where Corky attended Huntington Beach High School, the school closest to his home. He won his first surfing contest at the age of fifteen in 1962. The following year, he was named Junior

HONORS, AWARDS, AND MILESTONES	
1963	U.S. Junior Champion
1966-70	Overall U.S. Surfing Champion
1967	*Surfer* magazine Most Popular Surfer
1967-69	World International Surfing Champion
1969	International Pro-Am Champion

Vince Cavataio/Allsport

Champion. His fame began to grow beyond the scope of the local folklore, and Corky Carroll became a name heard often and the man to beat in international surfing circles.

Corky married for the first time when he was still in his teens. He fathered a son, Clint, when he was only nineteen years of age and about to become famous across the country and around the world.

Corky Carroll was the first professional surfer. Other than winning prize money from surfing contests and championships worldwide, he was the first surfer to be paid to do nothing other than surf and endorse products related to swimwear and surfboards. Corky has also designed surfboards, worked as advertising director at *Surfer* magazine, judged contests, and participated in other activities related to the sport in which he excelled.

Corky was the overall United States Surfing Champion for five years in a row, spanning 1966 through 1970. He complemented that achieve-ment with the title of International Surfing Champion for three of those years, 1967, 1968, and 1969. In a readers' poll, Corky Carroll was voted *Surfer* magazine's Most Popular Surfer in 1967.

That same year, only days before the international championship in Lima, Peru, Corky swallowed some contaminated ocean water and fell very ill. Being an extremely stubborn and determined individual, Corky went against his doctor's order, sneaked out of the Peruvian hospital, and went to the beach, where he surfed his way to another title in spite of his illness.

Continuing the Story

Corky won surfing contests based on his skill as a performance rider, or trick rider, rather than as a big-wave rider, although competing in the 1960's would differ from the contests to take place decades later. Corky has commented on the fact that surfing contests were far less organized when he competed than they are now. Complete objectivity in scoring this sport will al-

413

ways prove difficult because no two waves are exactly the same, but the professional surfing associations have made great strides in standardizing contest scoring. Whereas only two surfers will compete at the same time now, as many as six or seven would compete simultaneously in the earlier era of surfing.

Corky would continue to surf near his home in San Clemente, California. His son, Clint, has also surfed in the local pro-am contests. Corky would also play and teach tennis. He has written a book and a television script and made celebrity appearances in eleven television commercials. He has enjoyed performing as a comedian, a talent that was evident in his competitive surfing days.

In the years following his retirement from professional competition, Corky opened a surf school in Huntington Beach, launched a career in music, and created his own line of sportswear. He has remained an icon among younger generations of surfing professionals and enthusiasts.

Summary

Between seven and nineteen years of age, Corky Carroll won no fewer than fifty-two major surfing contests and was the first surfer who made his living from the sport. Whether long or short boards were the fashion, with them as his tools, Corky mastered the waves.

Leslie A. Pearl

Additional Sources:

Almond, Elliott. "He'd Still Rather Surf than Work." *Los Angeles Times* (Orange County edition), July 13, 1989, p. 6.

Carroll, Corky, with Joel Engel. *Surf-Dog Days and Bitchin' Nights.* Chicago: Contemporary Books, 1989.

Hicks, Jerry. "Surfer Corky Carroll Catches Wave of Fame." *Los Angeles Times* (Orange County edition), July 25, 1996, p. 1.

Weyler, John. "Carroll Might Return to Competitive Waters." *Los Angeles Times* (Orange County edition), June 24, 1993, p. 8.

DON CARTER

Sport: Bowling

Born: July 29, 1926
St. Louis, Missouri

Early Life

Donald James Carter was born on July 29, 1926, in St. Louis, Missouri. The youngest of two sons, Don was raised by his mother, Gladys Carter, because his father deserted the family while Don was still an infant.

As a boy, Don worked as a pinsetter for a local bowling alley in St. Louis. He first bowled at the age of thirteen, and later, while still in high school, built a lane in the basement of his house so that he could practice. Other sports held an interest for Don as well. During his years at Wellston High School, he earned seven varsity sports letters, four in baseball and three in football, before graduating in 1944.

Following graduation, Don joined the United States Navy and served as a ship radarman in the South Pacific for two years. He was discharged in June, 1946, with the rank of third-class petty officer.

The Road to Excellence

After leaving the Navy, Don was signed to play professional baseball by Bill Beckman of the Philadelphia Athletics. Don spent the 1947 season playing infielder and pitcher for a minor league team in Red Springs, North Carolina. Don, however, felt he was not a major league prospect and returned home to St. Louis at the end of the 1947 season.

Don was soon bowling in recreational leagues while holding various jobs. His work as a janitor, a bartender, and a plant worker left him little time for competitive tournament bowling. Gladys Carter was a source of encouragement for her son during these difficult years, allowing him to live at home and save money for bowling.

Eventually, Don's perseverance began to pay off. He became a bowling instructor at Silver Shield Lanes in St. Louis, then later at Floriss Lanes; both jobs gave him the opportunity to earn money and hone his bowling skills.

These developing skills caught the attention of the Pfeiffer bowling team of Detroit, which invited Don to join their ranks in 1951, offering him no salary but a chance to refine his skills in competition. Don accepted the invitation and took a job in the Detroit recreation department, making $60 a week to help cover his expenses.

Don received other recognition for his bowling ability in 1952; the *Bowlers Journal* named him to the All-American team. This was the first major award for Don, but it certainly would not be the last.

The Emerging Champion

Don went on to dominate the sport of bowling in the 1950's and early 1960's. He won more tournaments and money than any other bowler. His accomplishments earned him the nickname "Mr. Bowling."

The 1952 All-Star Championship became Don's first major title. He won the same tournament in 1953, as well as two team tournaments as a member of the Pfeiffer squad. For his efforts, the Bowling Writers Association of America honored Don as the Bowler of the Year.

In 1953, Don married LaVerne Haverly, a bowling champion from Los Angeles, California. Don and LaVerne eventually had two children, Cathy and Jimmy.

Meanwhile, the Pfeiffer bowling team continued to be successful, due in large part to Don, and other teams recognized this fact. In 1953, a newly formed team in St. Louis, sponsored by the Anheuser-Busch company, persuaded Don to join them. This crew was molded around Don, a smart move because the team proceeded to win six national team titles between 1955 and 1962.

Don also continued his individual excellence

HONORS AND AWARDS	
1952-54, 1957-63	*Bowlers Journal* All-American Team
1953-54, 1957-58, 1960, 1962	BWAA Bowler of the Year
1958-59, 1961-62	President of PBA
1970	Voted "Greatest Bowler of All Time" Inducted into ABC Hall of Fame
1975	Inducted into PBA Hall of Fame

RECORDS
Most top-five finishes in a year, 18 (1962)
Most consecutive top-five finishes, 7 (1962)

during this period. By 1964, Don had won five World's Invitational titles and six Bowler of the Year awards and had been named an All-American an amazing ten times. In addition to his prowess on the lanes, Don influenced bowling in other ways. He was a driving force in the development of the Professional Bowlers Association (PBA) in 1958, and when a rival association formed in 1961, featuring many top bowlers, Don stuck by the PBA. The rival group folded in less than a year.

Continuing the Story

Such achievements mark the long career of the man voted "Greatest Bowler of All Time" in 1970. Don continued to bowl until 1973, when he retired from competition. Don eventually moved to Miami, Florida, with his second wife, Paula, whom he had married in 1976.

The ability to concentrate was often cited as one of the factors that separated Don from other bowlers. He rarely spoke during his matches and his steely nerves allowed him to remain focused even when under great pressure. The pressure was so intense that Don often lost up to 8 pounds during a single match.

This intense temperament might be attributed to the criticism Don had to overcome early in his career because of his unusual bowling technique. Bowling purists believed the correct form was to crouch slightly when bowling and release the ball with an extended arm. Don, however, crouched very low on his approach, and when he released the ball, his arm was bent at the elbow. Criticism did not affect Don; he simply laughed

PBA TOUR VICTORIES	
1960	Paramus; National Championship at Memphis
1962	Houston; Seattle; Tucson; Rochester

OTHER MAJOR VICTORIES	
1953-54, 1957-58	U.S. Open
1957, 1959-62	World's Invitational
1961	ABC Masters

and said, "I guess I just learned to bowl wrong."

This winning personality, combined with his intense concentration, made Don a bowling favorite. He was popular among his peers, as was evident when Don was named the first president of the PBA.

Don was also popular among fans. They cheered his every strike at tournaments and groaned when things did not go so well. Perhaps they could identify with Don because of his background and his awkward bowling style.

Summary

From a humble beginning in the sport, Don Carter rose to be the best bowler of his time. Although his style may have seemed awkward, Don became a bowling legend. In 1970, he was elected to the American Bowling Congress (ABC) Hall of Fame, and in 1975, Don became a charter member of the PBA Hall of Fame.

Robert T. Epling

Additional Sources:

Brown, Gene, ed. *The New York Times Encyclopedia of Sports.* 15 vols. New York: Arno Press, 1979-1980.

Carter, Don. *Bowling the Pro Way.* New York: Viking Press, 1975.

Hickok, Ralph. *A Who's Who of Sports Champions.* Boston: Houghton Mifflin, 1995.

Porter, David L., ed. *Biographical Dictionary of American Sports: Basketball and Other Indoor Sports.* Westport, Conn.: Greenwood Press, 1989.

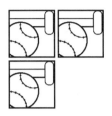

GARY CARTER

Sport: Baseball

Born: April 8, 1954
Culver City, California

Early Life

Gary Edmund Carter was born on April 8, 1954, in the Los Angeles suburb of Culver City, California, to James Carter, an aircraft parts inspector, and Inge Carter. He, along with his older brother, Gordon, grew up in nearby Fullerton, where Gary showed athletic ability even as a small child. When he was seven, he won the national Punt, Pass & Kick competition for his age group; as part of his prize, he was taken on tours of the Pro Football Hall of Fame and the White House, and he also filmed a television commercial for the contest. The next year, he finished as the national runner-up.

When Gary was twelve, his mother died of leukemia; as a result, he became very close to his father. Although deeply saddened by his mother's death, he developed an exuberant personality, and he would retain his outgoing nature as an adult.

Gary was a star athlete at Fullerton's Sunny Hills High School, captaining the baseball, basketball, and football teams and also earning selection to the National Honor Society for his academic performance. He was twice named a high school All-American in football, and he considered pursuing a football career. He suffered a severe knee injury in a scrimmage during his senior year, however, and he decided to concentrate on baseball. He turned down more than one hundred college scholarship offers to sign with the Montreal Expos of the National League (NL) after he was picked in the third round of the 1972 amateur draft.

The Road to Excellence

Gary started his professional career as a catching prospect with the Expos' low-level minor

New York Mets

STATISTICS

Season	GP	AB	Hits	2B	3B	HR	Runs	RBI	BA	SA
1974	9	27	11	0	1	1	5	6	.407	.593
1975	144	503	136	20	1	17	58	68	.270	.416
1976	91	311	68	8	1	6	31	38	.219	.309
1977	154	522	148	29	2	31	86	84	.284	.525
1978	157	533	136	27	1	20	76	72	.255	.422
1979	141	505	143	28	5	22	74	75	.283	.489
1980	154	549	145	25	5	29	76	101	.264	.486
1981	100	374	94	20	2	16	48	88	.251	.444
1982	154	557	163	32	1	29	91	97	.293	.510
1983	145	541	146	37	3	17	63	79	.270	.444
1984	159	596	175	32	1	27	75	**106**	.294	.487
1985	149	555	156	17	1	32	83	100	.281	.488
1986	132	490	125	14	2	24	81	105	.255	.439
1987	139	523	123	18	2	20	55	83	.235	.392
1988	130	455	110	16	2	11	39	46	.242	.358
1989	50	153	28	8	0	2	14	16	.183	.275
1990	92	244	62	10	0	9	24	27	.254	.406
1991	101	248	61	14	0	6	22	26	.246	.375
1992	95	285	62	18	1	5	24	29	.218	.340
Totals	2,296	7,971	2,092	371	31	324	1,025	1,225	.262	.430

Notes: Boldface indicates statistical leader. GP = games played; AB = at bats; 2B = doubles; 3B = triples; HR = home runs; RBI = runs batted in; BA = batting average; SA = slugging average

league teams in Florida. He made rapid progress through the Montreal farm system, reaching the Triple A level, just one step below the majors, by the end of his second season. After spending most of 1974 with Montreal's farm team in Memphis, he earned a late call up to the big leagues; he made the most of the opportunity, batting .407 in nine games and hitting a home run off future Hall of Famer Steve Carlton. Over the winter, he married his high school sweetheart, Sandy Lahm, with whom he would have two daughters.

In 1975, Gary was with the Expos from the start of the season, and he soon showed that his impressive performance the previous year was no fluke. While shuttling between catcher and the outfield, he hit 17 home runs and batted a solid .270, earned selection to the NL All-Star team, and won the league's Rookie of the Year Award.

The next season, though, Gary struggled. Bothered by injuries, he played in only ninety-one games, and he was also distracted by continued shifting between the outfield and the catcher's spot. His average dropped to .219, and he hit only 6 homers. With the help of special tutoring from coach Norm Sherry, however, he worked hard to improve his defense behind the

plate, and he opened the 1977 season as the Expos' full-time catcher.

Settled in at last, Gary came into his own. In April, he blasted 3 homers in a single game, and he stayed hot all year, finishing the season with 31 home runs and a .281 average. For good measure, he established himself as a top defensive player, leading NL catchers in total chances, putouts, and assists.

The Emerging Champion

The catcher's job is the most difficult in baseball. Catchers spend most of their on-field time in an uncomfortable crouch that takes a heavy toll on their backs and knees. Moreover, they suffer frequent injuries from such occupational hazards as errant pitches, charging base runners, and broken bats. Even the best catchers, therefore, are rarely consistent from year to year; for example, such greats as Roy Campanella and Johnny Bench alternated good years with lesser ones.

Gary, though, proved to be the rare exception. A rugged 6-foot 2-inch, 205-pounder, he stood up to the pounding of the position without letting it affect his performance. He continued to hit for power and for a good average, and he

419

MAJOR LEAGUE RECORDS

Most putouts by a catcher, career, 11,785
Most chances accepted by a catcher, career, 12,988
Fewest passed balls, season, 1 (1978)

HONORS AND AWARDS

1975	*Sporting News* National League Rookie Player of the Year
1975,1979-88	National League All-Star Team
1980-82	National League Gold Glove Award
	Uniform number 8 retired by Montreal Expos

refined his already impressive defensive skills, developing a feared throwing arm and earning a reputation as both a fierce plate blocker and a clever handler of pitchers. He earned All-Star status year after year and became the annual Gold Glove winner among NL catchers.

Gary's consistently excellent play and his openness with fans and the press soon made him the most popular Expo, and he was nicknamed "The Kid" for his boyish enthusiasm. Gary reciprocated the city's affection, moving his family to Montreal and taking courses to learn French, the area's primary language.

The Expos of the early 1980's were a talent-laden team that featured such other stars as pitcher Steve Rogers and outfielders Andre Dawson and Tim Raines. Year after year, experts predicted that Montreal would win the NL pennant—but year after year, the Expos fell short of expectations. As the team's biggest star, Gary came to feel the brunt of such disappointments. Teammates came to resent his popularity, and he began to draw criticism for failing to lead the Expos to a championship.

Continuing the Story

In the winter of 1984, Gary was traded to the New York Mets in exchange for four players, and the change of scene proved to be just what he needed. The Mets were another talented team, and they looked to Gary to provide veteran leadership for such young stars as Dwight Gooden and Darryl Strawberry.

This time, there were no disappointments. In 1986, the Mets dominated the NL, winning 108 games and stopping Houston in the playoffs before downing the Boston Red Sox in an exciting seven-game World Series. Gary was a big contributor all year, driving in 105 runs in the regular season, winning a playoff game with a twelfth-inning hit, and smacking 2 home runs in one game in the World Series.

Gary began to slip a little after the Mets' championship season, though he remained one of the game's better catchers. By 1989, however, his aching knees and other accumulated ailments had caught up with him, and he moved into a backup role. He left the Mets after the 1989 season and played briefly for the San Francisco Giants and the Los Angeles Dodgers before finishing his career back with the Expos in 1992. He retired as one of the all-time leaders among catchers in games played, home runs, and runs batted in, and he was regarded as a certain future Hall of Fame selection.

Summary

Gary Carter was one of only a handful of catchers in major league history to combine a powerful bat with top-notch defense. His long-term excellence at a demanding position made him one of the most valuable players of his era.
Robert McClenaghan

Additional Sources:

Buck, Ray. *Gary Carter, The Kid.* Chicago: Children's Press, 1984.

Carter, Gary, with Ken Abraham. *The Gamer.* Dallas, Tex.: Word, 1993.

Carter, Gary, with John Hough, Jr. *A Dream Season.* San Diego, Calif.: Harcourt Brace Jovanovich, 1987.

VINCE CARTER

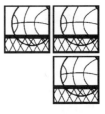

Sport: Basketball

Born: January 26, 1977
Ormond Beach, Florida

Early Life

Vince Carter was born on January 26, 1977, in Ormond Beach, Florida. Like many great athletes, he began his athletic career with great doubts. At age thirteen and less than 5 feet 5 inches, he was bowlegged and was cut from his basketball team because his coach thought he was too slow and too small despite his excellent shooting touch. As a high school freshman he was just an average 5-foot 7-inch player who dreamed of being a National Basketball Association (NBA) star.

During his sophomore year, however, Vince grew more than 6 inches and improved his jumping ability. By his senior year of high school, he was embraced as the best high school basketball player in the state of Florida. He played for Daytona Beach Mainland High School, near his hometown. He soon matured into a 6-foot 6-inch, 210-pound guard forward.

The Road to Excellence

After completing a high school career as an outstanding high school basketball player and a McDonald's All-American pick, Vince entered the University of North Carolina at Chapel Hill.

As a college basketball player, Vince was named to the National Collegiate Athletic Association (NCAA) Tournament All-East regional team in both 1997 and 1998. He was also named an Associated Press Second Team All-American and First Team All-ACC after his junior season as a North Carolina Tar Heel.

His college career was distinguished by weekly highlight films of his dunks and explosive athletic moves. His exploits in college were so impressive that on December 8, 2000, he was honored by the elevation of his jersey to the rafters at the Dean Smith Athletic Center in Chapel Hill, joining the jerseys of notable players Phil Ford, James Worthy, and Michael Jordan.

The Emerging Champion

After college Vince was drafted by the Toronto Raptors, a longtime under-performing team. In his NBA debut, he scored 16 points and 3 rebounds in a 103-92 victory over the Boston Celtics on February 5, 1999. He was the first Toronto Raptor in franchise history to be named NBA Player of the Week. By March, 1999, he was averaging 20 points per game, 7 rebounds per game, and 1.6 blocks per game. Just one week later he scored a game high of 32 points with 6 assists against the Houston Rockets.

The "invincible" Vince pushed the Raptors

STATISTICS

Season	GP	FGA	FGM	FG%	FTA	FTM	FT%	Reb.	Ast.	TP	PPG
1998-99	50	766	345	.450	268	204	.761	283	149	913	18.3
1999-00	82	1,696	788	.465	551	436	.791	476	322	2,107	25.7
2000-01	75	1,656	762	.460	502	384	.765	416	291	2,070	27.6
Totals	207	4,118	1,895	.460	1,321	1,024	.775	1,175	762	5,090	24.6

Notes: GP = games played; FGA = field goals attempted; FGM = field goals made; FG% = field goal percentage; FTA = free throws attempted; FTM = free throws made; FT% = free throw percentage; Reb. = rebounds; Ast. = assists; TP = total points; PPG = points per game

The Toronto Raptors' Vince Carter goes to the basket in a 1999 game.

the same weekend, scored 12 points as a starter for the 2000 NBA All-Star game. After that amazing rookie year, he scored more than 50 points in five games and scored multiple triple-doubles, the first occurring April 10, 2000, when he totaled 31 points, 11 rebounds, and 10 assists against the Cleveland Cavaliers. Chosen in 1999 as part of the new "Dream Team," Vince was a member of the gold medal winning 2000 U.S. Olympic team, which swept the competition in Sydney, Australia, in September, 2000.

Vince's third season in the NBA season was a turning point for both him and the Raptors. While raising his scoring average to 27.6 points per game, he led the Raptors back to the playoffs, where they shocked the New York Knicks in the first round. In the second round, they faced the top-seeded Philadelphia 76ers, led by league MVP Allen Iverson.

Observers who had criticized Vince for being too "quiet" in the first round swallowed their words in the second round as he and Iverson lit up the scoreboard in what became one of the marquee matches of the playoffs. After the Raptors stole a first-game victory on Philadelphia's home court, the 76ers stormed back in game two, led by Iverson's 54-point ex-plosion. In game three Vince countered by scoring 50 points and tied an NBA record with nine 3-point baskets, to lead the Raptors to a surprising 24-point victory. Two more 76er victories put the Raptors within one loss of elimination, but Vince scored 39 points in the sixth game to tie the series. The final game, however, was a heartbreaking loss for the Raptors. After trailing throughout the game, they rallied under Vince's leadership, only to lose by a single point as their final shot just missed as time ran out. Vince finished the series with an average of 30.4 points

into the playoffs. In his rookie year, he led the Toronto Raptors in scoring (18.3 points per game), blocked shots (1.54 per game), and field goal percentage (.450). In that year he also led all NBA rookies in scoring and blocked shots and was third in assists and double-doubles, fourth in rebounds, and fifth in steals. He was selected as Schick Rookie of the Year and was a unanimous selection to the 1998-1999 Schick All-Rookie First Team.

In 2000 he entered the NBA slam-dunk competition, which he won handily. He also, during

per game—one of the top performances of the playoffs.

Continuing the Story

On the eve of his last playoff game of the 2000-2001 season, Vince captured national headlines when the news media learned that he would be flying, by chartered jet, to North Carolina the next morning to attend his graduation at the University of North Carolina. When he left college to enter the NBA three years earlier, he had promised his mother he would complete his degree, and he was now fulfilling that promise. Some observers criticized him for mixing up his priorities, suggesting that he needed to stay focused on basketball. Others feared that an unexpected mishap—such as bad weather—might cause him to be late for the decisive game with the 76ers. However, calmer observers countered that Vince did, indeed, have his priorities right, and that his actions were a "spectacular" demonstration of the importance of education. As it turned out, Vince attended his graduation and returned to Philadelphia five and a half hours before the playoff game began.

The situation had an ironic twist: Throughout the entire season, the NBA had heavily promoted literacy during game broadcasts by having star players convey the message that "reading is *fundamental*." More than one observer wondered if those criticizing Vince's decision to attend his graduation might be destroying the positive message the league had been sending all year.

Summary

Vince Carter showed himself to be an outstanding player during his first three years in the NBA and is noted for his generous work in the community. A great athlete and a caring citizen, he is expected eventually to find a place among the greats in basketball history.

Culley C. Carson

Additional Sources:

Harris, Bill. *Vince Carter: The Air Apparent.* Toronto: Key Porter Books, 2000.

Stewart, Mark. *Vince Carter: The Fire Burns Bright.* Brookfield, Conn.: Millbrook Press, 2001.

Taylor, Phil, and David Sabino. "Fresh Vince." *Sports Illustrated* 92 (February 28, 2000): 36-43.

Winderman, Ira. "The Six Habits of the Highly Effective Vince Carter." *The Sporting News* 224 (January 24, 2000): 10-16.

VERA ČÁSLAVSKÁ

Sport: Gymnastics

Born: May 3, 1942
Prague, Czechoslovakia

Early Life

Vera Čáslavská was born on May 3, 1942, in the Czechoslovakian capital of Prague. As a small and pretty girl of ten, she began figure skating and became a student of former figure-skating champion Dagmar Lerchova. Vera spent her summers studying ballet, refining her instincts for grace and music.

Then one day she saw Eva Bosakova, the champion Czech gymnast, on television and was inspired to enter gymnastics. She began training under Bosakova and by the age of fifteen had shifted her entire focus to gymnastics.

The Road to Excellence

In 1958, Vera entered her first international competition at the World Championships in Moscow. At the age of sixteen, she was the youngest competitor. She did not fare especially well, but she saw the challenge before her as she witnessed the rivalry between Bosakova and the reigning champion, Soviet gymnast Larisa Latynina. The following year, at the European

424

Championships in Cracow, Poland, Vera began to make her name by taking first place in the balance beam and second in the vault, the two events that would remain her strongest throughout her career.

Over the following years, Vera continued training and developing her craft and style. During this period, she lived in a small flat in a Prague suburb and would train diligently for hours both before and after school. As well as following traditional women's gymnastics forms, she studied and adapted men's techniques from the Japanese gymnasts. At 5 feet 2 inches and 111 pounds, she had an ideal build for gymnastics, and her vivacious personality gave her immense audience appeal, even in the years before women's gymnastics gained popularity as a spectator sport. Vera was also a courageous, resilient gymnast who could accept challenges and bounce back from mistakes. During a warm-up on the uneven bars at the 1961 European Championships in Leipzig, East Germany, she fell and hit her head on the lower bar; though dazed, she went on to finish the competition and take a bronze medal in the all-around.

The Emerging Champion

In her first Olympic Games in Rome in 1960, Vera placed eighth in the all-around competition and left with only a silver medal for the Czech team. By the 1962 World Championships in her hometown, Prague, she was second only to Latynina and ready to move up. Unfortunately, when the 1963 European Championships in Paris arrived, diplomatic problems between France and East Germany provoked a Czech boycott—as so often before and since, politics intruded into the world of sports. Finally, in Tokyo at the 1964 Olympics, her moment came.

There, in spite of an attempted pirouette off the high bar that left Vera on the floor and in fifth place in uneven bars, she took first in vault and

STATISTICS					
Year	Competition	Event	Place	Event	Place
1959	European Championships	Balance beam	1st	Vault	2d
		All-Around	8th		
1960	Olympic Games	All-Around	8th	Team	Silver
		Balance beam	6th		
1961	European Championships	All-Around	3d	Balance beam	6th
		Floor Exercise	3d	Vault	6th
		Uneven parallel bars	5th		
1962	World Championships	All-Around	2d	Balance beam	5th
		Floor Exercise	3d	Vault	1st
		Uneven parallel bars	5th	Team	2d
1964	Olympic Games	All-Around	Gold	Balance beam	Gold
		Floor exercise	6th	Vault	Gold
		Uneven parallel bars	5th	Team	Silver
1965	European Championships	All-Around	1st	Balance beam	1st
		Floor exercise	1st	Vault	1st
		Uneven parallel bars	1st		
1966	World Championships	All-Around	1st	Balance beam	2d
		Floor exercise	2d	Vault	1st
		Uneven parallel bars	4th	Team	1st
1967	European Championships	All-Around	1st	Balance beam	1st
		Floor exercise	1st	Vault	1st
		Uneven Parallel bars	1st		
1968	Olympic Games	All-Around	Gold	Balance beam	Silver
		Floor exercise	Gold	Vault	Gold
		Uneven parallel bars	Gold	Team	Silver

balance beam and eclipsed Latynina for a gold medal in the all-around competition. Vera's supremacy was to continue for five years. At the 1966 World Championships in Dortmund, West Germany, Vera won two gold and two silver medals, and in the 1965 and 1967 European Championships in Sofia, Bulgaria, and Amsterdam, Holland, she accomplished a clean sweep of gold in all four events and the all-around.

Her greatest glory was yet to come, in Mexico City at the 1968 Olympics, when she became only the second woman to win two all-around Olympic titles. Her total of six medals—four gold and two silver—confirmed her claim to the top ranking in women's gymnastics in the world. Beyond the statistics, her blend of grace and attack, femininity and concentration, stillness and acrobatic artistry, all seen through her magnetic personality, captured the hearts of her audiences and helped to transform the world of women's gymnastics, a transformation that would be completed by Olga Korbut and Nadia Comăneci during the 1970's. Vera's choice of a "Mexican Hat

425

RECORDS
Won 140 career medals: 97 gold, 32 silver, and 11 bronze

HONORS AND AWARDS	
1968	Best Sportswoman of 1968, according to a worldwide poll Outstanding athlete, Olympic Games, Mexico
1990	Appointed head of all sports programs in Czechoslovakia by President Vaclav Havel
1991	Inducted into International Women's Sports Hall of Fame
1995	International Olympic Committee Czech Republic Medal of Merit, Second Grade
1998	Inducted into International Gymnastics Hall of Fame

Dance" for her floor exercise final thrilled the capacity crowds, and she was hailed as the "Queen of Mexico City."

Continuing the Story

Vera's Olympic victory came against a backdrop of unsurpassed joy and bitter agony. On the one hand, in an Olympic Village ceremony on the eve of the closing of the Games, she married Josef Odlozil, a Czech silver medalist in the 1,500-meter run. On the other hand, her time in Mexico City, as well as her wedding, were clouded over with the memory of the Soviet invasion of Czechoslovakia two months before the Games. Vera was a supporter of the rebellious Alexander Dubček regime crushed by the Soviets, and upon her return to Prague, she presented her four gold medals to the ousted leaders. She even feared for herself and went into hiding briefly, but she soon realized that her notoriety protected her from her oppressors.

She returned to her secretarial job and announced her retirement, at the age of twenty-six, from competitive gymnastics. She was, at her retirement, the most popular gymnast ever (once, upon mentioning in the press that she collected postcards, she received 3,500 cards from admiring fans within three days). The following year, a daughter, Radka, was born to Vera and Josef, and four years later, a son, Martin. Every year for five years after the 1968 Olympics, Vera tried to get a coaching job with the national team. She was denied a position because of her political attitudes and her refusal to denounce the 1968 "Manifesto of 2000 Words," a protest against the Soviet invasion. She fell out of official favor, which limited her professional and travel opportunities even after she started coaching in 1974.

Vera devoted her life to her family and to an old artistic pursuit, painting, while continuing her involvement in gymnastics as a coach at the Sparta Gymnastics Club, as an international judge, and as a member of the Technical Commission of the European Gymnastics Union well into the 1980's. With the dramatic political changes of late 1989, Vera was vindicated, and in early 1990 she was appointed as one of five advisers to the new Czech president Václav Havel. She was also named, in 1992, as the president of the Czech Republic's National Olympic Committee. In the 1990's, she was inducted into several halls of fame and expanded her role in the Olympic movement.

Summary

Vera Čáslavská, who was sometimes called "The Flower of Gymnastics," combined the stamina and precision of a diligent and well-trained technician with the charisma and zest of a true performer to bring excitement and grace to her routines. She set and achieved goals on a personal level and allowed her love of the sport to transform women's gymnastics from a secondary side event to a thrilling highlight of international athletic competition.

Barry Mann

Additional Sources:

"Čáslavská, Vera." In *The Continuum Dictionary of Women's Biography*, edited by Jennifer S. Uglow. 2d ed. New York: Continuum, 1989.

Harvey, Randy. "Blossoming in the Prague Spring." *Los Angeles Times*, April 5, 1990, p. C1.

Simons, Minot. *Women's Gymnastics, a History: Volume 1, 1966-1974*. Carmel, Calif.: Welwyn, 1995.

"Where Are They Now: Vera Čáslavská." *International Gymnast* Online. http://www.intlgymnast.com/paststars/psjanfeb00/psjanfeb00.html. January/February, 2000.

Zrala, Lenka. "Twenty Years Later." *International Gymnast*, August, 1989, 34.

BILLY CASPER

Sport: Golf

Born: June 24, 1931
San Diego, California

Early Life

William Earl Casper, Jr., was born June 24, 1931, in San Diego, California. His father, an amateur golfer, introduced him to the game when Billy was five. Billy showed a marked interest in golf from an early age and frequently practiced it at a small course on his grandfather's ranch in New Mexico.

As Billy matured, his concentration on golf increased. In his high school years, he was captain of the golf team, and he earned money by working as a caddy at the San Diego Golf Club. He won a golf scholarship to attend Notre Dame University but left after one year because of the severity of the winter weather. Rather than continue his college career elsewhere, he enlisted in the navy. His naval service proved a help to his aspirations to a career as a professional golfer. He managed golf courses, taught the game, and gave exhibitions, mostly around his native San Diego. He was fortunate that his period of military service, which ended in 1955, occurred during a period in which the United States was not involved in combat.

The Road to Excellence

The story told so far is of a young man with a more than average interest in golf—hardly suf-ficient to distinguish Billy from scores of his contemporaries. What made him stand out? The answer lies in a part of golf in which Billy demonstrated supreme excellence.

Golf in essence consists of two separate games: the play from tee-to-green and putting. Most pro-

Stephen Dunn/Allsport

427

fessionals are relatively equal in the first of these. Some golfers do indeed stand out even here: Jack Nicklaus drives with such power and accuracy that his second shot usually consists of a short iron to the green. For the most part, however, players before they reach the green are bunched together.

Putting is altogether another story. A par score of 72 strokes is based on 36 putts. A golfer who can score a significant number of one-putt greens can easily break par: The winner of a golf tournament will frequently turn out to be a player who is on an especially successful putting streak.

It was precisely in this area that Billy excelled. Since his early youth on his grandfather's ranch, he practiced putting incessantly. He much preferred it to drills in other types of shots, which he found to be both boring and hard work. His putting skill paid handsome dividends, and he became recognized as the best putter in golf.

His technique proved especially effective on long putts. He had a low, fast stroke reminiscent of the style of Bobby Locke, a South African golfer of the 1940's and 1950's who was another of golf's greatest putters. Billy's deadly accuracy on long putts enable him to achieve immediate success on the professional tour.

The Emerging Champion

Billy turned professional in 1955, soon after his discharge from the navy. To raise expenses, he arranged with a consortium of businesspersons for a loan of $1,000 a month. In return, he promised the group 30 percent of his winnings as well as repayment of the loan. Their investment proved a sound one; within a few years Billy had become one of the tour's leading money winners.

His march to success culminated in his 1959 victory in the United States Open, the premier American tournament. Over the very difficult New York course of Winged Foot, he needed only 114 putts for four rounds, an average of fewer than 30 per round. When one recalls that par in putting is 36, one can readily see why his ability in this area is so highly rated.

Billy's initial arrival at the pinnacle did not prove of long duration. He was confronted by several major problems. Although he was a genuine phenomenon in putting, other phases of his

MAJOR CHAMPIONSHIP VICTORIES	
1959, 1966	U.S. Open
1970	The Masters
1983	U.S. Senior Open
OTHER NOTABLE VICTORIES	
1957	Phoenix Open
1958, 1963	Bing Crosby National Pro-Am
1961, 1963, 1965, 1967, 1969, 1971, 1973, 1975	Ryder Cup Team
1962, 1964	Doral Open
1962, 1968	Greensboro Open
1964, 1968	Colonial National
1965-66, 1969, 1973	Western Open
1965, 1969	Bob Hope Classic
1967	Canadian Open
1968	Greater Hartford Open
1968, 1970	Los Angeles Open
1970	IVB-Philadelphia
1971	Kaiser International
1973	Sammy Davis, Jr.-Greater Hartford Open
1974	Lancome Trophy
1979	Ryder Cup captain
1982	Merrill Lynch/Golf Digest Commemorative Pro-Am/Senior tour
1984	Senior PGA Tour Roundup
1987	Del E. Webb Arizona Classic/Senior tour Greater Grand Rapids Open/Senior tour
1988	Mazda Senior Tournament Players Championship Vantage at the Dominion/Senior tour
1989	Transamerica Senior Golf Championship

RECORDS AND MILESTONES

Second player to reach $1 million in Official Tour earnings (1970)
PGA Tour's money leader (1966, 1968)
Won fifty-one events between 1956 and 1975, and was the money leader twice

HONORS AND AWARDS

1960, 1963, 1965-66, 1968	PGA Vardon Trophy
1966, 1968, 1970	*Golf Digest* Byron Nelson Award for Tournament Victories
1966, 1970	PGA Player of the Year
1968, 1970	GWAA Player of the Year
1971	GWAA Charlie Bartlett Award
1978	Inducted into PGA/World Golf Hall of Fame
1982	Inducted into PGA Hall of Fame

game were not as well developed. His fellow professionals frequently criticized him for his neglect of the tee-to-green part of golf. Not even Billy's near-miraculous putting would, in the long run, compensate for deficiencies elsewhere in his game.

This problem was difficult to remedy because Billy intensely disliked practice. Very unusual for a champion athlete, he was not a keen admirer of his own sport. Golf to him was a way of earning his living, not a vocation to be pursued with zest. He also suffered from an explosive temper and frequent attacks of nerves.

As if this were not enough, Billy's weight sharply increased during his first few years on the tour, and by 1964, he was more than 50 pounds overweight. He developed a number of allergies and in general became listless. It is hardly surprising that in the period from 1960 to 1963, he failed to match his United States Open triumph.

Continuing the Story

Billy showed that he had true championship quality by his manner of dealing with these problems. On the advice of a doctor, he embarked on a rigorous weight reduction program, and he soon managed to shed his excess pounds. His new diet featured unusual foods such as buffalo and elk meat, a fact that gained him much attention in the press.

Although he disliked practice, he realized its necessity and succeeded in improving his tee-to-green shotmaking. To his great delight, his skill in putting did not desert him during his period of illness and lethargy. When his acknowledged supremacy in the area was combined with his new-found physical fitness and an overall improved game, the result was readily predictable.

Once more Billy became one of golf's leading players. In 1966, he won the United States Open for a second time, defeating Arnold Palmer by 4 strokes in a play-off. For a number of years, he was at or near the top in money won, and he was a frequent tournament winner.

Billy joined the Senior PGA tour in 1981 and won the U.S. Senior Open two years later. He won his ninth senior tour victory in 1989 at the Transamerica Senior Golf Championship. Billy played in only three official events on the Senior Tour in 1999 and 2000 but made frequent appearances in Legends of Golf tournaments.

Summary

Billy Casper, like most golf champions, learned the game at an early age. Unlike most other outstanding players, his skill lay in one area—putting. He quickly became recognized as one of the greatest putters in the game, and his skill was sufficient to gain him two victories in the United States Open. After confronting serious health problems, he improved the remainder of his game and became one of the major golfers of the 1960's.

Bill Delaney

Additional Sources:

Allis, Peter. *The Who's Who of Golf*. Englewood Cliffs, N.J.: Prentice-Hall, 1983.

Casper, Billy. *Golf Shotmaking with Billy Casper*. Garden City, N.Y.: Doubleday, 1966.

_____. *The Good Sense of Golf*. Englewood Cliffs, N.J.: Prentice-Hall, 1980.

Editors of *Golf Magazine*. *Golf Magazine's Encyclopedia of Golf: The Complete Reference*. New York: HarperCollins, 1993.

Peery, Paul D. *Billy Casper, Winner*. Englewood Cliffs, N.J.: Prentice-Hall, 1969.

TRACY CAULKINS

Sport: Swimming

Born: January 11, 1963
Winona, Minnesota

Early Life

Tracy Caulkins was born in Winona, Minnesota, on January 11, 1963. Soon after, the family moved to Nashville, Tennessee, where Tracy's father, Tom, was employed by the Nashville/Metropolitan Davidson County schools and her mother, Martha, was an art teacher in the public schools. Tracy has an older brother, Tim, and an older sister, Amy. The family became involved in swimming as a competitive sport by joining the Seven Hills Swim Club, a year-round swim team.

The Road to Excellence

When Tracy was eight years old, the Westside Victory Club, where her brother and sister swam, needed some younger swimmers to compete in the "eight and under" age group. Tracy joined this group but at first would only swim the backstroke because she hated getting her face wet. That soon changed, and Tracy began to set local records. At age fourteen, she burst onto the international swimming scene by setting three new American records at the 1978 United States Women's International Swim Meet. These records were in the 200-yard breaststroke, the 200-yard individual medley, and the 400-yard individual medley. Tracy also swam on the 400-yard relay team, which set yet another record. That same year, Tracy set four individual records at the Amateur Athletic Union (AAU) National Short Course Championship and swam on the record-breaking 400-yard freestyle relay team. These AAU records were in the 100-yard breaststroke, 200-yard breaststroke, 200-yard individual medley, and 400-yard individual medley. Tracy's time of 1 minute 59.33 seconds in the 200-yard individual medley made her the first woman ever to swim this event in under 2 minutes.

Tracy Caulkins in 1991.

By the end of 1978, Tracy had set three world records at the World Aquatic Championships in Berlin and held three American records. Despite the training and travel, Tracy maintained a B-plus grade average at her high school, Harpeth Hall Academy. Because of her accomplishments, Tracy was chosen by the AAU to receive the James E. Sullivan Memorial Award as the top amateur athlete for 1978. She was the youngest person ever to win this outstanding honor. Yet Tracy was not perfect. She had been disciplined by the AAU for leaving her room after curfew at a swim meet to attend a birthday party in another swimmer's room.

430

The Emerging Champion

Before Tracy was sixteen years old, she was recognized as the top female amateur athlete in the United States. This had not been accomplished without hard work. Tracy was up by 5:00 A.M. six days a week, swam eight to ten miles a day, lifted weights three times a week, and once swam for six weeks with a broken leg in a fiberglass cast. Because she could not kick, this period gave Tracy tremendously strong arms and shoulders. Medical tests also showed that Tracy had an unusually efficient heart, which pumped oxygen-loaded blood so well that she was not out of breath at the end of her races.

As the top woman swimmer, Tracy was tremendously excited about going to Moscow to participate in the 1980 Olympics. Then international politics stepped in. The Soviet Union invaded Afghanistan, and the United States became one of the eighty nations to boycott the 1980 Olympic Games as a protest.

Although very disappointed, Tracy kept swimming and setting records. At the AAU Outdoor National Championships in 1980, when the times of the United States swimmers were compared with the women's times just set in Moscow, it was seen that the Americans would have won a great many gold medals. Yet the Olympic excitement was not there.

Continuing the Story

Usually people just graduating from high school are not considered "over the hill," but swim records are often held by people in their teens. Tracy was ready to enter the University of Florida, and the next Olympics were four long years of hard training away. Already some of her records were being lost to younger swimmers.

Yet Tracy did not give up. She continued to swim for the University of Florida and for the Nashville Aquatic Club, and she continued to win and to set records. By the end of her freshman year, she had set more swimming records than any American of either gender in history.

MAJOR CHAMPIONSHIPS

Year	Competition	Event	Place	Time
1978	World Championships	100-meter breaststroke	2d	1:10.77
		200-meter butterfly	1st	2:09.87 WR
		200-meter individual medley	1st	2:14.07 WR
		400-meter individual medley	1st	4:40.83 WR
		4×100-meter freestyle relay	1st	3:43.43
1979	Pan-American Games	400-meter freestyle	2d	4:16.13
		100-meter breaststroke	2d	1:12.52
		200-meter individual medley	1st	2:16.11 PAR
		400-meter individual medley	1st	4:46.05 PAR
		4×100-meter freestyle relay	1st	3:45.82
		4×100-meter medley relay	—	4:13.24
1981	U.S. Nationals	100-meter breaststroke	1st	1:10.77
		200-meter breaststroke	1st	2:32.48
		400-meter individual medley	1st	4:43.66
1982	World Championships	200-meter backstroke	6th	2:16.95
		200-meter individual medley	3d	2:15.91
		400-meter individual medley	3d	4:44.64
	NCAA Championships	100-yard butterfly	1st	53.91
		200-yard butterfly	1st	1:57.23
		100-yard individual medley	1st	55.74
		200-yard individual medley	1st	2:00.77
		400-yard individual medley	1st	4:12.64
		400-yard medley relay	1st	3:40.99
	U.S. Nationals	100-meter breaststroke	2d	1:11.62
		200-meter backstroke	1st	2:15.53
		200-meter individual medley	1st	2:15.66
		400-meter individual medley	1st	4:44.26
1983	Pan-American Games	100-meter breaststroke	4th	1:12.51
		200-meter butterfly	2d	2:14.15
		200-meter individual medley	1st	2:16.22
		400-meter individual medley	1st	4:51.22
	NCAA Championships	100-yard individual medley	1st	56.09
		200-yard individual medley	1st	2:00.34
		400-yard individual medley	1st	4:15.24
		400-yard medley relay	1st	3:43.00
	U.S. Nationals	100-meter breaststroke	2d	1:11.78
		200-meter butterfly	2d	2:11.57
		200-meter individual medley	1st	2:15.27
		400-meter individual medley	1st	4:45.71
1984	Olympic Games	200-meter individual medley	Gold	2:12.64 OR, NR
		400-meter individual medley	Gold	4:39.24
		400-meter medley relay	Gold	4:08.34
	NCAA Championships	100-yard breaststroke	1st	1:01.37
		200-yard butterfly	1st	1:55.55
		200-yard individual medley	1st	1:57.06
		400-yard individual medley	1st	4:08.37
		400-yard freestyle relay	1st	3:18.52
		800-yard freestyle relay	1st	7:06.98

Notes: OR = Olympic Record; WR = World Record; NR = National Record; PAR = Pan-American Record

At last it was 1984 and the Summer Olympic Games were to be held in Los Angeles. This time the Soviet Union led a boycott by Communist nations, so again some of the top women swimmers were not present. Tracy had qualified to swim three individual events and one relay event. Because of her ability and leadership, Tracy was made one of the captains of the United States swimmers for the Olympics.

In Los Angeles, Tracy's first event was the 400-meter individual medley, which she won by an astounding fifteen meters. Two days later, Tracy ended her competitive swimming career by winning the 200-meter individual medley and setting a new Olympic record, and then by helping the United States team win the 400-meter medley relay event.

The honors and recognition did not stop with the Olympics. United States Swimming, the directing body for the sport of swimming, named Tracy the 1984 Swimmer of the Year. The United States Olympic Committee named her Top Sportswoman of the Year, and, later, she was named to the Women's Sports Hall of Fame and the United States Olympic Hall of Fame.

Although various businesses were reputed to have offered Tracy up to $500,000 to make commercials endorsing their products, Tracy went back to the University of Florida, where she was graduated with honors in communications.

Since college graduation, Tracy has worked as a sports commentator and in public relations. She planned to marry Mike Stockwell of Australia, another swimmer. The Olympic Competition Pool at the Nashville Sportsplex is named for Tracy Caulkins. She was named the "Swimmer of the Decade" by *USA Today*.

Summary

Although both the 1980 and the 1984 Olympic Games were marred by boycotts, Tracy Caulkins has shown that champions can overcome obstacles in more areas than those in sports. Her ability as an athlete and her quiet, unassuming personality made Tracy not only the top record holder of either gender in United States swimming, but also a role model in every aspect of life.

Michael R. Bradley

Additional Sources:

Hickok, Ralph. *A Who's Who of Sports Champions.* Boston: Houghton Mifflin, 1995.

Levinson, David, and Karen Christenson, eds. *Encyclopedia of World Sport: From Ancient Times to Present.* Santa Barbara, Calif: ABC-CLIO, 1996.

Mallon, Bill, and Ian Buchanan. *Quest for Gold: The Encyclopedia of American Olympians.* New York: Leisure Press, 1984.

Wallechinsky, David. *The Complete Book of the Olympics.* Boston: Little, Brown and Company, 1991.

RECORDS

Won forty-eight national titles
Broke national records sixty times
United States record-holder in fourteen individual events

HONORS AND AWARDS

1977-79	Robert J. H. Kiphuth Award, Long Course Robert J. H. Kiphuth Award, Short Course
1978	Sullivan Award
1980	Robert J. H. Kiphuth Award, Indoors and Outdoors
1981	Women's Sports Foundation Amateur Sportswoman of the Year
1981-82, 1983-84	Honda Broderick Cup
1984	U.S. Swimming Swimmer of the Year Tri-Captain of the U.S. Olympic Swimming Team Southeast Conference Athlete of the Year U.S. Olympic Committee Top Sportswoman of the Year
1987	Inducted into Sudafed International Women's Sports Hall of Fame Inducted into Women's Sports Hall of Fame
1990	Inducted into International Swimming Hall of Fame Inducted into U.S. Olympic Hall of Fame

WILT CHAMBERLAIN

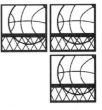

Sport: Basketball

Born: August 21, 1936
      Philadelphia, Pennsylvania
Died: October 12, 1999
      Bel-Air, California

Early Life

Wilton Norman Chamberlain was born on August 21, 1936, in Philadelphia, Pennsylvania. He was one of nine children of William and Olivia Chamberlain. His father worked as a handyman and his mother as a domestic worker. Wilt grew to dwarf his 5-foot 8-inch father and reached the height of 6 feet 10 inches by the age of fifteen. Even at that early age, he attracted considerable attention when he played basketball in junior high school. At Philadelphia's Overbrook High School, Wilt averaged 36.3 points per game over a three-year period. He also played during the summers at a resort in the Catskill Mountains of New York and competed in track and field events. In basketball, he scored 2,252 points in three years, including 90 points in one game. Overbrook was 58-3 and won two city championships. After his senior year, Wilt was drafted by the Philadelphia Warriors of the National Basketball Association (NBA).

The Road to Excellence

When Wilt graduated, he received more than two hundred offers for scholarships from colleges. He finally settled on the University of Kansas, under the legendary coach Forrest C. "Phog" Allen. Again Wilt participated in track as well as in basketball. As a sophomore at Kansas, Wilt opened his collegiate career on December 3, 1956, scoring 52 points against

Philadelphia 76er Wilt Chamberlain makes a shot in 1967.

Northwestern. He used his famed one-hand and two-hand dunk shots as well as short-range right-hand fade-away jumpers. The crowd of more than 17,000 went wild at Allen Fieldhouse.

Wilt earned seven All-American first-team

433

STATISTICS

Season	GP	FGM	FG%	FTM	FT%	Reb.	Ast.	TP	PPG
1959-60	72	1,065	.461	577	.582	**1,941**	168	2,707	37.6
1960-61	79	1,251	**.509**	531	.504	**2,149**	148	**3,033**	38.4
1961-62	80	1,597	.505	835	.613	**2,052**	192	**4,029**	50.4
1962-63	80	1,463	**.528**	660	.593	**1,946**	275	**3,586**	44.8
1963-64	80	1,204	.524	540	.531	1,787	403	**2,948**	36.9
1964-65	73	1,063	**.510**	408	.464	1,673	250	**2,534**	34.7
1965-66	79	1,074	**.540**	501	.513	**1,943**	414	**2,649**	33.5
1966-67	81	785	**.683**	386	.441	**1,957**	630	1,956	24.1
1967-68	82	819	**.595**	354	.380	**1,952**	702	1,992	24.3
1968-69	81	641	**.583**	382	.466	**1,712**	366	1,664	20.5
1969-70	12	129	.568	70	.446	221	49	328	27.3
1970-71	82	668	.545	360	.538	1,493	352	1,696	20.7
1971-72	82	496	**.649**	221	.422	1,572	329	1,213	14.8
1972-73	82	426	**.727**	232	.510	1,526	365	1,084	13.2
Totals	1,045	12,681	.540	6,057	.511	23,924	4,643	31,419	30.1

Notes: Boldface indicates statistical leader. GP = games played; FGM = field goals made; FG% = field goal percentage; FTM = free throws made; FT% = free throw percentage; Reb. = rebounds; Ast. = assists; TP = total points; PPG = points per game

berths as a sophomore. Kansas lost to the University of North Carolina, led by Lennie Rosenbluth, in a triple-overtime game, 53-52, for the 1957 National Collegiate Athletic Association (NCAA) Championship, played at Kansas City. Wilt played at Kansas through his junior year, when he signed for a year of basketball with the Harlem Globetrotters. He also won the Big Eight Outdoor High Jump crown at 6 feet 5 inches, and tied for first place at the Drake Relays with a jump of 6 feet 6½ inches in the spring of 1957.

Wilt was the most dominant player in college basketball history. He was dubbed "Wilt the Stilt," a name he disliked; he preferred being called "The Big Dipper." His presence changed the sport, and several rule changes were made in order to negate his overwhelming abilities.

The Emerging Champion

Wilt signed with the Philadelphia Warriors and played his first year as a professional in 1960, a year in which he was named NBA Rookie of the Year and also most valuable player. He possessed amazing power, coordination and stamina, and an unexpected grace that once led Red Auerbach, the Boston Celtics coach, to comment that the first time he saw Wilt he "just stood and watched him walk. Just watched him walk. It was incredible."

On March 2, 1962, in Hershey, Pennsylvania, Wilt scored 100 points in an NBA game against the New York Knicks. It was a remarkable feat: From the time of Wilt's effort through the 1990-1991 season, no two members of an NBA team had combined for 100 points in one game. Wilt's mark remains an almost unbelievable achievement for a single player.

In his 100-point game, Wilt had 25 rebounds, and his league-leading average that season for eighty games was 25.7. In comparison, Bill Walton of the Portland Trailblazers led the NBA in 1976-1977 with a 14.4 average. Yet it was in scoring that Wilt reached a peak that has never been approached. In the 1961-1962 season, he averaged 50.4 points per game. His dominance of the game during a career that lasted from 1959 through 1973 can best be understood by these comparisons: In the history of the NBA to that time, there were seven 70-point-plus performances, and Wilt made six of them. (Elgin Baylor made the other, a 71-point performance.) Of the forty-one 60-point-plus performances, thirty-two were achieved by Wilt and nine by others: four by Baylor, and one each by Rick Barry, Joe Fulks, Pete Maravich, Jerry West, and George Mikan.

Continuing the Story

Basketball styles and times have changed, but Wilt's dominance of the game is reflected when his statistics are compared with those of his contemporaries. When one player accounts for

434

more than 75 percent of all of the highest-scoring performances in thirty-three years, his accomplishments cannot be described as anything other than awesome. Before he retired, Wilt scored 31,419 points and grabbed 23,924 rebounds, both league records at the time.

In 1972, he led the Los Angeles Lakers to their first NBA championship. A year later, he left the Lakers and coached the San Diego Conquistadores of the American Basketball Association (ABA), which triggered a lengthy contract dispute. In February, 1979, Wilt was named to the Naismith Memorial Basketball Hall of Fame in his first year of eligibility.

After leaving the NBA, Wilt pursued a number of different interests. He played professional volleyball and sponsored a women's track team. He made many television commercials and played a role in the 1984 film *Conan the Destroyer.* In later

years, the Cleveland Cavaliers publicly confirmed that they were attempting to lure Wilt out of retirement. In 1978, there were rumors that he was considering signing to play with the Chicago Bulls, and he reportedly also held discussions with the Phoenix Suns. In the late 1970's, he even seriously considered challenging Muhammad Ali for the heavyweight boxing championship but later abandoned the idea.

Wilt wrote four books, including *A View from Above* (1992) and *Who's Running the Asylum: The Insane World of Sports Today* (1998). His writings range from recollections of his playing career to his opinions on sports, politics, and social issues in the 1990's. Large portions of the proceeds from the sale of his books were donated to Operation Smile to help provide health care for needy children. For many years, he sponsored the Wilt Chamberlain Rising Star Shootout Tournament in Florida to provide an environment where young basketball players could compete and showcase their skills.

Wilt made a fortune in the restaurant business, designed homes, owned race horses, sponsored youth track and volleyball teams, and developed land in countries all over the world. In 1996, Wilt was named to the NBA's 50 Greatest Players of All Time Team. In 1999, he was named as one of the twenty best NBA players of all time. He died of heart failure on October 12, 1999, at his home in Bel-Air, California.

Summary

Wilt Chamberlain's achievements on the basketball court are legendary and border on the mythical. Many NBA players, coaches, and experts say that Wilt was the strongest man and best athlete to ever play the game. His ferocious battles with Bill Russell of the Boston Celtics will remain engraved forever in NBA history. Wilt singularly dominated the game like no other NBA player

---

NBA RECORDS

Most rebounds, 23,924
Highest average in rebounds per game, 22.9
Most points in a season, 4,029
Highest scoring average in a season, 50.4
Most rebounds in a season, 2,149
Highest single-season average in rebounds per game, 27.2 (1960-61)
Highest field goal percentage in a season, .727
Most points in a game, 100 (1962)
Most field goals in a game, 36 (1962)
Most free throws made in a game, 28 (1962)
Most rebounds in a game, 55 (1960)

HONORS AND AWARDS

1957	NCAA Tournament Most Outstanding Player NCAA All-Tournament Team
1957-58	Consensus All-American
1960	NBA Rookie of the Year NBA All-Star Game most valuable player
1960-68, 1972	All-NBA Team
1960-69, 1971-73	NBA All-Star Team
1960, 1966-68	NBA most valuable player
1972	NBA Finals most valuable player
1972-73	NBA All-Defensive Team
1978	Inducted into Naismith Memorial Basketball Hall of Fame
1980	NBA 35th Anniversary All Time Team
1996	NBA 50 Greatest Players of All Time Team
1999	Named one of the twenty best NBA players of all time Uniform number 13 retired by Los Angeles Lakers

ever had. He was particularly proud of being the only non-guard to win an NBA assist title (1967-1968). When Wilt announced his retirement in 1972, Bob Cousy was reported to have remarked with relief that the NBA could then "go back to playing basketball."

Arthur F. McClure

Additional Sources:

Chamberlain, Wilt. *A View from Above*. New York: Dutton Books, 1992.

Frankl, Ron. *Wilt Chamberlain*. Broomall, Pa.: Chelsea House, 1994.

Kramer, Sydelle. *Basketball's Greatest Players*. New York: Random House, 1997.

Mallozzi, Vincent M. *Basketball: The Legends and the Game*. Willowdale, Ont.: Firefly Books, 1998.

FRANK CHANCE

Sport: Baseball

Born: September 9, 1877
Fresno, California
Died: September 14, 1924
Los Angeles, California

Early Life

Frank Leroy Chance was born into an affluent California family on September 9, 1877. His father, a bank president, sent him to Washington College in Irvington, California, to study medicine. There, starring as a catcher on the school baseball team, Frank was spotted by Bill Lange, who was nearing the end of a short but spectacular career as a major leaguer, and who persuaded Frank to leave college after two years and try his luck with a semiprofessional baseball team in Illinois. The tryout was successful, and the next year, 1898, found him reporting to Lange's team, the Chicago Cubs.

The Road to Excellence

Ruggedly handsome and large for his day at more than 6 feet tall and weighing close to 200 pounds, "Husk" (short for Husky) Chance spent his first five seasons in Chicago as a substitute catcher and outfielder. A promising right-handed hitter and a surprisingly agile base runner, he appeared by big league standards to be awkward behind the plate and clumsy out by the fences. In 1902, a new manager, Frank Selee, ordered Frank, over his protests, to play first base.

By the following season, he was a star at that position, quickly becoming a graceful fielder, batting .327, .310, .316, and .319 over a four-year period, and twice during that time leading the National League in stolen bases and once in runs scored.

Although he had the physical strength to be a power hitter, Frank preferred to hold a long, thin bat well up on the handle and hit line drives with a compact swing. Fearlessly crowding the plate,

he was hit by pitched balls thirty-six times, on many occasions in the head, resulting in a complete hearing loss in his left ear and, ultimately, in a serious brain operation. During one double-header, he was "plugged" five times by opposing pitchers, coming away with a black eye and a badly bruised forehead.

The Emerging Champion

When Selee became ill and was forced to resign as the Cubs' manager late in 1905, Frank took over the job at the age of twenty-seven. During the next five years, he became known as the "Peerless Leader," as he exhorted, threatened,

437

and cajoled his teammates, including future Hall-of-Famers Johnny Evers, Joe Tinker, and Mordecai Brown, to two world championships, four pennants, and an overall seasonal record of 116 wins and only 47 losses for a percentage of .693, a record unmatched by any other team in major league history.

With a .296 lifetime batting average and more than 40 stolen bases per season in his prime, Frank was also a dependable fielder and clever strategist. His players, many of them of German immigrant background, although generally heavy drinkers and brawlers with each other as well as with players on other teams, never disputed his authority and admired his leadership by example. Evers called him "the greatest first baseman of all time," and Tinker asserted that "Husk was always square . . . and smart." Brown admired him for his "stout heart" and keen mind.

Continuing the Story

In 1909, a broken shoulder limited Frank's playing time to ninety-three games. The following year, while managing the Cubs to another league championship, he appeared as a player in only eighty-eight regular season contests, although he hit .353 in the World Series that fall. Early in 1911, he badly fractured his ankle, an in-

jury that ended his playing career. Despite the loss of four of the eight position players from his 1910 pennant winners, Frank's 1911 club still finished second, only seven games behind John McGraw's New York Giants. In 1912, however, the Cubs could do no better than third place, and Frank, who quarreled with the team's owners over his relatively low salary, which was only about one-half of McGraw's, was dismissed from the team.

Signed to manage the New York Yankees at a salary two and one-half times more than the Cubs had paid him, Frank had his authority with the Yankee players undermined by the brilliant but dishonest Hal Chase, who had successfully purged three managers before Frank. Protesting that "Chase is throwing games on me," Frank finally persuaded the reluctant team owners to trade Chase to the White Sox, but Frank himself only lasted in New York through the 1914 season. Frequently incapacitated by severe headaches, probably resulting from the many "beanings" of his earlier years, and frustrated by the lack of home-team talent at the Hilltop Park on Washington Heights, Frank resigned to return to California and his investments in orange groves.

Feeling better in 1915, he managed the Los Angeles team to a Pacific Coast League title, but

STATISTICS

Season	GP	AB	Hits	2B	3B	HR	Runs	RBI	BA	SA
1898	53	147	41	4	3	1	32	14	.279	.367
1899	64	192	55	6	2	1	37	22	.286	.354
1900	56	149	44	9	3	0	26	13	.295	.396
1901	69	241	67	12	4	0	38	36	.278	.361
1902	75	236	67	9	4	1	40	31	.284	.369
1903	125	441	144	24	10	2	83	81	.327	.440
1904	124	451	140	16	10	6	89	49	.310	.430
1905	118	392	124	16	12	2	92	70	.316	.434
1906	136	474	151	24	10	3	**103**	71	.319	.430
1907	111	382	112	19	2	1	58	49	.293	.361
1908	129	452	123	27	4	2	65	55	.272	.363
1909	93	324	88	16	4	0	53	46	.272	.346
1910	88	295	88	12	8	0	54	36	.298	.393
1911	31	88	21	6	3	1	23	17	.239	.409
1912	2	5	1	0	0	0	2	0	.200	.200
1913	11	24	5	0	0	0	3	6	.208	.208
1914	1	0	0	0	0	0	0	0	—	—
Totals	1,285	4,294	1,272	199	79	20	797	596	.296	.393

Notes: Boldface indicates statistical leader. GP = games played; AB = at bats; 2B = doubles; 3B = triples; HR = home runs; RBI = runs batted in; BA = batting average; SA = slugging average

when he tried to make a major league comeback managing the 1924 White Sox, he was forced by ill health to resign the position before the season even began. He died on September 14, 1924, in Los Angeles, at a relatively young forty-seven. He left behind his wife, Edith, the only person to whom he had ever been really close.

Summary

In the 1923 edition of his memoir, *My Thirty Years in Baseball*, the formidable John McGraw placed Frank Chance at first base on his all-time National League team. "Frank Chance," declared the old New York Giant manager, "knew baseball from A to Z." Moreover, the "Peerless Leader" could always be relied upon to make key plays in important games, "as a hitter, a fielder and a baserunner." No greater praise could have been bestowed upon "Husk" than these expressions of admiration from his longtime rival, whose teams fought Frank's Cubs, with fists as well as with skilled play, for league domination for more than a decade. As Joe Tinker testified in his reminiscences, "Chance and McGraw were

HONORS AND AWARDS
1946   Inducted into National Baseball Hall of Fame

born to battle on baseball fields. If you didn't honestly and furiously hate the Giants, you weren't a real Cub." Frank, a true "gray-eyed man of destiny," was called by the eminent sports columnist Dan Daniel "the greatest Cub of all time."

Norman B. Ferris

Additional Sources:

Appel, Martin, and Burt Goldblatt. *Baseball's Best: The Hall of Fame Gallery.* New York: McGraw-Hill, 1977.

Hickok, Ralph. *A Who's Who of Sports Champions.* Boston: Houghton Mifflin, 1995.

Porter, David L., ed. *Biographical Dictionary of American Sports: Baseball.* Westport, Conn.: Greenwood Press, 1987.

Shatzkin, Mike, et al., eds. *The Ballplayers: Baseball's Ultimate Biographical Reference.* New York: William Morrow, 1990.

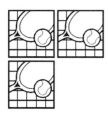

MICHAEL CHANG

Sport: Tennis

Born: February 22, 1972
      Hoboken, New Jersey

Early Life

Michael Chang was born to Joe and Betty Chang in Hoboken, New Jersey, on February 22, 1972, the younger of two tennis-playing brothers. It was Michael, however, who rose to tennis prominence.

His parents—both research chemists who met on a blind date in New York City in 1966—had a strong work ethic, which they instilled in both sons. Joe Chang taught himself tennis in 1974 and introduced the boys to the game. The Changs decided to relocate the family from New Jersey to St. Paul, Minnesota, in 1977, where the brothers quickly began defeating the local competition.

By the time the family moved to San Diego a few years later, Carl and Michael had developed reputations for being great tennis competitors. Dubbed "The Chang Gang," the brothers beat most of their age-group competition near their home in Placentia, California.

The Road to Excellence

Michael's movement on the court and tireless work ethic allowed him to compensate for his diminutive size. By the time he was ten years old, he had grown to 5 feet 7 inches tall, only 2 inches shorter than he would reach in adulthood. Most of the world's greatest tennis players have been taller.

By age fifteen, he had made a name for himself in the junior ranks by beating future American champions Pete Sampras and Jim Courier. In 1987, Michael became the youngest player since 1918 to win a main draw match at the U.S. Open (beating Paul McNamee in the first round) and the youngest to reach a tour semifinal.

The Emerging Champion

All eyes, however, turned to Michael when he entered the 1989 French Open as an unknown seventeen-year-old and si-

Michael Chang playing the first round of the Australian Open in 1999.

AP/Wide World Photos

440

lenced the naysayers who believed his size would hinder him from becoming a tennis champion. No American man had won the prestigious Grand Slam event since Tony Trabert in 1955, and Michael—ranked nineteenth in the world entering the tournament—was not the player most picked to end the losing streak.

With uncharacteristic grit and steely concentration, Michael bested his competition to set up a dramatic match against top-ranked Ivan Lendl in the Round of 16. In a marathon match that lasted more than three hours and had the crowd on its feet, Michael dove to the ground for balls, pumped his fists with each point won, and played through severe leg cramps in the fifth set to defeat Lendl 4-6, 4-6, 6-3, 6-3, 6-3, a match that Michael reportedly called the greatest of his career.

He went on to capture the French Open title, ending a thirty-four-year drought for the Americans in the tournament and catapulting Michael into the international spotlight. With his victory, Michael also became the first Asian American to win a Grand Slam tennis title. From 1989 until 1998, Michael compiled a 541-198 record, but has yet to duplicate the fantastic run he made in Paris.

Continuing the Story

During his career, Michael has earned nearly $20 million in prize money and has won thirty-three singles titles. Although the French Open was his greatest Grand Slam achievement, Michael has remained competitive. In 1994, he reached the quarterfinals of Wimbledon and in 1995 reached the quarterfinals of the U.S. Open. His best results outside of the French Open came in 1996, when he reached the finals of both the Australian Open and the U.S. Open. A year later, Michael reached the semifinals of the U.S. Open, only to lose in straight sets to eventual champion Patrick Rafter, a loss that was hard to swallow since Michael was ranked a career-high number two in the world that year and American rivals Sampras and Andre Agassi had already been knocked out of the tournament.

Michael, who has a career record of 609-247, remains competitive but has not been past the third round in a Grand Slam event since that 1997 loss to Rafter. In 1998, Michael suffered injuries to his left knee and right wrist that further

MAJOR CHAMPIONSHIPS	
1988	San Francisco
1989	French Open
	London Indoor
1990	Toronto
1991	Birmingham
1992	San Francisco
	Indian Wells
	Key Biscayne
1993	Jakarta
	Osaka
	Cincinnati
	Kuala Lumpur
	Beijing
1994	Jakarta
	Philadelphia
	Hong Kong
	Atlanta
	Cincinnati
	Beijing
1995	Hong Kong
	Tokyo Indoor
	Atlanta
	Beijing
1996	Indian Wells
	Washington
	Los Angeles
1997	Memphis
	Hong Kong
	Indian Wells
	Orlando
	Washington
1998	Boston
	Shanghai
2000	Los Angeles

knocked him back from his usual competitive results on the tour. In 1999 he fell to number fifty in the rankings.

Summary

Coached by brother Carl since 1991, Michael has traveled the tennis circuit with the same entourage that has been with him his entire life. His parents can often be seen in the players' box rooting him on, and Michael continues to work on his game and continues to enter tournaments. A devout Christian and bachelor, Michael often credits his faith and love of his family with helping him to overcome the hardships he has faced during his tennis career.

After losing in the first round of the 2000 Australian Open and failing to get past the Round of 16 at the French Open, Michael skipped Wimbledon for the first time in his career for undisclosed reasons, but was expected to play in the U.S. Open.

A. K. Ruffin

Additional Sources:

Collins, Bud, and Zander Hollander, eds. *Bud Collins' Modern Encyclopedia of Tennis.* 2d ed. Detroit: Visible Ink Press, 1994.

Dell, Pamela. *Michael Chang: Tennis Champion.* Chicago: Children's Press, 1992.

Dichfield, Christin. *Sports Great Michael Chang.* Springfield, N.J.: Enslow, 1999.

OSCAR CHARLESTON

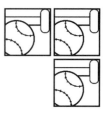

Sport: Baseball

Born: October 14, 1896
    Indianapolis, Indiana
Died: October 6, 1954
    Philadelphia, Pennsylvania

Early Life

Oscar McKinley Charleston was born on October 14, 1896, to Tom Charleston, a construction worker, and Mary (Thomas) Charleston, a homemaker. The seventh of eleven children, Oscar grew up playing baseball with his neighborhood friends. Tossing newspapers each day to his regular customers helped to develop his throwing arm; as a youth, Oscar also worked as a bat boy for the local black professional baseball team, the Indianapolis ABCs, and sometimes practiced with the club. Oscar attended Indianapolis public schools until age fifteen, when he ran away from home and joined the U.S. Army. While he was serving as a member of the all-black Twenty-fourth Infantry stationed in the Philippines, his natural athletic ability began to blossom.

The Road to Excellence

During his stint in the Philippines, Oscar excelled in both track and baseball. The underage soldier ran the 220-yard dash in 23 seconds and the120-yard high hurdles in 15.1 seconds, both excellent times for the era. As a baseball player, he was the only African American to play in the Manila League. At the time, black players were not allowed to play professional baseball for major league teams, so after his discharge from the Army in 1915, Oscar joined the Indianapolis ABCs of the National Negro League.

The Emerging Champion

The 6-foot 1-inch, 185-pound rookie quickly won a spot as the ABCs' starting center fielder. During the next two seasons, the left-handed hitting and throwing newcomer played an impor-

tant role for Indianapolis and helped the ABCs to defeat the Chicago American Giants in the 1916 Black World Series. Players in the Negro Leagues frequently shifted teams, and from 1918 to 1923, Oscar played for five different clubs. Although statistics for Negro League baseball are sketchy and unreliable, it is clear that Oscar compiled a very impressive record. In 1921, for example, he led the Negro National League (whose teams played about fifty games that year) in hitting (.446), triples (10), home runs (14), slugging percentage (.774), and stolen bases (28). From 1924 to 1927, he starred for the Harrisburg Giants of the Eastern Colored League, batting .411 in 1924 and .445 in 1925. In 1928 and 1929, he played for the Philadelphia Hilldales of the American Negro League, and he won the batting championship in 1929 with a .396 average. Throughout the 1920's, Oscar also played winter baseball in Cuba, hitting better than .400 three times.

During 1930 and 1931, Oscar was a member of the Homestead Grays team that included Josh Gibson, Ted Page, and Smoky Joe Williams. By this time, his weight had risen to 230 pounds, and he had moved from center field to first base. From 1932 to 1938, Oscar managed and played with the legendary Pittsburgh Crawfords, often considered the best Negro League team ever assembled. In addition to Charleston and Gibson, the squad also included legendary stars Satchel Paige, Judy Johnson, and James "Cool Papa" Bell. In 1932, the team compiled a 99-36 record, and Oscar batted .363 and hit 19 triples. For the next four years, the Crawfords dominated the tough Negro National Association. From 1939 until his death in 1954, Oscar managed various black teams, including the Philadelphia Stars and the Indianapolis Clowns, who he led to a Negro Leagues world championship in 1954. As the manager of the Brooklyn Brown Dodgers of the

443

United States League formed by Branch Rickey in 1945, he helped to scout, evaluate, and sign black players (including Roy Campanella) as part of Rickey's effort to integrate the major leagues.

Continuing the Story

Oscar was one of the most versatile players in baseball history. His blazing speed enabled him to play a very shallow center field and to often lead various leagues in stolen bases. Legendary black pitcher Satchel Paige insisted that Oscar, in his prime, could "outrun the ball." A born showman, Oscar would sometimes meander after a fly ball and make an acrobatic catch at the last second or even turn a somersault before snagging a routine fly. Teammates and opponents told many stories about his "miraculous" catches. As a publicity stunt, Oscar occasionally played all nine positions in a single game.

Oscar was more than a mere showman, however; he was part of a select group of players who could hit for a high average while driving the ball with power to all fields. Oscar's natural ability, excellent instincts, knowledge of the game, and competitive spirit all contributed to his greatness. His many accomplishments include an estimated .376 lifetime batting average in various Negro Leagues, a .361 mark for his nine seasons in the Cuban winter league (where he faced many top pitchers, both black and white, from the United States), and a .326 average in exhibition games against white major leaguers. He reputedly averaged 30 home runs a season in the Negro Leagues, and he hit 4 homers in a single exhibition game against the St. Louis Cardinals in 1921, two of them against Hall of Fame pitcher Jesse Gaines.

Oscar was often called the "black Babe Ruth" because of his home-run power, physique, personal popularity, and love of both life and baseball. Other sportswriters labeled him the "black Ty Cobb" because of his high batting averages, his base-stealing ability, and his habit of sliding hard with his spikes up high. His range and judgment in playing center field reminded many of major league defensive great Tris Speaker (at the time, only Speaker played as close to second base as Oscar did). Like Cobb, Oscar lost his temper quickly and participated in many fights. He fre-

HONORS AND AWARDS

1976	Inducted into National Baseball Hall of Fame

quently brawled with umpires, opponents, agents who tried to steal his players, and even a Ku Klux Klansman and several Cuban soldiers. Oscar died of a heart attack in Philadelphia on October 6, 1954, and was buried in Indianapolis.

Summary

Judged by many to be the greatest Negro League player of all time, Oscar was elected to the National Baseball Hall of Fame in 1976. A fierce competitor and a superb clutch hitter, Oscar was tremendously popular with black fans. One jour-nalist of the time wrote that Oscar was to thousands of black teenagers what Babe Ruth was to white children. Both New York Giants manager John McGraw and sportswriter Grantland Rice reportedly called the multitalented lefty the best all-around baseball player ever.

Gary Scott Smith

Additional Sources:

Porter, David L., ed. *African American Sports Greats: A Biographical Dictionary.* Westport, Conn.: Greenwood Press, 1995.

_____. *Biographical Dictionary of American Sports: Baseball.* Westport, Conn.: Greenwood Press, 1987.

Riley, James A. *The Biographical Encyclopedia of the Negro Baseball Leagues.* New York: Carroll & Graf, 1994.

BOBBY CHARLTON

Sport: Soccer

Born: October 11, 1937
Ashington, Northumberland, England

Early Life

Robert "Bobby" Charlton was born in Ashington, a bleak mining village in northeast England, on October 11, 1937. His father was a miner. Soccer had run in the family for four generations. Bobby's great-grandfather had six sons and five daughters, and they all played soccer. Bobby's uncle was Jackie Milburn, a famous Newcastle United and England star, and four of his other uncles played professionally for Football League clubs. Bobby's mother, Elizabeth, loved soccer and encouraged Bobby and his elder brother Jack (who also became a star player) in their early efforts. She even coached Bobby herself and managed to improve his sprinting ability.

Bobby's soccer skills came naturally to him, though. Even as a thin nine-year-old he was easily able to weave his way past boys five years his senior. He was soon captain of his high school soccer team.

The Road to Excellence

At high school, Bobby owed a great deal to the encouragement he received from his sports master, Norman McGuiness. McGuiness later commented that Bobby was so naturally talented he needed little coaching, and McGuiness was determined that he should play for the England schoolboy team.

This dream came true in 1953, when Bobby played for England in a schoolboys' international. He scored 2 goals.

Bobby was also indebted to Stuart Hemingway, the headmaster of Bedlington Grammar School, which Bobby began attending when he was eleven. Impressed by Bobby's potential,

Bobby Charlton before a match in 1965.

446

HONORS AND AWARDS

1957, 1965, 1967	English League champion
1963	English Football Association Cup champion
1966	World Cup champion European Player of the Year (Ballon d'Or) English Footballer of the Year
1968	European Cup champion
1969	Order of the British Empire
1974	English Professional Football Association Merit Award Commander of the British Empire
1994	Knighted by Queen Elizabeth II
2000	Inducted into first class of International Football Hall of Fame

MILESTONES

106 international appearances for England
49 international goals (English record)

Hemingway wrote to Matt Busby, the manager of Manchester United, one of the most famous soccer clubs in the land. Bobby was fifteen years old at the time, and no less than eighteen professional soccer clubs were interested in signing him. His brother Jack had already joined Leeds United. Bobby, however, chose Manchester United, and he left Ashington for Manchester in July, 1953. Two years later he signed as a professional. Joe Armstrong, Manchester United's chief coach, predicted that Bobby would play for England before he was twenty-one.

Bobby made his first appearance for the Manchester United first team against Arsenal in 1956. He had just celebrated his nineteenth birthday. More celebrations followed when Bobby scored 2 goals in United's victory. During his first season of top-class soccer, Bobby scored 10 goals in fourteen games, and he was considered to be a player to watch.

The Emerging Champion

In the mid-1950's, Matt Busby was developing a fine group of young players, and it looked as if Manchester United would become one of the great teams in English soccer history. They were known as the "Busby Babes," and Bobby Charlton was one of them.

Then tragedy struck in February, 1958. Manchester United was returning from a European match when their plane crashed on a runway at Munich, West Germany. Eight players were killed, but Bobby escaped with only minor injuries.

When he returned to the rebuilt team in March, Bobby was no longer a junior player. Even though he was only twenty, he was able to carry great responsibility, and his explosive shooting power won many games for his team. He also fulfilled Armstrong's prediction that he would play for England before he was twenty-one, scoring a brilliant goal in England's 4-0 victory over Scotland.

In spite of this success, Bobby was passed over for the England team that played in Sweden in the World Cup tournament of 1958. Although everyone agreed that Bobby was a soccer genius, his critics said that he was erratic and did not work hard enough. By the following year, however, he had forced his way back onto the England team. Bobby was by then playing at outside-left rather than inside-forward, and his speed and powerful shot, with either foot, could be devastating. He was one of England's outstanding players in the 1962 World Cup in Chile.

Continuing the Story

When Sir Alf Ramsey became the England team manager in 1962, he decided to build the England team around Bobby. Developing a new tactical formation that virtually eliminated wingers, Ramsey played Bobby as a deep-lying center-forward.

From this position, Bobby was able to utilize his newly developed passing abilities. He specialized in long, sweeping crossfield passes that could alter the pace and direction of a game. In addition, he was always dangerous when he set off on a powerful run from a deep position. Often he would cover 20 or 30 yards before unleashing an unstoppable shot from the edge of the penalty area. His game became far more consistent than before, and he rarely had a bad match. He also won a reputation for sportsmanship—he would never lose his temper or argue with referees.

Bobby's greatest moments came in 1966, when England won the World Cup. He scored a

447

typically spectacular goal against Mexico, and two more against Portugal in the semifinals. After England's success, Bobby was probably the most popular player in the country, and he was greatly admired all over the world. Along with Denis Law and George Best, he was part of the brilliant Manchester United forward line of the mid- and late 1960's, which helped Manchester to win the Football League championship twice. He was captain of the Manchester United team from 1968 to 1973.

Another great moment came in 1968. Bobby scored 2 goals in the European Cup final, steering Manchester United to a 4-1 victory over the Portuguese team, Benfica.

Bobby made 106 appearances for England in all, and scored 49 international goals, an English record. In 1969, in recognition of his services to soccer, he was awarded the Order of the British Empire (OBE), and in 1974 he received the Commander of the British Empire (CBE) award. In 1994 Bobby was knighted by Queen Elizabeth II.

Bobby finished his career as player-manager for Preston North End. He later became a director of Manchester United and organized schools for the training of young players.

Summary

Bobby Charlton was one of those rare players who could win a game in a few moments of supreme skill. His exciting style of play made the crowds roar with anticipation whenever he received the ball. When the film of the 1966 World Cup finals was released in England, Bobby's magnificent goal against Mexico would still bring audiences to their feet, even though everyone knew it was coming. Bobby's unflappable temperament and his loyalty to his club made him a great ambassador for the game.

Bryan Aubrey

Additional Sources:

Charlton, Bobby. *This Game of Soccer.* London: Cassell, 1967.

Charlton, Bobby, with Ken Jones. *Bobby Charlton's Most Memorable Matches.* London: St. Paul, 1984.

Henshaw, Richard. *The Encyclopedia of World Soccer.* Washington, D.C.: New Republic Books, 1979.

Hollander, Zander. *The American Encyclopedia of Soccer.* New York: Everett House, 1980.

Wilner, Barry. *Soccer.* Austin, Tex.: Raintree Steck-Vaughn, 1994.

JACK CHARLTON

Sport: Soccer

Born: May 8, 1935
Ashington, Northumberland, England

Early Life

John "Jack" Charlton was born in Ashington, Northumberland, in the northeast of England on May 8, 1935. The large town nearest to Ashington is Newcastle-upon-Tyne. Newcastle is not only the capital of the distinctive Tyneside region but also home to Newcastle United, one of the most prominent soccer teams in England during Jack's formative years. Newcastle United's success undoubtedly influenced young Jack's commitment to soccer, particularly since he was related to the star of the Newcastle team, the legendary forward Jackie Milburn.

The Road to Excellence

Like most soccer players of his generation, Jack began his soccer career by playing for amateur local teams. In 1951, he signed with the Leeds United amateurs, another typical step on the road to a soccer career in England. Football League clubs such as Leeds United have, in effect, their own farm systems: teams that compete at lower levels of competition than the so-called first team does.

In 1952, having proved himself at the amateur level, Jack signed as a professional with Leeds United, and he stayed with the club throughout his playing career. In all, Jack made 629 appearances for Leeds, a club re-cord. The fact that he stayed at Leeds is worth underlining, since Jack's career spanned the period when fees for transfers—or cash trades—skyrocketed.

The Emerging Champion

For most of Jack's career at Leeds, the club was a rather ordinary member of the Football

Jack Charlton in 1968.

League. Jack's gangly physique and strength as a header of the ball enabled him to retain his position of center-half, anchoring the defense. In particular, Jack became notorious for occupying a position on the opposition's goal line while corner kicks were being taken. His ability in the air eventually earned for him the nickname "The Giraffe."

Yet although Jack had proved himself as a thoroughly reliable professional and had adapted to the tactical revolution that took place in English soccer in the early 1960's, it was not until twelve years after he had become a professional that his career blossomed fully. One reason for his somewhat slow development was that much of his playing time was spent in the Football League second division (division numbers are intended to suggest level of player ability: Leeds United was promoted to the more competitive first division in 1964). Jack's breakthrough came when he was picked to play for England's international team against Scotland in 1965. In that game Jack and his brother Bobby, the renowned Manchester United forward, became the first two brothers to play for England in the twentieth century. Jack made the most of the opportunity to play internationally and quickly became the defensive mainstay of the English team that won the World Cup in 1966. In 1967, Jack was named English Footballer of the Year.

At about the same time, manager Don Revie was beginning to make his mark at Leeds United. Under his direction, Leeds became the dominant team in English soccer in the late 1960's and early 1970's. Although the Leeds team won fewer championships than expected, it compiled a record of consistency that was virtually unprecedented. In addition to winning the Football League Championship in 1969 and the Football Association Cup in 1972, the team met with considerable international success, winning what is now known as the Union of European Football Associations (UEFA) Cup in 1968 and 1971.

Jack's career as a player for England continued to flourish until the World Cup competition in Mexico in 1970. He played his last international game in that tournament, having been "capped" 35 times for his country (a "cap" refers to the piece of ceremonial headgear awarded international players upon their selection for the national team). Jack retired in 1973, having played professionally for twenty years, during which time he became a model of tenacity and tactical shrewdness, making up for deficiencies in speed and ball control by an almost legendary work ethic.

Continuing the Story

Jack continued to work in soccer after his retirement. He was manager of Middlesborough from 1973 to 1977, and in his first season led the team back to the first division. He was named Manager of the Year in 1974, and spent another successful term as manager of the Sheffield Wednesday club from 1977 to 1983. He also made a less productive managerial contribution at Newcastle United in 1983-1984.

In February, 1986, Jack was the surprise choice to manage the Republic of Ireland national team. He performed this task with outstanding success, leading the team to the finals of the 1988 European Championships and to the 1990 World Cup Group Finals. In the 1994 World Cup, Ireland was the only representative from the British Isles. Though they were defeated by Holland, Ireland defeated the eventual runner-up team, Italy, 1-0.

Jack's managerial style was reflected in the uncompromising, unfashionable, economical, defense-minded play of the Irish team. In the rare moments when he was not engaged in soccer, Jack indulged in his hobbies of shooting and fishing.

HONORS AND AWARDS	
1966	World Cup champion
1967	English Footballer of the Year
1968	English League Cup champion
1968, 1971	UEFA Cup champion
1969	English League champion
1972	English Football Association Cup champion
1974	English Football League Manager of the Year Order of the British Empire

MILESTONES
35 international appearances for England

Summary

Though Jack Charlton was by no means a naturally gifted athlete, his career is a classic example of how determination, dedication, and intelligence can enable a player not only to reach the highest levels of competition but also to compete with distinction on attaining them. His contribution to English national life was rewarded by enrollment in the Order of the British Empire by Queen Elizabeth in 1974.

George O'Brien

Additional Sources:

Henshaw, Richard. *The Encyclopedia of World Soccer.* Washington, D.C.: New Republic Books, 1979.

Hollander, Zander. *The American Encyclopedia of Soccer.* New York: Everett House, 1980.

Wolff, Alexander. "Here Come the Lads." *Sports Illustrated* 80, no. 23 (1994).

BRANDI CHASTAIN

Sport: Soccer

Born: July 21, 1968
San Jose, California

Early Life

Growing up in California, Brandi Chastain learned to love the game of soccer at an early age. She said that by the time she was six years old she knew this was the game for her. Her grandfather helped encourage her love of the game by offering an incentive for every goal she kicked and a bigger one for each assist she made. As a result of this lesson Brandi learned the importance of being a part of a team and not just a star.

Her parents, Roger and Lark, were among her biggest fans and supporters. She also loved to play all kinds of games with her younger brother. At the age of eight Brandi joined her first team, the Quakettes, and never looked back.

The Road to Excellence

Brandi played soccer for Archbishop Mitty High School in San Jose, winning three state championships. From the ages of twelve to sixteen she played for the Horizons, a team coached by her father. She also was noticed by the U.S. Olympic development group and played for her state team before moving on to a regional squad and then a national under-sixteen team. She excelled at soccer and her academics, receiving a number of scholarship offers including from the University of North Carolina. Brandi chose to stay closer to home and play for University of California, Berkeley.

The Emerging Champion

Brandi began her college career in 1986 at Berkeley but was hurt in 1987 and 1988. During her first year at Berkeley Brandi was named *Soccer America*'s freshman Player of the Year. After recovering from her injuries she transferred to Santa Clara University, graduating in 1990 with a degree in television and communications. While there she led the Broncos to two Final Four appearances. In 1990 she was named to the All-American First Team; the previous year she had been named All-Far West. The International Soccer Association of America named her National Player of the Year in 1990.

Brandi began play for the U.S. national team in 1991, seeing action in two games. In between her many travels with the national team Brandi worked as an assistant coach for the Santa Clara

Brandi Chastain celebrates by ripping off her jersey after scoring the game-winning penalty kick in the 1999 Women's World Cup final.

women's soccer team. Eventually, because of her traveling, she gave up the full-time position to serve as a volunteer.

In 1996 Brandi was a member of the gold-medal-winning Olympic team. When she joined the national team she was not a striker but a defender. In 1998 the team won the gold medal at the Goodwill Games, as well as the World Cup title in 1999. This victory brought much recognition to the team, as well as to women's sports in general, as millions watched the games and cheered the team to gold.

Brandi's name became a household word when her picture appeared on the cover of all the major sports magazines following the victory. Her picture as she removed her shirt in triumph, celebrating in her sports bra, became a symbol of the growing recognition of female athletes as strong, feminine, independent women. That single picture propelled Brandi and women's soccer to the forefront of the sporting world in 1999. The national team won a silver medal in the 2000 Olympics in Sydney, Australia.

NATIONAL TEAM STATISTICS

Year	Record	GP	G	Ast.	Pts.
1988	01-00-01	2	0	2	2
1991	07-05-01	13	7	1	15
1993	02-00-00	2	0	1	1
1996	20-01-02	23	2	7	11
1997	14-01-00	15	2	2	6
1998	21-01-02	24	5	5	15
1999	23-02-02	27	5	5	15
2000	23-05-07	34	4	3	11
Totals	111-14-15	140	25	26	76

Notes: GP = games played; G = goals; Ast. = assists; Pts. = points

leges, and other community centers. She has also been asked to endorse numerous products and has become a leading spokesperson for the game of soccer. Brandi and her husband, Jerry Smith, also continued to work with the Santa Clara University women's soccer team. Smith was the head coach, and Brandi was a volunteer.

Summary

Brandi Chastain brought much attention to the sport of women's soccer. Her excellence on the field was an inspiration to young women everywhere. The image of her taking off her shirt remains a strong statement of the power and confidence of female athletes.

Leslie Heaphy

Additional Sources:

"The 'Babe' Factor in Women's Soccer." *Business Week*, July 26, 1999, 118.

"Brandi's Brazen Celebration." *Maclean's*, July 26, 1999, 10.

Crothers, Tim. "Spectacular Takeoff." *Sports Illustrated* 93 (July 3, 2000): 64.

Wahl, Grant. "Out of This World." *Sports Illustrated* 91 (July 19, 1999): 38-44.

WORLD CUP STATISTICS

Year	Record	GP	G	Ast.	Pts.
1991	2-0-0	2	0	1	1
1999	5-0-1	6	1	2	4
Totals	7-0-1	8	1	3	5

Notes: GP = games played; G = goals; Ast. = assists; Pts. = points

Continuing the Story

Brandi's soccer resume, in addition to many championships with the national team, includes a year of playing professionally in Japan for Skiroke Serena. She was selected as the team's most valuable player. While she enjoyed that experience she would have preferred to play in her own country. This opportunity would come in the spring of 2001, with the creation of a new professional women's soccer league. Brandi joined the Cyber Rays in the Bay Area of California.

In addition to continuing her career on the field Brandi also became a highly sought after motivational speaker. She travels across the country giving talks to audiences at schools, col-

OLYMPIC GAMES STATISTICS

Year	Record	GP	G	Ast.	Pts.
1996	4-0-1	5	0	0	0
2000	3-1-1	5	1	0	2
Totals	7-1-2	10	1	0	2

Notes: GP = games played; G = goals; Ast. = assists; Pts. = points

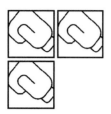

JULIO CÉSAR CHÁVEZ

Sport: Boxing

Born: July 12, 1962
Ciudad Obregón, Mexico

Early Life

Julio César Chávez was born on July 12, 1962, to Rodolfo and Isabel Chávez. Rodolfo, a railroad engineer, and Isabel, a homemaker, were the parents of a family that had very little money. Living in a city often referred to as the drug capital of Mexico, Julio grew up with the ever-present threat of violence. Early on, he began to feel a responsibility to care for and protect his family. He often took odd jobs, shining shoes, washing cars, and selling newspapers, to make extra money for them.

As a boy, Julio enjoyed playing soccer and baseball, but his brothers, Rodolfo and Rafael, were involved with boxing. Former boxer Juan Antonio López, who had once been ranked fifth in the world as a superbantamweight, recognized Julio's boxing skills and convinced him to begin training at a small gym in the suburb of Colonia Ejidal. Julio saw this as an opportunity to provide real financial security for his family.

The Road to Excellence

At the age of sixteen, Julio began training daily, going to fights on weekends and building his boxing skills. Motivated by the need to provide a good life for his family, he was determined and self-assured in the ring. It was during this time that Julio developed his skill at delivering devastating blows to the body, a skill that would be the key to his ability to dismantle an opponent. Supporters such as Augustin de Valdez promoted Julio within the boxing community and worked to ensure the continued growth of his career.

Julio's first professional fight, on February 5, 1980, ended in a win by knockout against Andres Felix. In the four years that followed, Julio had a fight almost every month. He added forty-two more victories to his record, thirty-five of them by knockout. He faced gradually greater opponents as his career progressed, and the boxing world began to take notice of him.

Finally, after four years with no losses, Julio got his first title shot. On September 13, 1984, Julio fought Mario Martinez for the superfeatherweight title of the World Boxing Council. Julio won by knockout in the eighth round and became the WBC superfeatherweight champion.

The Emerging Champion

In the next three years, Julio used his combination of punching power and boxing strategy to defend his WBC title ten times. Promoted exclusively by Don King, he was able to appear against a steady stream of top-ranked fighters while keeping his eye on more titles and higher weight divisions.

On November 21, 1987, Julio met with Edwin Rosario to battle for the lightweight title of the World Boxing Association (WBA). Using double and triple hook shots to the body, Julio gradually wore his opponent down in his usual fashion. Near the end of the eleventh round, Julio won by technical knockout and added a second world title to his record.

Julio moved on to unify the WBA and the WBC lightweight titles on October 29, 1988, against José Luis Ramírez. Ahead on points, Julio was declared the winner when the fight was called as the result of a bad cut on Ramírez's head.

Although some observers said that Julio was not at his best in the fight, his powerful combinations of punches had him well ahead when the fight was stopped.

Moving up in weight class, Julio next set his eye on the WBC super lightweight title. Fighting Roger Mayweather on May 13, 1989, Julio secured his fourth championship. Worn down by

Julio's persistent punches to the body, Mayweather quit before the eleventh round.

Going for his fifth championship against Meldrick Taylor for the juniorwelterweight title of the International Boxing Federation (IBF), Julio experienced one of the most controversial moments of his career. Throughout the fight, Taylor had been ahead of Julio, bewildering him several times with combinations. By the twelfth round, both fighters were tired. In the final round, Julio delivered several punches that staggered Taylor. The referee called the fight with only 2 seconds to go, claiming that Taylor was not in command of his senses and had been techni-

RECOGNIZED WORLD SUPERFEATHERWEIGHT CHAMPIONSHIP FIGHTS

Date	Loser	Result
Sept. 13, 1984	Mario Martinez	8th-round knockout
Apr. 19, 1985	Ruben Castillo	6th-round knockout
July 7, 1985	Roger Mayweather	2d-round knockout
Sept. 21, 1985	Dwight Pratchett	12th-round decision
May 15, 1986	Faustino Barrios	5th-round technical knockout
June 13, 1986	Refugio Rojas	7th-round knockout
Aug. 3, 1986	Rocky Lockridge	12th-round decision
Dec. 12, 1986	Juan La Porte	12th-round decision
Apr. 18, 1987	Tomás Da Cruz	3d-round technical knockout
Aug. 21, 1987	Danilo Cabrera	12th-round decision

RECOGNIZED WORLD LIGHTWEIGHT CHAMPIONSHIP FIGHTS

Nov. 21, 1987	Edwin Rosario	11th-round technical knockout
Apr. 16, 1988	Rodolfo Aguilar	6th-round technical knockout
Oct. 29, 1988	José Luis Ramírez	11th-round decision

RECOGNIZED WORLD SUPERLIGHTWEIGHT CHAMPIONSHIP FIGHTS

May 13, 1989	Roger Mayweather	10th-round knockout
Nov. 18, 1989	Sammy Fuentes	10th-round technical knockout
Dec. 16, 1989	Alberto Cortes	3d-round knockout

RECOGNIZED WORLD JUNIORWELTERWEIGHT CHAMPIONSHIP FIGHTS

Mar. 17, 1990	Meldrick Taylor	12th-round technical knockout
Dec. 8, 1990	Kyung-Duk Ahn	3d-round technical knockout
Mar. 18, 1991	John Duplessis	4th-round technical knockout
Sept. 14, 1991	Lonnie Smith	12th-round decision
Apr. 10, 1992	Angel Hernandez	6th-round technical knockout
Aug. 1, 1992	Frank Mitchell	4th-round technical knockout
Sept. 12, 1992	Hector Camacho	12th-round decision
Feb. 20, 1993	Greg Haugen	5th-round technical knockout
May 8, 1993	Terrence Ali	6th-round technical knockout
Sept. 10, 1993	(Pernell Whitaker, opponent)	12th-round draw
Dec. 18, 1993	Andy Holligan	5th-round technical knockout
Jan. 29, 1994	Julio César Chávez (Frankie Randall, winner)	12th-round decision
May 7, 1994	Frankie Randall	8th-round decision
Sept. 17, 1994	Meldrick Taylor	8th-round technical knockout
Dec. 10, 1994	Tony Lopez	10th-round technical knockout
Apr. 8, 1995	Giovanni Parisi	12th-round decision
Sept. 16, 1995	David Kamau	12th-round decision
June 7, 1996	Julio César Chávez (Oscar de la Hoya, winner)	4th-round technical knockout
Mar. 7, 1998	Miguel Angel Gonzalez	12th-round draw
July 29, 2000	Julio César Chávez (Kostya Tszyu, winner)	6th-round technical knockout

RECOGNIZED WORLD WELTERWEIGHT CHAMPIONSHIP FIGHTS

Sept. 18, 1998	Julio César Chávez (Oscar de la Hoya, winner)	8th-round technical knockout

cally knocked out by Julio. Despite the controversy, the decision stood, and Julio had taken his fifth world championship.

Continuing the Story

Julio defended his WBC super lightweight title against such competitors as Lonnie Smith and Hector Camacho. Against Camacho, he fought a long and difficult fight that left both fighters exhausted, with Julio finally earning the victory on points. He went on to face and defeat such fighters as Greg Haugen, retaining his title.

Controversy again arose on September 10, 1993, when Julio fought a close battle with Pernell Whitaker that ended in a draw. Many observers argued that Whitaker had clearly won the fight, but Julio retained his title.

On January 29, 1994, Julio lost his WBC super lightweight crown to Frankie Randall in a twelve-round split decision. Julio dominated the fourth through the seventh rounds, as well as the ninth and the tenth, on two of the judges' scorecards, but Randall ultimately overtook Julio on points. Although Julio won several of the rounds, the judges awarded more rounds to Randall; the defeat was Julio's first in ninety-one fights. A re-

match was scheduled almost as soon as the fighters left the ring. In May of 1994, Julio regained his title with a controversial eight-round technical split decision over Randall.

Julio defended his junior welterweight title two more times in 1994 with victories against Meldrick Taylor and Tony Lopez, both by technical knockouts. The thirty-two-year-old Julio was approaching an astounding one hundred victories.

In 1995 Julio won close decisions against Giovanni Parisi and David Kamau to retain his title in the junior welterweight division. In 1996, however, he faced the undefeated Oscar de la Hoya whose youth and power were too much for the aging champion. De la Hoya won the fight by a fourth-round technical knockout.

Julio and de la Hoya met again in 1998. After fighting Miguel Angel Gonzalez to a twelfth-round draw, Julio moved up one weight class to challenge de la Hoya for the WBC and lineal welterweight titles on September 18. Again, he lost by technical knockout, this time in the eighth round.

Julio returned to title contention in 2000, facing Kostya Tszyu for the WBC junior welterweight title. In a lopsided affair, the thirty-eight-year-old Julio was no match for Tszyu, suffering

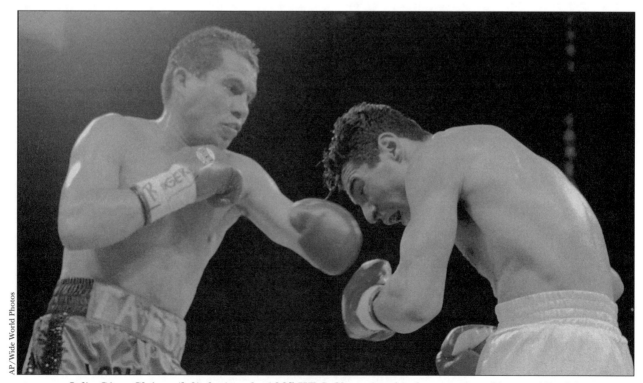

Julio César Chávez (left) during the 1995 WBC Championship bout against Giovanni Parisi.

only his second knockdown in his career, and eventually a sixth-round technical knockout. After the fight, Julio admitted that it was time for him to retire.

Summary

A hero among boxing fans in the United States and Mexico, Julio César Chávez's longevity in boxing was remarkable. His career record of 106-6-2 (with 83 knockouts) was testimony to the power of his fists and the strength of his chin. Though fans and analysts alike have criticized him for refusing to retire, his presence in the ring always drew genuine support, and his achievements rank him among boxing's best fighters.

Margaret Debicki

Additional Sources:

Goldman, Herbert G., ed. *The Ring 1985 Record Book and Boxing Encyclopedia.* New York: Ring Publishing, 1985.

Mullan, Harry. *The Ultimate Encyclopedia of Boxing: The Definitive Illustrated Guide to World Boxing.* Edison, N.J.: Chartwell Books, 1996.

Schulman, Arlene. *The Prize Fighters: An Intimate Look at Champions and Contenders.* New York: Lyons and Burford, 1994.

CUMULATIVE STATISTICS

Bouts, 111
Knockouts, 83
Bouts won by decision, 28
Bouts lost by decision, 3
Bouts lost by knockout, 3
Draws, 2

HONORS AND AWARDS

1987	Boxing Writers of America Fighter of the Year
1990	*Ring* magazine Fighter of the Year
1992	World Boxing Council Fighter of the Year

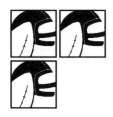

DUTCH CLARK

Born: October 11, 1906
Fowler, Colorado
Died: August 5, 1978
Canon City, Colorado

Courtesy of Amateur Athletic Foundation of Los Angeles

Early Life

Earl Harry "Dutch" Clark was born on October 11, 1906, on a farm near Fowler, Colorado. He was the fourth of five children born to Harry J. and Mary Etta Clark.

Earl was given the nickname "Dutch" at birth. His two older brothers were also called Dutch. They were referred to as "Big Dutch" (brother Carl), "Dutch" (brother Fred), and "Little Dutch" (Earl), but it was Earl who made the nickname famous. The Clark family moved to Pueblo, Colorado, when Dutch was very young.

The Road to Excellence

Dutch began his journey to excellence when he entered Central High School in Pueblo, Colorado, at the age of seventeen. In three years, Dutch earned a total of 16 letters in four sports. He made the Colorado All-State teams in football and basketball, and was named All-American in basketball. In 1926 Dutch's Central High School basketball team played in the Stagg National Interscholastic Finals in Chicago. It was football, though, that became Dutch's forte. The 175-pound center was converted to a back by his high school coaches. During his three seasons at Central, he scored a total of 298 points. The running back helped lead the Wildcats to South-Central League titles in 1924 and 1925. Going unbeaten in the 1925 season, Central met and defeated Littleton, Colorado, in the opening playoff game 58-3, with Dutch scoring 5 touchdowns. Dutch's accomplishments during his three seasons at Central gave him notoriety as the greatest high school athlete in the history of Colorado.

Dutch's philosophy helped make him a great athlete. His sister Pearl described Dutch as believing that he could never take anything for granted, that only through hard work and intense training could he excel in sports. Dutch was definitely serious about sports.

The Emerging Champion

After being recruited by football powers such as the University of Michigan, Dutch elected to attend Northwestern University. He left Northwestern after only one week with a bad case of homesickness. He then enrolled in small Colorado College, where he played freshman football in 1926, and joined the varsity in 1927. It was as a football player at Colorado College that Dutch became a national figure.

He was switched to quarterback by coach Hans Van de Graaff, and he began to make his name known in college football. In his junior year, he rushed for 1,359 yards in only 135 carries and earned All-American honors from the Associated Press, becoming the first Coloradoan so honored. In a game against the University of Wyoming, Clark carried for 381 yards, completed 8 of 15 passes for 200 more yards, and scored 36 points as Colorado won 48-25.

In his senior year, one memorable game took place when he scored all the points in a 3-2 victory over the University of Denver. Dutch's squad was unable to make any headway in the first half. In the second half, Dutch, who was also the team's punter, dropped back in the end zone to punt. He was tackled hard, giving Denver a safety and 2 points. Dutch tried in vain to move the ball

against Denver's defense, but with only 90 seconds remaining he drop-kicked from the 38-yard line. The ball traveled over the upright, not between, and the referee signaled the kick no good. Dutch called time out and got the referee's attention. Coach Van de Graaff convinced the referee that a field goal is good even if the kick does not split the upright, and persuaded the referee to reverse his decision, giving Colorado the win. Dutch ended his collegiate football career in 1930 by participating in the East-West Shrine Game, and was graduated from Colorado with a bachelor's degree in biology.

Dutch began his professional football career with the Portsmouth, Ohio, Spartans of the National Football League (NFL). Times were hard in Portsmouth during the Depression. More fans would show up for practice than for the games, and from time to time the players would get paychecks only to find there was no money in the bank to cover the checks.

Dutch led the NFL in scoring in 1932, 1935, and 1936. During the 1933 season he bowed out of professional football briefly to become the athletic director and football and basketball coach at the University of Colorado, but he soon returned to the NFL. In 1934, the Portsmouth franchise moved to Detroit and became the Detroit Lions. That year, Dutch was named All-Pro quarterback for the third time. In 1935 Dutch helped lead the Lions to an NFL title.

Dutch ended his playing career with the Lions in 1938 while serving as one of the last player-coaches in the NFL. Known as the "Flying Dutchman" during his professional playing days, he

STATISTICS

		Rushing				Receiving			
Season	GP	Car.	Yds.	Avg.	TD	Rec.	Yds.	Avg.	TD
1932	—	111	461	4.2	2	10	107	10.7	2
1934	—	123	763	6.2	6	7	72	10.3	2
1935	—	120	412	3.4	4	9	124	13.8	2
1936	—	123	628	5.1	6	1	5	5.0	1
1937	—	96	468	4.9	5	2	33	16.5	1
1938	—	7	25	3.6	0	0	0	0.0	0
Totals		580	2,757	4.8	23	29	341	11.8	8

Notes: GP = games played; Car. = carries; Yds. = yards; Avg. = average yards per carry or average yards per reception; TD = touchdowns; Rec. = receptions was often considered to be the greatest triple-threat back of his era. He was not only a running back but also the team's passer and field goal kicker. In addition, he was a safety on defense.

Continuing the Story

Dutch stayed in professional football for the next thirteen years. He coached the Cleveland Rams for four years before joining the coaching staff of the Seattle Bombers. Dutch ended his professional coaching career with the Los Angeles Dons.

In 1951, he was appointed head football coach

and athletic director at the University of Detroit. He stayed at the University until 1955, when he resigned to be a representative of a Detroit tool and die firm. He retired in 1963 and lived in Royal Oaks, Michigan, until 1976, when he decided to return to his native state. The Clarks built a home in Canon City, Colorado, where Dutch lived until his death on August 5, 1978.

Summary

Dutch Clark was a quiet, soft-spoken man off the field. He stayed out of the spotlight and avoided admiring fans. On the playing field, though, he was aggressive and confident, a bold leader who made decisions rapidly and with precision. He was a master strategist, constantly probing for a weakness in the opposition. When the Pro Football Hall of Fame opened in 1963, Dutch was made one of the original members in recognition of his many accomplishments.

Jessie F. Banks

Additional Sources:

Cope, Myron. *The Game That Was: The Early Days of Pro Football.* Cleveland: World, 1970.

LaBlanc, Michael L., and Mary K. Ruby, eds. *Professional Sports Team Histories: Football.* Detroit: Gale, 1994.

Porter, David L., ed. *Biographical Dictionary of American Sports: Football.* Westport, Conn.: Greenwood Press, 1987.

HONORS AND AWARDS

1926-30	All-Rocky Mountain Conference Team (football)
	All-Rocky Mountain Conference Team (basketball)
1928	Associated Press All-American
1930	East-West Shrine Game team captain
	All-Rocky Mountain Conference Team (baseball)
	All-Rocky Mountain Conference Team (track)
1931-32, 1934-37	NFL All-Pro Team
1951	Inducted into College Football Hall of Fame
1963	NFL All-Pro Team of the 1930's
	Inducted into Pro Football Hall of Fame
1973	Inducted into Greater Pueblo Sports Association Hall of Fame
1989	Inducted into Colorado High School Activity Association Hall of Fame
	Uniform number 7 retired by Detroit Lions

JIM CLARK

Sport: Auto racing

Born: March 14, 1936
     Kilmany, Scotland
Died: April 7, 1968
     Hockenheim, West Germany

Early Life

James Clark was born into a wealthy farming family on March 14, 1936, in Kilmany, Scotland. Jim was the youngest and only boy in a family of seven. Jim was always interested in farming, and on his holidays from boarding school, he became involved in the running of his father's farm. Interestingly, Jim's earliest experience of driving was on the farm's tractors. Jim's father always encouraged his young son's interest in driving, and, by the age of ten, Jim had his own car to drive around the farm.

The Road to Excellence

Jim's first contact with motor sports came in 1948, when his eldest sister married a local farmer whose hobby was car racing. Watching his brother-in-law race made Jim determined to be on the track.

At seventeen, Jim passed his driving test and, as a reward, was given the family Sunbeam. He entered the car in a precision driving contest, which he won. Jim gained more driving experience by entering driving competitions and minor rallies in the Scottish border country.

In June, 1956, Jim took part in his first proper race. Driving a DKW in Aberdeen, he finished last. Jim's initial failure did not deter him or the growing number of local backers who saw in him enough promise to sponsor his career. Later in the same month, Jim was on the winner's rostrum, having driven the family Sunbeam to victory in a local race.

Over the next few years, Jim won numerous races, but simply being involved in the sport gained him invaluable experience. By 1958, he had been successful enough for his backers to form the Border Reivers team, which would provide the cars for Jim's developing career.

Jim's sponsors were pressuring him to turn professional so he could make the break into bigtime motor racing. Because he was the only son in a farming

Jim Clark in 1964.

family, his parents wanted him to give up racing and devote his time to the farm. Jim was torn between these two options. In the end, he decided to pursue his dreams in motor racing.

The Emerging Champion

Jim drove his first professional race in a single-seater car in December, 1959, at Brands Hatch in England. News traveled fast about this talented young Scot, and he was signed by Team Lotus to drive in Formula Two and Formula Junior competitions.

Under the guidance of team manager Colin Chapman, Jim drove his Lotus to nine victories in the 1960 season, becoming joint Formula Junior World Co-Champion. Jim impressed Chapman sufficiently for the Lotus head to offer him a drive in the Formula One Dutch Grand Prix. At the age of twenty-four, Jim was driving in the highest level of motor racing. His fifth-place finish gave observers notice of the greatness that was to come.

Jim's first full season as a Formula One driver was 1961. Throughout this first year, Jim was criticized for being too young and inexperienced. Although his results were not outstanding, Jim practiced hard to develop his driving skills.

In 1962, Jim's efforts began to pay off. He won his first Grand Prix, in Belgium, and two other victories led to the runner-up spot in the drivers' championship. Jim's critics were silenced. For such a young driver, he showed an incredible ability to concentrate, which, in conjunction with his great enthusiasm and natural ability, made him a formidable competitor.

Everything came together for Jim in 1963. He had done his apprenticeship in Formula One, and, driving a powerful Lotus, he earned the World Championship of Drivers. During the course of the season, he won six Grand Prix championships, four in succession. Still only twenty-seven, Jim had reached the pinnacle of his sport.

Continuing the Story

Although Jim had reached the top in Formula One, he still was inquisitive and eager to learn everything about driving. As a result, Jim could often be found experimenting and exploring other types of motor racing. Jim's most famous venture into an unfamiliar form of racing came at the Indianapolis 500. He had finished second in his first race in 1963. Driving an Indy version of a Formula One race car, Jim dominated the race in 1965 and beat the second place finisher by more than a lap.

Having just failed to retain the Formula One drivers' championship in 1964, Jim would not be denied in 1965. His precision and superb reflexes were evident on all types of road surface. He won five consecutive Grand Prix and took the championship despite a series of mechanical failures toward the end of the season.

Jim had frustrating seasons in 1966 and 1967, plagued by more car troubles. By 1968, Jim and his Lotus car were back with a vengeance. In the opening South African Grand Prix, he thrilled the crowd with a stunning display that left the rest of the field trailing behind. This victory was Jim's twenty-fifth in the Formula One championship, and with it he broke the record number of victories set by the legendary Juan Manuel Fangio.

Jim was the driver to beat in the 1968 Formula One championship. He was at his peak, driving a fast car with supreme confidence. Because Jim was still thirsty for knowledge about driving, he frequently entered Formula Two races. On April 7, 1968, Jim was competing in such a race at

CART, GRAND PRIX, AND OTHER VICTORIES

1960	Formula Junior World Co-Champion
1961, 1963, 1965, 1968	South African Grand Prix
1962	Aintree 200
1962-65	Belgian Grand Prix
1962-65, 1967	British Grand Prix
1962, 1966-67	United States Grand Prix
1963	Milwaukee 200 Italian Grand Prix
1963-65, 1967	Dutch Grand Prix Netherlands Grand Prix
1963, 1965	French Grand Prix World Championship of Drivers
1963, 1967	Mexican Grand Prix
1965	Indianapolis 500 German Grand Prix
1965, 1967-68	Tasman Cup Series Championship

RECORDS

Most Tasman Cup Series Championships, 3
Most Tasman Cup Series victories, 14
Most Tasman Cup Series victories in a season, 5 (1967)

HONORS AND AWARDS

1963	Indianapolis 500 Rookie of the Year
1964	Order of the British Empire
1988	Inducted into Indianapolis Motor Speedway Hall of Fame
1990	Inducted into International Motor Sports Hall of Fame
	Inducted into Motorsports Hall of Fame of America

Hockenheim in West Germany. Light rain was falling when his Lotus went out of control at 175 miles per hour and crashed into some trees. Jim's neck was broken and he died instantly. The reason for Jim's fatal accident has never been conclusively established. The death of this great champion has remained a mystery.

Summary

Jim Clark was one of the greatest racing drivers of all time. The shy Scot possessed immense natural talent and felt most comfortable when behind the wheel. The greatest irony in Jim's life was that he died during a race that he had little chance of winning and which was of little importance to his career. Yet, this was simply a reflection of Jim's love of and dedication to his sport. Racing dominated Jim's life, and his insatiable passion for cars and driving made him the great driver that he was.

David L. Andrews

Additional Sources:

Clark, Jim. *Jim Clark at the Wheel: The World Motor Racing Champion's Own Story.* London: Arthur Barker, 1964.

Dymock, Eric. *Jim Clark: Tribute to a Champion.* Newbury Park, Calif.: Haynes North America, 1997.

Gauld, Graham. *Jim Clark Remembered.* New York: Arco, 1975.

Gauld, Graham, and Ian Scott. *Jim Clark: Portrait of a Great Driver.* New York: Arco, 1968.

Miller, Peter. *Man at the Wheel.* New York: Arco, 1965.

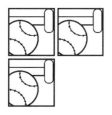

WILL CLARK

Sport: Baseball

Born: March 13, 1964
New Orleans, Louisiana

Early Life

William Nuschler Clark was born in New Orleans, Louisiana, on Friday, March 13, 1964, to Bill and Lottie Clark. When Will was just an infant, his father moved the family to Hattiesburg, Mississippi, to take a position as zone manager for International Harvester. It was there, when Will was four years old, that Flash, his black Labrador, retrieved first one and then another left-handed first-baseman's glove, as if to promote the boy's future in professional baseball.

Despite his dog's apparent foresight, Will's interest in playing professional baseball did not develop until after his family had moved back to New Orleans and he was in junior high school. His first love was hunting, especially with his father, a sharp-eyed pool player who had himself been an excellent athlete.

Will was still using those gloves when he started attending Jesuit High School and began mastering his career position at first base. It was there, with the help of good coaches, that he fashioned his classic, full swing, reminiscent of that of the great Stan Musial. He learned, too, from repeated readings of Ted Williams's *The Science of Hitting*.

The Road to Excellence

By the time Will entered Mississippi State University, he had already distinguished himself as a stellar player. He had been named a high school

St. Louis Cardinals' first baseman Will Clark hits a home run in an August, 2000, game.

All-American and had played in both the Babe Ruth and the American Legion World Series, but it was in college that he began to draw serious national attention. He helped propel his team into the College World Series, was named college All-American, and, in 1985, won the Golden Spikes Award as the nation's top college player. What drew greatest recognition, though, was his phenomenal performance in the 1984 Olympic competition. In forty games, Will hit 16 homers and batted in 43 runs. The self-styled "masher" simply outclassed fellow teammates Mark McGwire, B. J. Surhoff, and Barry Larkin.

The Emerging Champion

In June of 1985, the San Francisco Giants drafted Will and sent him to their Class A farm team in Fresno. Will hit 2 home runs in his first game, and in the sixty-five games he played, he helped Fresno to the California League title.

The next year he was with the Giants, and, as if to make it clear what opposing pitchers could expect from him, he hit a homer off Nolan Ryan in his first regular major league game. He went on that season to play in 111 games and compile a .287 batting average, but it was in the next season, 1987, that Will hit his true stride. He hit .308 and, with 35 homers, drove in 91 runs. In the process, he helped the Giants to their first Western Division title since 1971.

Continuing the Story

By 1988, Will, now dubbed "The Thrill" by catcher Bob Brenley, established himself as the premier first baseman in the National League (NL). Although that year his batting average dropped to .282, he drove in a league-leading 109 runs with a .508 slugging average. He also led the league in walks, a clear sign that opposing managers and pitchers were growing wary of him. Well they might, for Will was revealing a genius for doing his best in clutch situations. His percentages with men on base and the league's best pitchers opposing him were better than his total averages. Defying baseball odds, he was also batting better against southpaws than right-handed pitchers.

The next year, with teammate and friend Kevin Mitchell batting in the cleanup slot behind him, Will concentrated on hits instead of power. He amassed a .333 batting average and scored a league-leading 104 runs. With Mitchell, who had a banner year, Will led the Giants to their first National League pennant in twenty-nine years. Although their World Series performance against Oakland was poor, Will and Mitchell served notice that the Giants were going to be tough for the next several years, as they were in the heyday of Willie Mays, Orlando Cepeda, and Willie McCovey.

In 1990, pitching woes quickly dimmed the Giants' hopes of repeating their performance, but, with the addition of Matt Williams to the regular lineup, the Giants put together a "murderer's row" that caused sportswriters to make comparisons to great power-hitting teams of the past. Will, the key figure, set a personal goal to win baseball's triple crown by leading the league

STATISTICS

Season	GP	AB	Hits	2B	3B	HR	Runs	RBI	BA	SA
1986	111	408	117	27	2	11	66	41	.287	.444
1987	150	529	163	29	5	35	89	91	.308	.580
1988	162	575	162	31	6	29	102	**109**	.282	.508
1989	159	588	196	38	9	23	**104**	111	.333	.546
1990	154	600	177	25	5	19	91	95	.295	.448
1991	148	565	170	32	7	29	84	116	.301	.536
1992	144	513	154	40	1	16	69	73	.300	.476
1993	132	491	139	27	2	14	82	73	.283	.432
1994	110	389	128	24	2	13	73	80	.329	.501
1995	123	454	137	27	3	16	85	92	.302	.480
1996	117	436	124	25	1	13	69	72	.284	.436
1997	110	393	128	29	1	12	56	51	.326	.496
1998	149	554	169	41	1	23	98	102	.305	.507
1999	77	251	76	15	0	10	40	29	.303	.482
2000	130	427	136	30	2	21	78	70	.319	.546
Totals	1,976	7,173	2,176	440	47	284	1,184	1,205	.303	.497

Notes: Boldface indicates statistical leader. GP = games played; AB = at bats; 2B = doubles; 3B = triples; HR = home runs; RBI = runs batted in; BA = batting average; SA = slugging average

HONORS AND AWARDS

1984	U.S. Olympic baseball team member
1985	Golden Spikes Award
1988-92	National League All-Star Team
1989	National League Championship Series most valuable player
1989, 1991	Silver Slugger Award
1991	National League Gold Glove Award
1994	American League All-Star Team

in hitting average, homers, and runs batted in (RBIs).

Things remained good during the 1990's. Following the 2000 season, Will announced his retirement from baseball. He began the season with Baltimore but was traded to St. Louis at the end of July, helping the Cardinals make the NL championship series for the first time since 1996. In postseason play, he hit .345 with 12 home runs and 42 RBIs.

Between 1996 and 1999, Will underwent surgery that removed a total of thirty-six bone chips from his left elbow. Though his frequent surgeries affected his batting speed, he remained a formidable hitter, collecting 32 extra base hits during his final season. After a much-needed rest from the game, Will was expected to accept a position within the Cardinal organization.

Summary

Will Clark, the complete professional, is and always has been a winner. He cannot tolerate failure, especially in himself. Much of his exhibited fury on the field is self-directed, when, for example, he strikes out or boots an easy grounder. When in control of himself, Will has a single-mindedness and toughness reminiscent of Ted Williams. His great talent and aggressive style of play should make him one of the game's all-time greats.

John W. Fiero

Additional Sources:

DeMarco, Tony. "Will to Win." *Sport* 85, no. 5 (1994).

Kennedy, Kostya. "Catching Fire." *Sports Illustrated* 93, no. 15 (2000).

Knapp, Ron. *Sports Great Will Clark*. Hillside, N.J.: Enslow, 1993.

BOBBY CLARKE

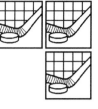

Sport: Ice hockey

Born: August 13, 1949
    Flin Flon, Manitoba, Canada

Early Life

Robert Earle Clarke was born on August 13, 1949, in Flin Flon, Manitoba, Canada.

Bobby learned the game and developed his lifelong love of ice hockey in the open-air rinks in Flin Flon. Playing in temperatures that dipped as low as 40 below zero, he developed a ruggedness and durability that people would marvel at during his entire career. He devoted all his attention to perfecting his stick-handling and skating abilities and admitted that his only ambition was to make the National Hockey League (NHL).

The Road to Excellence

Bobby's dream of making it into the NHL was sidelined on numerous occasions. After working through the local leagues in Flin Flon and gaining some early attention from local talent scouts, he suffered a setback. At the age of fourteen, Bobby was found to have diabetes, a disease in which a person's urine and blood contain excess sugar and that must be controlled by shots of insulin to control blood sugar levels. Extreme fatigue and other more serious complications, including blindness and coma, can develop if diabetes is not treated properly. Knowing the seriousness of the disease and the ambitions of his young patient, Bobby's doctor warned him to

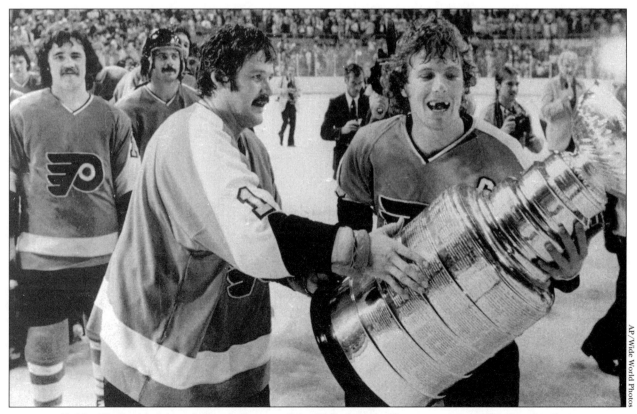

Bobby Clarke (right) and Bernie Parent of the Philadelphia Flyers carry the 1975 Stanley Cup.

467

quit hockey. He feared that the disease would drain the stamina Bobby would need to compete and would jeopardize his overall health. When those same talent scouts that had been tracking Bobby's progress learned of his condition, they too dismissed him as a medical risk.

Yet Bobby Clarke played on. Injecting 70 units of insulin each day to control his diabetes, he graduated to junior hockey with the Flin Flon Bombers. A tenth-grade high school dropout, Bobby saw hockey as an escape from the copper-zinc mines where his father had toiled for more than twenty-five years, and began serious pursuit of a profession in the sport. One of Western Canada's prized junior players, Bobby was nevertheless bypassed by most NHL scouts, who assumed that no diabetic could stand the rigors of professional hockey. The sole exception was Philadelphia scout Jerry Melnyk. Told that Bobby had been cleared by specialists to play, he double-checked and liked what he saw. In the 1969 amateur draft, ten NHL clubs bypassed Bobby before Philadelphia, an expansion team founded in 1967, chose him in the second round.

That fall, at training camp in Quebec City, Bobby collapsed twice because he had skipped breakfast before strenuous workouts. He soon learned that he needed to remain healthy to prove his strengths as a player and never again repeated that omission. Signed for $14,000 and a $5,000 bonus, Bobby posted 46 points and was named the top rookie in the NHL West Division during his first season, when the Flyers won just seventeen of seventy-six games.

The Emerging Champion

Bobby spent the summer honing a sharper shot and emerged in his sophomore season as one of the most aggressive players in the league.

For the next eleven years, Bobby earned a reputation as one of the most talented and hard-working players in NHL history. Named team captain at the age of twenty-three, he was instrumental, through his leadership, his

skill at face-offs, and his accuracy around the net, in leading the Flyers to back-to-back Stanley Cup Championship titles. He emerged as Philadelphia's all-time leading scorer, ranking fourteenth all-time in the NHL, with 358 goals and 852 assists for 1,210 points. He led the Flyers in scoring eight times and averaged more than a point per game during his career. Named to the NHL's first All-Star team twice and the second team twice, he received the league's Frank J. Selke Trophy as the top defensive forward in 1982-1983. Philadelphia retired his jersey number 16 in 1984. Three years later, Bobby was elected to the Hockey Hall of Fame.

Continuing the Story

Highly regarded in all facets of his profession, Bobby silenced skeptics early and throughout his career and earned numerous professional awards. He won the Bill Masterson Memorial Trophy for perseverance, sportsmanship, and dedication to hockey in 1971-1972, the Lester Pearson Award for outstanding service to hockey in the United States in 1979-1980, and three prestigious awards from the Philadelphia Sportswriters Association: Athlete of the Year (1974), Most Courageous Athlete (1980), and "Good Guy" Award (1983).

After fifteen years as a playing veteran with the Flyers, Bobby carried his mark of success to the

STATISTICS

Season	GP	G	Ast.	Pts.	PIM
1969-70	76	15	31	46	68
1970-71	77	27	36	63	78
1971-72	78	35	46	81	87
1972-73	78	37	67	104	80
1973-74	77	35	52	87	113
1974-75	80	27	**89**	116	125
1975-76	76	30	**89**	119	136
1976-77	80	27	63	90	71
1977-78	71	21	68	89	83
1978-79	80	16	57	73	68
1979-80	76	12	57	69	65
1980-81	80	19	46	65	140
1981-82	62	17	46	63	154
1982-83	80	23	62	85	115
1983-84	73	17	43	60	70
Totals	**1,144**	**358**	**852**	**1,210**	**1,453**

Notes: Boldface indicates statistical leader. GP = games played; G = goals; Ast. = assists; Pts. = points; PIM = penalties in minutes

post of general manager, spending six years, from May 15, 1984, to April 16, 1990, in that position. During his tenure, Philadelphia won three divisional titles and two conference championships and earned two berths in the Stanley Cup finals. His teams went 250-177-47 in regular season play and posted a 42-34 playoff record.

Bobby began the 1990-1991 hockey season as the vice president and general manager of the Minnesota North Stars, a post he held until 1992. Bobby later rejoined the Flyers as president and general manager in 1994 and served as the general manager for the Canadian Olympic hockey team during the 1998 Winter Olympics in Nagano, Japan. Team Canada lost to Finland in the bronze-medal round. Bobby was criticized in the late 1990's for numerous administrative decisions regarding the staff and players in Philadelphia, particularly in his handling of budding superstar Eric Lindros.

Summary

Modest in stature during his playing career, when he stood 5 feet 10 inches and weighed 185 pounds, Bobby Clarke survived in the tough world of professional hockey and hustled his way to super-stardom in spite of the odds. What he accomplished on ice, he equaled off the ice. He often took new players home to dinner, helped them get settled, and fostered team togetherness. He served as an inspiration to diabetics and hockey fans and players everywhere. He would continue to have an impact on the sport of ice hockey as a general manager and has rightfully earned recognition as one of the greatest players ever to have laced a skate.

Jan Giel

HONORS AND AWARDS	
1972	Bill Masterson Memorial Trophy Team Canada member
1973-74	NHL Second Team All-Star
1973, 1975, 1976	Hart Memorial Trophy
1974	Lester B. Pearson Award
1975-76	NHL First Team All-Star
1979	Challenge Cup team captain
1980	Lester Patrick Trophy
1983	Frank J. Selke Trophy
1987	Inducted into Hockey Hall of Fame Uniform number 16 retired by Philadelphia Flyers

Additional Sources:

Fischler, Stan. *Bobby Clarke and the Ferocious Flyers.* New York: Dodd-Mead, 1974.

Lapointe, Joe. "Clarke Has Buffed Away the Rough Edges." *The New York Times,* June 4, 1995, p. 3.

Wright, Jim. *Bobby Clarke: Pride of the Team.* New York: Putnam, 1977.

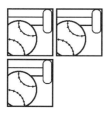

ROGER CLEMENS

Sport: Baseball

Born: August 4, 1962
Dayton, Ohio

Early Life

William Roger Clemens was born on August 4, 1962, in Dayton, Ohio. He moved with his parents to Houston, Texas, in 1966. His parents encouraged Roger and his older brother Randy to participate in athletics but insisted that they also concentrate on gaining an education. Randy played baseball and basketball at Mississippi College, then went on to a successful business career.

Roger starred in three sports at Springs Woods High School, winning 3 letters each in football and baseball and 2 more in basketball. He helped his American Legion team to a Texas state championship in 1979 and was named All-District defensive end for the Spring Woods football team the same year. Rather than immediately pursue a career in professional sports, Roger followed his parents' advice and accepted a baseball scholarship to attend San Jacinto Junior College.

The Road to Excellence

At San Jacinto, Roger was named Junior College All-American. Although he was drafted by the New York Mets after the 1981 season, he chose instead to attend the University of Texas, where he compiled a 25-7 record over the next two years, after each of which he was named All-American. When the Boston Red Sox made him their first-round draft choice in 1983, he decided to forgo his final year of college eligibility and enter professional baseball.

Roger spent little more than a year in the minor leagues before being called to the parent club in 1984. In 1983, he compiled a 3-1 record and an impressive 1.24 earned run average (ERA) in four games at Boston's Class A team at Winter Haven and a 4-1 record with a 1.38 earned run average in seven games at Class AA New Britain. He started the 1984 season with the Red Sox's Class AAA farm team at Pawtucket, but his performance in the first seven games (2-3 record, 1.93 earned run average) earned him a chance at the majors. In his rookie season, he compiled a 9-4 record with a 4.32 earned run average before being sidelined with an injury

New York Yankees pitcher Roger Clemens in June, 2000.

AP/Wide World Photos

STATISTICS

Season	GP	GS	CG	IP	HA	BB	SO	W	L	S	ShO	ERA
1984	21	20	5	133.1	146	29	126	9	4	0	1	4.32
1985	15	15	3	98.1	83	37	74	7	5	0	1	3.29
1986	33	33	10	254.0	179	67	238	**24**	4	0	1	**2.48**
1987	36	36	**18**	281.2	248	83	256	**20**	9	0	**7**	2.97
1988	35	35	**14**	264.0	217	62	**291**	18	12	0	**8**	2.93
1989	35	35	8	253.1	215	93	230	17	11	0	3	3.13
1990	31	31	7	228.1	193	54	209	21	6	0	**4**	**1.93**
1991	35	35	13	271.1	219	65	241	18	10	0	**4**	**2.62**
1992	32	32	11	246.2	203	62	208	18	11	0	**5**	**2.41**
1993	29	29	2	191.2	175	67	160	11	14	0	1	4.46
1994	24	24	3	170.2	124	71	168	9	7	0	1	2.85
1995	23	23	0	140.0	141	60	132	10	5	0	0	4.18
1996	34	34	6	242.2	216	106	**257**	10	13	0	2	3.63
1997	34	34	**9**	**264.0**	204	68	**292**	**21**	7	0	**3**	**2.05**
1998	33	33	5	234.2	169	88	**271**	**20**	6	0	3	**2.65**
1999	30	30	1	187.2	185	90	163	14	10	0	1	4.60
2000	32	32	1	204.1	184	84	188	13	8	0	0	3.70
Totals	512	511	116	3,666.2	3,101	1,186	3,504	260	142	0	45	3.07

Notes: Boldface indicates statistical leader. GP = games played; GS = games started; CG = complete games; IP = innings pitched; HA = hits allowed; BB = bases on balls (walks); SO = strikeouts; W = wins; L = losses; S = saves; ShO = shutouts; ERA = earned run average

and missing the last month of the season.

Roger continued to be plagued with injuries during the 1985 season, missing virtually the entire month of July because of a sore pitching shoulder and then missing the final month of the season when he reinjured the shoulder. The second injury necessitated an operation on August 30, and the Red Sox management feared that he might never regain the blazing fastball that had made him so effective as a pitcher. The operation was on the rotator cuff, a medical procedure that had failed with several other promising pitchers. Roger underwent a successful rehabilitation program with the help of his wife, Debbie, and returned in 1986 to have his finest year and lead his team to the World Series.

The Emerging Champion

Roger's season in 1986 was the sort of which most pitchers only dream. He led the major leagues in victories (24-4), winning percentage, and earned run average (2.48), for which he won the American League Cy Young Award, the highest honor that can be accorded to a pitcher. On April 29, he struck out an incredible 20 Seattle Mariners with his 95-mile-per-hour-plus fastball to set an all-time major league record for strikeouts in a single game (the old record was 18). In the All-Star Game, he pitched 3 perfect innings

and led the American League to victory. For his performance, he was voted the most valuable player in the All-Star Game.

The Red Sox rode Roger's arm to an American League Eastern Division Championship and victory in the League Championship Series against the California Angels. Roger was 1-1 with a 4.32 earned run average against the Angels in a series that the Red Sox won in dramatic fashion in seven games. Roger's dream season ended in disappointment, however, when the Red Sox lost a heartbreaking seven-game World Series to the New York Mets. Even that defeat could not tarnish the luster of Roger's regular season performance, for which he was voted the league's most valuable player and *The Sporting News* Major League Player of the Year (previously, only Sandy Koufax and Denny McLain had ever won those awards and the Cy Young Award in the same year). He had clearly established himself as the premier pitcher in the American League, perhaps in the majors, and potentially one of the greatest power pitchers of all times.

Continuing the Story

After his dream season of 1986, Roger "the Rocket" Clemens continued to terrorize major league batters. He led the major leagues in strikeouts (in 1988 with 291), and led both leagues in

471

HONORS, AWARDS, AND RECORDS

1982-83	College All-American
1986	American League most valuable player *Sporting News* Major League Player of the Year Joe Cronin Award Seagram's Seven Crowns of Sports Award Major league record for the most strikeouts in a game (20) All-Star Game most valuable player
1986-87	Associated Press Major League All-Star Team
1986-87, 1991, 1997-98	American League Cy Young Award
1986-88	United Press International American League All-Star Team *Sporting News* American League All-Star Team
1986, 1988, 1990-92, 1997-98	American League All-Star Team
1986, 1991, 1997-98	*Sporting News* Pitcher of the Year
1987	*Baseball America* American League Pitcher of the Year
1997-98	Players Choice Awards: American League Outstanding Pitcher
1999	MLB All-Century Team

shutout victories twice more (in 1987 with seven and in 1988 with eight). He also led the American League in complete games in 1987 with eighteen and tied for the league lead in that category with fourteen in 1988. In 1988 and 1990, he led the Boston Red Sox to the American League Eastern Division Championships, only to see his team fall both times in four straight games to the Oakland Athletics. He continued his phenomenal record in All-Star games by pitching 1 inning in the 1988 game and 2 innings in the 1990 game without giving up a hit or a run in either. In 1987, he won his second straight Cy Young Award, only the third pitcher ever to do so (the other two were Jim Palmer in 1975-1976 and Sandy Koufax in 1965-1966). Ten years later he would do the same, winning back-to-back Cy Young Awards in 1997 and 1998 with the Toronto Blue Jays, to bring his total to a record five awards.

In 1991 Roger signed a four-year, $21 million contract with Boston, making him the highest-paid pitcher in baseball history. That year, he earned his keep, posting an 18-10 record and an American League best 2.62 ERA, enough to secure his third Cy Young Award. After thirteen seasons with Boston, Roger became a free agent following the 1996 season and signed a three-year deal with the Toronto Blue Jays. In his two years with Toronto, he led the league in wins,

ERA, and strikeouts and captured two more Cy Young Awards.

Although he had accomplished so much in his career since 1984, Roger did not have a world championship. That would change in 1999, when he signed with the New York Yankees in a trade for David Wells. Bothered by a hamstring injury early in the season, Roger's regular season ERA was 4.60. He improved in the postseason, pitching 7 shutout innings against Texas in the division series and holding the Braves to 1 run and 4 hits to clinch his first world championship. That year, he was also selected for major league baseball's All-Century team. Putting to rest any speculation about his age and ability as a power pitcher, Roger finished the 2000 season with a 13-8 record and an ERA of 3.70, and won his second World Series ring.

In 2001, he began the season on a pace that pointed toward another Cy Young Award.

Summary

Roger Clemens overcame a potentially career-threatening injury through hard work and the support of his family to become one of the American League's all-time greatest pitchers. Although his volatile temper sometimes gets him into trouble both on and off the field, he seems poised to make an assault on many all-time career pitching records with his blazing fastball and his fierce competitiveness.

Paul Madden

Additional Sources:

Callahan, Gerry. "Commanding Presence." *Sports Illustrated* 86, no. 13 (1997).

Clemens, Roger, with Peter Gammons. *Rocket Man: The Roger Clemens Story*. New York: Penguin, 1988.

Macht, Norman L. *Roger Clemens*. Philadelphia: Chelsea House, 1999.

Schmuck, Peter. "Roger Clemens: He's Back in Command." *Baseball Digest* 56, no. 9 (1997).

ROBERTO CLEMENTE

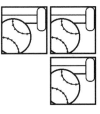

Sport: Baseball

Born: August 18, 1934
   Carolina, Puerto Rico
Died: December 31, 1972
   Near Carolina, Puerto Rico

Early Life

When Roberto Clemente y Walker was born on August 18, 1934, the small town of Carolina, Puerto Rico, was dominated by one industry: sugar. Residents toiled to harvest the cane; few other opportunities existed.

Yet, Roberto's parents were industrious and lived reasonably well according to the standards of the time and place. His father, Melchor, became a foreman for the local sugar company, and his mother, Luisa, went to work at the plantation house. Melchor also sold meat and later purchased trucks that enabled him to enter the construction trade on a part-time basis. The couple's children proved to be hard workers, too.

The Clementes valued education; they wanted their youngest child to be an engineer. A good student, Roberto nevertheless was destined for other spheres of activity. He frequently engaged in poor person's baseball practice: hitting tin cans with a stick. Roberto also habitually bounced rubber balls off the walls and clutched them very tightly to strengthen his arm.

The Road to Excellence

High school passed quickly for Roberto. In addition to baseball, he pursued track and javelin throwing to the extent that he was considered to be a potential Olympic competitor.

Many judged Roberto to be a natural athlete. Others claim that he purposefully used diverse sports to develop his baseball skills; javelin throwing may have aided his powerful arm. Theories aside, the young man demonstrated a supreme love of baseball while aiming for excellence in every chosen endeavor.

Baseball is a cultural treasure for Puerto Rico. The Winter Leagues, founded in 1938, drew professionals to the island during the off-season. Many cities also sponsored teams, and spectator enthusiasm fueled fierce competition and recognition of talented players.

Roberto's entry into the sport occurred when local businessman Roberto Marín spotted the fourteen-year-old whacking tin cans. Roberto was recruited for Marín's Sello Rojo Rice softball squad and then was acquired by the Juncos, a Double-A amateur baseball team.

Marín continued to be Roberto's unofficial publicist. The lad was unbelievable, he told his friend Pedrín Zorilla, Brooklyn Dodgers scout and owner of the Puerto Rican league team, the Santurce Crabbers. Soon afterward, Zorilla hap-

473

pened to watch a Juncos exhibition game. He inquired about one of the players and was surprised to discover that this was Marín's protégé.

Roberto signed on with the Santurce Crabbers for a $400 bonus and $40 a week. Breaking into the 1952-1953 lineup proved to be his biggest obstacle, as many of the players already were major league stars. Yet, the youth watched, learned, and constantly strived to improve his considerable talent. By the 1953-1954 season, he had become a regular, and nine professional ball teams approached him with contract offers that winter. Roberto chose the Brooklyn Dodgers; his $10,000 bonus was far above that of any other Hispanic professional.

The Emerging Champion

It had been seven years since the major leagues—specifically, the Dodgers—integrated baseball with the hiring of Jackie Robinson. Five African Americans currently played for Brooklyn, and the management feared fan reaction if more minorities joined the roster. Therefore, Roberto was relegated to the Montreal farm team.

According to baseball regulations of the time, his high bonus made him eligible for draft in the following year. The Dodgers wanted to keep Roberto, however, so they attempted to hide his

talents. During his first week, he hoisted a truly phenomenal home run. He was benched the next day. His errors resulted in more playing time, his successes yielded inactivity. The result was confusion and frustration.

Yet, Roberto's skills again managed to surface. The Pittsburgh Pirates, a perennial losing team, were searching for young talent upon which to build a respectable club. By virtue of their last-place standing, they were entitled to a first-round draft pick. Roberto Clemente was their choice.

His first season in Pittsburgh was one of transition. During the preceding winter, he had been involved in an automobile accident that permanently displaced three disks in his back. Although he was a regular player by his second week with the Pirates, he felt a deep loneliness.

Roberto barely spoke English, and Pittsburgh did not have a Hispanic community. When the rookie heard racial slurs against opposing players, he knew that similar comments also were being directed at him. Roberto combated such attitudes throughout his career.

Nor was Forbes Field, the Pirates' cavernous ball park, accommodating to home runs. Roberto adapted himself accordingly, becoming a stellar line-drive hitter. His batting average rose from .255 in 1955 to .311 in 1956. The Pirates slowly ac-

STATISTICS

Season	GP	AB	Hits	2B	3B	HR	Runs	RBI	BA	SA
1955	124	474	121	23	11	5	48	47	.255	.382
1956	147	543	169	30	7	7	66	60	.311	.431
1957	111	451	114	17	7	4	42	30	.253	.348
1958	140	519	150	24	10	6	69	50	.289	.408
1959	105	432	128	17	7	4	60	50	.296	.396
1960	144	570	179	22	6	16	89	94	.314	.458
1961	146	572	201	30	10	23	100	89	**.351**	.559
1962	144	538	168	28	9	10	95	74	.312	.454
1963	152	600	192	23	8	17	77	76	.320	.470
1964	155	622	**211**	40	7	12	95	87	**.339**	.484
1965	152	589	194	21	14	10	91	65	**.329**	.463
1966	154	638	202	31	11	29	105	119	.317	.536
1967	147	585	**209**	26	10	23	103	110	**.357**	.554
1968	132	502	146	18	12	18	74	57	.291	482
1969	138	507	175	20	**12**	19	87	91	.345	.544
1970	108	412	145	22	10	14	65	60	.352	.556
1971	132	522	178	29	8	13	82	86	.341	.502
1972	102	378	118	19	7	10	68	60	.312	.479
Totals	2,433	9,454	3,000	440	166	240	1,416	1,305	.317	.475

Notes: Boldface indicates statistical leader. GP = games played; AB = at bats; 2B = doubles; 3B = triples; HR = home runs; RBI = runs batted in; BA = batting average; SA = slugging average

quired new, more capable players, and the right fielder began to build his reputation as one of the game's strongest and most versatile talents.

Continuing the Story

During the 1960 season, the Pirates beat all odds to emerge as World Series champions. Roberto had been an All-Star team member that year. He batted .314 for the season, .310 in the Series. He had helped the Pirates win critical games. Yet, the most valuable player (MVP) award eluded him, and he felt berated by the press.

Roberto sustained physical—as well as emotional—injuries throughout his career: the car crash, two severe household-related accidents, and a bout with malaria. When he demanded to sit out, he often clashed with the stoical Pirate manager, Danny Murtaugh.

On the field, however, Pirate Number 21 erased all doubts. Announcer Vin Scully said, "Clemente could field a ball in Pennsylvania and throw out a runner in New York." He robbed his opponents of home runs, bare-handing high flys and colliding into stadium walls. Many of his triples were simply doubles extended through sheer speed and hustle.

In 1966, Roberto won the MVP award, an unusual tribute considering that the Pirates placed third in their division. The "Great One," as Pittsburgh fans called him, gradually turned an insular pride into team spirit. On May 15, 1967, he hit 3 home runs and a double, yet it was not his best game, he said, because the Pirates lost.

Roberto went home to Puerto Rico after each season. There, he met the beautiful Vera Zabala and married her in 1964; they had three sons. He continued to play in, then manage, Puerto Rican league teams. His charitable acts were legendary. Citizens asked Roberto to run for Mayor of San Juan, and in Pittsburgh, he was a mentor to young Hispanic ballplayers.

Summary

Roberto Clemente's 3,000th hit came on September 30, 1972; it was to be his last. An earthquake ravaged Managua, Nicaragua, that December. As honorary chair of the Nicaraguan Relief Committee, he decided to go there himself, in a small plane loaded with food and supplies. Shortly after takeoff, the craft sank into the Atlantic Ocean, killing everyone aboard.

One of Roberto's greatest dreams was realized through the tragedy. Thousands of memorial gifts arrived, generating enough money to build the Ciudad Deportiva, where Puerto Rican boys could cultivate their talents under the guidance of professional athletes. The National Baseball Hall of Fame also waived its rules to "prematurely" admit Roberto on August 6, 1973. He was the first Latin American player so honored.

Lynn C. Kronzek

MAJOR LEAGUE RECORDS
Most seasons leading in assists, 5 in 1958, 1960-61, 1966-67 (record shared)
Most triples in a game, 3 in 1958 (record shared)
Most hits in two consecutive games, 10 (1970)
Hit safely in all fourteen World Series games in 1960 and 1971 (record shared)

HONORS AND AWARDS	
1960-67, 1969-72	National League All-Star Team
1961-72	National League Gold Glove Award
1966	National League most valuable player
1971	World Series most valuable player Babe Ruth Award
1973	Inducted into National Baseball Hall of Fame
1975	Inducted into Black Athletes Hall of Fame Uniform number 21 retired by Pittsburgh Pirates

Additional Sources:

Bjarkman, Peter C. *Roberto Clemente*. New York: Chelsea House, 1991.

Markusen, Bruce. *Roberto Clemente: The Great One*. Champaign, Ill.: Sports Publishing, 1998.

Miller, Ira. *Roberto Clemente*. New York: Grosset & Dunlap, 1973.

Musick, Phil. *Who Was Roberto? A Biography of Roberto Clemente*. Garden City, N.Y.: Doubleday, 1974.

O'Brien, Jim. *Remember Roberto: Clemente Recalled by Teammates, Family, Friends and Fans*. Pittsburgh, Pa.: James P. O'Brien, 1994.

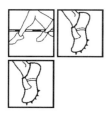

ALICE COACHMAN

Sport: Track and field (sprints and high jump)

Born: November 9, 1923
Albany, Georgia

Early Life

The daughter of Fred and Evelyna (Jackson) Coachman, Alice Coachman was born in Albany, Georgia, on November 9, 1923. To make extra money during the Great Depression years, Alice worked with her family, earning 50 cents per 100 pounds of cotton picked. Alice also tended her younger sisters and performed errands for her mother. Segregation prevented Alice from having access to public schools and athletic facilities. Considered a tomboy, she joined her brothers and their friends in vigorous games. Her parents disapproved of this activity, expecting her to conform to traditional feminine gender roles. Alice ran barefoot on dirt roads and learned to high jump over rags tied together. She enjoyed playground sports but wanted to become an actress or musician, specifically a saxophonist, after listening to Count Basie on her father's radio.

The Road to Excellence

After watching local track meets, Alice decided to compete. Despite encountering discrimination as an African American, Alice attracted national attention at Amateur Athletic Union (AAU) meets. She won the national outdoor high jump championship in 1939, and Tuskegee Institute in Alabama offered her a scholarship. At age sixteen, Alice moved to Tuskegee, where she enrolled at the institute's high school. A historic black college founded by Booker T. Washington, Tuskegee attracted many African American intellectuals and athletes.

The school's track team, trained by Cleve Abbott, a future National Track and Field Hall of Fame member, was considered one of the best in the United States. Alice won many honors during her years at Tuskegee. She participated in intercollegiate track meets, demonstrating

Alice Coachman after her 1948 Olympic gold medal win.

AP/Wide World Photos

her mastery of the high jump and sprints. She also played basketball (winning three consecutive Southern Intercollegiate Athletic Conference championships), studied dressmaking, and worked on campus to earn extra money. She sewed uniforms for the football team, maintained the tennis courts, and cleaned the pool and gymnasium.

The Emerging Champion

Competing at integrated AAU events, a barefoot Alice ran the 50-meter and the 100-meter dash. She competed in the national track championships, setting a new high jump record and winning the national outdoor high jump medal every year of the 1940's, a feat no others have accomplished. Alice was also indoor high jump champion three times, when that event was offered. She earned several sprinting national championships and was a member of Tuskegee Institute's 1941 and 1942 national champion 4×100-meter relay teams. She was the only African American female selected for the United States national AAU team that competed with Canada in 1946. There, she won the high jump and 100-meter race.

A versatile athlete, Alice sometimes won all of her races in addition to the high jump during

one meet and was named high-point athlete. During her athletic career, Alice tallied a total of twenty-five national AAU high jump and track titles. She might well have won two or more gold medals if the 1940 and 1944 Olympic Games had not been canceled because of World War II. Alice was disappointed that she could not compete internationally when she peaked athletically.

Continuing the Story

Alice waited eight years before the Olympics were restored in 1948. She attended Albany State College to supplement her Tuskegee degree. Despite back pain, she tried out for and secured a place on the United States track team, qualifying solely for the high jump competition. She admitted to feeling aches, which she attributed to her age and not being in superb condition. Sailing on a boat to London, England, Alice enjoyed a lack of the racial barriers prevalent in her home country. Previously, she had been denied rooms in hotels and forced to eat in segregated restaurants, even in northern states. During her Olympic travels, Alice shared sleeping spaces, bathrooms, and dining facilities with white teammates.

In August, 1948, she strained her hip during a practice jump, but the soreness did not interfere with her movement. She high-jumped 5 feet 6½ inches—a women's Olympic and world record that remained unsurpassed until 1956—to become the first black woman to win an Olympic gold medal. King George VI presented her with the gold medal. Alice toured Europe, where she was honored with parades. She met such notable people as future French president Charles de Gaulle, U.S. president Harry S. Truman, and former First Lady Eleanor Roosevelt. In New York, her childhood idol, Count Basie, hosted a party to celebrate Alice's triumph.

After returning home, Alice was honored along the 175-mile route from Atlanta to her hometown of Albany. In communities

MAJOR CHAMPIONSHIPS

Year	Competition	Event	Place
1939-1948	AAU National Championships	Outdoor high jump	1st
1941-1942	AAU National Championships	4×100-meter relay	1st
1941	AAU National Championships	Indoor high jump	1st
1942	AAU National Championships	100-meter dash	1st
1943	AAU National Championships	50-meter dash	1st
1944	AAU National Championships	50-meter dash	1st
1945	AAU National Championships	Indoor high jump	1st
1945	AAU National Championships	50-meter dash	1st
	AAU National Championships	100-meter dash	1st
1941-1948	AAU National Championships	Individual high-point trophy	Four-time winner
1946	AAU National Championships	Indoor high jump	1st
	AAU National Championships	50-meter dash	1st
	AAU National Championships	100-meter dash	1st
1947	AAU National Championships	50-meter dash	1st
1948	Olympic Games	High jump	Gold

477

HONORS AND AWARDS

1975	Inducted into National Track and Field Hall of Fame
1979	Inducted into Georgia Sports Hall of Fame
1996	Named one of 100 Greatest Living American Olympic Athletes Inducted into National Black College Alumni Hall of Fame
1999	Named one of Georgia's top 100 athletes of the 1900's Inducted into Albany State University Sports Hall of Fame

along the highway, people stood waiting to see Alice and to give her flowers and presents. Her victory, however, did not change segregated social traditions. At the ceremony held at the Albany Municipal Auditorium, blacks and whites were required to sit on separate sides.

Summary

Significant because she was the first black woman to win an Olympic gold medal, Alice Coachman also demonstrated that age did not necessarily impede the performance of a determined athlete. She broke both racial and gender barriers before retiring from athletic competition. Alice graduated from Albany State College with a home economics degree and began teaching physical education and coaching at Georgia and Alabama high schools. She became a role model for African Americans and female athletes. She was featured with Jessie Owens in a billboard advertisement for Coca-Cola, a Georgia-manufactured soft drink.

Despite the immediate acclaim Alice received after her victory, she is often omitted from histories of African American athletes. Sprinter Wilma Rudolph is frequently mistaken as the first black woman from the United States to have won an Olympic track and field gold medal. During the 1990's, the press finally rediscovered Alice, who was profiled as a pioneering athlete for publicity about the 1996 Atlanta Olympics, for which she was a torchbearer. Her team beret was displayed at an exhibit on Olympic women.

She established the Alice Coachman Track and Field Foundation to aid athletes and instructed at track and field clinics. Albany State hosts the annual Alice Coachman Invitational, and a local school was named for her. Alice has received numerous honors, including being inducted in athletic halls of fame and being named one of the one hundred greatest living American Olympic athletes.

Elizabeth D. Schafer

Additional Sources:

Davis, Michael D. *Black American Women in Olympic Track and Field.* Jefferson, N.C.: McFarland, 1992.

Jeansonne, John. "A Leap Past Prejudice." *Newsday,* May 6, 1996, p. A46.

Lee, D. T. "High Jumper." *American Legacy: Celebrating African-American History and Culture* 6 (Spring, 2000): 12, 14.

TY COBB

Sport: Baseball

Born: December 18, 1886
  Narrows, Georgia
Died: July 17, 1961
  Atlanta, Georgia

Early Life

Tyrus Raymond Cobb was born on December 18, 1886, in Narrows, Georgia. His father, W. H. Cobb, was a schoolteacher and hoped that his intelligent son would seek a higher education. Ty, however, was fascinated by baseball; he played in semiprofessional games throughout Georgia, Tennessee, and Alabama. When he was given a tryout by the Augusta, Georgia, team in 1904, he grabbed the opportunity to play professional baseball. His father was disturbed but thought that Ty would tire of the difficult life of a ballplayer and go back to school. Even though he was displeased at Ty's choice, he told him not to come home a failure.

The Road to Excellence

When Ty reported to the Augusta team, he was a very unskilled ballplayer. He was not a consistent outfielder and he made many errors; in addition, he only hit .237 that first year. When he returned the next year, however, he was a heavier and taller eighteen-year-old, if not a more mature one. He began showing signs of the Cobb style; he ran wildly on the bases and tried to stretch singles into doubles. His manager instructed him in the art of baseball: the hit and run, the bunt, the stolen base, and bat control. He began to bring his game together; baseball became a thinking game for him as well as a physical one. He soon improved his fielding and his batting average and became an outstanding player. The Detroit Tigers began to show an interest in him. Just before being called up by that major league team in August, 1905, Ty's father was shot by his wife when he attempted to sneak into the house. Many of Ty's later difficulties in getting along with teammates and others can be traced to his father's death. He became distrustful and seemed to see slights and insults in the most casual actions.

The Emerging Champion

Ty's first few months at Detroit were not successful; he fielded badly and hit only .240. In 1906 he began to come into his own; he hit a very respectable .320 and improved his base running and fielding. The year was, however, marked by a bitter feud between Ty and a group of veteran players. He did not overlook the rookie hazing they gave him but fought back. The feud continued in 1907, but Detroit won the pennant and Ty

had a splendid year. He hit .350 and led the league in batting average, runs batted in, and steals. His style was beginning to be defined; he flustered infielders by his daring moves and manufactured runs for his team.

The Tigers won two more pennants in 1908 and 1909, although they failed to win a World Series. Ty continued to dazzle fans with his batting and running. He won his second and third batting championships in these years, as well as the American League Triple Crown in 1909.

Continuing the Story

The years that followed were triumphant for Ty, although he was still dogged by controversy, and the Tigers were not to win another pennant while he played on the team. Some critics accused Ty of being interested only in his personal statistics and not in the team; but his achievement could not be faulted. In 1917, for example, he led the league in batting, steals, hits, doubles, triples, and slugging percentage. No other ballplayer in the history of baseball was so dominant in a single year. Ty approached this incredible

MAJOR LEAGUE RECORDS
Highest career batting average, .367 Most runs, 2,245

HONORS AND AWARDS
1911 American League most valuable player 1936 Inducted into National Baseball Hall of Fame

performance year after year. A rival, however, would emerge to challenge not only his dominance but also his popularity.

In 1919, the Red Sox traded Babe Ruth to the New York Yankees. Ruth became in a few short years the idol of America. Ty's aim was to strike fear in the heart of an opponent, to force him into making a mistake that Ty could take advantage of. His play was intense; he never let up. By contrast, Ruth played with an ease and grace that captured everyone. They still respected Ty but they loved the "Bambino."

In addition to winning the hearts of America, Ruth changed the game of baseball. His power

STATISTICS

Season	GP	AB	Hits	2B	3B	HR	Runs	RBI	BA	SA
1905	41	150	36	6	0	1	19	15	.240	.300
1906	98	350	112	13	7	1	45	41	.320	.406
1907	150	605	**212**	29	15	5	97	**116**	.350	.473
1908	150	581	**188**	**36**	**20**	4	88	**108**	.324	.475
1909	156	573	**216**	33	10	**9**	**116**	107	.377	.517
1910	140	509	196	36	13	8	**106**	91	**.385**	**.554**
1911	146	591	**248**	**47**	**24**	8	**147**	**144**	**.420**	**.621**
1912	140	553	**227**	30	23	7	119	90	**.410**	**.586**
1913	122	428	167	18	16	4	70	67	**.390**	.535
1914	97	345	127	22	11	2	69	57	**.368**	.513
1915	156	563	**208**	31	13	3	**144**	99	**.369**	.487
1916	145	542	201	31	10	5	**113**	68	.371	.493
1917	152	588	**225**	**44**	**23**	7	107	102	**.383**	**.571**
1918	111	421	161	19	**14**	3	83	64	**.382**	.515
1919	124	497	**191**	36	13	1	92	70	**.384**	.515
1920	112	428	143	28	8	2	86	63	.334	.451
1921	128	507	197	37	16	12	124	101	.389	.596
1922	137	526	211	42	16	4	99	99	.401	.565
1923	145	556	189	40	7	6	103	88	.340	.469
1924	155	625	211	38	10	4	115	74	.338	.450
1925	121	415	157	31	12	12	97	102	.378	.598
1926	79	233	79	18	5	4	48	62	.339	.511
1927	134	490	175	32	7	5	104	93	.357	.482
1928	95	353	114	27	4	1	54	40	.323	.431
Totals	3,034	11,429	4,191	724	297	118	2,245	1,961	**.367**	.513

Notes: Boldface indicates statistical leader. GP = games played; AB = at bats; 2B = doubles; 3B = triples; HR = home runs; RBI = runs batted in; BA = batting average; SA = slugging average

game was a direct challenge to Ty's finesse game. Ruth had no interest in the hit and run, the steal, or advancing the runner; one home run from Ruth could break open the game. The fans wanted to see the power game, and the teams soon altered their orientation. Ty Cobb had been the perfecter of a style of play that now seemed obsolete. He, of course, hated the power game and he hated Babe Ruth. He tried to defend the game that made him famous, the game that he loved.

Ty continued to win batting championships and to compile the most hits and the most steals, but something was missing. He tried to add to his formidable list of accomplishments by becoming player-manager for the Tigers in 1921. At first, he had some success as a manager; his instruction of individual players helped to enhance their performance. Yet, Ty could not understand why they could not perform the way he did after being instructed. The tension on the team increased, and the Tigers finished sixth. Ty could not perform the miracles for a team that he was able to do on his own. In addition, he narrowly lost the batting championship; he was no longer as dominant as he had been. The Tigers were able to finish second only once in the years that Ty managed them. The end of his career as a Tiger and a manager was stormy. He was accused of fixing a game.

Ty Cobb finished his career with the Philadelphia Athletics as an old man with tired legs, but one who could still hit. He was a bitter and isolated man who had given everything to excel in a career that had now come to an end. He died in Atlanta, Georgia, on July 17, 1961.

In 1994, actor Tommy Lee Jones portrayed Ty in the film *Cobb*, based on a book by journalist Al Stump. The film followed Sutmp's struggles to get the long-retired Ty to cooperate with him while he was writing his biography. Robert Wuhl played Stump.

Summary

Ty Cobb was one of the greatest baseball players of all time. He brought a dedication to the game that sometimes bordered on obsession. Many of his records that once seemed likely to stand forever have been broken, but the individual achievements of Ty remain unique; no one has matched him in his total mastery of the game.

James Sullivan

Additional Sources:

Alexander, Charles C. *Ty Cobb*. New York: Oxford University Press, 1984.

Bak, Richard. *Ty Cobb: His Tumultuous Life and Times*. Dallas, Tex.: Taylor Publishing, 1994.

Cobb, Ty. *My Life in Baseball: The True Record*. Edited by Al Stump. New York: Doubleday, 1961. Reprint. Lincoln: University of Nebraska Press, 1993.

McCallum, John D. *Ty Cobb*. New York: Praeger, 1975.

Stump, Al. *Cobb: A Biography*. Chapel Hill, N.C.: Algonquin Books of Chapel Hill, 1994.

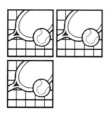

HENRI COCHET

Sport: Tennis

Born: December 14, 1901
      Lyons, France
Died: April 1, 1987
      St. Germain-en-Laye, France

Early Life

Henri Cochet was born on December 14, 1901, in Lyons, France. He was introduced to tennis at the age of seven. His father was the manager of the Lyons Lawn Tennis Club, and Henri would act as ball boy, so that he could get a closer look at the tennis matches. After the matches were over, he would pick up an old racket and practice against the wall. Henri practiced against a wall for two years before he was allowed to play on the courts with school friends. He loved the game and made steady improvement until he was the best young player in Lyons. Henri was thirteen when World War I started and the club was used by army trucks as a garage. After the war, he went back to playing tennis with more enthusiasm than ever.

The Road to Excellence

Henri stood only 5 feet 6 inches tall, and he usually found himself playing opponents who were larger and stronger. This challenge was very good experience for him, since it toughened his game and his resolve. Henri was becoming very adept at taking the ball early and rushing to the net. Touch and timing were his greatest assets. In 1920, he won the Lyons Championship for

the first time. His game was now ready for Paris and beyond.

Henri went to Paris in 1921 and entered its covered court championship. He and another unknown at the time, Jean Borotra, met in the final, and Henri prevailed easily. Borotra, along with Jacques Brugnon and René Lacoste, joined with Henri to become known as the Four Musketeers. These four players helped France to dominate the tennis world during the late 1920's and

the early part of the 1930's. Henri and Borotra became members of the French Davis Cup team in 1922, and a year later all the Four Musketeers were competing for their country on the team.

Henri won his first of five French Championships in singles in 1922. Always a very quiet man, and at times giving the impression of disinterest during a match, Henri surprised many an opponent with his capacity to turn the tide in his favor with his seemingly effortless strokes. He was not one for hard practice or for unnecessary movement during a match. Timing was the key to his game, and he was able—on numerous occasions in his career—to refine it to near perfection.

The Emerging Champion

In 1923, Henri played against Denmark, Ireland, and Switzerland for the Davis Cup team, but he did not travel to the United States or to Wimbledon to compete for the championships there. Lacoste defeated him in the 1924 French Championships and he lost to Vincent Richards in the finals of the Olympics. It was apparent to most observers that Henri was not himself and that he was not in good health. For some months

he suffered from influenza. As a natural player when his game was on, he was almost unbeatable; when his game was off, however, he became prey to many of lesser abilities. During 1925, Henri did not play any Davis Cup matches and entered a minimum number of tournaments. Journalists were even beginning to talk of him as being near the end of his career.

Henri was not on his way out, but about to start the greatest phase of his career. In 1926, he beat both Richards and Lacoste to capture the French Championship singles title. The most stunning match of the year was Henri's victory over Bill Tilden in the quarterfinals of the United States National Championship at Forest Hills, New York. Lacoste would eventually win the title, but Henri had served notice that he was back and playing inspired tennis.

He had won the Wimbledon doubles title that year, but it was not until 1927 that he broke through to take the singles title. He won Wimbledon in a dramatic fashion by rallying back from having lost the first two sets of each of his last three matches. He played Frank Hunter, Tilden, and Borotra in a row and snatched victory out of the jaws of defeat in each match. With Henri and the other Musketeers on the French Davis Cup team, France won its first Davis Cup by defeating the United States. France would not surrender the Cup until 1933.

Continuing the Story

The Four Musketeers dominated tennis in 1928. Henri won both the French and United States singles titles, while Borotra won in Australia, and Lacoste beat Henri to win Wimbledon. The French ruled the tennis world, and Henri was the greatest of the French. Tilden even went so far as to state that Henri Cochet was possibly the best ever to play the game. Henri became even more indispensable to the Davis Cup team in 1929 with the retirement of Lacoste. He also would capture his second Wim-

MAJOR CHAMPIONSHIP VICTORIES AND FINALS

1922, 1926, 1928, 1930, 1932	French Championship
1926, 1928	Wimbledon doubles (with Jacques Brugnon)
1927	U.S. National Championship mixed doubles (with Eileen Bennett)
1927, 1929	Wimbledon
1927, 1930, 1932	French Championship doubles (with Brugnon)
1927, 1931	Wimbledon doubles finalist (with Brugnon)
1928	Wimbledon finalist U.S. National Championship
1928-29	French Championship mixed doubles (with Bennett)
1932	U.S. National Championship finalist
1933	French Championship finalist

OTHER NOTABLE VICTORIES

1920-22	Lyons Championship
1927-32	On winning French Davis Cup team
1937	Professional World Doubles Tournament (with Bill Tilden)
1950	British Covered Court Championship doubles (with Jaroslav Drobny)

bledon singles title that year. His amateur career would last through 1932 after he had amassed two Wimbledon and five French Championship singles titles and one United States National Championship. Henri turned professional after France had lost to Great Britain in the Davis Cup competition in 1933.

His professional career could not live up to the standards he had set during his amateur days. Henri would get the chance to play Tilden again, since Tilden had already turned professional, but the natural gifts and inspiration that had taken him to the top of the amateur ranks were not there with the same intensity. His professional career was of little consequence, and after World War II, Henri was reinstated into the amateur ranks. The glory years were over, but he did manage to win a number of tournaments. He won his last title of significance in 1950, when he and Jaroslav Drobny captured the British Covered Court Championship doubles title.

Having run a successful sporting goods business and also having traveled as a French representative of the Ministry of National Education, Henri made the most of his time outside competitive tennis, without really ever giving up the hold that the game had on him, by being active in various tennis organizations. After a long illness, Henri died on April 1, 1987, in St. Germain-en-Laye, France.

Summary

Most experts agree that Henri Cochet was a tennis genius. His strokes looked effortless and his timing was impeccable. No one else could hit low volleys or half-volleys with the precision that Henri did. Along with the other members of the Four Musketeers, Henri took French tennis to the top during the late 1920's and early 1930's. Neither France nor any other country has produced another all-court player who looked as naturally suited to the game as Henri.

Michael Jeffrys

Additional Sources:

Brown, Gene, ed. *The New York Times Encyclopedia of Sports.* 15 vols. New York: Arno Press, 1979-1980.

Cochet, Henri. *The Art of Tennis.* New York: Hillman-Curl, 1937.

Collins, Bud, and Zander Hollander, eds. *Bud Collins' Modern Encyclopedia of Tennis.* 3d ed. Detroit: Gale, 1997.

Grimsley, Will. *Tennis: Its History, People, and Events.* Englewood Cliffs, N.J.: Prentice-Hall, 1971.

MICKEY COCHRANE

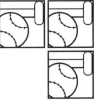

Sport: Baseball

Born: April 6, 1903
　　　Bridgewater, Massachusetts
Died: June 28, 1962
　　　Lake Forest, Illinois

Early Life

Gordon Stanley "Mickey" Cochrane was born on April 6, 1903, in Bridgewater, Massachusetts. The son of a proud Boston Irish father, he was called "Mickey" even as a young boy by everyone except his mother, Sarah. Mickey's father, John, worked as a coachman and caretaker for a wealthy family.

As a child, Mickey had an unusual dream—he wanted to be the manager of a baseball team. He was a good athlete and played several sports at Bridgewater High School. After graduation, he attended Boston University and was one of the finest all-around athletes the university had ever had.

In college, Mickey participated in basketball, boxing, track, football, and baseball. He was quite good in football. He played halfback and placekicker and was the captain of the 1923 team. His 53-yard field goal in 1921 was a school record for more than sixty years.

The Road to Excellence

In 1923, while he was still in college, Mickey started playing professional baseball to help pay his tuition. He played for the Dover team of the Eastern Shore League, using the name "Frank King" to protect his amateur status. Mickey preferred playing the outfield, but the only opening on the team was for a catcher, so he played that position. He remained a catcher for the rest of his career.

Mickey did not earn enough money to stay in school playing professional ball, so, because his education was important to him, he took on other jobs too, playing saxophone in a jazz band

and washing dishes. As a result, he was able to finish his degree.

After college, Mickey pursued his baseball career full time. He played well on the Dover team, batting over .300 and stealing 14 bases. He was only an average catcher, but he was fast and competitive and he earned a reputation as a hustler.

In 1924, Mickey signed with the Portland, Oregon, team of the Pacific Coast League, one step below the major leagues. Connie Mack, owner of the major league Philadelphia Athletics, wanted Mickey so badly that he bought controlling interest in the Portland team. A year later, Mickey joined the Athletics.

485

That first year with the Athletics was an important one for Mickey's career because it was the year he learned to be a better catcher. When he signed on with Philadelphia, the team already had a good catcher, Ralph "Cy" Perkins, who was nearing the end of his career. Perkins gave Mickey a considerable amount of coaching and helped him to improve his skills.

The Emerging Champion

The catcher's job is one of the most physically demanding of any on a baseball team, and it takes great stamina to play many games at that position. Mickey had that stamina.

In his first season in the majors, he caught in more than one hundred games, and he caught in one hundred or more games in each of the next ten seasons, from 1926 to 1935.

During those first eleven years, Mickey—now called "Black Mike" by many teammates and fans—also proved himself to be a great base runner and batsman. He batted .331 his first season, and dipped below .300 only three times in the next ten years. His lifetime batting average was an impressive .320.

One of his greatest years was 1928, when he was named the American League's most valuable player. Mickey batted only .293 that year, but the Athletics finished second in the league and Mickey's leadership was important to the team's overall success.

The Athletics won the American League pennant in 1929, 1930, and 1931, and won the 1929 and 1930 World Series. Owner Connie Mack said that Mickey was the most important reason for their success, although there were other big stars on the team (including Jimmie Foxx and Lefty Grove). Mickey had a way of encouraging his teammates and of soothing temperamental stars.

Mickey's abilities at bat, on the base paths, and behind the plate—and his ability to lead the team—helped make the Athletics winners. He batted a career-high .357 in 1930 and .349 in 1931, and drove in more than 80 runs both years.

Continuing the Story

In 1934, Mickey became a player-manager for the Detroit Tigers. He was still the league's best catcher, and now he was fulfilling his childhood dream of being a manager. That first year with Detroit, Mickey led the Tigers to the American League pennant.

Mickey's playing career ended on May 25, 1937, when he was hit in the head by a pitch thrown by Irving "Bump" Hadley of the Yankees. He was carried off the field and remained unconscious for ten days. He never played again.

Many people believe that if Mickey were playing today, the protective helmet that batters are now required to wear would have saved him from such serious injury.

The Tigers released Mickey the next year, but he returned to baseball in 1950 as general manager for his old team, the Athletics. He later

STATISTICS

Season	GP	AB	Hits	2B	3B	HR	Runs	RBI	BA	SA
1925	134	420	139	21	5	6	69	55	.331	.448
1926	120	370	101	8	9	8	50	47	.273	.408
1927	126	432	146	20	6	12	80	80	.338	.495
1928	131	468	137	26	12	10	92	57	.293	.464
1929	135	514	170	37	8	7	113	95	.331	.475
1930	130	487	174	42	5	10	110	85	.357	.526
1931	122	459	160	31	6	17	87	89	.349	.553
1932	139	518	152	35	4	23	118	112	.293	.510
1933	130	429	138	30	4	15	104	60	.322	.515
1934	129	437	140	32	1	2	74	76	.320	.412
1935	115	411	131	33	3	5	93	47	.319	.450
1936	44	126	34	8	0	2	24	17	.270	.381
1937	27	98	30	10	1	2	27	12	.306	.490
Totals	1,482	5,169	1,652	333	64	119	1,041	832	.320	.478

Notes: GP = games played; AB = at bats; 2B = doubles; 3B = triples; HR = home runs; RBI = runs batted in; BA = batting average; SA = slugging average

HONORS AND AWARDS

1928, 1934	American League most valuable player
1933-35	American League All-Star Team
1947	Inducted into National Baseball Hall of Fame

scouted for the Yankees and Tigers, and in 1960, he became a vice president in the Tigers organization, a job he held until his death.

In between baseball jobs, Mickey ran a dude ranch in Wyoming, worked for a trucking company, and, during World War II, served in the United States Navy's fitness program. Whenever an opportunity came along, he returned to baseball. He was between baseball jobs in 1947 when he was elected to the National Baseball Hall of Fame.

On June 28, 1962, suffering from a respiratory ailment, Mickey died in Lake Forest, Illinois. He was only fifty-nine years old. His life, like his playing career, had been suddenly cut short.

Summary

Mickey Cochrane was a powerful hitter, a fast and smart base runner, and a fine defensive catcher. Perhaps most important, he was a natural leader, able to help his teammates play their best too. In a career limited to only thirteen seasons because of injury, he led his team to the pennant five times.

Cynthia A. Bily

Additional Sources:

Appel, Martin, and Burt Goldblatt. *Baseball's Best: The Hall of Fame Gallery.* New York: McGraw-Hill, 1977.

Bevis, Charlie. *Mickey Cochrane: The Life of a Baseball Hall of Fame Catcher.* Jefferson, N.C.: McFarland, 1998.

Shatzkin, Mike, et al., eds. *The Ballplayers: Baseball's Ultimate Biographical Reference.* New York: William Morrow, 1990.

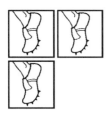

SEBASTIAN COE

Sport: Track and field (middle-distance runs)

Born: September 29, 1956
London, England

Early Life

Sebastian Newbold Coe, known as "Seb," was born on September 29, 1956, in Chiswick, a suburb of London, England. Peter Coe, his father, was an engineer who became an executive for a Sheffield cutlery company. Although not a runner himself, he became Seb's coach and played an important role in Seb's success. Some of Seb's running ability may have come from Peter's father, Seb's grandfather, who was a professional sprinter. Seb's mother, Angela, was an actress.

His name, Sebastian, was taken from a character in a play by William Shakespeare in which she had performed.

As a child, Seb was not an impressive athlete. He was frail, physically underdeveloped, and suffered severely from allergies. He was also prone to become very nervous in competitive situations. This caused him to do poorly in the examinations that determined which secondary school he would attend, and he was sent to a school where it was assumed students were not capable of college preparatory courses.

The Road to Excellence

Although he had always enjoyed running, Seb did not become a competitive runner until he joined the Hallamshire Harriers athletic club in Sheffield when he was twelve. Initially, he concentrated on cross-country running. In 1971, at age fourteen, he won his first major victory when he finished first in the Yorkshire School Colts division cross-country championship. Four years later, Seb won the English national junior 1,500 meters title, and he decided to concentrate on that event.

This decision had important consequences for his training. Because running 1,500 meters at world-class pace required speed more than endurance, Seb switched from long, slow training runs to repetitions of shorter distances at a fast pace.

Sebastian Coe won his second Olympic gold medal in the 1,500 meters in 1984.

Tony Duffy/Allsport

Also, after enrolling at the University of Loughborough in 1975, Seb used circuit training during the winter months, when it was difficult to run outdoors. This combined weightlifting with a series of jumping exercises, which strengthened his leg muscles.

The Emerging Champion

This training brought dramatic improvement in his times. In 1976, when he was only nineteen, Seb broke the 4-minute barrier in a mile race, finishing in 3 minutes 58.35 seconds. Three years later, in 1979, he set world records in the 800 and 1,500 meters and in the mile. He was ranked first in the world at both 800 and 1,500 meters that year, and *Track and Field News* declared Seb its World Athlete of the Year.

At the 1980 Olympic Games, Seb was the overwhelming favorite to win the gold medal in the 800-meter race. The pressure to live up to this expectation made him so nervous, however, that he ran a disappointing race, finishing second in a slow time. Unhappy with his performance, Seb was determined to use the 1,500-meter race to show what he was capable of doing. In that race, he conserved his energy until the last lap and then used a powerful finishing kick to win in 3 minutes 38.40 seconds.

Seb's running career reached its peak in 1981. He set a world record in the 800 meters in 1 minute 41.72 seconds, a time that was so much faster than what other runners were capable of doing that it remained the world record a decade after it was set. Twice during the year he set world records in the mile run, the second time lowering the record to 3 minutes 47.33 seconds. Because of his outstanding performance, Seb was once again ranked first in the world at 800 and 1,500 meters, and again chosen World Athlete of the Year by *Track and Field News*.

Continuing the Story

After this superb year, Seb was struck down by illness and injury, which made the following

STATISTICS				
Year	Competition	Event	Place	Time
1977	European Cup	800 meters	4th	1:47.61
	European Indoor Championships	800 meters	1st	1:46.5
1978	European Championships	800 meters	3d	1:44.8
1979	European Cup	800 meters	1st	1:47.28
1980	Olympic Games	800 meters	Silver	1:45.9
		1,500 meters	Gold	3:38.4
1981	European Cup	800 meters	1st	1:47.05
	World Cup	800 meters	1st	1:46.16
1982	European Championships	800 meters	2d	1:46.68
1984	Olympic Games	800 meters	Silver	1:43.64
		1,500 meters	Gold	3:32.53 OR
1986	European Championships	800 meters	1st	1:44.50
		1,500 meters	2d	3:41.67
1989	World Championships	1,500 meters	2d	3:35.79
1990	Commonwealth Games	800 meters	6th	1:47.24

Note: OR = Olympic Record

years a nightmare. A stress fracture in his foot prevented him from training for several months in 1982. Then he developed a mysterious illness that doctors were unable to identify. This weakened Seb to the point that he ran poorly in races and was repeatedly beaten by runners who were greatly inferior to him. After his illness was diagnosed as glandular toxoplasmosis, he spent several months in the hospital.

Determined to run in the 1984 Olympic Games in spite of his lack of training, Seb was only able to manage second in the 800 meters. As had been the case in 1980, this only strengthened his determination to do well in the 1,500-meter race. In that race, Seb defeated the favorite and finished first in the Olympic record time of 3 minutes 32.53 seconds. This made him the first person to win two Olympic 1,500-meter gold medals. His victory was especially important to Seb because many sports reporters had written before the Olympics that he was finished as a runner.

This fierce determination to prove himself best in the world at his events, even though handicapped by illness and injury, was one of the qualities that made Seb an outstanding athlete. He continued to race for several years after 1984, but repeated injuries prevented him from regaining the speed that he had had in 1979 when he set his first world records.

He retired from competition in 1990 and began a career in the Parliament following his election as a Conservative Party member in 1992.

Summary

During his running career, Sebastian Coe acquired an impressive collection of Olympic titles, world records, and victories against the world's best runners. Yet what made him a truly heroic figure in athletics was his refusal to give up in the face of severe illness and repeated injuries. It is for this as much as his world records that sports historians rank Seb among the greatest middle-distance runners of all time.

Harold L. Smith

Additional Sources:

The Lincoln Library of Sports Champions. 16 vols. Columbus, Ohio: Frontier Press, 1993.

Wallechinsky, David. *The Complete Book of the Olympics.* Boston: Little, Brown and Company, 1991.

Watman, Mel. *Encyclopedia of Track and Field Athletics.* New York: St. Martin's Press, 1981.

RECORDS
World record at 800 meters in 1981 (1:41.72)
World record at 1,000 meters in 1981 (2:12.18)
World record at 1,500 meters in 1979 (3:21.1)
Five world records at 1 mile: 1976 (3:58.35), 1979 (3:49.0), 1979 (3:48.95), 1981 (3:48.53), 1981 (3:47.33)
American indoor record at 800 meters in 1983 (1:44.91)
Ranked first in the world in 800 meters and 1,500 meters (1979, 1981)

HONORS AND AWARDS	
1979	World Trophy BBC Sports Personality of the Year
1979, 1981	*Track and Field News* World Athlete of the Year *Athletics Weekly World* Athlete of the Year

EDDIE COLLINS

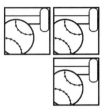

Sport: Baseball

Born: May 2, 1887
    Millerton, New York
Died: March 25, 1951
    Boston, Massachusetts

Early Life

Edward Trowbridge Collins was born May 2, 1887, in Millerton, New York, to John Collins, a railroad freight executive, and Mary (Trowbridge) Collins. He was brought up in nearby Tarrytown, a village southeast of New York City that had been made famous by the author Washington Irving as "Sleepy Hollow Country."

Although he was small as a boy (even as an adult, he grew to be only 5 feet 9 inches tall), Eddie was a natural athlete whose favorite sport was football. In 1903, he was graduated from high school in Tarrytown at the age of sixteen, and he enrolled at Columbia University in New York City, where he became quarterback of the school's football team. In order to earn tuition money, he played semiprofessional baseball in the summers. After Eddie's junior year, a scout for the Philadelphia Athletics of the American League (AL) saw him play and recommended him to Connie Mack, Philadelphia's owner and manager, as a fine professional prospect.

The Road to Excellence

Eddie struck a deal with the Athletics in 1906, but there was a hitch: He was still enrolled at Columbia, and he wanted to preserve his amateur standing so that he could continue to play college sports. Mack thus signed the young prospect to a contract under the name "Sullivan," and Eddie used the pseudonym while he spent the final part of the 1906 season with the Athletics, playing in six games as an infielder and batting .235. When he returned to school for his senior year, he found that he had lost his college eligibility anyway; Mack's ruse had been successful, but

it had been discovered that Eddie had played semiprofessional ball in New England.

Although he could not play for Columbia, Eddie was appointed manager of the school's baseball team, and after his graduation in 1907 he started playing professionally under his own name. He played four games with Newark in the Eastern League—the only minor league games of his career—and spent fourteen more games with Philadelphia before the season's end.

The Emerging Champion

In 1908, Eddie began his major league career in earnest. He played in 102 games for the Athletics, shuttling between second base, shortstop, and the outfield and batting a respectable .273. The next season, he came into his own, batting .346, stealing 61 bases, and winning a job as the A's regular second baseman. Before he retired, he would play more games at second than anyone else in major league history.

In 1910, Eddie hit .322 and led the AL with 81 stolen bases; he also led AL second basemen in every fielding category, helping the Athletics into the World Series against the Chicago Cubs. He was brilliant in the Series, batting .429 and setting a record with 9 hits—including 4 doubles—in Philadelphia's five-game victory. The next season, he continued to be one of the game's top stars, hitting .365 and leading AL second basemen in putouts as the Athletics cruised to a second consecutive pennant and World Series triumph. Together with star third baseman Frank "Home Run" Baker, first baseman Stuffy McGinnis, and shortstop Jack Barry, Eddie became famous as a member of the "$100,000 infield"—so called for their supposed cumulative value, which was staggering for the time.

The Athletics slumped to third place in 1912, but Eddie was, if anything, even better, hitting .348, stealing 63 bases, and leading the league in

491

STATISTICS

Season	GP	AB	Hits	2B	3B	HR	Runs	RBI	BA	SA
1906	6	17	4	0	0	0	1	0	.235	.235
1907	14	20	5	0	1	0	0	2	.250	.350
1908	102	330	90	18	7	1	39	40	.273	.379
1909	153	572	198	30	10	3	104	56	.346	.449
1910	153	583	188	16	15	3	81	81	.322	.417
1911	132	493	180	22	13	3	92	73	.365	.481
1912	153	543	189	25	11	0	**137**	64	.348	.435
1913	148	534	184	23	13	3	**125**	73	.345	.453
1914	152	526	181	23	14	2	**122**	85	.344	.452
1915	155	521	173	22	10	4	118	77	.332	.436
1916	155	545	168	14	17	0	87	52	.308	.396
1917	156	564	163	18	12	0	91	67	.289	.363
1918	97	330	91	8	2	2	51	30	.276	.330
1919	140	518	165	19	7	4	87	80	.319	.405
1920	153	601	222	37	13	3	115	75	.369	.489
1921	139	526	177	20	10	2	79	58	.337	.424
1922	154	598	194	20	12	1	92	69	.324	.403
1923	145	505	182	22	5	5	89	67	.360	.453
1924	152	556	194	27	7	6	108	86	.349	.455
1925	118	425	147	26	3	3	80	80	.346	.442
1926	106	375	129	32	4	1	66	62	.344	.459
1927	95	225	76	12	1	1	50	15	.338	.413
1928	36	33	10	3	0	0	3	7	.303	.394
1929	9	7	0	0	0	0	0	0	.000	.000
1930	3	2	1	0	0	0	1	0	.500	.500
Totals	2,826	9,949	3,311	437	187	47	1,818	1,299	.328	.410

Notes: Boldface indicates statistical leader. GP = games played; AB = at bats; 2B = doubles; 3B = triples; HR = home runs; RBI = runs batted in; BA = batting average; SA = slugging average

runs scored for the first of three consecutive seasons. In 1913, Philadelphia won yet another pennant, and Eddie was again a major contributor, batting .345 in the regular season and .421 in the Athletics' World Series defeat of the New York Giants.

Eddie earned the nickname "Cocky" for his hustling, aggressive style of play. If he was arrogant, he had good reason to be; there was little he could not do on a baseball field. He was a brilliant defensive player and a remarkable baserunner, and he ranked among the league leaders in batting average and walks drawn year after year. He did not have much home-run power—but in the dead-ball era of pre-1920's baseball, neither did anyone else. In 1914, his multiple talents were acknowledged with the Chalmers Award, the equivalent of the modern most valuable player award. That season, he led Philadelphia to a fourth pennant in five years, but the heavily favored Athletics lost the World Series to the Boston "Miracle Braves."

Continuing the Story

With its great infield and star pitchers Eddie Plank and Chief Bender, Philadelphia had become a baseball dynasty. Under financial pressure exacerbated by the emergence of the upstart Federal League, however, Connie Mack sold his stars to other teams. Eddie was sent to the Chicago White Sox in exchange for $50,000, and the decimated Philadelphia Athletics became the first team in major league history to go from first

MAJOR LEAGUE RECORDS

Most stolen bases, World Series, career, 14 (record shared)
Most seasons as active player, American League, career (25)
Most games played by a second baseman, career (2,650)
Most putouts by a second baseman, career (6,526)
Most assists by a second baseman, career (7,630)

HONORS AND AWARDS

1914	Chalmers Award
1939	National Baseball Hall of Fame

place to last in consecutive seasons.

With the White Sox, Eddie joined another powerful team that included star pitchers Red Faber and Ed Cicotte, slugging first baseman Jacques Fournier, and the brilliant outfielder "Shoeless" Joe Jackson. Eddie hit .332—second in the league to Ty Cobb—led the AL in walks drawn, and finished second in runs scored and third in stolen bases. The White Sox finished in third place, but they were clearly an up-and-coming team. In 1916 they climbed to second, and in 1917 Chicago took over the league, winning one hundred games and finishing nine games in front of second-place Boston. Eddie was again terrific in the World Series, hitting .409 and scoring the winning run on a dramatic play in the final game of Chicago's victory over the New York Giants.

Eddie played in only ninety-seven games in 1918, and his average dropped to .276. The Sox slumped badly, finishing in sixth place. World War I was raging in Europe, and Eddie enlisted in the Marines, but the war ended before he could be sent overseas. The next season, though, Chicago and Eddie came roaring back. The White Sox edged Cleveland for the pennant, and Eddie batted .319 and led the league in steals. In the infamous World Series of 1919, he was one of the few key Chicago players who did not join Jackson, Cicotte, and the other "Black Sox" in throwing the contest to the underdog Cincinnati Reds.

Major league baseball changed dramatically in the 1920's with the arrival of the "lively ball" era. Led by the example of Babe Ruth, players began hitting home runs in unprecedented numbers, and the speed-and-singles style of play that Eddie had mastered became obsolete almost overnight. Eddie, though, remained one of the

game's great players, hitting over .300 for nine of the decade's ten seasons, with a high of .360 in 1923. He also led the league twice more in steals, the last time at the advanced baseball age of thirty-seven.

In 1925, the White Sox named their respected veteran star to be the team's player-manager, but although Eddie hit .346 that year and .344 the next, the team finished in fifth place both times. After the 1926 season, Chicago released Eddie, and he finished his twenty-five-year career with four seasons as a part-time player and coach for

AP/Wide World Photos

the Athletics, who displaced Ruth's Yankees as the AL's top franchise.

After coaching for Philadelphia through the 1932 season, Eddie took a series of front-office jobs with the Boston Red Sox. He was instrumental in acquiring the young Ted Williams for Boston, and he remained with the Red Sox until his death from heart failure in 1951 at the age of sixty-three. In 1939, he was inducted into the National Baseball Hall of Fame.

Summary

Eddie Collins turned in one of the longest and most distinguished careers in major league history. He was a brilliant offensive and defensive player for more than two decades, and his multiple skills and hustling on-field leadership made him a key part of several of the best teams of the early century.

Robert McClenaghan

Additional Sources:

Hickok, Ralph. *A Who's Who of Sports Champions.* Boston: Houghton Mifflin, 1995.

Porter, David L., ed. *Biographical Dictionary of American Sports: Baseball.* Westport, Conn.: Greenwood Press, 1987.

Shatzkin, Mike, et al., eds. *The Ballplayers: Baseball's Ultimate Biographical Reference.* New York: William Morrow, 1990.

NADIA COMĂNECI

Sport: Gymnastics

Born: November 12, 1961
Onesti, Romania

Early Life

Nadia Comăneci was born on November 12, 1961, in Onesti, Romania. Nadia's father was an auto mechanic, and her mother a hospital caretaker. Nadia has one brother who is four years her elder.

Nadia was a lively child, but she was also very serious. She did not smile often and seemed emotionally strong. Nadia's release for her excessive energy was to run and jump and to pretend

Nadia Comăneci dismounts from the uneven bars in the 1976 Olympics.

to be a gymnast. In 1968, when Nadia was just six years old, she was discovered by Bela Karolyi. Karolyi was the Romanian Olympic gymnastics coach.

The Road to Excellence

Nadia's parents consented to the recruitment of their daughter by Karolyi. At the age of seven, Nadia competed in the Romanian National Junior Championships, where she placed thirteenth. After the meet, Coach Karolyi gave her a doll that was to remind her never to finish thirteenth again. The following year, Nadia won the National Junior Championships.

In 1975, Nadia was finally eligible to enter the senior international competition. The first competition she entered was the European Championships, in Skien, Norway. Many well-known gymnasts were in attendance, including Russian gymnasts Ludmila Turishcheva and Nelli Kim. Nadia placed first in the vault, uneven bars, beam, and all-around. She placed second to Nelli Kim in the floor exercises.

In March, 1976, Nadia entered the American Cup competition in New York City. In this competition one male and one female gymnast represent each of the participating nations. Nadia won the Cup for Romania.

The Emerging Champion

Nadia stood 5 feet tall and weighed 86 pounds when she won her position on the Romanian Olympic team. Nadia was just fourteen years old when the

495

1976 Olympics were held in Montreal, Canada. The Romanian team was the youngest gymnastics team in history to enter Olympic competition.

Although Nadia had won several major gymnastics meets, she still remained an unknown to the vast majority of sports fans. It was not long, however, before she would become a household word.

At the 1976 Olympics, the Romanian team received the beam as its first event in the team rotation. The beam is considered to be the least desirable event in which to begin a competition because of the balance and precise movement necessary. The rotation, however, did not bother Nadia. As the well-known and favored Russian gymnasts looked on, Nadia performed without apparent error. She received a 9.9 on a 10-point scale.

Nadia next moved to the uneven bars. Here she became the first gymnast in Olympic history to score a perfect 10 points. Led by Nadia, the Romanian team earned a silver medal in the team competition. The Soviet team won the gold.

During the individual competition, Nadia again scored a perfect 10 on both the uneven bars and the beam. She also won a gold medal in-

dividually in the all-around and a bronze medal in the floor exercises. When the competition was completed, Nadia had received the perfect score of 10 a total of seven times.

Nadia made Olympic history with her perfect scores. She also made history with her unique dismount from the uneven bars. What is now known as the Salto Comăneci dismount was first performed by Nadia at the 1976 Olympics. She improved the repertoire on the beam by doing three back handsprings in a row.

Continuing the Story

After the 1976 Olympics, Nadia returned to her Romanian homeland as a heroine. She and her family received many gratuities from the Romanian government, including vacations and an automobile. Nadia became the youngest Romanian to receive the Hero of Socialist Work Award, the highest honor bestowed by the Romanian government.

Over the next five years, Nadia grew four inches; struggled with illness, conditioning, and coaching changes; and continued to compete with varying degrees of success. In 1981 her coach Bela Karolyi and his wife defected to the United States, and Nadia competed in her last major competition: the World University Games in Bucharest, Romania. Nadia officially retired from the sport at age twenty-two, in 1984, shortly before the Olympic Games in Los Angeles.

She went on to become a judge and a coach of the Romanian national team. In 1989 she defected to the United States shortly before the fall of the Romanian government. In the early 1990's, Nadia renewed her friendship with American gymnast Bart Conner. The two became engaged in 1994 and married, in Romania, on April 26, 1996. Both are editors of and regular contributors to *International Gymnast* magazine, coach at Bart Conner's Gymnast Academy in Norman, Oklahoma, give public appearances and workshops, and are

STATISTICS

Year	Competition	Event	Place	Event	Place
1975	European Championships	All-Around	1st	Balance beam	1st
		Floor exercise	2d	Vault	1st
		Uneven parallel bars	1st		
1976	American Cup	All-Around	1st	Vault	1st
		Uneven parallel bars	1st		
	Chunichi Cup	All-Around	1st		
	Olympic Games	All-Around	Gold	Balance beam	Gold
		Floor exercise	Bronze	Vault	4th
		Uneven parallel bars	Gold	Team	Silver
1977	European Championships	All-Around	1st	Vault	2d
		Uneven parallel bars	1st		
1978	World Championships	All-Around	4th	Balance beam	1st
		Floor exercise	8th	Vault	2d
		Uneven parallel bars	5th	Team	2d
1979	European Championships	All-Around	1st	Balance beam	3d
		Floor exercise	1st	Vault	1st
		Uneven parallel bars	4th		
	World Championships	Team	1st		
1980	Olympic Games	All-Around	Silver	Vault	5th
		Floor exercise	Gold	Team	Silver
		Balance beam	Gold		

deeply involved in children's charities, especially the Muscular Dystrophy Association and the Canadian Quebec Agency for adopting Romanian children.

Summary

At the age of fourteen, Nadia Comăneci became the first gymnast in Olympic history to score a perfect 10. She dazzled the audience as they watched her receive a total of seven perfect scores before the 1976 Olympics were completed.

Her persistence and fearlessness allowed her to exhibit skills never performed before. The Salto Comăneci dismount bears her name as the initiator of the twisting backward dismount from the uneven bars. Nadia's personality, performance ability, and perfection of the most difficult moves helped to make women's gymnastics a premier event of the Olympic Games.

Joella H. Mehrhof

Additional Sources:

Comăneci, Nadia. *Nadia: The Autobiography of Nadia Comăneci.* New York: Proteus Books, 1981.

RECORDS AND MILESTONES
Achieved first perfect score (10) in the history of Olympic gymnastics competition, and went on to receive a total of seven perfect scores during the 1976 Montreal Olympic Games
Modern dismount off the uneven parallel bars, the "Salto Comăneci," is named after Nadia. She was the first to perform the maneuver in international competition (the 1976 Olympic Games)
Became the first woman to win the European All-Around title three times

HONORS AND AWARDS	
1976	Presented with the Hero of Socialist Work Award (she became the youngest Romanian ever to receive this honor) ABC *Wide World of Sports* Athlete of the Year
1990	Inducted into Sudafed International Women's Sports Hall of Fame
1993	Inducted into International Gymnastics Hall of Fame
1998	Flo Hyman Award
1999	World Sports Award

Connock, Marion. *Nadia of Romania.* London: Duckworth, 1977.

Gray, Kevin. "Head over Heels: For Gold Medal Gymnasts Nadia Comăneci and Bart Conner, Love Is Something to Flip For." *People Weekly,* March 27, 1995, 105-106.

Johnson, Anne Janette. "Nadia Comăneci." In *Great Women in Sports.* Detroit, Mich.: Visible Ink Press, 1996.

Miklowitz, Gloria D. *Nadia Comăneci.* New York: Grosset and Dunlap, 1977.

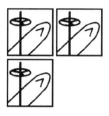

DEBORAH COMPAGNONI

Sport: Skiing

Born: June 4, 1970
Bormio, Italy

Early Life

Born a child of the mountains, Deborah Compagnoni grew up in Santa Caterina Valfurva, Italy, a small village on the northern border where her father was a ski instructor. As a child she learned to speak Italian, English, and German. Her hobbies were oil painting, reading, cooking, and studying flora. Her role model was Ingemar Stenmark, a skier from the flatlands of Sweden who had won a record eighty-six World Cup races.

The Road to Excellence

In 1987, Deborah began to enter various races in skiing. In that year, she came in fifth at Sestrière in the super-giant slalom, then fourth in the junior giant slalom World Champion Cup held in Val d'Isère, France. After this she began to train seriously in Italy, Austria, and the French Alps.

Deborah's first serious injury occurred in January, 1988. During a downhill race, she tore the anterior cruciate ligament in her right knee. In 1990, when she was almost fully recovered, she was again injured, this time with a fractured tibia. In addition, she endured a near-fatal intestinal block. By January, 1991, she was able to enter the World Cup race in Vail, Colorado, where she placed fourth in the giant slalom. During the 1991-1992 season, she entered six races and finished second in all but one. She was beginning to discover that her specialties were the slalom and the giant slalom.

The Emerging Champion

The year 1992 was important for Deborah. She won her first World Cup race, in the super-giant slalom, and collected several silver medals. She surprised everyone by winning the gold medal in the super-giant slalom in the Olympic Games held in Albertville, France. However, two days later, she fell during the giant slalom, tearing her left anterior cruciate ligament.

In the 1994 Winter Olympics in Lillehammer, Norway, Deborah again won the gold medal in the giant slalom. She dedicated her prize to her friend Ulrike Maier, an Austrian, who had died in a downhill crash shortly before the Olympics. Maier was known on the women's circuit as a role model for many women skiers. Deborah closed that season with a success in the Narvik World Cup. During the next four years, she continued racing.

Italian skiier Deborah Compagnoni at the World Championships in 1999.

498

A race in Park City on November 21, 1997, was especially memorable. During the Café de Columbia World Cup the ice on the slopes was treacherous and the light was flat, so that skiers could not see bumps ahead. The conditions caused twenty racers to either crash or miss gates and fall. Deborah skied well, however, beating runner-up Alexandra Meissnitzer of Austria by a combined 3.41 seconds over two runs and finishing nearly a full second in front of Germany's Martina Ertl in the American opening event. It was her second decisive giant slalom win of the season. Deborah said of the race, "My knees hurt, but that's nothing new, and everyone else has problems. I never made excuses and never will."

The 1997-1998 season saw Deborah ski with calculation rather than with instinct, and she was more efficient. On December 27, 1997, in Lienz, Austria, she experienced a disappointing loss by only 0.28 second to Ylva Nowen of Sweden. However, in Bormio, Italy, near her home in Santa Caterina, Deborah won the first giant slalom of 1998, her ninth consecutive victory in this event.

The best of this season was yet to come. On February 11, 1998, at the Winter Olympics in Nagano, Japan, the weather was rainy on Mount Higashidate, and Deborah was the last skier to start in the afternoon. Martina Ertl from Germany had won the giant slalom in the World Cup in 1996, but Deborah had an uncanny ability to peak under great pressure. She beat Ertl by 0.37 second and was almost 2 seconds in front of Anita Wachter of Austria, who had been the 1988 combined Olympic champion and overall World Cup winner in 1993. Deborah won the gold medal for the giant slalom and the silver for the slalom, making her the first woman to win three consecutive gold medals in Olympic skiing.

Continuing the Story

Deborah's quick smile and winning ways have made her the darling of Italian women's skiing. She can no longer lift heavy weights or put her knees through a standard training regimen, but she can handle pressure and steep, technically difficult slopes with stunning facility. One friend said of her that "she eats pressure for breakfast and never gives in." A small-town woman, in 1998 Deborah was working at her parents' Santa Caterina resort hotel. Deborah decided to give up her modeling career to concentrate on skiing and winning more medals in the 2002 Winter Olympics in Salt Lake City, Utah.

MAJOR CHAMPIONSHIPS

Year	Competition	Event	Place
1986	World Junior Championships	Downhill	3d
1987	World Junior Championships	Downhill	3d
		Giant slalom	1st
1992	Olympic Games	Super-G	Gold
1994	Olympic Games	Giant slalom	Gold
1996	World Championships	Giant slalom	1st
1997	World Championships	Giant slalom	1st
		Slalom	1st
	World Cup	Overall	4th
		Giant slalom	1st
		Slalom	3d
1998	Olympic Games	Giant slalom	Gold
		Slalom	Silver

Summary

From a small town in northern Italy, Deborah Compagnoni has gained world recognition to become the first woman ever to win a gold medal in three different Olympic Games: 1992, 1994, and 1998. She was able to overcome two serious knee injuries as well as several other critical surgeries on the way.

Winifred Whelan

Additional Sources:

Araton, Harvey. "New Champion Stops to Mourn an Old Friend." *The New York Times Current Events Edition,* February 25, 1994, p. B7, 9.

Chamberlain, Tony. "She's an Italian Heroine: Compagnoni Giant in Stature." *Boston Globe,* February 21, 1998, p. G3.

Clarey, Christopher. "With Styles Poles Apart, Italian Stars Seek Gold." *The New York Times,* February 8, 1998, p. 8.

Dufresne, Chris. "Winter Olympics 1998: This Hat Trick Is One for the Book, Alpine Skiing: Compagnoni Makes History." *Los Angeles Times,* February 20, 1998, p. 3.

Johnson, William Oscar. "The Alberto-Ville Games." *Sports Illustrated,* March 2, 1992, 22-27.

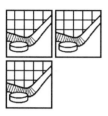

LIONEL CONACHER

Sport: Ice hockey

Born: May 24, 1900
Toronto, Ontario, Canada
Died: May 26, 1954
Ottawa, Ontario, Canada

Early Life

Born to working-class parents, Lionel Conacher entered the world amidst celebrations of the birthday of Queen Victoria. Although his parents were not in any way athletic, it was a different story with Lionel and his eight siblings. His brother Charlie played in the National Hockey League (NHL) and was elected to the Hall of Fame while another brother, Roy, also played professional hockey, leading the NHL one year in scoring. To the Conacher children, sport seemed one route to a better life.

The Road to Excellence

In his early years, Lionel's favorite game was road hockey, a game he frequently played with his brothers and sisters. His sporting world expanded in 1913 when he joined some neighborhood boys in a game of football. Lionel's problem soon became that he could not decide what sport to pursue. He added baseball and lacrosse to his sports, then began wrestling, winning the provincial championship of Ontario, and boxing, where he became light heavyweight champion of Canada in 1920. Football, however, became his main sport as he led his team to the championship of Toronto in 1914. He continued to pursue that game into the 1920's, excelling to the point where he became a household name across Canada when he led his Toronto Argonauts in capturing the Grey Cup, the national football championship of Canada. Hockey had also become one of his athletic pursuits, although it was not his best game.

The Emerging Champion

By 1920 there was no question that Lionel was the best athlete in the city of Toronto, having won both individual and team championships in a variety of sports. He had earned a nickname from a sportswriter that would stick with him for the remainder of his career. That the "Big Train," at twenty years of age, needed a way to earn a paycheck would determine the athletic path Lionel would follow. In an age where amateur athleticism was an ideal, few sports afforded Lionel the opportunity to make a living. One that did was hockey, as the National Hockey League had become a professional league. Once having followed that route, however, an athlete's opportunities to play amateur sports ended. Initially Lionel attempted to avoid this fate. He turned down offers to join the Toronto entry in the NHL and continued to excel in football. He also went to work for a bank and then opened a clothing store.

Hockey continued to beckon, however, and eventually Lionel, who had married and was reaching his athletic peak, changed course. In 1923 he joined the Pittsburgh Yellow Jackets, an amateur hockey team, but one that was on the brink of entering the professional world of the NHL. In November, 1925, Lionel signed a contract with the new Pittsburgh NHL franchise. The new professional starred for his team, and his fame over his skill in the positions of defenceman and winger grew. The quality of the Pittsburgh management did not match that of the star player and in December, 1926, Lionel was traded to the New York Americans.

After years of rave reviews in his new home, Lionel's game began to slip, in part because of

		STATISTICS			
Season	GP	G	Ast.	Pts.	PIM
1925-26	33	9	4	13	64
1926-27	39	8	9	17	93
1927-28	36	11	6	17	82
1928-29	44	5	2	7	132
1929-30	39	4	6	10	73
1930-31	35	4	3	7	57
1931-32	46	7	9	16	60
1932-33	47	7	21	28	61
1933-34	48	10	13	23	87
1934-35	40	2	6	8	44
1935-36	47	7	7	14	65
1936-37	45	6	19	25	64
Totals	498	80	105	185	882

Notes: GP = games played; G = goals; Ast. = assists; Pts. = points; PIM = penalties in minutes

excessive alcohol consumption. In 1930 he was traded to the Montreal Maroons from which, because of continued poor play, he was released. At the age of thirty, his hockey career appeared over. Inspired by the birth of a daughter and a battle with pneumonia, Lionel rallied to overcome his drinking problem and restore his hockey career. Montreal took another chance on him, re-signing him for the 1931-1932 season. A year later he made the NHL All-Star Team, and his career flourished for several more years.

Continuing the Story

By the late 1930's Lionel's hockey career had reached its conclusion. In 1937, after the NHL playoffs ended, he announced his retirement. His last game was on April 23 and, at the age of thirty-seven, his hockey career was over. Never one to stand still, he quickly entered a new arena, politics, and was elected later that year to the legislature of the Canadian province of Ontario.

With the outbreak of World War II in 1939, Lionel volunteered his time to the war effort, serving as an honorary member of the Royal Canadian Air Force and helping to raise funds on behalf of his country. He re-established his political career after the war and was elected to the federal parliament in Ottawa in 1949. It was in that city that Lionel died suddenly of a heart attack on May 26, 1954. Fittingly, the great Canadian athlete died in the midst of a softball game, just after he had slugged a triple.

HONORS AND AWARDS

1950	Canada's Male Athlete of the Half Century
1963	Inducted into Canadian Football Hall of Fame
1966	Inducted into Canadian Lacrosse Hall of Fame
1994	Inducted into Hockey Hall of Fame

Summary

Lionel Conacher was, first and foremost, a great athlete. While best known for his hockey career, he also excelled at several other sports, especially football and lacrosse. He was elected to the Canadian Football Hall of Fame in 1963, the Canadian Lacrosse Hall of Fame in 1966, and the Hockey Hall of Fame in 1994.

Steve Hewitt

Additional Sources:

Coleman, Jim. *Legends of Hockey: The Official Book of the Hockey Hall of Fame.* Toronto: Penguin, 1996.

Cosentuno, Frank, and Don Morrow. *Lionel Conacher.* Toronto: Fitzhenry & Whiteside, 1981.

Diamond, Dan, ed. *Hockey Hall of Fame.* Toronto: Doubleday Canada, 1996.

DAVID CONE

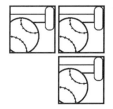

Sport: Baseball

Born: January 2, 1963
Kansas City, Missouri

Early Life

David Bryan Cone was the youngest of four children born to Ed Cone, who worked the graveyard shift in a meat-packing plant, and Joan Cone. David was coached in Little League by his father and by age seven or eight had already begun to display his infamous temper. He attended Rockhurst High, an all-boys Jesuit school, where he was quarterback of the district championship football team, and was an outstanding basketball player. As Rockhurst had no baseball team, David played in the Ban Johnson League. At sixteen, he entered an invitation-only tryout with the Kansas City Royals and, by seventeen, was throwing a strange 88-mile-per-hour fastball that befuddled batters.

The Road to Excellence

After high school, David enrolled at the University of Missouri but, in June, 1981, was selected in the third-round free-agent draft by the Royals. He signed for much less money than most new players received, but he was eighteen and eager to play. During the first year, David played rookie ball, going to A ball the following year with a record of 16-3 and a 2.08 earned run average (ERA). In 1983, in an exhibition game, David injured his left knee, requiring surgery and extensive rehabilitation.

After taking a year off from baseball and working in a company that produced conveyor belts, David summoned the fortitude to try baseball again. That was a turning point in his life. By 1985 he had progressed with the Royals up to the AAA class and in

1986 made it to the major league. In his first time out, he pitched one inning against the Milwaukee Brewers. He played in four games before be-

AP/Wide World Photos

The New York Yankees' David Cone pitches during a May, 1997, game.

STATISTICS

Season	GP	GS	CG	IP	HA	BB	SO	W	L	S	ShO	ERA
1986	11	0	0	22.2	29	13	21	0	0	0	0	5.56
1987	21	13	1	99.1	87	44	68	5	6	1	0	3.71
1988	35	28	8	231.1	178	80	213	20	3	0	4	2.22
1989	34	33	7	219.2	183	74	190	14	8	0	2	3.52
1990	31	30	6	211.2	177	65	**233**	14	10	0	2	3.23
1991	34	34	5	232.2	204	73	**241**	14	14	0	2	3.29
1992	35	34	7	249.2	201	111	261	17	10	0	**5**	2.81
1993	34	34	6	254.0	205	114	191	11	14	0	1	3.33
1994	23	23	4	171.2	130	54	132	16	5	0	3	2.94
1995	30	30	6	**229.1**	195	88	191	18	8	0	2	3.57
1996	11	11	1	72.0	50	34	71	7	2	0	0	2.88
1997	29	29	1	195.0	155	86	222	12	6	0	0	2.82
1998	31	31	3	207.2	186	59	209	**20**	7	0	0	3.55
1999	31	31	1	193.1	164	90	177	12	9	0	1	3.44
2000	30	29	0	155.0	192	82	120	4	14	0	0	6.91
Totals	420	390	56	2,745.0	2,336	1,067	2,540	184	116	1	22	3.40

Notes: Boldface indicates statistical leader. GP = games played; GS = games started; CG = complete games; IP = innings pitched; HA = hits allowed; BB = bases on balls (walks); SO = strikeouts; W = wins; L = losses; S = saves; ShO = shutouts; ERA = earned run average

ing sent back down to Omaha but was recalled two months later and allowed to finish the season.

The Emerging Champion

The day after David called his family to tell them he had made the 1987 opening-day roster for the Royals, he found out he had been traded to the New York Mets, the 1986 World Series champions. He filled in for a disabled pitcher but was himself later placed on the disabled list from May to August. In 1988 he soared with an amazing record of 20-3 and an ERA of 2.22, pitching a 6-0, one-hit, complete-game victory against San Diego on August 29, 1988.

Continuing the Story

David spent six years with the New York Mets. He won fourteen games in 1989 and another fourteen in 1990 and led the major league in strikeouts. In 1991 his salary catapulted to $2.35 million. He helped out his two brothers and sister financially and bought his parents a condominium in Florida. In August, 1992, he was traded to the Toronto Blue Jays, staying long enough to help the team win the World Series. He was granted free agency in October, 1992, and he signed with the Royals in a three-year, $18 million deal that made him the highest paid pitcher in the game.

David wanted to go back home to Kansas City, start a different life, and get involved in the community. He bought a house and considered marriage. He also worked on reprogramming his pitching, throwing one-pitch strikes rather than trying to overpower every hitter he faced, and at the same time amassing high pitch counts and high strikeout totals. By making the first pitch count, David won sixteen games and claimed the American League Cy Young Award in 1994.

At the beginning of the baseball strike in 1994, David began attending union meetings to educate himself about the issues. He became the American League representative because no one else wanted the job. David was surprised to gain no sympathy from the fans, who believed the players' greed caused the strike. Four days after the strike ended in 1995, the Royals traded David back to the Toronto Blue Jays, who traded him later that season to the New York Yankees.

In May, 1996, David, who had suffered from numbness in the fingers of his pitching hand, underwent surgery to repair an aneurysm in his right shoulder. Off the field for four months, David returned to the mound on September 3, to pitch 7 innings with no hits. In game 3 of the 1996 World Series, David, down 0-2 in Atlanta, outpitched Tom Glavine to get the Yankees back on track to win the Series.

David had shoulder surgery a second time in 1997, but in 1998 he had twenty wins and helped the Yankees win another World Series championship. In 1999 he pitched a perfect game, going 6-0 against Montreal with an exceptional slider that was a relic from the early career of the thirty-six-year-old. The second oldest pitcher to throw a no-hitter (Cy Young did so at thirty-seven), David threw only 88 pitches and struck out ten batters. Also that year, the Yankees won the World Series.

Suffering from chronic tendinitis, David had a 4-14 record in 2000 and, after fifteen years of service in the major league, was unsure about returning to the Yankees. Having reached a crossroads in his career, David filed for free agency and gave indications he was approaching retirement.

In 2001, he signed with the Boston Red Sox. By mid-season he was showing his old form and appeared headed toward a winning record, as the Sox challenged the Yankees in the American League East.

Summary

David Cone has had a long, fabled career in baseball. A brash, hot-tempered player who spent his early days and nights in baseball living recklessly, David caused himself many problems. However, his desire to master the thing he loved most and benefit others through it led him to improve. He excelled in all aspects of the game—from perfecting his arsenal of four pitches (slider, fastball, curveball, split-fingered fastball) and delivering them from an amazing variety of angles, to becoming one of the most knowledgeable individuals about the rights and responsibilities of baseball players—because of his commitment of time and attention to it.

Mary Hurd

Additional Sources:

Bradley, John Ed. "The Headliner." *Sports Illustrated* 78, no. 13 (April 5, 1993): 92.

Cannella, Stephen. "Masterpiece Theater." *Sports Illustrated* 91, no. 4 (July 26, 1999): 44.

Raab, Scott. "The Slow Boil." *Esquire* 131, no. 5 (May, 1999): 102.

Schwarz, Alan. "Roomful of Views." *Sport* 90 (September, 1999): 54.

Verducci, Tom. "A Moving Experience." *Sports Illustrated* 84, no. 1 (January 8, 1996): 57.

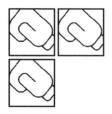

BILLY CONN

Sport: Boxing

Born: October 8, 1917
      Pittsburgh, Pennsylvania
Died: May 29, 1993
      Pittsburgh, Pennsylvania

Early Life

William David Conn, Jr., was born on October 8, 1917, in East Liberty, Pennsylvania, a blue-collar neighborhood of Pittsburgh. His parents were William David Conn, a steam fitter at a Westinghouse plant, and Margaret (McFarland)

Conn. At the age of thirteen, Billy began to take lessons from Johnny Ray, a former boxer who ran a nondescript gym for fighters in East Liberty. In exchange for the lessons, Billy swept up and did other jobs around the gym.

Ray saw that Billy had the potential to become a professional boxer, and he began to tutor Billy carefully. As Billy grew older, he spent hours each day working out and sparring at the gym and also watched many fights while at Ray's side. Never a good student, Billy dropped out of the parochial school he had been attending to concentrate on becoming a professional boxer. This seemed to make sense to Billy and his parents, given the depressed economic conditions of the 1930's. Billy made his professional debut at Fairmont, West Virginia, in January, 1935; Billy's share of the $2.50 purse was fifty cents.

The Road to Excellence

Billy fought more than three dozen times in 1935 and 1936, rarely traveling more than two hundred miles from Pittsburgh for a match. He lost six of his first fourteen professional fights, but he continued to work hard and developed an accurate jab, a great left hook, and a decent right cross. Realizing that Billy did not have a knockout punch, Ray especially wanted Billy to work on his combination punching and footwork.

Only six months after his pro debut, Billy began a twenty-seven-bout undefeated streak that stretched from August, 1935, to August, 1937. As he matured physically, he moved up from the lightweight to welterweight and then to the middleweight ranks, often fighting men four or five years older than himself. On December 28, 1936, Billy beat Fritzie Zivic, who would later win the welterweight crown; in 1937, he took on such quality middleweights as Teddy Yarosz, Young Corbett, and Solly Krieger, all three of whom made *Ring* magazine's list of top-ten middle-

RECOGNIZED WORLD LIGHT-HEAVYWEIGHT CHAMPIONSHIP FIGHTS

Date	Location	Loser	Result
July 13, 1939	New York, N.Y.	Melio Bettina	15th-round decision
Sept. 25, 1939	Pittsburgh, Pa.	Melio Bettina	15th-round decision
Nov. 17, 1939	New York, N.Y.	Gus Lesnevich	15th-round decision
June 5, 1940	Detroit, Mich.	Gus Lesnevich	15th-round decision

RECOGNIZED WORLD HEAVYWEIGHT CHAMPIONSHIP FIGHTS

June 18, 1941	New York, N.Y.	Billy Conn (Joe Louis, winner)	13th-round knockout
June 19, 1946	New York, N.Y.	Billy Conn (Joe Louis, winner)	8th-round knockout

weights in either 1937 or 1938. Billy lost to Corbett and Krieger the first time he fought them, but he beat each man in a rematch.

Except for one match each year in San Francisco, Billy continued to fight in Pittsburgh in 1937 and 1938. His success against such opponents as Krieger, a popular New Yorker, attracted the attention of the prominent New York promoter Mike Jacobs, who booked Billy for a fight on January 6, 1939, in the famous Madison Square Garden. There, Billy beat Fred Apostoli, recognized as the middleweight titleholder by the New York State Athletic Commission, in a thrilling nontitle bout before nearly eleven thousand fans. Only five weeks later, in what he regarded as his hardest fight ever, Billy won an even more exciting fifteen-rounder from Apostoli.

The Emerging Champion

Jacobs took a liking to Billy and believed that he could become an attraction at the box office. To sharpen Billy's image, Jacobs saw that the young fighter dressed well and met the right people, including show-business celebrities. Nicknamed the "Pittsburgh Kid," Billy did not let his growing prominence distract him from his mission of becoming champion. On July 13, 1939, Billy, who had outgrown the middleweight class, claimed the light-heavyweight title in a fight with Melio Bettina.

After defeating Bettina in a rematch, Billy defended his title in two memorable fights against top challenger Gus Lesnevich. Billy gained decisions over Lesnevich in a fifteen-round fight in New York on November 17, 1939, and in another fifteen-round battle in Detroit on June 15, 1940.

Billy, who was named Fighter of the Year in 1940, then stepped up to the heavyweight class, boxing's most publicized division and the only one where big money—perhaps $100,000 for a title match—could be earned. Ray and Jacobs both wanted to see Billy challenge the heavyweight champion, Joe Louis, who had held the title since 1937 and who so dominated the division that one writer referred to Louis's victims as members of the "Bum-of-the-Month Club." Fan interest in the heavyweights was declining, and Billy could revive it by challenging Louis, thought Ray and Jacobs.

Just over 6 feet in height and broad-shouldered, Billy rarely weighed as much as 175 pounds, the light-heavyweight limit, but for heavyweight fights his weight was usually announced as close to 180 pounds. Before he could fight Louis, Billy had to vacate his own light-heavyweight title. After beating rated heavyweights Lee Savold and Bob Pastor, he outclassed four consecutive opponents early in 1941. He met Louis for the title on June 18, 1941, at the Polo Grounds, a baseball park in New York City that could seat more than fifty thousand spectators.

Earlier in his career, Billy had sometimes been careless about his conditioning, but he had since learned to keep in good shape. Billy rarely won by a knockout, but he consistently went the distance to win his fights on points. He had never been knocked out. Although he was the underdog against Louis, several experts believed that Billy could outpoint the bigger, stronger Louis if he fought intelligently and took advantage of his nimble feet and remarkably quick hands.

The Polo Grounds was jammed for the contest, and for twelve rounds, Billy gave spectators and millions of radio listeners all the excitement they could want, taking seven rounds on points. Billy's cornermen told him to keep using his hit-and-run tactics and combination punching, but Billy, who had been dominating the fight since the eighth round and had nearly knocked the champion down in the twelfth, thought that Louis was weakening. Billy abandoned the tactics that had been working to try for a knockout. Billy's decision was a mistake, for Louis, who had won more than 80 percent of his fights by knock-out, staggered him with several hard blows. Billy went down for the count just before the end of the thirteenth round. In tears as reporters interviewed him after the fight, he said, "I lost my head and a million bucks."

To fans, however, Billy's near-upset of the champion enhanced his popularity. His curly hair and "toothpaste ad grin" made him perfect for Hollywood and earned him a contract soon after the Louis fight to star with actress Jean Parker in *The Pittsburgh Kid,* a 1941 film about boxing in which he played himself.

It was assumed that Billy and Louis would soon fight again, and fan and media anticipation of a rematch was high. In December, 1941, however, the United States entered World War II, and both Billy and Louis enlisted in the armed forces. On February 13, 1942, he took a twelve-round decision from Tony Zale, the "Man of Steel," in his last fight before entering the Army.

Continuing the Story

In the service, Billy visited hospitals for military personnel and led a group of boxers who fought exhibition matches to entertain the troops. In June, 1944, he led his group of boxers to England and around European battlefronts. While in Italy, Billy and some Army companions helped to rescue an American pilot from a flaming plane that had crashed near them. He later toured military bases in France with several popular entertainers headed by film star Bob Hope.

Both Louis and Billy were discharged from the Army in 1945. Billy resumed training and fought two exhibitions before fighting Louis for the heavyweight title in New York's Yankee Stadium on June 19, 1946. In their first battle, Billy had given fight fans much more than they had expected, but now he gave them less. Neither man had recaptured his 1941 form, but at one time in

his Army service, Billy had put on close to 25 pounds. For the fight with Louis, Billy could slim down only to 182 pounds, nearly 10 pounds above his normal prewar fighting weight. He could not regain the speed and timing that had been essential to his success. Billy realized this and tried to stay away from the champion; some disappointed fans in the capacity crowd booed. Louis knocked Billy out in the eighth round.

Billy no longer had the desire and the reflexes that had made him a great boxer. He did not fight at all in 1947, and had only a handful of bouts in 1948. After an exhibition match with Louis in December, 1948, he retired with a career record of sixty-three wins, eleven defeats, and one draw.

Billy, who had invested his earnings wisely, lived comfortably in Pittsburgh after his retirement, occasionally appearing as a referee at a boxing or wrestling match and for a while taking a job as a greeter at a Las Vegas casino. He was named to *Ring*'s Boxing Hall of Fame in 1965. In 1993, he died in Pittsburgh at the age of seventy-five.

Summary

Billy Conn is remembered more for his 1941 loss to Joe Louis than for the dozens of victories he earned in the ring with his deft footwork and quick hands. Win, lose, or draw, the "Pittsburgh Kid" was a popular fighter who dazzled the boxing world with his brash but appealing personality and prowess in the ring. Long after he retired, Billy Conn was still considered one of boxing's immortals.

Lloyd J. Graybar

CUMULATIVE STATISTICS

Bouts, 63
Knockouts, 14
Bouts won by decision, 49
Bouts lost by knockout, 2
Bouts lost by decision, 9
Draws, 1

HONORS AND AWARDS

1939	Edward J. Neil Award
1965	*Ring* magazine Boxing Hall of Fame
1990	International Boxing Hall of Fame

Additional Sources:

"Billy Conn." *Current Biography* 54, no. 8 (August, 1993): 60.

Blewett, Bert. *The A to Z of World Boxing.* London: Robson Books, 1996.

Deford, Frank. "The Boxer and the Blonde." *Sports Illustrated* 62 (June 17, 1985): 66-84.

Heller, Peter. *In This Corner: Forty World Champions Tell Their Stories.* New York: Simon & Schuster, 1973.

Mee, Bob. *Boxing: Heroes and Champions.* Edison, N.J.: Chartwell Books, 1997.

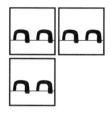

BART CONNER

Sport: Gymnastics

Born: March 28, 1958
Chicago, Illinois

Early Life

Bart Conner was born on March 28, 1958, in Chicago, Illinois, a city with a rich sports tradition and home to many championship teams and outstanding individual athletes.

Like many young people, Bart grew up participating in a variety of sports and recreational activities, and he was a skilled all-around athlete. At age seven, he began playing youth football and also took up the sport of speed skating, which was a very popular activity with the entire Conner family. Bart's parents were very supportive in helping him to pursue his interest in sports, letting him join an organized community sports program and encouraging him to try new activities at school and in the youth recreation programs in his hometown of Morton Grove, Illinois.

The Road to Excellence

Bart became interested in the sport of gymnastics at about the age of ten. The elementary school that he attended had a tumbling and gymnastics program, and Bart developed an immediate interest in the various exercises and routines that were a part of gymnastics. One of the teachers at his elementary school, Les Lang, helped Bart to learn the fundamentals of some of the gymnastics movements and events and encouraged him to practice. It was not long before Bart showed a great deal of potential at this sport and needed a higher level of coaching.

At age eleven, Bart began training at a local YMCA with other youngsters who

had gymnastic talent. He participated in his first meet later in that year at the Navy Pier Gymnasium in Chicago, on the lakefront of Lake Michigan. It was an important regional competition, and Bart participated in the tumbling and the pommel horse events. He won medals in both events, and he knew from that day on that gymnastics was the sport for him.

STATISTICS

Year	Competition	Event	Place	Event	Place
1977	NCAA Championships	All-Around	1st		
1978	NCAA Championships	All-Around	1st	Team	1st
	World Championships	All-Around	9th	Team	4th
		Parallel bars	5th		
1979	World Championships	All-Around	5th	Vault	3d
		Floor exercise	5th	Team	3d
		Parallel bars	1st		
1981	American Cup	All-Around	1st		
	World Championships	All-Around	11th	Team	5th
1982	American Cup	All-Around	1st		
	World Cup	All-Around	11th	Floor exercise	8th
1983	U.S. National Championships	All-Around	9th	Pommel horse	1st
		Parallel bars	3d	Rings	2d
1983	World Championships	All-Around	11th	Pommel horse	6th
		Floor exercise	5th	Team	4th
		Parallel bars	6th		
1984	Olympic Games	All-Around	6th	Team	Gold
		Floor exercise	5th	Parallel bars	Gold

Bart was a good all-around athlete, but he realized with the help of his coaches that becoming a successful gymnast meant a full-time commitment to the sport. Thus, he reluctantly gave up the other recreational sports activities in which he had been involved and put all of his energies into gymnastics. By the time he was a junior in high school, he was competing in meets sponsored by the Amateur Athletic Union (AAU) and had gained a national reputation in the junior division of the United States Gymnastics Federation (USGF).

The Emerging Champion

Bart attended Niles West High School in Morton Grove, Illinois, and under the coaching of John Burkell became nationally known. He won both the AAU and the USGF junior nationals as all-around champion and was voted the most outstanding Illinois high school gymnast in 1974.

Bart was attracted to the University of Oklahoma by coach Paul Ziert, who was building a strong program in both men's and women's gymnastics. Bart became an instant celebrity in Oklahoma, because he had already been identified for his potential as an Olympic athlete in the 1980 Games in Moscow, and he brought considerable attention to Oklahoma's athletic program.

Bart was a sensational college gymnast, receiving All-American honors as a freshman and leading the Oklahoma Sooners to the Big Eight championship and National Collegiate Athletic Association (NCAA) co-championship in his first year of competition. He went on to win many national and international awards while in college, yet his focus and dream was to be an Olympian and represent the United States in the 1980 Summer Games in Moscow.

In the international competition leading up to the selection of the U.S. Olympic team, Bart was nothing short of spectacular. He performed in all of the gymnastics events at the World Championships and captured first place in the parallel bars and third place in the vault and team event. His dream was realized when he was selected as a member of the 1980 U.S. Olympic gymnastics team.

In 1980, soon after the Soviet Union invaded Afghanistan, the United States, along with many other countries, decided not to send a team to Moscow for the Olympics as a protest to this invasion. President Jimmy Carter announced that the U.S. would not be participating, and for Bart and the other athletes this was a bitter disappointment, as they had spent years training and preparing just for the 1980 Olympics. Bart was angry and frustrated and had a difficult time accepting the fact that everything for which he had worked would be another four years away.

During the Olympic trials, Bart had sustained an injury to the muscles in his arm, and with the Olympic boycott in progress, he decided to sit

HONORS AND AWARDS

1980	Top qualifier for the men's U.S. Olympic gymnastics team
1984	Inducted into U.S. Gymnastics Hall of Fame (with the entire men's U.S. Olympic team)
1991	Inducted into U.S. Olympic Hall of Fame
1997	Inducted into International Gymnastics Hall of Fame

out a year and not compete in gymnastics. He returned to Oklahoma and took classes to complete his degree in journalism and public relations. Bart graduated from college and resumed his phenomenal athletic career by representing the U.S. in a series of international competitions. With his continuing success as a gymnast in meets around the world, Bart became an unofficial ambassador for the United States and at the same time resumed his quest for Olympic gold.

In addition to the disappointment of not participating in the 1980 Olympics, Bart had to overcome two operations on his upper arm and try to sustain his competitive interest while waiting for the 1984 Olympic trials. Without college competition, he had to look to international gymnastics for meets to compete in, and this meant getting a sponsor, traveling extensively, and performing at a level that would prepare him for the Olympic trials. Bart described this period of his life as the most difficult he had to endure and a time in which he matured in a hurry.

The year 1984, as it turned out, would be when Bart would realize his childhood dream of becoming an Olympic champion. In early August, in Los Angeles, the United States gymnastics team won the overall team title and the Olympic gold medal. Bart did his part by fininshing with high scores in all the events and scoring a perfect 10 on the horizontal bar. The gymnastics team was the sensation of the Olympics, and Bart became a sports legend.

Continuing the Story

Bart quickly turned his Olympic success into business success. He became part owner of *International Gymnast* magazine, to which he regularly contributes. He lined up lucrative endorse-ments, toured and did exhibitions, and, in 1991, opened Bart Conner's Gymnast Academy in Norman, Oklahoma. At this time, he also renewed his friendship with gymnastics legend Nadia Comǎneci, who had recently defected from Romania. In 1994 he proposed, and they were married in 1996. They both coach at his gym, do public appearances and workshops, have had a cable television show on exercise and nutrition, work out in the gym daily, and are deeply involved in children's charities, especially the Muscular Dystrophy Association and the Canadian Quebec Agency for adopting Romanian children.

Summary

For gymnastics fans, the accomplishments of the 1984 gymnastics team were monumental. They accomplished something a U.S. team had not done for eighty years by winning the team gold medal in gymnastics. For Bart Conner it was especially satisfying, because he had spent most of his life training for that moment, and the years of practice, pain, and frustration had ended in victory.

Henry A. Eisenhart

Additional Sources:

Conner, Bart, and Michael Haederle. "Hard Landing." *People,* August 7, 2000, 131-134.

Conner, Bart, with Paul Ziert. *Winning the Gold.* New York: Warner Books, 1985.

Gray, Kevin. "Head over Heels: For Gold Medal Gymnasts Nadia Comǎneci and Bart Conner, Love Is Something to Flip For." *People Weekly,* March 27, 1995, 105-106.

Lipsyte, Robert. "Two Gymnasts Flip and Fall for Each Other." *The New York Times,* April 5, 1996, p. B9.

DENNIS CONNER

Sport: Yachting

Born: September 16, 1943
San Diego, California

Early Life

Dennis Conner was born on September 16, 1943, in San Diego, California. He grew up in the Point Loma district, half a block from the prestigious San Diego Yacht Club. Dennis's father was a jet engineer who also fished commercially. The family was not poor, but Dennis did not have as much money as his yacht club friends, and this gave him something of an inferiority complex.

Dennis first sailed at the age of seven, and he began to spend so much time hanging around the San Diego Yacht Club that he was considered a bit of a pest. Eventually, at age twelve, Dennis was admitted to junior membership in the club, but, because of his lack of money, he crewed for other people rather than owning his own boat.

Dennis was an awkward, chubby child who nevertheless lettered in track, cross country, and basketball in high school. He was not outstanding in these sports, but in sailing, he realized that his physique was no handicap.

The Road to Excellence

While in high school, Dennis had a small Penguin sailboat and crewed in 18-foot Starlet keelboats. He also began crewing on many different larger boats. At first, he thought that not having his own big boat was a disadvantage. Later, he realized that this gave him the chance to learn from all the other crews what worked best. He saw that thorough preparation of the boat and the crew were the keys to success.

After high school, Dennis attended San Diego State University and majored in business. Most summers he worked in sail lofts. He began to crew regularly for a man who owned a carpet business. Later, Dennis went to work for him and eventually became his business partner.

In 1970, Dennis bought his first big boat, acquiring a seventeen-hundred-dollar half share in a 33-foot boat. In 1971, he bought a secondhand Star-class boat (23-foot keelboat) and won the world championship.

In the early 1970's, Dennis built a big boat reputation with wins both in fleet racing and in match racing (two boats only, racing head-to-head). The latter requires especially fine skills as the boats are rarely far apart. He won the Congressional Cup for the top U.S. sailors in round-robin match racing in 1973 and 1975, and the Southern Offshore Racing Conference (SORC), a series of offshore fleet races, in 1975. He helped the U.S. team to third place in the 1975 Admiral's Cup in Britain.

The Emerging Champion

In 1974, Dennis first sailed in the races that made him famous: the America's Cup series. He was the helmsman of the U.S. defender, *Courageous*, during the starting procedures (the most crucial part of match racing), and then he acted as tactician during the race. *Courageous* won the series 4-0 against the Australians.

At the Olympic Games in 1976, Dennis won a bronze medal in the Tempest class (a two-person 22-foot keelboat), and in 1977, he won the world Star Championship again with five straight first places against eighty-nine boats, a feat of which Dennis is most proud. When the America's Cup was held in 1980, Dennis was skipper of the U.S. defender, *Freedom*, winning the series 4-1.

The 1983 America's Cup was between the U.S. defender, *Liberty*, and the challenger, *Australia II*. At the time, the United States had held the America's Cup for 132 years, the longest winning streak in any sports event. Public attention was on *Australia II* because she had a revolutionary wing-shaped keel. This gave the boat superior performance. The American boat, by contrast, was badly designed, and the stage was set for the fight of Dennis's life.

In the best of seven series, *Liberty* won the first two races, and *Australia II* won the third. *Liberty* won the fourth race but in the fifth suffered gear failure. The Australian boat then won the sixth race to level the series 3-3. The final race was held in light winds, and Dennis Conner in *Liberty* led for much of the race. On the next-to-last leg, however, the Australian crew chose the breezier side of the course and won by 41 seconds, clinching the America's Cup.

Continuing the Story

Dennis did not want to be remembered as the man who lost the America's Cup, so preparations for the next series in 1987 were fantastically detailed. Unlike many helmsmen, Dennis did much of his own fund-raising, for it takes millions of dollars to mount a successful America's Cup campaign. He enjoyed the power of being

MAJOR CHAMPIONSHIP VICTORIES	
1971, 1977	World Championship (Star class)
1974	America's Cup (as helmsman)
1976	U.S. Olympic bronze medalist (Tempest class)
1980, 1987-88	America's Cup (as skipper)
1991, 1994	World Championship (Etchells class)
1993	National Championship (Australia Etchells class)

able to talk to the wealthiest people in the U.S. business world on equal terms.

Dennis demanded total dedication from all members of his organization. Dennis once said in an interview that he did not even particularly like sailing, but that it was the competition, drive, and winning that excited him. Many people in sailing thought this attitude took the fun out of the sport.

In the 1987 races, Dennis sailed to victory over the Australians. He won in four straight races,

Al Bello/Allsport

Skipper Dennis Conner in 1984.

and thus the first man to lose the America's Cup was also the first to regain the trophy. He was declared U.S. Yachtsman of the Year.

In 1988, a New Zealand crew challenged for the Cup in a huge 90-foot boat. At first, Dennis and his group tried to have so large a boat declared illegal in court, but this failed. He built a fast 60-foot catamaran in response. At this, the New Zealanders went to court to get a catamaran declared illegal in competition, but this too failed. The races were a hopeless mismatch. Dennis won the best of three series in two.

Though Dennis is well-known for his victories at the America's Cup, he has had great success in other national and international events. In 1993 Dennis set a transatlantic record of eleven days and eight hours in the Gold Cup race, the old record having stood since 1905. He also won the New Zealand Etcholls National Championship in 1997 and the Etcholls World Championship in 1991 and 1994.

Dennis skippered the *Stars and Stripes* in 1992, 1995, and 2000 without bringing home the Cup. Despite these overall losses, Dennis has won more than one hundred America's Cup races.

Summary

The 6-foot 1-inch, 200-pound Dennis Conner does not look like a sportsman, and ironically, he is a virtual nonswimmer. With grit and determination in place of money, the carpet salesman from San Diego made himself into a top ocean sailor. He became perhaps the most hard-driven, single-minded sailor of all time in his relentless pursuit of victory.

Shirley H. M. Reekie

HONORS AND AWARDS

1975, 1980, 1987	U.S. Yachtsman of the Year

Additional Sources:

Conner, Dennis, and Edward Claflin. *The Art of Winning.* New York: St. Martin's Press, 1988.

Conner, Dennis, and Michael Levitt. *The America's Cup: The History of Sailing's Greatest Competition in the Twentieth Century.* New York: St. Martin's Press, 1998.

Conner, Dennis, and John Rousmaniere. *No Excuse to Lose: Winning Yacht Races with Dennis Conner.* New York: Norton, 1978.

Hickok, Ralph. *A Who's Who of Sports Champions.* Boston: Houghton Mifflin, 1995.

Ryan, Patrick. *The America's Cup.* Mankato, Minn.: Creative Education, 1993.

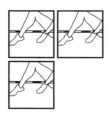

HAROLD CONNOLLY

Sport: Track and field (hammer throw)

Born: August 1, 1931
Somerville, Massachusetts

Early Life

Harold Vincent Connolly was born on August 1, 1931, in Somerville, Massachusetts, just outside Boston, to Harold and Margaret Connolly, both of whom were first-generation Americans. Young Hal began his life under the most adverse conditions. Just before his birth, doctors informed his father they could not save both mother and child. Mr. Connolly told them to do whatever they could, but to be sure to save his wife's life. Fortunately, they saved both, but the nerves in Hal's left arm were permanently injured. In spite of operations and constant therapy, Hal's left arm remained shorter and much weaker than his right. Yet, Hal became the first American since 1924 to win the Olympic hammer throw, an event that combines strength, coordination, speed, and single-minded purpose.

The Road to Excellence

At thirteen, Hal told his mother he would no longer go to therapy sessions because he was embarrassed to be considered handicapped; instead, he promised to do his own exercises. He discovered a weight-training magazine called *Strength and Health* and went to work, strengthening not only his damaged left arm but his entire body. Hal later said, "I wanted to prove myself as an athlete because I came from a family of athletes, mostly boxers."

Boxing was out of the question, but Hal became an overachiever in high school, where he ran the hurdles, put the shot, and played a very aggressive tackle on the football team. At Boston College, he continued with the shot put, but great shot-putters need their left arm to pull themselves through their motion, and Hal's did

Harold Connolly throwing the hammer during the 1960 Olympics.

STATISTICS

Year	Competition	Event	Place	Distance
1955	National AAU Championships	Hammer throw	1st	199′ 8″
1956	Olympic Games	Hammer throw	Gold	207′ 3″ OR
	National AAU Championships	Hammer throw	1st	205′ 10½″
1957	National AAU Championships	Hammer throw	1st	216′ 3″
1958	National AAU Championships	Hammer throw	1st	225′ 4″ WR
1959	Pan-American Games	Hammer throw	Gold	—
	National AAU Championships	Hammer throw	1st	216′ 10″
1960	Olympic Games	Hammer throw	8th	208′ 6″
	National AAU Indoor Championships	35-pound weight throw	1st	71′ 2½″
	National AAU Championships	Hammer throw	1st	224′ 4½″
1961	National AAU Championships	Hammer throw	1st	213′ 6½″
1964	Olympic Games	Hammer throw	6th	218′ 8½″
	National AAU Championships	Hammer throw	1st	226′ 5½″
1965	National AAU Indoor Championships	35-pound weight throw	1st	70′ ½″
	National AAU Championships	Hammer throw	1st	232′ 1″
1966	National AAU Indoor Championships	35-pound weight throw	1st	70′ 11″

Notes: OR = Olympic Record; WR = World Record

Hal's foremost competition in Melbourne came from the Soviet Union's Mikhail Krivonosov. At the Olympic level, competition is as much mental as physical, and in the months preceding the Games, Hal and Krivonosov not only traded the world record back and forth but traded verbal challenges as well. On the first day of practice Melbourne, Hal waited for his Soviet counterpart and immediately challenged him to see who was the better thrower. The Soviet coaches hurriedly pulled Krivonosov off the practice field, but by then Hal had made it clear that he welcomed the competition. A few days later, he defeated his Soviet rival, setting an Olympic record of 207 feet 3 inches.

not function that way. Quite by accident he took up the hammer. His Boston College coach, William Galligan, lived near the Connollys, so Hal always rode home with him after practice. The last athletes Galligan coached each day were the hammer throwers. To speed things up, Hal would retrieve the hammers and throw them back to the athletes. When he started throwing them over their heads, he had found his event.

The Emerging Champion

Strangely enough, Hal's withered left arm did not handicap him as much in the hammer as it did in the shot put. He compensated by shifting the emphasis down to his legs, with his arms functioning as a whip.

Because little emphasis is placed on the hammer throw in the United States, Hal traveled to Germany in 1954 to work with the legendary coach Sepp Christmann. Christmann had revolutionized the hammer throw by teaching athletes to turn on their heels and toes rather than toe turning and jumping around in the circle. Christmann told Hal that if he worked hard on this new technique, he would have a chance to win at the 1956 Olympics in Melbourne, Australia.

Continuing the Story

It was not just his Olympic victory that brought Hal fame in Melbourne. He had fallen in love with Olga Fikotová, the Czechoslovakian discus gold medalist. Their Cold War romance quickly caught the fancy of the international media, and people everywhere began to cheer for a happy ending to this improbable match between the Communist Czech Protestant and the free world American Catholic. Love won. In 1957, Hal and Olga married in Prague, with the great Czech distance runner, Emil Zatopek, serving as best man.

After considerable visa difficulties, Olga left with Hal to take up a new life in the United States. They eventually settled in Santa Monica, California, where Hal went into high school teaching and, later, administration. They both continued to compete. Hal extended the world record seven times, reaching a personal best of 233 feet 9½ inches in 1965. He was also a member of the United States Olympic team in 1960, 1964, and 1968 but did not win another medal. Olga became an American citizen, gave birth to four children, and was on each of the American Olympic teams with Hal, plus the 1972 team, when her teammates selected her to be the American flag-bearer in the opening ceremonies, an honor Hal

517

had earned in 1968 but turned down because he thought the Olympics had become too political.

Summary

Between 1956 and 1965, Harold Connolly raised the world record in the hammer throw seven times and won nine national Amateur Athletic Union titles. Hal will be best remembered for overcoming physical adversity to become an Olympic champion and for the storybook Cold War romance with Olga Fikotová that transcended the political problems of a troubled world.

Lewis H. Carlson

Additional Sources:

Bateman, Hal. *United States Track and Field Olympians, 1896-1980*. Indianapolis, Ind.: The Athletics Congress of the United States, 1984.

Hickok, Ralph. *A Who's Who of Sports Champions*. Boston: Houghton Mifflin, 1995.

Wallechinsky, David. *The Complete Book of the Olympics*. Boston: Little, Brown and Company, 1991.

Watman, Mel. *Encyclopedia of Track and Field Athletics*. New York: St. Marti's Press, 1981.

MAUREEN CONNOLLY

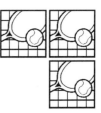

Sport: Tennis

Born: September 17, 1934
    San Diego, California
Died: June 21, 1969
    Dallas, Texas

Maureen Connolly won the women's title at Wimbledon in 1952.

Early Life

Maureen Catherine Connolly was born on September 17, 1934, in San Diego, California. Her parents were Martin J. Connolly and Jassamine Connolly. Horses were her chief childhood passion until, at ten years of age, her family moved to a house near some municipal tennis courts. The pro there, Wilbur Folsom, became so accustomed to seeing a small, curly-haired girl peeking through the fence watching people play that he invited her inside and hit some balls to her.

Folsom was so impressed with the girl's natural ability that he offered to give her lessons. He switched her from a left-handed to a right-handed player, and after several months of coaching, he entered her in a tournament where she reached the finals. From then on tennis became the main dedication of Maureen Connolly.

The Road to Excellence

The next year the famous Eleanor Tennant became Maureen's teacher and coach. "Teach" Tennant had developed such champions as Helen Wills, Alice Marble, and Pauline Betz. Teach, well known not only for her coaching but for also her skills as an analyst and psychologist, brought Maureen along slowly and deliberately. Besides the tennis coaching, she gave Maureen exercises to strengthen her arm and wrist. These exercises are considered routine coaching today but were a novelty back in the 1940's. Teach also had her take dance lessons to improve her footwork.

519

Maureen practiced hard, usually three to four hours a day, until she had molded herself into a highly capable player. By the time Maureen was fifteen, she not only had won fifty titles but also had become the youngest girl up to that time to win the coveted National Junior Championships, for players eighteen years of age and under. She won that title again the next year in 1950, when she was sixteen, and also competed on the women's circuit. She did so well that she was tenth in the women's rankings of 1950.

Noticed by the press, she was dubbed "Little Mo" or "Mighty Little Mo," in contrast to the then most powerful battleship, the *Missouri*, or "Big Mo." Her nickname was attributed to the fact that even though she was only 5 feet 5 inches in height, similar to the guns of the *Missouri*, she mowed down her opponents with her outstanding powerful forehand and backhand drives.

The Emerging Champion

In 1951, she did not defend her National Junior title because the date of the championship conflicted with the United States National Championship at Forest Hills, New York. She won this tournament and at seventeen was the second youngest player at the time to win the title. That year she was selected for the Wightman Cup team and was the youngest to that date to make the team. Moreover, she repeated as a member of the team in 1952, 1953, and 1954, and in four years of Wightman Cup play, she never lost a match.

Many wondered what made this teenager so successful against more experienced players. Not only was Maureen skillful, but her outstanding concentration, coupled with her tremendous drive to win, noticed by everyone who watched her play, made her the great champion that she was.

Continuing the Story

In 1952, Maureen not only retained her United States title but won Wimbledon, and the Associated Press (AP) named her Female Athlete of the Year. In addition, she was presented the Service Bowl Award by the United States Lawn Tennis Association (USLTA), given to the person who makes the most noticeable contribution to the sportsmanship, fellowship, and service of tennis.

MAJOR CHAMPIONSHIP VICTORIES AND FINALS	
1951-53	U.S. National Championship
1952-54	Wimbledon
1953	Australian Championship Australian Championship doubles (with Julia Sampson)
1953-54	French Championship
1954	French Championship doubles (with Nell Hall Hopman) French Championship mixed doubles (with Lew Hoad)

OTHER NOTABLE VICTORIES	
1951-54	Member of winning U.S. Wightman Cup team
1953	Italian Championship doubles (with Sampson)
1953-54	U.S. Clay Court Championship
1954	Italian Championship U.S. Clay Court Championship doubles (with Doris Hart)

The next year, 1953, after winning the Australian Championship, Maureen won the French Championship, repeated as winner at Wimbledon, and was victorious again at the United States National Championship at Forest Hills. By winning these four major championships in one year she won the Grand Slam of tennis and accomplished what only one other person (Don Budge) had ever done. It is significant to note that Maureen lost only one set in achieving this feat.

At the end of 1953 Maureen was selected again by the AP as the Female Athlete of the Year, was ranked number one by the USLTA, and was listed as number one in the world.

At the age of twenty, in 1954, she won her second French Championship and her third consecutive Wimbledon and was predicted to repeat her victory at Forest Hills. Unfortunately, however, as Maureen was riding her new horse before the tournament, a speeding truck frightened the animal and Maureen was thrown against the truck, broke her right leg, and severed all the muscles in the calf. Even though she could not compete in the remaining tennis tournaments that year, for the third straight year the AP voted her Female Athlete of the Year.

Maureen tried every form of rehabilitation, but it soon became obvious that her leg was severely damaged. In January, 1955, the sad announcement was made that she would never play competitive tennis again.

It is speculation what Maureen would have achieved had she not been injured before she was twenty-one years of age. What is amazing is that from September, 1951, when she won her first United States National Championship, to July, 1954, when she won her third Wimbledon title, she had lost only one match anywhere in the world, and that was in 1954 in California.

Most authorities believe that had she competed the normal years of a tennis champion, her record might have been unparalleled. Even so, she is regarded as one of the greatest women tennis players who have ever played the game.

Summary

In 1955, Maureen Connolly married Norman Brinker, a former member of the United States equestrian team, whom she had met several years before while she was out riding. They settled in Dallas, Texas, and had two daughters.

Maureen was elected to the National Lawn Tennis Hall of Fame in 1968, and in 1969, knowing she had terminal cancer, she created the Maureen Connolly Brinker Foundation to help promote promising junior players. Also in 1969, the USLTA established the Maureen Connolly Brinker Award to be presented each year at the Girls' Nationals to the player who has had an outstanding year and who is exceptional in ability, sportsmanship, and competitive spirit. Maureen hoped to present the first award to be given in August, but she died of her cancer on June 21, 1969, at the age of thirty-four.

Perhaps the best tribute to her brief career is by Lance Tingay, the tennis authority of the *London Telegraph*: "Whenever a great player comes along, you have to ask, Could she have beaten Maureen? In every case the answer is, I think not."

Joanna Davenport

RECORDS AND MILESTONES

First woman to win the Grand Slam (1953)
U.S. Wightman Cup team (1951-54)
Nationally ranked number one (1951-53)
Ranked number one in the world (1952-54)

HONORS AND AWARDS

1952	Service Bowl Award
1952-54	Associated Press Female Athlete of the Year
1968	Inducted into National Lawn Tennis Hall of Fame

Additional Sources:

Collins, Bud, and Zander Hollander, eds. *Bud Collins' Modern Encyclopedia of Tennis.* 3d ed. Detroit: Gale, 1997.

Frayne, Trent. *Famous Women Tennis Players.* New York: Dodd, Mead, 1979.

Grimsley, Will. *Tennis: Its History, People, and Events.* Englewood Cliffs, N.J.: Prentice-Hall, 1971.

Sherrow, Victoria, ed. *Encyclopedia of Women and Sports.* Santa Barbara, Calif.: ABC-CLIO, 1996.

Woolum, Janet. *Outstanding Women Athletes: Who They Are and How They Influenced Sports in America.* Phoenix, Ariz.: Oryx Press, 1998.

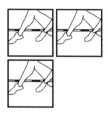

OLGA CONNOLLY

Sport: Track and field (discus throw)

Born: November 13, 1932
Prague, Czechoslovakia

Early Life

Olga Connolly was born Olga Fikotová on November 13, 1932, in Prague, the capital city of Czechoslovakia. Her childhood joys included dancing to the lively music of Czechoslovakian folk songs and long walks with her parents through the Prague countryside.

Olga began her sport career at a very young age. She learned to ice-skate at just four years of age. Although she never had formal skating lessons, Olga learned quickly by watching the older children. Even as a young girl, she seemed to appreciate the "beauty of perfect motion." Olga Fikotová seemed destined to become an athlete.

The Road to Excellence

When Olga was about fourteen, some of the neighborhood children invited her to learn team handball. Team handball, also known as European handball, is a sport that is a mix of basketball and soccer. The first position Olga tried was that of goalie. She practiced that position for the next three and a half years. At age seventeen, Olga became the youngest member of the Czechoslovakian national women's handball team.

Although she was very good at team handball, Olga decided to give it up to try the challenge of a new sport. When a basketball team was formed at her school, she joined it. In just two years, she was good enough to be selected to play on the Czechoslovakian national women's basketball team.

In 1952, Olga began studies at the Charles University Medical School in Prague. Studying to become a doctor severely limited Olga's time on the basketball court. When she found herself sitting on the bench most of the time, Olga began to look around for another sport.

In 1955, one of Olga's classmates found an old rubber discus. Knowing what a good athlete Olga was, he challenged her to learn to throw the discus. Jokingly, he told Olga, "Learn to throw this, and you will go to the Olympics in Australia next year." Olga accepted his challenge. Little did she know then that this sport would gain her international athletic fame.

The Emerging Champion

Olga rearranged her schedule to add two hours of track and field workouts to each day. She trained each morning before school from 5 A.M. to 7 A.M. Evenings were spent on her medical studies. She fell into bed, exhausted, at about 1 A.M. The next morning at 5 A.M., she was back out on the practice field.

When the summer vacation from school came, Olga moved to a small town outside Prague where her parents were then living. Olga's parents were very supportive. Her father, a former athlete himself, attended every workout. Her workouts included sprinting, jumping, throwing, gymnastics, and lots of push-ups.

Olga entered her first track and field meet that summer. Even as a relative beginner in discus, Olga finished among the leaders in each meet.

That fall, she surprised even herself with a throw of 156 feet. This feat won her the 1955 championship of Czechoslovakia. It also won her a place on her third national athletic team, the Czechoslovakian national track and field team.

Olga returned to her medical studies that same fall. The studies were even more demanding. Olga performed rather poorly in a series of pre-Olympic competitions in the spring of 1956. Nevertheless, she continued her training routine. After finishing her course examinations, she turned her full attention to the discus.

522

MAJOR DISCUS COMPETITIONS

Year	Competition	Place	Distance
1956	Olympic Games	Gold	176′ 1″
	Czechoslovakia Nationals	1st	—
1957	National AAU Championships	1st	147′ 8″
	Czechoslovakia Nationals	1st	—
1960	Olympic Games	7th	—
	National AAU Championships	1st	159′ 6½″
1962	National AAU Championships	1st	172′ 2″
1964	Olympic Games	12th	—
	National AAU Championships	1st	158′ 4″
1968	Olympic Games	6th	—
	National AAU Championships	1st	170′ 10″

feet. (The Olympic record for women was then 168 feet 8½ inches.)

In November of 1956, Olga boarded a ship bound for the Olympics in Melbourne, Australia. She had always performed her best when the stands were filled with many spectators, so people who knew her predicted a good performance at the Olympics.

In front of more than a hundred thousand spectators, Olga threw the discus farther than she had ever thrown it. Her throw was measured at 176 feet 1 inch. Olga won the gold medal and instantaneously became a heroine across all of Czechoslovakia.

Continuing the Story

The Melbourne Olympic Games were to change Olga's life in many ways. Besides becoming an internationally renowned athlete, Olga

After a few days of rest and relaxation, Olga's discus prowess seemed to return. All through that summer, she regularly threw more than 160

Olga Connolly in 1956.

Tony Duffy/Allsport

met her future husband in Melbourne. One morning soon after arriving in Melbourne, Olga bumped into Hal Connolly outside an equipment shack on one of the practice fields for the Olympic track and field athletes.

Connolly was there to compete for the United States in the hammer throw. Olga had studied English in school, so she and Hal were able to struggle through a ten-minute conversation that morning. In the days that followed, they spent as much time together as possible. They realized that they were in love.

Four months later, Hal Connolly and Olga Fikotová, both gold medal winners at the Olympics, were married in Prague. It did not seem to matter that he was an American and she was from a Communist country. Nor did it matter that he was Catholic and she was Protestant. Their love affair pleased the world. After the wedding, the Connollys moved to Boston, Massachusetts.

Despite the difficulties of being amateur athlete in minor sports in the United States, both Olga and Hal continued to compete in their respective sports of discus and hammer throw. Olga won five Amateur Athletic Union titles between 1957 and 1968. She also represented the United States in the next four Olympic Games.

Olga finished seventh in the 1960 Olympics, twelfth in 1964, and sixth in 1968. In 1972, at age thirty-nine and as the mother of four children, she was selected to carry the United States flag at the opening ceremonies in Munich, Germany. Olga had thrown a record distance of 185 feet

---

RECORD

World record in discus in 1972 (185′ 3′)

---

3 inches earlier in 1972, but she failed to qualify for the finals of the Olympics that year.

Olga resigned from competition after the 1972 Olympics. She did not, however, give up her interest in sports. She went on to become the Director of Intramural Sports at Loyola Marymount University in Los Angeles.

Summary

Olga Connolly was an outstanding athlete, competing on national teams in team handball, basketball, and track and field. She is best known, though, for her excellence in the discus throw. She always seemed to love the beauty of movement and worked hard at her sport. Long after many athletes had retired, Olga was still competing in discus and working to promote physical education and sports for women in the United States.

Kathleen Tritschler

Additional Sources:

Hanley, Reid M. *Who's Who in Track and Field.* New Rochelle, N.Y.: Arlington House, 1971.

Wallechinsky, David. *The Complete Book of the Olympics.* Boston: Little, Brown and Company, 1991.

Watman, Mel. *Encyclopedia of Track and Field Athletics.* New York: St. Martin's Press, 1981.

JIMMY CONNORS

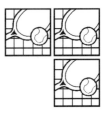

Sport: Tennis

Born: September 2, 1952
East St. Louis, Illinois

Jimmy Connors plays at Wimbledon in 1985.

Early Life

James Scott Connors was born on September 2, 1952, in East St. Louis, Illinois. Jimmy was the second son of Gloria (Thompson) Connors, a tennis pro, and James Connors, Sr., an automobile bridge toll booth manager. Jimmy and his brother John, a year and a half older, grew up in East St. Louis and Belleville, Illinois.

Jimmy was first encouraged to play tennis as a preschooler, when his small hand could barely grasp a sawed-off racket. His mother and grandmother, the late Bertha Thompson, a tournament player, were his major tennis supporters. Jimmy has always been known to have a passion for the game of tennis and from the very beginning has credited his love for the sport as his greatest motivation.

The Road to Excellence

Jimmy practiced constantly and would play from morning until night if allowed. His dedication from the outset was tireless, and absolutely nothing would stand in his way to improve.

Split-second timing and a two-handed backhand became the left-handed Jimmy's trademarks, as he was taught by his mother. Jimmy was taught during his early involvement to strike the tennis ball on the rise to keep his opponent from getting prepared. Jimmy was small for his age and his success was largely dependent on speed, agility, and quickness.

525

At the age of eight, Jimmy entered major tournaments for boys. His first championship was in the ten-and-under category in the Southern Illinois tournament.

During his sophomore year at Assumption High School in St. Louis, Jimmy chose to play amateur tennis on the junior United States Lawn Tennis Association (USLTA) circuit. Jimmy believed he would improve faster on this circuit than if he played for his high school team.

In 1968, Jimmy won the sixteen-and-under U.S. National title against a much more experienced opponent, 6-3, 6-1. Jimmy then moved up to the junior level a full year early, to continue to challenge himself against the toughest possible opponents. It was at this point that Jimmy decided he needed a coach as well as the opportunity to play more.

Francisco (Pancho) Segura became Jimmy's coach. Jimmy, now seventeen, and his mother moved to Los Angeles to be close to Segura. Jimmy attended Rexford High School in the mornings and played tennis in the afternoon.

The year 1970 was a great one for Jimmy. He won the Junior National Hardcourt Championship and the Junior National Clay Court Championship that year. He was also a member of the Junior Davis Cup team and went to the semifinals in the Junior Outdoor Nationals.

Attending the University of California at Los Angeles (UCLA) in 1970-1971, Jimmy won the National Collegiate Athletic Association (NCAA) Championship against Roscoe Tanner. Jimmy was the first freshman ever to win the NCAA title. At the time, Jimmy was ranked first nationally in junior tennis and fourteenth as an adult.

HONORS AND AWARDS

1972	Rolex Rookie of the Year
1974	Player of the Year Award
1974-78	Ranked number one by the Association of Tennis Professionals
1982	International Tennis Federation Player of the Year
1991	Domino's Pizza Team Tennis Male Rookie of the Year
1998	Inducted into International Tennis Hall of Fame

MILESTONES

109 professional titles
10 Grand Slam titles
U.S. Davis Cup team (1972, 1976, 1981, 1984)

The Emerging Champion

After winning the NCAA Championship as a freshman, great things were expected of Jimmy Connors. A slumping second year in college and his passion for greatness caused him to consider turning professional.

Playing in a tournament in Maryland, Jimmy made it to the finals against Ilie Nastase. Jimmy lost, yet had to turn down a large prize check to retain his amateur status. The experience helped convince him to turn professional. After discussing the move with his mother, Jimmy competed in Jacksonville, Florida, the next week as a professional.

Showing the mark of a future superstar, Jimmy won his first tournament as a professional and took home a check for three thousand dollars for four days' work. The next tournament, in Virginia, again showed the outstanding talent of this young man, as he again won. Jimmy quickly became the hottest player on the circuit, and his years of hard work and determination were paying off.

By March of 1972, Jimmy had made the Davis Cup team, representing the United States. Jimmy played his first Wimbledon that same year, bowing out in the quarterfinals. In his first year as a professional, Jimmy had seventy-five victories, the highest total among all American male professionals. Jimmy also finished second on the money list with $90,000 in prize money that year.

With Jimmy's quick start and enormous success his first year as a professional, 1973 provided increasing challenges. A roller-coaster year was highlighted by his victory in the United States Pro Championship. Jimmy was the youngest winner ever of this championship.

The year 1974, perhaps Jimmy's best, resulted in many important victories. Jimmy won 99 of 103 matches that year. Among these were his first Wimbledon, United States Open, and Australian Open titles. His play in 1974 seemed to establish the Connors style of play: always attacking, intense concentration, crisp ground strokes, great return of service, and precision timing.

Between the years 1974 and 1978, Jimmy was known as the most consistent player in men's tennis. "Jimbo" won more than fifty tournaments. In 1984, he became the first player to win one hundred singles titles.

MAJOR CHAMPIONSHIP VICTORIES AND FINALS

1973	Wimbledon doubles (with Ilie Nastase)
1974	Australian Open
1974, 1976, 1978, 1982-83	U.S. Open
1974, 1982	Wimbledon
1975	U.S. Open doubles (with Nastase)
1975, 1977	U.S. Open finalist
1975, 1977-78, 1984	Wimbledon finalist

OTHER NOTABLE VICTORIES

1971	NCAA Championship
1973	U.S. Pro Championship
1973-75, 1978-79, 1983-84	U.S. Indoor Championship
1974	U.S. Clay Court Championship doubles (with Nastase)
1974, 1975	U.S. Indoor Championship doubles (with Frew McMillan; with Nastase)
1974, 1976, 1978-79	U.S. Clay Court Championship
1975	U.S. Indoor Championship doubles (with Nastase)
1976, 1978-80	U.S. Pro Indoor Championship
1977, 1980	WCT Finals
1978	The Masters
1978-79	U.S. National Indoor Championships
1979	WCT Tournament of Champions
1980	Seiko World Super Tennis Classic
1982	Pacific Southwest Open

Continuing the Story

Although the emergence of tennis greats Björn Borg and John McEnroe in the late 1970's and early 1980's made Jimmy less dominant, he remained ranked in the top five in the world for many years. Jimmy Connors had certainly made his mark as one of the greatest U.S. players ever.

A trademark of Jimmy, along with his aggressiveness and spirited play, was his "fiery" attitude on the tennis courts. Along with Jimmy's loner status within the tennis world, he also created a "bad boy" image. This eventually became his greatest strength, as people would always be guaranteed a gutsy performance if Jimbo was participating.

Jimmy's driving spirit kept him more than competitive throughout the 1980's, well past his physical prime. He extended his tennis involvement as a television commentator during the latter part of his competitive career.

Jimmy will always be remembered in the tennis world for being a great return of server, having a tireless attack, spirited play, and a "never-say-die" attitude every time he stepped on the court. His competitive instinct was once again demonstrated in dramatic fashion at the 1991 U.S. Open. Through the first several rounds, thirty-nine-year-old Jimmy electrified the crowd—who by then had every reason to think that he might actually go on to win his sixth Open title. In the quarterfinals, however, Jimmy ran out of miracles, losing in three sets to American Jim Courier. Jimmy began playing on the Worldwide Senior Tennis Circuit in 1993.

Summary

Jimmy Connors's competitive fire kept burning brightly throughout the 1980's and into the 1990's. Even though his play was a few notches below that of the Jimbo of old, he remained an inspiration for younger players. Jimmy's style of play made him as successful as an entertainer as he once was as a competitor.

There is no doubt that Jimmy's personality and determination will live on in the tennis world. Along with his long record of accomplishments, his spirit and drive will long be remembered. Many youngsters will undoubtedly copy his style and aggressive approach to playing tennis.

Hal J. Walker

Additional Sources:

Burchard, Marshall. *Sports Hero, Jimmy Connors.* New York: Putnam, 1976.

Busch, Jim, and Diane Busch. *Jimmy Connors, a Biography: Eye of the Tiger.* Pittsburgh, Pa.: Dorrance, 1998.

Collins, Bud. "Jimmy Connors." In *Bud Collins' Tennis Encyclopedia,* edited by Bud Collins and Zander Hollander. 3d ed. Detroit: Visible Ink Press, 1997.

Sabin, Francene. *Jimmy Connors, King of the Courts.* New York: Putnam, 1978.

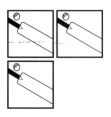

LEARIE CONSTANTINE

Sport: Cricket

Born: September 21, 1901
  Petit Valley, Diego Martinez, Trinidad
Died: July 1, 1971
  London, England

Early Life

Learie Nicholas Constantine was born on September 21, 1901, at Petit Valley, Diego Martinez, on the island of Trinidad in the West Indies. His family was not poor, but his father did not make much money working as an overseer on a local estate.

Learie's father, Lebrun, was an exceptional man. He was able to combine his workload at the estate and his duties as a father, and still managed to be one of the finest batsmen in the West Indies. Learie was certainly fortunate to have a great cricketer for a father. Lebrun Constantine instilled in his children a great passion for the game.

The Road to Excellence

Learie's father soon recognized that his son had an outstanding talent. He developed upon this by teaching Learie the finer points of the game and always insisted that he maintain the highest standard of play. Learie was a good learner; he was exceedingly bright and picked up things very quickly.

At school, Learie was recognized as being the son of "Old Cons," and he became known as "Young Cons." Learie did not live long in his father's shadow. His exploits as a schoolboy cricketer alerted everybody to his great potential.

Upon leaving school, Learie took a job as a solicitor's clerk. While he was glad to be working, his whole life revolved around the weekends. Learie joined his father's club, Shannon, which had the most competitive cricket league in Trinidad. Learie had a fair degree of success and became viewed by knowledgeable Trinidadians as a promising player.

In 1921, Learie followed his father into the Trinidad side. Indeed, in 1923, both the Constantines were to play in the same Trinidad side in a match against British Guiana at Georgetown. Also in 1923, Learie was selected for the West Indies team to go to England. He was still very young and woefully inexperienced, but the West Indian cricket authorities believed this young all-around player had abundant talents that they simply could not overlook.

The trip to England in 1923 changed Learie's entire life. In terms of cricket he had an average tour, excelling only as a fielder. Nevertheless, the experience he gained in England opened his eyes to the unequal world in which he lived. Learie realized that cricket was the only stepping-stone he had to the kind of life he wanted to live.

The Emerging Champion

In the seasons following his tour to England, Learie worked diligently to improve his game. By the late 1920's, he was a lightning-fast bowler, a dashing batsman, and a supreme fielder. His performances and warm personality made him the darling of the Trinidadian people. Despite his cricketing successes, Learie was still dismayed at being unable to find the kind of employment he was seeking. As a lower-middle-class black man he was constantly faced with racial discrimination when it came to finding jobs. It was not sufficient for Learie to be a solicitor's clerk all of his life; now he wanted to be the solicitor.

Learie's only solution was to leave Trinidad and try to get educated somewhere else. Realizing there were professional cricket leagues in England, he decided to go there to play cricket and study law. The meager income he could earn from cricket would, he hoped, give him enough to go through school.

As luck would have it, the West Indian team were due to tour England in 1928. In the months

CAREER STATISTICS

First-Class Cricket

Batting:
Runs: 4,451
Centuries: 5
Average runs-per-inning: 24.32
Bowling:
Wickets: 424
Average 20.60

Test Match Cricket

Matches: 18
Batting:
Runs: 641
Centuries: 2
Average runs-per-inning: 19.42
Bowling:
Wickets: 58
Average: 30.10

Nelson did his popularity little harm. Learie was the Nelson cricket team, and he dominated the batting, bowling, and fielding. In his ten seasons with the club, Nelson won the competitive Lancashire League on eight occasions.

World War II effectively put an end to Learie's cricket career. He remained in London, however, and worked at the Ministry of Labour Welfare Office, in a department that dealt specifically with West Indians. The war returned Learie to the attention of the British public, and he was frequently asked to do radio broadcasts to the nation. After the war he was made a Member of the British Empire (M.B.E.) for his services during the conflict.

Throughout his time in England, Learie continued his education. The distractions of profes-

leading up to the tour, Learie trained like never before. He was determined that he should reach England in peak physical condition, so that he would be a prized acquisition for any professional league club.

Although he performed moderately in test matches, Learie captured the imagination of the English population through his dashing exploits against the county sides. He was the perfect league cricketer. His explosive batting and bowling were winning matches in a matter of minutes, and his peerless fielding was a joy to watch.

During the 1928 tour, he agreed to join the Nelson Club in the Lancashire League in the following summer. The people of Trinidad were disheartened, but no one could blame their hero for wanting to make a better life for himself. As things were, this never could have happened back home in Trinidad.

Continuing the Story

In 1929, Learie and his wife, Norma, moved to Nelson, a small, mainly working-class mill town. Few people in the town had ever seen black people before, but the Constantines settled in very quickly and were always made to feel welcome. Of course, Learie's commanding displays for

Sir Learie Constantine in 1939.

529

sional cricket, however, and later the war, diverted Learie away from his chosen career in law. It was only after years of studying that he eventually qualified as a lawyer in 1954. After qualifying, Learie returned to Trinidad and became a leading figure in the government of the island. Learie eventually returned to London in 1962 (the same year in which he was knighted) as the High Commissioner for the Government of Trinidad and Tobago.

As his people's representative in London, Learie had reached a position of importance he could only ever have dreamed of. He never forgot his commitment to eradicating the discrimination he had faced due to the color of his skin. As a result of his ceaseless work in fighting for the rights of the disadvantaged classes of society, Learie was created a Life Peer in 1969. Learie died in London on July 1, 1971.

Summary

When Learie Constantine died, he was officially known as Baron Constantine, of Maraval in Trinidad and Tobago, and of Nelson in the County Palatine of Lancaster. This title demonstrates that Learie had a lasting impact on both sides of the Atlantic. Although a fine cricketer, Learie realized there were far more important things in life than scoring runs, taking wickets,

and holding catches. His popularity brought him to the public's attention, and he used his widespread appeal to influence popular opinion on the rights of black people throughout the world. Learie became one of the most influential figures of his time.

David L. Andrews

HONORS AND AWARDS	
1945	Member of the British Empire
1962	Knight of the British Empire
1969	Life Peer

Additional Sources:

Constantine, Learie. *Colour Bar.* London: Stanley Paul, 1954.

_____. *Cricketers' Cricket.* London: Eyre & Spottiswoode, 1949.

_____. *The Young Cricketer's Companion.* London: Souvenir, 1964.

Constantine, Learie, and Denzil Batchelor. *The Changing Face of Cricket.* London: Eyre & Spottiswoode, 1966.

Howat, Gerald M. *Learie Constantine.* London: Allen & Unwin, 1975.

CYNTHIA COOPER

Sport: Basketball

Born: April 14, 1963
Chicago, Illinois

Early Life

Cynthia Cooper grew up in a big family, with three brothers and four sisters. She was the middle child. Her mother, Mary Cobb, taught them all the importance of hard work and trusting in the Lord. Her mother was their example, as she raised eight children by herself, working for the Rapid Transit Department in Los Angeles. The family had moved from Chicago when Cynthia was just about a year old. They lived for a number of years in the area known as Watts. Cynthia faced tough times living in that area, and she desired to someday get out of the neighborhood.

The Road to Excellence

While attending Gompers Junior High School, Cynthia had her first introduction to the game of basketball while watching others practice. Cynthia convinced one of the high school coaches, Lucias Franklin, to teach her how to play the summer before she entered Locke High School. As a result, Cynthia made the varsity team her first year in high school. In addition to developing as a basketball star, Cynthia also ran track, devoting her energies to the 400 meters. During her senior year the Locke Saints won the California AAAA state championship. She was named

the league's most valuable player and Los Angeles City Player of the Year in 1981.

The Emerging Champion

Cynthia attended the University of Southern California (USC), graduating as a physical education major in 1986. While at college she led the

Cynthia Cooper (right) dribbles by Teresa Weatherspoon in an August, 2000, game against the New York Liberty.

531

STATISTICS

Season	GP	FGA	FGM	FG%	FTA	FTM	FT%	Reb.	Ast.	TP	PPG
1997	28	406	191	.470	199	172	.864	111	131	621	**22.2**
1998	30	455	203	.446	246	210	.854	110	131	680	**22.7**
1999	31	458	212	.463	229	204	.891	87	162	686	**22.1**
2000	31	392	180	.459	168	147	.875	85	156	550	17.7
Totals	120	1,711	786	.459	842	733	.871	393	580	2,537	21.1

Notes: Boldface indicates statistical leader. GP = games played; FGA = field goals attempted; FGM = field goals made; FG% = field goal percentage; FTA = free throws attempted; FTM = free throws made; FT% = free throw percentage; Reb. = rebounds; Ast. = assists; TP = total points; PPG = points per game

USC Lady Trojans to three Final Four competitions and to national championships in 1983 and 1984. After the victory in 1983, Cynthia and her teammates received an invitation to the White House to meet President Ronald Reagan.

Cynthia's basketball career took a backseat to family obligations in 1985 when she dropped out of school to go to work for a bank in Inglewood, California. After spending a season away from the game Cynthia began playing pickup games and joined a local touring team that played in Mexico. From this experience came an offer to play professionally in Austria. Instead, Cynthia reenrolled in college to finish her senior year and graduate.

While at USC Cynthia never really had the chance to shine, playing in the backcourt and being overshadowed by stars like Cheryl Miller. Never being named to an All-American team seemed to confirm her lower status, but Cynthia did make the All-Pac West team in 1985-1986. When she graduated, her choices of avenues to continue playing basketball were fairly limited and outside the United States. In 1986 and 1987 Cynthia played in Segovia, Spain, followed by more than a decade of playing in both Parma and Alcamo, Italy. While in Italy Cynthia was named Rookie of the Year and Player of the Year in 1987.

Cynthia did play in the Goodwill Games in 1986 and 1990, as well as the Pan-Am Games in 1987, when her team won the gold. In addition, she played in the 1986 World Championships with the U.S. national team. Cynthia also had the joy of representing her country in the Olympics in 1988, 1992, and 2000, winning three medals, two gold and one bronze. She did not get asked to play in 1996, when the call seemed to go to younger, more well-known players.

Continuing the Story

In 1997 Cynthia finally had the chance to play professionally in the United States following the creation of the Women's National Basketball Association (WNBA). Cynthia joined the Houston Comets in 1997, and the team won all four WNBA championships it played. She was named most valuable player in each of those four series. Cynthia was selected to the All-WNBA First Team for four straight years and was a Western Conference All-Star in 1997 and 1998. She led the league in scoring from 1997 to 1999. Finally Cynthia was a star in her own country. In 1997-1998 Cynthia won the ESPY Award for Female Basketball Player of the Year. That same year she was second in the voting to soccer star Mia Hamm for the Woman Athlete of the Year award. Cynthia also won an Arete Award for courage in sports in 1998.

HONORS, AWARDS, AND MILESTONES

1987	Most valuable player, European All-Star Game
1988, 2000	Gold Medal, Olympic Basketball
1992	Bronze Medal, Olympic Basketball
1996	Leading scorer (37.5 ppg) in European Cup
1997-98	WNBA Most Valuable Award
1997-2000	Most valuable player of the WNBA Championship All-WNBA First Team
1998	First WNBA player to top 1,000 career points
1999-2000	All-Star Team

In 1999 Cynthia wrote a book about her basketball journey, *She Got Game*. In this book Cynthia talks about her life from humble beginnings in Watts to her later stardom in the WNBA. She also discusses her family and the people in her life who helped and inspired her to become the best she could be. In December, 2000, Cynthia was named the head coach of the Phoenix Mercury, replacing Cheryl Miller.

Summary

Cynthia Cooper retired at the end of the 2000 season, after winning four straight WNBA championships with the Houston Comets. She left behind much more than that legacy, however. Cynthia played the game of basketball with all her skill and talent laid on the line. She saw herself as a role model for others, showing them what could be possible if they worked hard enough. She used her time in the WNBA to become a positive example for others from the inner city and beyond. Cynthia also became a spokesperson for breast cancer awareness and research both on and off the field, wearing a pink ribbon on her uniform as a constant reminder of the disease that killed her mother in 1999.

Leslie Heaphy

Additional Sources:

"A League of Her Own." *Sports Illustrated* 93, no. 9 (September 4, 2000): 27.

Berkow, Ira. "Cooper Leaving Behind a Legacy of Greatness." *The New York Times*, August 28, 2000, p. D4.

Cooper, Cynthia. *She Got Game: My Personal Odyssey*. New York: Warner Books, 1999.

Howard, Johnette. "Comet's Tale." *Sports Illustrated* 87, no. 8 (August 25, 1997): 34-35.

ANGEL CORDERO, JR.

Sport: Horse racing

Born: November 8, 1942
San Juan, Puerto Rico

Early Life

Angel Tomas Cordero, Jr., was born on November 8, 1942, in San Juan, Puerto Rico. Angel, according to his father, was born to race. The Puerto Rico racing encyclopedia includes an entire page of jockeys with the surname Cordero, and there is an equally long list of riders with the surname Hernandez, which is Cordero's mother's maiden name.

Angel's father and grandfather were famous jockeys in Puerto Rico, and, from the time he could walk, he wanted to race horses. He did not even know that a world existed outside racing until he went to school at age five. Angel's father wanted him to be a doctor because of the danger in horse racing but eventually accepted his son's desire to be a jockey. Angel would go to the track to work and learn about racing before and after school until he graduated from high school. From then on, however, it was racing and nothing else.

The Road to Excellence

He began to race at a local track in San Juan. Six months before his eighteenth birthday, he took a terrible fall in a race: Five jockeys in all went down and were injured. Although he was only slightly injured, Angel was very shaken up and quit racing. Yet five days later he returned to the track, ready to resume riding.

He was a determined jockey and rode like a man on fire. People began to say that he was too dangerous—such was his obsession with winning. Another hard fall resulted in two broken ribs, but he was riding again as soon as he was healthy.

The next year at the El Comandante race track brought Angel much success; after being the leading apprentice rider, he became the top journeyman rider in Puerto Rico with 124 wins. This record number of wins is amazing because, first, the track was open only three days a week

Jockey Angel Cordero, Jr., shortly before the 1995 Breeders' Cup.

AP/Wide World Photos

534

MAJOR CHAMPIONSHIP VICTORIES

Year	Race	Horse
1974	Kentucky Derby	Cannonade
1976	Belmont Stakes	Bold Force
	Kentucky Derby	Bold Force
1980	Preakness Stakes	Codex
1984	Preakness Stakes	Gate Dancer
1985	Kentucky Derby	Spend a Buck
	Breeders' Cup Distaff	Life's Magic
1988	Breeders' Cup Juvenile Fillies	Open Mind
	Breeders' Cup Sprint	Gulch
1989	Breeders' Cup Sprint	Dancing Spree

and, second, Angel had been suspended from racing for five months for dangerous tactics.

The Emerging Champion

Angel arrived in New York in 1962 to try his hand at American horse racing. He had no friends or family and could not speak English. After several months of fighting for mounts and having only forty-one rides and one winner, he returned to Puerto Rico totally disappointed. He got married, regained his confidence and drive, and returned with his wife to New York in 1965.

At first his races were peppered with successes, but he still felt like quitting. Angel knew a lot about racing—he knew how to give orders but did not like taking them. Even though he had more talent than anyone else, he was treated by other jockeys as though he was not good enough to clean stables. Once Angel learned to channel this anger and intensity into racing, however, he began to win more races.

In America, as in Puerto Rico, Angel became known for his aggressive and daring riding style. He also became famous for his style of dismount. Once, at Belmont, before the race, the horse bucked and Angel was hurled through the air. Somehow he managed to land on his feet, smiling. Since then he has dismounted by leaping off the horse as if it was a trampoline and landing with both feet on the ground.

In 1974, Angel rode a spectacular race in the Kentucky Derby. Many jockeys decided to take the outside rail, but Angel was aggressive and went for the inside rail. He was on a horse that was not given much of a chance, but he survived two bumpings and won from fourteen lengths back.

Continuing the Story

Angel was a fixture in the New York Racing Association for more than twenty years. He was the leading rider in New York six times during his career. Several times he led the nation in wins and money won. His mounts earned more than $150 million, including a North American record of more than $10 million in 1983. In 1983 he was also honored with his second consecutive Eclipse Award, the most respected award in horse racing. Most important, he won the Kentucky Derby three times, the Preakness Stakes twice, and the Belmont Stakes once.

Through the years, Angel's drive to win only became stronger. He became an athlete who gave something back to the sport of horse racing. Talented and successful, Angel shared his skills with many young jockeys from his homeland. He retired from racing in 1992.

Summary

Angel Cordero, Jr., finished his racing career with 7,057 wins (fourth all-time) in 38,646 starts, including three Kentucky Derby victories. Upon his retirement in 1992, he ranked sixth all-time in career winnings, with $164.5 million. A two-time winner of the Eclipse Award, Angel was one of the most dominant jockeys in horse racing.

Brooke K. Zibel

MILESTONES

Annual money leader in 1976
His 7,057 victories rank sixth all-time

HONORS AND AWARDS

1982-83	Eclipse Award, Outstanding Jockey
1988	Inducted into National Horse Racing Hall of Fame

Additional Sources:

Reed, W. F., and R. Demak. "The End of the Ride." *Sports Illustrated* 76, no. 19 (1992).

FRED COUPLES

Sport: Golf

Born: October 3, 1959
Seattle, Washington

Early Life

Fred Couples was born in Seattle, Washington, on October 3, 1959. He was an enthusiastic soccer and baseball player as a youth. During his teens, Jefferson Park, a municipal golf course about two blocks from his home, became the center of his interest in golf.

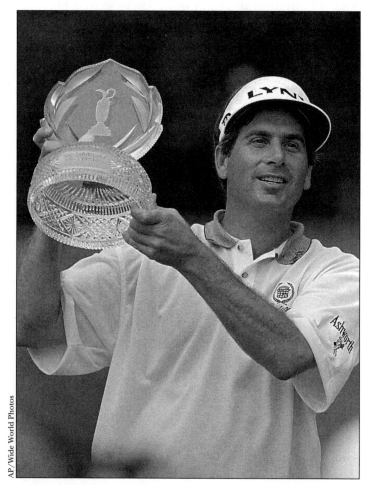

Fred Couples displays the Memorial Tournament trophy in May, 1998.

As his golf skills developed, Fred enjoyed the fun and challenge of playing in competitive golf games with older boys and men. When he and his friend Jay Turner got jobs at the Jefferson Park driving range, he was allowed to hit golf balls for free. He loved to blast them as far as he could.

After completing St. George grade school, he attended O'Dea Catholic High School for Boys, a small school that was run by the Irish Christian Brothers. The school's golf coaches, Brothers Patitucci and O'Grady, took the team to courses in the Seattle area and occasionally took members across the Puget Sound to play. Fred enjoyed these trips to new courses and became a skilled player.

The Road to Excellence

At the age of eighteen, Fred won the Washington State Open Golf Tournament as an amateur. He chose to attend the University of Houston and made the golf team as a freshman. He improved each year, and his college roommate, Jim Nantz, who later became a network television sports announcer, predicted that some day Fred would win the Masters Tournament. Fred laughed and told Jim that he played golf solely for enjoyment. As he played against the best college players, however, and saw professionals play in Texas, he began to believe that he could compete at the professional level.

Fred met Deborah Morgan, his future wife, while they were students at Houston. During the summer of 1980, before his senior year, Fred went to California to visit her. While there, he inquired about playing in the Queen Mary Open Tournament in Long Beach. He was told that all the amateur openings

AP/Wide World Photos

MAJOR CHAMPIONSHIP VICTORIES

1992	The Masters

OTHER NOTABLE VICTORIES

1983	Kemper Open
1984	Tournament Players Championship
1987	Byron Nelson Golf Classic
1990,1992	Nissan Los Angeles Open
1991	B.C. Open Federal Express St. Jude Classic
1991,1995	Johnnie Walker World Championship
1992	Nestlé Invitational
1992-1995	World Cup Team
1993	Honda Classic
1994	World Cup Championship (Individual) Buick Open
1995	Dubai Desert Classic
1996	Players Championship
1998	Bob Hope Chrysler Classic

were filled but that he could play as a professional. A friend paid his entry fee. Fred tied for sixth place. He repaid the loan, and his professional career had begun.

After finishing in fifty-third place on the Professional Golf Association (PGA) tour list of money winners in both 1981 and 1982, Fred won his first PGA tournament, the Kemper Open, in 1983. The following year, he won the prestigious Tournament Players Championship and gained recognition as a bright young prospect. His smooth swing, powered by strong calf and thigh muscles, generated drives that made him one of the longest hitters on the tour.

Although he did not win again until the Byron Nelson Golf Classic in 1987, by the end of that year he had earned more than a million dollars since joining the tour in 1981. He finished nineteenth in earnings in 1987, joining the elite players on the tour.

In 1989, Fred was chosen as a member of the U.S. Ryder Cup team. The Ryder Cup competition matches two teams of top-ranking professionals, one from

the United States and one from Europe. He lost all of his matches. The European team retained the Ryder Cup, as the U.S. team was only able to tie it in total match points. Fred was disappointed that he was not able to help the U.S. effort, but his fellow professionals Tom Watson and Raymond Floyd encouraged him to use the experience as motivation to become a tougher competitor. With golf instructors Paul Marchand and Dick Harmon, Fred worked earnestly on his swing and on his mental approach to the game.

The Emerging Champion

Fred realized that he needed to develop a reliable putting stroke, one that he could depend on under pressure. His improved putting helped him to build confidence in his game. That confidence led to one tournament victory in 1990 and three wins in 1991. Even more satisfying was his performance in the 1991 Ryder Cup matches. He won three matches and contributed to the close victory of the U.S. team. His consistent play on the PGA tour also won him the Vardon Trophy for the lowest scoring average per round on the tour.

Fred continued his strong play as the 1992 season began, winning the Nissan Los Angeles Open and the Nestlé Invitational. In April, he achieved the goal that his friend Jim Nantz had predicted by winning the Masters Tournament at the Augusta National course in Georgia. During 1992, his three-year cumulative record earned him the top position in the Sony World Rankings of players. He was also recognized as Player of the Year on the PGA Tour and again won the Vardon Trophy.

Continuing The Story

In the midst of his rise to golf prominence, Fred and his wife, Deborah, separated in 1992, after a marriage of eleven years. Fred's career could have taken a downturn, but with the sup-

HONORS AND AWARDS

1989,1991,1993,1995,1997	Ryder Cup Team
1991-92	PGA Tour Player of the Year Vardon Trophy for lowest scoring average on tour
1992	PGA of America Player of the Year

port of his father, Tom, his mother, Violet, his sister Cindy, and loyal friends on the tour, Fred rededicated himself to the philosophy of making golf his life and his source of enjoyment. During 1993, he won the Honda Classic tournament and again represented the United States as a member of the Ryder Cup team.

Fred played on five Ryder Cup teams, won the World Cup Championship (individual) in 1996, and became the first player to win two Players Championships. He also recorded back-to-back victories on the PGA European tour in 1995, the first American to do so since Charles Coody in 1973. In nineteen events entered in 2000, Fred had five top-ten finishes and eleven top-twenty-five finishes, and he earned nearly $1 million for the season.

Summary

Fred Couples's skill, backed by the confidence that his talent, experience, and determination gave him, enabled him to compete successfully with the best players in his profession. His honesty, down-to-earth attitudes, and desire to enjoy a simple, private lifestyle reflected his basic values.

Ray Sobczak

Additional Sources:

Bissell, Kathlene. *Fred Couples: Golf's Reluctant Superstar.* Lincolnwood, Ill.: Contemporary Books, 1999.

Couples, Fred, with John Andrisani. *Total Shotmaking: The Golfer's Guide to Low Scoring.* New York: HarperCollins, 1994.

Couples, Fred, Guy Yocum, and Stephen Szurlej. "Fred Couples' Guide to Life." *Golf Digest* 51, no. 11 (2000).

Feinstein, John. "Semi-Retired." *Golf Magazine* 42, no. 9 (2000).

Wilner, Barry. *Golf Stars of Today.* Philadelphia, Pa.: Chelsea House, 1998.

JIM COURIER

Sport: Tennis

Born: August 17, 1970
Sanford, Florida

Early Life

James Spencer Courier, Jr., was born on August 17, 1970, in Sanford, Florida, to James Spencer Courier, Sr., a marketing executive, and Linda Courier, an elementary-school media specialist. Jim was the second of three children in a family that included an older sister, Audra, and a younger brother, Kris. Growing up in Dade City, Florida, Jim got his competitive spirit from his father, who had been a baseball pitcher at Florida State University.

Baseball was Jim's first love until the age of seven, when his great-aunt, Emma Spencer, introduced him to tennis. Aunt Emma, who had been a women's tennis coach, ran the Dreamworld Tennis Club out of her home in Sanford. In addition to the fundamentals of the game, she taught Jim how to behave on a tennis court. By the time Jim was eleven, he was ready for formal tennis training. He was sent to the legendary Australian tennis instructor Harry Hopman, who ran a tennis academy in Largo, Florida.

Jim Courier plays at the 1999 Davis Cup.

AP/Wide World Photos

The Road to Excellence

Hopman was so impressed with how Jim hit the ball that he waived all fees and decided to instruct the boy for free. Jim remained under Hopman's tutelage for two years. The intense training paid off when Jim reached the finals of the fourteen-and-under division of the Orange Bowl Junior Championships, the pinnacle of junior tennis. Famous coach Nick Bollettieri was so impressed with Jim's game that he offered him a full scholarship to his tennis academy in Bradenton, Florida. While attending the academy, Jim trained with another future tennis great, Andre Agassi. Jim sometimes became frustrated at all the personal attention that Agassi got from Bollettieri, but he continued to work hard.

Power was the main component of Jim's tennis game when he was a teenager. He patterned his two-handed backhand stroke on a baseball swing. There was nothing subtle about his game.

MAJOR CHAMPIONSHIP VICTORIES AND FINALS

1991	U.S. Open finalist
1991-92	French Open
1992-93	Australian Open
1993	French Open finalist
	Wimbledon finalist

OTHER NOTABLE VICTORIES

1989	Swiss Indoors
1991	Lipton International
1991,1993	Newsweek Champions Cup
1992,1995	Winning U.S. Davis Cup team member
1992	Japan Open
	Salem Open
1992-93	Italian Open
1993	Kroger/St. Jude International
	RCA/U.S. Hardcourts

Jim would hit the ball hard, and if that did not work, he would hit the ball even harder. By winning in his age group at the 1986 and 1987 Orange Bowl Junior Championships, Jim became the first player since Björn Borg to win consecutive Orange Bowl titles. He was winning some matches on desire alone; he had not learned yet how to win by playing the intelligent shot instead of the power shot. In 1988, Jim decided it was time to join the professional tour. Although he did not win any tournaments that year, he raised his Association of Tennis Professionals (ATP) ranking to forty-third in the world.

The Emerging Champion

Jim finally broke through and won his first professional tournament in 1989, defeating Stefan Edberg in the finals of the Swiss Indoors in Basel, Switzerland. With the victory, his world ranking rose to number twenty-four. Although Jim was steadily moving up in the rankings, his game was too one-dimensional for him to rise much above twentieth in the world. Jim was a fierce competitor, but he would get so tense on the court during a match that it became impossible for him to adjust his game to his opponent or to a particular situation in a match. Jim understood that a change was necessary, but he needed some expert guidance.

Although he was still taking instruction from Bollettieri, Jim knew that the association was not benefiting him. Early in 1990, he formally cut his ties with Bollettieri and looked to find a coach who could devote himself to improving his chances of cracking the top ten. In José Higueras, Jim found a coach who was up to the task. Under Higueras' guidance, Michael Chang had won the 1989 French Open. Jim began training with Higueras and college coach Brad Stine in 1990, and they set out to transform Jim's tennis strategy.

Jim had won or lost matches based on his powerful baseline game. Higueras and Stine wished to make Jim an all-court player. They wanted him to introduce variety into his game and to learn to employ tactics to defeat an opponent. In 1991, Jim began to make successful use of what his new coaches had taught him. He won three tournaments that year, including the prestigious French Open, one of tennis' four Grand Slam tournaments. In the French Open final, Jim defeated Andre Agassi in a thrilling five-set match (3-6, 6-4, 2-6, 6-1, 6-4).

Continuing the Story

Because of his strong showing in 1991, Jim became the second-ranked player in the world. His willingness to work hard and never quit had pushed him to the top of the tennis game. In Jim, Higueras and Stine had found a student who was willing to learn, willing to put in long hours to get results. In January, 1992, Jim won the Australian Open, another Grand Slam event, by defeating the then-number-one player in the world, Stefan Edberg, in four sets (6-3, 3-6, 6-4, 6-2).

With the help of this victory, Jim became the first American to be ranked number one since John McEnroe in 1985. Jim solidified his number-one ranking with the winning of a second French

HONORS AND AWARDS

1991	ATP Most Improved Tour Player
1992	ATP Tour Player of the Year
	Jim Thorpe Player of the Year

Open, and he capped off the year by helping the United States to defeat Switzerland to win the Davis Cup.

Jim started 1993 by defending his Australian Open title. At the French Open, however, he was stunned by little-known Sergei Bruguera in a dramatic five-set final. In June, 1993, Jim reached his first Wimbledon final, but he lost a tough four-set match to fellow American Pete Sampras. By the end of September, Jim had lost his number-one ranking to Sampras, who had also won the U.S. Open. Jim finished the year ranked third in the world behind Sampras and Germany's Michael Stich. Although he had lost his number-one ranking, he had established himself as a tough, down-to-earth champion who would remain an important force in professional tennis. In May, 2000, Jim decided to retire from competitive tennis. He was hired in 2000 to be a tennis analyst by Turner Network Television (TNT) and CNN/ Sports Illustrated.

Summary

Jim Courier combined a wonderful work ethic with raw athletic talent to rise to the top of the tennis world. Always willing to give his best effort on the court, Jim will be remembered both as one of the best tennis players of the 1990's, and as a champion who had great heart.

Jeffry Jensen

Additional Sources:

Feinstein, John. "Why Tennis Needs Jim Courier." *Tennis* 33 (January, 1998): 14.

Forrest, Christine. "Jim Courier." In *World of Tennis*, edited by John Barrett. Chicago: Triumph Books, 1994.

Martin, James. "Lord Jim." *Tennis* 34 (June, 1999): 138.

Trabert, Tony, and Mark Preston. "Courier's Ripping Runaround Forehand." *Tennis* 32 (March, 1997): 53-55.

Wolverton, Brad. "Courier's Last Stand." *Tennis* 34 (September, 1998): 54-59.

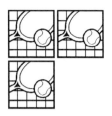

MARGARET COURT

Sport: Tennis

Born: July 16, 1942
Albury, New South Wales, Australia

Early Life

Margaret Smith was born in the small town of Albury, New South Wales, Australia, on July 16, 1942. Albury is located approximately two hundred miles north of the city of Melbourne, Australia. Margaret was the youngest of the four children of Lawrence and Maud Beaufort Smith. Her father worked as a foreman for a plant that produced dairy products. Margaret was good in a number of sports as a child. Tennis is a very popular sport in Australia, and many have played it at one time or another.

The Smiths lived across the street from the Albury and Border Lawn Tennis Association tennis courts. Because Margaret and her friends were not allowed to play on the grass courts of the club, they would have to sneak onto the courts. They would attempt to play out of sight of the club professional, Wal Rutter, who would chase them off the premises. The friends whom Margaret played against were all boys. It was possible for them to remain out of sight of Rutter if they would play on a court that he could only partially view. Because Margaret was a girl, she was placed at the net on one side of the court while the boys would blast balls toward her from the other side. This early introduction to net play helped Margaret become a confident volleyer.

The Road to Excellence

Margaret first played tennis left-handed, but her friends teased her so much that she was forced to learn how to play tennis with the racket in her right hand. At the age of ten, Margaret started attending a tennis clinic on Saturday mornings at the club across the street. She was so good that the instructors used her to show the other students how to hit the ball. Rutter organized competition among the students, and Margaret was good enough to win her age division the next four years. She was starting to believe that tennis was going to play a large part in her future.

Courtesy of the International Tennis Hall of Fame

As a teenager, Margaret won most of the senior divison tennis championships in New South Wales and Victoria. More and more of her attention was focused on improving her tennis strokes and away from her schoolwork. Every chance she got, Margaret would hit with Rutter or any other adult who would take the time to play with this promising teenager.

A major turning point in her development came when she was invited to be coached by one of Australia's great tennis players, Frank Sedgman. Margaret would have to move to the Melbourne area where her sister June lived. That was a big move for her, since she was an extremely shy young woman. Margaret made the move to live with her sister in the Melbourne suburb of Auburn and started an intensive training regime under the watchful eye of Sedgman. The program included the lifting of weights and sprinting. By the time of the Australian Championships in 1960, Margaret had developed powerfully toned arms and legs. At the age of seventeen, she won her first Australian Championship by defeating the talented Brazilian Maria Bueno. It was a tough, three-set victory; with the victory in hand, Margaret became the youngest player to win the tournament.

The Emerging Champion

Sedgman was somewhat surprised at what his pupil had accomplished. He now knew for sure that Margaret could conquer the wider tennis world through hard work and emotional maturity. Following his advice, she would not travel outside Australia for another year, at which time he felt she would finally be ready to

MAJOR CHAMPIONSHIP VICTORIES AND FINALS

1960-66	Australian Championship
1961, 1962-63, 1965	Australian Championship doubles (with Mary Carter Reitano; with Robyn Ebbern; with Lesley Turner)
1961, 1962, 1965, 1963, 1964	U.S. National Championship mixed doubles (with Robert Mark; with Fred Stolle; with Ken Fletcher; with John Newcombe)
1962, 1964	French Championship
1962, 1965, 1968, 1969	U.S. National Championship
1963	U.S. National Championship finalist
1963-64	Australian Championship mixed doubles (with Fletcher)
1963-64	Australian Open mixed doubles (with Fletcher)
1963-65	French Championship mixed doubles (with Fletcher)
1963, 1968	U.S. National Championship doubles (with Ebbern; with Maria Bueno)
1963, 1965-66, 1968, 1975	Wimbledon mixed doubles (with Fletcher; with Marty Riessen)
1963, 1965, 1970	Wimbledon
1964-65, 1966	French Championship doubles (with Turner; with Judy Tegart)
1964, 1969	Wimbledon doubles (with Turner; with Tegart)
1964, 1971	Wimbledon finalist
1965	French Championship finalist
1966, 1971	Wimbledon doubles finalist (with Tegart; with Evonne Goolagong)
1968, 1969, 1973, 1970	U.S. Open doubles (with Bueno; with Virginia Wade; with Tegart-Dalton)
1969-71, 1973	Australian Open
1969-70, 1971, 1973	Australian Open doubles (with Tegart-Dalton; with Goolagong; with Wade)
1969-70, 1972	U.S. Open mixed doubles (with Reissen)
1969-70, 1973	U.S. Open French Open
1969	French Open mixed doubles (with Riessen)
1971	Wimbledon mixed doubles finalist (with Riessen)
1973	French Open doubles (with Wade)

OTHER NOTABLE VICTORIES

1961, 1964	Italian Championship mixed doubles (with Roy Emerson; with John Newcombe)
1962-64	Italian Championship
1963, 1964	Italian Championship doubles (with Ebbern; with Turner)
1964-65, 1968, 1971	On winning Australian Federation Cup team
1968	Italian Open doubles (with Wade) Italian Open mixed doubles (with Riessen)
1970	Canadian Open
1970, 1972, 1975	Canadian Open doubles (with Rosie Casals; with Goolagong; with Julie Anthony)

543

handle the pressure that was sure to present itself outside the isolated Australian environment. Margaret made her first appearance at Wimbledon in 1961, where she reached the quarterfinals. She was not disappointed with the results, but she was more determined than ever to do better the next time. The experience of playing Wimbledon was somewhat unsettling for someone still very shy and not used to the pageantry involved.

In 1962, after capturing her third Australian title and winning both the French and Italian championships, the twenty-year-old Margaret was ready to make a serious run for the Wimbledon crown. She lost to the young American, Billie Jean Moffitt (later Billie Jean King), in their first-round match. The pressure of being seeded number one at Wimbledon had been too much for Margaret. She went on to win her first United States National Championship in September of 1962. Because she had won three of the Grand Slam tournaments (the Australian, French, and U.S. championships), she was ranked first in the world at the end of the year. The only Grand Slam championship that had eluded her was Wimbledon. Margaret would finally win her first Wimbledon singles title the next year by defeating Moffitt by the scores of 6-3, 6-4.

From 1960 to 1966, Margaret won seven consecutive Australian singles titles and four Australian doubles titles. She would win Wimbledon again in 1965, which meant that during the early 1960's Margaret captured two French Championships, two U.S. National Championships, and two Wimbledon titles. By the end of 1966, Margaret had won everything for which a tennis player could hope. The years of playing had taken their toll, but she still shocked the tennis world when she announced that she was retiring from tennis.

Continuing the Story

After retiring from tennis, Margaret went back to Australia and, with Helen Plaisted, she opened a boutique by the name of "Peephole." The shop was located in the Western Australian city of Perth. Margaret met wool broker and yachtsman Barry Court, and they were married on October 28, 1967. Through the encouragement of

---

MILESTONES
Australian Federation Cup team (1962-65, 1968-69, 1971)
Grand Slam mixed doubles (1963,with Ken Fletcher)
Grand Slam (1970)
66 Grand Slam titles

HONORS AND AWARDS
1979   Inducted into International Tennis Hall of Fame
1986   Inducted into Sudafed International Women's Sports Hall of Fame

her husband, she decided to return to active tennis competition in 1968. Traveling with her husband, Margaret was more relaxed, and playing the game of tennis was not as all-consuming as it had been in the past. She regained her top form in 1969 when she won all the Grand Slam singles titles except for Wimbledon. The next year, however, was to be her greatest. Her newfound confidence helped Margaret to become only the second woman in the history of tennis to win all the major championship singles titles in one calendar year. She played one of her greatest matches against Billie Jean King in the Wimbledon final. The match lasted almost three hours before Margaret prevailed by the score of 14-12, 11-9.

In 1972, Margaret gave birth to a son, Daniel, and resumed her tennis career as soon as she could later that year. The next year is remembered for her match with Bobby Riggs in what was billed as the "Battle of the Sexes." The aging tennis great and hustler got the better of Margaret and defeated her on May 13, 1973. Always a reserved individual, she felt ill at ease in such a circuslike event. In more familiar surroundings, she won her ninth Australian title, her fifth French, and her fifth U.S. title. Margaret retired from tennis in 1977 with a total of sixty-six Grand Slam titles, including singles, doubles, and mixed doubles. After retiring, she served as a minister for a nondenominational Christian church in Australia.

Summary

Margaret Court was inducted into the International Tennis Hall of Fame in 1979. During her career, she was ranked number one in the world seven times. There is no doubt that this quiet woman from Australia is one of the all-time greatest champions, and in some experts' minds, Margaret was the best woman player to ever walk onto a tennis court.

Michael Jeffrys

Additional Sources:

Collins, Bud. "Margaret Smith Court." In *Bud Collins' Tennis Encyclopedia,* edited by Bud Collins and Zander Hollander. 3d ed. Detroit: Visible Ink Press, 1997.

Court, Margaret, with George McGann. *Court on Court, a Life in Tennis.* New York: Dodd, Mead, 1975.

"Margaret Court." In *The Lincoln Library of Sports Champions.* 6th ed. Columbus, Ohio: Frontier Press, 1993.

Oldfield, Barbara. *A Winning Faith: The Margaret Court Story.* Tonbridge, England: Sovereign World, 1993.

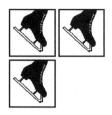

ROBIN COUSINS

Sport: Figure skating

Born: August 17, 1957
Bristol, England

Early Life

Robin John Cousins was born on August 17, 1957, in Bristol, England. The son of Fred and Jo Cousins, Robin had two elder brothers and was brought up in a typically comfortable, middle-class household.

The whole Cousins family was sports-crazy. Robin's father, a motor tax officer by trade, had played soccer for Millwall, and his mother had been a long-distance swimmer. The sporting environment certainly influenced Robin's brothers. Martin, the eldest brother, excelled at rugby and cricket, while middle brother Nick became a physical education teacher.

It was little surprise that the young Robin became involved in sport. What was a surprise was the sport that he chose. It was purely an act of fate that led Robin to ice skating. On a family holiday to the south coast resort of Bournemouth in August, 1965, Robin and his mother ventured into a local ice arena to get shade from the stifling heat, and Robin's skating career was started.

The Road to Excellence

Robin was a natural on skates, and, from the beginning, he was intent upon developing his natural talent for skating. Robin's skating career nearly ended virtually before it had started. On his return to Bristol from his holiday in Bournemouth, and much to his dismay, Robin realized that he would not be able to practice his newfound hobby because Bristol did not have an ice arena. Luckily for Robin, an ice arena opened in Bristol in 1966. He now had the facilities and the desire to develop his skating talent.

Pamela Davis was the senior resident skating tutor at the Bristol rink and immediately took Robin under her wing. Pamela was very strict with Robin because she saw in him great potential. She set extremely high standards so that Robin would realize his promise.

Over the next year, Robin dedicated himself to skating. He developed an individualistic, flowing style, and both his jumping and spinning were accomplished for one so tall. Robin's first big test came in December, 1967, when he took three proficiency tests—in figure skating, free skating, and ice dancing—on the same day. Robin prepared for months beforehand, but on that day he was very nervous. Robin need not have worried, for he passed all three tests with excellent marks.

Between 1967 and 1972, Robin became better known as a promising skating talent in the Bristol area. He won numerous trophies and kept striving to improve. Robin's exploits first created national interest in 1972, when he won the British junior championship and finished in a remarkable third place in his first national senior championship. A fifteen-year-old British prodigy had arrived on the skating scene.

The Emerging Champion

Robin debuted in international competition in the 1973 European Championships, held in Cologne, West Germany. He finished in a creditable fifteenth place. In the same year, Robin also took second place in the British championship. In his home country, Robin was bettered only by John Curry, who was destined to win the World, European, and Olympic titles in 1976.

In the next few years, Robin's career was hampered by injuries, first to his ankle and then to his knees, which required cartilage operations. Despite these setbacks, Robin continued to improve his skating techniques. This process was enhanced by Robin's move to London, where he was coached by Gladys Hogg at Queen's Skating Club. Robin worked even harder while in London, waking at 6:00 A.M. to get as much time as possible before the crowded public skating sessions.

Fellow Briton John Curry captured the skating headlines in 1976. Robin, however, was making steady progress, which resulted in his finishing sixth in the European, ninth in the world, and tenth in the Olympic championships of that year. Robin was widely acclaimed as one of the finest young free skaters in the world, but, unfortunately, his poor figure skating put him at an immediate disadvantage in international competitions.

Following the Olympic year, Robin made a momentous decision that enabled him to dominate the world of skating. Taking his lead from Curry, Robin decided to move to Denver, Colorado. Relocating to the United States enabled Robin to obtain more time on the ice than he could have had at home. Perhaps more important, the move also brought him into contact with the influential skating coaches Carlo and Christa Fassi, who had guided Curry to his numerous triumphs.

MAJOR CHAMPIONSHIPS		
Year	Competition	Place
1975	World Championships	12th
1976	European Championships	6th
	Olympic Games	10th
	World Championships	9th
1977	European Championships	3d
1978	European Championships	3d
	World Championships	3d
1979	European Championships	3d
	World Championships	2d
1980	European Championships	1st
	World Championships	2d
	Olympic Games	Gold

As a result of training in Denver, Robin's skating became stronger. His goal was to dominate skating in 1980 to the same extent that Curry did in 1976. The 1977 season saw Robin win his first international event, the Skate Canada competition. He also gained a bronze medal at the

Hulton Getty/Archive Photos

547

HONORS AND AWARDS	
1980	Member of the British Empire BBC Sports Personality of the Year
1989	Gordon's Gin Good Guy Award (for charity work)
1992	Professional Skater of the Year

European Championships in Helsinki.

In 1978 and 1979, Robin never finished lower than third in any competition. Indeed, in all events, Robin emerged as the top free skater. This not only demonstrated the relative weakness of his figure skating but also underlined that he was without question the most creative skater in the world. As of 1979, however, despite an abundance of artistic grace, Robin had yet to win a major championship.

At the 1980 European Championships held in Gothenburg, Sweden, Robin finally won his first major crown. Despite finishing only third in the figures section, he dominated the free program and took the gold.

The skating caravan then moved to the Olympic Games, which were held at Lake Placid, New York. Here was Robin's opportunity to prove his greatness. The Olympic competition began with Robin finishing in a distant fourth place in the compulsory figures. To have any chance at the gold, Robin would have to produce the free-skating performance of his life. After the short program, he had moved up to second place behind the experienced East German Jan Hoffman. Everything rested on the long program. Skating thirteenth, Robin produced a near-faultless performance and won the gold by the narrowest of margins.

Continuing the Story

Following his Olympic triumph, Robin attempted a hat trick of victories at the World Championship in Dortmund, West Germany. This time, a poor performance in the figures put him out of contention from the start, and despite a spellbinding performance in the free skate, Robin had to be content with the silver medal.

In June, 1980, Robin was made a Member of the British Empire for services to skating. Following the 1980 season, Robin embarked upon a successful and lucrative professional skating career. Because of his tremendous artistry and creativity, Robin dominated professional competitions until 1988, when a third knee operation seriously impaired his jumping ability. He was the first top-level skater to perform a back flip in a layout position in competition. Throughout his professional career he pushed the boundaries of creativity and innovation.

During the 1980's and 1990's he was also active in other aspects of figure skating: He was a television commentator for the BBC and NBC, choreographer, coach, costume designer, and producer of ice shows and television specials. His dancing and singing abilities gained him leading and featured roles in musical theater and as a British pantomime artist. In January, 2000, after giving more than thirty years of routines to audiences, Robin retired from ice performance.

Summary

Robin Cousins was a naturally gifted athlete, but to reach the top, he and his family had to make considerable sacrifices. He eventually emerged from the shadows of John Curry's triumphs and ended with a career of equal greatness. Like Curry, Robin became an English national hero and greatly enhanced the popularity of skating throughout the world. His widespread popularity was a tribute not only to his skating expertise but also to his humble and amiable personality.

David L. Andrews

Additional Sources:

Cousins, Robin. "A Conversation with Robin Cousins." Interview by K. Shively. *Cricket*, December, 1990, 30-36.

Kimball, Martha Lowder. *Robin Cousins*. Baltimore, Md.: Gateway Press, 1998.

Milton, Steve. *Skate Talk: Figure Skating in the Words of the Stars*. Buffalo, N.Y.: Firefly Books, 1998.

BOB COUSY

Sport: Basketball

Born: August 9, 1928
New York, New York

Early Life

Robert Joseph Cousy was born on August 9, 1928, the only child of immigrant parents who had recently settled in the Upper East Side of Manhattan Island. Bob spent his early years in an urban ghetto. Like his parents, he spoke French. He did not master the English language until he began attending elementary school in New York City.

At age twelve, Bob and his parents left the inner city for St. Albans, Queens. Before moving to the suburbs, Bob had demonstrated his athletic abilities in games of handball and stickball, but he had never played basketball. At Andrew Jackson High School in St. Albans, however, basketball was socially popular, and the varsity players were treated as heroes. At this time, Bob became determined to learn the game that was to alter his life.

The Road to Excellence

As a high school freshman, Bob failed to make even the junior varsity team. Although disappointed, he became even more determined to develop his inborn basketball skills. His hard work soon paid off. By the time he graduated from high school, Bob was among the most highly recruited basketball players in the country.

In selecting a college to attend, Bob had two requirements. To fulfill a promise he had made to his grandmother, the school had to be a Catholic college. To satisfy his own sense of adventure, the school had to be away from home. Bob narrowed his choices to Boston College and Holy Cross. At the persuasion of Ken Haggerty,

a high school buddy already playing at Holy Cross, Bob decided to attend Holy Cross.

During Bob's freshman and sophomore years at Holy Cross, the school's team, the Crusaders, twice made it to the National Collegiate Athletic Association Final Four, defeating Oklahoma for

Boston Celtic Bob Cousy in 1953.

549

STATISTICS

Season	GP	FGM	FG%	FTM	FT%	Reb.	Ast.	TP	PPG
1950-51	69	401	.352	276	.756	474	341	1,078	15.6
1951-52	66	512	.369	409	.808	421	441	1,433	21.7
1952-53	71	464	.352	479	.816	449	**547**	1,407	19.8
1953-54	72	486	.385	411	.787	394	**518**	1,383	19.2
1954-55	71	522	.397	460	.807	424	**557**	1,504	21.2
1955-56	72	440	.360	476	.844	492	**642**	1,356	18.8
1956-57	64	478	.378	363	.821	309	**478**	1,319	20.6
1957-58	65	445	.353	277	.850	322	**463**	1,167	18.0
1958-59	65	484	.384	329	.855	359	**557**	1,297	20.0
1959-60	75	568	.383	319	.791	352	**715**	1,455	19.4
1960-61	76	513	.371	352	.779	331	587	1,378	18.1
1961-62	75	462	.391	251	.754	261	584	1,175	15.7
1962-63	76	392	.397	219	.735	193	515	1,003	13.2
1969-70	7	1	.333	3	1.000	5	10	5	0.7
Totals	924	6,168	.375	4,624	.803	4,786	6,955	16,960	18.4

Notes: Boldface indicates statistical leader. GP = games played; FGM = field goals made; FG% = field goal percentage; FTM = free throws made; FT% = free throw percentage; Reb. = rebounds; Ast. = assists; TP = total points; PPG = points per game

the championship in 1947 and losing to the eventual champions, Kentucky, in 1948. Although pleased with his team's successes, Bob was frustrated with his lack of playing time. After becoming a starter in his junior year, however, the self-confident Bob began to impress others with his court wizardry. An Honorable Mention All-American in 1949 and a Consensus All-American in 1950, Bob ended his collegiate career in a sensational fashion. Although lacking in size and leaping ability, Bob proved that a good shooter with quickness, exceptional court vision, and a masterful knowledge of the game could compete with the best of the nation's collegiate stars.

The Emerging Champion

Although a local favorite in the Boston area, Bob was overlooked in the professional draft by his beloved Boston Celtics, a team whose scouting reports labeled him as too small to make it big in the National Basketball Association (NBA). Selected instead by the Tri-Cities Black Hawks, and then promptly traded to the Chicago Stags, Cousy made his way back to Boston when the Stags franchise folded and its players were distributed around the league. When the Boston Celtics drew Cousy's name out of the hat, they had some hopes that Cousy's popularity would bring additional fans to the Boston Garden. At the start of the 1950-1951 season, however, few basketball minds—including Boston's new

coach, Red Auerbach—were optimistic that the 6-foot 1-inch guard could contribute much on the court.

In the NBA, as in high school and college, it did not take the court magician long to prove that he could play with the big boys. As the NBA's Rookie of the Year in 1951, Bob averaged 15.6 points per game (ninth best in the league) and helped to turn the last-place Celtics into division contenders. Throughout the next decade, Bob dazzled both fans and opponents with his ball-handling and backcourt skills. Early in his career, when the Celtics desperately needed a scorer, Bob proved he could score. A long-distance shooter in the days before the three-point shot, Bob placed among the top three in scoring for four consecutive years (1951-1952 through 1954-1955) and became the first player to score 50 points in a playoff game. It was as a playmaker and backcourt artist, however, that Bob achieved his greatest fame. As the NBA's assist leader for eight consecutive seasons (1952-1953 through 1959-1960), Bob, at the time of his retirement, held NBA records for most career assists (6,955) and most career minutes played (30,230).

While amassing these career statistics, Bob performed a number of amazing basketball stunts that stand among the great moments in NBA history. Once in 1954, with Boston trailing by 4 points with half a minute remaining, Bob pulled a Celtic victory out of defeat with 2 steals in the final 30 seconds. On another occasion in 1960, Bob preserved a dramatic one-point Boston victory by killing the final 23 seconds with a fabulous dribbling exhibition around and between five frustrated New York Knicks. In 1963, Bob ended his playing career in razzle-dazzle style by dribbling off the final seconds to preserve a hard-fought victory in the seventh game of the NBA finals. This victory marked the fifth consecutive NBA title for the Celtic franchise led by the man known by sport enthusiasts as "Mr. Basketball."

Continuing the Story

After retiring as a player, Bob did not leave basketball. In 1963, he became coach of the Boston College team. Over the next six years, Bob took the Eagles to five national tournaments while compiling a record of 117 wins against 38 losses. Upon leaving collegiate coaching, he spent five years as coach of the Cincinnati Royals and the Kansas City Kings in the NBA. In 1973, he coached the United States national team, which successfully avenged the controversial defeat by the Soviet Union in the 1972 Olympics. Elected to the NBA Hall of Fame in 1971, Bob was selected to the NBA Silver Anniversary Team, which recognized the ten best players during the NBA's first quarter century. Bob has served as a general goodwill ambassador for the sport.

Bob began broadcasting games for the Celtics in 1974. He wrote an acclaimed book on the game of basketball titled *Basketball: Concepts and Techniques* (1970). He ran unsuccessfully for a seat in the United States Congress, served as the commissioner of the American Soccer League from 1974 to 1979, and was a Big Brother. He has conducted basketball clinics in Europe and in Asia.

In 1980, Bob was selected to the NBA's Thirty-fifth Anniversary team. Possessing exceptional peripheral vision, large hands, and extremely sturdy legs, Bob is still known as the "Houdini of the Hardwood," the ultimate point guard. In 1996, he received the prestigious honor of being named to the NBA's 50 Greatest Players of All Time Team. In 1999, he was named as one of the

twenty best NBA players of all time. Beginning in the early 1980's, Bob provided color commentary on Celtics telecasts and was one of the most respected NBA analysts on television.

Summary

One of the greatest playmakers of all time, Bob Cousy was selected to every All-Star Game throughout his thirteen-year career and made the All-NBA First Team for ten consecutive years. A living legend, Bob demonstrated that there was room for the average-sized player who has the talent and determination to make it.

Terry D. Bilhartz

Additional Sources:

Bjarkman, Peter C. *The Boston Celtics Encyclopedia.* Champaign, Ill.: Sports Publishing, 1999.

Cousy, Bob, Frank G. Power, Jr., and William E. Warren. *Basketball: Concepts and Techniques.* 2d ed. Boston: Allyn & Bacon, 1983.

Ryan, Bob. *The Boston Celtics—The History, Legends, and Images of America's Most Celebrated Team.* New York: Gallery Books, 1989.

Shouler, Kenneth A. *The Experts Pick Basketball's Best Fifty Players in the Last Fifty Years.* Lenexa, Kans.: Addax, 1998.

HONORS, AWARDS, AND RECORDS	
1950	Consensus All-American
1951	NBA Rookie of the Year
1951-63	NBA All-Star Team
1952-63	All-NBA Team
1953	NBA record for the most free throws made in a playoff game (30) (four overtimes)
1954, 1957	NBA All-Star Game most valuable player
1957	NBA most valuable player
1970	Inducted into Naismith Memorial Basketball Hall of Fame NBA 25th Anniversary All Time Team
1980	NBA 35th Anniversary All Time Team
1996	NBA 50 Greatest Players of All Time Team
1999	Named one of the twenty best NBA players of all time ESPN Sports Century top 100 Athletes of the 20th Century Uniform number 14 retired by Boston Celtics

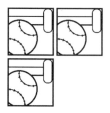

STAN COVELESKI
Stanislaus Kowalewski

Sport: Baseball

Born: July 13, 1889
Shamokin, Pennsylvania
Died: March 20, 1984
South Bend, Indiana

Early Life

Stanislaus Kowalewski, born on July 13, 1889, was the youngest of five boys born to the Kowalewski family in the coal-mining town of Shamokin, near Scranton, Pennsylvania. All the Kowalewski boys played baseball. Brother Harry, who was the first to change his surname to Coveleski, reached the major leagues with the Philadelphia Phillies and was known as the "Giant Killer" by the age of twenty-one. The oldest boy in the family, Jacob, was a pitcher, but he never had a chance to play professional baseball, as he was killed during the Spanish-American War. Another pitcher in the family, Frank, played with the "outlaw" Union League, a league that was never officially recognized by organized baseball. The fifth brother, John, made it only to the minor leagues. Stanley Anthony Coveleski, however, made it all the way.

Stan grew up working in the coal mines. At the age of twelve, he worked for a nickel an hour for up to seventy-two hours a week. He had no time to play ball, so after work he enjoyed throwing stones at tin cans to improve his pitch.

The Road to Excellence

Over time, Stan gained a reputation for his accuracy in knocking down tin cans. His reputation was aided by his brother Harry, who had reached the major leagues. In 1908, Stan was asked to become a member of a team in his hometown. He made a 6-2 record for the Shamokin team in the Atlantic League during his first year of play. The next year, he joined the team in Lancaster, Pennsylvania, in the Tri-State League. He went on to lead that league as well with 23 victories.

STATISTICS

Season	GP	GS	CG	IP	HA	BB	SO	W	L	S	ShO	ERA
1912	5	2	2	21.0	18	4	9	2	1	0	1	3.43
1916	45	27	11	232.0	247	58	76	15	13	3	1	3.41
1917	45	36	24	298.1	202	94	133	19	14	4	9	1.81
1918	38	33	25	311.0	261	76	87	22	13	1	2	1.82
1919	43	34	24	296.0	286	60	118	24	12	4	4	2.52
1920	41	37	26	315.0	284	65	**133**	24	14	2	3	2.49
1921	43	40	29	315.2	341	84	99	23	13	2	2	3.36
1922	35	33	21	276.2	292	64	98	17	14	2	3	3.32
1923	33	31	17	228.0	251	42	54	13	14	2	5	**2.76**
1924	37	33	18	240.1	286	73	58	15	16	0	2	4.04
1925	32	32	15	241.0	230	73	58	20	5	0	3	**2.84**
1926	36	34	11	245.1	272	81	50	14	11	1	3	3.12
1927	5	4	0	14.1	13	8	3	2	1	0	0	3.14
1928	12	8	2	58.0	72	20	5	5	1	0	0	5.74
Totals	450	384	225	3,092.2	3,055	802	981	215	142	21	38	2.88

Notes: Boldface indicates statistical leader. GP = games played; GS = games started; CG = complete games; IP = innings pitched; HA = hits allowed; BB = bases on balls (walks); SO = strikeouts; W = wins; L = losses; S = saves; ShO = shutouts; ERA = earned run average

When he became restless in Lancaster in 1912, he got himself transferred within his league to a team in Atlantic City. That year he played ball so well, posting a 20-13 mark, that the manager of the Philadelphia Athletics, Connie Mack, took note.

Mack watched the young Stan play. He assessed the 178-pound boy as a pitcher who showed good control, throwing the standard slowball, fastball, and curve. He decided to let him play in the major leagues starting in September. Stan did well enough, finishing his first month with a 2-1 record for five games.

It was obvious to both Mack and Stan that Stan had no future as a pitcher with the Philadelphia Athletics because there were four other fine pitchers ahead of him. Mack therefore sent Stan to the Northwest League in Spokane in 1913. In his eighth minor league season, Stan led this league with 214 strikeouts.

The Emerging Champion

The year that made a difference in Stan's playing career was 1915. He learned how to throw a spitball, a pitch that was later outlawed but which served him well throughout his years of playing. As a result of his ability to make the ball break up or down, thus adding two more pitches to his repertoire, he was promoted to the major leagues at last.

Joining the Cleveland Indians in 1916, Stan became known for his control. Rather than try to strike out his opponents, he chose to allow them to hit his first pitch. In one game, however, he pitched nothing but strikes for the first 7 innings. As a result of his talented pitching, the Indians climbed from sixth place to third in 1917.

It was not until 1920 that the Indians enjoyed their banner year. Stan compiled a 24-14 record and led the league in strikeouts, thereby earning the pennant for the Indians by two games against Chicago. Now the Indians had to play the Brooklyn Dodgers in the World Series.

Stan played his best and became the first pitcher since 1905 to win three Series games. He only had to throw 72, 78, and 82 pitches, respectively, in each of those games. He allowed only 2 runs, and each victory was a 5-hitter. The Indians had won the Series at last.

Continuing the Story

By 1920, a major decision changed the nature of organized baseball as Stan and many pitchers of his time had known it: The spitball pitch was outlawed. There was one exception to this decision, however. Sixteen pitchers who depended on that pitch for their livelihood, including Stan, were allowed to continue using the spitball.

In the year following the outlawing of the spitball, Stan went on to record his fourth 20-win season in a row. In 1924, however, his earned run average suddenly increased to 4.04. In addition,

553

he posted a poor 15-16 record that year. This slump caused the Indians' manager to consider Stan finished.

By December of that year, Stan found himself traded to the Washington Senators, where critics thought he would be unlikely to make the team. To their surprise, he led the league with a 20-5 record and a 2.84 earned run average. He and his team made it to the second contest of the 1925 World Series but lost to Pittsburgh.

In the course of his career, Stan recorded some impressive achievements. He led the American League in shutouts (9) in 1917, strikeouts (133) in 1920, and winning percentage (.800) in 1925.

Eventually, Stan drew his release from professional baseball and moved to South Bend, Indiana, with his wife. There he operated a filling station, which, in time, he gave up for fishing and doing occasional repair work in his garage. Stan was elected to the National Baseball Hall of Fame in 1969. He was also inducted into both the Polish American and Cleveland Indians halls of fame. Stan died on March 20, 1984, in South Bend, Indiana.

Summary

Although Stan Coveleski's pitch was deadly, fans called him the "Silent Pole" because he was so quiet. He was not always silent, however, being a fellow who enjoyed a good laugh at times.

During his fourteen-year career, Stan reached the 20-victory mark five times. His trademark was control, for he pitched consistently into the strike zone. At various times, he led the American League in shutouts, strikeouts, and winning percentage.

Nan White

HONORS AND AWARDS	
1966	Inducted into Cleveland Indians Hall of Fame
1969	Inducted into National Baseball Hall of Fame
1976	Inducted into Polish American Hall of Fame

Additional Sources:

Appel, Martin, and Burt Goldblatt. *Baseball's Best: The Hall of Fame Gallery.* New York: McGraw-Hill, 1977.

Hickok, Ralph. *A Who's Who of Sports Champions.* Boston: Houghton Mifflin, 1995.

Porter, David L., ed. *Biographical Dictionary of American Sports: Baseball.* Westport, Conn.: Greenwood Press, 1987.

Shatzkin, Mike, et al., eds. *The Ballplayers: Baseball's Ultimate Biographical Reference.* New York: William Morrow, 1990.

DAVE COWENS

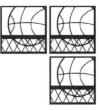

Sport: Basketball

Born: October 25, 1948
Newport, Kentucky

Early Life

David W. Cowens learned the game of basketball early, and by the age of eight he joined his first basketball team. He planned to play for his high school, Newport Catholic High; however, a conflict with his coach during his freshman year caused him to quit. Instead of basketball, the 6-foot 1-inch freshman joined the swimming and track and field teams. By his junior year, Dave was five inches taller, and the basketball team had a new head coach. He decided to play basketball again. During his senior year Dave was averaging 13 points and 20 rebounds per game, and Newport, boasting a 29-3 record, headed for the state tournament.

The Road to Excellence

Many universities actively sought to recruit Dave. Ultimately, he chose Florida State University (FSU). As promised by coach Hugh Durham, Dave was a starter during his sophomore year. The now 6-foot 9-inch, red-haired left-hander—highly energetic, consistent in performance, and a master playmaker—helped develop FSU's fast break offense. With an 11-15 record in Dave's sophomore year, FSU brought the record to 18-8 his junior year and finally 23-3 his senior year. His soft jump shot from the 15- to 20-foot range and his driving layup provided Dave with a 19-point average and shooting percentage of 52 percent, for a total of 1,479 career points. Dave ranked eighth in total points for the Seminoles. However, it was his remarkable 17.2 rebounds per game and aggressive playmaking that made Dave unique. He remained the Seminole leader in total rebounds and per-game rebounds more than forty years later. To honor his accomplishments, Dave's number, 13, was retired by FSU.

On the recommendation of retiring center Bill Russell, the Boston Celtics sought Dave. He was fourth overall in the 1970 National Basketball Association (NBA) draft. Although Dave, at 6 feet 9 inches, lacked Russell's size as a center, he more than compensated by nonstop hustle and

Dave Cowens of the Boston Celtics in 1973.

555

STATISTICS

Season	GP	FGM	FG%	FTM	FT%	Reb.	Ast.	TP	PPG
1970-71	81	550	.422	273	.732	1,216	228	1,373	17.0
1971-72	79	657	.484	175	.720	1,203	245	1,489	18.8
1972-73	82	740	.452	204	.779	1,329	333	1,684	20.5
1973-74	80	645	.437	228	.832	1,257	354	1,518	19.0
1974-75	65	569	.475	191	.783	958	296	1,329	20.4
1975-76	78	611	.468	257	.756	1,246	325	1,479	19.0
1976-77	50	328	.434	162	.818	697	248	818	16.4
1977-78	77	598	.490	239	.842	1,078	351	1,435	18.6
1978-79	68	488	.483	151	.807	652	242	1,127	16.6
1979-80	66	422	.453	95	.779	534	206	940	14.2
1982-83	40	136	.444	52	.825	274	82	324	8.1
Totals	**766**	**5,744**	**.460**	**2,027**	**.783**	**10,444**	**2,910**	**13,516**	**17.6**

Notes: GP = games played; FGM = field goals made; FG% = field goal percentage; FTM = free throws made; FT% = free throw percentage; Reb. = rebounds; Ast. = assists; TP = total points; PPG = points per game.

resourcefulness. His 32 points and 12 rebounds in the preseason Maurice Stokes Benefit Game in August, 1970, earned Dave the title of most valuable player and set the tone for his rapid acceptance by the Celtics.

The Emerging Champion

During his first year with the Celtics, Dave averaged 17.0 points and 15.4 rebounds, setting a Celtic record second only to that of Bill Russell. He shared Rookie of the Year honors with Geoff Petrie of the Portland Trail Blazers. Dave's aggressive ball playing also had its drawbacks. He committed a league-high 350 fouls. During his first year Dave was up and down court, setting picks, making daring passes, diving after loose balls, and continually getting in the faces of the opposing team by blocking shots. His daring aggressiveness and dogged determination quickly won over the hearts of normally tough Boston fans.

During his second season, Dave improved his average to 18.8 points per game, shooting .484 on field goals. He was selected to appear in the first of six All-Star games. In his first game, Dave scored 14 points and grabbed 20 rebounds, playing against giants such as Wilt Chamberlain and Kareem Abdul-Jabbar. At the end of Dave's second season, Boston won the Atlantic Division title with a 56-26 record.

In his third season (1972-1973), Dave averaged a career high 20.5 points per game and averaged 16.2 rebounds. For his performance he was awarded the league's most valuable player award, joining the two Celtic greats Bob Cousy and Bill Russell. That year Dave also received the All-Star game MVP award for his 15 points and 13 rebounds during the game. The Celtics went on to a 68-14 record in 1972-1973, which was unrivaled in the league.

Dave averaged 19.0 points and 15.7 rebounds during his fourth season (1973-1974). Boston finished with an impressive 56-26 record and faced the Milwaukee Bucks for the championship. In the seventh game, Dave scored 28 points and made 14 rebounds to give Boston an easy 102-87 victory over the Bucks.

The Celtics won sixty games during the 1974-1975 season, with Dave averaging 20.4 points and 14.7 rebounds. However, they fell to the Washington Bullets in the Eastern Division championship. The next season (1975-1976) Dave averaged 19.0 points with 16.0 rebounds per game. Boston went on to the finals, winning against the Phoenix Suns in game 5, a 128-126 triple-overtime basketball classic. Fortunes for both Boston and Dave had peaked.

Continuing the Story

Following the championship, Boston traded Paul Silas, a close friend of Dave, to the Denver Nuggets. Following this, Dave announced his plans to retire from basketball. He was only twenty-eight and was leaving at the peak of his career, giving as his only reason that the game was no longer fun. The retirement lasted only thirty games. However, when he returned in the 1976-1977 season, Dave was not in his old form. He averaged 16.6 points and 11.4 rebounds. This would be a bad season for Boston, and the next season was even worse. After a miserable start in the 1978-1979 season, Dave became player coach. He had never coached before, and Boston finished the season with only 29 victories. The Celtics had fallen from great heights. Dave headed for his second retirement; his uniform number, 18, was retired in 1981.

Dave emerged in the 1982-1983 season playing for the Milwaukee Bucks. He averaged 8.1 points and 6.9 rebounds per game. At the end of the season, he entered his third and final retirement as a player. In 1990, Dave was selected for the Basketball Hall of Fame and ranked among the NBA's top fifty players. Reacting to these honors, a humble Dave commented: "I never considered myself a superstar. I feel I represent the working class of the NBA."

In August, 1994, Dave was hired as assistant coach by the San Antonio Spurs. In 1996, he moved to the head coach position for the Charlotte Hornets. He led the Hornets to two consecutive 50-win seasons. However, with a 4-11 record in the 1998-1999 season he quit, dissatisfied with being one of the NBA's lowest paid coaches. One month later he announced he would take over from Garry St. Jean as coach of the Golden State Warriors, a position he took up in January, 2000.

Summary

Dave Cowens played ten seasons for the Boston Celtics and one season for the Milwaukee Bucks, scoring 13,516 points in 766 regular sea-son games and averaging 17.6 points per game. He had 10,444 rebounds and 2,910 assists. His nonstop hustle led Boston to two NBA championships and helped earn for him a place among the NBA's top fifty players. After 1994, his career in basketball continued in a coaching capacity.

Irwin Halfond

Additional Sources:

Bjarkman, Peter C. *The Boston Celtics Encyclopedia.* Champaign, Ill.: Sports Publishing, 1999.

Borstein, Larry. *Dr J/Dave Cowens.* New York: Tempo Books, 1974.

Shaughnessy, Dan. *The Boston Celtics: A History in the Words of Their Players, Coaches, Fans, and Foes, from 1946 to Present.* New York: St. Martin's Press, 1991.

Sullivan, George. *Dave Cowens: A Biography.* Garden City, N.Y.: Doubleday, 1977.

HONORS AND AWARDS

1970	*Sporting News* All-America Second Team
1971	NBA Co-Rookie of the Year
1972-1978	NBA All-Star Game
1973	NBA most valuable player NBA All-Star Game most valuable player
1973, 1975, 1976	All-NBA Second Team
1975, 1980	NBA All-Defensive Second Team
1976	NBA All-Defensive First Team
1990	Inducted into Naismith Memorial Basketball Hall of Fame
1996	NBA 50 Greatest Players of All Time Team

LYNNE COX

Sport: Swimming

Born: January 2, 1957
Boston, Massachusetts

Early Life

Lynne Cox was born on January 2, 1957, in Boston, Massachusetts. She spent her first twelve years in New Hampshire, where she and her brother and sisters began swimming. Although her early years were spent on the East Coast, in 1969, Lynne moved with her entire family to the suburban community of Los Alamitos, just south

Nordisk Pressefoto/Archive Photos

of Los Angeles, California. The move west gave the Coxes an opportunity to enjoy their favorite sport year-round. The sport was swimming, and Lynne's specific event would be long-distance and channel swimming.

Lynne learned to swim when she was five years old. She, along with her brother, Dave, and sisters, Laura and Ruth, enjoyed swimming at an early age. By the time she and her sisters were in high school, they swam competitively on the swim team or water polo team. Lynne's older brother Dave attended Brigham Young University on an athletic scholarship and was also an accomplished channel swimmer. Lynne would later challenge Dave's Catalina Channel swim off the coast of Los Angeles.

Lynne, like her sisters, began swimming competitively in standard pools but found the 50-meter laps boring. She was also being passed by younger kids. Lynne found that ocean swims were more rewarding. She found pleasure in feeling the kelp pass through her fingers or swimming with a school of dolphins. She also found that she excelled at long-distance swimming.

The Road to Excellence

In 1971, when Lynne was fourteen, she, along with four friends, swam across the 20-mile Catalina Channel between Catalina Island and the coast of California. Her goals for the future were to swim the English Channel, to break her brother's Catalina Channel record, and to attempt a number of swims around the world.

Lynne's first English Channel attempt was in July, 1972, when she broke both the men's and women's records by finishing the 19-mile distance in 9 hours 57 minutes. Her record swim was broken three weeks later. The next summer, Lynne entered from the

STATISTICS

Year	Place	Milestones	Time
1971	Catalina Channel: 20 miles	First attempt, 14 years of age	12 hrs 30 mns
1972	English Channel: 19 miles	Broke both men's and women's records	9 hrs 57 mns
1973	English Channel: 19 miles	Broke men's and women's records	9 hrs 36 mns
1974	Catalina Channel: 20 miles	Broke men's and women's records	8 hrs 48 mns
1975	Cook Strait, New Zealand: 11 miles	First woman to swim between New Zealand's North and South Islands	12 hrs
1976	Strait of Magellan, Chile 4.5 miles	First person to swim across the 42 degrees Fahrenheit waters of Strait of Magellan	1 hr
	Oresund Strait: 12 miles	First person to swim strait between Denmark and Sweden	Under 5 hrs 30 mns
	Skagerrak Strait: 15 miles	First person to swim strait between Norway and Sweden	Under 6 hrs 30 mns
1977	Aleutian Channels	First person to swim channels separating three Aleutian islands	
	Cape of Good Hope, South Africa: 10 miles	First person to swim the Cape of Good Hope; crew members had to fend off sharks with spear guns	4 hrs 30 mns
1980	Joga Shima, Japan: 5 miles	A swim around the island of Joga Shima	
1983	Southern Alps, New Zealand	First person to swim across Lakes Ohau, Tekapo and Pukaki on New Zealand's South Island	
1984	Across America	Series of swims including Lake Tahoe, Boston Harbor, the Detroit River, and 9 other cold and difficult waterways	
1985	Around the world	Series of swims around the world in 80 days	
1987	Bering Strait: 2.7 miles	Water temperatures ranged from 38 to 44 degrees F	
1988	Lake Baikal, Soviet Union: 10 miles	First person to swim across the world's deepest lake; temperatures recorded between 48 and 50 degrees F	
1990	Spree River, Germany	First person in 45 years to swim between the two Germanies	
	Beagle Channel	First person to swim the channel between Argentina and Chile	
1994	Gulf of Aqaba: 15 miles	First person to swim the Gulf between Israel, Egypt, and Jordan. Water temperature was 80 degrees Fahrenheit	
1992	Lake Titicaca	Swam across the world's highest navigable lake, located in the Andes mountains	

England coast and arrived on the French coast in 9 hours 36 minutes. She held a three-year record as the fastest female swimmer to cross the English Channel at sixteen years of age.

In early September of 1974, Lynne began her first attempt at breaking her brother's Catalina record. She began late in the evening, at 11:21 P.M., as channel swimmers normally do. On this night, the conditions were particularly difficult because the evening was so dark and a thick fog blanketed the ocean's surface. Visibility in Lynne's immediate surrounding was so obscured that she lost contact with her parents, who traveled in an escort boat alongside their daughter. Dr. Albert and Mrs. Estelle Cox found her two hours later, frightened and disoriented. They halted the swim attempt.

The Emerging Champion

A few weeks later, Lynne returned to the Catalina Channel, entering from the Marineland Pier en route to Santa Catalina Island. With the help and encouragement of family and friends, Lynne finished the swim from the direction opposite her brother's record swim. Lynne managed to beat her brother's record by two minutes, with a time of 8 hours 48 minutes.

Lynne's training regimen required that she swim five to fifteen miles a day. While a senior at Los Alamitos High School, she attended school during the day and swam in the afternoons at Long Beach. Lynne attended the University of California, Santa Barbara (UCSB), where she could complete her academic studies in history and psychology and continue her workouts in

559

the Pacific Ocean. Later in her career, Lynne would attempt swims in 43-degree-Fahrenheit waters and would therefore train and prepare in low-temperature waters.

At the age of eighteen, Lynne became the first woman to swim Cook Strait, one of the more difficult straits, which is located in New Zealand between the South and North Islands. Although Cook Strait was a shorter distance than her local Southern California swims, Lynne had to contend with the natural forces of unpredictable tides and frigid submarine currents. From the North Island's Ohau Point to the South Island's Perano Head, she had to swim a series of S curves and make seven changes of direction. She completed the 20 miles in 12 hours 3 minutes.

Continuing the Story

After the New Zealand swim, Lynne continued to set goals for herself by attempting several cold-water swims. She was the first person to swim the Oresund Strait between Vedbaek, Denmark, and Landskrona, Sweden, and the Skagerrak Strait, a 15-mile swim from Askedapstander, Norway, to Stromstad, Sweden. Lynne's additional Southern Hemisphere swims included the Strait of Magellan in 1976 and the Cape of Good Hope in 1977. Amid her travels and swimming, Lynne graduated from UCSB in 1979. She stayed at the university an additional year to teach and coach swimming.

In the 1980's and 1990's, Lynne continued to plan and train for long-distance swims. She combined her swimming feats with statements of political and social goodwill. In 1987, she crossed the Bering Strait, leaving from Alaska's Little Diomede Island and swimming to the Soviet Union's Big Diomede Island. Lynne considered this swim her riskiest and most difficult. The water temperature was recorded at 43 degrees. Lynne swallowed an internal electronic sensitive thermos capsule so doctors could monitor her body temperature during the swim.

In 1988, Lynne swam the deepest lake in the world, Lake Baikal in the Soviet Union. In early 1990, Lynne continued to promote goodwill between two political rival nations, Argentina and Chile. In June, 1990, she completed a historic 10-mile swim across the Spree River. This river is between what were then the separated nations of East Germany and West Germany.

Lynne has traveled extensively and has contributed to a number of magazines, such as *Triathlon Magazine* and the *Los Angeles Times Magazine*. She shares her experiences by delivering speeches to audiences all over the country. Lynne encourages others to reach their goals and believes a positive attitude can overcome any barrier.

Lynne continued to find new challenges in the early 1990's. She swam the Beagle Channel between Argentina and Chile, crossed the chilly waters of the world's highest navigable lake, Lake Titicaca in the Andes Mountains, in 1992, and swam the warmer waters of the Gulf of Aqaba in the Red Sea in 1994.

Inducted into the International Swimming Hall of Fame in 2000, Lynne became a successful author, motivational speaker, and swimming instructor.

HONORS

2000	Inducted into International Swimming Hall of Fame

Summary

Lynne Cox's training goes beyond the physical by including the knowledge and understanding of ocean conditions, weather and climatic situations, and the human body. Her later swims required an understanding of international and political cultures of various countries around the world. Lynne has developed her talents as a trained and skilled world-class swimmer. Although her choice of event is not the most popular, she is a true athlete dedicated to understanding and appreciating the sport of long-distance and cold-water swimming.

Shirley Ito

Additional Sources:

Besford, Pat. *Encyclopedia of Swimming*. New York: St. Martin's Press, 1976.

Cox, Lynne. "Swimming at the Bottom of the World." *Swim Magazine* 15, no. 6 (1999).

Libman, Gary. *An Interview with Lynne Cox*. Mankato, Minn.: Creative Education, 1977.

Sprawson, Charles. "Swimming with Sharks." *The New Yorker* 75, no. 24 (1999).

BUSTER CRABBE

Sport: Swimming

Born: February 17, 1908
Oakland, California
Died: April 23, 1983
Scottsdale, Arizona

Early Life

Clarence Lindon Crabbe was born on February 17, 1908, in Oakland, California. The Crabbe family had its roots in the Hawaiian Islands, and before Clarence's second birthday, his father moved the family back to Hawaii.

Clarence's father had a variety of jobs, none at which he was particularly successful. As a result, the Crabbe family was usually struggling to make ends meet. Edward Crabbe encouraged his sons to play sports, however, and he taught Clarence to swim before he was five years old. From this time onward, Clarence's life was dominated by swimming.

The Road to Excellence

Living in Hawaii, the young Clarence spent most of his time at the beach. He became a powerful swimmer and an excellent surfer. Clarence attended Punahou High School in Honolulu, which was famed for producing superb swimmers. He continued the tradition of swimming excellence, winning three varsity letters and ultimately being inducted into the school's hall of fame.

Swimming was by no means the only high school sport at which Clarence excelled. In football, basketball, track, and swimming, he demonstrated his athletic versatility. In all, Clarence won an amazing sixteen varsity letters.

The famed Hawaiian swimmer Duke Kahanamoku was Clarence's boyhood idol, and he dreamed of emulating Kahana-

moku's win of three gold medals and one silver medal in Olympic swimming competition. When the Hawaiian swimmers, including Kahanamoku, left the islands for the 1924 United States Olympic trials, Clarence was there to wave them on. He was determined that, in four years' time, he would be on the United States team for the Olympics in Amsterdam.

STATISTICS

Year	Competition	Event	Place	Time
1927	AAU Outdoor Championships	1-mile freestyle (ocean)	1st	22:52.4
1928	Olympic Games	1,500 freestyle	Bronze	—
	AAU Outdoor Championships	800-yard freestyle	1st	10:29.2
		1-mile freestyle	1st	21:35.6
		300-meter individual medley	1st	4:16.0
1929	AAU Outdoor Championships	440-yard freestyle	1st	5:04.0
		800-yard freestyle	1st	10:27.0
		1-mile freestyle	1st	22:09.8
		300-meter individual medley	1st	4:12.2
1930	AAU Outdoor Championships	800-yard freestyle	1st	10:20.4 WR
		1-mile freestyle	1st	21:27.0
		300-meter individual medley	1st	4:06.8
	AAU Indoor Championships	220-yard freestyle	1st	2:16.8
		300-yard freestyle	1st	3:41.0
1931	NCAA Championships	440-yard freestyle	1st	5:02.0
	AAU Outdoor Championships	440-yard freestyle	1st	4:49.8
		880-yard freestyle	1st	10:37.6
		1-mile freestyle	1st	22:14.8
		300-meter individual medley	1st	4:05.8
	AAU Indoor Championships	300-yard individual medley	1st	3:58.5
1932	Olympic Games	400-meter freestyle	Gold	4:48.4 OR
	AAU Indoor Championships	1,500-meter freestyle	1st	19:45.6
		300-yard individual medley	1st	3:36.4

Notes: OR = Olympic Record; WR = World Record

Over the next four years, Clarence trained with the single-minded goal of gaining a place on the United States team. Success came quickly, and by the age of nineteen, he had already become the holder of the American 1-mile title. Clarence's place on the boat to Amsterdam was assured; all he had to do was follow the victorious footsteps of his great Hawaiian hero.

The Emerging Champion

The 1928 Olympics were a great disappointment to Clarence. The grueling boat trip across the Atlantic took its toll on him and the rest of the Olympic team. He arrived in Amsterdam weak and feeble, having lost more than 10 pounds. Practicing conditions were also far from ideal. Taking these problems into account, Clarence's fourth-place finish in the 400-meter free-style and bronze medal in the 1,500-meter free-style were fine achievements. Clarence, however, felt he had let himself and his country down.

Clarence's experiences in Amsterdam strengthened his resolve to do better in the next games. After leaving high school, Clarence returned to the United States mainland and enrolled at the University of Southern California (USC). At USC, Clarence successfully combined his swimming career with that of being a full-time law student. Swimming successes came frequently, as Clarence went on to win four indoor and eleven outdoor national titles and to set sixteen world and thirty-five national records.

The Los Angeles Olympic Games of 1932 came around very quickly for Clarence. In the state of his birth, he had the perfect opportunity to avenge his earlier disappointments. The only obstacle between Clarence and Olympic glory was the seemingly invincible swim team from Japan.

As captain of a humiliated United States team, Clarence had seen the might of Japanese swimming in a Tokyo meet in 1931. The Japanese similarly dominated the Olympic swimming events, winning five gold, three silver, and three bronze medals. It was left to Clarence in the 400-meter freestyle to regain some pride for the home nation.

In the 400-meter finals, Clarence was very conscious of the threat posed by the three young Japanese swimmers. Surprisingly, his biggest challenge came from the French swimmer, Jean Taris. Taris quickly built a substantial lead and, at the 300-meter mark, was still in front. Then, willed on by a 10,000-strong partisan crowd, Clarence made his move and began to cut down Taris's lead. The finish was incredibly close, but Clarence just edged it, winning by one-tenth of a second in a time of 4 minutes 48.4 seconds. The crowd went wild, and at that very instant Clarence became a national hero.

Continuing the Story

Winning a gold medal thrust Clarence into the attention of the American public, particularly because all the other events were won by Japan. His victory changed his whole life. He had intended to return to Hawaii and use his law degree to secure employment. As a result of his Olympic triumph, Clarence came to the attention of the movie moguls from Paramount Pictures, who were seeking an alternative attraction to MGM's athletic film star, Johnny Weissmuller.

Paramount offered Clarence a screen test, and in it he dazzled the camera with his blond good looks and finely tuned physique. Following a second test, Clarence was immediately signed to a $100-a-week contract. Nothing would ever be the same in Clarence's life again.

The first thing Paramount did was to change Clarence's name. A few days after Clarence Crabbe's swimming victory, "Buster" Crabbe started a movie career that was to include more than 190 films and 8 film serials. During the course of his career, Buster played numerous roles including Buck Rogers, Flash Gordon, Captain Gallant, and Tarzan. In most of his films, Buster played the athletic hero who always ended up with the girl, a story replicated in real life, as his wife, Adah, would testify.

After World War II, Buster turned away from movies and became involved in television and his numerous business interests, most of which revolved around swimming or swimming pools. In his later years, he also served on the Olympic Organizing Committee for the Los Angeles Games of 1984. Unfortunately, Buster never lived to see the Olympics return to California, as he died of a heart attack on April 23, 1983, in Scottsdale, Arizona.

Summary

Buster Crabbe's life was dominated by swimming, even into his later years, and even when he assumed the persona of Buster the movie star. Swimming gave him the chance to get an education and provided him with the leverage to enter the acting profession, in which he developed a successful career. Clarence never forgot that swimming got Buster to the top, and he was always grateful for that.

David L. Andrews

Additional Sources:

Dawson, Buck. *Weissmuller to Spitz: An Era to Remember.* Fort Lauderdale, Fla.: International Swimming Hall of Fame, 1988.
Johnson, William O. "A Star Was Born." *Sports Illustrated* 61 (July 18, 1984): 137-146.
Leiner, Katherine. *The Real Flash Gordon.* La Jolla, Calif.: Oak Tree Publications, 1980.

RECORDS AND MILESTONES

Set sixteen world records and thirty-five national records

Starred in the World's Fair Aquacade in New York before World War II

Aquacade star and film star (played Flash Gordon, Buck Rogers, and Tarzan)

Toured the United States and Europe for five years with his Aquaparade

HONOR

| 1965 | Inducted into International Swimming Hall of Fame |

BEN CRENSHAW

Sport: Golf

Born: January 11, 1952
Austin, Texas

Early Life

Ben Daniel Crenshaw was born January 11, 1952, in Austin, Texas. His family was well-off, his father, an attorney prominent in local politics, and his mother, a schoolteacher. Ben's father, Charles Crenshaw, was an ardent amateur golfer, and he often took his young son with him when he played. Ben was already playing golf in elementary school and won his first tournament in the fourth grade. The Crenshaws were a very close family, and Ben carefully followed the instruction of his father.

The Road to Excellence

An athlete cannot achieve excellence without inborn talent, and Ben demonstrated from an early age that he had what it takes. He shot a 74, a score many golfers never reach in their lives, when he was ten years old. In his midteens, he won a number of local and city championships.

A considerable gap exists between a talented youngster and a golfer with championship potential. Ben was able to bridge that gap because of several factors. Among the people he grew up with was Tom Kite, who went on to become one of the world's best golfers. Few things match the stimulus of competition in bringing out a young athlete's best efforts. Several other people whom he played against in high school, including Bill Rogers, also became leading professionals.

Ben had an outstanding teacher, Harvey Penick, the head professional at the Austin Country Club and one of the leading golf teachers in the United States. Many instructors have elaborate theories about the proper swing and detailed prescriptions on the grip, weight shift, pivot, and other facets of the game. Penick did not. He emphasized improvement of the swing the golfer had already developed. When coaching Ben, he basically left things alone, providing useful tips and diagnosing the source of any problems.

Ben was lucky to have topflight competition and instruction so early in his life, but to take advantage of these opportunities, more than luck

Ben Crenshaw at the 1995 Masters.

MAJOR CHAMPIONSHIP VICTORIES

1984, 1995	The Masters

OTHER NOTABLE VICTORIES

1971, 1972, 1973	NCAA Championship
1972, 1988	World Cup Team
1973	San Antonio-Texas Open World Open Western Amateur
1976	Bing Crosby National Pro-Am Irish Open
1977	Colonial National
1979	Phoenix Open
1980	Texas State Open
1981, 1983, 1987, 1999	Ryder Cup Team
1983	Byron Nelson Classic
1986	Buick Open
1988	Doral Ryder Open
1990	Southwestern Bell Colonial
1992	Central Western Open
1993	Nestlé Invitational
1994	Freeport McMoran Classic

was needed. Fortunately, he had the necessary dedication for hours of daily practice. Although he participated in a number of sports besides golf in high school, golf was his first priority. He played one or two rounds every day for ten months a year.

By Ben's senior year in high school, his golfing talent began to attract wide public notice. In his first United States Open, he finished thirty-second, tied for top amateur. In his college years, Ben played successfully on the University of Texas team and won or finished near the top in a number of tournaments.

The Emerging Champion

Ben turned professional in 1973 and immediately surpassed expectations. He won his first tournament, the San Antonio-Texas Open, and three weeks later won the prestigious World Open in North Carolina. His fellow professinals, usually a skeptical lot, joined in the chorus that acclaimed the young man as the next Arnold Palmer or Jack Nicklaus.

Unfortunately, Ben's early promise encountered obstacles. In his next few years on the tour, he went into a slump; his best performance was a tie for third in the 1975 United States Open. His record was by no means a bad one, but he had not yet succeeded in becoming one of the game's superstars.

Ben's reaction to his problems showed he had an essential quality of a true champion. He did not give up, but resolved to correct the defects that held him back. To do so, he sought instruction from Bob Toski, a former winner of the United States Open. Toski's teaching method stresses how the proper swing feels. By making a few changes in Ben's swing, Toski helped him to regain an outstanding swing rhythm. Toski also gave him valuable pointers on the mental side of golf.

Even the best instruction does not suffice to ensure success, and Ben had to drill his muscle memory until it became second nature. He was willing to pay the price of success, and his persistence paid off. By 1976, he was again viewed as an emerging superstar. In that year, he won three tournaments, finished second in the Masters, and placed second among the year's money winners, topped only by Nicklaus.

Continuing the Story

From 1976 to 1982, Ben established a solid if not spectacular reputation as one of the tour's leading players. He won a number of tournaments, including the 1977 Colonial National Invitational, and always finished high on the annual money-winners list. Yet the highest mark of success eluded him: He failed to win a major championship. The golf "majors" consist of four tournaments: the United States Open, British Open, Masters, and Professional Golfers' Association (PGA) Championship. Golfers' positions among the immortals of the game are determined by their record of success in these events.

Ben found it particularly upsetting that he was unable to win the British Open. He was an avid student of golf, and the British Open, the oldest major tournament, is the most traditional of all golf tournaments. The British courses on which it is played are among the most difficult in the world.

After 1982, the situation worsened. Ben went

into another period of decline, and his career seemed over. He called anew on his dedication and determined to overcome his problems. This time, he returned to his original instructor, Harvey Penick.

His comeback left no doubt about his status as one of golf's great players. In 1983, he finished second in the Masters, and in 1984, he won the same tournament, defeating his arch-rival from high school years, Tom Kite. He at last had succeeded in winning a major.

After his triumph at the Masters, Ben's career continued in a pattern of slumps and comebacks. In spite of temporary difficulties, however, he continued throughout the 1980's to be recognized as an outstanding golfer. In 1989, he led the Masters after three rounds but was overtaken by Nick Faldo in the last round.

Between 1992 and 1995, Ben had a victory each year. In one of his most memorable performances, Ben won his second Masters championship in 1995 by 1 stroke over Davis Love III a week after serving as pallbearer for longtime friend and teacher Harvey Penick.

After undergoing foot surgery in 1997 and disappointing performances in 1998 and 1999, Ben was named the team captain for the 1999 Ryder Cup team. In the greatest comeback performance in the history of the Ryder Cup Tournament, the U.S. team scored 8½ points on the final day of competition to overcome a 4-point deficit and claim the victory.

Ben played in eleven PGA tournaments in 2000, including the Masters and PGA Championships, but he only made the cut in the GTE Byron Nelson Classic, where he finished in a tie for seventy-seventh place.

Summary

Few golfers have demonstrated their talent as early as Ben Crenshaw, who was playing top-flight golf in his teens. He did not rely solely on his inborn gifts but practiced incessantly. He announced his arrival as a professional in dramatic fashion, winning several tournaments in his first year. Although slumps have impeded his career, his persistence secured him a place among the outstanding golfers of the 1970's and 1980's and his leadership during the 1999 Ryder Cup Championship provided one of the most exciting tournaments in the history of the event.

Bill Delaney

MILESTONES

Placed second in the Masters (1976, 1983)
Placed second in the British Open (1978-79)
Placed second in the PGA Championship (1979)
Placed third in the U.S. Open (1975)

HONORS AND AWARDS

1974	*Golf Digest* Rookie of the Year
1976	*Golf Digest* Byron Nelson Award for Tournament Victories *Golf Digest* Most Improved Golfer
1989	GWAA Richardson award PGA Ed Dudley Award
1991	Bobby Jones Award

Additional Sources:

Barkow, Al. *The History of the PGA Tour*. New York: Doubleday, 1989.

Callahan, Tom, and Scott Smith. "The Perfect Gentleman." *Golf Digest* 50, no. 9 (September, 1999): 76-77.

Crenshaw, Ben, with Melanie Hauser. *A Feel for the Game*. New York: Doubleday, 2001.

Feinstein, John. "Gently, Ben." *Golf Magazine* 37 (June, 1995): 183-186.

Sampson, Curt. "Ben Crenshaw." *Golf Magazine* 32 (August, 1990): 58-63.

Strange, Curtis. "Twenty Questions with Crenshaw." *Golf Magazine* 41 (October, 1999): 120-124.

JOHAN CRUYFF

Sport: Soccer

Born: April 25, 1947
Amsterdam, Netherlands

Early Life

Johan Cruyff was born on April 25, 1947, in Amsterdam, Holland, The Netherlands. Growing up in Holland, Johan had an interesting choice of winter sports—ice-skating, field hockey, and soccer. In all these sports, Holland has enjoyed a degree of international success. However, fate determined that it would be soccer that would attract Johan.

As Johan's father, a grocer, was deceased, Johan's mother had to find work, and she found employment as a cleaning lady in the Ajax Stadium, Amsterdam. The stadium was the home of a professional soccer team called Ajax.

The Road to Excellence

European soccer is based on a vast grassroots movement, drawing its players from the immediate community and tapping and channelling the talents of very young players. Johan trained and practiced diligently from the age of four. He

Johan Cruyff in 1974.

HONORS AND AWARDS

1966-68, 1970, 1972-73, 1982-84	Dutch League champion
1967-69	Dutch Player of the Year
1971-73	European Cup champion
1971, 1973-74	European Player of the Year (Ballon d'Or)
1974	Spanish League champion World Cup most valuable player
1979	NASL Player of the Year
1986	World Soccer Manager of the Year
1998	Inducted into International Football Hall of Fame

MILESTONES

48 international appearances and 33 goals for Holland

knew that to be accepted as a soccer apprentice would take a degree of good fortune and an enormous amount of hard work.

At the age of ten, Johan was selected to be a member of the elite Ajax Juniors after a grueling selection process that eliminated two hundred other hopeful players. Rinus Michels, a famous Dutch coach, later said of Johan that even "as a baby he was an exceptional player." What was always remarkable about Johan was that, in addition to his skill and deftness, he had physical strength and stamina out of all proportion to his natural build. At fifteen years of age he was only 5 feet 3 inches tall and weighed just 115 pounds.

The Emerging Champion

In 1965, when Johan joined the senior Ajax team as a forward, Ajax had been finishing in the lower half of their league. Johan proved to be more than a dynamo. He scored goals, led by example, and was an inspiring player.

He followed up the consecutive awards of Dutch Player of the Year with two European Player of the Year awards in 1971 and 1973. Johan seemed to have the Midas touch. He starred for Ajax and the Dutch national team, and although Holland lost the World Cup Final to West Germany in 1974, he was voted the tournament's most valuable player.

One year earlier, in 1973, Johan had left Ajax of Amsterdam to join El Club de Futbol de Barcelona in Spain. Sporting superstars are frequently

motivated by complex reasons in their decisions to switch clubs. Among Johan's reasons for leaving Holland was that he wanted to join up with his former coach, Rinus Michels; he also was unhappy with Holland's 80 percent level of income tax for people earning what he did. Barcelona paid Ajax the sum of $2,250,000 for Johan, which was the highest transfer sum in soccer history up to that time.

European professional soccer clubs in the 1970's were willing to invest huge amounts of money in attempts to create championship teams. Johan in his first year with Barcelona was paid a basic sum of $10,000 a month, and once incentives, bonus, and endorsements were added to that, it was not surprising that the Spanish press came to name Johan not the "Flying Dutchman" but the "Golden Dutchman."

Perhaps Johan's greatest asset was his ability to motivate and transform his teammates. Just as he had with Ajax in 1965, he turned a losing team (fourth from the bottom in their league) into an incredible power that won or drew its next twenty-six games. At the end of the season, Barcelona was the Spanish League champion, and Johan was well on his way to being a major Spanish folk hero.

Johan's inspiring leadership continued into 1974, with Barcelona winning the Spanish League title again. In 1976 and 1977, Barcelona was runner-up. Sadly, the pressure of being a public celebrity always hounded by the press took its toll on Johan and his family. In June, 1978, he announced his retirement. He commented bleakly that "even if you go to the toilet, somebody's marking you."

Happily, Johan's retirement was short-lived. He decided to play some exhibition games for the New York Cosmos of the North American Soccer League (NASL), who had done a brilliant job of resurrecting the career of the Brazilian star Pelé. However, it was the chance to play again under Michels that took Johan to the NASL's Los Angeles Aztecs. In July of 1979, Johan signed a two-year contract with the Aztecs worth, in total, over $2 million.

Although he was thirty-two years of age, Johan proved that he still possessed magical skills. Players in the NASL described in awe Johan's ability to beat defender after defender. Just as with Ajax and Barcelona, Johan was such a dangerous threat that opposing teams had to devise two-player formations to defend against the Dutchman.

Continuing the Story

Johan was the NASL's Player of the Year in 1979, but he never really enjoyed playing with the Aztecs, who played some of their games indoors on artificial turf. He negotiated a sizable contract with the NASL's Washington Diplomats and announced that soccer, for it to be "real" soccer, should be played on proper grass. The Diplomats had a natural grass soccer field.

In 1980 and 1981, Johan found himself moving from the Washington Diplomats (the franchise closed down) to the New York Cosmos, and then to the Levante club in Spain.

One goal that is still talked about took place on August 16, 1981. Johan, playing for the Diplomats, with three defenders in tow banged in a goal from 40 yards out against the Toronto Blizzard.

At the end of 1981, Johan returned to Europe and again signed with Ajax of Amsterdam. Many soccer players keep on playing into their late thirties with skills and speed that erode and then evaporate. That was not the case with Johan. Although his blinding pace and acceleration were diminished, his artistry and technical ability remained untarnished. He took Ajax to two championship titles, and then as a swan song joined Feyenoord (another Dutch professional soccer team) and saw them succeed as league champions. In 1985, Johan was appointed as Ajax's technical director, and one year later he was named European Manager of the Year.

Later, Johan replaced Terry Venables as the coach of Barcelona, and in 1989 he led them to the European Cup Winner's Cup. In 1992 he added the World Cup championship to his list of accomplishments, helping Barcelona step out of the shadow of national rival Real Madrid. By 1994, he had won four successive Spanish Championships. In 1996, however, he was replaced after two disappointing seasons. During his tenure with Barcelona, he won eleven trophies in eight years, successfully making the transition from player to coach.

Summary

Johan Cruyff was the world's top player through much of the 1970's, and some experts rank him even with Pelé among soccer's all-time greats. Like the Brazilian superstar, Johan turned his teams into winners wherever he played.

Scott A. G. M. Crawford

Additional Sources:

Adler, Larry. *Heroes of Soccer.* New York: J. Messner, 1980.

Brenner, David. *Love of Soccer.* New York: Crescent Books, 1980.

Henshaw, Richard. *The Encyclopedia of World Soccer.* Washington, D.C.: New Republic Books, 1979.

Hollander, Zander. *The American Encyclopedia of Soccer.* New York: Everett House, 1980.

Janssen, Roel. "Hail Number Fourteen." *Europe* no. 367 (1997).

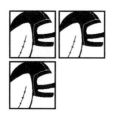

LARRY CSONKA

Sport: Football

Born: December 25, 1946
Stow, Ohio

Early Life

Lawrence Richard Csonka was born on Christmas Day in 1946 in the working-class town of Stow, Ohio. He was raised on a farm near Stow along with his older brother, Joe, by his mother, Mildred, and his father, Joseph.

Larry was known for his hard work around the farm. His crooked nose was first broken by a steer

that spooked while Larry was tending to it. His nose was broken eight more times in football.

When Larry was nine years old, his father took him to watch his brother, Joe, play in a high school game. Joe played end, and when he caught a pass, Larry was instructed by his dad to take a dollar to Joe on the sideline as a reward. The excitement of the sideline and being around the players under the lights caught Larry's attention. He wanted to be a football player.

The Road to Excellence

Larry was quite large for his age, so when it came time for football, the coaches put him on the line. Larry wanted to carry the football, though. He had a fight his way, literally, into the backfield of his high school team. One of his teammates told Larry to go play as a lineman when he came over to the running backs to practice. An argument and a fight followed, and Larry remained mostly on the line until he ran back a kickoff in a varsity game as a sophomore. Larry ran over everyone in his path. From then on, he was the varsity fullback.

After high school, Larry attended Syracuse University. There, too, the coaches wanted Larry to be a lineman on defense. One Syracuse coach later said putting Larry on the line was the worst mistake he ever made. He also said that the smartest move he ever made was to put Larry back on offense.

Larry was not a great student in college. He overcame obstacles with hard work. He married during his sophomore year in college and supported his family by working nights, even dur-

STATISTICS

Season	GP	Rushing					Receiving			
		Car.	Yds.	Avg.	TD	Rec.	Yds.	Avg.	TD
1968	11	138	540	3.9	6	11	118	10.7	1
1969	11	131	566	4.3	2	21	183	8.7	1
1970	14	193	874	4.5	6	11	94	8.5	0
1971	14	195	1,051	**5.4**	7	13	113	8.7	1
1972	14	213	1,117	5.2	6	5	48	9.6	0
1973	14	219	1,003	4.6	5	7	22	3.1	0
1974	12	197	749	3.8	9	7	35	5.0	0
1975	7	99	421	4.3	1	5	54	10.8	1
1976	12	160	569	3.6	4	6	39	6.5	0
1977	14	134	464	3.5	1	2	20	10.0	0
1978	16	91	311	3.4	6	7	73	10.4	0
1979	16	220	837	3.8	12	16	75	4.7	1
NFL-AFL Totals	148	1,891	8,081	4.3	64	106	820	7.7	4
WFL Totals	7	99	421	4.3	1	5	54	10.8	1

Notes: Boldface indicates statistical leader. GP = games played; Car. = carries; Yds. = yards; Avg. = average yards per carry *or* average yards per reception; TD = touchdowns; Rec. = receptions

ing football season. There would be no pampering for Larry Csonka, the Syracuse football star.

Larry broke all the rushing records at Syracuse, including those set by Jim Brown, Ernie Davis, and Floyd Little. He was All-American as a junior and senior, and he was the first player named the outstanding player in both the 1968 College All-Star Game and the Coaches' All-American Game.

The Emerging Champion

Larry was the first running back chosen in the 1968 American Football League (AFL) draft. The Miami Dolphins signed him to be their fullback. After the 1969 season, Don Shula became head coach of the Dolphins and began to build a football dynasty. Larry was the cornerstone. His powerful running forced opponents to play tight defenses, which allowed Larry's talented Dolphin teammates Bob Griese, Paul Warfield, Mercury Morris, and Jim Kiick more room to operate.

Shula worked the team very hard, especially Larry. They developed a mutual respect. Larry would say that the games were fun, but it was the practices that they paid him for.

Larry became known as the finest fullback ever, on one of the best teams ever. He reminded people of Bronko Nagurski with his power, quickness, and aggressiveness. He would often carry would-be tacklers with him as he ran. At times he seemed to look for an opponent to run over as he carried the ball. His battering style resulted in several injuries to his head, elbow, and back. Even when Larry was hobbled, his team could still count on him to help them win. He claimed the pain did not bother him much, because it proved he had contributed in the game.

Continuing the Story

In 1972, the Dolphins went undefeated and won the Super Bowl. The next year they lost only

HONORS, AWARDS, AND RECORDS

1967-68	College All-American
1968	Chicago College All-Star Game Outstanding Player
	Coaches' All-American Game Outstanding Player
	Overall first choice in the AFL Draft
1971-73	*Sporting News* AFC All-Star Team
1971-75	NFL Pro Bowl Team
1973	NFL record for the most touchdowns in a postseason game (3) (record shared)
1974	NFL Super Bowl most valuable player
1980	NFL All-Pro Team of the 1970's
1987	Inducted into Pro Football Hall of Fame
1989	Inducted into College Football Hall of Fame

571

two games and again won the Super Bowl, and "Zonk" was named the game's most valuable player. With all of his success, Larry remained humble. After the 1974 Super Bowl, Larry said "What I do around here is no big deal. We have a great offensive line." He and Jim Kiick became known for a time as "Butch Cassidy and the Sundance Kid." They were close friends and exciting athletes. Even so, when Kiick was replaced by Mercury Morris, Larry remained a team player and helped Morris to succeed just as he had helped Kiick.

In 1974, Larry and two of his teammates were signed away from the Dolphins by a team in the newly formed World Football League (WFL). Larry played one season for the Memphis Southmen of the WFL, but the new league had immediate financial troubles. When the league folded, Larry returned to the NFL and signed with the New York Giants. He played very little with the Giants as a result of a severe knee injury. Larry finished his career by playing one final season with the Dolphins in 1979. He made a great comeback by rushing for 837 yards and 12 touchdowns, and he helped lead Miami to a division title. He finished his career with 8,081 yards rushing in eleven pro seasons. Larry was voted into the Pro Football Hall of Fame in 1987.

Summary

Larry Csonka was arguably the best fullback ever to play football. He was a powerful and bruising ball carrier, a team player, and a champion. After his retirement Larry became involved in professional football's labor disputes, and in that arena, too, his forcefulness helped make him one of the game's most respected figures.

Kevin R. Lasley

Additional Sources:

Aaseng, Nathan. *Football's Breakaway Backs*. Minneapolis: Lerner, 1980.

Csonka, Larry, and Jim Kiick. *Always on the Run*. New York: Random House, 1973.

Gutman, Bill. *Csonka*. New York: Grosset & Dunlap, 1974.

BILLY CUNNINGHAM

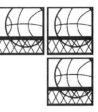

Sport: Basketball

Born: June 3, 1943
Brooklyn, New York

Early Life

William (Billy) John Cunningham was born on June 3, 1943, in Brooklyn, New York. Billy's father was a fire chief. Billy's early basketball experience was gained on the outdoor courts of Manhattan Beach, New York. Billy and a boyhood friend, Lewis Schaffel, spent many hours shooting baskets, and Schaffel helped Billy perfect his slashing style. Billy played in all kinds of weather on the playgrounds, where windy conditions encouraged players to drive to the basket rather than shoot outside jump shots. Billy's strong competitive spirit soon earned him the nickname "Billy the Kid." The highlight of Billy's early career was leading Erasmus Hall High School to an undefeated season and New York City title in 1961.

The Road to Excellence

Billy was recruited by the legendary Coach Frank McGuire to play college basketball at the University of North Carolina (UNC). McGuire, originally from New York, was very successful at luring many outstanding high school stars to UNC. Although recruited by McGuire, Billy played for Coach Dean Smith, after McGuire took a coaching position in the professional ranks.

During Billy's time at UNC, Smith was trying to develop his program and establish a winning basketball tradition. The UNC basketball team did not experience great success those first years of Smith's coaching, but Billy was an instant star. He is remembered by Smith as a dedicated and intelligent player who always gave 100 percent. At UNC, Billy earned the nickname the "Kangaroo Kid" for his tremendous leaping ability. He is thought of as the first of Smith's many great play-

ers. Billy still holds many UNC scoring and rebounding records, which is particularly impressive because he played in an era when freshmen were ineligible.

Billy's collegiate accomplishments include selections as UNC's most valuable player (1963-1965), All-Atlantic Coast Conference (ACC) (1963-1965), and first-team All-American (1964-1965). Billy's hard work in the classroom also was

Billy Cunningham takes a shot during a game with the St. Louis Hawks in 1966.

573

STATISTICS

Season	GP	FGM	FG%	FTM	FT%	Reb.	Ast.	TP	PPG
1965-66	80	431	.426	281	.634	599	207	1,143	14.3
1966-67	81	556	.459	383	.686	589	205	1,495	18.5
1967-68	74	516	.438	368	.723	562	187	1,400	18.9
1968-69	82	739	.426	556	.737	1,050	287	2,034	24.8
1969-70	81	802	.469	510	.729	1,101	352	2,114	26.1
1970-71	81	702	.462	455	.734	946	395	1,859	23.0
1971-72	75	658	.461	428	.712	918	443	1,744	23.3
1972-73	84	771	.487	472	.789	1,012	530	2,028	24.1
1973-74	32	253	.471	149	.797	331	150	656	20.5
1974-75	80	609	.428	345	.777	726	442	1,563	19.5
1975-76	20	103	.410	68	.773	147	107	274	13.7
ABA Totals	116	1,024	.483	621	.791	1,343	680	2,684	23.1
NBA Totals	654	5,116	.446	3,394	.720	6,638	2,625	13,626	20.8

Notes: GP = games played; FGM = field goals made; FG% = field goal percentage; FTM = free throws made; FT% = free throw percentage; Reb. = rebounds; Ast. = assists; TP = total points; PPG = points per game

rewarded, for in 1965 he was selected to the Academic All-American team. He is one of the few athletes to receive All-American and Academic All-American selection in the same season.

The Emerging Champion

Billy's professional career began in 1965, when he was drafted in the first round by the Philadelphia 76ers of the National Basketball Association (NBA). Early in his professional career, he proved his ability by being named to the NBA's 1966 All-Rookie team. Billy spent seven seasons (1966-1972) with the 76ers, establishing himself as one of the NBA's top players. In Philadelphia, Billy was fortunate to play with some of the greatest players in NBA history; his teammates included Wilt Chamberlain, Hal Greer, and Chet Walker. In 1966-1967, the 76ers won the NBA championship. The 1966-1967 team won a league-record sixty-eight games while losing only thirteen and is considered by some experts to be the greatest team in the history of professional basketball.

Billy became a free agent after the 1971-1972 season and signed with the Carolina Cougars of the American Basketball Association (ABA). In his first season, he captured the MVP Award and led Carolina to the best ABA regular season record. The year before Billy arrived, the Cougars were only a fifth-place team. Billy showed all-around ability by leading the Cougars in scoring, rebounding, assists, and steals. Billy was just what a new professional basketball league needed—an established star who could put people in the seats at arenas around the league.

After two ABA seasons, Billy returned to the 76ers. His playing time was limited in 1976 by a kidney ailment, and he sustained a serious knee injury and was forced to retire before the start of the 1976-1977 season. During his professional career, which lasted eleven years. Billy averaged more than 20 points and 10 rebounds per game and played in more than eight hundred games. He was a starter on the NBA All-Star team from 1969 to 1971 and played on the ABA All-Star team in 1973.

Continuing the Story

Following his retirement from the NBA, Billy was named as head coach of the 76ers in 1977. His success continued as a coach. He won two hundred and three hundred games faster than any coach in NBA history. During Billy's tenure, the 76ers compiled a record of 454 wins and 196 losses for a winning percentage of .698. He also guided the 76ers to the NBA championship series in 1980 and 1982 and won the NBA championship in 1983.

Billy's numerous accomplishments have been recognized by many. The 76ers have retired his jersey (number 32), and in 1986, he was elected to the Naismith Memorial Basketball Hall of Fame. In 1989, Billy was one of the ten initial inductees into the New York Sports Hall of Fame.

574

Never one to rest, Billy took on a new challenge when he became a CBS television commentator for the NBA. Because of his insights into the game and his ability to verbally express himself, he received recognition as one of the top television analysts for NBA games.

Following his stint with CBS, Billy took on another new challenge. He began working with the city of Miami to acquire an NBA franchise. As in the past, Billy's hard work paid off, and he became vice president and part owner of the Miami Heat, an NBA expansion team. The Heat made the playoffs in the 1991-1992 season.

Still known as the "Kangaroo Kid" for the leaping ability he displayed as a player, Billy was named to the NBA's 50 Greatest Players of All Time Team in 1996. A well-known basketball personality, Billy is a strong advocate for the values of the game and is a respected goodwill ambassador for the NBA.

Summary

Whether as a player, coach, broadcaster, or team owner, Billy Cunningham has always been known for his desire to excel and his complete dedication to the game. His success comes from a combination of the intensity of a New York City playground kid and the intelligence of a Wall Street business executive. Billy knows the fundamentals of success and uses them in all aspects of his life.

Joe McPherson

Additional Sources:

Bjarkman, Peter C. *The Biographical History of Basketball.* Chicago: Masters Press, 1998.

Dolin, Nick, Chris Dolin, and David Check. *Basketball Stars: The Greatest Players in the History of the Game.* New York: Black Dog and Leventhal, 1997.

Mallozzi, Vincent M. *Basketball: The Legends and the Game.* Willowdale, Ont.: Firefly Books, 1998.

Sachare, Alex. *One Hundred Greatest Basketball Players of All Time.* New York: Simon and Schuster, 1997.

Shouler, Kenneth A. *The Experts Pick Basketball's Best Fifty Players in the Last Fifty Years.* Lenexa, Kans.: Addax, 1998.

HONORS AND AWARDS

1963-65	All-ACC Team
1964-65	College All-American
1965	Academic All-American
1966	NBA All-Rookie Team
1969-71	NBA All-Star Team
1969-72	All-NBA Team
1973	ABA most valuable player ABA All-Star Team
1986	Inducted into Naismith Memorial Basketball Hall of Fame
1989	Inducted into New York City Sports Hall of Fame
1996	NBA 50 Greatest Players of All Time Team Uniform number 32 retired by Philadelphia 76ers

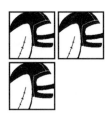

RANDALL CUNNINGHAM

Sport: Football

Born: March 27, 1963
Santa Barbara, California

Early Life

Randall Cunningham was born on March 27, 1963, in Santa Barbara, California, to Samuel Cunningham, a porter on the Southern Pacific Railroad, and Mabel Cunningham, a nurse. He spent his childhood in Santa Barbara, a coastal city about one hundred miles north of Los Angeles.

The Cunninghams were an athletic family. Randall's brother Sam played at the University of Southern California (USC) as a running back and later had a long professional career. At Santa Barbara High, Randall became a star quickly. He played quarterback and defensive back and also punted for the team, which won a league championship in Randall's junior year.

The Road to Excellence

Randall had already developed his wide-open, scrambling style of quarterbacking in high school. Many college recruiters were wary of his flashy style, however, fearing he was too undisciplined to run a college-level offense. USC offered him a scholarship as a defensive back, but Randall wanted to play quarterback, so he chose to attend the University of Nevada at Las Vegas (UNLV), the only school that guaranteed him a chance to compete for the starting job at that position.

The college years were difficult at first for Randall. His mother died

of cancer in November of 1981, and his father passed away a year later after a heart attack.

On the football field, Randall was beginning to adjust to the rigors of the college game. He continued to be a versatile player, handling the quarterbacking duties and the punting for the Rebels during his varsity career. Randall became one of only three players to pass for more than 2,500 yards for three straight seasons in college; the other two were former Heisman Trophy win-

Randall Cunningham of the Dallas Cowboys in an October, 2000, game.

576

STATISTICS

Season	GP	PA	PC	Pct.	Yds.	Avg.	TD	Int.
1985	6	81	34	42.0	548	6.77	1	8
1986	15	209	111	53.1	1,391	6.66	8	7
1987	12	406	223	54.9	2,786	6.86	23	12
1988	16	560	301	53.8	3,808	6.80	24	16
1989	16	532	290	54.5	3,400	6.39	21	15
1990	16	465	271	58.3	3,466	7.45	30	13
1991	1	4	1	25.0	19	4.75	0	0
1992	15	384	233	60.7	2,775	7.23	19	11
1993	4	110	76	69.1	850	7.73	5	5
1994	14	490	265	54.1	3,229	6.59	16	13
1995	7	121	69	57.0	605	5.00	3	5
1997	6	88	44	50.0	501	5.69	6	4
1998	16	**425**	**259**	60.9	**3,704**	8.72	34	**10**
1999	7	200	124	62.0	1,475	7.38	8	9
2000	6	125	74	59.2	849	6.79	6	4
Totals	157	4,200	2,375	56.5	29,406	7.00	204	132

Notes: Boldface indicates statistical leader. GP = games played; PA = passes attempted; PC = passes completed; Pct. = percent completed; Yds. = yards; Avg. = average yards per attempt; TD = touchdowns; Int. = interceptions

ner Doug Flutie of Boston College and Stanford's John Elway, who went on to become a top professional quarterback.

The Emerging Champion

A professional career awaited Randall as well. Following his standout career at UNLV, Randall was selected by the Philadelphia Eagles in the second round of the 1985 National Football League (NFL) draft.

The Eagles were a team in transition. They had been to the Super Bowl in 1980, but many of the players from that team were getting old, and younger players such as Randall were coming in to replace them. Randall played only occasionally in his first two seasons, backing up aging veteran Ron Jaworski. Eagles coach Buddy Ryan would often use Randall as the quarterback on third-and-long plays, on which he could often use his scrambling ability and strong arm to pick up the necessary yardage for a first down.

In 1986, Randall first began to learn about the excitement—and the pain—that goes along with being a starting quarterback in the NFL. He was named the starter at the beginning of the season and played in twelve of the sixteen games. He completed almost 55 percent of his passes, threw for 23 touchdowns, and rushed for 505 yards and 3 more touchdowns. Yet the news was not all good. The Eagles' young offensive line did not

provide much protection, and he was sacked 72 times that season, an NFL record at the time. Still, his 23 touchdown passes were the third-best mark in the conference, and his 505 rushing yards led the team.

Continuing the Story

The 1988 season was Randall's breakthrough year. He played in all sixteen games as the Eagles' starter, tossed 24 touchdown passes, and threw for more than 3,800 yards. He also rushed for more than 600 yards and added another half-dozen touchdowns on the ground. For his efforts, he was selected to the NFC Pro Bowl team,

HONORS AND AWARDS

1984	College All-American
1988	Professional Football Writers Associations NFL Player of the Year
1988, 1990, 1998	Bert Bell Trophy
1988-90	NFL Pro Bowl Team
1989	NFL Pro Bowl most valuable player
1990	United Press International Player of the Year
1992	Comeback Player of the Year
1993	NFC Offensive Player of the Month, September
1998	Pro Bowl Team

and he was voted the most valuable player in the annual postseason contest in Hawaii.

Randall was rapidly becoming known throughout the league as a dangerous runner and passer. Opponents simply could not get to him the way they had in years past. When he had time to pass, Randall was deadly; if the pass rush forced him out of the pocket, Randall could hurt teams with his running. "He may be the best athlete ever to play the (quarterback) position," said Buddy Ryan, the Eagles' head coach at the time. To let everyone know how much he valued his prize quarterback, Ryan jokingly began to refer to Randall as "The Boss" and then designed his whole offensive scheme to take advantage of his star quarterback's abilities.

Randall also was voted to the Pro Bowl after the 1989-1990 and 1990-1991 seasons. He continued to improve; in 1990-1991, he completed 58 percent of his passes, tossed a career-best 30 touchdowns, and rushed for an amazing 942 yards. The 1,000-yard milestone is considered the mark of an excellent running back, and Randall nearly reached that level while playing at quarterback.

Randall lost the 1991-1992 season to a knee injury, but he rebounded in 1992-1993 to throw 19 touchdown passes and run for 5 more touchdowns. The talented Eagles were expected to contend for the Super Bowl title in 1993-1994 and got off to a fast start, but Randall was again injured in the fourth game. He missed the remainder of the season, and the Eagles stumbled to an 8-8 record, leaving fans to hope for better things when he returned.

Randall sat out the 1996 season in retirement but came back in 1997, playing for the Minnesota Vikings. He led the Vikings to new heights, especially in 1998, when he passed for more than 3,000 yards. That same year Randall led the league with a 106.0 quarterback rating. He won the Bert Bell Trophy, making him and Johnny Unitas the only players to receive the trophy three times. On June 2, 2000, Randall was released by the Vikings, but he was signed a few days later by the Dallas Cowboys to a three-year deal that included a $500,000 signing bonus and a $500,000 salary for the 2000 season.

Summary

Randall Cunningham brought to professional football a combination of passing and running ability not often seen in a quarterback. Those abilities have helped him to become one of the most exciting offensive weapons in the NFL.

John McNamara

Additional Sources:

Cunningham, Randall, and Steve Wartenberg. *I'm Still Scrambling*. New York: Doubleday, 1993.

King, Peter. "Pro Football: On the Rocks It's Good That Randall Cunningham Now Has a Marble and Granite Shop, Because Employment as a Starting Quarterback May Be Over." *Sports Illustrated* 84, no. 11 (March 18, 1996): 78-79.

Murphy, Austin. "Pro Football: Second Coming Rejuvenated After a Year in Retirement, Randall Cunningham Is Setting the League on Its Ear and Leading the Vikings to New Heights." *Sports Illustrated* 86, no. 23 (December 7, 1998): 36-41.

TOM CURREN

Sport: Surfing

Born: July 3, 1964
        Santa Barbara, California

Early Life

Tom Curren was born on July 3, 1964, in Santa Barbara, California, on the coast north of Los Angeles. It was no accident that Tom's parents chose to live in a place that was near some of the best surfing spots in the United States. Tom's father, Pat Curren, was an avid surfer, surfboard designer, and skin diver. He loved the ocean and the life that went with riding waves.

Pat Curren had dropped out of high school at age sixteen to pursue surfing. He met Tom's mother, Jeanine Curren, while watching a surfing film in La Jolla, California, and soon after they were married in Hawaii. Pat rode the biggest waves on the north shore of Oahu, 30-foot monsters that made every ride a gamble with serious injury or even death.

As a child in Santa Barbara, Tom would push a skiff out into the surf and watch his father dive for abalone. During a family vacation in Hawaii, Pat Curren bought six-year-old Tom his first surf-

STATISTICS

Year	Competition
1978	Western Surfing Association Championship, Boys 14-and-under
1978-79	U.S. National Junior Championship
1980	World Junior Championship
1982	World Amateur Championship
1982-83, 1990	Marui Pro
1983	Straight Talk Tyre Hang Ten California
1983-84, 1988	Op Pro
1984	Rip Curl Bell's Classic
1984-85	Stubbies Classic
1985	Philishave Tracer BHP Steel International
1985-86	Fosters Surfmasters
1985-86, 1990	ASP World Tour Championship
1986	Gotcha Pro Lacanau Pro
1986-88	Marui Japan Open Stubbies Pro
1989	Rip Curl Pro Landes
1990	O'Neill/Pepsi Cold Water Classic Bundaberg Rum Masters Rip Curl Coca-Cola Classic Quicksilver Lacanau Pro Arena Surfmasters Buondi Pro
1992	Lyland galleries Pro

board. Later, back in California, Tom would surf after school at a place called Hammonds Reef. Tom also loved to play the drums, and when he was not surfing, he often could be heard pounding out a rock rhythm in his room.

The Road to Excellence

As Tom grew up, he and his father would spend hours surfing together. Although Pat Curren was a legend as a big-wave rider, he never pushed Tom to surf competitively. The urge to surf well had to come from within. It was obvious, however, that Tom had more than average talent.

As a young teenager, the developing surfer was faced with problems. Tom got involved with drinking and marijuana use. His mother began taking him to church with her and encouraging him to channel his energy into surfing. When

Tom was to compete in a local contest, Jeanine would drive him there, stay until the contest was over, then drive him home.

Gradually, her attentiveness and understanding of Tom's rebelliousness paid off. In 1978, at the age of fourteen, Tom won the boys fourteen-and-under Western Surfing Association title. He won the 1978 and 1979 United States National Junior Championship, and in 1980, at sixteen, he won the World Junior Championship.

The Emerging Champion

Pat Curren left his family in 1981, an event that cast a shadow on Tom's life. Even before Pat moved away, communication between father and son had been strained. Leaving his problems on the beach, however, Tom continued to perfect his wave-riding skills, and in 1982, he won the World Amateur title. He also entered his first contests on the professional tour.

In his first year surfing as a professional, he won the Marui Pro in Japan and was ranked eighteenth overall. In 1983, Tom married another avid surfer, Marie, a Frenchwoman whom he had met in a surf shop in Santa Barbara.

Tom's quiet single-mindedness as well as his ability to flow with the wave's energy and perform amazing maneuvers led him to further victories against the dominant Australian surfers in the early 1980's. Competitors and friends alike attributed much of his success to the stabilizing effects of his marriage and religious beliefs.

Yet there would be difficulties to overcome. Although he won four major events in 1983 and three in 1984, his overall world ranking was only ninth. The pressures of the tour included long stretches away from home, frequent travel to distant countries, and an increasingly competitive atmosphere as contest prize money grew.

The promise Tom showed in his first seasons as a professional was finally realized in 1985. Surfing against the best in the world, he began the year by winning several major events, among them the Stubbies Classic and the Fosters Surfmasters. He ended the season by winning the Association of Surfing Professionals (ASP) World Tour Championship. No American had done that before. In case there was any doubt about his ability, he returned to win a second ASP World Tour Championship in 1986.

Continuing the Story

Tom Curren was on his way to becoming a surfing legend. After a string of victories and two world titles in the mid-1980's, his following had grown to include youngsters just beginning to surf. Suddenly, parents and their children began showing up for surf contests. Tom's image as a clean-living, focused athlete had changed the attitudes of many people who considered surfing part of a marginal lifestyle.

One of the high points in Tom's surfing career came in 1985, when he traveled to Costa Rica to star in a surfing film. During his two-week stay, he was reunited with his father, Pat, who was living there on a banana and cacao farm. After years of separation and noncommunication, father and son surfed together as they had years before.

In 1989, Tom decided to take a rest from the pressures of touring. He and his wife spent the year at their home in southern France with Lee Ann, their newborn daughter. During his time off, he played music and surfed for the pure fun of it.

When Tom returned to the contest circuit in 1990, he was ranked fifty-fifth and had to qualify for each event by going through trials, or "heats." Although coming from behind, he put on a tremendous display of surfing skill and won seven events. In doing so, he broke several ASP records and regained his ASP World Tour title.

Following a victory at the Wyland Galleries Pro in Hawaii, Tom's interest in professional competition waned again. His sponsor, Rip Curl, launched a promotional video series called The Search, which featured Tom and a crew of other surfers traveling across the globe in search of the perfect wave.

In 1999 Tom returned to the professional circuit and demonstrated that he was ranked among the world's best surfers. He placed third in the 2000 Biarritz Surf Trophée in France.

Summary

Tom Curren won his first major contest at the age of fourteen. Some years later, he captured a world championship. In the years since, he has shown the same quiet grace yet fearless enthusiasm for his sport that he did as a young man. Surfing is more than just recreation, he has said. To Tom, the importance of surfing goes far deeper than that, to a search for the perfect relationship between surfer and wave. It is a search to which he has given new meaning and direction.

Francis Poole

Additional Sources:

Barilotti, S. "Tom Curren: The Surfer's Surfer." *Boy's Life* 82, no. 2 (1992).

Nunn, K. "Surfing Champion." *Rolling Stone*, July 16, 1987.

ASP WORLD TOUR RECORDS

Most events won, 31
Most events won in a season, 7, 1990
Most money won, $398,230
Most money won in a season, $132,800
Best ratings improvement in a season, 54 places
Most man-on-man heat victories, 298
Best man-on-man winning percentage, 80.71 percent
Most Consecutive Victories to open a season, 3
Only trialist to capture the ASP World Tour Championship
First surfer to recapture the ASP World Tour Championship
At 26 years, 5 months of age, the oldest ASP World Tour title holder

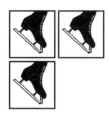

JOHN CURRY

Sport: Figure skating

Born: September 9, 1949
    Birmingham, England
Died: April 15, 1994
    near Stratford-upon-Avon, England

Early Life

John Curry was born on September 9, 1949, in Birmingham, England, and grew up in Manchester. Even as a toddler, he wanted to take dance lessons, but the idea was unacceptable to the working-class family in which he was reared. When he was seven, however, his parents allowed him to take skating lessons because they felt that skating was more masculine than dancing.

John took his skating lessons very seriously. As a youth, he spent most of his time after school training himself for competitions. Whenever he had free time, he secretly studied dance. Eventually, his interests in dance and skating merged into one preoccupation. As a result, he lost points in the first competitions that he entered for "over-artistry." His desire to win was so strong, though, that he began incorporating the traditional costume and required steps into his routine.

The Road to Excellence

By the time John was in his early twenties, he had won so many championships that he began to think seriously about entering the Olympics. Even though John could skate well enough to win the local figure skating competitions, he realized that he had to add a spectacular element to his skating in order to become a world champion. In the early 1970's, he enlisted the help of skating coach Gustav Lussi, who taught John to jump by putting him in a confined space and telling him to "leap." This strenuous exercise forced him to develop his muscle coordination.

John's extensive preparation finally paid off in 1976. He started the year by winning the European Championships. Then, at the 1976 Olympics at

John Curry competes in the European Skating Championships in 1976.

582

MAJOR CHAMPIONSHIPS

Year	Competition	Place
1971	European Championship	7th
	World Championship	14th
1972	European Championship	5th
	Olympic Games	11th
	World Championship	9th
1973	European Championship	4th
	World Championship	4th
1974	European Championship	3d
	World Championship	7th
1975	European Championship	2d
	World Championship	3d
1976	European Championship	1st
	Olympic Games	Gold
	World Championship	1st

Innsbruck, Austria, John dazzled the crowd by skating to a piece entitled "After All" that had been choreographed especially for him by dancer and choreographer Twyla Tharp. His performance, which one judge compared to ballet on ice, won for him the gold medal in men's figure skating. John rounded out the year's achievements by winning the World Championship. His feats on ice prompted former champion Dick Button to call him "one of the greatest skaters of all time."

The Emerging Champion

Like other figure skating champions before him, John turned professional after winning the Olympic gold. He was offered high-paying jobs with various ice shows, but he turned them down to pursue his own vision. Bored with the spectacle that most ice shows offered, John wanted to transform ice skating into a physical representation of music.

To accomplish his dream, John created a new art form that combined skating and dancing. After showcasing his "ice dancing" in a television spectacular, John decided to create an even more elaborate production. He choreographed two numbers himself and then commissioned choreographers such as Jean-Pierre Bonnefous and Peter Martins from the New York City Ballet to stage eight other numbers. He also formed a troupe of energetic young skaters, such as JoJo Starbuck. The result was "John Curry's Ice Dancing," which

performed to rave reviews in London, New York, Los Angeles, and San Francisco in 1978. John's impressive range was most effectively displayed in Claude DeBussy's "Afternoon of a Faun." Although this piece had been the trademark of the ballet star Vaslav Nijinsky, John proved that it could be equally exciting when performed on ice.

In 1979, John decided to take his concept of ice dancing a step further. He started a school to train skaters who wanted to learn to dance on ice. His approach was based on one concept. He believed that every step, movement, and gesture had equal value. Thus, to John, jumping, which is a vital element of the routines of most figure skaters, was no more important than a slow glide. John had to evolve an entirely new series of exercises in order to get his point across to his students.

This school eventually produced an entire company of performers called "The John Curry Skating Company." In 1984, John decided to return to the format that had made "John Curry's Ice Dancing" so successful. On July 25, the John Curry Skating Company brought its new revue to the Metropolitan Opera House in New York, where sold-out performances earned standing ovations. Of the twenty-four works on the program, John had choreographed fifteen. By this time, he had developed into such a fine ice choreographer that many critics felt that his work was better than that of the other choreographers who were featured in the production. Aside from an adventuresome piece called "Glides," John's best work was generally agreed to be the pieces that he wrote for soloists such as David Santee, Dorothy Hamill, and JoJo Starbuck.

The company's 1985-1986 tour was launched at the Kennedy Center Opera House. One of the new works on the program, "Skating Class," was based on the company's daily workout. This was said to be the first group exercise for figure skaters.

Continuing the Story

At the end of the 1985-1986 tour, John's company fell apart. Its collapse can be attributed to the public's changing attitude toward skating. Audiences seemed to value competition over expressiveness. Disillusioned by the failure of his

583

company, John temporarily abandoned skating for an acting career.

For the remainder of the decade, John made occasional performances in various productions. In 1988, he presented two solos on a one-time-only program by the Ice Theatre of New York, which is a nonprofit skating organization. Then, in 1989, he upstaged all the other performers in a television performance entitled "The Ice Stars' Hollywood Revue." Even though he was rapidly approaching middle age, John seemed to be as agile as ever. However, John—an open member of New York City's gay community—contracted AIDS and succumbed to a heart attack when he was only forty-four.

Summary

John Curry will be remembered primarily as one of the greatest figure skaters of all time who won the Olympic gold medal in men's figure skating in 1976. Yet, John was also an innovator who added his own unique touch to both teaching techniques and choreography. Like all men of vision, he had the courage to depart from the mainstream and do things his own way.

Alan Brown

Additional Sources:

Brennan, Christine. *Edge of Glory: The Insider's Story of the Quest for Figure Skating Olympic Gold Medals.* New York: Scribner, 1998.

_____. *Inside Edge: A Revealing Journey into the Secret World of Figure Skating.* New York: Scribner, 1996.

Money, Keith. *John Curry.* New York: Alfred A. Knopf, 1978.

Oglanby, Elva. *Black Ice: The Life and Death of John Curry.* London: Gollancz, 1995.

Smith, Beverley. *Figure Skating: A Celebration.* Toronto: McClelland & Stewart, 1994.

BETTY CUTHBERT

Sport: Track and field (sprints)

Born: April 20, 1938
Merrylands, near Sydney, Australia

Early Life

Australian sport historians Reet Howell and Max Howell have described the period from 1950 to 1970 as the "Golden Age of Australian Sport." During that period, Australian runners, swimmers, and tennis players (men and women) won several Olympic gold medals and Wimbledon tennis crowns. Betty Cuthbert, born on April 20, 1938, in Merrylands, near Sydney, Australia, was raised in a country where sporting activities, especially in the outdoors, were vigorously supported by home, community, and the nation itself. The climate of Sydney, New South Wales, bears some resemblance to that of California. Betty found, in her high school years, that she possessed genuine ability as a sprinter in the 100 and 200 meters. Role modeling plays a key role in determining why certain adolescents pursue certain athletic goals. With Betty Cuthbert, there were the performances of fellow Australian Marjorie Jackson. Jackson, at the 1952 Olympics in Helsinki, Finland, won the 100/200 meter double.

The Road to Excellence

For eighteen-year-old Betty, the excitement of running for Australia was equaled by the fact that the Olympics, for the first time, were to be held on the continent of Australia. The games were held in Melbourne, the capital of the state of Victoria. Just as the United States consists of fifty states, Australia is a federation of six states.

There were four thousand athletes from sixty-three countries, and the opening day attendance in the Melbourne Stadium was 103,000.

Betty set an Olympic record in the first round of the 100 meters with a time of 11.4 seconds. In the semifinals, however, she was beaten by the powerful Christa Stubnick from the country then known as East Germany. The final was a different story. Betty led from the start and won the

Four-time Olympic gold medal winner Betty Cuthbert in 1963.

gold medal in 11.5 seconds. Four days later, Betty won the finals of the 200 meters in 23.4 seconds to equal the Olympic and world records. Once again in second place was East Germany's Christa Stubnick.

On the final day of the Games, Betty found herself suited up for an attempt at triple gold medals. She had won the 100 and 200 meters. The sternest challenge of all was to be the 4×100-meter relay. In the opening heat, the Australians set a world record of 44.9 seconds. In the final, Betty, who by this time had been dubbed "The Golden Girl" by the international press corps, ran the anchor leg. Despite being hard pressed by Heather Armitage of Great Britain, Betty passed her in the home straight and reached the finishing line in a world record of 44.5 seconds.

The Emerging Champion

Betty was far from Australia's only gold medalist at the Melbourne Olympics. Yet her youthful vivacity, her blonde hair, and her rare acceleration made her Australia's darling. Overnight she became a celebrity and a folk heroine. Here was a winsome, talented athlete who had taken on the world's best and proved that she was the greatest female sprinter in the world.

The next eight years, however, were to be a period of frustration, injury, seeming recovery, and setback for Betty.

Four years later at the Rome Olympics, she suffered a hamstring pull and had to withdraw from competition after completing only one race. Melvin Watman, in his *Encyclopedia of Track and Field Athletics*, commented on her post-1956 career: "She was overshadowed by team-mate Marlene Willard at the 1958 Commonwealth Games, injured at the 1960 Olympics and showed indifferent form at the 1962 Commonwealth Games. . . ."

Still, at the conclusion of the 1962 Commonwealth Games, it seemed as if Betty was on the way back. She ran the last leg of the 4×110-yard relay for Australia and won a gold medal. The Commonwealth Games, originally called the British Empire Games, are to the old remnants of the colonial British Empire (Canada, parts of South Africa, Australasia, and India) what the Pan-American Games are to North and South America. In other words, they are a major athletic festival but not on the same global scale as the Olympics. It seemed as if Betty was firmly back as a possible Olympic contender for the 1964 Tokyo Olympics. She still possessed great speed. Indeed, two years earlier, in 1960, she broke a world record that had stood for twenty-six years. She ran 7.2 seconds for the 60 meters. The record of 7.3 seconds had been set as far back as 1933.

Continuing the Story

Known to her teammates as "The Beaut" because of her film star looks, at the 1964 Olympics Betty followed a different path from the one she had followed at Melbourne. Still coached by Australian June Ferguson (who had won a silver medal at the 1948 Olympics), Betty decided to attempt a new Olympic distance for women, the 400 meters. She had won an Australian national title in the 440 yards in 1963. That was unquestionably one of the wisest decisions that she ever made in her career. It is unlikely that she would have been a medalist in either the 100 or 200 meters. In the 400 meters, however, she added strength, stamina, and staying power to her leg speed. In the 1964 400-meter final, although Betty was highly regarded because of her Melbourne gold medals and her 1964 times in the 400 meters, Ann Packer of Great Britain was also seen as the possible champion. Betty won the remarkably close one-lap race in a time of 52.0 seconds. David Wallechinsky, in his *The Complete Book of the Olympics* (1988), observed that, after the race, Betty described it as "the only perfect race I have ever run."

STATISTICS

Year	Competition	Event	Place	Time
1956	Olympic Games	100 meters	Gold	11.5 OR
		200 meters	Gold	23.4 WR, OR
		4×100-meter relay	Gold	44.5 WR, OR
1962	Commonwealth Games	4×100-yard relay	Gold	46.6
1964	Olympic Games	400 meters	Gold	52.0 OR

Notes: OR = Olympic Record; WR = World Record

With this last gold medal, Betty became only the second woman to win four Olympic gold track medals. The other was Fanny Blankers-Koen of the Netherlands at the 1948 London Olympics.

In such a career, it is difficult to suggest what might have been the high point. For Betty, and indeed for Australia, it might have been her sensational gold medal victory in the 100 meters at the Melbourne Cricket Ground. As Allison Danzig reported in *The New York Times* of November 27, 1956, "the spectators hailed Betty with an ovation surpassing any other at the games."

Betty Cuthbert retired in 1964 at the age of twenty-seven. In 1981 she was diagnosed with multiple sclerosis. She remained an ardent advocate for continued research to find a cure for this debilitating muscular disorder.

Summary

Betty Cuthbert continued to be actively involved in track and field in Australia despite severe illnesses. Named one of the Australian "Golden Girls" with teammates Shirley Strickland-de la Hunty, Marjorie Jackson-Nelson, and Marlene Matthews-Willard, Betty's performances have remained etched indelibly in the national

RECORDS
Set a total of 16 world records from 60 meters to 440 yards World record at 60 meters in 1960 (7.2) Best times: 100 meters (11.4), 200 meters (23.2), 400 meters (52.0) Only second woman to win four Olympic gold medals in track

HONORS AND AWARDS	
1964	World Trophy

consciousness of Australia. The land portrayed by the stereotype of the outback and the sun-tanned athlete produced a charming, attractive, and engaging personality who was also a four-time Olympic champion.

Scott A. G. M. Crawford

Additional Sources:

Hanley, Reid M. *Who's Who in Track and Field.* New Rochelle, N.Y.: Arlington House, 1971.

Wallechinsky, David. *The Complete Book of the Olympics.* Boston: Little, Brown and Company, 1991.

Watman, Mel. *Encyclopedia of Track and Field Athletics.* New York: St. Martin's Press, 1981.

TAMAS DARNYI

Sport: Swimming

Born: June 3, 1967
Budapest, Hungary

Early Life

Tamas Darnyi was born in Budapest, Hungary, on June 3, 1967. His father, a worker in a steel plant, got six-year-old Tamas involved in a swimming lesson program advertised in a local newspaper. After showing promise, Tamas joined the Central Sports Club, led by the renowned Hungarian coach Tamas Szechy.

Tamas excelled in backstroke but was a strong swimmer in all strokes and began showing prowess in the individual medley events. In 1983 Tamas suffered a setback: A friendly snowball fight turned tragic as an errant snowball accidentally hit him in the left eye, detaching his retina. After four operations, Tamas retained 50 percent of his vision in the left eye. Doctors advised him against swimming again, but against this advice he returned to the sport in 1984.

The Road to Excellence

Coach Szechy's training method was characteristically regimented in terms of training distance and tapering methods; in addition, Hun-

Tamas Darnyi in 1991 during the World Championships in Perth, Australia.

garian swimmers did not compete in all big meets, leading the competition to wonder what the small yet powerful Hungarian team had in store at its next showing. Tamas returned to competition in 1985, making an unexpected showing at the European Championships by winning both the 200- and 400-meter individual medleys. This was the beginning of complete domination of these two events for many years to come.

In 1986 Tamas competed in the World Championships, taking the 200- and 400-meter individual medley gold medals from Canadian swimmer Alex Baumann and setting a new European record in the 200. In 1987 he again took both events at the European Championships, this time breaking the world record in both distances. In this year he was also named Hungary's Athlete of the Year.

The Emerging Champion

Tamas's first Olympic victory was at the 1988 Seoul Games. Now established as the leader in both medley events, exhibiting little or no weakness in any stroke, Tamas was poised to grab both golds in the individual medleys. The first gold came on September 21, 1988: Tamas went out fast in the butterfly and backstroke, and by the halfway mark he was more than 2 seconds ahead of American contender David Wharton. He finished strongly and ahead of the pack, setting a new world record of 4:14.75.

Days later, on September 25, Tamas swam to victory in the 200-meter individual medley, setting another world record of 2:00.17. The world began noticing his interesting racing method; while many swimmers race against the clock, Tamas claimed to race instead against the competition.

The following year, twenty-two-year-old Tamas won three gold medals at the European Championships in Bonn, Germany. In addition to the individual medleys, he also won the 200-meter butterfly. In January, 1991, at the World Championships in Perth, Australia, Tamas set a startling new world record in the 400-meter individual medley of 4:12.36, more than 2 seconds faster than his previous world record. Several days later he placed third in the 200-meter butterfly, not his top event but nevertheless one in which he was a strong contender.

STATISTICS

Year	Competition	Event	Place
1985	European Championships	200-meter medley	1st
		400-meter medley	1st
1986	World Championships	200-meter medley	1st
		400-meter medley	1st
1987	European Championships	200-meter medley	1st WR
		400-meter medley	1st WR
1988	Olympic Games	200-meter medley	Gold
		400-meter medley	Gold
1989	European Championships	200-meter medley	1st
		400-meter medley	1st
		200-meter butterfly	1st
1991	World Championships	200-meter medley	1st WR
		400-meter medley	1st WR
		200-meter butterfly	3d
1992	Hungarian National Championships	200-meter medley	2d
		400-meter medley	2d
	Olympic Games	200-meter medley	Gold
		400-meter medley	Gold
1993	European Championships	400-meter medley	1st

Note: WR = World Record

The following day he swam the 200-meter individual medley, winning the gold and setting a new world record of 1:59.36. This marked several firsts in swimming: Tamas was the first swimmer to break the two-minute barrier in the 200 and was the first swimmer to keep winning consecutive titles at the Worlds.

At the conclusion of the competition, Tamas was voted Best Swimmer of the Games. The presentation of the award was odd: Officials were handed the name of the wrong person, and they announced this individual as the winner, but the real winner was Tamas. After the trophy was retrieved from the false winner as she was awaiting her plane at the airport, Tamas was given the award. After these games, a German sports paper accused Tamas and another Hungarian swimmer of using performance-enhancing drugs, an allegation that was refuted by coach Szechy. Tamas never tested positive for any drug use during his career.

Tamas declined participation in the next European Championships and set his sights on the 1992 Olympic Games in Barcelona. He did, however, compete in the Hungarian National Championships in June, 1992, at which he was defeated in the medleys by a younger teammate, Attila Czene. This did not stop him from a strong showing at the Olympics. Although his times were slower than in previous Olympic Games, in both races he was forced to swim extremely fast freestyle legs to edge out his competition. Tamas won gold medals in both medleys.

Continuing the Story

Despite rumors that Tamas would retire after the Barcelona Games, he continued swimming for another year. In 1993 he competed in the European Championships in Sheffield, England, racing to victory in the 400-meter individual medley He narrowly beat Finnish swimmer Jani Sievinen and withdrew from the 200-meter medley, which Sievinen won. In late July, 1994, just two months before the World Championships, Tamas announced on Hungarian national television that he was retiring from swimming. He expressed a desire to finish his career as a winner. The European Championships were his last major international competition.

In March, 1992, he was awarded the Amateur Athletic Foundation's World Trophy, which is given to international athletes from six different regions. He was European Swimmer of the Year three times (1987, 1988, 1991), Hungarian Sportsman of the Year four times, and World Swimmer of the Year in 1991. In his personal life, Tamas also finished a degree at the College of Catering and the College of Physical Education in Budapest, Hungary.

Summary

Tamas Darnyi is one of the world's most decorated and accomplished individual medley swimmers. Overcoming a vision challenge, he won both the 200- and 400-meter medley events at major international competitions for nearly a decade. He set six world records in the medleys and one in the 200-meter backstroke. He won gold medals in the medleys at the 1988 and 1992 Olympics and was the first swimmer to break the two-minute mark in the 200-meter individual medley.

Michelle C. K. McKowen

Additional Sources:

"A Clash of Wills." *Sports Illustrated,* September 14, 1988, 138.

"He's Boffo in Budapest." *Time* 132 (September 19, 1988): 61.

Lidz, Franz. "A Hungarian Who's Still Hungry." *Sports Illustrated* 73 (July 30, 1990): 6-7.

LINDSAY DAVENPORT

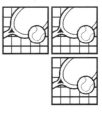

Sport: Tennis

Born: June 8, 1976
Palos Verdes, California

Early Life

Lindsay Davenport was born on June 8, 1976, the third child of Ann and Wink Davenport. Her parents were both volleyball players; her father, Wink, was a member of the United States volleyball team in the 1968 Olympics. Both of Lindsay's older sisters, Shannon and Leiann, played volleyball in college. As a child, however, Lindsay was drawn to tennis. At age seven she began playing on the hard courts of Southern California near her home. With her natural athletic ability, she developed the classic hard, flat ground strokes that became the foundation of her game.

The Road to Excellence

As Lindsay started competing in junior tennis matches, her abilities became recognized. In 1991, when she was fifteen, she was named female junior player of the year by *Tennis* magazine. In 1992 she fulfilled her promise in international junior competition, winning the U.S. Open junior singles and doubles titles as well as the Australian Open junior doubles. She was a finalist in junior singles at the Australian Open and in junior doubles at the French Open. Lindsay participated in the player development program sponsored by the United States Tennis Association.

By 1993, Lindsay had reached a level that made turning professional a logical step, which she took on February 22, 1993. Her first two seasons were learning experiences. She divided her time between tennis and school until she graduated from Murrieta Valley High School in 1994. At the same time, she was becoming accustomed

Lindsay Davenport reacts to a good match during the 2000 U.S. Open.

to life on professional tennis tours. She won her first professional tournament, the European Open, in Strasbourg in 1993, moving her ranking into the top thirty players. She was named 1993 Rookie of the Year by *Tennis* magazine. By 1994, she was ranked among the top ten female professional tennis players.

The Emerging Champion

Although Lindsay was successful as a professional tennis player, she still had much unrealized potential. She was tall, almost 6 feet 3 inches. She had penetrating hard ground strokes and a good net game. At the same time, she was not quick around the court, and her serve did not utilize the natural asset of her height.

During 1996, several things happened that helped Lindsay raise the level of her game to championship status. First, she started working with a new coach, Robert Van't Hof. He helped her improve her conditioning and strengthen her serve. Second, she won her first Grand Slam title, the French Open doubles, paired with Mary Joe Fernandez. Her confidence received a great boost when she participated in the 1996 Olympic Games in Atlanta, Georgia. The coach for the U.S. women's tennis team was the legendary tennis star Billie Jean King. She bolstered Lindsay's belief in her ability as a tennis player. Lindsay won the gold medal in women's singles at the 1996 Olympics. En route to her victory, she defeated a number of highly ranked players, including Arantxa Sanchez-Vicario in the finals.

During 1997 she continued to play, winning several tournaments. At the U.S. Open she took the title with Jana Novotna. In 1998, her game began to peak. She was a semifinalist at the Australian Open and the French Open, and a quarterfinalist at Wimbledon, but she was still shy of a Grand Slam victory. Later in the summer she began playing the best tennis of her life, feeling like she was "in the zone." She won three hard-court tournaments in California and defeated Martina Hingis, the number one ranked player in one of them. Her confidence was brimming as she came into the U.S. Open. At this Grand Slam tournament, she finally achieved her breakthrough by defeating Hingis in the finals. About six weeks later, in October, 1998, she became the top-ranked singles player in women's tennis.

Continuing the Story

Lindsay had hoped to carry her high level of play into the next season. She reached the final of the year-ending Chase Championships but lost to Hingis. In January of 1999 she reached the semifinals at the Australian Open but lost in a tight three-set match. A wrist injury hampered her for several months, but she put in a good performance to reach the quarterfinals at the French Open.

At the 1999 Wimbledon tournament, Lindsay surprised everyone by capturing her second Grand Slam on grass courts, not her favorite surface. She won convincingly, not losing a set and defeating Jana Novotna, the defending champion, in the quarterfinals, and Steffi Graf, a seven-time Wimbledon winner, in the final. She and her partner, Corina Morariu, also captured the doubles title.

She was not able to defend her 1998 U.S. Open victory, losing in a close match in the semifinals to the eventual champion, Serena Williams. She ended the year by winning the Chase Championships, dominating Martina Hingis in three (out of five) sets. In addition, she began the

MAJOR CHAMPIONSHIPS	
1996	Olympics, Singles
1997	U.S. Open, Doubles Chase Championships, Doubles
1998	U.S. Open, Singles Chase Championships, Doubles
1999	Wimbledon, Singles Wimbledon, Doubles Chase Championships, Singles
2000	Australian Open, Singles Indian Wells, Singles Indian Wells, Doubles Federation Cup

HONORS AND AWARDS	
1991	*Tennis* magazine Female Junior Player of the Year
1993	*Tennis* magazine Rookie of the Year
1993-2000	United States Federation Cup Team
1996	Gold Medal, Olympic Women's Singles Tennis
1998	WTA Tour Player of the Year Diamond Aces Award *Tennis* magazine Player of the Year

2000 season by winning her third Grand Slam event, the Australian Open. By late spring, she had regained the number-one ranking.

Summary

Lindsay Davenport was a commanding presence in women's tennis during the 1990's. She was not a teenage phenomenon; rather, her game matured at a steady pace. She has not sought attention and publicity but has let her athletic talent and achievement speak for itself. Her results in 2000, particularly her third Grand

Slam title, demonstrate that she has earned a place among the great players of women's tennis.

Karen Gould

Additional Sources:

Greer, Jim. "The Nice Girl Who Finished First." *Tennis,* September, 1999, 52-56.

Price, S. L. "Standing Tall." *Sports Illustrated* 89, no. 12 (September 21, 1998): 60-63.

Wertheim, L. Jon. "Lissome Lindsay." *Sports Illustrated* 89, no. 8 (August 24, 1998): 51-53.

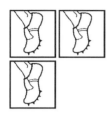

WILLIE DAVENPORT

Sport: Track and field (hurdles)

Born: June 8, 1943
       Troy, Alabama

Early Life

Willie Davenport was born in Troy, Alabama, on June 8, 1943. Like many young black Americans growing up in the 1950's, Willie had a number of athletic role models to look up to. In track there was the legendary Jesse Owens, winner of an amazing four gold medals at the 1936 Olympics. In baseball there was Jackie Robinson, who, in 1947, was signed by the Brooklyn Dodgers and became the first black man in the major leagues.

Willie came from a modest background but early on demonstrated great speed in high school track competitions. He had relatively little high hurdling experience until he accepted a track scholarship at Southern University in Baton Rouge, Louisiana.

The Road to Excellence

As a twenty-one-year-old, Willie was selected to run the high hurdles for the United States at the 1964 Olympics. Arriving at the Olympic Village in Tokyo, Japan, Willie found himself with a serious leg injury. Nevertheless, he pressed on and

Courtesy of Amateur Athletic Foundation of Los Angeles

594

ran in 14.4 seconds in that first heat to make it through the semifinals. In the semifinals, however, his injury clearly restricted the necessary flexibility needed to step over ten barriers, each 3 feet 6 inches in height. He came in seventh and was eliminated.

As with many highly successful athletes, early failure and setback turned into a driving determination to persevere and do well. Willie won the American Athletic Union (AAU) outdoor 110-meter hurdles title in 1965, clocking 13.6, fractionally outside the then world record. Realizing that year-round training and a commitment to high-level competition were critical for success, Willie took part in a full indoor season. He won the AAU indoor 60-yard hurdles championship in both 1966 and 1967.

In 1968, benefiting from the intensive training and coaching of Southern University, Willie romped through the Olympic trials and was seen as a major contender for the Olympic crown. Still, the leg injury that had plagued his run for the gold at the 1964 Olympics had continued to interrupt his career from 1964 to 1968. In the 1968 Olympic finals, held at high altitude (seven thousand feet above sea level) at Mexico City, Willie lined up for the 110-meter hurdles with seven other competitors, including two other Americans.

The Emerging Champion

The United States has dominated the high hurdles in Olympic history. From 1896 to 1980, America brought home sixteen gold medals out of a possible twenty, and thirteen silver and thirteen bronze medals.

Willie was by no means the confirmed favorite to win. In the semifinals, teammate Ervin Hall had run an outstanding race, setting a new Olympic record. Perhaps no other track race requires such precision and the ability to retain form in the face of pressure. In the intermediate 400-meter hurdles, a poor hurdles clearance or an un-

STATISTICS

Year	Competition	Event	Place	Time
1965	National AAU Outdoor Championships	110-meter high hurdles	Gold	13.6
1966	National AAU Outdoor Championships	110-meter high hurdles	Gold	13.3
	National AAU Indoor Championships	60-yard high hurdles	Gold	6.9
	NAIA Indoor Championships	60-yard hurdles	1st	7.1
1967	National AAU Outdoor Championships	110-meter high hurdles	Gold	13.3
	National AAU Indoor Championships	60-yard high hurdles	Gold	7.0
	NAIA Indoor Championships	60-yard hurdles	1st	7.0
1968	Olympic Games	110-meter high hurdles	Gold	13.3 OR
1969	National AAU Outdoor Championships	110-meter high hurdles	Gold	13.3
	National AAU Indoor Championships	60-yard high hurdles	Gold	7.0
1970	National AAU Indoor Championships	60-yard high hurdles	Gold	7.1
1971	National AAU Indoor Championships	60-yard high hurdles	Gold	7.0
1972	Olympic Games	110-meter high hurdles	4th	13.5
	National AAU Championships	110-meter high hurdles	2d	13.6
1976	Olympic Games	110-meter high hurdles	Bronze	13.38

Note: OR = Olympic Record

even landing can be overcome because of the distance and the reliance upon power and endurance. In the "highs," everything comes down to rhythm and setting a tempo that maximizes contact with the ground and minimizes time spent in the air. The hurdle is shaved by the athlete, and the winner is the fastest sprinter able to skim over all ten hurdles.

In the finals, Willie ran the perfect race and won by a meter in an Olympic record of 13.3 seconds in front of eighty thousand spectators. Neil Admur, writing in an October 18, 1968, issue of *The New York Times*, observed that, for Willie, the triumph "wiped out four years of frustration." The victory was not as easy as it appeared. David Wallechinsky, in his *The Complete Book of the Olympics* (1988), recounts an anecdote about Willie. He was so wound up by the race preliminaries that he almost tripped when taking off his tracksuit and had no recollection of moving into the "set" position. The joy of Mexico City did not repeat itself four years later at the Munich Games, where Willie was only able to manage a fourth place in 13.5 seconds.

Continuing the Story

Although track dominated Willie's early life, it was his interest in exercise and physical fitness

HONORS AND AWARDS

1982	Inducted into National Track and Field Hall of Fame
1991	Inducted into U.S. Olympic Hall of Fame

that came to the fore toward the end of his career as an active runner. He successfully completed academic studies at Southern University in 1970 and 1974, earning a bachelor's and then a master's degree. At his alma mater, Southern University, he was head track coach from 1971 to 1974. Another responsibility was serving as executive director of a community council for youth opportunity from 1970 to 1980. He then became Director of the Governor's Council on Physical Fitness and Sports for the Louisiana Department of Health and Human Resources. In short, an early search for athletic excellence led to a career in providing sporting challenges and opportunities for young Americans in the Bayou State.

Summary

For Willie Davenport, the sadness of injury and defeat in 1964 turned into the euphoria of victory at the Mexico Olympics in 1968. Although his subsequent appearance at the Olympics did not translate into a medal, the fact that he ran in a third consecutive Olympics elevated him to an elite group of "repeating" Olympians. His track career has reflected his passionate desire to get young people actively involved in athletics.

Few Olympians come out of retirement and succeed. At the 1980 Winter Olympics, Willie achieved a memorable first. He was selected for his country's bobsled team because of his rare acceleration ability and competitive edge. The United States came in twelfth place, and since that time, other black American runners such as Willie Gault and Herschel Walker have tried their hand at the bobsled event.

Scott A. G. M. Crawford

Additional Sources:

Bateman, Hal. *United States Track and Field Olympians, 1896-1980.* Indianapolis, Ind.: The Athletics Congress of the United States, 1984.

Hickok, Ralph. *A Who's Who of Sports Champions.* Boston: Houghton Mifflin, 1995.

The Lincoln Library of Sports Champions. 16 vols. Columbus, Ohio: Frontier Press, 1993.

Wallechinsky, David. *The Complete Book of the Olympics.* Boston: Little, Brown and Company, 1991.

Watman, Mel. *Encyclopedia of Track and Field Athletics.* New York: St. Martin's Press, 1981.

BOB DAVIES

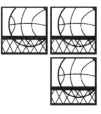

Sport: Basketball

Born: January 15, 1920
Harrisburg, Pennsylvania

Early Life

Robert Edris Davies was born on January 15, 1920, in Harrisburg, Pennsylvania, the state capital. Robert grew up in a middle-class neighborhood, the younger of two brothers. His father, Edris, was a sales executive, and his mother, Esther, a homemaker.

Young Bob learned about sports from his father and brother at an early age. With a loving family and comfortable lifestyle, he found plenty of time to devote to a variety of sporting activities.

Bob first learned baseball while playing catch in the family's backyard at age five. He soon discovered football and basketball and enjoyed many hours of play on neighborhood sandlots and playground courts.

The Road to Excellence

Bob's first organized sport was baseball, which he began playing at age nine on a Harrisburg recreation league team.

By the time Bob entered John Harris High School in Harrisburg, he was developing into a fine all-around athlete. In addition to being an excellent fielder and hitter in baseball, running back in football, and guard in basketball, Bob added track and field to his sporting interests. Upon graduation in 1937, he was the second four-sport letterman in the school's history.

Bob's enthusiasm for basketball soon began to overshadow his interest in other sports. He read magazine articles about Hank Luisetti and copied the Stanford star's behind-the-back dribble and one-handed shooting style.

Bob's basketball prowess during high school did not attract college recruiters. His baseball ability, however, attracted professional baseball scouts. After his high school graduation, Bob at-tended Seton Hall University on a baseball scholarship arranged by the Boston Red Sox.

In his first year of college, Bob played baseball and basketball, but he chose to concentrate on basketball the remainder of his collegiate career. His decision voided the scholarship arrangement with the Red Sox, but basketball coach John "Honey" Russell recognized Bob's basketball ability and granted him a scholarship.

Coach Russell moved Bob to a starting guard position in his sophomore year. Although barely 6 feet tall, blond-haired and baby-faced, Bob was an intimidating figure. With his defense, shooting, passing, and free-lance play, the Seton Hall

597

Pirates won their last twenty games of the 1939-1940 season.

As team captain in 1940-1941, Bob led the Pirates to a 23-0 season and a National Invitational Tournament (NIT) bid. The Pirates won their first-round NIT game over Rhode Island State 70-54. In their second game against Long Island University, however, Bob was held scoreless in the first half and scored only 4 points in the second half before fouling out with 7 minutes left in the game. Without Bob's leadership, Seton Hall lost 49-26, ending the team's forty-three-game win streak.

Twice during his college career, in 1940-1941 and 1941-1942, Bob earned All-American honors. He was named most valuable player of the 1942 College All-Star Game following his senior season.

The Emerging Champion

Bob's outstanding collegiate basketball career did not go unnoticed by professional basketball scouts, and the Boston Red Sox baseball scouts still showed interest. Following graduation in 1942, however, Bob felt a strong duty to serve his country during World War II.

Bob joined the United States Navy in late summer of 1942. Before reporting for duty at the Great Lakes Naval Training Station, Bob married his collegiate sweetheart, Mary Helfrich. They were to have four children: James, Robert, Richard, and Carole. During his first year of military service, Bob spent most of his time playing basketball. In 1943, he led his Great Lakes Naval

Training Station team to the service title.

Following his discharge in 1945, Bob joined the Rochester Royals of the National Basketball League (NBL), which soon merged with another league to form the National Basketball Association (NBA). Bob played ten seasons with the Royals, leading them to championships in 1946 and 1951.

As a professional, Bob did not score with the same proficiency as he did in college. In 569 career games, Bob scored 7,771 points for a 13.7 points-per-game average.

To compensate for his point production, Bob became an excellent playmaker. A magician with a basketball, he led the NBA in assists with 321 in 1949 and set a single-game record for assists with 20 in 1951. Bob led the league in assists seven times and finished his career with 2,250 total assists.

In 1947, Bob was named to the All-NBL team and received the league's most valuable player award. After the merger, Bob received All-NBA honors five times from 1949 to 1953, and he played in the NBA's first four All-Star games, from 1951 to 1954.

Continuing the Story

In 1947, while playing with the Royals, Bob joined the college coaching ranks, guiding his Seton Hall alma mater to a 24-3 season. After retiring from professional basketball at the end of the 1954 season, Bob spent two seasons as coach of six sports at Gettysburg College in

STATISTICS

Season	GP	FGM	FG%	FTM	FT%	Reb.	Ast.	TP	PPG
1945-46	27	86	—	70	.680	—	—	242	9.0
1946-47	32	166	—	130	.783	—	—	462	14.4
1947-48	48	176	—	121	.752	—	—	473	9.9
1948-49	60	317	.364	270	.776	—	**321**	904	15.1
1949-50	64	317	.357	261	.752	—	294	895	14.0
1950-51	63	326	.372	303	.795	197	287	955	15.2
1951-52	65	379	.383	294	.776	189	390	1,052	16.2
1952-53	66	339	.385	351	.753	195	280	1,029	15.6
1953-54	72	288	.371	311	.718	194	323	887	12.3
1954-55	72	326	.415	220	.751	205	155	872	12.1
Totals	569	2,720	—	2,331	.758	—	—	7,771	13.7

Notes: Boldface indicates statistical leader. GP = games played; FGM = field goals made; FG% = field goal percentage; FTM = free throws made; FT% = free throw percentage; Reb. = rebounds; Ast. = assists; TP = total points; PPG = points per game (complete records not available.)

HONORS AND AWARDS

1941-42	College All-American
1942	College All-Star Game most valuable player
1947	NBL most valuable player All-NBL Team
1949-53	All-NBA Team
1951-54	NBA All-Star Team
1966	Inducted into Pennsylvania Sports Hall of Fame
1969	Inducted into Naismith Memorial Basketball Hall of Fame
1970	NBA 25th Anniversary All Time Team Uniform number 11 retired by Sacramento Kings

Gettysburg, Pennsylvania: basketball, baseball, football, soccer, tennis, and track and field.

In 1957, Bob left coaching and joined the Converse Rubber Company to take charge of promotion and sales of athletic footwear.

Summary

For his size, Bob Davies was an exceptional athlete. He probably could have played several sports professionally, but his love for and dedication to basketball helped to establish the game at the professional level and to ensure the success of today's National Basketball Association.

Jerry Jaye Wright

Additional Sources:

Groliers Educational Corporation. *Pro Sports Halls of Fame.* 8 vols. Danbury, Conn.: Groliers Educational Corporation, 1996.

Hickok, Ralph. *A Who's Who of Sports Champions.* Boston: Houghton Mifflin, 1995.

LaBlanc, Michael L., and Mary K. Ruby, eds. *Professional Sports Team Histories: Basketball.* Detroit: Gale, 1994.

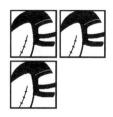

ERNIE DAVIS

Sport: Football

Born: December 14, 1939
New Salem, Pennsylvania
Died: May 18, 1963
Cleveland, Ohio

Early Life

Ernest Davis was born on December 14, 1939, in New Salem, a small town in the coal-rich southwest corner of Pennsylvania. Ernie's father was killed in an accident before Ernie was born, and so, when Ernie was fourteen months old, his mother had to leave him to live with his grandparents in nearby Uniontown, Pennsylvania, while she searched for a job to support her only child.

Although Ernie's grandfather worked as a coal miner, it was difficult for the grandfather to support the family. He had twelve children of his own, and the family lived in poverty.

Ernie dreamed, as a child, of becoming a professional athlete. His heroes were baseball star Stan Musial and Chicago Bears quarterback Johnny Lujack, men whose athletic skills had helped them escape the coal mines and steel mills of western Pennsylvania, where Ernie grew up.

The Road to Excellence

When Ernie was twelve years old, his mother settled in Elmira, New York, a community that became his adopted home. Even as early as grade school, Ernie was displaying the talents that would eventually lead to greatness. He could run faster, throw harder, and kick farther than anyone else in the school.

Ernie attended Elmira Free Academy High School, where he won eleven varsity letters. Many believed that he was a better basketball player than a football player, and his basketball statistics were certainly impressive. He set the All-Southern Tier Conference career scoring record with 1,605 points, averaging 18.4 points per game. In addition, his team won 52 consecutive games during his last two years at the school.

National Football Foundation Hall of Fame

Ernie was a great player who could control a game. However, if his team had a sizable lead, he would not shoot or rebound or, sometimes, play defense. He would let other players (even his opponents) have the opportunity to score points and to perform well in the game.

Ernie's ambition, in spite of his basketball successes, had always been to be the best professional football player anywhere. Ernie therefore chose to concentrate on football instead of basketball.

The Emerging Champion

Although he had always dreamed of playing halfback for Notre Dame, Ernie chose to attend Syracuse University from among the thirty colleges that offered him a football scholarship, because he felt that Syracuse would provide him with the best opportunity to run with the football. Once at Syracuse, he quickly became known as the "Elmira Express" because of his running ability.

Ernie wore number 44, the same number worn by a previous Syracuse great, Jim Brown. During the three years that Ernie played, he broke most of Brown's records, including marks for total rushing yards (2,386), yards per carry (6.6), total touchdowns (35), and total points (220).

In his sophomore year, Ernie gained 686 yards and scored 64 points. Those numbers represented totals greater than the combined totals of all ten of Syracuse's opponents that year. Playing both offense and defense, Ernie led the Orangemen to a 23-14 victory over Texas in the Cotton Bowl that year. In that game, he scored 16 of Syracuse's points on 2 touchdowns and two 2-point conversions, and set up the other touchdown with a pass interception. The win completed an undefeated season and enabled Syracuse to gain the number-one ranking in the country.

In his senior year, Ernie was awarded the Heisman Trophy as the best college football player in the United States. He was the first black player ever to receive the award. Perhaps his biggest thrill, though, occurred when President John F. Kennedy shook his hand following the Heisman ceremonies.

Ernie set an example of excellence for others, not only in athletics, but in character as well. His

STATISTICS

| | | Rushing | | | |
Season	GP	Car.	Yds.	Avg.	TD
1959	—	98	686	7.0	—
1960	—	114	877	7.7	—
1961	—	150	823	5.5	—
Totals	—	362	2,386	6.6	35

Notes: GP = games played; Car. = carries; Yds. = yards; Avg. = average yards per carry or average yards per reception; TD = touchdowns; Rec. = receptions

grandfather, who had raised him until he was twelve years old, had been a strict disciplinarian, and Ernie's character reflected this upbringing.

Ernie was thoughtful and polite. He did not smoke, swear, or drink, and he willingly helped others when they needed assistance. He was a hero to many children, but especially to those in Elmira. At his college graduation, he was honored by his fellow senior students by being selected as marshal and leading his classmates into graduation ceremonies.

Continuing the Story

Playing in the National Football League (NFL) had always been Ernie's dream. When he was drafted by the Cleveland Browns and was going to join Jim Brown in the same backfield, his dream seemed to be realized.

Unfortunately, Ernie never got to play in the NFL. In July of 1962, Ernie was diagnosed as having leukemia, and he died from this disease in Cleveland, Ohio, on May 18, 1963, at the age of twenty-three.

People still remember his funeral. He was so well respected and liked that thousands of people attended his funeral, including almost the entire Cleveland Browns football team. There were lines of mourners two blocks long waiting to pay their respects.

The people of Elmira have never forgotten Ernie or the courage, sportsmanship, and other good qualities that he displayed. Elmira Free Academy was renamed Ernie Davis Junior High School, and in 1988, to commemorate the twenty-fifth anniversary of Ernie's death, a life-sized bronze statue of him was dedicated in front

HONORS AND AWARDS

1961	Heisman Trophy
	Camp Award
1962	Overall first choice in the NFL Draft
1979	Inducted into College Football Hall of Fame
1987	Inducted into Pro Football Hall of Fame
	Uniform number 45 retired by Cleveland Browns

Heisman Trophy as the best college football player in the United States. His courage and outstanding character made him a hero and an inspiration to many people, but especially to children. Unfortunately, his death at a very young age prevented him from playing in the NFL and took away the opportunity for him to reach even greater heights of achievement.

Stephen Schwartz

of the school. A city park, located across the street from the school, is also named after him.

The sport of football has not forgotten Ernie either. In 1987, in spite of never having played a down in professional football, Ernie was voted into the Pro Hall of Fame.

Summary

Ernie Davis was one of the greatest players in college football history. He set many records at Syracuse University, and in his senior year he became the first black player ever to win the

Additional Sources:

Clark, Steve. *Fight Against Time: Five Athletes—a Legacy of Courage.* New York: Atheneum, 1979.

Gallagher, Robert C. *Ernie Davis, the Elmira Express: The Story of a Heisman Trophy Winner.* Silver Spring, Md.: Bartleby, 1983.

Nack, William. "A Life Cut Short." *Sports Illustrated* 71, no. 10 (September 4, 1989): 136-146.

Savage, Jeff. *Top Ten Heisman Trophy Winners.* Springfield, N.J.: Enslow, 1999.

GLENN DAVIS

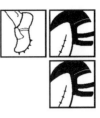

Sport: Football and Track and field

Born: December 26, 1924
Claremont, California

Early Life

Irma and Ralph Davis received a double surprise on the day after Christmas in 1924. Irma gave birth to twin boys, Ralph, Jr., and Glenn, in Claremont, California, on December 26, 1924. Glenn, who was born nine minutes after his brother, was later nicknamed "Junior." As a teenager growing up in Southern California, Glenn developed into a fine all-around athlete. He was a fast sprinter in track, a strong-armed center fielder in baseball, and a swift runner in football. At Bonita High School, he played four varsity sports, baseball, football, basketball, and track, and earned sixteen varsity letters. Glenn was not

Courtesy of Amateur Athletic Foundation of Los Angeles

only chosen to a high school All-Star team in baseball, but he also won the Knute Rockne Trophy as Southern California's best high school track performer in 1943.

Football was Glenn's ticket to greatness, however. In his senior year, he scored a remarkable 236 points and was chosen football player of the year in his conference.

The Road to Excellence

After graduating from high school, Glenn and twin brother Ralph were appointed to the U.S. Military Academy at West Point in 1943. There, Glenn quickly established himself as one of the greatest athletes to enter West Point. He scored a record 962.5 points out a possible 1,000 in the Army Master of the Sword physical fitness test. Unfortunately, in his first year, Glenn failed a mathematics course and was forced to drop out. He was disappointed, but he worked hard in mathematics at another college to catch up. His work paid off, and Glenn was permitted to reenter West Point in 1944.

By 1944, Army football coach Earl "Red" Blaik had assembled a powerful football team, including gifted quarterbacks Doug Kenna and Arnold Tucker, as well as strong tackle DeWitt "Tex" Coulter and talented end Barney Poole. A powerful fullback from South Carolina, Felix "Doc" Blanchard, also joined the team. Glenn and Blanchard formed a running duo that became legendary in college football. Glenn, an all-around player, was known for excelling at receiving, passing, blocking, and defending. With his exceptional speed and powerful leg drive, he was superb at shedding tacklers, leaving them floundering in his wake.

The Emerging Champion

Glenn and Blanchard complemented each other perfectly. Glenn, smaller than Blanchard

603

COLLEGE FOOTBALL STATISTICS

| | | | Rushing | | | | Receiving | | |
Season	GP	Car.	Yds.	Avg.	TD	Rec.	Yds.	Avg.	TD
1943	95	634	6.7	7	—	—	—	—	1
1944	58	667	11.5	14	—	—	—	—	4
1945	82	944	11.5	15	—	—	—	—	3
1946	123	712	5.8	7	—	—	—	—	6
Totals	358	2,957	8.3	43	—	—	—	—	14

Notes: GP = games played; Car. = carries; Yds. = yards; Avg. = average yards per carry or average yards per reception; TD = touchdowns; Rec. = receptions

at 5 feet 9 inches and 170 pounds, was a fast and elusive open-field runner. At 6 feet and 205 pounds, Blanchard was a classic power fullback and blocker who shredded opposing defensive lines for yardage. Later known as "Mr. Inside" (Blanchard) and "Mr. Outside" (Davis), this remarkable pair's glory days had just begun.

In their sophomore year, Glenn and Blanchard led Army to an undefeated season. They destroyed opposing teams by scores of 83-0, 76-0, 69-7, and 59-0. Glenn and Blanchard became known as the "Touchdown Twins." Glenn scored 20 touchdowns that year and averaged an incredible 11 yards each time he carried the ball. In other words, he gained a first down nearly each time he ran. Glenn's spectacular year earned him the Maxwell Award and Walter Camp Award as player of the year. He also made the Helms Athletic Foundation All-Time All-American team.

The next two seasons were more of the same. Army was the national champion in 1945 and tied for the title in 1946. Glenn starred in every game. In fact, he never once played in a losing game during his three years with the team. As a result, he was repeatedly chosen as an All-American and won the coveted Heisman Trophy in 1946. Glenn scored 59 touchdowns, an average of nearly 2 per game. His coach, Earl Blaik, hailed him as the best player he had ever seen. In addition, many football authorities have rated the 1945 Army team as the best college team ever to play the game.

After finishing second in Heisman Trophy balloting two years in a row, Glenn finally won the trophy in 1946. That same year he was also named College Player of the Year by *The Sporting News* and was voted Male Athlete of the Year by the Associated Press.

Continuing the Story

Glenn was a dedicated athlete who trained hard. He was the epitome of the clean-cut, All-American athlete. Because of his tremendous running speed, he was offered a contract to play baseball with the Brooklyn Dodgers in 1947, but Glenn turned it down.

After graduating from West Point, Glenn was required to serve in the U.S. Army until 1950. Consequently, his professional football career was postponed. After serving in Korea, Glenn resigned his Army commission in 1950 to give pro football a try.

As the best running back in college football history, Glenn joined the Los Angeles Rams and became an important part of a great team. He led the team in rushing and receiving and was a runner-up for the Rookie of the Year award. Unfortunately, an old knee injury began to hamper him, and he retired from football in 1952.

A year later, Glenn married Harriet Lancaster. He has one son, Ralph, and a stepson, John Slack. After retiring from pro football, Glenn accepted a position as promotions director for the *Los Angeles Times* newspaper. He directed special events for the paper and administered the paper's charitable fund-raising activities. He was also an Olympic gold medalist in 1956 and 1960, winning the 400-meter hurdles in Olympic-record time. In 1961, he was chosen to the National Football Foundation College Football Hall of Fame. A contented man, Glenn considered himself lucky to have accomplished all that he did.

TRACK STATISTICS

Year	Competition	Event	Place	Time
1956	Olympic Games	400-meter hurdles	Gold	50.1 OR
1960	Olympic Games	400-meter hurdles	Gold	49.3 OR

Note: OR = Olympic Record

HONORS, AWARDS, AND RECORDS

1944	Associated Press Outstanding College Football Player
	Maxwell Award
	Camp Award
	Consensus All-American
	Helms Athletic Foundation All-Time All-American
1944, 1946	Citizens Savings College Football Player of the Year
1945	World Trophy
	Citizens Savings Southern California Athlete of the Year
1945-46	Unanimous All-American
1946	Heisman Trophy
	Sporting News College Player of the Year
	Associated Press Male Athlete of the Year
1951	NFL Pro Bowl Team
1956, 1958	World record in the 400-meter hurdles (49.5 in 1956; 49.2 in 1958)
1958	Sullivan Award
1960	World record in the 4×400-meter relay (3:02.21)
1961	Inducted into College Football Hall of Fame
1974	Inducted into National Track and Field Hall of Fame
1986	Inducted into U.S. Olympic Hall of Fame

Summary

One of the fastest running backs in college football history, Glenn Davis was also one of the best. He and Doc Blanchard combined to form one of the most potent running combinations of all time. Between them, they led Army to three straight undefeated football seasons. Glenn's great talent, combined with his dedication, made him a terrific athlete and an inspiration to all players of the game.

Nan White

Additional Sources:

Fimrite, Ron. "Mr. Inside and Mr. Outside." *Sports Illustrated* 69, no. 23 (November 21, 1988): 76-87.

LaBlanc, Michael L., and Mary K. Ruby, eds. *Professional Sports Team Histories: Football.* Detroit: Gale, 1994.

Sugar, Burt R. *The One Hundred Greatest Athletes of All Time.* New York: Citadel Press, 1995.

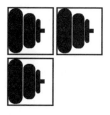

JOHN DAVIS

Sport: Weightlifting

Born: January 12, 1921
      Smithtown, New York
Died: July 13, 1984
      Albuquerque, New Mexico

Early Life

John Henry Davis was born on January 12, 1921, in Smithtown, New York, and was reared in Brooklyn. Of slight build, he was interested in all forms of sports to build his body. He enjoyed gymnastics, handball, running, and swimming. Like most boys, John also tried to emulate many of the strong men of the day. One day as he was playing, John lifted a large rock over his head on a dare. A local weightlifter named Steve Wolsky saw the feat, recognized the raw power in the young boy, and invited him to his gym to try his hand at lifting barbells.

John took quickly to the sport of weightlifting. During John's athletic career, Olympic-style weightlifting competitions consisted of three lifts: the press, in which the barbell is lifted, or cleaned, to the chest and then pressed overhead with the legs kept straight; the snatch, in which the barbell is lifted overhead from the floor in one motion; and the clean and jerk, in which the barbell is lifted to the chest and then, with the use of the legs, thrust overhead. Within a year, John began winning competitions against more seasoned lifters and was attracting the attention of those in the sport. By age sixteen, he could clean and jerk 300 pounds over his head.

The Road to Excellence

The most dominant weightlifting club of the period was the York Barbell Club in York, Pennsylvania. Bob Hoffman, the owner of the York Barbell Company and the coach of the York Barbell Club, noticed the teenager's natural strength and talent. Under Hoffman's direction, John's progress was rapid.

His first national meet was the 1938 Junior National Championships held in Cleveland, Ohio. Following that meet, he competed in the 1938 National Championships in Woonsocket, Rhode Island, where John, weighing 194 pounds, finished second in the heavyweight division. The competition was the last time John would be beaten for fifteen years.

That same year, 1938, John, then only seventeen years old, was selected as an alternate on the U.S. team competing in the World Championships in Vi-

Weight lifter John Davis won his fifth world championship here in 1951.

enna, Austria. While en route to the competition, the team's light-heavyweight lifter became ill and was not able to compete, and John immediately lost fifteen pounds to compete as a light-heavyweight. Miraculously, he won the world championship with a total lift of 815 pounds. In so doing, the teenager defeated Louis Hostin of France, the 1932 and 1936 Olympic champion, and former world champion and world-record holder Fritz Haller of Austria. Soon after the championships, John proved that his victory was not just luck when he set a new world record in the clean and jerk by lifting 352 pounds.

MAJOR CHAMPIONSHIPS	
1938	World Light-heavyweight Champion
1939-40	U.S. Light-heavyweight Champion
1941-43, 1946-48, 1950-53	U.S. Heavyweight Champion
1948, 1952	Gold Medalist, Olympic Weightlifting (heavyweight division)
1951, 1955	Gold Medalist, Pan-American Games Weightlifting (heavyweight division)

HONORS AND AWARDS	
1989	U.S. Olympic Hall of Fame
	Black Athletes Hall of Fame
	Helms Hall of Fame

The Emerging Champion

When John returned to Brooklyn, he took jobs that allowed him to dedicate more time to training. The dedication paid off, with John easily winning light-heavyweight national titles in 1939 and 1940. In 1941, he moved up to the heavyweight class and immediately broke the world record total of 1,000 pounds by ten pounds. He repeated as national heavyweight champion in 1942 and 1943.

John received the praise and respect of the sporting world, and he was offered full citizenship by Egypt, England, France, Germany, Sweden, and Spain. At home, however, he still had to fight for the consideration given so freely elsewhere. An African American, John did not enjoy many of the privileges that his fellow American competitors appreciated. While traveling throughout the United States, he had to abide by segregation laws that did not allow him to mingle freely with his white teammates and competitors in many public places. Yet he used this prejudice to his advantage by developing a strength and dignity that allowed his accomplishments to speak for themselves.

In 1943, John was sent to the South Pacific as a member of the U.S. Army. While serving, he contracted malaria that would haunt him the rest of his life. Had World War II not caused the cancellation of the 1940 and 1944 Olympic Games, John would surely have added two Olympic med-

als to his many titles. As it was, he had to wait until 1948 to win the only title that had eluded him.

With the war over in 1945, John returned home some forty-five pounds lighter from his bouts with malaria. The World Championships were scheduled to resume in Paris the next year, however, so he immediately began training. After winning the U.S. heavyweight title in 1946, John defended his world title in Paris and successfully defended it the next year in Philadelphia. In 1948, he added the elusive Olympic title to his collection by winning the gold medal in the heavyweight division at the London Games.

Continuing the Story

After defending his title for the fifth time at the 1949 World Championships in The Hague, John gave a demonstration in Paris. It was here that he became only the third man in history to lift the Apollon Bell, a 365-pound railroad axle and wheels. As John's popularity on the world sporting stage grew, it became apparent that he was no one dimensional athlete. An ardent fan of classical music and the possessor of a rich baritone voice, John took singing lessons in hopes of breaking into opera. One of John's personal highlights of the 1949 championships was not the competition but the chance to see the largest collection of recordings by his musical idol Richard Tauber.

At the 1950 World Championships, once again in Paris, John gave a memorable display of the strength not only of his body but of his character as well. During an intense competition with

607

Jakov Kutsenko of the Soviet Union, John snatched 325 pounds, a total that would easily have won him the competition. Yet, although all the judges ruled that it was a fair lift, John acknowledged that his knee had touched the floor, a violation, and refused to accept the judges' decision. On his next attempt, he successfully completed the lift again. He earned not only his sixth world championship but also the respect of the lifting world, including the Soviets.

John's undefeated string would stretch another three years to include the 1952 Olympic title and a fifth-place finish in the Sullivan Award balloting for the nation's top amateur athlete. His fifteen-year winning streak came to an end at the 1953 U.S. National Championships when he was beaten by Norm Schemansky. John continued lifting until a severe leg injury at the 1956 Olympic trials forced his retirement at the age of thirty-seven.

Following his competitive career, John was employed as a corrections officer with the New York State penal system, establishing fitness programs for juvenile delinquents. He retired in 1984 when it was discovered that he had inoperable cancer brought on by a long-time cigarette habit. He faced his death as he had lived his life, with dignity and strength, acknowledging that this was his reward for such excess. He was honored as a special representative for the 1984 Olympics in Los Angeles, but died only days before the start of the Games.

Summary

Pound for pound, John Davis was the first weight lifter who truly deserved the title strongest man in the world. For many years, he was the model for young weight lifters to emulate, and he remains a genuine legend in the sport of weight-lifting.

Rusty Wilson

Additional Sources:

Brown, Gene, ed. *The New York Times Encyclopedia of Sports*. 15 vols. New York: Arno Press, 1979-1980.

Hickok, Ralph. *A Who's Who of Sports Champions*. Boston: Houghton Mifflin, 1995.

TERRELL DAVIS

Sport: Football

Born: October 28, 1972
San Diego, California

Early Life

Denver Broncos running back Terrell Davis has achieved football stardom despite taking a perilous road to the National Football League (NFL). Born on October 28, 1972, Terrell was the youngest of six boys. Growing up in east San Diego, California, Terrell at first played Little League. Then he discovered the joys of Pop Warner League football, earning the nickname "Boss Hog" for his tenacious playing style. In 1986, when Terrell was fourteen, his father, John, died of lupus, leaving his mother, Kateree, to raise the rambunctious boys all alone.

Money, according to Terrell's recollections, was hard to come by, but he always believed that sports would be his ticket to bigger and better things. His first chance to prove that came when he transferred from Morse High School to Lincoln Prep in San Diego. He played six different positions at Lincoln, including nose guard, before he graduated in 1990. Although he was destined to become a running back in college, Terrell scored only 3 touchdowns during his whole high school career.

The Road to Excellence

Encouraged by his older brother, Reggie, Terrell earned a scholarship to California State University, Long Beach, where, as a redshirt freshman, he played for legendary coach George Allen. Allen took notice of Terrell's running ability and tenacity and began to groom him. Adversity struck when Allen died of a heart attack after the 1990 season, and the Long Beach football program was dismantled. Terrell reluctantly transferred to the University of Georgia, which used a passing offense that did not showcase his speed. Playing for three sea-

Denver Bronco Terrell Davis celebrates after a win in November, 2000.

AP/Wide World Photos

609

STATISTICS

Season	GP	Car.	Rushing Yds.	Avg.	TD	Rec.	Receiving Yds.	Avg.	TD
1995	14	237	1,117	4.7	7	49	367	7.5	1
1996	16	345	1,538	4.5	13	36	310	8.6	2
1997	15	369	1,750	4.7	15	42	287	6.8	0
1998	16	392	**2,008**	**5.1**	**21**	25	217	8.7	2
1999	4	67	211	3.1	2	3	26	8.7	0
2000	5	78	282	3.6	2	2	4	2.0	0
Totals	70	1,488	6,906	4.6	60	157	1,211	7.7	5

Notes: Boldface indicates statistical leader. GP = games played; Car. = carries; Yds. = yards; Avg. = average yards per carry *or* average yards per reception; TD = touchdowns; Rec. = receptions

sons, the 5-foot 11-inch, 210-pound Terrell still finished his career at Georgia with 1,657 yards on 317 carries (a 5.2 average) and 15 touchdowns. He also caught 46 passes for 529 yards and 4 touchdowns. As a senior, he led the team with 445 yards and 7 touchdowns on 97 carries (a 4.6 average), in addition to 31 receptions for 330 yards.

Nevertheless, Terrell did not leave Georgia as a top NFL prospect. In fact, he was selected by the Broncos as the 196th player in the sixth round of the 1995 draft, a placement that usually relegates one to practice-player status on a team, not superstardom.

The Emerging Champion

Undaunted, Terrell took his rookie season by storm, starting fourteen games in the season and rushing for 1,117 yards on 237 carries and 7 touchdowns. He also caught 49 passes for 367 yards and 1 touchdown. For his efforts, he was voted by his teammates as the club's offensive most valuable player (MVP) and he was voted second for NFL offensive Rookie of the Year. Terrell's output landed him in the record books as well. He became the lowest drafted player in NFL history to rush for over 1,000 yards in his rookie season.

Terrell's numbers continued to improve. In his second season on the team, he led the American Football Conference (AFC) and was second in the NFL in both rushing yards (1,538 on 345 carries) and total yards from scrimmage (1,848). He led the NFL in first downs earned, with 108, and was second in the AFC and third in the

league in both rushing touchdowns (13) and total touchdowns (15). He also set franchise single-season records in rushing attempts, rushing yards, and total yards.

By 1997, Terrell began to show the brilliance that led him to the upper echelons of the game. Starting the first fifteen games, Terrell finished his third season with 1,750 yards on 369 carries (4.7 average) and 15 rushing touchdowns. All his rushing numbers were career and franchise highs. He won the AFL rushing title and finished second in the league that year.

Continuing the Story

Terrell's greatest triumph came on January 23, 1998, in his hometown, when he rushed for 157 yards and scored a Super Bowl record 3 touchdowns to lead the Broncos to a Super Bowl victory. Terrell started at halfback in all sixteen games that season and won his first rushing title with 2,008 yards and 21 touchdowns on 392 carries. In doing so, Terrell became only the fourth player in league history to top the 2,000-yard mark in a single season. His total also ranked third-best behind Hall of Famer Eric Dickerson's 2,105 in 1984 and Barry Sanders's 2,053 in 1997. The season also helped Terrell become the Broncos' all-time career rushing leader with 6,413 yards, surpassing Floyd Little's mark of 6,323 set between 1967 and 1975.

Terrell continued his triumphant play in 1998 by helping Denver win a second consecutive Super Bowl title. Terrell rushed for 102 yards against the Atlanta Falcons in Super Bowl XXXIII. After five seasons' work, Terrell had earned two Super Bowl rings, had appeared in three Pro Bowls, and had been voted MVP of Super Bowl XXXII. He also became the first 2,000-yard rusher to win a Super Bowl.

Injuries spoiled his 1999 and 2000 seasons, but he expected to return to playing at full strength in 2001.

Summary

Never considered gifted in the field of football, Terrell Davis has surpassed many expectations by displaying grit and drive. His determined attitude is a staple of his playing style.

Terrell has not forgotten his roots, continuing to remain a part of his San Diego community. In 2000, Terrell—whose performances have garnered him a nine-year, $56.1 million contact that essentially keeps him in Denver until he retires—returned to Lincoln Prep to a hero's welcome, complete with marching band and ceremony in which his number 7 jersey was retired. In kind, Terrell donated a check for $10,000 to the school.

A. K. Ruffin

Additional Sources:

Peterson, Brian C. *Terrell Davis*. New York: Dorling Kindersley, 2000.

Saunders, Patrick. "Davis Carries Himself as Well as He Does the Football." *The Denver Post*, September 12, 1999.

Sherman, Josepha. *Terrell Davis*. Chicago: Heinemann Library, 2001.

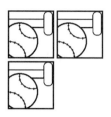

ANDRE DAWSON

Sport: Baseball

Born: July 10, 1954
Miami, Florida

Early Life

Andre Fernando Dawson, the oldest of eight children, was born on July 10, 1954, in Miami, Florida, where he was reared. Athleticism ran in Andre's family. His uncle, Theodor Taylor, had played minor-league baseball for the Pittsburgh Pirates organization from 1967 to 1969; another uncle, Curtis Taylor, started a South Miami Little League program when Andre was seven years old.

Andre loved baseball from an early age. He played at Southwest Miami High School, from

which he was graduated in 1972. That fall, Andre attended Florida A&M University.

The Road to Excellence

At Florida A&M, Andre played baseball for three years. His play attracted the attention of professional scouts, and he was chosen by the Montreal Expos of the National League (NL) in the 1975 amateur draft. Andre, a trim, strong, 6-foot 3-inch outfielder, was not, however, considered a top prospect; he was the 251st player chosen in the 1975 draft.

Andre worked hard and proved himself in one short year in the Expos' minor-league system. He played seventy-two games at Lethbridge, Alberta, Canada, in the Class A Pioneer League, hitting 13 home runs, batting in 50 runs, and compiling a .330 average. In 1976, he was promoted to Quebec City in the Class AA Eastern League, where he hit .357 in only forty games. He was then sent to Denver to play AAA ball, and he hit 14 home runs and batted in 28 runs in his first month with Denver. He was named player of the month in the American Association, and at the end of the season he was called up to the Expos.

Andre's batting average dropped only briefly after he entered the majors. He averaged .235 in twenty-four games during what was left of the 1976 season. The Expos started Andre in 1977 as a part-time outfielder, and he did not perform well at the plate until Expos manager Dick Williams placed him in center field full-time.

The Emerging Champion

In June, 1977, Andre was installed as the Expos' starting center fielder, and his performance improved immediately. He batted .282 for the season, hitting 19 homers and knocking in 65 runs. His great speed allowed him to steal 21 bases, and he was named the NL Rookie of the Year.

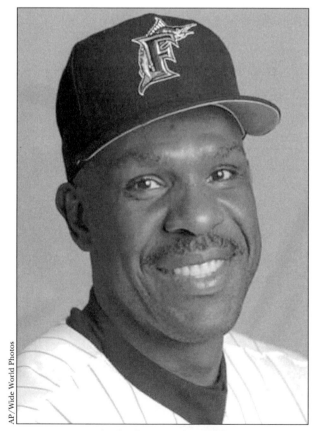

Andre Dawson in 1995.

STATISTICS

Season	GP	AB	Hits	2B	3B	HR	Runs	RBI	BA	SA
1976	24	85	20	4	1	0	9	7	.235	.306
1977	139	525	148	26	9	19	64	65	.282	.474
1978	157	609	154	24	8	25	84	72	.253	.442
1979	155	639	176	24	12	25	90	92	.275	.468
1980	151	577	178	41	7	17	96	87	.308	.492
1981	103	394	119	21	3	24	71	64	.302	.553
1982	148	608	183	37	7	23	107	83	.301	.498
1983	159	633	**189**	36	10	32	104	113	.299	.539
1984	138	533	132	23	6	17	73	86	.248	.409
1985	139	529	135	27	2	23	65	91	.255	.444
1986	130	496	141	32	2	20	65	78	.284	.478
1987	153	621	178	24	2	**49**	90	**137**	.287	.568
1988	157	591	179	31	8	24	78	79	.303	.504
1989	118	416	105	18	6	21	62	77	.252	.476
1990	147	529	164	28	5	27	72	100	.310	.535
1991	149	563	153	21	4	31	69	104	.272	.488
1992	143	542	150	27	2	22	60	90	.277	.456
1993	121	461	126	29	1	13	44	67	.273	.425
1994	75	292	70	18	0	16	34	48	.240	.466
1995	79	226	58	10	3	8	30	37	.257	.434
1996	42	58	16	2	0	2	6	14	.276	.414
Totals	2,627	9,927	2,774	503	98	438	1,373	1,591	.279	.480

Notes: Boldface indicates statistical leader. GP = games played; AB = at bats; 2B = doubles; 3B = triples; HR = home runs; RBI = runs batted in; BA = batting average; SA = slugging average

For the rest of the 1970's, Andre developed and refined his baseball skills. He could do everything—hit powerfully, run, field, and throw. He tied a major league record on July 30, 1978, when he hit 2 home runs in one inning (he repeated the feat on September 24, 1985). He hit 25 homers in 1978 and 25 more in 1979, and he earned a reputation as a slugging, smooth-fielding player with a powerful throwing arm. In 1980, he hit better than .300 for the first time in his major league career and won the first of eight Gold Glove Awards for fielding excellence.

In 1981, Andre took another step forward, playing in the first of eight All-Star games. Although his batting statistics were severely hurt by the fact that Olympic Stadium, the Expos' home field, was a tough park for a hitter, he nevertheless developed into one of the most feared sluggers in the NL. He could hit for both power and average, and he continued his stellar defensive play, leading NL outfielders in putouts and total chances in 1981, 1982, and 1983.

Accolades for Andre poured in throughout the 1980's. From 1980 through 1985 and again in 1987 and 1988, he won Gold Gloves. In 1981, *The Sporting News* magazine named him the Player of the Year, and in both 1981 and 1983 he was runner up in the voting for the NL most valuable player award. Other players, too, appreciated both Andre's professional attitude and his great athletic skills; in a poll conducted by *The New York Times* in 1983, major leaguers chose him as the game's best all-around player.

Continuing the Story

Despite Andre's success in the field and at bat in Montreal, however, star catcher Gary Carter was the most popular Expo with the fans. Moreover, the artificial turf at Olympic Stadium was damaging Andre's knees. In 1984, knee injuries began to take their toll. His average dropped more than 50 points, and his home-run and stolen-base totals plummeted. Although he remained an effective player, for three seasons he did not approach his prior level of excellence. Andre had corrective surgery on both his knees, but there was really only one solution to his problems: He needed to play baseball on natural grass.

Andre was a free agent after the 1986 season, and he wanted desperately to play for the Chicago Cubs, who played day baseball on the natu-

MAJOR LEAGUE RECORDS

Most intentional bases on balls, game, 5
Most home runs, inning, 2 (twice; record shared)
Most runs batted in, inning, 6
Most total bases, inning, 8 (twice; record shared)

HONORS AND AWARDS

1977	National League Rookie of the Year
1980-85,1987-88	National League Gold Glove Award
1981-83,1987-91	National League All-Star Team
1981,1987	*Sporting News* National League Player of the Year
1987	National League most valuable player
1995	Hutch Award Uniform number 10 retired by Montreal Expos

ral grass of Wrigley Field, where he had always hit well. At the time, however, the owners of the twenty-four major league teams had made a secret agreement not to bid for free-agent players in an illegal attempt to hold down salaries. Andre received no contract offers, and the Cubs took him on only after he signed a blank contract and allowed the club to determine his salary. The Cubs chose to pay him $500,000 for the 1987 season—a fraction of what he had made in Montreal, and far less than comparable players were paid. (Several years later, an arbitrator found the owners guilty of colluding to suppress salaries, and Andre and other players were awarded millions in damages.)

Andre repaid the Cubs well for their relatively small investment. With his knees revitalized by the grass field, he had his best season in years, blasting 49 homers and driving in 137 runs to lead the NL in both categories. Although the Cubs finished last in the NL Eastern Division, Andre's achievements were recognized with the most valuable player Award.

Andre's brilliant and steady play continued at Chicago, and he continued to add to his impres-

sive list of achievements. In 1989, he had 8 consecutive hits in two days. In 1990, he stole his 300th base; on September 13 of that year, he played in his 2,000th major league game. In 1993, after six successful seasons with the Cubs, he signed with the Boston Red Sox of the American League (AL), for whom he could play as a designated hitter. In his first season with Boston, Andre hit his four hundredth home run, only the twenty-fifth player in history to reach that mark.

As Andre approached the twilight of his career, he joined the Florida Marlins in 1995, playing only seventy-nine games with 8 home runs and an average of .257. The following year, he played only forty-two games before announcing his retirement on August 14, 1996. His character as a ballplayer, as much as his statistics, makes Andre a certain candidate for the Cooperstown Hall of Fame.

Summary

A little-heralded prospect when he left college, Andre Dawson shot through the minor leagues and soon proved himself to be one of the most potent combinations of power and speed in major league history. A fearsome hitter who also excelled in the field, he impressed fans and opponents alike as one of the best all-around players of his generation.

Alicia Neumann

Additional Sources:

Dawson, Andre, with Tom Bird. *Hawk: An Inspiring Story of Success at the Game of Life and Baseball.* Grand Rapids, Mich.: Zondervan, 1994.

"Hall Material." *Sports Illustrated* 78, no. 16 (1993): 53.

Kurkjian, Tim. "No Room in the Hall." *Sports Illustrated* 85 (August 26, 1996): 121.

Sheinin, Dave. "Dawson Retires from Playing Career, but Seeks Job in Marlins' Front Office." *Knight-Ridder/Tribune News Service,* August 15, 1996, p. 815K8578.

LEN DAWSON

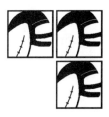

Sport: Football

Born: June 20, 1935
Alliance, Ohio

Early Life

The son of English immigrants James and Annie Dawson, Leonard Ray Dawson was born on June 20, 1935, in Alliance, Ohio. Lenny's father worked as a machinist in a pottery factory in order to feed his eleven children. Lenny's childhood was like that of many youngsters who grew up during the Depression, and who came from a small town and a very large family. Such children developed remarkable survival skills in order to get their share at the dinner table.

Since Lenny was the runt of the Dawson litter, he soon learned to live by his wits. As a fourteen-year-old, he calculated that at his weight of only 125 pounds, he had better go in for baseball rather than football. Lenny went out and hit .400 in American Legion baseball.

He was also a talented basketball player. His football-player brothers would not leave him alone until he played their sport as well, so he did, but he did not enjoy it. Playing football meant facing mammoth linemen whom he feared, and he hated the violence, hated getting hit. Lenny came up with his own way of coping. He developed a quick release that enabled him to pass the ball before defenders could get close to him, and he managed to complete 100 out of 200 passes in his high school years for 1,615 yards and 19 touchdowns. His senior year, he was the first athlete at Alliance High to earn All-State honors in both football and basketball. Players nicknamed him "Lenny the Cool" for his calm, calculating ability to survive and triumph.

The Road to Excellence

After graduating from high school in 1953, Lenny attended Purdue University, where he lettered in basketball and starred in football as a quarterback. He worked with assistant coach Hank Stram, who would later play an

615

important role in Lenny's professional career. For three years, Lenny led the Big Ten Conference in passing and total offense. By 1956, he was graduated with a degree in physical education and was an Academic All-American, having finished his college career with a B average and with 3,325 yards passing.

Then began the most difficult phase of Lenny's career. Although the Pittsburgh Steelers selected him in the first round of the National Football League (NFL) draft, the team already boasted Bobby Layne as its premier quarterback. So Lenny spent most of his time on the bench as reserve quarterback. From Layne, the quiet Lenny learned to be more aggressive with his teammates, to chew them out when they erred. Yet this was not in keeping with his personality, and his new toughness eventually backfired.

In 1960, Pittsburgh's coach, Buddy Parker, traded Lenny to the Cleveland Browns. Sadly, Lenny's jinx continued, for he was benched most of the time. Coaches seemed to feel he lacked the competitive spark—that he was there to serve time, not to win. Consequently, in Lenny's first year with Cleveland he played so rarely that he threw only 13 passes; in his second, only 15. After five frustrating years as a pro, Lenny had thrown

a total of only 45 passes. He felt that he had wasted all those years.

The Emerging Champion

Luckily, Lenny's former coach from college, Hank Stram, invited him to join the Dallas Texans of the American Football League (AFL), where Stram was then coaching. When Lenny arrived, he had been inactive for so long that his footwork was clumsy, his passing arm weak. Stram did not recognize him as the player he had coached at Purdue and had second thoughts about keeping him. He did, however, figuring time would sharpen Dawson's skills. Meanwhile, the team's promoters had a difficult time attracting fans to watch a quarterback who had never been more than a sub. Consequently, only a few thousand spectators came to Lenny's first game.

Given the chance at last to perform, Lenny became an immediate star. He showed what a daring play-caller he was, how deadly accurate his passing arm could be. He was also great at scrambling. Soon, he set a league record by completing 61 percent of his passes. Throughout the season, Lenny the Cool was the player who either made every big play or brought it out of his teammates. By year's end, Lenny had led the Texans to the

STATISTICS

Season	GP	PA	PC	Pct.	Yds.	Avg.	TD	Int.
1957	3	4	2	.500	25	6.3	0	0
1958	4	6	1	.167	11	1.8	0	2
1959	12	7	3	.429	60	8.6	1	0
1960	2	13	8	.615	23	1.8	0	0
1961	6	15	7	.467	85	5.7	1	3
1962	14	310	189	**.610**	2,759	8.9	**29**	17
1963	14	352	190	.540	2,389	6.8	**26**	19
1964	14	354	199	**.562**	2,879	8.1	30	18
1965	14	305	163	**.534**	2,262	7.4	**21**	14
1966	14	284	159	**.560**	2,527	8.9	**26**	10
1967	14	357	206	**.577**	2,651	7.4	24	17
1968	14	224	131	**.585**	2,109	9.4	17	9
1969	8	166	98	**.590**	1,323	8.0	9	13
1970	13	262	141	.538	1,876	7.1	13	14
1971	14	301	167	.555	2,504	8.3	15	13
1972	14	305	175	.574	1,835	6.0	13	12
1973	9	101	66	.653	725	7.2	2	5
1974	14	235	138	.587	1,573	6.7	7	13
1975	12	140	93	.664	1,095	7.8	5	4
Totals	209	3,741	2,136	.571	28,711	7.7	239	183

Notes: Boldface indicates statistical leader. GP = games played; PA = passes attempted; PC = passes completed; Pct. = percent completed; Yds. = yards; Avg. = average yards per attempt; TD = touchdowns; Int. = interceptions

championship and was chosen AFL Player of the Year. After all it had taken to get there, Lenny felt like he had been reborn.

Nevertheless, the Dallas Texans were not receiving enough support from local fans. The franchise soon moved to Kansas City, renamed the Chiefs. The Chiefs got off to a slow start in their new home, losing as many games as they won. They improved rapidly, though, winning AFL championships in 1966 and 1969, and compiling the highest winning percentage in pro football.

Dawson's greatest triumph came in 1970. First, though, the AFL's top-rated quarterback had to go through a very difficult test. On the eve of Super Bowl IV, when the Chiefs were to face the Minnesota Vikings, television newscasters reported that Lenny and other quarterbacks were friendly with a professional sports gambler who bet on football games illegally. Although Dawson's teammates called him "the Puritan," he was distressed. He knew his fans considered him a marked man. If he gave anything but a flawless performance during the following day's Super Bowl—if he fumbled or was intercepted—he would appear guilty of such unwarranted charges.

Len gave that game all of himself. He pitched to one teammate for a 46-yard touchdown, completed 12 of 17 passes for 142 yards, and led the Chiefs to three field goals. They won the championship, 23-7, and Lenny won the most valuable player award.

Continuing the Story

Len's Kansas City coach, Stram, should take some credit for Len's success. Since Len's arm was not strong enough to throw long passes, Len compensated by becoming the most accurate passer football had known. It was Stram's innovative offense of "play-action" passes and a movable pass pocket that enabled Len to shine as a quarterback, highlighting his strengths without exposing his weaknesses. Len was noted not only for his passing accuracy but also for his quick release in throwing the ball. He always remained "Lenny the Cool" when under pressure. He was never the kind to raise his voice—if a fellow player did anything wrong, Lenny would simply give him a look that meant he should shape up. Usually he did.

HONORS AND AWARDS	
1956	Academic All-American
1962	*Sporting News* AFL Player of the Year Newspaper Enterprise Association AFL Player of the Year
1962, 1966	*Sporting News* AFL All-Star Team All-League Team
1963, 1965, 1967-70	AFL All-Star Team
1969	AFL All-Star Game Co-Outstanding Offensive Player
1970	NFL Super Bowl most valuable player
1972	NFL Pro Bowl Team
1973	NFL Man of the Year
1987	Inducted into Pro Football Hall of Fame Uniform number 16 retired by Kansas City Chiefs

By the time he retired in 1975, Lenny held impressive professional career statistics. He ranked eighth in completions and passing yardage, seventh in games played, fourth in passing efficiency and touchdown passes, and third in seasons as an active player. Named to the AFL All-Star team six times, he also held AFL career records for passing efficiency, touchdown passes, total passing yardage, yards gained per pass, and lowest interception percentage.

Lenny's achievements did not end with his NFL career, though. After his retirement he worked briefly as a commentator on televised NFL games; later, he worked for a time as a football analyst on radio. At the same time, Lenny worked for many charities and civic organizations, in recognition of which he was honored as the NFL's Man of the Year for 1973. In 1987, he was elected to the Pro Football Hall of Fame. Lenny married Jacqueline Puzder in 1953; they have two children, Len, Jr., and Lisa. In the 1990's Len worked as a commentator for HBO Sports' weekly *Inside the NFL*.

Summary

Len Dawson went from being a bench-warmer to become the number-three passer in professional football history. Although many doubted his ability for the first five years of his professional career, Lenny the Cool proved himself as the AFL's top-rated quarterback. Playing for the Dallas Texans and later the Kansas City Chiefs, he was the player who either made every big play or brought it out of his teammates. After leading the Texans to the championship, Lenny was chosen AFL Player of the Year. For leading the Chiefs to victory in Super Bowl IV, Lenny was honored with the most valuable player award.

Nicholas White

Additional Sources:

Dawson, Len. *Len Dawson: Pressure Quarterback.* New York: Cowles, 1970.

Maule, Tex. "Hank Stram's Superchiefs." *Sports Illustrated* 32, no. 3 (January 19, 1970): 10-15.

Shapiro, Milton J. *The Pro Quarterbacks.* New York: J. Messner, 1971.

PAT DAY

Sport: Horse racing

Born: October 13, 1953
Brush, Colorado

Early Life

Pat Day grew up in the small ranching town of Eagle, Colorado. His father was an avid horseman who taught him basic horsemanship. As a youth, Pat excelled in sports, particularly wrestling and rodeo, despite his diminutive stature. In summers, he performed in the Little Britches Rodeo and during the school year was a member of his high school rodeo team. His dream of becoming a rodeo cowboy became a reality after graduating from high school in 1971. Though skilled on horseback, bull riding left the 4-foot 11-inch, 100-pound Pat bruised and beaten. In January, 1973, he abandoned rodeo riding for horse racing. He moved to Riverside Thoroughbred Farm in California to train as a jockey.

The Road to Excellence

In July of 1973 at Prescott Downs, Arizona, the nineteen-year-old Pat first tasted victory, in a 7-furlong claiming race atop a colt named Forblunged. Pat was a natural. During his first few years as a jockey, he won numerous races on tracks in Illinois, Louisiana, and Massachusetts. Early success went to his head, and he was considered arrogant both on and off the track.

In the mid-1970's he married Deborah Bailey. Her father, a former jockey, convinced Pat to try his skill at the top-ranked New York tracks; Pat tried but failed.

The temptation of the big city proved overwhelming, and he turned to alcohol and drugs. By the late 1970's, he had ruined his marriage and all but destroyed his career. He left New York for Miami, but nothing changed. Drugs eventually caused him to stop riding altogether.

Then, in the early 1980's, Pat turned his professional life around. A friend convinced him to return to the track. He did, and in 1982 he won more races than any rider in the United States: 399. He would repeat this feat in 1983. In 1984, his personal life also changed. In 1979, he had

Jockey Pat Day after his seven thousandth career win, in 1997

AP/Wide World Photos

619

married Sheila Johnson, who opposed his drug use. In early 1984 he became a born-again Christian, and his new disciplined life had a positive influence on his racing career. In 1984, he not only won his third consecutive victories title, with 399, but also won his first big race, the $3 million Breeders' Cup Classic, aboard Wild Again. For the first time he won the Eclipse Award as the country's outstanding jockey of the year.

The Emerging Champion

In the 1980's, Pat emerged as one of horse racing's best jockeys. In 1985, he captured his first Triple Crown victory riding Tank's Prospect in the Preakness (the second leg of the Triple Crown). The next year was one of his best, with Pat winning his second Eclipse Award, leading the nation in victories for the fourth time—with 429—and riding the Breeders' Cup Distaff winner and Horse of the Year Lady's Secret. In 1987, Pat again won the Eclipse Award.

He had another stellar year in 1989. His favorite mount that year was Easy Goer, a horse often compared to the great Triple Crown winner Secretariat. Easy Goer, favored to win the Triple Crown, was beaten in the first two legs by SunPat Silence, but in the Belmont Stakes, Pat and Easy Goer prevailed. Pat, who rode Easy Goer in all 20 of his career starts, considered this champion thoroughbred the best horse he had ever ridden. In that same year, he became the only jockey to ever win 8 out of 9 races in one day. When the decade ended, Pat had won 3,270 races, more than any other jockey. In 1989, Lucien Laurin, the trainer of Secretariat, stated that he considered Pat "the greatest rider today, bar none."

In 1990, Pat won his second Breeders' Cup Classic with Unbridled, won his second Preakness Stakes astride Summer Squall, and again led the country in wins, with 364. Perhaps his greatest year as a jockey was 1991. Although he did not win any leg of the American Triple Crown, he did win the Canadian Triple Crown aboard Dance Smartly. In that year he set a record for most stakes won in a single season, won his fourth Eclipse award, and for the sixth time in his career led the nation in victories (430). This amazing year was topped off by Pat's induction into racing's Hall of Fame.

Continuing the Story

In 1992, Pat had one of his most emotional wins. Prior to 1992, Pat was 0 for 9 in the Kentucky Derby. That year he rode the 17-1 longshot, Lil E. Tee. He visited a children's hospital the day before the Derby, met a young boy recovering from a bone marrow transplant, and promised him he would win the Kentucky Derby and would wear a hat in the winner's circle displaying the hospital's name. Lil E. Tee won, and Pat kept his promise.

Following the 1992 Kentucky Derby, Pat continued winning Triple Crown races. In 1994, 1995, and 1996, he won the Preakness Stakes, the only jockey to win this race three consecutive times. In 1994, he won his second Belmont Stakes aboard Preakness winner Tabasco Cat. His third Belmont win came in 2000 on the longshot Commendable. Pat holds the record for most victories ever at Churchill Downs.

MAJOR CHAMPIONSHIP VICTORIES

Year	Race	Horse
1984	Breeders' Cup Classic	Wild Again
1985	Preakness	Tank's Prospect
1986	Breeders' Cup Distaff	Lady's Secret
1987	Breeders' Cup Juvenile Fillies	Epitome
	Breeders' Cup Turf	Theatrical
1989	Belmont Stakes	Easy Goer
1990	Breeders' Cup Classic	Unbridled
	Preakness	Summer Squall
1991	Breeders' Cup Distaff	Dance Smartly
	Canadian Triple Crown	Dance Smartly
1992	Kentucky Derby	Lil E. Tee
1994	Breeders' Cup Juvenile Fillies	Flanders
	Breeders' Cup Juvenile	Timber Country
	Preakness	Tabasco Cat
	Belmont Stakes	Tabasco Cat
1995	Preakness	Timber Country
1996	Preakness	Louis Quatorze
1997	Breeders' Cup Juvenile	Favorite Trick
1998	Breeders' Cup Classic	Awesome Again
1999	Breeders' Cup Classic	Cat Thief
2000	Kentucky Oaks	Secret Status
	Belmont Stakes	Commendable

HONORS, AWARDS, AND RECORDS

1982-84, 1986, 1990-91	Nation's winningest jockey
1984, 1986-87, 1991	Eclipse Award as Outstanding Jockey
1985	George Woolf Memorial Jockey Award
1991	Set record for most Stakes won in a single season
	Canadian Triple Crown Winner
	Inducted into Racing Hall of Fame
1995	Mike Venezia Award
2000	All-time winningest rider: Keeneland Race Track
	2,000 wins at Churchill Downs

Through December, 1999, Pat ranked second in highest lifetime earnings among all jockeys. As of June, 2000, Pat had 7,747 lifetime wins. Only two riders, Laffit Pincay, Jr., and Willie Shoemaker, have posted more victories than Pat.

Summary

From a childhood dream of becoming a rodeo champion, Pat Day has emerged as one of America's greatest jockeys. By his own account, his religious conversion in the 1980's is greatly responsible for his success. With perseverance, he could well become only the third rider in racing history to break the eight-thousand-win barrier.

Ken Millen-Penn

Additional Sources:

Duke, Jacqueline. "A Long Journey into the Light for Day." *The Racing Times*, October 11, 1991, p. 3.

Nack, William. "Great Day." *Sports Illustrated* 76, no. 18 (May 11, 1992): 16.

Reed, William F. "Night and Day." *Sports Illustrated* 84, no. 21 (May 27, 1996): 56.

Vader, J. E. "Day of Reckoning." *Sports Illustrated* 70, no. 19 (May 1, 1989): 74-75.

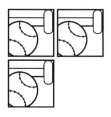

DIZZY DEAN

Sport: Baseball

Born: January 16, 1911
Lucas, Arkansas
Died: July 17, 1974
Reno, Nevada

Early Life

Jay Hanna Dean was born on January 16, 1911, in Lucas, Arkansas, but spent much of his early years on the move, following his father, Albert Dean, who picked cotton for a living. Jay and his two brothers, Elmer and Paul, were raised by their father after their mother, Alma (Nelson) Dean, had passed away. When the boys were old enough to pick their weight in cotton, they earned two dollars a day working alongside their father. Albert Dean had played semiprofessional baseball and taught his sons the game.

The Road to Excellence

Jay really learned to play baseball in the army. Even though the tall, husky youngster was too young to join the service legally at sixteen, he convinced the recruiting sergeant that he was eighteen. Jay soon became the ace pitcher for the Twelfth Field Artillery at Fort Sam Houston in San Antonio, Texas. Realizing that he had a future in baseball, he tried to get out of his four-year commitment to the service. Because at that time soldiers could purchase their release, Jay convinced his father to give him $120 to buy his discharge from the service.

After pitching semiprofessional ball in San Antonio, his reputation as a hard-throwing right-hander spread. In 1930, a bird-dog scout for the St. Louis Cardinals, Don Curtis, saw Jay pitch a few times in a San Antonio industrial league and quickly signed him to a contract. The nineteen-year-old hurler received a salary of three hundred dollars a month, which must have seemed like a princely sum for the impoverished Dean

Dizzy Dean of the St. Louis Cardinals pitches in 1935.

622

STATISTICS

Season	GP	GS	CG	IP	HA	BB	SO	W	L	S	ShO	ERA
1930	1	1	1	9.0	3	3	5	1	0	0	0	1.00
1932	46	33	16	**286.0**	280	102	**191**	18	15	2	**4**	3.30
1933	**48**	34	26	293.0	279	64	**199**	20	18	4	3	3.04
1934	50	33	24	311.2	288	75	195	**30**	7	7	**7**	2.66
1935	50	**36**	29	**325.1**	324	77	190	**28**	12	5	3	3.04
1936	51	34	28	**315.0**	310	53	195	24	13	**11**	2	3.17
1937	27	25	17	197.1	206	33	120	13	10	1	4	2.69
1938	13	10	3	74.2	63	8	22	7	1	0	1	1.81
1939	19	13	7	96.1	98	17	27	6	4	0	2	3.36
1940	10	9	3	54.0	68	20	18	3	3	0	0	5.17
1941	1	1	0	1.0	3	0	1	0	0	0	0	18.00
1947	1	1	0	4.0	3	1	0	0	0	0	0	0.00
Totals	317	230	154	1,967.1	1,925	453	1,163	150	83	30	26	3.02

Notes: Boldface indicates statistical leader. GP = games played; GS = games started; CG = complete games; IP = innings pitched; HA = hits allowed; BB = bases on balls (walks); SO = strikeouts; W = wins; L = losses; S = saves; ShO = shutouts; ERA = earned run average

during the heart of the Depression. Jay created a stir in the minor leagues, carousing on and off the field, all the while pitching sensationally. It was here that Jay acquired his nickname, "Dizzy," as he got in scrapes with his teammates, opposing players, and the law.

Dizzy pitched so well in his first year in the minors that he earned a shot with the parent club in September. Although Dizzy did not pitch for the Cardinals until late September, after the ball club had clinched the pennant, he impressed management when he held the hard-hitting Pittsburgh Pirates to only 3 hits.

Charging expenses to the club without permission and addressing his superiors by first name did not endear Dizzy to the Cardinals front office. Even though Dizzy was clearly ready to pitch in the majors during the 1931 season, the Cardinals management felt that he was too brash and sent him down to the minors—a clear message that his antics were not appreciated. Dizzy had another excellent season in the minors in 1931, winning twenty-six games while posting an impressive earned run average of 1.53. Dizzy married Patricia Nash that summer.

The Emerging Champion

After that great season, the Cardinals could not keep Dizzy down in the minors any longer, and he immediately became one of the most valuable members on the team. The ball club was nicknamed the "Gashouse Gang" for its outra-

geous antics on and off the field, and Dizzy fit the team's character. Dizzy and teammate Pepper Martin regularly played practical jokes in dugouts and hotels. Between the white lines, Dizzy won eighteen games in his first full year in the big leagues (1932), aided by his high hard one, a fast curve he called his "crooky," and by pinpoint control. During one five-day stretch in August, he won three games. During the 1933 season, Dizzy won twenty games, striking out a then record 17 batters in one game. An irrepressible character, Dizzy made predictions, missed games, and generally created outrageous publicity (and headaches for management) throughout his career. He also convinced the Cardinals to sign his hard-throwing younger brother, Paul.

In 1934, Dizzy brazenly predicted that "me and Paul" would win forty-five games between them during the upcoming campaign. Dizzy was wrong: They combined to win forty-nine games, as Dizzy collected thirty victories, garnered the National League most valuable player award, and led the team to a pennant and a World Series triumph against the Detroit Tigers.

Dizzy's off-the-field antics created as much notoriety as his accomplishments on the mound. At one point in 1934, Dizzy and Paul missed an exhibition game. Manager Frankie Frisch fined Dizzy and Paul one hundred dollars and fifty dollars, respectively. In response, the Deans went on a two-man strike. Frisch reacted by

623

suspending them and, during a heated shouting match, told them to take off their uniforms if they were not going to play. Dizzy and Paul complied by ripping their home uniforms into shreds in front of their incredulous manager. When wire-service photographers lamented that they had missed the uniforms episode, Dizzy and Paul promptly tore up their road uniforms for the benefit of the photographers. The Deans were summoned to the office of the Commissioner of Baseball, Judge Kennesaw "Mountain" Landis, who publicly admonished the brothers, docked them one week's pay, and then reinstated them.

A fitting climax to the bizarre 1934 season was the World Series against the Detroit Tigers. In the Series, Dizzy won two games, pitching a shutout in the deciding game. During the series he bragged incessantly, took batting practice with the Tigers, played a tuba, and squeezed the tail of an oversized toy tiger. During the fifth game, Dizzy was beaned while running the bases by a throw from Detroit shortstop Billy Rogell. He was taken to the hospital, and the famous headline that appeared the next day read, "X-Ray of Dean's Head Shows Nothing."

Continuing the Story

Over a four-year span (from 1932 to 1935) Dizzy averaged a stunning twenty-four wins a season. He not only led the National League each year in strikeouts, but in two of those four years, he also led the league in innings pitched. In 1936, Dizzy started in the regular rotation and, amazingly, also came out of the bullpen to relieve on 17 occasions, notching 11 saves. The tireless hurler started the 1937 campaign by pitching 20 scoreless innings in a row.

When the team went to Boston in 1937, Dizzy predicted he would strike out outfielder Vince DiMaggio four times in one game. After fanning the first three times at bat against Dizzy, Vince, Joe DiMaggio's brother, managed to lift a weak foul pop behind the plate. When catcher Bruce Ogrowdowski was just about to catch it, Dizzy screamed at the confused catcher to let the fly drop. The catcher complied, and then Dizzy fulfilled his boast by striking out the forlorn DiMaggio for a fourth time. In another wacky incident during May, 1937, Dizzy,

HONORS AND AWARDS	
1934	National League most valuable player Associated Press Male Athlete of the Year
1934-37	National League All-Star Team
1953	Inducted into National Baseball Hall of Fame
1976	Inducted into National Sportscasters and Sportswriters Hall of Fame Uniform number 17 retired by St. Louis Cardinals

upset over a balk called against him several days earlier, began a protest strike of sorts on the mound against the balk rule. Dizzy stalled so long that it took him more than 10 minutes to throw three pitches.

Unfortunately, in the 1937 All-Star Game, Dizzy was hit on the toe by a batted ball. After he was removed from the game, he learned that the toe was broken. Dizzy stayed sidelined for only two weeks and resumed pitching too soon. Because he still had to favor his sore toe, he altered his pitching motion. The result of the change in pitching mechanics was a sore arm that never really improved. After that point, Dizzy lost the speed on his fastball and was a shadow of his former self. He continued to pitch until 1941 on guile and guts, with only mixed results.

After his early retirement in 1941 at the age of thirty, Dizzy became a radio and television broadcaster, giving new meaning to the expression "color" commentary. A born self-promoter, Dizzy relied on his "down-home," folksy humor and colorful syntax to regale baseball fans. A runner did not slide into a base, he "slood." When, in turn, a runner was thrown out, Dizzy informed listeners that the player "got throwed out." At one point, the St. Louis Board of Education criticized him for his repeated use of the substandard expression "ain't." Dizzy's response was typical: "A lot of folks that ain't saying ain't, ain't eatin'."

Summary

The best way to summarize Dizzy Dean is to say that they broke the mold when they created him. Although his career was cut short by arm miseries, he was unstoppable in his prime. Full of himself, he entertained fans while unnerving teammates and infuriating opponents (not to mention management).

During his shortened career, he won 150 games and compiled a 3.02 earned run average. In 1953, he was elected to the National Baseball Hall of Fame. After his baseball career, he endeared himself to millions of Americans on radio and television broadcasts over the course of the next quarter-century. In addition to his work with the St. Louis Cardinals, he also did play-by-play for the New York Yankees and the CBS and NBC Game of the Week telecasts. He died in Reno, Nevada, on July 17, 1974.

Allen Wells

Additional Sources:

Feldman, Doug. *Dizzy and the Gas House Gang: The 1934 St. Louis Cardinals and Depression-Era Baseball.* Jefferson, N.C.: McFarland, 1998.

Fleming, G. H. *The Dizziest Season.* New York: William Morrow, 1984.

Gregory, Robert. *Diz: Dizzy Dean and Baseball During the Great Depression.* New York: Viking, 1992.

Kavanagh, Jack. *Dizzy Dean.* New York: Chelsea House, 1991.

Smith, Curt. *America's Dizzy Dean.* St. Louis: Bethany Press, 1978.

INGE DE BRUIJN

Sport: Swimming

Born: August 24, 1973
Barendrecht, Netherlands

Early Life

Inge De Bruijn was born in Barendrecht, Netherlands, on August 24, 1973. She has a twin sister, Jakline; an older sister, Yvette; and a younger brother, Matthijs. Inge swam her first competitive laps at age seven, after joining a local swim team at the encouragement of a friend. "Inky de inktvis," or "Inky the octopus," as her teammates nicknamed her, showed an early natural proficiency for the sport, turning her coaches'

comments on technique into immediate changes in her stroke. At age twelve, Inge boarded a plane for the first time, headed for her first overseas competition, in London. This was a motivating force in continuing her budding swimming career.

The Road to Excellence

In 1991 Inge earned four medals at the European Championships in Athens, Greece. She placed second in the 100-meter butterfly, third in the 50-meter freestyle, first in the 4×100-meter free relay, and third in the 4×100-meter medley relay. At the World Championships that year, she placed eighth and tenth in the 100-meter butterfly and 100-meter freestyle, respectively. At the 1992 Olympic Games in Barcelona, she took eighth place in the 50-meter freestyle, ninth in the 100-meter butterfly, and eighth with the 4×100-meter medley relay team.

The next year, 1993, was also important; Inge swam her personal best 100-meter butterfly time of 1:00.21, which placed her twelfth in the world. Throughout the early 1990's, Inge had moments of great success, in which she placed as high as the top three, but she dropped to eighth or tenth at other meets.

In 1996, Inge qualified for the Dutch Olympic team. Her drive and practice habits, however, were not stellar. Her times were not improving, her interest had waned, and she held a reputation at the pool as a somewhat lazy swimmer, talented enough to

Dutch swimmer Inge De Bruijn after winning her 50-meter freestyle heat in the 2000 Olympics. She went on to win the gold medal in the event.

AP/Wide World Photos

score well in competition but lacking the drive to continue improving and excelling. Before the Olympic Games rolled around, Inge's boyfriend and coach of the Dutch team, Jacco Verhaeren, advised her to stop attending practice. Inge did just that, leaving her swimming career and tough practice schedule behind and enjoying the more relaxed pace and activities of a non-swimming lifestyle.

The Emerging Champion

The time off was successful. Though common belief held that Inge had retired, her thoughts returned to swimming. The 1996 Olympics were difficult for her to watch on television and probably served as motivation to begin anew.

An American swimming friend of Inge's recommended she train with American, Paul Bergen, coach to former Olympian Tracy Caulkins, among others. Inge moved to Virginia, where she began a grueling training program very different from the Dutch style. In addition to pool training, which made up the majority of her training hours in the Netherlands, Bergen started Inge on an extensive dry-land schedule, including weightlifting, rope climbing, sit-ups and push-ups, bike riding, martial arts, Tae-Bo boxing (at the recommendation of American swimmer Dara Torres), and running. In the water, her workouts were made tougher by occasionally swimming with shoes, to create drag.

Inge's new workouts not only were longer and more demanding but also brought her into a different environment and demanded a new attitude toward the sport. She attacked the training with great vigor, proving herself a hard worker, punctual with practice and attentive to instruction. Physically, Inge grew much stronger; mentally, she became focused and driven. When her grandfather died in 1997, Bergen asked her to remain in the United States to train for an up-

STATISTICS			
Year	Competition	Event	Place
1991	European Championships	100-meter butterfly	2d
		50-meter freestyle	3d
		4×100-meter freestyle relay	1st
		4×100-meter medley relay	3d
1992	Olympic Games	50-meter freestyle	8th
		100-meter butterfly	9th
		4×100-meter medley relay	8th
1993	European Championships	50-meter freestyle	3d
		100-meter butterfly	4th
1995	European Championships	50-meter freestyle	4th
		100-meter butterfly	4th
1998	European Championships	50-meter freestyle	1st
		50-meter butterfly	1st
		100-meter butterfly	3d
		4×50-meter freestyle relay	2d
		4×50-meter medley relay	3d
1999	European Championships	50-meter freestyle	1st
		100-meter butterfly	1st
		100-meter freestyle	2d
	World Championships	50-meter freestyle	1st
		50-meter butterfly	3d
		4×100-meter freestyle relay	2d
2000	Olympic Games	50-meter freestyle	Gold
		100-meter freestyle	Gold
		100-meter butterfly	Gold WR
		4×100-meter freestyle relay	Silver

Note: WR = World Record

coming meet rather than return to the Netherlands and interrupt her mental focus with the emotional trauma of a death.

Continuing the Story

Inge followed Bergen to Beaverton, Oregon, where he began coaching the Tualatin Hills Swim Club. The training regimen, coupled with Inge's newfound drive, proved itself gradually and steadily, within a relatively short time. In the December, 1997, United States Open, she took second place in the 100-meter butterfly and fourth in the 100-meter freestyle. Her times were the best she had attained since 1993. At this meet, Bergen noted Australian swimmer Michael Klim's straight-arm recovery freestyle technique and began working with Inge on changing her stroke. This helped her as well.

At the 1998 Long Course World Championships Inge placed seventh in the 100-meter butterfly and eighth in the 100-meter freestyle. Later

627

that year at the Short Course European Championships she took a gold in the 50-meter butterfly and a bronze in the 100-meter butterfly. In 1999 she continued her ascent: At the Long Course European Championships she took two golds, in the 50-meter freestyle and the 100-meter butterfly, and a silver in the 100-meter freestyle.

In this same year she raised her world rankings to first in the 50-meter freestyle, second in the 100-meter freestyle, second in the 50-meter butterfly, and second in the 100-meter butterfly. Many of these times were personal bests, and Inge was now competing against the best in the world. Unlike in the past, in which her performances were more likely to be sporadic, she began consistently scoring high.

In the spring of 2000 Inge's prowess began to stun the world. She competed in several European meets in Sheffield, England; Monaco, Monte Carlo; and Amsterdam, the Netherlands. During this short time she set six world records and broke and reset three of them, including the 1994 50-meter freestyle record set by China's Li Jingyi. She dropped the 50-meter butterfly record by a half-second, remarkable for this short sprint event. Perhaps most remarkable was her 100-meter butterfly race in May, 2000; Mary T. Meagher's eighteen-year-old record had been broken just one year previously by Jenny Thompson, who shaved .05 second off the time. Inge, however, swam 1.19 seconds faster.

By the time the 2000 Sydney Olympics came around, Inge was in top physical and mental shape. She was also the topic of rumors. Various swimmers and coaches were suspicious of her amazing times, and there were rumors that Inge was using performance-enhancing drugs. She was compared to Irish swimmer Michelle Smith, who had risen to quick fame and fast times and later tested positive for drug use, resulting in sus-

pension from the sport. Inge underwent a series of drug tests, none of them positive. She credited her performances to "ruthless training" and pointed out that she had been an elite swimmer for many years but had never trained at her current, tough level. Many of those skeptical of Inge came to apologize or change their views after learning more about her training and becoming more familiar with her as a hard-working, ethical, and tough-minded athlete.

Despite the negative effect these rumors might have had on her performance, Inge swam to her all-time bests at Sydney. She took first in the 50-meter freestyle with a time of 24.32 seconds. Another gold came in the 100-meter freestyle (53.83), and a third gold was scored in the 100-meter butterfly (56.61), a new world record. She also helped the Dutch team to a silver in the 4×100-meter freestyle relay (3:39.83).

Summary

Inge De Bruijn has, through extremely hard work and dedication, gone from being a talented swimmer to a top-level performer. She was the world's most prolific female swimmer in 2000, breaking or tying eight world records over the span of a few months.

Michelle C. K. McKowen

Additional Sources:

Jeffrey, Josh. "Dutch Treat." *Swimming World and Junior Swimmer,* November 1, 1999, 25.

Michaelis, Vicki. "Rededicated to Winning De Bruijn Makes a Splash in Comeback." *USA Today,* September 5, 2000, p. Cl.

Whitten, Phillip. "Trouble de Bruijn?" *Sports Illustrated* 92 (June 19, 2000): 33.

"World and European Swimmers of the Year." *Swimming World and Junior Swimmer,* December 1, 2000, 30.

DAVE DeBUSSCHERE

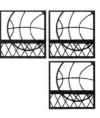

Sport: Basketball

Born: October 16, 1940
Detroit, Michigan

Early Life

Born October 16, 1940, in Detroit, Michigan, David Albert DeBusschere would spend the next twenty years of his life in the Motor City. He developed some of his physical strength by spending his afternoons and summers unloading boxcars for his father's business.

Dave attended Austin High School, a Catholic, all-boys school. He found his place as a top-notch athlete, successful in any sport he tried. "From as early as I can remember," Dave once recalled, "I just had the drive to excel in sport—football, baseball, basketball, you name it."

The Road to Excellence

Over the course of his career at Austin, Dave became the most highly publicized basketball player in the state of Michigan up to that time. As a senior, he led Austin to a state championship victory over Benton Harbor. In that game, Dave went up against Benton Harbor's star, Chet Walker. Their rivalry continued over the years, as both Dave and Walker became stars in the National Basketball Association (NBA) much later.

Dave decided to stay home to attend college, receiving an athletic scholarship from the University of Detroit. Detroit got quite a bargain in Dave, for not only was he an excellent basketball player, but he was equally talented on the baseball diamond, where he was a star pitcher. By the time his collegiate career was over, Dave was Detroit's all-time leading scorer, and, despite standing only 6 feet 6 inches tall, was also the top rebounder in school history.

Shortly after graduation in 1962, Dave was given a baseball contract with the Chicago White Sox that included a $160,000 bonus, and also signed a contract with the Detroit Pistons to play

basketball. Over the next four years, Dave played both sports professionally. The forty-eight consecutive months of competition were very strenuous, and Dave had doubts about his curve ball and control on the major league baseball level. He was quite successful on the basketball court, however. In his first four seasons with Detroit, he averaged nearly 15 points per game. When the Pistons, hoping he would play basketball exclusively, offered him a new contract as both player and coach, Dave accepted.

The Emerging Champion

At twenty-four, Dave was the youngest head coach in professional sports. With his additional responsibilities of coaching, Dave's record at the helm of the Pistons was less than spectacular. It

New York Knickerbockers

629

was a great relief for him when he was traded to the New York Knicks on December 19, 1968.

Dave broke the hearts of Detroit fans during his first game with the Knicks. Although he had yet to practice with New York, he scorched his former teammates for 21 points and 15 rebounds on the Pistons' home court.

Now in the media spotlight of New York, Dave, although an All-Star in Detroit, began to gain recognition as one of the best forwards in the National Basketball Association (NBA). He was much more comfortable on the Knicks, a more balanced and talented team than the Pistons. He did not score as much as he had in Detroit, but now he was able to excel in the areas in which he was most comfortable: rebounding and scoring. An intense, tough player, Dave almost always guarded the opposing teams' best forwards, usually holding them well below their scoring averages. His outstanding defensive efforts were appreciated by other players and coaches, as he was named to the NBA's All-Defensive team every year he played with the Knicks.

New York certainly benefited from Dave's team-oriented play, and he was a vital member of the teams that won NBA championships in 1970 and again in 1973, when Dave had his best scoring season with the Knicks up to that point, 16.3 points per game. It was during the 1973 playoffs, with Knick captain Willis Reed, the center, out with an injury, that Dave truly proved his worth.

Without Reed at center, New York coach Red Holzman turned to Dave to guard the great Wilt Chamberlain, who towered over Dave by seven inches. The unorthodox move paid off, and the Knicks won the contest. Dave, Paul Zimmerman, and Dick Schaap wrote an insightful book about the 1970 champion Knicks titled *The Open Man: The Championship Diary of the New York Knicks* (1970).

Continuing the Story

Dave's high standards of play continued despite his advancing age. When the Knicks needed someone to help pick up the scoring load in the 1973-1974 season, Dave responded with a remarkable 18.1 points per game at thirty-three years of age.

That was Dave's last season as a professional basketball player, but his presence was still felt off the court, as he put to good use his degree in business administration. Dave was named commissioner of the American Basketball Association (ABA) following his retirement, overseeing spectacular performances from the likes of Julius Erving and George McGinnis. Following the 1976 season, the ABA merged with its longtime rival, the NBA.

Without a league to head, Dave moved to the front office of a team close to where he had won two NBA championships with the Knicks, becoming general manager of the New Jersey Nets. In

STATISTICS

Season	G	FGM	FG%	FTM	FT%	Reb.	Ast.	PPG
1962-63	80	406	.430	206	.718	694	207	12.7
1963-64	15	52	.391	25	.581	105	23	8.6
1964-65	79	508	.425	306	.700	874	253	16.7
1965-66	79	524	.408	249	.659	916	209	16.4
1966-67	78	531	.415	361	.705	924	216	18.2
1967-68	80	573	.442	289	.664	1,081	181	17.9
1968-69	76	506	.444	229	.698	888	191	16.3
1969-70	79	488	.451	176	.688	790	194	14.6
1970-71	81	523	.421	217	.696	901	220	15.6
1971-72	80	520	.427	193	.728	901	291	15.4
1972-73	77	532	.435	194	.746	787	259	16.3
1973-74	71	559	.461	164	.756	757	253	18.1
Totals	**875**	**13,249**	**.432**	**2,609**	**.699**	**9,618**	**2,497**	**16.1**

Notes: GP = games played; FGM = field goals made; FG% = field goal percentage; FTM = free throws made; FT% = free throw percentage; Reb. = rebounds; Ast. = assists; TP = total points; PPG = points per game

HONORS, AWARDS, AND RECORDS

1963	NBA All-Rookie Team
1966-68, 1970-73	NBA All-Star Team
1967	NBA record for the most field goals in one quarter of an All-Star Game (18)
1969	All-NBA Team
1969-74	NBA All-Defensive Team
1982	Inducted into Naismith Memorial Basketball Hall of Fame
1996	NBA 50 Greatest Players of All Time Team Uniform number 22 retired by New York Knicks

1982, he received one of the greatest honors a basketball player can receive: election to the Naismith Memorial Basketball Hall of Fame.

Between 1982 and 1986, Dave served as the general manager of the Knicks. He was responsible for choosing Patrick Ewing from Georgetown as the first overall draft pick in the 1985 NBA lttery. After his days as general manager, he became involved in the commercial real estate business. In 1996, Dave was named to the NBA's 50 Greatest Players of All Time Team. He serves as a vice president in charge of corporate real estate development for Williamson, Picket, and Gross, which is located in lower Manhattan, New York.

Summary

It takes not only great talent to play two sports professionally, but a great work ethic and desire as well. Dave DeBusschere possessed all these qualities, as he was able to play both professional baseball and professional basketball for four years. Once dedicated solely to basketball, Dave's attributes were obvious, and he will always be remembered as one of the grittiest forwards ever to play the game.

Stephen T. Bell

Additional Sources:

Bjarkman, Peter C. *The Biographical History of Basketball.* Chicago: Masters Press, 1998.

Dolin, Nick, Chris Dolin, and David Check. *Basketball Stars: The Greatest Players in the History of the Game.* New York: Black Dog and Leventhal, 1997.

Kalinsky, George, and Phil Berger. *The New York Knicks: The Official Fiftieth Anniversary Celebration.* New York: Macmillan, 1996.

Mallozzi, Vincent M. *Basketball: The Legends and the Game.* Willowdale, Ont.: Firefly Books, 1998.

Shouler, Kenneth A. *The Experts Pick Basketball's Best Fifty Players in the Last Fifty Years.* Lenexa, Kans.: Addax, 1998.

MARY DECKER-SLANEY

Sport: Track and field (middle- and long-distance runs)

Born: August 4, 1958
Flemington, New Jersey

Early Life

Mary Decker was born on August 4, 1958, in Flemington, New Jersey. Soon after, her family moved to Huntington Beach, California, where she graduated from high school in 1976.

Childhood for Mary was not always easy and at times was full of stress. Mary's parents divorced when she was young, leaving Mary, her sister Denise, and brother John with her mother, while her father took care of her younger sister, Christine.

Mary turned to running as her outlet from the stress she experienced at home. She entered and won her first cross-country race without even knowing what the sport was, and soon was winning all the local road races in her area.

The Road to Excellence

The first track club Mary ran for was the Long Beach Comets, which she joined at the age of eleven. Even as a young girl, Mary was a natural at distance running. Her racehorse-like form and great heart for competition quickly led her to become an international competitor.

The summer of 1973 was the first exposure of the "Pigtailed American Darling" to the newspaper headlines, when she beat the Soviet standout Niele Sabaite in the half-mile in Minsk. In this one race, "little Mary Decker" found a place in the hearts of all Americans.

Mary continued to press on, and while still in pigtails and braces, she began an extensive training regime in order to reach her goal of the 1976 Olympic competition. Although her heart was with the 1976 Olympic team, her body had virtually collapsed beneath her. Because of the stressful training and large number of competitions, Mary developed lower-leg ailments and needed two operations to relieve her of constant pain.

Mary's legs healed and she continued to train and reset her goal for the 1980 Olympic team, only to be sidelined again because of the American boycott of the 1980 Olympic Games.

The Emerging Champion

In the early 1980's, Mary began working with Athletics West coach and physiologist Dick Brown. He was able to channel Mary's passion for running into limited, intense training and to reduce her injuries. Her perseverance paid off, and in 1982 she set eight world records and

Mary Decker-Slaney running in a 5,000-meter heat at the 1996 Olympics.

AP/Wide World Photos

632

STATISTICS

Year	Competition	Event	Place	Time
1974	National AAU Outdoor Championships	440-yard	1st	2:05.20
	National AAU Indoor Championships	880-yard	1st	2:07.10
1983	World Championships	1,500 meters	1st	4:00.90
	World Championships	3,000 meters	1st	8:34.62
1988	Olympic Games	1,500 meters	8th	—
	Olympic Games	3,000 meters	10th	—

eleven American records in distances ranging from the 1 mile to the 10,000 meters. In the summer of 1983, she won two gold medals in the 1,500 meters and 3,000 meters at the World Championships in Helsinki. Everything was finally on track for Mary as she pursued her now longtime obsession, to compete in the 1984 Olympic Games in Los Angeles.

The Los Angeles Games were to be Mary's time for triumph. When the gun went off in the 3,000-meter race, the fans were entranced as Mary led a tight lead pack of four runners, including the young, barefoot runner, Zola Budd, South Africa's version of Mary Decker. The crowd and runners were completely unprepared for what happened next. At 1,700 meters, Mary's swift legs entangled with Zola's bare heel and Mary tumbled to the infield in agony. Tears of anguish came to the competitor who had once again been stripped of her long-awaited chance for Olympic gold.

Continuing the Story

Shortly after the "Great Fall" of the 1984 Olympic Games, Mary married Richard Slaney, an Olympic discus thrower from England. With his support and confidence, Mary continued to train and pursue her running goals. In 1985, a year after the memorable Olympic Games, Mary set the world record in the mile at 4 minutes 16.7 seconds.

With running going well again, motherhood was her next goal. She hoped that childbearing would increase her strength for the 1988 Olympic Games, but pregnancy was difficult and Mary was unable to train during much of the nine months. Within two weeks of delivery, Mary started to make up for her time missed, but ended up injured and sidelined for more than a

year in 1986-1987. Again she healed, and again set out, determined to win in the 1988 Olympics.

In the 3,000-meter race in Seoul, Mary tore from the starting line in pursuit of her elusive gold. She led with a furious pace that eventually had to slow down around the 1,000-meter mark. With only five laps to go, Vicki Huber of the United States made a move and passed the fading Mary, who finished a disappointing tenth. Later that week, Mary flirted briefly with the lead in the 1,500-meter race, but again her pace was too quick and she ended, unsatisfied, in eighth place.

Olympic gold continued to elude Mary. She failed to advance past the trials for Barcelona in 1992. She spent the next three years recovering from various injuries, including a number of stress fractures. In 1996, however, she competed

RECORDS

Two world indoor records in 1980: 1,500 meters (4:00.8), 800-yard (1:59.7)

World indoor record at 1,000 yards in 1978 (2:23.8)

Three American outdoor records in 1985: 800 meters (1:56.90), 1 mile (4:16.17) WR, 3,000 meters (8:25.83)

American outdoor records at 1,000 meters in 1988 (2:34.65), 1,500 meters in 1983 (3:57.12), 2,000 meters in 1984 (5:37.7), 10,000 meters in 1982 (31:35.3)

American indoor records at 800 meters in 1980 (1:58.9), 1,000 meters in 1989 (2:37.6), 1 mile in 1982 (4:20.5), 2,000 meters in 1985 (5:34.52)

Collegiate best at 880 yards in 1978 (2:03.5)

Collegiate best at 1,000 yards in 1978 (2:23.8)

Set 8 world records and 11 American records in 1982 at distances ranging from 1 mile to 10,000 meters

HONORS AND AWARDS

1980	Today's Sportswoman Award Saettel Award, Track
1980, 1982	Track and Field News Indoor Athlete of the Year
1980, 1982-83	Women's Sports Foundation Amateur Sportswoman of the Year
1982	Associated Press Female Athlete of the Year Sullivan Award
1983	Sports Illustrated Sportswoman of the Year Jesse Owens Award

633

in her final Olympic Games, finishing the 5,000-meter qualifying heat in seventh place and failing to advance.

Summary

Many track and field fans who have watched Mary Decker-Slaney grow up have been dismayed by the struggles and setbacks in her career. Yet Mary herself has come to terms with both her talent and her upsets. She has become a role model to all young athletes by proving that love for a sport and competitiveness can keep one going against all odds.

Elizabeth Jeanne Alford

Additional Sources:

Bateman, Hal. *United States Track and Field Olympians, 1896-1980.* Indianapolis, Ind.: The Athletics Congress of the United States, 1984.

Hickok, Ralph. *A Who's Who of Sports Champions.* Boston: Houghton Mifflin, 1995.

The Lincoln Library of Sports Champions. 16 vols. Columbus, Ohio: Frontier Press, 1993.

Wallechinsky, David. *The Complete Book of the Olympics.* Boston: Little, Brown and Company, 1991.

Watman, Mel. *Encyclopedia of Track and Field Athletics.* New York: St. Martin's Press, 1981.

ANITA DeFRANTZ

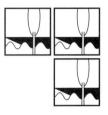

Sport: Rowing

Born: October 4, 1952
Philadelphia, Pennsylvania

Early Life

Anita DeFrantz was born October 4, 1952, in Philadelphia, Pennsylvania, and grew up in Indianapolis, Indiana. Anita's parents were always active in the community. Her father worked for Community Action Against Poverty, and her mother was a teacher who eventually became a professor of education at the University of San Francisco.

Anita always liked sports and played football with her three brothers when she was young. When she was nine, she became a competitive swimmer, competing for two years. Anita could not train as much as her competitors, however, because the swimming pool at which she trained opened in June and closed in August. Anita's more well-off competitors could swim year-round in indoor pools.

Because swimming was out of the question, Anita became a basketball fan. In her own words, she could "watch basketball for hours," and she gave up any hope of becoming a competitive athlete.

The Road to Excellence

One day when Anita was strolling on the Connecticut College campus in New London, rowing coach Bart Gulong invited her to try out for his team. Gulong believed that Anita, at 5 feet 11 inches, could be an excellent rower. Soon after, Gulong could tell that Anita had a feeling for the sport. He recommended that she begin rowing in the summers at the Vesper Boat Club in Philadelphia and that she try out for the United States rowing team.

Anita took his advice and moved to Philadelphia in 1974 to row. At the same time, she studied law at the University of Pennsylvania Law School. In 1975, she raced her way into the coxed four that won the National team trials and placed sixth at the World Championships Coxed Four.

Anita enjoyed racing at the World Championships and set her sights on the Montreal Olympics in 1976. This was a critical time for Anita,

U. S. Olympic rower Anita DeFrantz at a news conference in New York, where she announced a suit against the U. S. Olympic Committee because of the American boycott of the 1980 Olympics in Moscow.

635

when her skills as both a lawyer and a rower were developing. Her training went well, and Anita earned a bronze medal on the 1976 United States Eight, placing third behind East Germany and the Soviet Union.

That same year, she enjoyed her first success in the political arena. Anita served on the United States Olympic Committee's Athletes Advisory Council, where she forcefully argued at congressional hearings that athletes should be free to compete when and where they choose. Prior to this time, athletes could compete only with the permission of the Amateur Athletic Union (AAU) or the National Collegiate Athletic Association (NCAA). In 1976, Anita established herself as one who would fight for the needs of athletes.

The Emerging Champion

Anita continued her training in Philadelphia and set her sights on a gold medal at the 1980 Olympics, which were scheduled to be held in Moscow, the Soviet Union. At the United States Nationals in 1977, she placed first in the straight pair, a two-person racing shell that is the most difficult boat to row. In the 1978 World Championships, she raced in both the coxed four and the eight-oared shell, winning a silver in the coxed four and placing fourth in the eight. Her ninth-place finish in the coxed four in 1979 was disappointing, but inspired her to work especially hard for the 1980 Olympics. That would be her final year in world championship competition.

One evening in January, 1980, Anita was at a friend's birthday party when she heard President Jimmy Carter announce that the United States Olympic team would not compete in Moscow because of the Soviet invasion of Afghanistan. Carter believed that the best way to tell the world that this invasion was wrong was for the United States Olympic team to boycott the Olympics. Suddenly, Anita's training as a lawyer and an athlete made her an invaluable asset to athletes in sport politics. She knew the law and she knew sport. Once again, Anita would fight for the rights of athletes to determine when and where they compete.

Anita knew that the United States Olympic Committee (USOC) could enter a team in Moscow over the objections of President Carter. Athletes in Great Britain had done just this and were successful. Anita became the representative of American Olympic athletes and was so persuasive that President Carter sent Vice President Walter Mondale to meet with the USOC. Mondale argued that a United States boycott of the Moscow Olympics was crucial to the nation.

Anita's speech to the USOC House of Delegates drew cheers, but it was not enough. They voted 2 to 1 not to go to Moscow, and Anita and her fellow Olympians were not allowed to compete. Her dream of an Olympic gold medal had ended.

Continuing the Story

The end of Anita's athletic career was the beginning of her career as one of the most powerful people in the world of Olympic sports. In 1981, Peter Ueberroth, Chair of the Los Angeles Olympic Organizing Committee, asked Anita to work with the Olympic Committee to keep nations from boycotting the 1984 Olympics. She was incredibly successful, talking forty-three of the forty-four black African nations out of boycotting the 1984 Olympics.

Anita did not stop there. She was named to the International Olympic Committee in 1986, only the fifth woman ever to hold a committee position. She also became president of the Amateur Athletic Foundation of Los Angeles, the group that administers the profits from the 1984 Olympics. Both positions allow Anita to help athletes begin the

MAJOR CHAMPIONSHIPS

Year	Competition	Event	Place
1975	U.S. Nationals	Elite four-oared shell with coxswain	1st
	World Championships	Four-oared shell with coxswain	6th
1976	Olympic Games	Eight-oared shell	Bronze
1977	U.S. Nationals	Elite pair shell	1st
	U.S. Nationals	Elite eight-oared shell	1st
1978	U.S. Nationals	Elite pair shell	1st
	U.S. Nationals	Elite four-oared shell with coxswain	1st
	World Championships	Four-oared shell with coxswain	2d
1979	U.S. Nationals	Elite four-oared shell with coxswain	1st
	World Championships	Four-oared shell with coxswain	9th

HONORS AND AWARDS

Bronze Medal of the Olympic Order
Jackie Robinson Sports Achievement Award
NAACP Black Woman of Achievement Award
Named to *Sporting News* "100 Most Powerful People in Sports" list

journey toward their Olympic dreams.

Anita played a crucial role in getting women's soccer and softball recognized as medal sports in the Atlanta Games in 1996. In 1997, Anita achieved another milestone when she became the first woman to serve as vice-president of the IOC executive committee. She was expected by many to become the president of the IOC when the current president retired. However, when a new president was elected in mid-2001, she received a disappointing number of votes.

Summary

Anita DeFrantz has continued to represent that part of Olympic sport that seems to need it the most: the athletes. Surprising as it seems, most political decisions regarding sport do not consider the needs of athletes. Although Anita never won an Olympic gold medal herself, her efforts are making it possible for others to do so. Indeed, Anita's beliefs are best summarized by her motto: "Sport belongs to everybody."

Steven G. Estes

Additional Sources:

Johnston, David. "Anita DeFrantz: Putting Her Oar In." *American Visions* 3 (1988): 12-14.

Lamb, Yanick Rice. "Olympic Legends." *Essence* 26 (January, 1996): 89-97.

Lewis, Linda. *Water's Edge: Women Who Push the Limits in Rowing, Kayaking, and Canoeing.* Seattle, Wash.: Seal Press, 1992.

Moore, Kenny. "An Advocate for Athletes." *Sports Illustrated* 69 (August 29, 1988): 132-135.

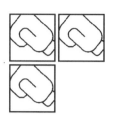

OSCAR DE LA HOYA

Sport: Boxing

Born: February 4, 1973
Los Angeles, California

Early Life

Oscar de la Hoya was born on February 4, 1973, in East Los Angeles, California, to Joel de la Hoya, a shipping and receiving clerk, and Cecilia de la Hoya.

Boxing was a part of several generations of Oscar's large and close-knit Mexican American family. Before moving to the United States, Oscar's grandfather, Vincente de la Hoya, had been an amateur featherweight boxer in Durango, Mexico, and Joel had been a professional boxer in Los Angeles in his youth.

Oscar's first experience in the ring was at the age of six, when Joel entered him in Pee-Wee boxing tournaments at the neighborhood Resurrection Boys Club. In his debut fight, young Oscar knocked out his opponent in the first round.

In addition to being a family tradition, boxing shielded Oscar from the tensions of a notoriously dangerous city. The pressures of gangs, drugs, and crime were widespread in East Los Angeles. Once, Oscar was mugged by gang members as he walked home from his girlfriend's

Oscar de la Hoya (left) fights Hector Camacho in a 1997 championship bout.

RECOGNIZED JUNIOR-LIGHTWEIGHT CHAMPIONSHIP FIGHTS

Date	Location	Loser	Result
Mar. 5, 1994	Los Angeles, Calif.	Jimmi Bredahl	10th-round technical knockout
May 27, 1994	Las Vegas, Nev.	Giorgio Campanella	3rd-round technical knockout

RECOGNIZED LIGHTWEIGHT CHAMPIONSHIP FIGHTS

Date	Location	Loser	Result
July 29, 1994	Las Vegas, Nev.	Jorge Paez	2d-round knockout
Nov. 18, 1994	Las Vegas, Nev.	Carl Griffith	3rd-round knockout
Dec. 10, 1994	Los Angeles, Calif.	John Avila	9th-round technical knockout
Feb. 18, 1995	Las Vegas, Nev.	John-John Molina	12th-round decision
May 6, 1995	Las Vegas, Nev.	Rafael Ruelas	2d-round technical knockout
Sept. 9, 1995	Las Vegas, Nev.	Genaro Hernandez	6th-round technical knockout
Dec. 15, 1995	New York, N.Y.	Jesse James Leija	2d-round technical knockout
June 7, 1996	Las Vegas, Nev.	Julio César Chávez	4th-round technical knockout
Jan. 18, 1997	Las Vegas, Nev.	Miguel Angel Gonzalez	12th-round decision
Apr. 12, 1997	Las Vegas, Nev.	Pernell Whitaker	12th-round decision
Jun. 14, 1997	San Antonio, Tex.	David Kamau	2d-round knockout
Sept. 13, 1997	Las Vegas, Nev.	Hector Camacho	12th-round decision
Dec. 6, 1997	Atlantic City, N.J.	Wilfredo Rivera	8th-round technical knockout
June 13, 1998	El Paso, Tex.	Patrick Charpentier	3rd-round technical knockout
Sept. 18, 1998	Las Vegas, Nev.	Julio César Chávez	8th-round technical knockout
Feb. 13, 1999	Las Vegas, Nev.	Ike Quartey	12th-round decision
May 22, 1999	Las Vegas, Nev.	Oba Carr	11th-round technical knockout
Sept. 18, 1999	Las Vegas, Nev.	Oscar De La Hoya (Felix Trinidad, winner)	12th-round decision
Feb. 26, 2000	New York, N.Y.	Derrel Coley	7th-round knockout
Jun. 17, 2000	Los Angeles, Calif.	Oscar De La Hoya (Shane Mosely, winner)	12th-round decision

house. Frequently, he could hear the sounds of gunshots echoing just a few blocks away. Unlike some of his peers who became caught up in this violent street life, Oscar went directly to the Resurrection Gym on South Lorena Street every day after school.

The Road to Excellence

The long hours spent sparring in the ring paid off quickly for Oscar. His trainer during these first years was former Los Angeles policeman Al Stankie. Stankie had guided another boxer from East Los Angeles, Paul Gonzalez, to an Olympic gold medal in 1984.

Oscar won his first national championship, the 119-pound Junior Olympic title, in 1988 at the age of fifteen. His skill was widely recognized, especially his confident way of moving and punching with a powerful left hook. Many people called the 5-foot 11-inch lightweight a "natural" at the sport. They marveled at his rapid development inside the ring and noticed his likable spirit outside it. In 1989, he earned the national Golden Gloves 125-pound title. One year later,

he won the 125-pound division of the United States Boxing Championships.

Indeed, 1990 was a pivotal year for Oscar. As the youngest participant at the Goodwill Games in Seattle, he brought home his first gold medal. He also returned home knowing for the first time that his mother was terminally ill.

The day after the Goodwill Games ended, the de la Hoya family told Oscar that Cecilia had breast cancer. Until then, he was unaware that she had been receiving radiation therapy for many months. The news was devastating for Oscar, who thought of Cecilia as his best friend. When she died at the age of thirty-nine in October, 1990, the young champion vowed to win her the highest honor, a gold medal, at the Olympic Games in Barcelona.

The next year brought other changes in Oscar's life. He was graduated from Garfield High School, where he had been a good student and had particularly enjoyed classes in art and architecture. He also switched coaches, replacing Stankie with Robert Alcazar. Frequent victories followed at home and abroad, including gold

639

CUMULATIVE STATISTICS

Bouts, 34
Knockouts, 26
Bouts won by decision, 1

HONORS AND AWARDS

1991-92	USA Boxing Boxer of the Year
1992	Gold Medal, Olympic Boxing
1995	*Ring* magazine Fighter of the Year
	Edward J. Neil Trophy

medals at the 1991 U.S. Olympic Sports Festival and the 1991 U.S. Amateur Boxing tournament. USA Boxing voted Oscar the 1991 Boxer of the Year.

That fall, Oscar also suffered his first defeat in four years. After thirty-six consecutive victories in international competition, Oscar lost to Marco Rudolph of Germany at the World Championships in Sydney, Australia. Initially, the loss confused Oscar, who had grown accustomed to winning. Before long, however, he realized that the experience had helped him to rediscover his determination for the sport. With renewed enthusiasm, Oscar prepared for his greatest challenge yet: the 1992 Summer Olympic Games.

The Emerging Champion

Making the U.S. Olympic boxing team was easy for Oscar. Tryouts in Massachusetts and Arizona earned him a place among other American amateur athletes bound for Barcelona, Spain, in July. Once he was there, however, the thrill of Olympic competition was diminished by judging that sometimes seemed unfair to Oscar and his coaches. Still, Oscar steadily advanced from one round to the next in the 132-pound class.

In his first match, he knocked out Adison Silva of Brazil. He then outpointed Moses Odion of Nigeria and Dimitrov Tontchev of Bulgaria to advance to the semifinals. In that round, South Korean boxer Hong Sung Sik proved to be a difficult opponent. His wrestling-like style distracted Oscar, but the young American won by a single point.

This narrow triumph was critical. Because of it, Oscar advanced to a gold-medal bout against the only boxer to defeat him since childhood:

Marco Rudolph of Germany. On August 8, he avenged the loss that had bothered him in Australia by beating Rudolph. By a convincing score of 7-2, Oscar fulfilled his promise to his mother and won the U.S. team's only gold medal in boxing of the 1992 Games.

Continuing the Story

While Oscar was sad that Cecilia could not share his triumph, there were many reasons for happiness after winning the Olympic gold. As an amateur, Oscar had achieved an astonishing record: 225 wins and only 5 losses, with 153 knockouts. Because of this record, Oscar signed one of the richest deals in boxing history, a million-dollar contract with New York managers Bob Mittleman and Steve Nelson. The package included cash, cars, and a new house in Montebello, California, for his family. Oscar also signed contracts with a promoter and an agent, who would handle endorsement deals.

Oscar's professional debut occurred on November 23, 1992, at the Los Angeles Forum. Wearing a black sombrero and carrying both an American and a Mexican flag as he walked into the ring, East L.A.'s "Golden Boy" knocked out competitor Lamar Williams after only one minute and forty-two seconds. More than ever, observers said that Oscar was destined for stardom. After running off eleven wins—ten by knockout—in less than a year, Oscar met Jimmi Bredahl for the World Boxing Organization (WBO) junior-lightweight title. In the tenth round, Oscar scored a technical knockout (TKO) to capture his first professional championship. In 1994, he moved up to the lightweight division and knocked out Jorge Paez for the WBO's vacant lightweight title.

On May 6, 1995, Oscar added the IBF lightweight title to his collection by scoring a second-round TKO against Rafael Ruelas. In that year, he was also named *Ring* magazine's Fighter of the Year. By April of 1996, Oscar had abandoned his lightweight titles as he moved up in weight to the junior welterweight division. He faced the aging but still dangerous Julio César Chávez on June 7, overpowering him with a fourth-round TKO.

In 1997, Oscar moved up in weight again, this time to face Pernell "Sweet Pea" Whittaker for the WBC welterweight title. In a very close fight,

640

which many thought Whittaker should have won, Oscar took a twelfth-round decision and began a lengthy reign at the top of the welterweight division.

Oscar's reign ended controversially on September 18, 1999, when he suffered his first loss in a close decision to Felix Trinidad. Oscar seemed to have the fight well in hand going into the final rounds, but his failure to seal the victory convincingly and Trinidad's aggressive approach in the final rounds swayed the judges in Trinidad's favor.

After defeating Derrel Coley to win the IBF welterweight title on February 26, 2000, Oscar faced the undefeated Sugar Shane Mosely on June 17 in Los Angeles. In a much anticipated bout, both fighters electrified the crowd with their speed and power. Mosely won by split decision after landing 45 of 88 punches in the final round, handing Oscar his second loss in three fights.

Summary

Oscar de la Hoya overcame the obstacles of childhood in East Los Angeles and his mother's death to win the United States' only gold medal in boxing at the 1992 Olympics. His quick rise to the forefront of the sport led him to be called "the pride of East L.A." and the "Golden Boy." Though he suffered two disappointing losses, he remained one of boxing's most popular and powerful fighters and one of the most dominant welterweights in boxing history.

Alecia C. Townsend Beckie

Additional Sources:

Mullan, Harry. *The Ultimate Encyclopedia of Boxing: The Definitive Illustrated Guide to World Boxing.* Edison, N.J.: Chartwell Books, 1996.

Schulman, Arlene. *The Prize Fighters: An Intimate Look at Champions and Contenders.* New York: Lyons and Burford, 1994.

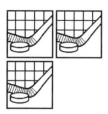

ALEX DELVECCHIO

Sport: Ice hockey

Born: December 4, 1931
Fort Williams, Ontario, Canada

Early Life

Alex Peter Delvecchio was born on December 4, 1931, in Fort Williams, Ontario, Canada. Like most of the youth in the area where he grew up, Alex spent his winters playing hockey on the frozen outdoor rinks of Ontario. The weather was never too cold to be outdoors practicing. Hockey seemed like the most natural thing in the world to Alex. The determination for excellence and love of the game would show up later in

Alex's life. He would become one of the few professionals to play in the National Hockey League (NHL) for twenty or more seasons. The amazing thing about Alex's career is that he played on only one team, the Detroit Red Wings.

The Road to Excellence

Alex started his professional ascent with the Oshawa Generals of the Ontario Hockey Association Junior A League. After one highly successful season there and six games with the Indianapolis Caps of the American Hockey League, Alex was called up to the big-league team during the 1950-

Alex Delvecchio, right, celebrates a victory with Detroit Red Wings teammates Ted Lindsay, left, and Gordie Howe, center.

1951 season. In his first full year with Detroit, Alex scored 15 goals and impressed both coaches and fans alike with the style of hockey that he played. Once established as a player who could hold his own, Alex starred on left wing and center for the next twenty-three years. During this time, he would become recognized as one of the great players of the game. Alex was not only a great player but also one who would be lucky for most of his career. Aside from his own talent, which was impressive, he had the good fortune to play with some of the greatest stars ever to put on skates. For most of his career, Alex played with the immortal Gordie Howe, possibly the best hockey player ever. Add to that the goaltending of Terry Sawchuk, and the nucleus of a formidable team was established in Detroit. No one man can carry a team for a whole season, but the assembly of stars that played together in Detroit provided the fans with great hockey for many years. Alex was always an important member of that team.

The Emerging Champion

In 1962, when the great Gordie Howe stepped down, the team captaincy was passed on to Alex. It was recognized that Alex had the ability and leadership qualities to carry on the great Detroit tradition. Also, some long-deserved recognition would come his way. It was not easy being a player of Alex's caliber and yet not being the star of his team. Detroit had the legendary Howe and a supporting cast of All-Stars.

In 1962, Alex became only the third Red Wing to score 200 goals in a career. That was in a time when the league had only six teams and goals were harder to score. It would be another four years before Alex would pass the 300 career goal mark. In 1969, Alex became only the third skater to pass the 1,000 career point total, joining Gordie Howe and Jean Beliveau. In 1970, Alex became only the fifth player to score 400 goals. The other players who preceded him into the 400-goal club were teammate Howe, Maurice "Rocket" Richard, Beliveau, and Bobby Hull.

Whereas other players had a great year or two, Alex put together a great career. In thirteen separate seasons, he scored at least 20 goals. He never accumulated more than 37 penalty minutes in any one season, thus showing great sportsman-

STATISTICS

Season	GP	G	Ast.	Pts.	PIM
1950-51	1	0	0	0	0
1951-52	65	15	22	37	22
1952-53	70	16	43	59	28
1953-54	69	11	18	29	34
1954-55	69	17	31	48	37
1955-56	70	25	26	51	24
1956-57	48	16	25	41	8
1957-58	70	21	38	59	22
1958-59	70	19	35	54	6
1959-60	70	19	28	47	8
1960-61	70	27	35	62	26
1961-62	70	26	43	69	18
1962-63	70	20	44	64	8
1963-64	70	23	30	53	11
1964-65	68	25	42	67	16
1965-66	70	31	38	69	16
1966-67	70	17	38	55	10
1967-68	74	22	48	70	14
1968-69	72	25	58	83	8
1969-70	73	21	47	68	24
1971-72	75	20	45	65	22
1972-73	77	18	53	71	13
1973-74	11	1	4	5	2
Totals	1,549	456	825	1,281	383

Notes: GP = games played; G = goals; Ast. = assists; Pts. = points; PIM = penalties in minutes

ship along with his ability. He was a three-time winner of the Lady Byng Trophy, which is handed out to the league's most gentlemanly player. One season, the offensive trio of Alex and teammates Gordie Howe and Frank Mahovlich produced a then record 114 goals.

Continuing the Story

In 1973, with the Red Wings in despair, Alex was hired as the new head coach. He had appeared in eleven games as a player that season before hanging up his skates and taking over the bench duties. He had ended his playing days with 456 goals and 825 assists in 1,549 hockey games; he also scored 35 goals and 69 assists during 121 playoff games.

In 1974, the task of general manager was added to Alex's coaching job. When an offer came from the rival World Hockey League, Alex chose to stay with his "family," the Detroit Red Wings. Things did not progress as Alex had envisioned, however. The team was not playing like it should and the fans were clamoring for more. As is sometimes the case when a team does not play well, the coach loses his job. In 1977, Alex was

643

HONORS AND AWARDS

1953	NHL Second Team All-Star
1959, 1966, 1969	Lady Byng Memorial Trophy
1974	Lester Patrick Trophy
1977	Inducted into Hockey Hall of Fame

fired. In that same year, he was elected into the Hockey Hall of Fame. Also, the city of Thunder Bay, Ontario, honored the great player with an Alex Delvecchio Day.

Summary

Consistency and reliability were the trademarks of Alex Delvecchio's career. He was able to play a tough game yet handle it like a gentleman. Alex was fortunate to play on some great Red Wing teams, loaded with tremendous talent. That, however, should not distract from the amount of natural ability and leadership qualities that he possessed. He was a great addition to a fine team and proved his on-ice worthiness each time he stepped onto the rink. His induction into the Hall of Fame was a justly deserved accolade at the end of his brilliant career.

Carmi Brandis

Additional Sources:

Fischler, Stan, and Shirley Walter Fischler. *The Hockey Encyclopedia.* New York: Macmillan, 1983.

Kariher, Harry C. *Who's Who in Hockey.* New Rochelle, N.Y.: Arlington House, 1973.

JIMMY DEMARET

Sport: Golf

Born: May 25, 1910
     Houston, Texas
Died: December 28, 1983
     Houston, Texas

Early Life

James Newton Demaret was born May 25, 1910, in Houston, Texas. He was one of nine children of a carpenter. Unlike many golfers who learn the game from their fathers, Jimmy was not in a position to take up hobbies. He was faced early in life with the need to earn enough money to live on.

Occasionally people who rise to success from a difficult background are hard-driving and ruthless. Having known poverty, they will allow nothing to place them at risk of a return to that state. Jimmy had an entirely different attitude. He was a happy-go-lucky, friendly person who enjoyed parties and continually engaged in banter.

The Road to Excellence

Jimmy became interested in golf as a means of earning money, not as an activity valued for its own sake. Money was available through local tournaments and through gambling in rounds with wealthy amateurs. The game was not Jimmy's main source of funds, however: He worked as a nightclub singer with a band.

The Texas courses had low, rolling areas near the green that encouraged, and demanded, a delicate touch. Like his friend Jack Burke, Jimmy developed into an excellent wedge player. Because of the flat surfaces of the courses, one's putter would often be used in shots to approach the green—the so-called "Texas wedge." Jimmy added this technique to his repertoire, further enhancing his skill in the short game. He was also superb with long irons.

His ability and technique enabled him early to dominate Texas professional golf. He won a number of local tournaments, including the Texas

Jimmy Demaret during the 1949 Ryder Cup tournament.

Professional Golfers Association (PGA) Championship five times in succession. He decided to turn full-time professional in 1938. It was at once apparent that his decision was sound. He won the important Los Angeles Open in his first full year on the circuit, 1939.

The Emerging Champion

As Jimmy rose to national prominence in the late 1930's, golf fans encountered a player the likes of whom they had never before seen. He specialized in colorful clothes—bright orange or blue trousers were favorites. To Jimmy, a golf cap was no mere article of convenience but an opportunity to display a riot of colors. Conservative golfers, who might otherwise have protested, would only shake their heads. By his constant good-natured conversation on the course, he charmed both galleries and his fellow professionals. Throughout his career, Jimmy was among the best-liked players in the game.

Jimmy demonstrated that he was much more than a comedian on the course. Quite the contrary, he soon proved to be one of the best golfers in the country. In 1940, he won the Masters Tournament, establishing a tournament record in the process. In the final 18 holes of the tournament, he scored an incredibly low 60. The Masters was the most important of the seven tournaments he won in 1940, six of them in row.

His ability reached its peak just before the United States entered World War II, and Jimmy served in the Navy during the years—the early 1940's—in which he would have had the best chance of dominating the game. As always, Jimmy was not discouraged. He emerged from

military service with both his personality and his golf game intact.

He immediately resumed his rank among the leaders. He won the Masters Tournament again in 1947, and in 1948, he finished second in the United States Open. He became the first three-time winner of the Masters in 1950: He won the tournament with a strong closing round of 69. In 1947, he was the leading money winner. His purses totaled $27,936, a very high amount for golfers in the 1940's.

In spite of his success, two weaknesses plagued his game. He devoted little time to practice. He much preferred late-night parties and dancing, no doubt reflecting his earlier career as an entertainer. Sam Snead once suggested that Jimmy's lack of practice made him play far below his potential.

Continuing the Story

This weakness raises a question. Why did Jimmy fail to discipline himself adequately to take a commanding place among his contemporaries? He lacked the driving intensity characteristic of most champions: As long as he did well and enjoyed himself, he was content. His lack of aggressiveness made him especially vulnerable in match play. He was uninterested in struggling against an opponent face-to-face, and players more intent on victory could usually beat him. Once, after losing a match to Ben Hogan in the PGA Championship, he joked that the turning point of the match was Hogan's appearance on the course. Nevertheless, his ability enabled him to reach the semifinals of the PGA four times.

A further obstacle confronted him. Jimmy had the misfortune to play his golf at the same time as three of the foremost players of all time: Sam Snead, Byron Nelson, and Ben Hogan. Owing to the unusually difficult competition, Jimmy was unable to win a major title besides the Masters. An illustration of the forces with which he had to contend is the outcome of the 1948 United States Open. Jimmy broke the previous course record for the Open by three strokes, but Hogan broke it by five. Jimmy's best finish in the Open was his second place in the 1948 tournament; he finished fourth or better three times. Altogether, he won some forty tournaments in his career.

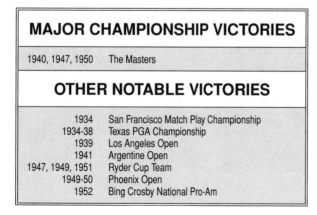

MAJOR CHAMPIONSHIP VICTORIES	
1940, 1947, 1950	The Masters

OTHER NOTABLE VICTORIES	
1934	San Francisco Match Play Championship
1934-38	Texas PGA Championship
1939	Los Angeles Open
1941	Argentine Open
1947, 1949, 1951	Ryder Cup Team
1949-50	Phoenix Open
1952	Bing Crosby National Pro-Am

RECORDS AND MILESTONES

Credited with forty-four tournament wins, not all of which are recognized by the U.S. PGA

In 1950, became the first golfer to collect three Masters titles

Came close to winning the U.S. Open several times: sixth (1946), second (1948), fourth (1953), third (1957)

Reached the PGA Championship semifinals four times

HONORS AND AWARDS

1947	PGA Vardon Trophy
1960	Inducted into PGA Hall of Fame
1983	Inducted into PGA/World Golf Hall of Fame

Jimmy did not resent having to play second fiddle to other golfers. He became Ben Hogan's closest friend in golf and won six tournaments playing with Hogan as his partner. (These events, called Four-Balls, are matches in which the low scorer wins the hole for the two-person team.) The two players were utterly opposed in temperament: Hogan was grim and taciturn and had a desire to win stronger than any other player of his time. Nevertheless, the two were fast friends.

After Jimmy's tournament days were over, he developed the Champions Golf Club with his life-long friend Jack Burke. He suffered a fatal heart attack in Houston, Texas, on December 28, 1983.

Summary

Jimmy Demaret honed his exceptional short-game play on the Texas semiprofessional circuit. He attracted national attention by his colorful dress and pleasant personality, but these should not hide the fact that he was one of the best golfers of the 1940's. Ben Hogan and others eclipsed him, but he did not mind. Had he required consolation, he could have looked to his three wins in the Masters.

Bill Delaney

Additional Sources:

Demaret, Jimmy. *My Partner, Ben Hogan.* New York: McGraw-Hill, 1954.

Grimsley, Will. *Golf: Its History, People, and Events.* Englewood Cliffs, N.J.: Prentice-Hall, 1966.

Porter, David L., ed. *Biographical Dictionary of American Sports: Outdoor Sports.* Westport, Conn.: Greenwood Press, 1988.

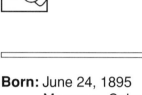

JACK DEMPSEY

Sport: Boxing

Born: June 24, 1895
Manassa, Colorado
Died: May 31, 1983
New York, New York

Early Life

William Harrison Dempsey was born June 24, 1895, in Manassa, Colorado, the town that is the origin of his nickname, "The Manassa Mauler." (He adopted the name "Jack" in his teens.) His parents were sharecroppers, and he was one of eleven children. The family moved to Utah during Jack's early youth, but their fortunes did not improve.

Jack had little formal education, never getting beyond the eighth grade. He held a number of jobs, all of which involved heavy physical labor: He was variously a fruit picker, a lumberjack, and a miner. At this stage of his life, his future prospects appeared dim. He spent much of his spare time in pool halls and bars and appeared to be no more than a local ne'er-do-well.

The Road to Excellence

One fact made Jack stand out from other young men of his limited social background: his fierce determination to succeed. He liked to fight and was good at it; he therefore decided to put all his effort into becoming a top-flight boxer.

He adopted a rigorous program of training. In addition to the usual sparring and running,

he soaked his hands, face, and upper body in brine to toughen them. He also did exercises to strengthen his jaw muscles.

Jack's determination and training paid off. After turning professional in 1915, he began to win all his bouts, almost always by knockout. Starting from a crouch, he would carry the fight to the opponent with relentless punching. Although thor-

Library of Congress

RECOGNIZED WORLD HEAVYWEIGHT CHAMPIONSHIPS

Date	Location	Loser	Result
July 4, 1919	Toledo, Ohio	Jess Willard	4th-round technical knockout
Sept. 6, 1920	Benton Harbor, Mich.	Billy Miske	3d-round knockout
Dec. 14, 1920	New York City, N.Y.	Bill Brennan	12th-round knockout
July 2, 1921	Jersey City, N.J.	Georges Carpentier	4th-round knockout
July 4, 1923	Shelby, Mont.	Tommy Givvons	15th-round referee's decision
Sept. 14, 1923	New York City, N.Y.	Luis Firpo	2d-round knockout
Sept. 23, 1926	Philadelphia, Pa.	Jack Dempsey (Gene Tunney, winner)	10th-round unanimous decision
Sept. 22, 1927	Chicago, Ill.	Jack Dempsey (Gene Tunney, winner)	10th-round unanimous decision

oughly acquainted with ring technique, he was much more a slugger than a boxer.

His relentless aggression placed him at risk of tiring, but this problem rarely arose. Jack was a incredibly hard puncher, ranking, according to most authorities, among the most devastating of all time. Few opponents could withstand one of Jack's assaults.

At the end of 1916, the young fighter faced a challenge. He had proved himself against all local competition. How was he to emerge into the light of national recognition?

The Emerging Champion

The answer to this question came in 1917, when Jack acquired a new manager. Jack Kearns was a boxing expert, and Jack benefited from the manager's training. Even more important, Kearns was a master of publicity and promotion.

He matched his young charge against a number of prominent fighters. Jack continued to knock out almost all his opponents. The combination of his ability and Kearns's promotion secured him a national reputation. Only one setback marred his rise to the top. For the first time in his career, he was knocked out in a match with "Fireman" Jim Flynn, a veteran heavyweight who was often understimated because he appeared to be fat and out of shape.

Jack did not let this defeat interfere with his progress. By 1919, he was clearly the leading contender for the heavyweight title, and a match between him and the champion, Jess Willard, was held on July 4 of that year.

Jack was tall and muscular, standing 6 feet tall and weighing 190 pounds. Willard towered 6 inches over him and outweighed him by 70 pounds, but Willard's size and strength did him little good. Jack utterly demolished Willard, knocking him out in four brutal rounds. As a result of the beating, the left side of Willard's face was permanently caved in.

Jack's slashing style made him a popular champion, and he successfully defended the title five times until defeated by Gene Tunney in September, 1926. He easily defeated the French champion, Georges Carpentier, in a match held in Jersey City, New Jersey, in 1921, the first million-dollar gate in boxing history.

Jack's 1923 match against the "Wild Bull of the Pampas," Argentine boxer Luis Firpo, proved much more exciting. The fight lasted only 3 minutes and 57 seconds. Firpo's style was an exaggerated version of Jack's: He floored Jack in the first round and, at the round's close, hit him so hard that Jack was knocked out of the ring. Showing his iron determination, Jack retaliated in the second round by knocking out his wild-swinging opponent.

Continuing the Story

By 1926, Jack had passed his peak as a fighter. He signed for a match against Gene Tunney, whose approach to boxing differed strikingly from his own. Tunney lacked Jack's killer instinct and power but made up for this with a careful study of boxing technique. In their fight, held in September, 1926, in Philadelphia, Tunney avoided Jack's charges, scoring heavily with jabs. Jack had not trained very hard for the bout. Tunney's steady pressure wore him down, and by the end of the tenth round the match was over. Tunney was awarded the world's title by unanimous decision.

As one might anticipate, Jack was by no means finished. He trained hard to regain his title, and

649

```
┌─────────────────────────────────────────────────┐
│                  STATISTICS                      │
├─────────────────────────────────────────────────┤
│ Knockouts, 49                                    │
│ Bouts won by decision, 12                        │
│ Bouts won by fouls, 1                            │
│ Knockouts by opponents, 1                        │
│ Bouts lost by decision, 5                        │
│ Draws, 10                                        │
├─────────────────────────────────────────────────┤
│              HONORS AND AWARDS                   │
├─────────────────────────────────────────────────┤
│ 1923  Citizens Savings Southern California Athlete of the Year │
│ 1938  Neil Trophy                                │
│ 1954  Inducted into Ring magazine Boxing Hall of Fame │
│ 1957  Walker Memorial Award                      │
│ 1990  Inducted into International Boxing Hall of Fame │
└─────────────────────────────────────────────────┘
```

the rematch in Chicago in 1927 made boxing history. Tunney repeated his tactics of the preceding year and by the seventh round had established a comfortable lead. Jack then charged at Tunney and battered him to the canvas with a series of seven punches. Instead of retreating to a neutral corner, as the rules of boxing mandated, Jack stood over his dazed foe.

The length of time that elapsed before Jack moved away and the referee began his count is uncertain, but Tunney gained at least 3 or 4 crucial seconds. He beat the ten count, lasted out the round, and came back strongly in the remaining few rounds to win the fight.

The former champion made a few attempts at a comeback but eventually recognized that his time in the ring had passed. After his retirement, he enjoyed a long career as a successful businessman and restaurant owner. He died in New York City in 1983.

Summary

Jack Dempsey's aggressiveness and punching power made him one of the greatest of all heavyweight boxers. He owned his success not only to natural talent but also to hard work and study. Strong and fast boxers are not unusual, but few if any have equaled Jack in his desire to win and willingness to sacrifice to attain his goals.

Bill Delaney

Additional Sources:

Dempsey, Jack, and Bob Considine. *Dempsey: By the Man Himself.* New York: Simon & Schuster, 1960.

Dempsey, Jack, and Myron M. Stearns. *Round by Round: An Autobiography.* New York: McGraw-Hill, 1940.

Kahn, Roger. *A Flame of Pure Fire: Jack Dempsey and the Roaring '20s.* New York: Harcourt Brace, 1999.

Roberts, Randy. *Jack Dempsey: The Manassa Mauler.* Baton Rouge: Louisiana State University Press, 1984.

Smith, Toby. *Kid Blackie: Jack Dempsey's Colorado Days.* Ouray, Colo.: Wayfinder Press, 1987.

DONNA DE VARONA

Sport: Swimming

Born: April 26, 1947
San Diego, California

Early Life

Donna Elizabeth de Varona was born in San Diego, California, on April 26, 1947. When she was three, her family moved to San Francisco, and, when she was six, they moved to Lafayette, California, where she grew up. She comes from a family of athletes. Her father, Dave, was an out-

Gold medalist Donna de Varona at the 1964 Olympics.

standing football player for the University of California, Berkeley, and later for the San Diego Bombers. He was also a rower for the University of California crew team, and later he became a high school football coach. Her brother David was a football and baseball player, and her sister Joanne was a competitive diver.

The Road to Excellence

As a youngster, Donna was adventurous, riding horses and playing with her older brother. She soon entered competitive sports as a diver, but she then began to swim with her brother at the Las Lomas High School pool. She entered her first race at the age of ten and placed tenth in the Far Western Amateur Athletic Union (AAU) meet in San Francisco.

Her early competitive years were difficult. She was small for a competitive swimmer, 5 feet 2 inches and weighing barely 100 pounds. Her early training was also difficult because she moved from one club to another and one coach to another. She therefore received little systematic, consistent coaching.

Donna wanted to swim for the Berkeley City Club, but the coach did not want her. She swam at the Berkeley YMCA, where she first trained with Jack Barkley, and when she became ten years old, she trained with coach Weikko (Finn) Ruuska, who she claimed taught her how to work. In 1960, however, she and Ruuska had difficulties. After Donna defeated his daughter, Sylvia, who was among the best swimmers in the 400-meter individual medley, Ruuska accused Donna of taking pep pills. Although the pills proved to be iron pills, Ruuska was no longer Donna's coach.

Donna continued her training at the Berkeley YMCA with Tatto Yamashita, who became the coach there. In April of 1960, she went to her first nationals in Bartlesville, Oklahoma, made alter-

651

nate on the United States Olympic swimming team, and became the youngest American, at the age of thirteen, at the Rome, Italy, Olympics in 1960.

It was at the meet in Oklahoma that Donna met George Haines, the coach of the Santa Clara Swim Club, who was to become her coach.

The Emerging Champion

Donna continued to train hard, swimming every day before and after school for four hours, believing that success in competition depended on two things—physical condition and mental attitude. On July 15, 1960, she set her first world record of 5 minutes 36.5 seconds in the 400-meter individual medley event at the National AAU Championships in Indianapolis, Indiana. The event, which consisted of the butterfly, the backstroke, the breaststroke, and the freestyle, was her favorite race.

She defended her national title in the 400-meter individual medley in 1961, again setting a world record of 5 minutes 34.5 seconds in Philadelphia, Pennsylvania, on August 11, 1961. She lost the title the following year to Sharon Finneran. She won the national title in the 100-

meter backstroke, however, with a time of 1 minute 10.4 seconds. Later in 1962, in Osaka, Japan, Donna and Finneran broke the world record in the 400-meter medley three times in three days, with Finneran emerging victorious, clocking 5 minutes 21.9 seconds.

Although Donna preferred the medley race and was devoted to regaining the title, she continued to win in the 100-meter backstroke. On July 28, 1963, she swam a world-record 1 minute 8.9 seconds in Los Angeles, lowering the record by one-tenth of a second.

In 1964, at the age of seventeen, Donna peaked in her last competitive season. On March 10, 1964, she reclaimed the world 400-meter individual medley with a 5-minute 16.5-second effort at Lima, Peru. With three other members of the Santa Clara Swim Club, she also won the 400-meter medley relay.

For the first time, the 400-meter individual medley was included in the 1964 Olympic Games at Tokyo, Japan. In preparation for this, Donna again lowered her world record with a time of 5 minutes 14.9 seconds.

In Tokyo, she won the first gold medal ever awarded to a woman in the Olympic 400-meter medley. Her time was 5 minutes 18.7 seconds. She earned a second gold medal as a member of the 400-meter freestyle relay team, which set a world record of 4 minutes 3.8 seconds.

STATISTICS

Year	Competition	Event	Place	Time
1960	AAU Outdoor Championships	400-meter individual medley	1st	5:36.5 WR
1961	AAU Outdoor Championships	400-meter individual medley	1st	5:34.5 WR
1962	AAU Outdoor Championships	100-meter backstroke	1st	1:10.4
	AAU Indoor Championships	100-yard backstroke	1st	1:04.0
1963	Pan-American Games	4×100-meter freestyle relay	—	4:15.7
	AAU Outdoor Championships	100-meter backstroke	1st	1:08.9 WR
		200-meter individual medley	1st	2:31.8
		400-meter individual medley	1st	5:24.5
	AAU Indoor Championships	200-yard individual medley	1st	2:15.0
		400-yard individual medley	1st	4:47.3
1964	Olympic Games	400-meter individual medley	Gold	5:18.7
		4×100-meter freestyle relay	Gold	4:03.8 WR, OR
	AAU Outdoor Championships	200-meter individual medley	1st	2:29.9 WR
		400-meter individual medley	1st	5:17.7
	AAU Indoor Championships	200-yard butterfly	1st	2:10.5
		200-yard individual medley	1st	2:12.4
		400-yard individual medley	1st	4:42.9

Notes: OR = Olympic Record; WR = World Record

Continuing the Story

During her years as a successful, competitive swimmer in the 1960's, Donna was regarded as "The Queen of Swimming" and was featured on the covers of *Sports Illustrated, Time, Life,* and *The Saturday Evening Post.* In 1964, her most successful year, she was voted America's Outstanding Athlete by Associated Press and United Press International. In 1965, she was selected by the National Association of Swimmers as the Greatest Woman Athlete. She was inducted into the International Swimming Hall of Fame

RECORDS

Won 37 individual national championships medals, including 18 golds

Held world records in 8 long course events, and American records in 10 short course events

First woman on network television in the sports broadcasting field in 1965

HONORS AND AWARDS

1964	Voted America's Outstanding Woman Athlete by the Associated Press and United Press International
	Outstanding American Female Swimmer
	National Academy of Sports Award
	San Francisco's Outstanding Woman of the Year
	Mademoiselle Award
1965	Greatest Woman Athlete
1969	Inducted into International Swimming Hall of Fame
1983	Inducted into Sudafed International Women's Sports Hall of Fame
1987	Inducted into U.S. Olympic Hall of Fame
	Inducted into Women's Sports Hall of Fame

in 1969 and the Women's Sports Hall of Fame in 1987. She was also chosen as San Francisco's Outstanding Woman of the Year in 1964 and was honored with the *Mademoiselle* Award.

After retiring from competition, Donna studied political science at the University of California at Los Angeles and became the first woman sportscaster on network television for ABC Sports. She has continued to promote sports for women as president and founding member of the Women's Sports Foundation, as a former member of President Jimmy Carter's Advisory Committee for Women, and as a special consultant to the United States Senate, where she was instrumental in the passage of Title IX legislation, designed to offer women equality in sports opportunities. She has worked as well to promote amateur sport in the United States with her support of the Amateur Sports Act and as a member of the President's Council on Physical Fitness and the 1984 Olympic Organizing Committee.

Summary

At the age of thirteen, Donna de Varona became the youngest member of the United States Olympic team in 1960. For five years, she dominated the 400-meter individual medley, setting six world records. At one time she also held the 100-meter backstroke record. She captured two gold medals at the 1964 Olympic Games in Tokyo, winning the first gold medal ever awarded to a woman for the 400-meter individual medley and a gold medal as a member of the 400-meter freestyle relay team. Throughout her career, she won thirty-seven individual national championship medals and held eighteen national and world records.

Susan J. Bandy

Additional Sources:

Besford, Pat. *Encyclopedia of Swimming.* New York: St. Martin's Press, 1976.

Bortstein, Larry. *After Olympic Glory: The Lives of Ten Outstanding Medalists.* New York: F. Warne, 1978.

Hickok, Ralph. *A Who's Who of Sports Champions.* Boston: Houghton Mifflin, 1995.

Schapp, Dick. *An Illustrated History of the Olympics.* New York: Alfred A. Knopf, 1975.

Thomas, Bob. *Donna de Varona: Gold Medal Swimmer.* New York: Doubleday, 1968.

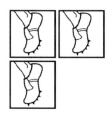

GAIL DEVERS

Sport: Track and field (sprints and hurdles)

Born: November 19, 1966
Seattle, Washington

Early Life

Yolanda Gail Devers was born on November 19, 1966, in Seattle, Washington, to Larry Devers, a Baptist minister, and Alabe Devers, a teacher's aide. Her career as a runner began when her brother Parenthesis teased her after he beat her in a foot race. Determined not to lose to him again, she practiced and won the next time they raced. From that time forward running was all that mattered to Gail.

The Road to Excellence

At Sweetwater High School in National City, California, near San Diego, Gail tried running middle distances, but during her junior year she switched to sprints. In 1984 she single-handedly earned her team fourth place in the state championship meet with wins in the 100 meters and the 100-meter hurdles and a second-place finish in the long jump. She attracted the attention of coach Bob Kersee, who recruited her for the University of California at Los Angeles (UCLA) track team. At UCLA she ran both 100-meter events; her training partner and best friend was Jackie Joyner-Kersee. During her senior year, 1988, Gail set the American record in the hurdles with a time of 12.61 seconds; the record stood for three years.

The year 1988 was significant in Gail's personal life. She married former UCLA miler Ron Roberts and graduated with a de-gree in sociology. On the track she qualified for the U.S. Olympic team in the 100 meters but opted not to run that event so she could concentrate on the hurdles. At the Olympics she finished eighth in the hurdle semifinals.

While training for the Olympics, her health had begun to deteriorate. She suffered migraine headaches, fainting spells, vision loss, and extreme exhaustion. Doctors diagnosed her condition as Graves' disease, a chronic thyroid disorder. Her feet became blistered and swollen, and she faced possible amputation of them. Pain and radiation treatment for the disease caused her to give up running for two years, but Gail was determined not to quit. With the help of medication, a careful diet, and a workout plan she was able to return to training. In 1991 she won the U.S.

Gail Devers clears a hurdle in a second-round heat of the women's 100-meter hurdles during the Olympic team trials in Atlanta in 1996.

Championships in the hurdles and second place in the event at the World Championships.

The Emerging Champion

At the 1992 Olympics in Barcelona, Spain, only seventeen months after doctors considered amputating her feet, she won the gold medal in the 100 meters, with a time of 10.82, and the title "world's fastest woman." Although she was the favorite for the gold in the 100-meter hurdles, Gail hit the final hurdle and fell. As the other contestants ran by, she crawled across the finish line for fifth place.

During 1993 she won seven titles, including the U.S. and world indoor 60 meters, the U.S. 100 meters (10.82 wind-aided), the world 100 meters (10.82 seconds), and the world 100-meter hurdles (12.46 seconds). Her double 100-meter wins at the World Championships were the first time such a feat had been accomplished in forty-five years.

Continuing the Story

Hamstring problems in 1994 kept Gail from competing in the hurdles, but she won the U.S. title in the 100 meters in 11.12 seconds. The following year she participated in only the hurdles and won the U.S. and World Championships in the event with times of 12.77 and 12.68 seconds, respectively. Fully recovered from injuries, Gail prepared for the 1996 Olympics. She won the U.S. trials in the hurdles and placed second in the 100 meters. In Atlanta she repeated as the Olympic champion in the 100 meters. Her leaning forward at the finish gave her the gold medal when she and Jamaican sprinter Merlene Ottey recorded the same time of 10.94 seconds. Gail finished fourth in the hurdles and earned a second gold medal as a member of the American 4×100-meter relay team. In 1996 a made-for-television movie, *Run for the Dream: The Gail Devers Story*, told the story of her triumph over Graves' disease.

During 1997 Gail's competitions were very limited. She won the 60-meter U.S. and world indoor titles and anchored the winning American 4×100-meter relay team at the World Championships. The following year she did not compete at all. The capture of the 1999 U.S. and World Championships in the 100-meter hurdles

MAJOR CHAMPIONSHIPS			
Year	Competition	Event	Place
1988	NCAA	100 meters	1st
1991	U. S. Championships	100-meter hurdles	1st
	World Championships	100-meter hurdles	2d
1992	Olympic Games	100 meters	Gold
		100-meter hurdles	5th
1993	U. S. Indoor Championships	60 meters	1st
	World Indoor Championships	60 meters	1st
	U. S. Championships	100 meters	1st
		100-meter hurdles	2d
	World Championships	100 meters	1st
		100-meter hurdles	1st
1994	U. S. Championships	100 meters	1st
1995	U. S. Championships	100-meter hurdles	1st
	World Championships	100-meter hurdles	1st
1996	Olympic Games	100 meters	Gold
		4×100-meter relay	Gold
1997	U.S. Indoor Championships	60 meters	1st
	World Indoor Championships	60 meters	1st
1999	World Championships	100-meter hurdles	1st

in 1999 earned Gail the number-one ranking in the world in that event, and a second-place finish in the 100 meters in the U.S. Championships placed her fifth in the world at that distance.

At the 2000 U.S. Olympic trials Gail lowered her American record to 12.33 seconds. She was the favorite for a long-awaited gold in the 100-meter hurdles in Sydney, but unfortunately she injured her hamstring in the semifinals and was forced to withdraw.

Gail devoted much of her free time to two projects close to her heart—Graves' disease and the Gail Devers Foundation. She spoke extensively about thyroid disease among women and received an achievement award from the American Medical Women's Association for her efforts. Her foundation supports scholarships and community programs to help youths achieve their fullest potential.

Summary

Gail Devers is a champion on and off the track. Her faith and determination helped her overcome not only a serious disease but also disappointments in competitions. The world watched as she fell then courageously crawled

655

across the finish line in the 100-meter hurdles at the 1992 Olympics. She did not give up competition but returned stronger than ever to capture gold in another Olympics and several U.S. and World Championships titles in the 100 meters and the 100-meter hurdles.

Marlene Bradford

Additional Sources:

Gutman, Bill. *Gail Devers.* Austin, Tex.: Raintree Steck-Vaughn, 1996.

Lessa, Christian. *Stories of Triumph: Women Who Win in Sport and in Life.* New York: Universe, 1998.

Mead, Katherine. *Gail Devers: A Runner's Dream.* Austin, Tex.: Steck-Vaughn, 1998.

KLAUS DIBIASI

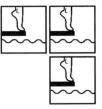

Sport: Diving

Born: October 6, 1947
Solbad Hall, Austria

Early Life

The Italian super-diver Klaus Dibiasi was born on October 6, 1947, in Austria of Italian parents who moved back to Bolzano in the Italian Alps (the Dolomites) when he was very young. It is quite cold in the mountainous northern parts of Italy, and Klaus learned to dive outdoors at age ten.

His father was his coach, and his mother was his chaperon on diving trips. Carlo "Papa" Dibiasi had been springboard diving champion of Italy from 1933 to 1936 and was still competing at the age of fifty-three, when he retired from diving to become a full-time coach.

The Road to Excellence

In 1963, Klaus was Papa's star pupil at sixteen when he won his first of many Italian diving championships. It is seldom that a father can coach his own son to become the best in the world, and yet Carlo Dibiasi was on the verge of doing just that with Klaus. The Italian team of Papa, Klaus, and Giorgio Cagnotto became the best diving team Italy ever had.

Klaus Dibiasi and his best friend, talkative and handsome Franco "Giorgio" Cagnotto, traveled around Europe and the world representing Italy. Giorgio had great ability and a macho flair that not only won him spots on five Olympic teams but also made him the perfect compan-

ion to the quiet, almost shy dignity of the taller Klaus. The world of diving loved all three of them.

The Emerging Champion

From 1964 until 1976, Klaus was king of the high dive. He proved to be the most durable world-class diver in history, winning three gold medals in the tower diving events (1968, 1972, and 1976 Olympics). Not only was he the star on the high diving tower, or platform, as it is also called, but he also was a star on the springboard, taking a silver medal in the 1968 Olympic Games.

Courtesy of the International Swimming Hall of Fame

657

No other diver has ever won three straight Olympics, and no other Olympic athlete has won three straight golds and a silver in a fourth.

When an athlete is the best and stays the best, people often wonder about the athlete's motivation to keep training and winning. Says Klaus Dibiasi in commenting on Greg Louganis, his only rival, who began his fabulous career just as Klaus was finishing at the 1976 Montreal Olympics: "He must think just of the contest. He must block everything else out of his mind, including the newspaper reports that he'll get a gold medal for sure. Only the coach and diver know the problems that can happen in a contest. Every Olympic Games I was in there was a big question in my mind of whether I'd be good or not. You never know until the last dive."

As a diver, Klaus made rip entries famous and had the long legs to make this no-splash style popular. Two unique characteristics were Klaus's trademarks that won over the diving judges and the public: his patrician bearing and his relaxed, personable manner. He never complained about the judging, although he would say later, as a coach, that judging is the weak point in modern diving. Klaus very nearly won the Olympic diving title four times, narrowly missing his first by 1.04 points to the United States' Bob Webster at Tokyo in 1964. In his last gold in 1976 at Montreal, Klaus beat out Greg Louganis, who, after this defeat, learned a few of Klaus's tricks. After taking a silver to Klaus's gold in Montreal, Greg went on to capture the diving world during the 1980's.

Continuing the Story

From 1964 to 1976, twelve years, Klaus was the dominant diver of the world and Italy's top athlete and first gold medal winner in swimming or diving. The 5-foot 11-inch, fair-haired Austro-Italian weighed 165 pounds before he succeeded his father as Italian national diving coach in

1977. He has coached many top divers and made regular appearances at the International Swimming Hall of Fame International Diving Meet held each year in Fort Lauderdale, Florida.

Summary

Klaus Dibiasi was Italy's greatest tower diver of all time. He won three straight Olympics (1968, 1972, and 1976) and was second in a fourth (1964). He was inducted into the International Swimming Hall of Fame in 1981.

Buck Dawson

MAJOR CHAMPIONSHIPS				
Year	Competition	Event	Place	Points
1964	Olympic Games	10-meter platform	Silver	147.54
1966	European Championships	10-meter platform	1st	—
1968	Olympic Games	3-meter springboard	Silver	159.74
		10-meter platform	Gold	164.18
1970	World University Games	3-meter springboard	—	564.90
		10-meter platform	—	485.73
	European Championships	3-meter springboard	2d	—
		10-meter platform	2d	—
1972	Olympic Games	10-meter platform	Gold	504.12
1973	World Championships	3-meter springboard	2d	615.18
		10-meter platform	1st	559.53
1974	European Championships	3-meter springboard	1st	—
		10-meter platform	1st	—
1975	World Championships	3-meter springboard	2d	588.21
		10-meter platform	1st	547.98
1976	Olympic Games	10-meter platform	1st	60.51

HONOR
1981   Inducted into International Swimming Hall of Fame

Additional Sources:

Levinson, David, and Karen Christenson, eds. *Encyclopedia of World Sport: From Ancient to Present*. Santa Barbara, Calif.: ABC-CLIO, 1996.

Schapp, Dick. *An Illustrated History of the Olympics*. New York: Alfred A. Knopf, 1975.

Wallechinsky, David. *The Complete Book of the Olympics*. Boston: Little, Brown and Company, 1991.

ERIC DICKERSON

Sport: Football

Born: September 2, 1960
Sealy, Texas

Early Life

On September 2, 1960, in the small town of Sealy, Texas, a son was born to Robert Johnson and his sixteen-year-old wife. The boy was named Eric Demetric. Because his mother was so young at the time, Eric was legally adopted by his great-aunt and great-uncle, Viola and Kary Dickerson, and became known as Eric Demetric Dickerson. The Dickerson family also lived in Sealy, a town of

fewer than 5,000 people located 50 miles from Houston, and there Eric grew up.

Eric had a simple childhood. He did not grow up in the lap of luxury and developed early on a habit of living frugally. He learned to do with what he had and to be happy. This inner contentment sprang from his happy family life and was to spill over into the rest of his later life, when he came to be known for his friendliness, charm, and a balanced sense of self-esteem.

As a boy, Eric was an athlete with high standards. He used to feel disappointed whenever he

Indianapolis Colts running back Eric Dickerson (29) eludes New England Patriots defenders during a game in 1987.

watched O. J. Simpson run and yet fail to gain 100 yards in a game. Eric was a fine runner himself. Even as a boy, his legs barely seemed to move when he ran, and he looked as though he were gliding. His running talent was to serve him well in the future.

The Road to Excellence

When Eric was old enough to attend Sealy High School, he participated in track, basketball, and football. In track, he won the state 100-yard dash championship in the excellent time of 9.4 seconds. Eric's track success came as no surprise to those who had watched him run as a child. In football, he became a running back. Eric found he liked football more than other sports, because he enjoyed sneaking up on people.

By the time Eric was a high school senior, he had become a superb running back, and he rushed for 2,653 yards that year. In the state high school championship game, he scored four touchdowns and led Sealy to the title. For his achievements, Eric was *Parade* Magazine's choice as All-American and the best high school running back of 1978.

The next fall, Eric enrolled in Southern Methodist University (SMU). There, he had many injuries playing football as a freshman. As a sophomore, though, he played five games in which he rushed for more than 100 yards. After two years at SMU, Eric wanted to drop out, but his adopted mother, Viola, talked him out of it.

In Eric's junior year, he was selected as Southwest Conference (SWC) Player of the Year after he had rushed for the second-best yardage total in SWC history. He also set scoring records at SMU with 114 points and 19 touchdowns.

More records came Eric's way as a senior. His 48 career touchdowns alone set a record at SMU. That year, he made consensus All-American and ranked third nationally with 147 rushing yards per game. As a result of his success in college football, Eric was the second choice in the National Football League's (NFL's) 1983 draft. Eric was drafted by the Los Angeles Rams, and he joined them before the 1983 NFL season.

The Emerging Champion

In several respects Eric was fortunate that the Rams had chosen him. The team had a good offesive line, and its coach, John Robinson, was a strong proponent of the running game. Still, Eric did not become a hero overnight. During his first three games, he fumbled six times—and one of the fumbles set up a field goal that caused the Rams to lose the game.

Eric's fourth game was another matter, though. He made an 85-yard touchdown that was the longest NFL run so far that year. He went on breaking records that year, setting the rookie rushing record while leading the Rams into the playoffs. Other 1983 honors earned by Eric included unanimous Pro Bowl selection and the United

STATISTICS

| Season | GP | Rushing | | | | | Receiving | | | |
		Car.	Yds.	Avg.	TD	Rec.	Yds.	Avg.	TD
1983	16	390	**1,808**	4.6	18	51	404	7.9	2
1984	16	379	**2,105**	5.6	**14**	21	139	6.6	0
1985	14	292	1,234	4.2	12	20	126	6.3	0
1986	16	404	**1,821**	4.5	11	26	205	7.9	0
1987	12	283	**1,288**	4.6	6	18	171	9.5	0
1988	16	388	**1,659**	4.3	14	36	377	10.5	1
1989	15	314	1,311	4.2	7	30	211	7.0	1
1990	11	166	677	4.1	4	18	92	5.1	0
1991	10	167	536	3.2	2	41	269	6.6	1
1992	16	187	729	3.9	2	14	85	6.1	1
1993	4	26	91	3.5	0	6	58	9.7	0
Totals	146	2,996	13,259	4.4	98	281	2,137	7.6	6

Notes: Boldface indicates statistical leader. GP = games played; Car. = carries; Yds. = yards; Avg. = average yards per carry *or* average yards per reception; TD = touchdowns; Rec. = receptions

NFL RECORDS

Most consecutive seasons with at least 1,000 rushing yards, 7
Most rushing touchdowns in a rookie season, 18 (1983)
Most rushing yards in a season, 2,105 (1984)
Most rushing yards in a rookie season, 1,808 (1983)
Most rushing yards in a postseason game, 248 (1985)

HONORS AND AWARDS

1980	All-Southwest Conference Team
1981	Southwest Conference Player of the Year College All-American
1982	Hula Bowl All-Star Team Japan Bowl All-Star Team Consensus All-American
1983	*Sporting News* NFL Player of the Year Associated Press Offensive Rookie of the Year United Press International NFC Rookie of the Year Bell Trophy Seagram's Seven Crowns of Sports Award *Sports Illustrated* NFL Player of the Year
1983-84, 1986	United Press International NFC Offensive Player of the Year
1983-84, 1986-88	*Sporting News* NFL All-Star Team
1984-85, 1987-90	NFL Pro Bowl Team
1984, 1986	All-NFL Team
1999	Inducted into Pro Football Hall of Fame

Press International National Football Conference (NFC) Player of the Year award.

The following season, Eric learned to be more patient on the field and to choose the holes through which he rushed more carefully. He began to recognize his limits, realizing he could not possibly gain 100 yards every week, as many people expected. The more selective approach helped Eric break O. J. Simpson's 1973 NFL record for single-season rushing in 1984. That season, Eric gained at least 100 yards in a game 11 times. For his performance, he was chosen as NFC Offensive Player of the Year, named to the All-NFL team, and selected to play in the Pro Bowl.

Continuing the Story

Dickerson became best known for his remarkable speed and durability. Size helped him, too. He stood 6 feet 3 inches and weighed 218 pounds. Together, these qualities made Eric one of the finest running backs ever. Whenever he ran, he would start out slowly, but somehow he always seemed to be six yards or so downfield before any opponent could reach him. Then he would switch to overdrive and glide by the defense, his legs barely seeming to move. People enjoyed just watching Eric run, because he did it so beautifully.

Off the field, too, Eric was popular with fans. Articulate and charming, he made frequent appearances on television and acted in several commercials. In 1987, though, a long-simmering salary dispute between Eric and the Rams' management boiled over, and Eric was traded to the Indianapolis Colts in one of the biggest deals in NFL history. The Rams received eight players from the Colts in return for Eric.

Eric had an immediate effect on the hapless Colts. In 1986, Indianapolis had gone 3-13 and finished last in the American Football Conference's (AFC's) Eastern Division. With Eric in the backfield, the next season the Colts improved to 9-6 and won the Eastern Division title. Eric finished his playing career in 1992 in Los Angeles with the Rams and in 1993 with the Atlanta Falcons. As of late 2000, he was the NFL's third leading career rusher. In 1999 Eric was inducted into the Pro Football Hall of Fame. The following year he joined the broadcasting team of *Monday Night Football* as a field commentator.

Summary

Eric Dickerson combined speed, power, and grace in a way few other running backs ever have. Eric was often described as the "prettiest" runner in the game, and even the great O. J. Simpson, whose single-season rushing record was broken by Eric, conceded that Eric may have been the best running back ever.

Nan White

Additional Sources:

Dickerson, Eric, and Steve Delsohn. *On the Run.* Chicago: Contemporary Books, 1986.

Nielsen, Nancy J. *Eric Dickerson.* Mankato, Minn.: Crestwood House, 1988.

Roberts, Rich. *Eric Dickerson: Record-Breaking Rusher.* Chicago: Children's Press, 1985.

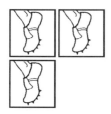

HARRISON DILLARD

Sport: Track and field (hurdles)

Born: July 8, 1923
Cleveland, Ohio

Early Life

William Harrison Dillard was born on July 8, 1923, in Cleveland, Ohio, the hometown of Jesse Owens, the winner of four gold medals at the 1936 Berlin Olympic Games. The first time Harrison saw Owens was when Owens returned to Cleveland for a parade held in his honor following his Olympic victories. The youngster ran home and told his mother that he was going to be just like Owens. It was in 1936, at the age of thirteen, that Harrison began to dream about sprinting to an Olympic victory like his hero had done.

A year later, as a student at Cannard Junior High, Harrison began to run in organized track competition. His track coach discouraged him from being a sprinter because Harrison was so small and weighed only 85 pounds—hence his nickname "Bones."

Harrison's idol, Owens, who worked on Cleveland's East Side, dropped by track practice one day to encourage and instruct the young athletes. Owens left Harrison with two things, a pair of track shoes and some advice—try the hurdles.

The Road to Excellence

Harrison attended East Technical High School in Cleveland, just like Owens had done years before. He also took Owens's suggestion and began to run the hurdles. In fact, he ran the hurdles so well that he won the Ohio state championships in both the high and low hurdles his senior year.

In the fall of 1941, Harrison planned to attend Ohio State University, where Owens had run collegiate track. At the last minute, however, he decided to go to Baldwin-Wallace, a college of seventeen hundred students in Berea, Ohio, a town not far from Harrison's home. There he ran track under the direction of Coach Eddie Finnegan.

Together, Harrison and Coach Finnegan made hurdling an exact science. Harrison's speed had helped him win hurdle races in high school. Now speed and technique were joined together to make hurdling history.

An explosive start and great speed allowed Harrison to reach the first hurdle in exactly eight steps. Because of his somewhat short stature (5 feet 10 inches) for a high hurdler, Harrison developed a new hurdling technique using his phenomenal leaping ability. He took off eight feet from the hurdle and landed

Harrison Dillard, left.

STATISTICS

Year	Competition	Event	Place	Time
1946	NCAA Outdoor Championships	120-yard high hurdles	1st	14.1
		220-yard low hurdles	1st	23.0
	National AAU Outdoor Championships	110-meter high hurdles	1st	14.2
1947	NCAA Outdoor Championships	120-yard high hurdles	1st	14.1
		220-yard low hurdles	1st	22.3
	National AAU Outdoor Championships	110-meter high hurdles	1st	14.0
	National AAU Indoor Championships	60-yard high hurdles	1st	7.4
1948	Olympic Games	100-meter	Gold	10.3 OR
		4×100-meter relay	Gold	40.6
	National AAU Indoor Championships	60-yard high hurdles	1st	7.2
1949	National AAU Indoor Championships	60-yard high hurdles	1st	7.2
1950	National AAU Indoor Championships	60-yard high hurdles	1st	7.3
1951	National AAU Indoor Championships	60-yard high hurdles	1st	7.4
1952	Olympic Games	110-meter hurdles	Gold	13.7 OR
		4×100-meter relay	Gold	40.1
	National AAU Outdoor Championships	110-meter high hurdles	1st	13.7
	National AAU Indoor Championships	60-yard high hurdles	1st	7.4
1953	National AAU Indoor Championships	60-yard high hurdles	1st	7.3
1955	National AAU Indoor Championships	60-yard high hurdles	1st	7.3

Note: OR = Olympic Record

rison had won 201 out of 207 sprints and hurdle race finals. From May, 1947, to June, 1948, Harrison scored eighty-two consecutive victories, a record that was not surpassed until Edwin Moses's dominance in the 400-meter hurdles in the 1970's and 1980's.

His consecutive victory streak ended at the Olympic trials in the summer of 1948. Harrison wanted to "clean up" in the London games like Jesse Owens had done in Berlin, so he tried to make the United States team in three events—the 110-meter hurdles, the 100-meter dash, and the 4×100-meter relay.

Continuing the Story

Because he finished third in the 100-meter dash, behind Barney Ewell and Mel Patton, Harrison went to the 1948 London Olympics an underdog. Having run the race in 10.3 seconds, which was one-tenth of a second off the world record, Harrison was confident of his chances and believed that he could run with any sprinter in the world on a given day.

The 100-meter Olympic final was close. Both Harrison and Ewell claimed victory in a photo finish. The official photograph showed that Harrison had won the race by one foot. Harrison tied the Olympic record of 10.3 seconds, set by his hero Owens in 1936, and by another great black sprinter, Eddie Tolan, in the 1932 Olympic Games. Harrison also won another gold medal as part of the 4×100-meter relay team.

Two gold medals could not compensate for the disappointment Harrison felt at not being the Olympic hurdles champion. After graduating from college in 1949, he began training for the 1952 Helsinki Olympics and his anticipated gold medal in the 110-meter hurdles.

At the age of twenty-nine, Harrison made the Olympic team and won the gold in the hurdles. The race was decided at the last hurdle, where he touched down first and sprinted to the finish line. Another gold medal in the 4×100-meter re-

five feet beyond it, about two feet farther than most hurdlers. Generally, the longer time in the air would slow down the hurdler, but Harrison was able to use his speed to get his trail leg down almost as quickly as his lead leg. The Baldwin-Wallace trackster was something that most track fans had never seen before—a great hurdler who was also a great sprinter.

The Emerging Champion

While Harrison was competing in track during his first two years at Baldwin-Wallace, the United States was fighting in World War II. In 1943, after his sophomore year, Harrison was drafted into the United States Army.

At the end of the war, Harrison participated in the GI Olympics held in Frankfurt, Germany, and won four gold medals in the sprints and the hurdles. After viewing Harrison's performance, General George S. Patton, Jr., himself a medalist in the decathalon in the 1912 Olympics, remarked that Harrison was the best athlete he had ever seen.

Harrison returned to Baldwin-Wallace to finish his education and continue to run track. At the conclusion of his collegiate career, Har-

---

RECORDS

World record at 110-meter hurdles in 1948 (13.6)

World record at 220 yards in 1947, 1948

First man to win gold medals in sprints (100 meters) and hurdles (110 meters)

Three-time world record holder in the 110-meter hurdles

HONORS AND AWARDS

1955	Sullivan Award
1974	Inducted into National Track and Field Hall of Fame
1983	Inducted into U.S. Olympic Hall of Fame

---

lay brought Harrison's career gold medal total to four, the same total as Owens.

Summary

After the 1952 Olympics, Harrison Dillard continued to hurdle and win championships. His heroics were acknowledged in 1955, when he received the James E. Sullivan Memorial Award as the nation's outstanding amateur athlete. Harrison became a charter member of the National Track and Field Hall of Fame in 1974, and in 1983, he was inducted into the United States Olympic Hall of Fame.

After his track career ended, Harrison returned to where it began—the Cleveland Public School System—and served as an administrator in charge of business affairs. In 1984, Harrison returned to his alma mater, Baldwin-Wallace, and received an honorary doctorate of human letters for his track achievements as well as his contributions to the Cleveland community.

William G. Durick

Additional Sources:

Bingham, Walter. "Track and Field: Pathways to the Olympics." *Sports Illustrated* 69, no. 1 (July 4, 1988): 47-54.

Carlson, Lewis H., and John J. Fogarty, eds. *Tales of Gold: An Oral History of the Summer Olympic Games Told by American Gold Medal Winners.* Chicago: Contemporary Books, 1987.

Findling, John E., and Kimberly D. Pelle, eds. *Historical Dictionary of the Modern Olympic Movement.* Westport, Conn.: Greenwood Press, 1996.

JOE DiMAGGIO

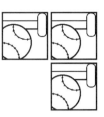

Sport: Baseball

Born: November 25, 1914
      Martinez, California
Died: March 8, 1999
      Hollywood, Florida

Early Life

Joseph Paul DiMaggio, Jr., was born on November 25, 1914, in Martinez, California, across the bay from Fisherman's Wharf in San Francisco, where he grew up. His immigrant family was poor and spoke only Italian at home. Joe was one of nine children supported by a fisherman father. The children all worked at odd jobs to help out at home. Joe hated the smell of fish and sold newspapers rather than work on the boat.

Joe DiMaggio in 1941.

Joe was extremely shy then, as he remained all his life. Shyness may have been one of the reasons he left high school. The others were his love of baseball and his great natural ability.

The Road to Excellence

Joe broke into professional baseball at age eighteen with the San Francisco Seals of the Triple-A Pacific Coast League. His brother Vince was already on the roster. A third brother, Dominic, later took up the sport, and all three played in the majors.

Joe's statistics as a Seal speak for themselves: In 1933, his rookie season (he played in one game in 1932), he drove in 169 runs and hit safely in sixty-one straight games. Despite Joe's broken knee, sustained when he was hurrying out of a taxi, Yankee scouts Joe Devine, Bill Essick, and George Weiss urged Jacob Ruppert, owner of the Yankees, to take a chance on this natural ballplayer. The price was twenty-five thousand dollars and five players.

Joe came back strong from this first of many injuries he was to suffer in his career. He played out 1935, his third and last season with the Seals. He was named most valuable player in the Pacific Coast League, batting .398 with 270 hits and 154 runs batted in. These mammoth figures propelled him into a New York Yankee uniform in 1936.

Babe Ruth had left the Yankees in 1934, but Joe joined Lou Gehrig, Lefty Gomez, and other great players to form a new Yankee dynasty. They would win ten pennants in thirteen years. His closest friend was Gomez. Manager Joe McCarthy was a stern father-figure who insisted on dignified dress and behavior by all Yankees.

The Emerging Champion

From 1936 to 1942, Joe nearly became a legend in his time. His greatest achievement came

665

in 1941, when he hit safely in fifty-six consecutive games, a record that has not been surpassed. The streak was stopped only by two fine fielding plays by third baseman Ken Keltner of Cleveland, but Joe started a 16-game streak the very next game. He was nicknamed "Joltin' Joe" and the "Yankee Clipper."

One almost forgets that Joe DiMaggio was one of the game's great center fielders as well. His play in the field was nearly flawless. Like Tris Speaker before him, Joe played dangerously shallow, but his instincts allowed him to get the jump on balls hit deep, and he always arrived in time to make the catch. In fact, he rarely had to dive for the ball; he made hard plays look "routine" and gained a reputation for gracefulness in the field. Players who knew him agree that he never threw to the wrong base. These are attributes that do not appear in the statistics. Statistics do, however, record his marvelous list of league leaderships in fielding percentage and assists.

Joe was rarely called upon to steal bases. Sportswriters note, however, that they never saw Joe thrown out when stretching a single to a double or going from first to third on a hit.

He was not asked to bunt often either; he was too good a hitter. Manager Joe McCarthy was asked if DiMaggio even knew how to bunt. He replied, "I don't know and I don't intend to find out." His skills as a hitter and fielder have over-

shadowed the fact that Joe was one of the great students of the game of baseball. Constantly alert on the field, he rarely missed a sign.

Just as Joe was reaching his prime, World War II took three years from Joe's career and his statistics, as it did from many major leaguers. In Joe's case, these statistics are significant because he ranks near the top in so many areas. Three additional productive years at his prime would have placed him ahead of many others in home runs and in every other department at the plate.

He was one of the first men drafted into the Army. He returned in 1946 but was beset by injuries and played in great pain until his retirement after the 1951 season. Still, his performance on the field inspired the Yankees to four pennants in his last six seasons. Worst of all his injuries was the bone spur in his heel, which kept him out of half of the 1949 season. Reentering the lineup in a crucial June series against the Boston Red Sox, Joe hit 4 home runs and had 9 runs batted in and a game-saving catch in the three-game series. He regarded this as the high point of his career. The Yankees won the pennant over the Red Sox by one game.

Continuing the Story

In 1951, the year Joe retired, the Yankees offered him $100,000 to stay, but his poor .263 season convinced Joe that he could no longer perform up to his own standard of excellence.

STATISTICS

Season	GP	AB	Hits	2B	3B	HR	Runs	RBI	BA	SA
1936	138	637	206	44	**15**	29	132	125	.323	.576
1937	151	621	215	35	15	**46**	**151**	167	.346	**.673**
1938	145	599	194	32	13	32	129	140	.324	.581
1939	120	462	176	32	6	30	108	126	**.381**	.671
1940	132	508	179	28	9	31	93	133	**.352**	.626
1941	139	541	193	43	11	30	122	**125**	.357	.643
1942	154	610	186	29	13	21	123	114	.305	.498
1946	132	503	146	20	8	25	81	95	.290	.511
1947	141	534	168	31	10	20	97	97	.315	.522
1948	153	594	190	26	11	**39**	110	**155**	.320	.598
1949	76	272	94	14	6	14	58	67	.346	.596
1950	139	525	158	33	10	32	114	122	.301	**.585**
1951	116	415	109	22	4	12	72	71	.263	.422
Totals	1,736	6,821	2,214	389	131	361	1,390	1,537	.325	.579

Notes: Boldface indicates statistical leader. GP = games played; AB = at bats; 2B = doubles; 3B = triples; HR = home runs; RBI = runs batted in; BA = batting average; SA = slugging average

HONORS AND AWARDS

1936-42, 1946-51	American League All-Star Team
1939	*Sporting News* Major League Player of the Year
1939, 1941, 1947	American League most valuable player
1941	Associated Press Male Athlete of the Year Major league record for the longest consecutive- game hitting streak (56)
1955	Inducted into National Baseball Hall of Fame
1969	Voted baseball's Greatest Living Player in a nationwide poll
1999	MLB All-Century Team Uniform number 5 retired by New York Yankees

Incredibly, Joe was not elected to the National Baseball Hall of Fame until his second year of eligibility in 1955.

Upon his return from military service, Joe and his first wife, actress Dorothy Arnold, were divorced. In 1954, Joe married Marilyn Monroe, but the marriage lasted less than a year. They remained close friends, however, and Joe took care of her funeral arrangements in 1962 and secretly placed flowers on her grave every year. He became part-owner of DiMaggio's Restaurant in San Francisco and was a vice president of the Oakland Athletics for a time in 1968. Golf became his passion in retirement. Joe was hospitalized in Florida in October, 1998, and diagnosed with lung cancer. After struggling on life support for several months, the eighty-four-year-old Yankee Clipper died on March 8, 1999.

In his controversial biography, *Joe DiMaggio: The Hero's Life*, published in 2000, Pulitzer Prize-winning author Richard Ben Cramer challenged many of the public's notions about Joe, revealing a number of indiscretions in Joe's personal life. Though Cramer's book has demythologized Joe's life to a certain extent, it has done little to alter his status as one of baseball's all-time finest players.

Summary

Joe DiMaggio is named in every discussion of the greatest players in the game of baseball. In 1969, he was voted by a nationwide poll as baseball's Greatest Living Player. Besides that, Joe's life, on and off the field, was conducted with a dignity rarely seen among great athletes. Joe's autobiography, *Lucky to Be a Yankee* (1946), is an excellent source for understanding his mind, motivation, and attitude. The book's title represents Joe's most sincere sentiment.

Daniel C. Scavone

Additional Sources:

Cramer, Richard Ben. *Joe DiMaggio: The Hero's Life.* New York: Simon & Schuster, 2000.

Dunn, Herb. *Joe DiMaggio, Young Sports Hero.* New York: Aladdin Paperbacks, 1999.

Moore, Jack B. *Joe DiMaggio, Baseball's Yankee Clipper.* New York: Praeger, 1987.

Seidel, Michael. *Streak: Joe DiMaggio and the Summer of '41.* New York: Penguin Books, 1989.

PYRROS DIMAS

Sport: Weightlifting

Born: November 13, 1971
Chimarra, Albania

Early Life

Born Pirro Dhima to ethnically Greek parents in southern Albania in 1971, Pyrros Dimas first began weightlifting and competing in his native country. By the time he was twenty he was ranked twentieth in the world. The following year he and his grandfather crossed the newly opened Greek-Albanian border. Once across the border he adopted the Greek spelling and pronunciation of his name, Pyrros Dimas.

As an immigrant he found it difficult to find a job or a real place in his new homeland. Initially he lugged concrete blocks at a construction site before finally finding a job in an electronics shop. At the same time he began looking for friends and fellow sports enthusiasts by joining a weightlifting club.

The Road to Excellence

In 1992 Pyrros qualified to lift as a light heavyweight on the Greek Olympic team to compete in Barcelona, Spain, and secured his first Greek passport. He had a difficult task in front of him, facing serious competition from both Poland and the Commonwealth of Independent States (CIS). Ibragim Samadov of the Commonwealth was favored to win. Pyrros and the others all lifted the same weight; however, Pyrros won the gold because he reached the final weight total with the fewest number of lifts.

His adopted nation was ecstatic. Excluding the first modern Olympics in 1896, when only nine nations competed, Greece's only gold medals were won in 1960 and 1980. Suddenly Pyrros was no longer an immigrant; he was, instead, a Greek hero, receiving gifts, money, and job offers. He did not have to worry about his place in Greek society.

The Emerging Champion

Now with a secure place in his new homeland and as an important part of the Greek athletic community, he began setting his sights on the next Olympics. All his training and competing was directed toward ensuring his place on the Olympic team. Along the way he also won world titles in 1993 and 1995.

Greek weight lifter Pyrros Dimas won the gold medal in his weight class at the 2000 Olympics.

He made a brilliant showing at the 1996 Atlanta Games. He had already clinched the gold medal with his first lift; then he added more weight to the bar. He made five more lifts, setting three world records. On his final attempt, when he lifted the 396.8 pounds over his head,he broke his own world record. Pyrros set world records in the snatch (396.8 pounds) and the clean-and-jerk (469.6 pounds). He and three other Greek gold medalists returned to Athens heroes and received another gold medal from the mayor of Athens.

Continuing the Story

Having won two Olympic gold medals and set three world records, Pyrros now had an additional goal. He wanted to win a third Olympic gold medal to tie the record of Turkish weightlifter Naim Suleymanoglu, who won gold in three consecutive Olympics.

The road to this goal was not smooth, however. In 1999 at the World Championships he again seemed assured of the gold when he set a new world record in the snatch. Several moments later he saw the gold snatched away when an Iranian weightlifter won the overall contest. In 2000 at the European Championships he performed poorly because of an injured shoulder.

At the 2000 Olympics in Sydney, Australia, it seemed as if this bad luck might have followed him. The Greek fans who filled the stadium to show Pyrros their support cheered wildly for him. When he stepped to the bar and began to lift, one fan next to the podium yelled at the same time that a cell phone rang. This disrupted his concentration, and he dropped the bar. He later said that he could not really blame the fans, that he should have been professional enough to ignore the distractions.

Still distracted, however, Pyrros also missed his second attempt. His coach took him aside to berate him for the missed opportunities. His third attempt was now crucial. He calmed himself before stepping to the bar. He easily lifted 385.75 pounds,

MAJOR WEIGHTLIFTING CHAMPIONSHIPS							
Year	Competition	Snatch in kg	Place	Clean & Jerk in kg	Place	Total in kg	Place
1992	European Championships	165.0	3d	202.5	3d	367.5	3d
1992	Olympic Games	167.5		207.5		370.0	Gold
1993	European Championships	170.0	2d	200.0	5th	370.0	3d
1993	World Championships	177.5	1st	205.0	4th	377.5	1st
1994	World Championships	178.5	3d	200.0			
1995	European Championships	177.5	1st	210.0	1st	387.5	1st
1995	World Championships	175.0	2d	212.5	1st	385.0	1st
1996	Olympic Games	180.0		213.0		392.5	Gold
1998	European Union Championships	167.5	1st	200.0	1st	350.0	1st
1998	European Championships	172.5	2d	210.0	3d	377.5	2d
1998	World Championships	178.0	2d	212.5	2d	387.5	1st
1999	World Championships	182.5	1st	212.5	3d	387.5	2d
2000	European Championships	170.0	4th	205.0	7th	370.0	4th
2000	Olympic Games	175.0		218.5		390.0	Gold

following this feat with a clean-and-snatch of 473.75 pounds to win the gold. Although unable to set a new world record at 481 pounds, he was happy to have won the gold medal.

Having won his third gold medal he returned to Athens to spend time with his wife and two children. The Greek government showed its appreciation by offering him almost $420,000 for bringing home the gold. The money was only a small part of the motivation to win, however. After winning the gold he set his sights on another record, hoping to win his fourth consecutive gold in the 2004 Olympics, in his adopted city of Athens.

Summary

Pyrros Dimas never let adversity stand in his way. After he left his native Albania to settle in Greece, he took whatever job he could find in order to support himself while he pursued his training. He went to Greece ranked twentieth in the world and only one year later was chosen to compete on the Greek men's weightlifting team. He walked into the arena in Barcelona in 1992 facing stiff competition. He not only won the gold medal but also won the first gold Greece had seen in years. Four years later at the 1996

669

Olympics in Atlanta, Georgia he outdid himself by winning gold and setting three world records.

The immigrant became a hero in his adopted country. World records and gold medals were no longer the goal Pyrros dreamed of achieving. He achieved the unique distinction of winning gold medals at three consecutive Olympics after Sydney in 2000.

Deborah Service

Additional Sources:

"Barcelona '92 Olympics/Day 7 Daily Report." *Los Angeles Times*, August 1, 1992, p. 9.

"Dimas Wins at 187 Pounds for Third Straight Lifting Gold." *The Atlanta Journal-Constitution*, September 24, 2000, p. F7.

Passy, Charles. "Music Jazzes up the Most Obscure of Olympic Sports." *The Atlanta Journal-Constitution*, July 29, 1996, p. S40.

"Pyrros Dimas: Greece/Weightlifting." *Time International* 156, no. 11 (September 18, 2000): 86.

Wangrin, Mark. "Weightlifting Dimas' Gold Comes Mighty Quick." *The Atlanta Journal-Constitution*, July 27, 1996, p. S24.

RAIMONDO D'INEZEO

Sport: Equestrian

Born: February 8, 1925
Rome, Italy

Early Life

Raimondo d'Inezeo was born on February 8, 1925, in Rome, Italy, with two assets: a talented and helpful older brother, Piero, who became his riding companion, and a father, Sergeant-Major Carlo Constante d'Inezeo, who had a riding school near Rome and was known as one of the best horse trainers and teachers of riding and showjumping in Italy. A third advantage was that Raimondo's father taught the new Caprilli method of showjumping. Named for the Italian cavalry officer Federico Caprilli, it basically was a change of position for the rider. Instead of leaning back into the saddle during the jump and letting the weight of the rider interfere with the natural movement of the horse, Caprilli shortened the stirrups so the rider could rise up out of the saddle, lean forward, raise the seat, and thus conform rather than work against the horse's natural jumping arc. Another of Raimondo's father's gifts passed on to his sons was his understanding of horses and how to make them obedient, cooperative, and balanced. Even as a boy, Raimondo had developed a real understanding of horses, an asset that would make him a world-class champion.

Raimondo at first felt he could not compete with his talented older brother and decided to go to the University of Rome. The brothers in fact were quite different: Piero was open and confident; Raimondo was more quiet and less confident. Yet, riding and showjumping were in Raimondo's blood. After two years, he left the university and joined the Italian cavalry, which had adopted the Caprilli method so that Raimondo could continue his father's teaching.

Raimondo left the cavalry so he could be part of the Italian jumping team at the 1948 London Olympics. The Italian team did not score, but the contest was valuable experience.

The Road to Excellence

In 1950, Raimondo joined the *carabinieri*, or Italian mounted police, where, as in the cavalry, he could train with excellent horses and equipment. The Italian government supported the

Raimondo d'Inezeo (left), with Hans Winkler and Piero d'Inezeo.

671

MAJOR CHAMPIONSHIPS

Year	Competition	Event	Place
1956	World Championship	Showjumping	1st
	Olympic Games	Individual jumping	Silver
		Team jumping	Silver
1960	Olympic Games	Individual jumping	Gold
		Team jumping	Bronze
1964, 1972	Olympic Games	Team jumping	Bronze
1974	Dublin Horse Show, Guiness Gold Cup	—	Winner

buying of the best jumping horses, most of which came from Ireland. Raimondo practiced every spare moment he could find, and in 1952, together with his brother Piero, was part of the Italian jumping team at the Helsinki Olympics. Although the Italian team was ahead, Piero missed his turn in the jumping and the team was eliminated.

Raimondo and his brother did better at the 1956 Stockholm Olympics. Although the Germans, under Hans Günter Winkler, placed first in both individual and team jumping, Raimondo, on his horse Merano, was second in individual jumping, winning the silver medal. His brother Piero, on Uruguay, was third, winning the bronze medal. Both brothers were part of the Italian jumping team that was second, winning another silver medal. Raimondo won the title of World Showjumping Champion at Aachen, Germany, that same year. He was now in fact a world-class showjumper.

The Emerging Champion

Although Raimondo never had the style of his older brother, he had a better understanding of horses, giving them every assistance possible. In the end, he became the better jumper. This was obvious at the 1960 Rome Olympics, where the Italians, because of Raimondo, swept the field. Against a background of his wildly cheering countrymen, Raimondo, on Posillipo, won the gold medal in individual jumping. His brother Piero, on The Rock, was second, winning the silver. The Italian jumping team, with both Raimondo and Piero as members, won the bronze medal. It was an exciting moment in Olympic history—one that Raimondo never forgot.

Continuing the Story

Raimondo's young daughter was killed in a tragic skiing accident, and for a while he thought he would never jump again. In his daughter's memory, however, Raimondo became more determined than ever to win. He took part in the equestrian event in the next four Olympics, winning in two. In 1964, at the Tokyo Olympics, the Italian jumping team, with Raimondo as captain on Posillipo, placed third, winning the bronze medal. In 1968, at the Mexico City Olympics, the Italian jumping team, with Raimondo as captain on Bellevue, failed to win a medal, placing fifth. The team made a comeback at the Munich Olympics in 1972, placing third and winning a bronze medal. Raimondo's horse this time was Fiorello. These were the last Olympic Games in which Raimondo participated. Although he won no medals in 1968, Raimondo set a record by participating in eight consecutive Olympic Games, from 1948 to 1976. In recognition of the service of the d'Inezeo brothers to their country, the Italian government asked Raimondo to carry the Italian flag at the opening ceremonies.

Summary

Although Raimondo d'Inezeo had advantages, he also faced handicaps such as a talented older brother and the loss of a child. Through constant practice and a willingness to learn, to adopt new methods, and to make the most of natural talents such as understanding horses, Raimondo became one of the greatest showjumpers of the twentieth century.

Nis Petersen

Additional Sources:

Brown, Gene, ed. *The New York Times Encyclopedia of Sports.* 15 vols. New York: Arno Press, 1979-1980.

Wathen, Guy. *Great Horsemen of the World.* North Pomfret, Vt.: Trafalgar Square, 1991.

Wise, Michael T., Christina Bankes, and Jane Laing, eds. *Chronicle of the Olympics, 1896-1996.* New York: DK Publishing, 1996.

MARCEL DIONNE

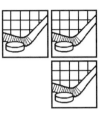

Sport: Ice hockey

Born: August 3, 1951
Drummondville, Quebec, Canada

Early Life

Marcel Elphege Dionne was born on August 3, 1951, in Drummondville, a steel mill town 60 miles northeast of Montreal in Canada's largely French-speaking Quebec province. His father, Gilbert, was a 6-foot 2-inch, 230-pound ex-lumberjack, and his mother, Laurette, a talented figure skater.

Marcel was the oldest of eight children in a tightly knit French-Canadian family. Numerous relatives frequented their home, a seventeen-room stucco house with a grocery store business in the front. Young Marcel worked here after school hours, delivering cartons of beer to customers on his bicycle.

When he was only two, Marcel's mother bought him a pair of ice skates. Each winter, his father turned the backyard into a hockey practice rink. Here, beside a snowbank, the boy sharpened his skills in freezing temperatures.

The Road to Excellence

By age nine, Marcel was an attraction in the town's youth hockey program. The Montreal Canadiens expressed interest in Marcel's future when he was barely a Pee-Wee-level player. Promoting Marcel's career became a family project for his parents and thirteen uncles. His parents bought him very expensive skates when he was thirteen, and appreciative fans donated money after games to buy equipment. At sixteen, Marcel was lured away from his Drummondville Rangers Junior A amateur team by the St. Catharines Junior A Black Hawks of Ontario, a club that has prepared many famous National Hockey League (NHL) stars.

This decision to leave Drummondville and Quebec to play for an English-speaking team at age sixteen angered some French-Canadians and hometown folks. When they threatened legal action, Marcel's parents pretended to separate. The mother left to live in St. Catharines for three months. This ploy ensured that Marcel could legally play there. Three years later, when the Black Hawks met the Quebec Remparts for the 1971 national amateur championship, the Quebec press called Marcel a "traitor" and fans threw garbage at his parents and physically attacked the Ontario team.

In Ontario, where he also attended school, Marcel overcame the language barrier and learned English. During this three-year apprenticeship, he set a league scoring record of 375 ca-

Courtesy of Amateur Athletic Foundation of Los Angeles

673

reer points. In the 1971 NHL draft, Montreal, with first choice, picked another French-Canadian sensation, Guy Lafleur. The Detroit Red Wings, having second choice and seeking a replacement for the famous Gordie Howe, selected Marcel.

The Emerging Champion

Marcel spent four hectic seasons with Detroit. His 77 points in 1971-1972 was an NHL record for rookies. In these first four seasons, Marcel scored 366 points, a higher total than any previous NHL player. The Red Wings' management, however, branded him a troublemaker and selfish player when he spoke his mind too often, criticizing the constant replacement of coaches and uninspired play of teammates. After the 1974-1975 season, Marcel decided not to sign a new contract. Many teams were after him, and the Los Angeles Kings won the bidding war with the best offer.

The Kings wanted a superstar center who could improve their chances and attract more fans in an area where hockey was an unfamiliar sport. Marcel made a difficult adjustment to fit in with the disciplined, defense-oriented style favored by his new coach. He worked hard on his defensive game, bombarded the net with goals as expected, and was praised for being an unselfish playmaker.

Only 5 feet 7½ inches tall and 185 pounds, Marcel, who was called "Little Beaver," made up for his small, stocky build by being one of hockey's fastest and most agile skaters. He would duck under checks by big defensemen and streak past them toward their goal. His dazzling footwork would leave defenders sprawling as he skated around them on breakaways. The sight of Marcel coming at top speed was unnerving to goalies because he had so many unpredictable moves. He kept goaltenders guessing up to the last instant whether he would try to fake them off position and slam the puck by, or pass to an oncoming wing.

Continuing the Story

In 1977, a computer picked Marcel as hockey's most consistent player from game to game. Moreover, in seven seasons, from 1976-1977 to 1982-1983, he only once failed to score 50 or more goals and more than 100 points; the single exception was because of an injury. Marcel won the league scoring title in 1979. The players' association picked him as the league's best in 1979 and 1980. Marcel drew fewer penalties than most players and twice won the Lady Byng Trophy for good sportsmanship.

In Los Angeles, Marcel earned a handsome salary and lived contentedly in a splendid house with his wife, Carol, a French-Canadian girl he met in St. Catharines, and their three children. Sometimes the team's lack of success led to disputes with management and other players. In his sixteen seasons with Detroit and Los Angeles, Marcel's teams had only four winning years. The Kings drew progressively smaller crowds in their sixteen thousand capacity Forum. In Los Angeles, hockey seemed to be as out of place as surfing in Drummondville. Local sportswriters virtually ignored the Kings' superstar, although he was an accessible and colorful personality. If Marcel had played in Montreal, Boston, or New York, his accomplishments would have received the recognition they deserved. Stars who were less consistent but played on winning teams in cities where hockey was popular received much more media exposure than Marcel.

STATISTICS					
Season	GP	G	Ast.	Pts.	PIM
1971-72	78	28	49	77	14
1972-73	77	40	50	90	21
1973-74	74	24	54	78	10
1974-75	80	47	74	121	14
1975-76	80	40	54	94	38
1976-77	80	53	69	122	12
1977-78	70	36	43	79	37
1978-79	80	59	71	130	30
1979-80	80	53	84	**137**	32
1980-81	80	58	77	135	70
1981-82	78	50	67	117	50
1982-83	80	56	51	107	22
1983-84	66	39	53	92	28
1984-85	80	46	80	126	46
1985-86	80	36	58	94	42
1986-87	67	24	50	74	54
1986-87	14	4	6	10	6
1987-88	67	31	34	65	54
1988-89	37	7	16	23	20
Totals	**1,348**	**731**	**1,040**	**1,771**	**600**

Notes: Boldface indicates statistical leader. GP = games played; G = goals; Ast. = assists; Pts. = points; PIM = penalties in minutes

HONORS AND AWARDS

1975, 1977	Lady Byng Trophy
1977, 1980	Seagram's Seven Crowns of Sports Award
1977, 1981	NHL First Team All-Star
1979	Challenge Cup Team member
1979, 1980	NHL Second Team All-Star Lester B. Pearson Award
1980	Art Ross Trophy *Sporting News* NHL Player of the Year
1992	Inducted into Hockey Hall of Fame Uniform number 16 retired by Los Angeles Kings

In March, 1987, the Kings traded their aging superstar to the New York Rangers. Marcel played two more seasons. When he hung up his skates, Marcel's career point total of 1,771 (731 goals, 1,040 assists) in 1,348 games was second only to Gordie Howe's record of 1,850 points (801 goals, 1,049 assists) in 1,767 games. Drummondville has the right to be proud of its contribution to professional hockey. After his retirement in 1990, Marcel became involved in team ownership and administration in the NHL with the expansion North Stars team and in minor league hockey with the ECHL's South Carolina Sting Rays.

Summary

Marcel Dionne's career statistics speak for themselves. They were the result of playing longer and more consistently at a superior level than many other stars who enjoy only five or six such seasons. The fact that Marcel constantly had to make adjustments to playing with new personnel on his line in Los Angeles makes his accomplishment even more impressive. Marcel's career is also proof that a little man with the proper skills and attitude can succeed in a bigger man's physical game.

David A. Crain

Additional Sources:

Fischler, Stan, and Shirley Walter Fischler. *The Hockey Encyclopedia.* New York: Macmillan, 1983.

O'Donnell, Chuck. "King Without a Crown." *Hockey Digest,* 26, no. 2 (1997).

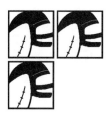

MIKE DITKA

Sport: Football

Born: October 18, 1939
Carnegie, Pennsylvania

Early Life

Michael Keller Ditka was born October 18, 1939, in Carnegie, Pennsylvania. He and his younger brothers and sisters grew up in a government housing project in Aliquippa, Pennsylvania, where the only future that lay ahead for most children was a life in the steel mills.

Mike's father, the son of a Ukrainian immigrant, worked in the Jones and Laughlin steel mill and on the railroad. He instilled in his children a belief in the value of hard work.

As a boy, Mike excelled in sports, primarily because of his hatred of losing. He started out playing Little League baseball because he was too small for most sports. By the time he was in fifth grade, he joined the football team because he enjoyed the head-to-head contact. He was so determined to become a good football player that he lifted weights and did push-ups through junior high and high school. As a result of his grueling workouts, Mike played offensive end on the Aliquippa High School team that won the state championship in his junior year.

In high school, Mike's fierce desire to win a college athletic scholarship was fueled by his refusal to work in the mills as his father and grandfather had. Although he wanted to attend Notre Dame, Mike went to the University of Pittsburgh, because he wanted to enter its dental school. While playing defense for the Pitt Panthers, he earned a reputation as an aggressive player who expected every player to give 100 percent to the game.

The Road to Excellence

After his senior year in college, Mike signed a $12,000 contract with the Chicago Bears of the National Football League (NFL). Soon afterward, the Houston Oilers of the rival American Football League (AFL) offered him a $50,000 contract. Still, Mike had no regrets about joining the Bears, because he wanted to be part of a hard-hitting team.

Mike had no sooner joined the Bears than he began making a name for himself as an exceptional offensive tight end. In 1961, he was voted NFL Rookie of the Year. In 1963, he helped the Bears to win the NFL title.

However, Mike's determination and commitment to doing his best did not become fully apparent until he became injured. In 1965, he played every game and caught 36 passes, even though he had severely injured his right foot just prior to the season's opening day. The following year, he caught 32 passes, despite the fact that his injury was slowing him down.

Mike believes that God arranged for him to be traded to the Philadelphia Eagles at the end of the 1966 season so that he could "learn a little humility." Mike spent most of the 1967 and 1968 seasons on the bench because of his pulled muscles and torn ligaments. He was also forced to sit out as punishment for his public criticism of his team, and he began drinking to escape his depression.

In 1969, the Eagles traded Mike to the Dallas Cowboys. Under the influence of Dallas coach Tom Landry, Mike worked hard to get himself back into shape. Mike's renewed enthusiasm helped propel the Cowboys to the Super Bowl in the 1970 and 1971 seasons. However, when back pain robbed him of his former strength and speed, Mike decided to retire as a player in 1972.

The Emerging Champion

Mike loved football so much that he accepted a position as a Dallas assistant coach under Tom Landry in 1973, even though his salary was cut in half. Still, he accepted his pay cut because of the invaluable lessons that he was learning from Landry about analyzing game films and dealing with individualistic players. He served eight years as an offensive coordinator for the Cowboys.

In 1981, Mike's patience was rewarded with his appointment as head coach of the Chicago Bears, a team that had had only two winning seasons in the previous thirteen. Mike tried so hard to justify the team owners' faith in him that he often flew into fits of rage. He even broke his hand punching a steel trunk in the Bear's locker room.

By 1984, Mike had completely revamped the team by firing lazy players and hiring new ones. The new Bears were a team of strong-willed individualists. Fortunately, Mike had the ability to mold a group of such distinct personalities as

STATISTICS

Season	GP	Rec.	Yds.	Avg.	TD
1961	14	56	1,076	19.2	12
1962	14	58	904	15.6	5
1963	14	59	794	13.5	8
1964	14	75	897	12.0	5
1965	14	36	454	12.6	2
1966	14	32	378	11.8	2
1967	9	26	274	10.5	2
1968	11	13	111	8.5	2
1969	12	17	268	15.8	3
1970	14	8	98	12.3	0
1971	14	30	360	12.0	1
Totals	**144**	**410**	**5,614**	**13.7**	**45**

Notes: GP = games played; Rec. = receptions; Yds. = yards; Avg. = average yards per reception; TD = touchdowns

quarterback Jim McMahon and defensive coordinator Buddy Ryan into a formidable team. Fans across the nation turned Mike and his players into celebrities.

Mike piloted the Bears to a 15-1 season in 1984, and the Bears went on to crush the New England Patriots in the Super Bowl 46-10. Mike, who was by then the best-known football coach in America since Vince Lombardi, was named Coach of the Year by the Associated Press, United Press International, and *The Sporting News*.

Continuing the Story

After the Super Bowl, Mike became Chicago's most famous citizen. He appeared on more billboards and made more television commercials than any public figure in Chicago's history. He became so well known throughout the entire nation that sportswriter Peter Gent dubbed him "the John Wayne of the NFL."

Mike retained his determination to keep winning after the Super Bowl. He did perhaps his best coaching job in 1988, when he coached a 12-4 season out of an aging team. By the end of the decade, his team had won five National Football Conference (NFC) Central Division titles.

In 1988, though, Mike found that he could no longer maintain his volatile coaching style. At the end of a disappointing season in 1988, Mike suffered a minor heart attack just before he was supposed to introduce former vice president George Bush at a campaign rally in Lake Forest, Illinois. Only eleven days later, Mike was back on

677

HONORS AND AWARDS

1960	*Sporting News* College All-American
1961	United Press International NFL Rookie of the Year Bell Trophy *Sporting News* NFL Rookie of the Year
1961-65	*Sporting News* NFL Western Conference All-Star Team
1962-66	NFL Pro Bowl Team
1985	Associated Press Coach of the Year *Sporting News* Coach of the Year
1985, 1988	United Press International NFC Coach of the Year
1986	Inducted into College Football Hall of Fame
1988	Inducted into Pro Football Hall of Fame

the sidelines of a Bears game with the Washington Redskins. He later explained that he "coaches by crisis," and that he would never be happy unless he had something to fight and overcome.

Still, Mike seemed to have learned that he was not invulnerable. He started a cholesterol-free diet and curtailed his drinking. He also has an artificial hip, the result of his football injuries. He still smokes his trademark cigars, though.

At the end of the 1989 season, Mike was so embittered by the fact that his team had lost ten of its last twelve games that he almost quit. Mike's frustration surfaced in front of television cameras in 1990, when he yanked the clipboard out of the Bears' defensive coordinator's hand and began calling the plays himself. Once again, he had made the point that only winning would satisfy him. In 1992 Mike was fired as head coach of the Chicago Bears. In 1997 he was hired as head coach of the New Orleans Saints. Mike continued his hard-driven coaching style, but the Saints did not do well. During Mike's three seasons as the Saints' head coach, the team's record was 15-33. He was fired from that club in January, 2000. He then purchased and operated a restaurant in Chicago.

Summary

Mike Ditka has become a folk hero, the champion of the all-American work ethic. As a player, he was one of the toughest men in the history of the sport. As a coach, he pushed his players as hard as he had pushed himself when he played. He has emerged as a hard-driven man who is fueled by the courage of his convictions.

Alan Brown

Additional Sources:

Ditka, Mike, and Don Pierson. *Ditka: An Autobiography*. Chicago: Bonus Books, 1986.

Keteyian, Armen. *Ditka: Monster of the Midway*. New York: Pocket Books, 1992.

Silver, Michael. "Sound and Fury." *Sports Illustrated* 85, no. 12 (September 22, 1997): 28-33.

Stamborski, Jim. *Don't Get Me Wrong*. Chicago: Chicago Review Press, 1988.

ALEXANDER DITYATIN

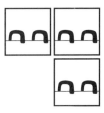

Sport: Gymnastics

Born: August 7, 1957
        Leningrad, Soviet Union

Early Life

Alexander Dityatin was born in Leningrad (now Saint Petersburg), Soviet Union, on August 7, 1957. His father worked as a repairman and his mother as an assembly worker in a plant in Leningrad. As a boy, Alexander developed a problem with stooped shoulders; it was to remedy this condition that he began doing gymnastics exercises at the age of eight. He liked the sport, did well, and continued training at the Leningrad Dynamo Club, under the coaching of Anatoli Yarmovski. A stubborn, intelligent, and hard-working student, by the age of sixteen, younger than the usual age for qualification, he was awarded his title as Master of the Sport. He looked to his predecessors for models and inspiration—to the courage of Victor Tchoukarine and the elegance of Mikhail Voronin.

The Road to Excellence

Alexander appeared on the gymnastics scene under the shadow of Nikolai Andrianov, who dominated Soviet and much of world gymnastics throughout the 1970's. In 1974, Alexander showed great promise at his first international meets, the Eastern Bloc "Tournament of Friendship" in Pyongyang, North Korea, and a Dynamo Club match against the home squad in Hamburg, West Germany. The following year, Alexander established himself on the international scene with bronze medals in all-around competitions at the European Championships in Bern, Switzerland, the World Cup in London, England, the Pre-Olympics in Montreal, Canada, and the Chunichi Cup in Nagoya, Japan.

Alexander grew a dramatic five inches during his seventeenth year; at 5 feet 9¾ inches he was appreciably taller than most

Alexander Dityatin, the all-around gold medalist at the 1980 Games, performs on the parallel bars.

of his competitors. His greater stature, which might have been viewed as a liability, he turned to his advantage, finding a wider range of amplitude and movement than was available to smaller men. His long legs gave him elegance and helped him to excel on such apparatus as the rings and the vault. In all events, he exhibited great consistency in landing solidly on his dismounts. On the other hand, he developed a weakness in the floor exercises that he was to overcome later in his career only through steady hard work. Alexander was a handsome man, and his cheerful disposition and native charisma always charmed and pleased audiences.

The Emerging Champion

At the 1976 Olympics in Montreal, Alexander took fourth in the all-around competition, be-

hind his teammate Andrianov and the Japanese champions Sawao Kato and Mitsuo Tsukahara. He left Montreal with his hopes fixed on the Moscow Olympics in 1980. In the intervening years, he traveled with the Soviet team to Great Britain for an exhibition tour, where his passable English must have come in handy. While enrolled as a student at the Leningrad Institute of Physical Culture, he continued to grow in international competition. In 1977, he was ranked ninth in the world in standings based on overall performance, and by 1978 he had moved up to third. He won a bronze medal in the all-around at the World Championships in Strasbourg, France, in 1978, but once again it was his teammate Andrianov who took the gold.

The older gymnast faltered the following year at the World Championships in Fort Worth, Texas, however. In Fort Worth, Alex's somewhat conservative strategy, taking few chances but executing his customary moves with elegance and perfection, reflected the temperament of a diligent and intelligent student and showed the even, consistent performances across the various events of a complete gymnast. Alexander eclipsed Andrianov and the rising American Kurt Thomas for first in the all-around, and set himself up for ascendancy at the coming Olympics in Moscow.

Alexander married a student in track and field at the Physical Culture Institute in Leningrad, and in the fall of 1979 he and Elena became parents to a son, Alyosha. The family lived in Leningrad, where Alexander served as a member of the city government. When not in the arena, he pursued numerous avocations, including reading science fiction and detective stories, fishing, synchronized swimming, ballet, and the theater.

With the boycott of the 1980 Moscow Olympics by the United States, Japan, China, and other

				STATISTICS		
Year	Competition	Event	Place	Event	Place
1975	Moscow Cup	All-Around	4th	Pommel horse	1st
		Floor exercise	6th	Rings	2d
		Parallel bars	6th		
	European Championships	All-Around	3d	Rings	3d
		Parallel bars	2d	Vault	2d
	World Cup	All-Around	3d	Pommel horse	4th
		Floor exercise	5th	Rings	4th
		Horizontal bar	5th	Vault	6th
		Parallel bars	4th		
	Chunichi Cup	All-Around	3d		
1976	Olympic Games	All-Around	4th	Rings	Silver
		Pommel horse	6th	Team	Silver
1978	World Championships	All-Around	3d	Rings	2d
		Floor exercise	3d	Vault	4th
		Pommel horse	4th	Team	2d
	World Cup	All-Around	1st		
1979	European Championships	Parallel bars	2d	Rings	1st
		Pommel horse	1st		
	World Cup	All-Around	1st	Parallel bars	2d
		Floor exercise	4th	Rings	1st
		Horizontal bar	4th	Vault	2d
	World Championships	All-Around	1st	Rings	1st
		Horizontal bar	3d	Vault	1st
		Parallel bars	4th	Team	1st
		Pommel horse	4th		
1980	Olympic Games	All-Around	Gold	Pommel horse	Silver
		Floor exercise	Bronze	Rings	Gold
		Horizontal bar	Silver	Vault	Silver
		Parallel bars	Silver	Team	Gold
1981	World Championships	Parallel bars	2nd	Rings	1st
		Team	1st		
1982	World Cup	All-Around	5th		

680

nations, Alexander's accomplishments there lose some of their shine, yet his domination over the Eastern European gymnasts, and especially Andrianov, was certainly impressive. He not only took the all-around and rings, but also, in placing in each individual event and being on the first-place team, won eight medals in all, breaking the standing record of seven set by Soviet gymnast Boris Shakhlin in Rome in 1960 and matched by American swimmer Mark Spitz in Munich in 1972 and Andrianov in Montreal in 1976. In addition, harking back to Nadia Comăneci's glory in women's gymnastics in Montreal, Alexander became the first male gymnast in Olympic history to receive a perfect score when judges awarded him a 10 for his vault. With the 1980 Olympics, he was acknowledged as the world's best male gymnast and had become something of a media star—a "pin-up boy"—in his native Russia.

Continuing the Story

Following his glory in Moscow, Alexander decided not to attend the 1980 World Cup in Toronto, Canada—possibly, it has been suggested, as a retaliation for the American boycott of the Olympics. An ankle injury at the 1981 World Championships in Moscow caused him, after stepping onto the mat for his floor exercises, to salute, turn around, and drop out of the event. While taking a gold medal on the rings and a silver on parallel bars, he finished last in the overall competition. Over the following year, he lost much weight and strength: His reappearance at the 1982 World Cup in Zagreb, where he took fifth in the all-around but made no finals in individual events, was disappointing. Competing and exhibiting sporadically despite troubling injuries well into 1983, Alexander at last retired from active work, passing on the leadership of Soviet men's gymnastics to Dmitri Belozerchev.

HONORS, AWARDS, AND RECORDS

1979	*International Gymnast* magazine Most Successful Man of 1979
1980	Decorated with the Order of Lenin
	Voted the third-ranked Soviet Sportsman of the Year
	First gymnast to win a medal in all eight categories in a single Olympiad
	Set record for the most medals won in a single Olympiad (8)
	First male gymnast to receive a perfect score (10) in Olympic history

---

Having graduated as a sports teacher from Leningrad's Lesgaft Institute, the oldest sports institute in the Soviet Union, Alexander turned to coaching after his retirement.

Summary

In an age when smaller was better, Alexander Dityatin showed that a gymnast of greater than ordinary size could achieve extraordinary elegance and formal perfection. He assumed a position in a continuing dynasty of Soviet gymnasts and became, through his athletic performances and his warm personality, one of the best-loved gymnasts ever.

Barry Mann

Additional Sources:

"Alexander Dityatin." Yahoo! Sport: Olympic Games 2000. http://uk.sports.yahoo.com/oly/oldgames/bio/3199.html. November 9, 2000.

Haycock, Kate. "Alexander Dityatin." In *Gymnastics*. New York: Crestwood House, 1991.

Srebnitsky, Alexei. "Alexander Dityatin: A Profile." *Soviet Life* (October, 1981): 62-64.

"Where Are They Now: Alexander Ditiatin." *International Gymnast* Online. http://www.intlgymnast.com/paststars/psfeb99.html. February, 1999.

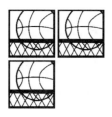

VLADE DIVAC

Sport: Basketball

Born: February 3, 1968
Prijepolje, Serbia, Yugoslavia

Early Life

Son of Milenko, an executive of an electronics firm, and Rada Divac, Vlade Divac (pronounced VLAH-day DEE-vahtch) was born in the small town of Prijepolje, in the republic of Serbia. When he was twelve years old, he left Prijepolje to play on a club team in Kraljevo, a larger town about four hours away. He quickly moved through the ranks, and by the time he was sixteen he had already advanced to the senior leagues of the Yugoslavian basketball system and signed a contract with the team Sloga. This feat would be comparable to a sixteen-year-old joining the ranks of the National Basketball Association (NBA). As a member of the national team, Vlade's travels took him all over Europe.

The Road to Excellence

In 1985, at the age of seventeen, Vlade helped lead the Yugoslavian Junior Olympic team to the gold medal in the World University Games, beating a group of soon-to-be superstars from America including Gary Payton and Larry Johnson. When he was eighteen, he began playing for Belgrade Partizan, one of the leading teams in the Yugoslavian league. During his seasons with Partizan, Vlade averaged approximately 20 points and 10 rebounds per game. Three years later, he was the starting center on the Yugoslavian Olympic team at Seoul, Korea, and averaged 11.7 points and 6.5 rebounds per game. That year, his team brought home the silver medal.

The Emerging Champion

When Vlade was drafted by the Los Angeles Lakers in 1989, he was filling a huge gap: Kareem

Vlade Divac of the Sacramento Kings passes the Denver Nuggets' Keon Clark in a 1999 game.

682

STATISTICS

Season	GP	FGA	FGM	FG%	FTA	FTM	FT%	Reb.	Ast.	TP	PPG
1989-90	82	549	274	.499	216	153	.708	512	75	701	8.5
1990-91	82	637	360	.565	279	196	.703	666	92	921	11.2
1991-92	36	317	157	.495	112	86	.768	247	60	405	11.3
1992-93	82	819	397	.485	341	235	.689	729	232	1,050	12.8
1993-94	79	895	453	.506	303	208	.686	851	307	1,123	14.2
1994-95	80	957	485	.507	382	297	.777	829	329	1,277	16.0
1995-96	79	807	414	.513	295	189	.641	679	261	1,020	12.9
1996-97	81	847	418	.494	259	177	.683	725	301	1,024	12.6
1997-98	64	536	267	.498	188	130	.691	518	172	667	10.4
1998-99	50	557	262	.470	255	179	.702	501	215	714	14.3
1999-00	82	764	384	.503	333	230	.691	656	244	1,005	12.3
2000-01	81	755	364	.482	350	242	.691	673	231	974	12.0
Totals	878	8,440	4,235	.502	3,313	2,322	.701	7,586	2,519	10,881	12.4

Notes: GP = games played; FGA = field goals attempted; FGM = field goals made; FG% = field goal percentage; FTA = free throws attempted; FTM = free throws made; FT% = free throw percentage; Reb. = rebounds; Ast. = assists; TP = total points; PPG = points per game

Abdul-Jabbar had just retired from the Lakers the year before. As NBA basketball tends toward a much rougher style of play than its European counterpart, Vlade also had to adjust to a different set of rules. He had the benefit of excellent teachers: Magic Johnson, James Worthy, Michael Cooper, and Byron Scott were all NBA champions, and coach Pat Riley was also willing to teach Vlade the ropes of NBA basketball. His playing experience and athleticism earned him a spot on the All-Rookie First Team, and his obvious love for the game and his impressive agility and speed quickly endeared him to Los Angeles fans.

The summer after his first season in the NBA, he married his girlfriend, Snevana. As a testament to his popularity in his homeland, their wedding was filmed by a television crew and later broadcast on Yugoslavian national television. His apprenticeship in the NBA continued, and during the next five seasons, his production steadily increased in all areas. In the 1994-1995 season, starting all eighty games for the Lakers, Vlade averaged 16 points, 10.4 rebounds, 4.1 assists (leading all NBA centers that year), and 2.17 blocks. Following this impressive season, he helped the Yugoslavian team to a victory in the European Championships in the summer of 1995.

Continuing the Story

After the 1995-1996 season, Vlade was traded to the Charlotte Hornets for superstar-to-be Kobe Bryant and an opportunity to hire Sha-

quille O'Neal. Before playing with the Hornets, however, Vlade helped the Yugoslavian Olympic team win a silver medal in Atlanta, Georgia, in 1996. While disappointed to leave Los Angeles, he performed well during his first year on the Hornets, averaging 12.6 points, 9 rebounds, 3.7 assists (again leading the league for centers), and a career-high 2.22 blocks per game. During his two years as a Hornet, he led his team in blocked shots, setting a Hornets record for blocks in one game, with 12. In a statistic that demonstrates Vlade's quick-handedness, he led the team in steals his first year and ranked second on the team his next.

As a free agent, he was able to return to the state of California, moving to the Sacramento Kings for the 1998-1999 season. In his first year on the Kings, he averaged 14.3 points, 10 rebounds, and 4.3 assists per game. His experience served the Kings well as they challenged the much-favored Utah Jazz in a strong first-round playoff match. During the playoff series, he led the Kings in points, rebounds, and assists. After that season, he signed a contract to play for an-

MILESTONES

1993	Matched Lakers franchise record of 13 offensive rebounds
1997	1,000th career blocked shot 5,000th career rebound

HONORS AND AWARDS

1989-1990	NBA All-Rookie First Team
1988, 1996	Silver Medal with Yugoslav Olympic team

other five years with the Kings. Once a student of the NBA game, Vlade became a wily veteran, bringing eleven years of experience to a young Sacramento team.

In 2000-2001, Vlade and teammate Chris Webber led the Kings to their best-ever record and a tie for first place in the NBA's Pacific Division. When the Lakers' Shaquille O'Neal could not play in the all-star game, Vlade was named to replace him.

Despite the considerable wealth and fame that comes with being an NBA star, Vlade has not forgotten his roots. The violence in the Federal Republic of Yugoslavia during the 1990's was always present in his mind, as he left many family members and friends behind when he moved to the United States. He has used his status as a professional athlete to bring some attention to the human side of the political confrontation.

Aside from his two sons, Luka and Matia, the Divacs adopted a Yugoslav orphan girl, Petra. In 1995 Vlade, along with teammates from his Yugoslav basketball days, founded the Divac Childrens' Foundation/Group 7, which raises funds for children of all ethnic backgrounds impacted by the war in Yugoslavia. He has also been active in a number of activities dedicated to disadvantaged children in the United States. Thanks to his work in these fields, he was awarded the J. Walter Kennedy Citizenship Award for the 1999-2000 season, becoming the first foreign-born player to earn the honor.

Summary

Vlade Divac is a player who has matured during his eleven years in the NBA. He began his NBA career barely able to speak English and has since performed in a number of commercials, television programs, and films. Once unaccustomed to the pace and the physicality of the NBA game, he has learned the various tricks of the NBA, and he passes his knowledge and experience to his younger teammates. While he has learned a number of things, Vlade came into the league with many of the skills that continue to make him one of the great players in the NBA. For a center, he is an excellent shooter, passer, and ball-handler. His enthusiasm and love for the game have always been primary in his career and have earned him the respect of his teammates and his opponents.

Alexander Jordan

Additional Sources:

Reilly, Rick. "Vlade Divac's Private War." *Sports Illustrated* 90, no. 21 (May 24, 1999): 114.

"Vlade Divac, Kings." *Sports Illustrated* 90, no. 18 (May 3, 1999): 76.

Wolff, Alexander. "Prisoners of War; Nine Years Ago, as Yugoslavs and Friends, They Beat the U.S. to Win the World Junior Basketball Title." *Sports Illustrated*, June 3, 1996, 80.

LARRY DOBY

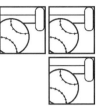

Sport: Baseball

Born: December 13, 1924
Camden, South Carolina

Early Life

Lawrence Eugene Doby was born to David and Etta Doby in South Carolina in 1924. Larry's father, who had a reputation as a great baseball hitter, worked away from home most of the time, grooming horses. With his mother also working away from home, Larry's grandmother, Amanda Brooks, reared him during most of his early years, teaching him strict discipline, reading and writing skills, and the importance of church attendance. When his grandmother developed a mental illness, Larry's mother placed him under the tutelage of her sister, where he spent four very happy years. Larry attended Mather Academy in Camden, South Carolina, where he played organized baseball for the first time in his life.

In 1938, Larry graduated from the eighth grade, and his mother insisted that he move with her to Paterson, New Jersey, to attend high school. Larry lettered in four sports at Paterson East Side High School, then entered Long Island University on a basketball scholarship in 1942. He later transferred to Virginia Union University prior to joining the U.S. Navy in 1943.

The Road to Excellence

While still in high school, Larry played a few games of professional baseball with the Newark Eagles of the Negro National League under the alias "Larry Walker" in order to protect his college eligibility. Following graduation, he played with the Eagles during the summer of 1942, batting .391 in twenty-six games. While in the Navy, Larry played for the Great Lakes Naval Training School team, where he encountered racial discrimination.

Discharged from the Navy in early 1946, Larry returned to professional baseball, playing the

winter in Puerto Rico and then rejoining the Newark Eagles. In the 1946 season, Larry hit .348 for the team and helped lead it to the Negro World Series title. In 1947, Larry married his teenage sweetheart, Helyn Curvy, and they reared five children.

STATISTICS

Season	Games	AB	Hits	2B	3B	HR	Runs	RBI	BA	SA
1947	29	32	5	1	0	0	3	2	.156	.187
1948	121	439	132	23	9	14	83	66	.301	.490
1949	147	547	153	25	3	24	106	85	.280	.468
1950	142	503	164	25	5	25	110	102	.326	.545
1951	134	447	132	27	5	20	84	69	.295	.512
1952	140	519	143	26	8	**32**	**104**	104	.276	**.541**
1953	149	513	135	18	5	29	92	102	.263	.487
1954	153	577	157	18	4	**32**	94	**126**	.272	.484
1955	131	491	143	17	5	26	91	75	.291	.505
1956	140	504	135	22	3	24	89	102	.268	.466
1957	119	416	120	27	2	14	57	79	.288	.464
1958	89	247	70	10	1	13	41	45	.283	.490
1959	39	113	26	4	2	0	6	13	.230	.301
Totals	1,533	5,348	1,515	245	55	253	960	970	.283	.490

Note: Boldface indicates statistical leader. GP = games played; AB = at bats; 2B = doubles; 3B = triples; HR = home runs; RBI = runs batted in; BA = batting average; SA = slugging average

During the first half of the 1947 season, Larry was leading the Negro National League with a .458 average and 14 home runs, when the challenge came to play in the major leagues. After weeks of rumors, Larry was told that he had been purchased by Bill Veeck's Cleveland Indians on July 3, 1947. On July 5, he made his major league debut, striking out as a pinch hitter. Larry had become the first African American to play in the American League, and only the second African American to play major league baseball, following Jackie Robinson of the National League Brooklyn Dodgers by eleven weeks. During his first half-season with the Indians, Larry received very limited playing time.

The Emerging Champion

After being converted from an infielder to an outfielder in 1948, Larry batted .301, hit 14 home runs, and led the Cleveland Indians to the American League title. In the World Series against the Boston Braves, Larry hit .318 and became the first African American to hit a home run in the World Series, blasting a 400-foot game winner off of Braves pitching star Johnny Sain in game 4. Larry helped lead the Indians to the series win over the Braves and became the first African American to play on a World Series champion team.

After leading major league outfielders with 14 errors in 1948, Larry worked very hard to become an excellent fielder. In 1950, he was selected as the top center fielder in the major leagues, ahead of Joe DiMaggio and Duke Snider. During one stretch of his career, Larry made no errors in 164 consecutive games.

Continuing the Story

During the 1952 season with the Indians, Larry became the first former Negro League player to win a major league home run title, leading the American League with 32 homers. In 1954, he led the American League in home runs with 32 and in runs batted in with 126, finishing second to Yogi Berra in the most valuable player voting. He helped the 1954 Indians win 111 games and return to the World Series, where they lost to the New York Giants.

Larry played in every major league All-Star game from 1949 through 1954 and was the first African American to hit a home run in the All-Star game. After a successful career playing for the Indians, Chicago White Sox, and Detroit Tigers, Larry retired from the major leagues in 1959 after breaking an ankle while sliding into third base. His final major league statistics boast a .283 average, with 253 home runs and 970 runs batted in.

MILESTONES

1952	First former Negro League player to win a major league home run title (32 home runs)
1952	First African American to hit a home run in an All-Star Game

In 1969, Larry reentered professional baseball as a hitting coach for the Montreal Expos. He later coached for the Indians and the White Sox. Because of his ability to communicate with the players and adapt instruction to their styles and abilities, Larry proved to be a very effective coach. In 1978, he became the second African American to manage a major league baseball team, when he was selected to pilot the White Sox for much of the season. Although he was able to improve the team's performance, his players could not win a pennant, and Larry was released at the end of the season.

In the 1990's, Larry received some well-earned rewards. On July 3, 1994, the Cleveland Indians retired his jersey, number 14. In 1997, Larry was hired as an assistant to American League president Gene Budig. In addition, the 1997 All-Star game played in Cleveland was dedicated to Larry, and he acted as honorary American League captain. Finally, on July 26, 1998, Larry was inducted into the Baseball Hall of Fame after being selected by the Veterans Committee.

Summary

Possessing exceptional athletic ability and a staunch constitution, Larry Doby made his mark in baseball as the first African American to break the color barrier in the American League. Fur-

HONORS AND AWARDS	
1949-1955	American League All-Star Team
1994	Uniform number 14 retired by Cleveland Indians
1997	All-Star Game dedicated to Doby; he acts as American League captain
1998	Inducted into National Baseball Hall of Fame

thermore, he was the first African American player to lead the major leagues in home runs, to hit a home run in the World Series, and to hit a home run in an All-Star game. He is one of only four players to play in both a major league and Negro League World Series.

Alvin K. Benson

Additional Sources:

Gardner, Robert, and Dennis Shortelle. *The Forgotten Players: The Story of Black Baseball in America.* New York: Walker, 1993.

Holway, John, ed. *The Sluggers.* Alexandria, Va.: Redefinition, 1989.

Koppett, Leonard. *Koppett's Concise History of Major League Baseball.* Philadelphia, Pa.: Temple University Press, 1998.

Moore, Joseph Thomas. *Pride Against Prejudice: The Biography of Larry Doby.* New York: Praeger, 1988.

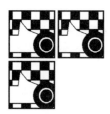

MARK DONOHUE

Sport: Auto racing

Born: March 18, 1937
  Summit, New Jersey
Died: August 19, 1975
  Graz, Austria

Early Life

Mark Donohue, Jr., born on March 18, 1937, grew up in Summit, New Jersey. Before the age of ten, he was able to drive the family car through the awkward and difficult driveway into the garage. The family barn became his auto shop. Once when the barn caught fire, Mark ran for help, then rushed back into the barn to put out the fire. This act was not sheer recklessness: He knew exactly the location of the fire extinguisher, the path the burning gasoline would take, and

how to escape if he could not douse the fire. The flames were extinguished before the fire department arrived.

Mark was also a survivor; he was not stopped by scarlet fever, a tonsillectomy, vein cauterizations, an appendectomy, or even polio. These early traumas taught him to adopt a stoic attitude, which freed him to think rationally and sensibly even in the midst of pain and confusion.

The Road to Excellence

In 1959, Mark graduated with a degree in mechanical engineering from Brown University. Soon after, Mark sold his souped-up Corvette and, with this money, bought an Elva Courier with an MG engine. While working as a mechanical engineer, he entered the Elva in various regional amateur races. By 1961, he was racing all over the country and winning frequently. He won three national amateur sports car championships before turning professional in 1966.

Mark joined the team headed by Roger Penske, a former amateur driving champion. Mark began by test-driving cars for Penske but soon was racing for him. In 1967 and 1968, Mark won the United States Road Racing Championship. When that series of races was discontinued, Mark successfully raced a modified Chevrolet Camaro in the Trans-American Sedan Series for small, sporty cars. He also competed successfully in a different arena: the Canadian-American Challenge Series (Can-Am). The Formula Seven cars in these races were "technically unlimited": virtually no rules governed the engine or bodywork, allowing creativity in the design.

The Emerging Champion

By 1969, Penske had convinced Mark that the new goal was the Indianapolis 500. (Indy-type cars, unlike Can-Am cars, have defined maximum engine sizes and other technical restric-

tions and run on a mixture of methanol and nitromethane.) The Indianapolis 500 is the biggest event in American auto racing and perhaps the most widely attended annual event in the country. At Indianapolis, Mark's quiet disposition earned him a new nickname: Captain Nice. Mark finished seventh and was voted Rookie of the Year.

Mark and Penske concentrated their efforts on Indy the next year, but a disappointed Mark Donohue finished a distant second, behind Al Unser, who had led nearly the entire race. By this time, however, the long hours Mark spent preparing for races had taken a toll on his personal life. He separated from his wife and two children.

Mark set his sights on Indy for 1971. During a practice run, he broke the track record by going 177 miles per hour, and, about a week later, he ran 180 miles per hour. Winning Indy, however, did not depend solely on speed; it also entailed completing the race. Mark had built up an almost unbeatable lead when a gearbox broke and he had to drop out of the race. Worse yet, his car, a McLaren M16, was soon destroyed in a freak accident. Later that year, Mark won the first Schaefer 500-mile race, and the experience of winning a long, Indy-type race helped him the next year.

In 1972, Mark and Penske were ready. Their plan was to race with an "underpowered" car that would give them good speed but, more importantly, was reliable enough to endure the grueling 500 miles. Mark finally succeeded in winning the Indianapolis 500, setting a new Indy record at more than 163 miles per hour.

A few weeks later, Mark was testing a new Porsche prototype at Road Atlanta when the steering disintegrated on the track. He badly injured his left knee. While he recuperated, he kept thinking of racing. In particular, he wanted to challenge Team McLaren, who had dominated the past five or six years of the Can-Am se-

SPORTS CARS AND OTHER VICTORIES	
1966	Can-Am Challenge Cup Race (Mosport Park)
1967-68	U.S. Road Racing Overall Driving Champion
1968	Can-Am Challenge Cup Race (Bridgehampton Race circuit) Trans-Am Race (Sebring Road Course)
1968-71	Trans-Am Race (Mont-Treblant circuit)
1968-69, 1971	Trans-Am Overall Driving Champion
1969	The 24 Hours of Daytona Trans-Am Race (Laguna Seca Raceway) Trans-Am Race (Riverside International Raceway)
1969, 1971	Watkins Glen Grand Prix
1970-71	Trans-Am Race (Road America)
1971	USAC 200-Mile Trans-Am Race (Edmonton International Speedway) Michigan 200
1971-72	USAC 500-Mile
1972	Indianapolis 500
1972-73	Can-Am Challenge Cup Race (Edmonton International Speedway)
1973	Winston Western 500 Watkins Glen Grand Prix Champion Can-Am Challenge Cup Race (Laguna Seca Raceway) Can-Am Challenge Cup Race (Riverside International Raceway) Can-Am Challenge Cup Race (Road America) Can-Am Challenge Cup Series Championship
1974	International Race of Champions Champion Driver

ries. The next season, Mark returned to racing and won most of the Can-Am races and the overall championship, then abruptly retired. As far as American auto racing was concerned, Mark had done it all.

Continuing the Story

In February, 1974, Mark briefly emerged from retirement for the International Race of Champions designed to determine who was the greatest of the great drivers. The competitors in this race were each given a Porsche Carrera to drive. Mark won it easily, beating Bobby Unser, A. J. Foyt, Peter Revson, David Pearson, and George Follmer.

Mark retired from driving again to engineer a Grand Prix (Formula One) car for young driver Peter Revson. Engines of Grand Prix cars are smaller than those of Indy-type cars, run on ordinary gasoline, and are rear-mounted in cigar-shaped cars. When Revson was killed in a crash, Mark came out of retirement and began racing

RECORDS

Most victories on the Trans-Am circuit, 29

HONORS AND AWARDS

1968	Driver of the Year
1969	Indianapolis 500 Rookie of the Year
1990	Inducted into International Motor Sports Hall of Fame Inducted into Motorsports Hall of Fame of America

Summary

Some race car drivers, many of whom never finished high school, complained that Mark Donohue had an unfair advantage because he was trained in engineering. Despite his technical expertise, he showed that champions win because of careful planning, precise execution, cool nerves, and, above all, driving instinct. Mark was the consummate race car driver and a champion in all racing categories.

Frank Wu

the Formula One car that he had helped design. Grand Prix racing was the "missing link," the racing category that Mark had yet to master. It was a type of racing dominated by Europeans such as Jackie Stewart. Mark's best Grand Prix showing with this new car was fifth, but he was looking forward to a better season the following year.

While he was doing 160-mile-per-hour practice laps for the Austrian Grand Prix, his left front tire lost air and his Penske March 751 crashed. Mark died in a hospital two days later, on August 19, 1975. At his bedside were his father, Mark Sr.; Penske; and his second wife of eight months, Eden. He was a champion to the end; two weeks before his death, he had set a world speed record on a closed track in a turbocharged Porsche, driving at more than 221 miles per hour.

Additional Sources:

Berger, Phil, and Larry Bortstein. *The Boys of Indy.* New York: Corwin Books, 1977.

Breton, Tracy. "The Donohue Death: Will a $20 Million Judgment Against Goodyear Signal the Beginning of the End of Racing as We Know It?" *Car and Driver* 30 (August, 1984): 123-128.

Donohue, Mark, with Paul Van Valkenburgh. *The Unfair Advantage.* New York: Dodd, Mead, 1975.

Jones, Robert F. "Good Show, Charlie Brown!" *Sports Illustrated* 36, no. 23 (June 5, 1972): 22-25.

Posey, Sam. "Magnificent Obsession: A Personal Look at Mark Donohue—Talent and Tragedy." *Road and Track* 43, no. 10 (June, 1992): 146-153.

TONY DORSETT

Sport: Football

Born: April 7, 1954
    Aliquippa, Pennsylvania

Early Life

Anthony (Tony) Drew Dorsett was born on April 7, 1954, in Aliquippa, Pennsylvania. The sixth of seven children, Tony grew up in a conservative churchgoing family.

His mother, Myrtle Dorsett, instilled in him the values of respecting other people and getting a first-rate education. His father, Westley Dorsett, supported the family by working in a steel mill. His father gave Tony the nickname "Hawkeye" (often abbreviated to "Hawk"), and the name has stuck with fans and sportswriters.

Tony worked at developing muscle strength and aggressiveness during his childhood years. Many believe that this determination was spurred by his rejection from a "midget" league football team when he was twelve.

The Road to Excellence

Tony's determination to build himself into an athlete paid off. As an outside linebacker for Hopewell High School, Dorsett was known as "monster man" who streaked out of nowhere to make crushing tackles. As a junior, Tony was made a running back by Coach Butch Ross.

Dorsett led Hopewell to the Midwestern Athletic Conference Championship. As a senior, he rushed for 1,238 yards and 23 touchdowns and was named first-team All-State and Scholastic All-

American by *Parade, Scholastic,* and *Coach and Athlete* magazines.

A top college prospect, Tony was finally convinced by coach Johnny Majors to attend the University of Pittsburgh. Tony was convinced that the Panthers, who had gone through nine losing seasons, could go nowhere but up with his help at running back. Nothing could have been more true.

Coach Majors observed that Dorsett was "like a man possessed in his dedication." Tony added

power to his 5-foot 10-inch frame by working with weights, and grew from 157 to 190 pounds. The increased power was evident in his freshman season, as he rushed for 1,586 yards and led the Pittsburgh Panthers to a 6-4-1 record in 1973. For that, Tony became the first freshman All-American since 1944, when Doc Blanchard won the same honor.

The next season, Pittsburgh improved its record to 8 wins and 4 losses, and Tony increased his total yards accumulated in college to 2,590. Tony's proudest achievement that year was a 303 yard rushing performance against Notre Dame.

The Emerging Champion

Tony's greatest season in a University of Pittsburgh uniform came in 1976, his senior year. The Panthers finished that season undefeated and went on to the Sugar Bowl, where they defeated the University of Georgia.

Including his performance in the Sugar Bowl, Tony rushed for 2,050 yards in his senior year. The Panthers were named national champions in both the Associated Press and United Press International polls, and Tony was awarded the Heisman Trophy, the Maxwell Award, and numerous Player of the Year citations.

After being selected in the first round of the National Football League (NFL) draft by the Dallas Cowboys, Tony signed a five-year $1.1 million contract. Immediately, Tony exceeded expectations, as he surprised the Dallas Cowboy coaches with his excellent catching and blocking abilities.

A position on the first team of the Cowboys would have to wait, however. At first, Dorsett was used sparingly, warming the bench while veteran Preston Pearson played at the running back position. Though Tony was on the second team, playing half of each game, he still led the team in touchdowns and rushing at midseason. By the tenth game of the season, Tony was put on the first team. He won the Rookie of the Year award easily, and in the 1978 Super Bowl he was the leading rusher, contributing 1 touchdown in the win over the Denver Broncos.

Among the Dallas club records Tony held are longest scoring catch of the 1978 season (91 yards); most yards gained in a season (1,325 yards); 484 yards rushing and 5 touchdowns in the playoffs; and 101 yards rushing in the NFC championship game.

When the Cowboys' passing game slumped, they turned to Tony's running to pick up the slack. In a 1979 game against the New York Giants, Tony carried the ball 29 times for 108 yards, a career high. The Cowboys won that game 28-7 and later that season won their fifth straight divisional championship.

STATISTICS

| Season | GP | Rushing | | | | Receiving | | | |
		Car.	Yds.	Avg.	TD	Rec.	Yds.	Avg.	TD
1977	14	208	1,007	4.8	12	29	273	9.4	1
1978	16	290	1,325	4.6	7	37	378	10.2	2
1979	14	250	1,107	4.4	6	45	375	8.3	1
1980	15	278	1,185	4.3	11	34	263	7.7	0
1981	16	342	1,646	4.8	4	32	325	10.2	2
1982	9	177	**745**	4.2	5	24	179	7.5	0
1983	16	289	1,321	4.6	8	40	287	7.2	1
1984	16	302	1,189	3.9	6	51	459	9.0	1
1985	16	305	1,307	4.3	7	46	449	9.8	3
1986	13	184	748	4.1	5	25	267	10.7	1
1987	12	130	456	3.5	1	19	177	9.3	1
1988	16	181	703	3.9	5	16	122	7.6	0
Totals	173	2,936	12,739	4.3	77	398	3,554	8.9	13

Notes: Boldface indicates statistical leader. GP = games played; Car. = carries; Yds. = yards; Avg. = average yards per carry or average yards per reception; TD = touchdowns; Rec. = receptions

Continuing the Story

Whenever Tony got the ball he left a wake of dazed defensive backs. About his incredible running ability, he has said, "I see a guy, and if I can spin on him, I spin. If you do it wrong, you get hit dead center in the back." His college coach said Tony could "Stop on a dime . . . take three little bitty steps and be off again." The fastest tacklers who pursued him were often left grasping air.

After eleven stellar seasons in Dallas, Tony was traded by the Cowboys to the Denver Broncos shortly before the start of the 1988 season. Tony played one season with the Broncos and appeared in all sixteen of the team's games before retiring at the season's end. In 1994 Tony was inducted into the Pro Football Hall of Fame.

Tony has been described as affable and articulate, walking with a fluid bounce. He has a son, Anthony Drew Dorsett, Jr., who attended the University of Pittsburgh and played wide receiver on its football team.

Summary

Not since O. J. Simpson had there been a greater breakaway running back in professional football than Tony Dorsett. Tony was a four-time All-American at the University of Pittsburgh, where he led the team to a national championship and claimed for himself the Heisman Trophy. As a Dallas Cowboy he used his great offensive ground speed to break rushing records, and he helped the team to a world's championship in the Super Bowl.

Rustin Larson

NCAA DIVISION 1-A RECORDS	
Most rushing yards, 6,082	

HONORS AND AWARDS	
1973-76	College All-American
1976	Heisman Trophy
	Maxwell Award
	Camp Award
	Sporting News College Player of the Year
	Citizens Savings College Football Player of the Year
	Sporting News College All-American
1977	Associated Press Offensive Rookie of the Year
	United Press International NFC Rookie of the Year
	Sporting News NFC Rookie of the Year
	Bell Trophy
1979, 1982-84	NFL Pro Bowl Team
1981	United Press International NFC Player of the Year
	Sporting News NFL All-Star Team
1994	Inducted into Pro Football Hall of Fame

Additional Sources:

Aaseng, Nathan. *Football's Breakaway Backs*. Minneapolis: Lerner, 1980.

Barber, Phil. "NFL: Football's One Hundred Greatest Players: The Hit Men." *The Sporting News* 223 (November 1, 1999): 12-16.

Conrad, Dick. *Tony Dorsett*. Chicago: Children's Press, 1979.

Dorsett, Tony, and Harvey Frommer. *Running Tough: Memoirs of a Football Maverick*. New York: Doubleday, 1989.

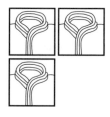

DAVID DOUILLET

Sport: Judo

Born: February 17, 1969
Rouen, France

Early Life

From his early years, David Douillet showed interest and potential in sports. Born in northwestern France in 1969, David weighed in at some 10 pounds and measured 22 inches in length. His home life was not perfect. His father deserted the family before David turned one year old. This departure left David's mother as the sole provider for herself and her son. To meet her responsibilities, she accepted employment in Switzerland and was forced to leave her son in the care of his grandmother in the Normandy region of France.

By the age of eight, David had become enamored with the horses that ran freely through the Normandy countryside and made known his desire to become a jockey. However, his large size made this dream an impossibility, so his interests eventually fell upon the mat sport of judo. His grandmother bought him his first gi when he was only eleven years old. Following his introduction to judo, David began training in earnest at a Neufchatel en Bray judo club.

The Road to Excellence

David's long hours of work paid off when he won his first major championship, the French Junior Championship, at the age of seventeen. The young, growing, and improving *judoka* then entered the public eye. While training in Rennes, David came to the attention of Jean-Luc Rougé, who brought France its first world judo championship in 1975. Impressed with the young athlete, Rougé secured a spot for David at France's premier sports training facility, the National Institute for Sport and Physical Education (INSEP), much like the United States Olympic Training Facility at Colorado Springs, Colorado.

The Emerging Champion

From the beginning, David showed great potential in all aspects of judo. However, he found his strength in *uchi-mata*, or the inner thigh throw, and *hara goshi*, or the sweeping hip technique. David's name soon became known beyond the world of French judo mats when he began winning wide-ranging titles. In 1989 he won the bronze medal in the Junior European Championships. In 1991 and 1992, he placed first in the French judo championship.

David narrowly missed winning his first European championship in 1993, having to settle for

David Douillet celebrates after winning a gold medal in judo at the 2000 Olympics.

MAJOR JUDO CHAMPIONSHIPS

Year	Competition	Place
1989	Junior European Championships	3d
1991-92	French Judo Championships	1st
1992	Olympic Games	Bronze
1993	European Club Cup	1st
	European Championship	2d
1993-95, 1997	World Championship	1st
1994	European Championship	1st
1996, 2000	Olympic Games	Gold

the silver medal. In that same year, he won his first world title in Hamilton, Canada, and he piloted the French judo team to the European Club Cup Championship in Frankfurt, Germany. In 1994 David captured his first European Championship and headed the French team, which won that country's first world team championship.

In 1995 David was forced to prove his strength when he defended his world title in Chiba, Japan. By the end of the tournament, David had risen to the top of the *judokas* by taking gold in both the over-95 kilogram and the open categories. His fierce competition and eventual success won David a place in the annals of Japanese judo, the titular home of the sport. He would echo this success in 1997, when he won his fourth world title, in Paris, in the over-95 kilogram category. The French were ecstatic with David's win, validating their long support and adoration of this countryman who had won all that there was to win.

Continuing the Story

Regardless of the French, European, and world titles that he would amass, David's place in sports history became assured after his performances at the Olympic Games. David began his quest for Olympic medals at the 1992 Barcelona Olympics. Although some had questioned the sense of placing David on the French national team, he took a bronze medal.

David's second Olympic appearance, at the 1996 Atlanta Olympic Games, was also surrounded by a bit of controversy. World champion David Khakhaleichvili of the Republic of Georgia was disqualified for not appearing for the official weigh-in. This placed David Douillet in a front-seat position from which he did not falter, taking the heavyweight gold medal. David became only the fourth French Olympic judo champion, the others being Thierry Rey, Angelo Perisi, and Marc Alexandre.

Douillet's third Olympic medal came when he took the gold at the Sydney 2000 Olympic Games. However, David's win was a controversial one. He successfully threw Japanese competitor Shinohara, who then attempted a counterthrow. The match judge, Craig Monaghan of New Zealand, ruled Shinohara's effort unsuccessful and awarded the match to David. Because of this ruling Monaghan received not only criticism from Japanese fans but also several death threats.

Summary

The story of David Douillet is almost stereotypical in that it is the story of a young man who learned a foreign sport and rose to the position of world champion, even defeating Japanese competitors and achieving the ranking of Sixth Dan from the International Judo Federation. His French, European, and World championships would have been enough to assure him a place in sports posterity, but his Olympic victories made him a household name around the world and a national hero in his native France. For his achievements, David was immortalized by having his wax figure placed with other French elite in the Paris wax museum the Museé Grevin.

Tom Frazier

Additional Sources:

Douillet, David, with Jean-Michel Rascol and Jean-Louis Korb. *L'Âme du conquérant.* Paris: R. Laffont, 1998.

695

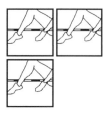

STACY DRAGILA

Sport: Track and field (pole vault)

Born: March 25, 1971
Auburn, California

Early Life

Stacy Dragila was born Stacy Mikaelson on March 25, 1971, in the Northern California town of Auburn. Her parents, Bill and Irma Mikaelson, owned and operated a ranch, where as a child Stacy helped with the chores and developed an affection for animals.

Stacy's older brother was an accomplished athlete, and Stacy would accompany him to Little League baseball games, soccer matches, and track meets, running in her first meet at age six. Stacy participated in several sports as a youth, in-cluding basketball and rodeo (in which she competed in breakaway roping and team roping), but excelled in track, drawing inspiration and influence from female track stars such as Jackie Joyner-Kersee and Florence Griffith-Joyner. While in high school, Stacy went to the California state track meet twice as a hurdler and finished second in the 400-meter hurdles at the 1990 Golden West Invitational.

The Road to Excellence

Although she was an outstanding hurdler in high school, Stacy realized the need to work with an expert coach who could help her to sharpen her technique. During her senior year, she began working with John Orgonen, a track coach at nearby Yuba College. Orgonen saw a great deal of potential in Stacy and recruited her for the Yuba track team. While at Yuba College, Stacy competed in the heptathlon, a series of seven events that includes the 100-meter hurdles, the 200- and 800-meter dashes, jumping, the shot put, and the javelin throw. After two years at Yuba (a junior college), Stacy enrolled at Idaho State University in 1993, where she competed in the heptathlon under coach Dave Nielsen. Stacy married Brent Dragila in 1993, assuming the name by which she has been known for most of her athletic career.

By the time she arrived at Idaho State, Stacy was an accomplished athlete but knew that she was not a good enough heptath-lete to compete at the national level. During her junior year,

In 2000, American Stacy Dragila was the first to win the women's pole vault gold medal in the Olympics.

MAJOR POLE VAULT CHAMPIONSHIPS

Year	Competition	Place
1996	USA Indoor Championships	1st
	USA Outdoor Championships	1st
1997	World Indoor Championships	1st
	USA Indoor Championships	1st
1998	USA Indoor Championships	1st
1999	World Championships	1st
2000	USA Olympic Trials	1st
	Olympic Games	Gold
2001	World Championships	1st

Nielsen, a former collegiate pole vaulter, suggested that his female heptathletes try pole vaulting. Stacy later described her first attempts at pole vaulting as frightening and disorienting, but Nielsen encouraged her to continue training for the event, which was increasing in popularity among women. She became doubly determined to master the pole vault after a male teammate at Idaho State told her that women were too weak ever to excel at the event. Recognizing the opportunity to carve a niche for herself in a relatively new and competitively open event, Stacy began training intensively to be a pole vaulter.

The Emerging Champion

Stacy continued competing as a heptathlete until her graduation from Idaho State in 1995, but by then had also begun to vault competitively. At an indoor meet in 1994, she set an American record by vaulting more than 10 feet, but she was not aware of what she had done until she read about it in *Track and Field News*. Setting a record motivated Stacy to intensify her training, and, although she finished second in the heptathlon at the 1995 Big Sky Championships, she had begun to build a reputation as a promising women's pole vaulter. *Track and Field News* ranked her second among American women pole vaulters in 1995, and she finished second in the vault at the U.S. Outdoor Championships that year. In 1996 Stacy won both the U.S. Indoor and U.S. Outdoor Championships and was ranked number one in the U.S. She would remain the top-ranked American women's pole vaulter for the rest of the decade.

Continuing the Story

During the late 1990's, Stacy continued to build steadily upon her record-setting marks, raising the standard in women's pole vaulting by 13 inches between 1998 and 2000. During much of this time she traded the world record with Emma George of Australia, but on several occasions she set new records by breaking her own. After winning the 1999 World Championship with a record-tying vault of 15 feet 1 inch (which earned her the first gold medal in women's pole vault history), Stacy broke the world indoor record in February of 2000 with a vault of 15 feet 1½ inches, only to break it again the following month with vault of 15 feet 1¾ inches at the U.S. Track and Field Championships in Atlanta. In July, 2000, Stacy once again broke the world record with a vault of 15 feet 2¼ inches at the U.S. Olympic trials. It was the sixth time that she had tied or broken the American or world record that year.

When the International Olympic Committee announced that women's pole vaulting would be a medal sport in the 2000 Olympics in Sydney, Australia, Stacy was the first athlete mentioned as a favorite for the gold medal in the event. Her record-setting performances leading up to the games had helped to popularize the event in the United States, as Stacy became the subject of numerous magazine articles, interviews, photographic features, and television commercials.

Nevertheless, Stacy experienced some difficulty in the Olympic finals, missing her first two attempts of 14 feet 9 inches. Having struggled with anxiety before the games, she was left with one last vault to keep her dream of a gold medal alive. Stacy cleared the third vault at a height of 15 feet 1 inch, then watched as Australia's Tatiana Grigorieva missed her next four attempts, making Stacy the first Olympic gold medalist in the women's pole vault.

Summary

Although she claimed that she is "not a natural athlete," Stacy Dragila was a multisport competitor as a youth, and as an adult became the world's first women's pole vaulting champion. A heptathlete in college, Stacy took up pole vaulting at the relatively late age of twenty-two but quickly became one of the top female vaulters in

697

the world by compiling an incredible string of victories and records during the 1990's. Her career totals include four U.S. indoor championships, four U.S. outdoor championships, one world championship, numerous world records, and the first Olympic gold medal ever awarded in the women's pole vault. A series of phenomenal performances leading up to the 2000 Games, combined with her charming personality and photogenic appearance, drew the attention of the media, making Stacy an ambassador for her sport and a symbol of the modern female athlete.

Michael H. Burchett

Additional Sources:

Donnelly, Sally. "Meet the Power Sisters." *Time* 156 (July 24, 2000): 70.

"Meet the Power Sisters: Weight Lifter Cheryl Haworth and Vaulter Stacy Dragila Star in Two New Strength Events for Women." *Time* 156, no. 4 (July 24, 2000): 70.

"Meet the Stars." *Track and Field News*, November 1, 1999, 13.

"Vaulters Climbing Higher." *Track and Field News*, August 1, 2000, 36.

HEIKE DRESCHLER

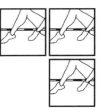

Sport: Track and field (long jump)

Born: December 16, 1964
　　　 Gera, East Germany

Early Life

Born Heike Daute on December 16, 1964, in Gera, East Germany, Heike Dreschler lost her father in an untimely accident at a fairground when he was only thirty-one years old. Her mother, a shift worker, was left to raise Heike and her three siblings alone. Heike was groomed for greatness as part of the old East German sports system. Throughout her long, successful career as a long jumper, sprinter, and heptathlete, the Olympic star seldom failed to live up to her country's expectations.

Behind the Iron Curtain, success in sports translated into money, privilege, and even power. Knowing that, Heike's family encouraged her to pursue sports. Tall, agile, and strong for her age, she was spotted by German coaches when she was a schoolgirl and was recruited for track and field. She quickly established herself as an international star.

The Road to Excellence

At age seventeen, Heike made her international debut in 1981 by setting a world junior record in the heptathlon (5,812 points), then set two in the long jump—22.67 feet and 22.90 feet—with the latter standing as the world junior record for at least nineteen years. She was 5 feet 11 inches tall, and her athletic build and world-class speed made her an immediate threat in the senior ranks.

After moving up to face elite competition at her first World Championships in 1983, Heike won her first world title in the long jump, at 23.42 feet, and became the youngest athlete, at age nineteen, to win a gold medal. She also upset reigning world-record holder Anisoara Cusmir of Romania in the process.

The Emerging Champion

Heike continued her winning streak by racking up more titles and more places in the record books—not only in long jumping but also in sprinting. In 1986, she won the indoor 100-meter title at the country's national championships and equaled countrywoman Marita Koch's world record time of 21.71 in the 200 meters. From 1982 through 1996, she won 206 of 245 long jump competitions, including her one hundredth victory at the 1992 Olympic Games in Barcelona, Spain.

Heike Dreschler won her second long jump gold medal at the 2000 Olympics.

699

STATISTICS

Year	Competition	Event	Place
1983	World Championships	Long jump	1st
1987	World Championships	Long jump	3d
	World Championships	200 meters	2d
1988	Olympics	Long jump	Silver
1990, 1994, 1998	European Championships	Long jump	1st
1991	World Championships, Tokyo	Long jump	2d
1991, 1992, 1994, 1995, 1998, 1999	German Championships	Long jump	1st
1992	Olympic Games	Long jump	Gold
1993	World Championships, Stuttgart, Germany	Long jump	1st
1995	World Championships, Gothenburg, Sweden	Long jump	9th
1997	World Championships, Athens, Greece	Long jump	4th
1998	European Championships	Long jump	1st
	Olympic Games	Long jump	Silver
	Olympic Games	100 meters	Bronze
	Olympic Games	200 meters	Bronze
2000	Olympic Games	Long jump	Gold

Perhaps Heike's claim to fame as an athlete is her spirited rivalry with some of America's best, both past and present. Between Jackie Joyner-Kersee and Heike, Heike has five of the top ten all-time best jumps, while Joyner-Kersee has only three. Joyner-Kersee won their head-to-head contest at the 1988 Olympic Games in Seoul, South Korea, however, with a record-breaking performance while Heike settled for the silver medal.

Heike continued her competitive streak against American superstar Marion Jones in the long jump. She beat Jones in 1999 with jump of 22.41 feet over Jones's 22.24 feet and was the only women to beat Jones at any event during the 1998 season. Heike ended Jones's winning streak of thirty-six competitions at the World Cup in Johannesburg, South Africa, when she beat her by 2.76 inches with a jump of 23.20 feet.

Continuing the Story

Few athletes have had Heike's longevity in the sports world, yet at age thirty-five she continued to compete, more than fifteen years after joining the elite level. In 1999 in Seville, Spain, Heike competed in her seventh consecutive World Championships. Only German discus thrower Jurgen Schult and Jamaican sprinter Merlene Ottey have equaled Heike's mark.

In 2000 she won her second Olympic gold medal in the long jump, eight years after her first. Her jump of 22.93 feet beat Italian Fiona May's and Jones's jumps of 22.70 feet. She never expected to win the gold and stated it would be her final Olympic appearance.

Once the Iron Curtain fell, Heike capitalized on her fame by signing lucrative endorsement deals. She left her club, Jena, after fifteen years at the start of 1995 to take up an attractive offer at Chemnitz, which included a deal with a health insurance company to be a spokeswoman.

Heike, who once held a seat in East Germany's parliament, married soccer-player husband Andreas Dreschler and petitioned the German sports federation for permission in the prime of her competitive career to have a baby. After much debate, the German officials relented, and Heike gave birth to her only child, Toni, on November 1, 1989, eight days before the fall of the Berlin Wall. Now divorced from Dreschler, the long jumper and her son moved to Karlsruhe, Germany, with French decathlete and former European champion Alain Blondel, but continued to train with her father-in-law, Erich Dreschler.

Summary

In a career admittedly tainted by her years as the wunderkind of an East German regime that employed systematic doping and her time, of which details are minimal, as an informer for the *Stasi*—the state secret police—Heike Dreschler's long jumping has earned her three world titles, two Olympic gold medals, four European titles, and three world records. She was the first woman to jump beyond 25 feet (wind aided) and has cleared 22.97 feet more than four hundred times during her career.

Additional Sources:

Knight, Tom. "Rivalry That Stirs Dreschler's Desire." *Track & Field Magazine* 1548 (August 21, 1999).

"Long Jump All Time Records." International Amateur Athletic Federation. http://www.iaaf.org.

"Olympic Games: Dreschler Pulls Out with Knee Injury." http://www.eurosport.com. July 16, 1996.

Wolff, Alexander. "Katrin the Great." *Sports Illustrated Magazine* 75, no. 17 (October 21, 1991): 84.

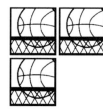

CLYDE DREXLER

Sport: Basketball

Born: June 22, 1962
New Orleans, Louisiana

Early Life

Clyde Drexler was born on June 22, 1962, in New Orleans, Louisiana. His family moved to Houston, Texas, when he was four years old. Clyde grew up in a family of five children. His mother, Eunice Drexler Scott, was a single parent who stressed education as the first priority for her children.

Like most of his friends, Clyde played Little League baseball and basketball during his early adolescence. Although he enjoyed sports and games and loved the thrill of competing and winning, he also spent a great deal of time on his schoolwork.

The Road to Excellence

Clyde, like most playground youths who participate in basketball, was fascinated with the dunk shot, which was to become one of his most thrilling, powerful, acrobatic moves. The first time he dunked was on the playground behind Albert Thomas Junior High School; he was fifteen years old and 6 feet 1 inch tall. Two tall youths who were guarding the basket scared him as he drove for the basket, but he made the shot. It was a special moment. Clyde was to recall an-other remarkable aspect about that first dunk: The basket was a foot higher than a regulation basket.

As a sophomore, Clyde declined an invitation to play for Sterling, his high school team. His height increased to 6 feet 4 inches by his junior year. He was again invited by the coach to join the school's team. Deep down he wanted to play, but, because of the hard practices and time involved,

Clyde Drexler of the Houston Rockets during a 1995 game.

702

STATISTICS

Season	GP	FGM	FG%	FTM	FT%	Reb.	Ast.	TP	PPG
1983-84	82	252	.451	123	.728	235	153	628	7.7
1984-85	80	573	.494	223	.759	476	441	1,377	17.2
1985-86	75	542	.475	293	.769	421	600	1,389	18.5
1986-87	82	707	.502	357	.760	518	566	1,782	21.7
1987-88	81	849	.506	476	.811	533	467	2,185	27.0
1988-89	78	829	.496	438	.799	615	450	2,123	27.2
1989-90	73	670	.494	333	.774	507	432	1,703	23.3
1990-91	82	645	.482	416	.794	546	493	1,767	21.5
1991-92	76	694	.470	401	.794	500	512	1,903	25.0
1992-93	49	350	.429	245	.839	309	278	976	19.9
1993-94	68	473	.428	286	.777	445	333	1,303	19.2
1994-95	76	571	.461	364	.824	480	362	1,653	21.8
1995-96	52	331	.433	265	.784	373	302	1,005	19.3
1996-97	62	397	.442	201	.750	373	354	1,114	18.0
1997-98	70	452	.427	277	.801	346	382	1,287	18.4
Totals	**1,086**	**8,335**	**.472**	**4,698**	**.788**	**6,677**	**6,125**	**22,195**	**20.4**

Notes: GP = games played; FGM = field goals made; FG% = field goal percentage; FTM = free throws made; FT% = free throw percentage; Reb. = rebounds; Ast. = assists; TP = total points; PPG = points per game

he could not make the decision. All his life he was told by family members to go to school and get a good education. After talking with Clyde's mother, however, the coach persuaded Clyde to play.

Clyde's basketball ability improved with each practice and with each game. He worked hard to improve his game, playing almost every position on the team. His hard work, dedication, and patience began to pay off. His improvement was steady, but he was not yet a complete ballplayer. He was recruited by only three major colleges: Texas Tech, New Mexico State, and the University of Houston. Although he was overlooked by most college recruiters in high school, he was a two-year starter, the team's most valuable player, and an All-Houston Independent School District selection as a senior.

The Emerging Champion

One of Clyde's friends, Michael Young, attended Jack Yates High School and was the most sought-after basektball player in the state. When the University of Houston signed Michael, he told Coach Guy Lewis that Clyde Drexler was the best player he had played against. That convinced Coach Lewis to sign Clyde. Clyde and Michael were roommates as freshmen, but their friendship had begun long before, on the playgrounds of MacGregor Park, an inner-city park

less than one mile south of the University of Houston's campus.

During Clyde's freshman year, a Houston sports reporter said that Clyde treated the fans to moves similar to those of Julius Erving, who was one of Clyde's idols. Coach Lewis said that Clyde was improving all the time and that the only time that he had played like a freshman, if he ever had, was in high school.

After Clyde's third season at the University of Houston, the team record was eighty-six wins and twelve losses. Clyde's individual play was remarkable during that period. He was called "Clyde the Glide" because of his style of play. He would often glide down the basketball court, steal the ball, and score with an improbable open-court move. His versatility as a player was evident; he became the first Houston player to score at least 1,000 points, collect at least 800 rebounds, and pass for at least 3,000 assists.

Continuing the Story

The 1983 season was truly thrilling for all Houston Cougar basketball fans. Clyde was joined by future NBA star Akeem Olajuwon on one of the best college teams of the decade. The team was nicknamed "Phi Slamma Jamma" because of the powerful assortment of dunk shots it inflicted upon opponents. Clyde was the most creative and spectacular of the fraternity of

703

Slamma Jammas. The team advanced to the finals of the National Collegiate Athletic Association (NCAA) Championship Tournament, only to lose to North Carolina State.

After the NCAA loss, Clyde decided to forgo his senior year and turn professional. He agonized for weeks over his decision to remain in school or declare himself eligible for the National Basketball Association (NBA). Becoming a professional basketball player was one of Clyde's childhood dreams. His mother wanted him to stay in school to get his degree, but she left the decision to Clyde.

When Clyde declared himself eligible for the professional draft in 1983, he was chosen in the first round by the Portland Trail Blazers. His on-court displays thrilled the fans in the NBA. Magic Johnson has ranked Clyde with other stars of the NBA such as Larry Bird, Michael Jordan, and himself, considering Clyde a tremendous player on both ends of the court. Clyde had seasons where he averaged more than 25 points, 7 rebounds, 6 assists, and 2 steals per game for his team.

During his playing years, Clyde worked in a Houston bank during the off-season to gain the experience and finance background to help him to handle his investments. He also continued to be involved with community activities during the off-season. He sponsored a summer inner-city youth basketball camp for eight- to eighteen-year-olds in Houston.

The 1991-1992 season was one of Clyde's most memorable. He averaged 25.0 points per game, became only the second player in Trail Blazers history to make the All-NBA First Team, finished second to Michael Jordan for the most valuable player award, and took the Trail Blazers to the NBA finals against Jordan and the Chicago Bulls. Later in 1992, he earned a gold medal as a member of the 1992 U.S. "Dream Team" at the Summer Olympics in Barcelona, Spain.

Near the middle of the 1994-1995 season, Clyde was traded to the Houston Rockets. He left Portland as the team's all-time leader in scoring, games played, minutes played, field goals, free throws, rebounds, and steals. The trade reunited him with his former college teammate Hakeem Olajuwon, and the two led the Rockets to the 1995 NBA championship. In 1996, Clyde was

HONORS AND AWARDS

1981	Southwest Conference Newcomer of the Year
1982-83	Consensus All-Southwest Conference Team
1983	Consensus All-American Dallas Times-Herald Southwest Conference Player of the Year
1988, 1990-92	All-NBA Team
1992	Gold Medal, Olympic Basketball
1996	NBA 50 Greatest Players of All Time Team
1999	All-Star 2ball Championship (with Cynthia Cooper) Inducted into Texas Sports Hall of Fame Inducted into Houston Hall of Fame
2001	Uniform number 22 retired by Portland Trail Blazers

named to the NBA's 50 Greatest Players of All Time Team.

Because of a number of injuries and the addition of Charles Barkley to the Rockets, Clyde's output began to diminish. He announced his retirement during the 1997-1998 season. He ended his NBA career ranked seventeenth on the all-time scoring list with 22,195 points and fourth in steals with 2,207. He, Oscar Robertson, and John Havlicek are the only players in NBA history to amass over 20,000 points, 6,000 rebounds, and 6,000 assists in a career.

On March 18, 1998, Clyde announced his acceptance of the head coaching job with his alma mater, the Houston Cougars. Although his first year of coaching produced only a 10-17 record, Clyde seldom changed his calm courtside demeanor in games. His ultimate goal was to have the best collegiate team in the nation. In 1999, Clyde was inducted into the Texas Sports Hall of Fame, as well as Houston's Hall of Fame.

Summary

"Clyde the Glide" Drexler was a superstar in the NBA. He exhibited genuine concern for his teammates and was considered a team player even when he had achieved superstar status. He has contributed to the community by sponsoring basketball camps and making frequent personal appearances. His strong commitment to continuing education is shown by his work toward a banking career after his playing days in the NBA.

Thurman W. Robins

Additional Sources:

Bjarkman, Peter C. *The Biographical History of Basketball.* Chicago: Masters Press, 1998.

Dolin, Nick, Chris Dolin, and David Check. *Basketball Stars: The Greatest Players in the History of the Game.* New York: Black Dog and Leventhal, 1997.

Kelly, J., and Brian Silverman. *Clyde Drexler.* Broomall, Pa.: Chelsea House, 1997.

Mallozzi, Vincent M. *Basketball: The Legends and the Game.* Willowdale, Ont.: Firefly Books, 1998.

Shouler, Kenneth A. *The Experts Pick Basketball's Best Fifty Players in the Last Fifty Years.* Lenexa, Kans.: Addax, 1998.

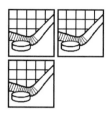

KEN DRYDEN

Sport: Ice hockey

Born: August 8, 1947
Hamilton, Ontario, Canada

Early Life

On August 8, 1947, Kenneth Wayne Dryden was born in Hamilton, Ontario, Canada, to Murray Dryden, a successful businessman, and his wife, Margaret. Ken has a younger sister, Judy. His elder brother Dave, born in 1941, later played thirteen professional seasons at goal with National Hockey League (NHL) and World Hockey League (WHL) teams.

In 1949, the family moved to metropolitan Toronto, settling in the Islington sector of Etobicoke in the western suburbs. When Ken was five, the Drydens bought a house with a large back-yard. Ken's father had part of this area paved and regulation goals installed at each end. Dave and Ken manned the nets and got experience stopping flying tennis balls in neighborhood tournaments. Murray Dryden encouraged his boys' participation in sports, faithfully attending their games and coaching and sponsoring youth teams. School came before athletics in this household, however.

The Road to Excellence

Ken started playing organized hockey at seven, always playing with boys several years older as he progressed through each age division. In addition to hockey, he excelled in baseball and basketball. In 1963, Ken joined the Etobicoke In-

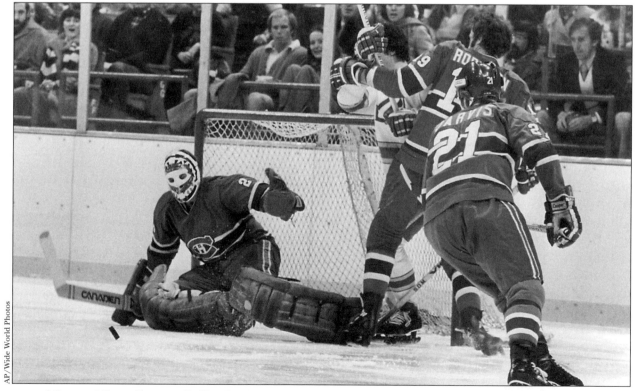

Montreal Canadiens goalie Ken Dryden prepares to block a shot against the Atlanta Flames in 1978.

dians of the Metro Toronto Junior B amateur hockey league. Considered the league's best goalie, Ken was drafted that same year by the Montreal Canadiens, who wanted him to play for their Junior A Petersborough, Ontario, team. To their surprise, Ken stayed with the local team so he could concentrate on doing well in grade thirteen, the most important school year for college preparation in Canada. Ignoring the advice of scouts, who believed he was discarding an NHL career opportunity, Ken chose in 1965 to attend Cornell University, an Ivy League school in New York, and to play hockey on the college team.

At Cornell, Ken excelled in the classroom and the rink. According to coach Ken Harkness, "Ken was a splendid student as a history major, a brilliant goaltender, and an excellent team player." Harkness inspired Ken with pride in winning. Ken was an All-American selection in each of his three varsity seasons. During this period, Cornell lost only four of eighty-three games with Ken at goal, and he compiled a sensational average of 1.60 goals allowed per game. Some considered Ken to be the best goalie in the history of college hockey. Montreal still had first rights to Ken, and the Canadiens' interest in him revived when he graduated in 1969.

The Emerging Champion

Following graduation, Ken married Lynda Curran, a Cornell student. Again, he spurned the Canadiens by joining Canada's national team so he could study law in Winnipeg, the team's home base. After this amateur team folded in midseason, the Canadiens gave Ken an opportunity to combine law school and hockey the next season in Montreal. Ken could attend classes at McGill University while practicing once a week and playing mostly home games with the AHL Montreal Voyageurs. Near the close of the 1970-1971 season, the Canadiens called up Ken.

Montreal surprised the hockey world. Ken, with only six games of NHL experience, was to start Montreal's first game of Stanley Cup action against highly favored Boston. The Bruins

STATISTICS						
Season	GP	W	L	T	GAA	PIM
1970-71	6	6	0	0	1.65	0
1971-72	64	**39**	8	15	2.24	4
1972-73	54	**33**	7	13	**2.26**	2
1974-75	56	30	9	16	2.69	0
1975-76	62	**42**	10	8	**2.03**	0
1976-77	56	**41**	6	8	**2.14**	0
1977-78	52	37	7	7	**2.05**	0
1978-79	47	30	10	7	**2.30**	4
Totals	397	258	57	74	2.24	10

Notes: Boldface indicates statistical leader. GP = games played; W = wins; L = losses; T = ties; GAA = goals against average; PIM = penalties in minutes

won 3-1, but Ken played well. In game 2, with Ken at goal, Montreal fell behind 5-1 but managed a stunning 7-5 comeback victory. The team's confidence surged.

As the series progressed, Ken's great skill became evident. At 6 feet 4 inches and 210 pounds, he nearly filled the goal opening. His 83-inch reach and tremendous catching hand repeatedly stopped sure goals. The deciding seventh game in Boston was a one-man spectacle. The Canadiens triumphed 4-2 as Ken withstood a 48-shot barrage. Even when Ken was caught far off position, the big glove came from nowhere to make unbelievable saves. Boston forwards who raised their sticks, anticipating a victory dance after scoring, ended by gesturing in disbelief when Ken robbed them. Bruins star Phil Esposito, a frequent victim, declared it was Ken who beat them.

Behind Ken's 20-game performance, Montreal went on to beat Minnesota in the semifinal round, then defeat arch-rival Chicago in an exciting seven-game series to win the Stanley Cup in a historic upset. Ken was chosen the most valuable playoff performer. The next season, he proved that this showing was no fluke. Ken earned the Calder Memorial Trophy as the league's top rookie with an average of 2.24 goals allowed per game and 8 shutouts.

Continuing the Story

The scholarly goaltender was a unique NHL superstar. Ken spent the summer of 1971 doing volunteer work for consumer advocate Ralph Nader's organization. He enlisted other athletes

707

HONORS AND AWARDS

1967-69	NCAA All-American
1971	Conn Smythe Trophy
1972	Calder Memorial Trophy NHL Second Team All-Star
1973, 1976-79	NHL First Team All-Star Vezina Trophy
1978	Seagram's Seven Crowns of Sports Award
1983	Inducted into Hockey Hall of Fame

in a campaign to clean up polluted waterways. Dividing time between studies and hockey was difficult, but Ken completed his law degree in December, 1972.

In the nets, "the human octopus" continued to frustrate opponents. After assisting Team Canada's difficult series victory over the Soviets in September, 1972, Ken went on to win the Vezina Trophy as the NHL's best goaltender of 1972-1973. In another surprising move, Ken sat out 1973-1974 after a contract dispute, working as a law clerk. Montreal gave him a good contract the next year, and Ken performed respectably, although below previous standards. Over the next five seasons, however, Ken regained his superior form in both the regular season and the playoffs. In 1978, a computer selected Ken as hockey's best player. The next season, however, Ken found himself blinking at slap shots and enjoying hockey less. Still in his prime as a superstar, Ken retired in 1979.

Playing seven full NHL seasons, Ken won or shared five Vezina awards. His career 2.24-goals-per-game average is seventh among all netminders but tops for NHL goalies playing since the 1930's. The earlier, low-scoring era of hockey enhanced goaltenders' statistics. During Ken's eight postseason playoffs, the Canadiens won six Stanley Cups. In 1983, Ken was elected to the Hockey Hall of Fame.

Ken's success in hockey has extended to his life off the ice. In the years after his retirement, Ken authored several books, served as educator-in-residence at the University of Toronto's faculty of education, and along with Al Michaels served as the commentator during Team USA's "miracle on ice" against the U.S.S.R. in the 1980 Winter Olympics.

Ken returned to the NHL in 1996 as the president and general manager of the Toronto Maple Leafs. In 1999, Ken was named one of the inaugural inductees to the International Scholar-Athlete Hall of Fame, housed on the campus of the University of Rhode Island.

Summary

Some consider Ken Dryden as the best goaltender in NHL history. Moreover, he is living proof that scholastic achievement and sports need not be separate worlds. Ken's route to NHL stardom indicates that college and hockey can be meshed without lowering the quality of the game. In a sport where many Canadian youth quit school in pursuit of a professional career, Ken's successful example is a healthy contribution.

David A. Crain

Additional Sources:

Dryden, Ken. *The Game.* New York: Penguin Books, 1984.

Dryden, Ken, with Mark Mulvoy. *Face-off at the Summit.* Boston: Little, Brown, 1973.

Swift, E. M. "Tough Save." *Sports Illustrated* 87, no. 23 (1997).

DON DRYSDALE

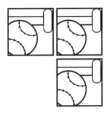

Sport: Baseball

Born: July 23, 1936
　　　　Van Nuys, California
Died: July 3, 1993
　　　　Montreal, Canada

Early Life

Donald Scott Drysdale was born on July 23, 1936, in Van Nuys, California, a Los Angeles suburb in the San Fernando Valley. He was the only son born to Scott and Verna Ruth Drysdale; he had a younger sister, Nancy.

Don profited from his father's love for baseball. Scott Drysdale, a supervisor with the Pacific Telephone and Telegraph Company, had been a minor league pitcher and continued to play on semiprofessional teams in Southern California, often taking young Don along for the weekend games.

Even at an early age, Don enjoyed the feel of a bat and ball in his hands. When he was old enough, he joined a youth baseball league, where he played just about every position but pitcher.

The Road to Excellence

Later, as coach of Don's American Legion baseball team, Scott Drysdale helped launch his son's future career by putting him in to replace the starting pitcher, who did not show up for the game one day. As luck would have it, visiting Brooklyn Dodgers scouts were impressed enough to invite him for a private tryout, and he showed them a strong, accurate arm.

In Don's senior year at Van Nuys High School, his first season as a pitcher gained him All-City honors and the notice of several major league teams and two universities. Among the teams vying for his attention were the Dodgers, who had made Scott Drysdale a part-time scout, partly in order to maintain contact with Don.

On his father's advice, Don opted in 1954 for the Dodgers' farm team system. He was sent to play on the Class C team in Bakersfield, California, where he had an 8-5 record.

The next season, he was elevated to the team's Triple-A squad in Montreal, where the lanky right-hander managed to salvage an 11-11 record after breaking his hand when he punched a soft-drink machine in a fit of temper.

Once again, good fortune stepped in on Don's side. In 1956, the major league club found itself lacking pitchers following

Don Drysdale, pitcher for the Dodgers, in 1962.

some injuries. Don was called up and showed himself to be a hard-throwing strikeout artist, gaining a 5-5 record. He appeared briefly as a relief pitcher in a World Series game; the Dodgers lost the series to the Yankees.

The Emerging Champion

During the club's 1957 season, its last before moving to Los Angeles, Don began showing the intimidating form that would become his legacy. At 6 feet 6 inches tall, he was an imposing presence on the mound, especially when he hurled pitches at 94 to 95 miles per hour, intended to scare batters away from the plate. Don was effective as well as fearsome, compiling a 17-9 record and a 2.69 earned run average.

The Dodgers' new, temporary home field at the Coliseum in Los Angeles gave him trouble. It was not built for baseball, and its short left-field fence made it easier to hit home runs off a hard thrower.

In the next four seasons there, Don won fifty-seven games and lost fifty, although he led the league in strikeouts in 1959, with 242, and in 1960, with 246. He also distinguished himself as a good hitter; in 1958, he hit 7 home runs to tie the record for National League pitchers.

Don's temper often got the better of him. The home runs in the Coliseum would rattle his concentration and hurt his pitching. By the early 1960's, he was frequently accused of deliberately hitting batters with mean sidearm pitches; in response, he once threatened to sue the league for hiring umpires who said he threw "beanballs."

Continuing the Story

Don never considered himself a "mean" player. He was determined to win, doing whatever it took, and most often his temper was directed at himself for making mistakes on the mound. His determination paid off over a bright career with two memorable highlight years: 1962 and 1968.

In 1962, Don bounced back from several mediocre seasons with his best year ever, right after the team moved into its new home at newly built Dodger Stadium. That year, with the help of a slight change in his pitching style, Don struck out 232 batters while winning twenty-five games and losing only nine, the best in the major leagues. He was honored with the Cy Young Award. His extraordinary effort came at the right time for the Dodgers, who had lost their other star pitcher, Sandy Koufax, for much of the season because of an injury.

In the next three years, Don compiled sixty wins in helping the team to two World Series titles.

Don worked his way into the record books early in the 1968 season by pitching six straight shutouts and holding opponents scoreless in 58⅔

STATISTICS

Season	GP	GS	CG	IP	HA	BB	SO	W	L	S	ShO	ERA
1956	25	12	2	99.0	95	31	55	5	5	0	0	2.64
1957	34	29	9	221.0	197	61	148	17	9	0	4	2.69
1958	44	29	6	211.2	214	72	131	12	13	0	1	4.17
1959	44	36	15	270.2	237	93	**242**	17	13	2	4	3.46
1960	41	36	15	269.0	214	72	**246**	13	14	2	5	2.84
1961	40	37	10	244.0	236	83	182	13	10	0	3	3.69
1962	43	**41**	19	**314.1**	272	78	**232**	**25**	9	1	2	2.83
1963	42	**42**	17	315.1	**287**	57	251	19	17	0	3	2.63
1964	40	**40**	21	**321.1**	242	68	237	18	16	0	5	2.18
1965	44	**42**	20	308.1	**270**	66	210	23	12	1	7	2.77
1966	40	40	11	273.2	279	45	177	13	16	0	3	3.42
1967	38	38	9	282.0	269	60	196	13	16	0	3	2.74
1968	31	31	12	239.0	201	56	155	14	12	0	8	2.15
1969	12	12	1	63.0	71	13	24	5	4	0	1	4.43
Totals	518	465	167	3,432.1	3,084	855	2,486	209	166	6	49	2.95

Notes: Boldface indicates statistical leader. GP = games played; GS = games started; CG = complete games; IP = innings pitched; HA = hits allowed; BB = bases on balls (walks); SO = strikeouts; W = wins; L = losses; S = saves; ShO = shutouts; ERA = earned run average

HONORS, AWARDS, AND RECORDS

1958, 1965	National league record for the most home runs hit by a pitcher in one season (7) (record shared)
1959, 1961-65, 1967-68	National League All-Star Team
1962	National League Cy Young Award *Sporting News* Major League Player of the Year *Sporting News* National League All-Star Team
1968	Major league record for the most consecutive shutouts in one season (6)
1984	Inducted into National Baseball Hall of Fame Uniform number 53 retired by Los Angeles Dodgers

consecutive innings. "The Streak" secured Don's place in baseball annals and in the memories of fans.

Don retired as a player in 1969 and started a new career as a broadcaster. Over the next two decades, he was an announcer for various organizations, including the Montreal Expos, St. Louis Cardinals, Texas Rangers, California Angels, Chicago White Sox, ABC Sports, and the Dodgers. He was married twice and the father of three children. Don died of a heart attack on July 3, 1993 while in Montreal to broadcast a game.

Summary

Don Drysdale's induction into the National Baseball Hall of Fame in 1984 was a salute to his famous scoreless-innings record—broken by Orel Hershiser of the Dodgers in 1988—and to his competitiveness during fifteen years as a player. The plaque in the Hall of Fame noted his "intimidating" style of play.

Along with Bob Gibson and Juan Marichal, Don was among the best-known of the modern pitchers who gained fame by battling hitters with hard throws meant to hit or scare them.

Although he was often overshadowed by teammate Sandy Koufax, Don enjoyed his own share of the spotlight. Handsome and gregarious, Don was suited to glamour-conscious Los Angeles; he even acted on television shows.

Kenneth Ellingwood

Additional Sources:

Drysdale, Don, and Bob Verdi. *Once a Bum, Always a Dodger: My Life in Baseball from Brooklyn to Los Angeles.* New York: St. Martin's Press, 1990.

Shapiro, Leonard. *The Don Drysdale Story.* New York: Julian Messner, 1964.

Shatzkin, Mike, et al., eds. *The Ballplayers: Baseball's Ultimate Biographical Reference.* New York: William Morrow, 1990.

HERB DUDLEY

Sport: Softball

Born: December 19, 1919
Youngstown, Florida

Early Life

Herbert L. Dudley was born December 19, 1919, on the family farm in Youngstown, Florida, 20 miles north of Panama City, Florida. He was the second youngest of eight children, four boys and four girls, born to his parents, Nathan and Millie Dudley.

The family moved to Clearwater, Florida, in 1928, where Herb attended and graduated from local elementary, junior high, and senior high schools.

In high school, Herb played football, baseball, and softball. In his senior year, he was elected captain of the baseball team and also won First Team honors as All-County guard in football.

After the family moved to Clearwater, Herb participated in various sports offered through the recreation department headed by Ralph Van-Fleet, who organized age-group leagues for most sports. Herb started out as a shortfielder, then moved to first base, then to pitcher, and then to pitcher/catcher.

In 1939, Herb caught a ride home from one of his older friends, Charlie Grace, whose team had a softball game to play. Herb told Charlie he would ride along if he did not mind because he had played some softball and liked the game. Herb went to the game with Charlie. Charlie's team built up a large lead and the team's manager, Mike Tsacrios, also a pitcher, asked Herb if he would like to pitch. Herb did, and the manager asked Herb to join the team as a pitcher.

Herb's team won the first half of the recreation league while he was still in high school. During the summer, he went to Panama City to live with his sister and play softball while working at the local paper mill.

When Herb returned to school, he found out his team (Whetstone's Texaco) had lost the second half championship. Whetstone's did win the playoffs, however, beating the Lions Club for the championship of the recreation league.

The following year, Herb and four of his teammates moved to the Senior League and played for a newly formed team sponsored by the Blackburn Lumber Company. This team eventually became the Blackburn Bombers and then the Clearwater Bombers, and won ten Amateur Softball Association (ASA) Men's Major Fast Pitch national championships.

In 1941, Herb and his catcher participated in the ASA Men's Championship after being added to the roster of the state champions, Rieck and Fleece of St. Petersburg, Florida.

The Road to Excellence

The national championship was held in Detroit. The Rieck and Fleece All-Stars played the Deep Rock Oilers of Tulsa, Oklahoma, in their first game and lost. The loss eliminated them from the tournament. Herb pitched the last 2 innings of the game, striking out five of six batters.

Besides playing in his first national championship that year, Herb also married Lucille D. Futch on August 15, 1941.

In 1942, Herb and his wife moved to Chickasaw, Alabama, where he worked at the Navy Shipyard. On July 22, 1944, Herb entered the Army and was sent to New Guinea after completing basic training. He then spent sixteen months in Leyte, Philippines, serving ten months as a scuba diver and six as a chaplain's assistant.

Herb returned to the United States on April 30, 1946, and entered Stetson University. He graduated four years later, majoring in Bible with a minor in physical education. Herb later entered the University of Florida, and in February of 1952 he received a master's degree in physical education with a minor in history.

The Emerging Champion

After returning to Florida following his service in the army, Herb and some of his former teammates joined the Blackburn Lumber Company team, managed by Eddie Moore. The team won the district and state titles but lost in the regionals. Herb had a 25-0 record that year, pitching 7 no-hitters and 16 shutouts, and striking out 429 batters in 211 innings pitched.

In 1947, the team again captured the district and state titles and finally won the regionals to earn a spot in the ASA National Championship Tournament. In the championships, Herb compiled a 3-2 record. He finished the 1947 season with a won-lost record of 23-3 and 17 shutouts. He fanned 543 batters in only 239 innings.

In 1948, the name of Herb's team was changed from the Blackburn Bombers to the Clearwater Bombers. In years to come, the Bombers would

HONORS AND AWARDS	
1949-50, 1957, 1964, 1966	ASA All American
1957	ASA National Championship Tournament most valuable player
1981	Inducted into Stetson University Sports Hall of Fame
1985	Inducted into National Softball Hall of Fame
	Inducted into Florida Sports Hall of Fame

become as famous in softball as the New York Yankees in baseball.

Continuing the Story

In 1949, Clearwater emerged as the runner-up in the national tournament, with Herb setting records for strikeouts in one game (55) and total strikeouts (130). He recorded the single-game record against the Phillips Oilers of Okmulgee, Oklahoma, winning 1-0 in a game that took 3 hours and 20 minutes.

In 1950, Clearwater won its first of a record ten ASA national championships, beating Austin, Texas. Herb was named to the All-American team. He finished the year with a 36-4 record. From 1946 to 1950, Herb won 142 games and lost 10 for Clearwater.

In addition to 1949 and 1950, Herb also earned All-American honors in 1957, 1964, and 1966. In 1957, he also earned the championship tournament's most valuable player award.

Herb played two years for the famed Fort Wayne Zollner Pistons, of Fort Wayne, Indiana, before he returned to Clearwater in 1953. By then he had also completed an Educational Specialist's Program at the University of Florida, which led to a Rank I teacher's certificate in the field of administration/supervision.

In September of 1953, Herb was assigned to Clearwater Senior High School as a teacher and coach. He was an instructor in physical education and served as chair of the physical education department for twenty-eight years before retiring in January, 1982. He also coached football, basketball, and baseball.

During the summers, he continued to play softball before retiring in 1981. Ironically, the last team Herb played for was the team with whom he started out his career—the Clearwater Bombers. In 1981, at age sixty-one, he competed

713

in the ASA National Championship Tournament and saved two games, pitching 2⅔ innings of scoreless relief. He finished the year with a 13-1 record, including pitching a no-hitter.

Summary

After retiring, Herb Dudley remained active in softball, traveling throughout the United States, giving clinics to youngsters interested in learning how to pitch.

Herb was inducted into the Florida Sports Hall of Fame (1985), the Stetson University Hall of Fame (1981), and the National Softball Hall of Fame (1985).

Although records are incomplete, it is estimated that Herb won more than one thousand games during his career, striking out between 13,000 and 14,000 and hurling more than 100 no-hitters. In ASA National Championship play,

Herb compiled a record of twenty-eight wins and seven losses in sixteen ASA national championships.

His records are impressive, but more impressive is how he has lived his life. The three things Herb really cares about are religion, family, and softball. Herb never played softball on Sunday: "I can play softball every other day of the week, I don't need to play on Sunday," he said.

Bill Plummer III

Additional Sources:

Bealle, Morris A. *The Softball Story: A Complete, Concise, and Entertaining History.* Washington, D.C.: Columbia, 1957.

Dickson, Paul. *The Worth Book of Softball: A Celebration of America's True National Pastime.* New York: Facts on File, 1994.

CHARLEY DUMAS

Sport: Track and field (high jump)

Born: February 12, 1937
Tulsa, Oklahoma

Early Life

Charles Everett Dumas was born on February 12, 1937, in Tulsa, Oklahoma, one of six children—two girls and four boys—of Monroe and Nancy Dumas. When Charley was four, his father moved the family to Los Angeles, a crucial moment in his life that exposed him to the climatic and sporting advantages of Southern California. As a junior high school student, he began his track and field career as a hurdler and jumper, and, when he set the school high jump record, he began to focus upon that event.

The Road to Excellence

Charley's decision to concentrate on high jumping turned out to be a good one, as he surprised nearly everyone in his first major meet. Competing as a ninth-grader in the Los Angeles City High School meet, held at the Los Angeles Coliseum, the site of the 1932 Summer Olympic Games, he tied for second place in the high jump. By his senior year, 1955, he further demonstrated his potential by winning the California Interscholastic Federation high jump. That same year, he gained national prominence by tying Ernie Shelton for the national Amater Athletic Union (AAU) title. Following graduation from high school, Charley enrolled at Compton Junior College, where he was undefeated in his event. He captured the second of five consecutive AAU high jump titles, and his outstanding performance garnered him an invitation to the U.S. Olympic trials, an invitation that would dramatically affect the world of track and field.

The Emerging Champion

When the 1950's began, there were four supposedly "unbreakable barriers" in the world of track and field: the 4-minute mile, the 60-foot shot put, the 16-foot pole vault, and the 7-foot high jump. It should be noted that these records were truly significant only in the United States, Great Britain, and other non-metric nations. On May 6, 1954, Roger Bannister ran a time of 3:59.4 to break the 4-minute barrier in the mile. Just two days later, Parry O'Brien put the 16-pound shot more than 60 feet. The 7-foot high jump and the 16-foot pole vault records remained unbroken.

The high jump record had inched upward slowly with the progressive techniques of the "scissors," the "Eastern" roll, the "Western" roll, and the straddle used by Charley. It was not until 1976 that the "Fosbury flop" changed high jumping forever. In fact, from 1941 to 1956, the record had gone up only half an inch. Then, on June 29, 1956, at the Olympic trials in Los Angeles, Charley, who had already won the event and qualified for the Olympic team with a leap of 6 feet 11¾ inches, had the bar raised to 7 feet ½ inch. On his second attempt he cleared the bar, and one more mythical barrier fell, although *The New York Times* observed that "it was a moment comparable to, if not as dramatic as the moment the 4-minute mile barrier was broken."

In October, Charley traveled to the Olympics in Melbourne, Australia, with the American team. In one of the most dramatic competitions in the history of the event, Charley and another nineteen-year-old, Charles "Chilla" Porter, an Australian from Brisbane, dueled into the night long after the day's other events were completed. Porter exceeded his personal best by 3 inches. Finally, both jumpers missed twice at 6 feet 11½ inches. On his third and final attempt, Charley cleared the bar and won the gold medal, setting a new Olympic record in the process. The disappointed but appreciative Australian fans gave him a three-minute ovation.

Continuing the Story

Those two days in 1956 were to represent the high point of Charley's athletic career, although that career was to continue with some success for several more years. On his return to Los Angeles, he transferred to the University of Southern California (USC), after considering many offers. Although he failed to capture a National Collegiate Athletic Association title while at USC, he did win the gold medal at the 1959 Pan-American Games and continued his hold on the Amateur Athletic Union title for four consecutive years.

In 1960 Charley again qualified for the American Olympic squad, but in Rome he shared the disappointment of the American track and field team in general in jumping only 6 feet 7⅞ inches to finish sixth. Upon receipt of his baccalaureate degree from USC in 1960, he decided to retire from active track and field competition. Four years later, at twenty-seven years old, he staged a comeback and made a leap of 7 feet ½ inch at the Coliseum Relays in Los Angeles. Since his first 7-foot jump eight years earlier, however, a new breed of jumpers, such as American John Thomas and Valery Brumel of the Soviet Union, had raised the bar for serious competition to 7 feet 4 inches. Charley failed to make the 1964 Olympic team and retired for good after that.

He subsequently earned a master's degree from University of California, Los Angeles, and turned his talents to teaching and coaching high school students in Inglewood, California. He and his wife, Gloria, had two children, and Charley continued as an inspirational speaker to young people. He was named to the National Track and Field Hall of Fame in 1990, and in February of 2000 he joined Bill Toomey, Evelyn Ashford, and Tommie Smith to honor founder Al Franken on the fortieth anniversary of the Los Angeles Indoor Track Meet.

Summary

Of the three great track and field record breakers of the 1950's, Charley Dumas remains perhaps the least well known, yet his record lasted longer than Bannister's and was certainly the equivalent of O'Brien's. In fact, unlike Bannister, Charley added an Olympic gold medal to his name. His relative anonymity may have to do with the fact that his reign at the top was relatively brief. Whatever the reason, his story remains an inspiring one. For four months in 1956, the sports world belonged to Charley Dumas.

Daniel J. Fuller

MAJOR CHAMPIONSHIPS

Year	Competition	Event	Place
1955	AAU	High jump	1st (tie)
1956	Olympic Trials	High jump	1st WR
	Olympic Games	High jump	Gold
1956-1959	AAU	High jump	1st

Note: WR = World Record

Additional Sources:

Bateman, Hal. *United States Track and Field Champions.* Indianapolis, Ind.: Athletics Congress of the United States, 1984.

Hickok, Ralph. *A Who's Who of Sports Champions.* New York: Houghton Mifflin, 1995.

Melton, Bill, and Ian Buchanon. *Search for Gold: The Encyclopedia of American Olympians.* New York: Leisure Press, 1984.

Porter, David. *Biographical Dictionary of American Sports: Outdoor Sports.* Westport, Conn.: Greenwood Press, 1988

Wallechinsky, David. *The Complete Book of the Olympics.* New York: Viking, 1988.

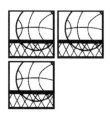

TIM DUNCAN

Sport: Basketball

Born: April 25, 1976
St. Croix, Virgin Islands

Early Life

Tim Duncan was born in St. Croix in the Virgin Islands on April 25, 1976, and only came to the attention of National Basketball Association (NBA) scouts when he came to play ball at Wake Forest University. Tim's father, William, was a mason and hotel employee, while his mother, Ione, was a midwife.

Interestingly enough, Tim's favorite sport when he was growing up was swimming, not basketball. He seemed to be following in the steps of his sister Tricia, who swam in the 1988 Olympics in the 100- and 200-meter backstroke. Tim's best event was the 400-meter freestyle. His participation in swimming ended when Hurricane Hugo swept through the islands and destroyed the swimming complex where he trained. At the same time Tim's mother lost her battle with breast cancer, passing away in April, 1990. She had always been Tim's biggest fan at his swimming meets.

Tim turned to basketball his freshman year of high school and never looked back. He played for St. Dunstan's Episcopal High School, where he averaged 25 points, 12 rebounds, and 5 blocked shots per game during his senior season. Tim was discovered by an alumnus of Wake Forest, Chris King, when an exhibition team toured the island. King had the chance to watch Tim play well against Alonzo Mourning. Wake Forest coach Dave Odom visited Tim at his home, and Tim went on to enjoy a great college career for the Demon Deacons.

The Road to Excellence

Once Tim committed to playing basketball for Wake Forest he steadily improved, so that by his senior year in college he was named National

Tim Duncan of the San Antonio Spurs shoots in game 5 of the 1999 NBA finals.

718

STATISTICS

Season	GP	FGA	FGM	FG%	FTA	FTM	FT%	Reb.	Ast.	TP	PPG
1997-98	82	1,287	706	.549	482	319	.662	977	224	1,731	21.1
1998-99	50	845	418	.495	358	247	.690	571	121	1,084	21.7
1999-00	74	1,281	628	.490	603	459	.761	918	234	1,716	23.2
2000-01	82	1,406	702	.499	662	409	.618	997	245	1,820	22.2
Totals	288	4,819	2,454	.509	2,105	1,434	.681	3,463	824	6,351	22.1

Notes: GP = games played; FGA = field goals attempted; FGM = field goals made; FG% = field goal percentage; FTA = free throws attempted; FTM = free throws made; FT% = free throw percentage; Reb. = rebounds; Ast. = assists; TP = total points; PPG = points per game

Collegiate Athletic Association (NCAA) Player of the Year and the National Defensive Player of the Year for the third straight year. Some had thought Tim might leave after his junior year and enter the NBA, but Tim returned to Wake Forest for his final season. He wanted to earn his degree, as he had promised his mother he would. He also wanted one more chance to lead his team to an NCAA championship.

He ended his career as the all-time leading shot blocker in Atlantic Athletic Confence (ACC) history. To honor his achievements, the Demon Deacons retired Tim's number, 21, at the Joel Coliseum. While at Wake Forest Tim earned a degree in psychology.

The Emerging Champion

In 1997 the San Antonio Spurs picked Tim first in the NBA draft. Their faith was rewarded when Tim won Rookie of the Year honors, beating out New Jersey's Keith Van Horn with 113 points out of a possible 116. Tim was also named to the Schick All-Rookie First Team. Tim and Van Horn were the only unanimous selections, receiving all twenty-eight first-place votes. In his rookie year Tim averaged 21.1 points, 11.9 rebounds, and 2.51 blocked shots in just over thirty-nine minutes a game. He started all eighty-two games for San Antonio as a rookie and played in the All-Star game.

In his second season Tim played in only fifty games because of the strike-shortened season, but he still averaged over 21 points a game and 11 rebounds a game. In addition to playing in the All-Star game he went on to help his team win the NBA championship; he was named the most valuable player (MVP) of the championship series. After the Spurs eliminated the Lakers from

the playoffs in a 4-game sweep, some reporters began referring to Tim as basketball's newest and best player.

During the summer of 1999 Tim was named to Team USA and played in the Tournament of the Americas in preparation for the Olympics. The team finished 10-0 and won the gold medal over Canada.

Continuing the Story

During the 1999-2000 season Tim picked up where he finished the previous year. He started in seventy-four games, averaging nearly thirty-nine minutes a game. Injuries kept him sidelined during some games in that season and prevented him from participating in the playoffs, from which the Spurs were quickly eliminated. After the season, Tim became a free agent and negotiated with the Orlando Magic. However, he chose to remain with the Spurs.

Tim and his teammate David Robinson have become one of the most feared tandems in the NBA. Their skills and style complement each other, though at times some have criticized Tim for being too laid-back and easygoing. Tim plays with a quiet style that does not fit with many of the younger players in the NBA who are vocal and emotional, but he gets the job done.

Summary

Tim Duncan began playing in the NBA in

MILESTONES

1997	Finished his college career first in Atlantic Coast Conference and second in NCAA history with 481 blocked shots, and third all-time in the ACC in rebounds (1,570)

HONORS AND AWARDS

1997-1998	Schick Rookie of the Year
	Schick All-Rookie First Team, unanimous selection
	Schick Rookie of the Month for all six months of the season
1997-1999	All-NBA First Team
1998	NBA Player of the Week for week ending March 1
	NBA All-Star Team
1998-1999	All-NBA First Team
1998-2000	NBA All-Defensive First Team
1999	NBA Player of the Month: March
	U.S. Basketball Men's Senior National Team for 1999 Americas Qualifying Tournament for the 2000 Olympic Games
1999-2000	All-NBA First Team
2000	NBA Player of the Week ending April 2
	NBA All-Star Game, co-most valuable player

1997, and he made his mark on the game in a short time. His accomplishments with the San Antonio Spurs have placed him among the league's best. Wherever Duncan's career takes him he will most likely be a player to watch for years to come.

Leslie Heaphy

Additional Sources:

Byman, Jeremy. *Tim Duncan*. Greensboro: Morgan Reynolds, 2000.

Kernan, Kevin. *Tim Duncan: Slam Duncan*. Sports Publishing, 2000.

Thornley, Stew. *Super Sports Star Tim Duncan*. Berkeley Heights, N.J.: Enslow, 2001.

MARGARET OSBORNE duPONT

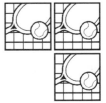

Sport: Tennis

Born: March 4, 1918
　　　Joseph, Oregon

Early Life

Margaret Evelyn Osborne was born on March 4, 1918, in Joseph, Oregon, to Charles Marcus St. Lawrence Osborne, a farmer and garage manager, and Eva Jane Osborne. Margaret spent her early years on the family farm in Oregon. When she was nine, the family moved to Spokane, Washington, where Margaret saw tennis played for the first time. She became fascinated with the game, so her mother bought her a racket and encouraged her to play.

When Margaret was ten years old, the family moved to San Francisco. There she played tennis on the public courts at Golden Gate Park. As Margaret's tennis began to improve, her mother suggested that they find a coach who could help to develop and refine her game. They hired a coach, and Margaret received her first formal tennis lessons when she was seventeen. Since the family had little money, Margaret helped to pay for the lessons by writing tennis articles for her coach.

The Road to Excellence

One day while Margaret was practicing, Hazel Wightman—a tennis champion, teacher, and founder of the Wightman Cup championship—saw her play. Hazel commented that Margaret was "too nice" and that she lacked the "killer instinct" to be a top competitor. Rather than be dis-

couraged, Margaret was challenged by Hazel's comments. She vowed to improve her game and enter a national competition. In 1936, at eighteen, she won the national girls' singles and doubles titles. By the time she was twenty, Margaret was ranked seventh among women players.

Even though Margaret had won national titles and received national ranking, she was always calm and steady when competing. These were the character traits that would later help her to cope with the rigorous demands of top-level competition. Her game continued to improve,

Margaret duPont competes at Wimbledon in 1948.

721

and she developed a reputation for playing her best tennis under pressure.

Between 1940 and 1945, just as Margaret's game began to reach its peak, several important tennis competitions were suspended because of World War II. One competition that continued was the United States National Championship. During the war, many women tennis stars worked in factories and offices or served as volunteers. Margaret worked as a shipbuilding clerk eight hours a day, six days a week, practicing tennis after work. She joined another California tennis player, Louise Brough, entertaining soldiers with tennis exhibitions at more than fifty military bases.

The Emerging Champion

Margaret's style of play surprised competitors and tennis fans unfamiliar with California-style tennis. Unlike many women champions before her, she was a serve-and-volley player, rather than a baseline player. She developed a hard, fast serve, which she combined with well-placed net volleys that featured slices and topspins. She was known for tactical ability, and her skilled shot placement won many points.

During the 1940's and 1950's, Margaret ranked among the top players in the world. Her years of training, excellent skills in all phases of the game, love of tennis, and calm disposition placed her in championship company.

In 1941, teamed with Sarah Palfrey Cooke, Margaret won her first U.S. National Championship in doubles. From 1942 to 1950, she joined Louise Brough in winning the U.S. women's doubles title for an unprecedented nine consecutive

years. During her career, she was ranked in the world's top ten fourteen times; she was ranked number one in the United States from 1948 to 1950.

Margaret continued her winning ways in mixed doubles, playing with tennis champions William Talbert, Kenneth McGregor, Ken Rosewall, and Neale Fraser. Her championship play extended to Europe, where she won the French Open singles championship in 1946 and 1949 and the French doubles title with Louise Brough in 1946, 1947, and 1949.

Margaret's success continued in England, where she won the Wimbledon doubles title in 1946 and the singles title in 1947. In 1949 and 1950, she lost the singles championships to her doubles partner, Louise Brough. Their singles rivalry did not affect their play as a team, however; from 1946 to 1954, they won five Wimbledon doubles championships.

In 1947, Margaret married William duPont, Jr., a wealthy businessman, avid horseman, and tennis enthusiast. Marriage provided Margaret with additional personal and financial support to sustain a successful career in competitive tennis.

In 1946, she was selected for the Wightman Cup team, captained by the same Hazel Wightman who had previously questioned Margaret's championship ability. During the 1940's and 1950's, the Wightman Cup players were known for their powerful serves and "killer" overhead shots. A writer for *The Times* of London commented that perhaps no other woman's serve had ever traveled as fast as Margaret's. From 1946 to 1962, she achieved one of the finest Wightman Cup records, remaining unbeaten in ten singles and eight doubles competitions. She did not play on a losing side from 1946 to 1962; during this time, she was captain for the U.S. Wightman Cup team nine times.

Margaret's style of play helped to launch a new era in women's tennis. Her strong forehand, powerful serve, precise volleys, and attacking style of net play would become the standard for future women's competition.

	MAJOR CHAMPIONSHIP VICTORIES AND FINALS
1941	U.S. National Championship doubles (with Sarah Palfrey Cooke)
1942-1950,1955-57	U.S. National Championship doubles (with Louise Brough)
1943-46	U.S. National Championship mixed doubles (with William Talbert)
1944,1947	U.S. National Championship finalist
1946,1949	French Open
1946-47,1949	French Open doubles (with Louise Brough)
1946,1948-50,1954	Wimbledon doubles (with Louise Brough)
1947	Wimbledon
1948-50	U.S. National Championship
1949-50	Wimbledon finalist
1950	U.S. National Championship mixed doubles (with Kenneth McGregor)
1956	U.S. National Championship mixed doubles (with Ken Rosewall)
1958-60	U.S. National Championship mixed doubles (with Neale Fraser)
1962	Wimbledon mixed doubles (with Neale Fraser)

Continuing the Story

Margaret dominated United States women's singles from 1948 to 1950; her doubles and mixed doubles titles success extended from 1941 to 1962. Her record in the U. S. championships may never be surpassed. In all, she won twenty-five U.S. titles—three in singles, thirteen in doubles, and nine in mixed doubles. Another of her records is the twenty-one-year span between her first U.S. title, in 1941, and her last in 1962—when she was forty-four years old.

Although Margaret had humble beginnings playing on public courts and paying for her own lessons, she had the talent and temperament to make her a champion. Her mother, her husband, and Hazel Wightman greatly influenced Margaret in her rise to the top, a position she held for more than two decades.

Summary

Margaret Osborne duPont's strong serve and forehand, aggressive volley, and net play com-

HONORS AND AWARDS	
1945	USLTA Service Bowl
1946-50,1953-55,1957-59,1961-63	Wightman Cup Team
1967	International Tennis Hall of Fame

bined to make her successful. Her mastery of tennis basics, calm temperament under pressure, and exceptional skill made her a top individual competitor and a perfect doubles partner.

Barbara J. Kelly

Additional Sources:

Grimsley, Will. *Tennis: Its History, People, and Events.* Englewood Cliffs, N.J.: Prentice-Hall, 1971.

Jacobs, Helen H. *Gallery of Champions.* New York: A. S. Barnes, 1949.

Johnson, Anne J. *Great Women in Sports.* Detroit: Visible Ink Press, 1996.

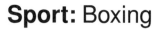

ROBERTO DURAN

Sport: Boxing

Born: June 16, 1951
Panama City, Panama

Early Life

Roberto Carlos Duran was born on June 16, 1951, in Panama City, Panama, a short distance from the Canal Zone. Roberto was the third of nine children of Clara Samaniego, a domestic, and Margarito Duran, a cook who was serving in the United States Army in the Canal Zone. His father left the family and moved to the United States when Roberto was three, and Roberto did not see his father again until he was twenty-three years old.

Roberto grew up on the streets fending for himself. He helped his mother and his brothers and sisters by working and entertaining in bars as a youth. Growing up on the streets meant that

Roberto had to defend himself against tough neighborhood kids. He often got into fights when others tried to take away the tips he earned at work.

The Road to Excellence

When Roberto was twelve years old, he walked into a boxing gymnasium. Sammy Medina, a former boxing champion of Panama, was impressed by Roberto's fighting abilities and became Roberto's first boxing manager and trainer. Roberto fought sixteen amateur fights, winning thirteen, before he turned professional.

Many young boxers do not have the money to pay for the expenses connected with training for fights. Managers and trainers have to be paid, and money is needed for the gymnasiums where fighters work out. Fortunately for Roberto, a

Panamanian boxer Roberto Duran (right) with Pat Lawlor in a 2000 National Boxing Association title fight.

RECOGNIZED WORLD LIGHTWEIGHT CHAMPIONSHIPS

Date	Location	Loser	Result
June 26, 1972	New York City, N.Y.	Ken Buchanan	13th-round technical knockout
Jan. 20, 1973	Panama City, Panama	Jimmy Robertson	5th-round knockout
June 2, 1973	Panama City, Panama	Hector Thompson	8th-round technical knockout
Sept. 8, 1973	Panama City, Panama	Ishimatsu Suzuki	10th-round technical knockout
Mar. 16, 1974	Panama City, Panama	Esteban De Jesus	11th-round technical knockout
Dec. 21, 1974	San Juan, Puerto Rico	Masataka Takayama	1st-round technical knockout
Mar. 2, 1975	Panama City, Panama	Ray Lampkin	14th-round technical knockout
Dec. 14, 1975	San Juan, Puerto Rico	Leoncio Ortiz	15th-round knockout
May 22, 1976	Philadelphia, Pa.	Lou Bizzarro	14th-round knockout
Oct. 15, 1976	Miami, Fla.	Alvaro Rojas	1st-round knockout
Jan. 29, 1977	Miami, Fla.	Vilomar Fernandez	13th-round knockout
Sept. 17, 1977	Philadelphia, Pa.	Edwin Viruet	15th-round decision
Jan. 21, 1978	Las Vegas, Nev.	Esteban De Jesus	12th-round knockout

RECOGNIZED WORLD WELTERWEIGHT CHAMPIONSHIPS

Date	Location	Loser	Result
June 20, 1980	Montreal, Canada	Sugar Ray Leonard	15th-round decision
Nov. 20, 1980	Los Angeles, Calif.	Roberto Duran (Sugar Ray Leonard, winner)	8th-round knockout

RECOGNIZED WORLD JUNIOR MIDDLEWEIGHT CHAMPIONSHIPS

Date	Location	Loser	Result
Jan. 20, 1982	Las Vegas, Nev.	Roberto Duran (Wilfredo Benitez, winner)	15th-round decision
June 16, 1983	New York City, N.Y.	Davey Moore	8th-round knockout
June 15, 1984	Las Vegas, Nev.	Roberto Duran (Thomas Hearns, winner)	2d-round knockout

RECOGNIZED WORLD MIDDLEWEIGHT CHAMPIONSHIPS

Date	Location	Loser	Result
Nov. 10, 1983	Las Vegas, Nev.	Roberto Duran (Marvin Hagler, winner)	15th-round decision
Feb. 24, 1989	Atlantic City, N.J.	Iran Barkley	12th-round decision

RECOGNIZED WORLD SUPER MIDDLEWEIGHT CHAMPIONSHIPS

Date	Location	Loser	Result
Dec. 7, 1989	Las Vegas, Nev.	Roberto Duran (Sugar Ray Leonard, winner)	12th-round decision

wealthy Panamanian, Carlos Eleta, took the young boxer under his wing and took care of him. "Papa," as Roberto affectionately calls Eleta, met Roberto years before under difficult circumstances. He had caught the tough boy stealing coconuts on his estate. Instead of calling the police or punishing him, Eleta brought him into his home and gave him breakfast. When Roberto needed a sponsor, Eleta remembered him and helped him out financially.

Eleta never signed a contract with Roberto as many managers do; they have a handshake agreement. Eleta, who is a millionaire, has never taken any of Roberto's money. Instead, he has invested Roberto's earnings so that Roberto would not squander his money like many boxers who experience success at a young age. Eleta also tried to keep the rough youngster out of trouble, counseling him to stay out of nightclubs.

The Emerging Champion

Eleta, recognizing the youngster's raw potential, wisely found Roberto an excellent trainer, Ray Arcel, who had trained nineteen boxing champions. On June 26, 1972, the twenty-one-year-old Panamanian boxer made the most of

725

Arcel's counsel and in his first major test defeated lightweight champion Ken Buchanan of Scotland for the title in Madison Square Garden in New York City.

Over the next six years, Roberto defended his lightweight title twelve times, knocking out almost every challenger. The 5-foot 7-inch, 135-pound slugger earned his nickname, "Manos de piedra," or "Hands of Stone," by pounding his opponents relentlessly to the body and the head. Roberto was a vicious fighter who knew only one strategy, to keep pressing forward and never step back. He absorbed a tremendous number of punches with his street-fighting style, but he always gave more than he received in these encounters.

Despite Eleta's advice, when Roberto was not defending his title he lived like a playboy, frequenting bars and night clubs in Panama City. He loved to eat steaks, drink whiskey, and dance to salsa music. A national hero in Panama, Roberto was treated like royalty wherever he went.

In 1979, Roberto gave up his lightweight crown to move up to a higher weight class, the welterweight division (147-pound maximum). He made that move for three reasons: He had defeated nearly all the lightweight contenders, he was having trouble keeping his weight to the 137-pound lightweight maximum because of his penchant for high living, and he wanted to earn more money by fighting well-known welterweights like Carlos Palomino and Sugar Ray Leonard.

Continuing the Story

Roberto defeated Palomino easily in 1979, and then fought Leonard in Olympic Stadium, Montreal, Canada, for the welterweight title on June 20, 1980. Leonard was undefeated and was the classic boxer, jabbing, feinting, and moving constantly. Roberto was the quintessential brawler. It was a classic confrontation. Roberto won a hard-fought fifteenth-round decision as Leonard abandoned his usual style to slug it out with the Panamanian. Leonard paid the price, but he would learn from his mistake and avenge his defeat later that year in a rematch. Meanwhile, Roberto was honored for his victory in Panama, and the day he returned to Panama was declared a national holiday.

STATISTICS
Bouts, 95
Knockouts, 60
Bouts won by decision, 26
Knockouts by opponents, 2
Bouts lost by decision, 7

MILESTONES
Captured recognized world titles at four weight classifications

Leonard's victory in the rematch in late 1980 was Roberto's worst defeat. He was out of shape for the fight, and Leonard shrewdly elected to box and not brawl this time. Leonard, recognizing that Roberto could not hurt him, taunted the Panamanian mercilessly throughout the fight, and in the eighth round, Roberto simply stopped fighting, telling the referee, "no más, no más," ("no more, no more"). Roberto later claimed he had stomach cramps from gorging himself before the fight on steak, eggs, french fries, and fried chicken. From that point on, despite all his accomplishments, Roberto was labeled a quitter—in Panama and around the world—the worst thing that a fighter, especially a proud man like Roberto, could be called. He wanted revenge.

To make matters worse for Roberto, Leonard refused to give him a rematch for a long time. Roberto kept busy and won a third title in 1983 by defeating Davey Moore for the junior middleweight title. His skills were diminished, however, after years of battering in the ring wars. He lost a fifteenth-round title bout against Marvin Hagler and was knocked out unceremoniously by Thomas Hearns. Roberto claimed that what he really wanted was to fight Sugar Ray Leonard and avenge the "no más" episode. Even though it was clear he was not the fighter he once was, as he told Pat Putnam in *Sports Illustrated* in 1988, "I was born to fight. I do not know what else to do." Another problem Roberto had was with the Internal Revenue Service, which claimed that he had not paid two million dollars in taxes on his earnings. Roberto had to keep fighting to pay off his debts.

Finally, Roberto got his rematch with Sugar Ray Leonard on December 7, 1989, for the world super middleweight title. Roberto had to wait nine years for his second chance. Both fighters by this time in their careers were diminished in their abilities. Leonard boxed and threw a few punches that did little damage, but he was too fast and elusive for Roberto. Leonard won an easy victory, but this time Roberto fought nobly to the end and did not quit, redeeming his reputation even in defeat.

Long after contemporaries like Sugar Ray Leonard and Marvin Hagler retired from the ring, Roberto remained despite his age and diminishing ability. Following his rematch with Leonard in 1989, Roberto fought only three title bouts, losing two by decision and the third by knockout in the third round against William Joppy in 1998. Roberto's performance against Joppy was so bad that the Nevada Boxing Commission suspended his license. Shortly after, he announced his retirement, but he was not long in returning to the ring.

Roberto lost a decision to Omar Gonzalez in Buenos Aires in 1999 and won a decision against Pat Lawler in Panama City, both non-sanctioned fights that served as little more than a tune-up for his return to professional boxing. His license was reinstated in August of 2000, and Roberto returned to the United States to face P. J. Gossen in Yakima, Washington. Looking well-trained and trim, the forty-nine-year-old Roberto won an easy tenth-round decision and vowed that he would continue to box well into his fifth decade in the sport.

Summary

Some athletes choose to retire when they are at the peak of their careers. Others, swayed by the promise of lucrative offers, extend their careers too long. Perhaps Roberto Duran boxed too long, but no one can take away the storied accomplishments throughout his career. He makes his home in his native Panama with his wife, Felicidad del Carmen Iglesias, his three daughters, Dalia, Jovani, and Irichelle, and his son, Roberto, Jr. "Manos de piedra" would continue to fight after more than ninety prize fights and four world championship belts. His rise from the streets of Panama City to international celebrity status was not a smooth one, but it brought him a place in boxing history.

Allen Wells

Additional Sources:

Goldman, Herbert G., ed. *The Ring 1985 Record Book and Boxing Encyclopedia.* New York: Ring Publishing, 1985.

Mullan, Harry. *The Ultimate Encyclopedia of Boxing: The Definitive Illustrated Guide to World Boxing.* Edison, N.J.: Chartwell Books, 1996.

Odd, Gilbert E. *Encyclopedia of Boxing.* New York: Crescent Books, 1983.

Schulman, Arlene. *The Prize Fighters: An Intimate Look at Champions and Contenders.* New York: Lyons and Burford, 1994.

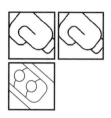

EDDIE EAGAN

Sport: Boxing and Bobsledding

Born: April 26, 1897
　　　Denver, Colorado
Died: June 14, 1967
　　　Rye, New York

Early Life

Edward Patrick Francis Eagan was born on April 26, 1897, in Denver, Colorado. Edward, who was called Eddie, was the son of John and Clara Eagan. His father was killed in a railroad accident when Eddie was just one year old. Mrs. Eagan raised Eddie and his four brothers. She spoke five languages and supported her children by teaching German and French. Eddie became interested in boxing while in high school. The family had moved to Longmont, Colorado, a cattle town. His boxing coach, Abe Tobin, encouraged him to continue his education instead of seeking a career as a professional boxer.

The Road to Excellence

Eddie won a number of amateur boxing matches in tough competition in mining towns throughout Colorado. After his boxing tour, he enrolled at the University of Denver and spent one year there. He won the Western Amateur Middleweight title while a student.

He decided to enlist in the United States Army and was commissioned as an artillery lieutenant. After he was discharged, he entered Yale University in New Haven, Connecticut.

During his first year at Yale, he entered the 1919 Amateur Athletic Union (AAU) boxing championships. He fought seven bouts in two days. Eddie lost a close decision in the light heavyweight class; however, he returned later that evening and won the heavyweight title.

Later in 1919, Eddie competed in the Inter-Allied Games in Paris, France, and won the middleweight championship. In 1920, Eddie tried out for the U.S. Olympic boxing team. He represented the United States at the 1920 Antwerp Olympics in the light heavyweight division. He defeated boxers from South Africa, Great Britain, and Norway to win the gold medal.

Eddie returned to the United States and graduated from Yale University. He enrolled in law school at Harvard University, but he

HONORS, AWARDS, AND MILESTONES	
1919	Amateur Athletic Union heavyweight champion
	Inter-Allied Games middleweight champion
1920	U.S. Olympic gold medalist (light heavyweight boxing)
1932	U.S. Olympic gold medalist (four-person bobsled)
1983	Inducted into U.S. Olympic Hall of Fame

dropped out of law school to try out for the 1924 Olympic Games. He made the U.S. Olympic team again and sailed to Paris, but he was eliminated in the first round of the heavyweight division.

The Emerging Champion

Apparently, Eddie had been influenced by Coach Tobin's encouragement to pursue an education rather than a professional boxing career. He was awarded a Rhodes scholarship and continued his studies at Oxford University in England. He competed on Oxford's boxing team and participated in several exhibitions with the American heavyweight champion, Jack Dempsey.

After completing his studies at Oxford, Eddie toured the world. He participated in numerous boxing matches during his world tour.

When Eddie returned to the United States, he helped Gene Tunney train for a rematch with Jack Dempsey. Gene had become the new heavyweight champion.

In 1932, Eddie tried out for the U.S. Olympic bobsled team. The 1932 Olympic Winter Games were held in Lake Placid, New York. Eddie made the four-person bobsled team.

The finals of the four-person bobsled were delayed because of a severe winter storm. Despite poor weather conditions, a crowd of twenty thousand arrived for the competition and were disappointed when just two of the four runs could be completed. The snow was so deep that sleds slowed down and very poor times were recorded. The competition had to be postponed until the following day.

The Olympic Games were actually over when two bobsled heats were run. Billy Fiske was the pilot of the team, Eddie was the number-two man, and Clifford Gray was the third man. Jay O'Brien

was the brakeman. A fast start is essential for a good bobsled time, and the American team, led by Fiske, worked well together.

Very few people turned out in the bitter cold to view the last two runs. Eddie's team had the best time for each of the first three runs and the best overall time and claimed the Olympic championship. Eddie and his teammates were each presented with a gold medal. Eddie became the first Olympic athlete to win gold medals in both the Winter and Summer Olympic Games. He distinguished himself as a true competitor in two sports at the international level.

In 1932, Eddie entered private law practice. He served as Assistant Attorney for Southern New York for five years. He returned to his law practice, but joined the Army Air Force when World War II began. He was chief of special services in the Air Transport Command and visited nearly every part of the world where American planes were based. He retired from the Army as a lieutenant colonel.

Continuing the Story

When Eddie returned to civilian life in 1945, he was appointed head of the New York State Athletic Commission, which governed boxing. Because of his boxing background, Eddie was well suited for the job.

He served as head of the commission for six years. He made a major contribution by developing a scoring system for boxing that became the basis of the modern system. He also required strict physical examinations of boxers before and after their bouts. In 1956, President Dwight Eisenhower appointed Eddie chairman of the People-to-People Sports Committee. He also served as director of the sports program at the 1964 New York World's Fair. He headed the Boys' Athletic League of New York for two years.

Eddie's involvement in sports organizations gave him many opportunities to express his belief that sports serve as a "common denominator" of all people. He viewed sports activities as a way to bring people of different backgrounds together.

Eddie died of a heart attack on June 14, 1967, at Roosevelt Hospital in New York. He was living in Rye, New York, and was survived by his wife, his son, Sidney, and a daughter, Caroline.

729

Summary

Eddie Eagan's athletic ability and his educational background served him well. His interest in reading about a Yale student introduced him to Yale University, and his involvement in boxing and bobsledding led him to international competition in the Olympic Games. He was the first athlete to win gold medals in both the Winter and Summer Olympic Games.

Paula D. Welch

Additional Sources:

Blewett, Bert. *The A to Z of World Boxing.* London: Robson Books, 1996.

Eagan, Eddie. *Fighting for Fun: The Scrap Book of Eddie Eagan.* New York: Macmillan, 1934.

Herzog, Brad. "Modeled on a Myth." *Sports Illustrated* 87, no. 26 (December 29, 1997): 6-7.

DALE EARNHARDT

Sport: Auto racing

Born: April 29, 1951
     Kannapolis, North Carolina
Died: February 18, 2001
     Daytona Beach, Florida

Early Life

Ralph Dale Earnhardt was born on April 29, 1951, in Kannapolis, North Carolina, a small town in a part of the southern United States that has produced many stock car race drivers. His father, Ralph Earnhardt, was one of these drivers. From very early childhood, Dale was often at the track with his mother, Martha, and his brothers and sisters Kay, Cathy, Randy, and Danny, to watch "Ironheart," as his father was called, race. Sometimes there were as many as three races a week. Dale's father was not a superstar, but his hard work supported the family, and he was on his way up the ranks of drivers when he was killed in a racing accident in 1973 at age forty-four.

Dale grew up as much in the garage as he did in the house and was knowledgeable about auto mechanics before he was out of the sixth grade. He always remembered his father's advice to "stay cool on the race track."

The Road to Excellence

Dale was so interested in racing stock cars that he quit school in the ninth grade. This was something that later concerned him because he often found himself in situations where, as he would say, "I miss an education." Also, his father strongly opposed Dale's quitting school, and Dale's dropping out damaged their relationship for a time.

Dale was a good mechanic and pit crew member, and his father began to teach him about driving. By age nineteen, Dale had his own racer and was gaining experience on the dirt tracks so frequently found in the South.

The driving style developed by Dale was much like that of his father, fiercely aggressive and never giving an inch to a competitor. In fact, Dale soon earned for himself the title "Ironfoot." Dirt track racing, however, is not a sport with big purses for winners, so Dale had to work as a welder and a mechanic to support his family. Just at the time it appeared he would have to give up racing to work at another job full time, he was hired by Rod Osterlund to drive for the 1979 season.

This was a chance Dale would not miss. At the end of 1979, the National Association for Stock Car Auto Racing (NASCAR) named him Rookie of the Year. Dale would not stay a rookie for long. In 1980, he won the NASCAR Winston Cup Championship, the only second-year driver ever to win the title.

The Emerging Champion

This championship was far from an easy victory. Going into the final race of the year, Dale led Cale Yarborough by only 29 points out of a possible 4,000. For the last several races, Yarborough had been steadily closing the gap, which had been as wide as 230 points. Also, Dale's pit crew chief had quit in the middle of the season, and Dale's young, inexperienced crew were not thought to be good enough to carry him through to victory.

For the first 365 miles of the 500-mile race, Dale fought high winds and hard luck. He had to finish fifth to win the championship. One by one, other cars broke down or dropped out until Yarborough and Dale were dueling it out. Then, on a pit stop, Dale seemed to run out of luck. He sideswiped the pit wall, scattering his pit crew and, as they were finishing changing tires, he roared out of the pit with his car still on the jack. By the time all this was straightened out, Dale was in fifth place again, but Yarborough had also lost ground and was running third. That is where the race ended, with Dale earning the title by a whisker.

Continuing the Story

Being an aggressive driver is a good way to win races, but it is also a good way to be involved in controversies. In 1983 and 1984, Dale won the Talladega 500, and both times it was his strong driving that helped him break into the lead literally at the end of the race. He was the first driver ever to win this race twice in a row, and Dale's 1984 win helped him set a NASCAR record by winning twelve of nineteen events.

In 1986, Dale was fined five thousand dollars for reckless driving during a race and was briefly placed on probation. In a race at Richmond, Virginia, Dale collided with Darrell Waltrip when Waltrip tried to pass near the end of the race. During the 1987 season, Dale won nine races, but in three of them

NASCAR CIRCUIT VICTORIES

1979-80	Southeastern 500
1979-80, 1985, 1987	Valleydale 500
1980	Coca-Cola 500 Champion Old Dominion 500 National 500 Nashville 420
1980, 1986	Mello Yello 500
1980, 1986-87, 1990-91, 1993-94	NASCAR Winston Cup Champion
1982, 1986-87, 1990	Transouth 500
1983, 1986, 1990	Daytona 500 Twin 125 Qualifying Race
1983-84, 1999	Talladega 500
1984, 1986, 1989	Atlanta Journal 500
1985	Goody's 500
1985, 1987	Miller High Life 400
1985, 1987-88	Busch 500
1986	Coca-Cola 600
1986-87, 1989	First Union 400
1987	Virginia National Bank 500 Goodwrench 500 Summer 500 Miller American 400 Wrangler Jeans Indigo 400
1987, 1989-90	Heinz Southern 500
1988, 1990	Motorcraft 500 Sovran Bank 500
1989	Budweiser 500 Peak Performance 500
1990	Motorcraft 500 Miller Genuine Draft 400 Pepsi 400 Busch Pole Award Checker 500
1990-91	Die Hard 500
1990, 1995, 1999	International Race of Champions
1990, 2000	Winston 500 Champion
1991	Champion Spark Plug 300 Tyson 400
1998, 2000	Daytona 500
1999	Bristol 5000
2000	Cracker Barrel Old Country Store 500

he bumped the leaders and then passed. At the 1987 Winston Invitational, an All-Star race at Charlotte, North Carolina, Dale was involved in five bumping incidents. He also won the NASCAR Winston Cup Championship again in 1986, 1987, and 1990 and collected more than one million dollars in winnings.

Dale did not see himself as a careless driver or one who took unfair advantage of anybody. He saw stock car racing as a tough sport that calls for drivers who are tough, both physically and mentally. Off the track, Dale was an easy person to get along with. He prefered to deal truthfully with every person, to pull no surprises and to have none pulled on him.

As a result of being a competitive driver, Dale had several excellent seasons. After winning seasons in 1988 and 1989, Dale won eleven races in 1990, including the International Race of Champions title. In 1990, and again in 1991, he came close to winning the prestigious Daytona 500, but each year, an accident frustrated his goals. In 1991, he was charging up from second place when a multicar crash took him out of the race with only 3 laps to go.

Dale won back-to-back Winston Cup Championships in 1990-1991 and 1993-1994, bringing his total to seven and securing a place in stock car racing history. In 1995, Dale ended the season with five first-place finishes and over $3 million in earnings.

Dale struggled in 1997, with no wins and only seven finishes in the top five. Although he won only one event the following year, it was a big one—the 1998 Daytona 500. He improved even more in 1999, winning three NASCAR events, including the International Race of Champions. In 2000, Dale added a third win at Daytona to his long list of victories. He finished the season in second place with 4,690 points, just 265 shy of winning his eighth Winston Cup Championship.

Tragically, Dale was killed on February 18, 2001, in a high-speed crash that occurred in the

HONORS AND AWARDS

1979	NASCAR Rookie of the Year
1998	Fifty Greatest Drivers in NASCAR history

final lap of the final race of his twenty-third Daytona 500. His death at age forty-nine threw fans into mourning and forced NASCAR to reconsider issues concerning driver protection.

Dale, a husband and father of four, ended his career with seventy-six wins and seven Winston Cup championships. In 1998, the man nicknamed "The Intimidator" was honored as one of the Fifty Greatest Drivers in NASCAR history. It was an honor he shared with his father. It was left to Dale's son, Dale Earnhart, Jr., to continue the family legacy.

Summary

A hard competitor, Dale Earnhardt liked winning and did not shy away from the hard work and mental preparation necessary. While he competed all-out on the track, he was a friendly person off it. Dale liked to work on a farm he bought in North Carolina, where he enjoyed raising cattle. Yet, to Dale, racing was as natural as breathing. That is why he was exceptional at it.

Michael R. Bradley

Additional Sources:

Garfield, Ken. *Dale Earnhardt: The Intimidator.* Champaign, Ill.: Sports Publishing, 2000.

Lucido, Jerome. *Racing with the Hawk: The Man Behind Dale Earnhardt.* Grand Rapids, Mich.: F. H. Revell, 1998.

Moriarity, Frank. *Dale Earnhardt.* New York: Friedman/Fairfax, 2000.

Owens, Tom, and Diana Star Helmar. *NASCAR.* Brookfield, Conn.: Twenty-First Century Books, 2000.

Steenkamer, Paul. *Dale Earnhardt, Star Race Car Driver.* Berkeley Heights, N.J.: Enslow, 2000.

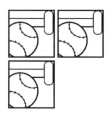

DENNIS ECKERSLEY

Sport: Baseball

Born: October 3, 1954
Oakland, California

Early Life

Dennis Lee Eckersley was born on October 3, 1954, in Oakland, California. Dennis's father, a warehouse supervisor, settled in the San Francisco Bay Area while working for the United States Navy during World War II, and Dennis and his two siblings were brought up in Fremont, an Oakland suburb.

Dennis excelled in sports as a child, and in high school he played quarterback for the school's football team. He did not care for the contact of football, though, and he dreamed of pitching someday for the San Francisco Giants. When the Giants sent a scout to watch him pitch for his high school team, however, Dennis had a terrible day, and the opposing team hit him hard. The Giants passed on the chance to draft him.

The Road to Excellence

In June, 1972, when Dennis was still seventeen, the Cleveland Indians of the American League (AL) made him a third-round draft choice. Dennis had expected to be drafted sooner, perhaps even in the first round, and he was not entirely happy about being picked by the Indians, a perennially weak club that had not won a pennant since 1954. He was reconciled to the idea of playing for the Indians, though, both by the team's offer of a thirty-two-thousand-dollar signing bonus and by the realization that he could progress to the major-league level much faster with a poor team than with a good one.

Dennis was correct in supposing that he could make it to the majors in a hurry. He tore through the Indians' minor-league system, posting records of 12-8 at Reno in the Class A California League in 1973 and a sizzling 14-3 at San Antonio of the Double-A Texas League in 1974. In 1975, at the age of twenty, Dennis found himself in the Indians' starting rotation.

In his first big-league start, Dennis faced the powerful Oakland A's, who had won their third consecutive World Series title the previous October. Dennis shut out the defending world champions and went on to set a record for rookies by not allowing a single run in his first 28 innings in the majors. At the season's end, Dennis had compiled a 13-7 record and a fine 2.60 earned run average (ERA), and he was named the American League's Rookie Pitcher of the Year.

In 1976, he won thirteen more games for the hapless Indians and accomplished the remark-

Boston Red Sox relief pitcher Dennis Eckersley in a 1998 game.

734

STATISTICS

Season	GP	GS	CG	IP	HA	BB	SO	W	L	S	ShO	ERA
1975	34	24	6	186.2	147	90	152	13	7	2	2	2.60
1976	36	30	9	199.0	155	78	200	13	12	1	3	3.44
1977	33	33	12	247.0	214	54	191	14	13	0	3	3.53
1978	35	35	16	268.1	258	71	162	20	8	0	3	2.99
1979	33	33	17	247.0	234	59	150	17	10	0	2	2.99
1980	30	30	8	198.0	188	44	121	12	14	0	0	4.27
1981	23	23	8	154.0	160	35	79	9	8	0	2	4.27
1982	33	33	11	224.1	228	43	127	13	13	0	3	3.73
1983	28	28	2	176.1	223	39	77	9	13	0	0	5.61
1984	33	33	4	225.0	223	49	114	14	12	0	0	3.60
1985	25	25	6	169.1	145	19	117	11	7	0	2	3.08
1986	33	32	1	201.0	226	43	137	6	11	0	0	4.57
1987	54	2	0	115.2	99	17	113	6	8	16	0	3.03
1988	60	0	0	72.2	52	11	70	4	2	**45**	0	2.35
1989	51	0	0	57.2	32	3	55	4	0	33	0	1.56
1990	63	0	0	73.1	41	4	73	4	2	48	0	0.61
1991	67	0	0	76.0	60	9	87	5	4	43	0	2.96
1992	69	0	0	80.0	62	11	93	7	1	**51**	0	1.91
1993	64	0	0	67.0	67	13	80	2	4	36	0	4.16
1994	45	0	0	44.3	49	13	47	5	4	19	0	4.26
1995	52	0	0	50.3	53	11	40	4	6	29	0	4.83
1996	63	0	0	60.0	65	6	49	0	6	30	0	3.30
1997	57	0	0	53.0	49	8	45	1	5	36	0	3.91
1998	50	0	0	39.2	46	8	22	4	1	1	0	4.76
Totals	1,071	361	100	3,285.2	3,076	738	2,401	197	171	390	20	3.50

Notes: Boldface indicates statistical leader. GP = games played; GS = games started; CG = complete games; IP = innings pitched; HA = hits allowed; BB = bases on balls (walks); SO = strikeouts; W = wins; L = losses; S = saves; ShO = shutouts; ERA = earned run average

able feat of averaging more than one strikeout an inning by striking out 200 batters in 199 innings of pitching. In 1977, he threw a no-hitter against the California Angels during a streak in which he did not allow a hit in 22-1/3 innings, the longest such streak in the major leagues since Cy Young had thrown 25-1/3 consecutive no-hit innings in 1904. Though he was still just twenty-three years old, Dennis had established himself as one of the game's top pitchers. He had posted a winning record in each of his three big-league seasons despite the handicap of playing for one of the majors' poorest teams, and baseball fans wondered how good he would be with a good team behind him.

The Emerging Champion

Dennis got his chance to show everyone in 1978, after the Indians sent him to the Boston Red Sox in exchange for four players. The 1978 Red Sox were loaded with talent, including future Hall-of-Famer Carl Yastrzemski and young stars Fred Lynn, Jim Rice, Dwight Evans, and Carlton Fisk. Dennis posted 20 victories against only 8 losses, and the Red Sox led the American League Eastern Division for most of the season before faltering in a heartbreaking four-game September series against the New York Yankees.

Although the Red Sox missed the playoffs, it seemed as though Dennis was on top of the world. He was a young 20-game winner for a contending club and the recipient of a large multiyear contract from the Red Sox; it was no surprise that opposing players called him "cocky" and grew irritated at his behavior on the mound, where Dennis would sometimes seem to dance in celebration after retiring a hitter. In fact, though, Dennis was unhappy.

Dennis had been married when he was only eighteen, and by 1978 he and his wife, Denise, had separated. In late 1978, they were divorced. To make matters worse, Dennis had developed a drinking problem during his years in Cleveland. Although his personal troubles had not seemed to hurt his on-field performance, they would soon take their toll.

In August of 1979, Dennis was cruising through another fine season with a 16-5 record when his arm suddenly grew tired. Pitching had always seemed effortless to him, but now it began to hurt. Dennis lost five of his last six decisions that year, and the next season he had his first losing record while his ERA soared to 4.27. For three more seasons with the Red Sox, Dennis continued to drink and his career continued to flounder. By 1983 he had hit bottom, finishing 9-13 and posting an ugly 5.61 ERA. The Red Sox sent him to the Chicago Cubs in the National League (NL), and his once-bright future seemed only a memory.

Dennis had some success in Chicago, winning ten games for the Cubs' 1984 division-champion team. He had begun using a Cybex exercise machine to strengthen his pitching shoulder, and the exercises helped; however, he was drinking more than ever. In 1985, though he posted an 11-7 record, his arm troubles returned, and the next season he slumped again to 6-11. Though he had managed to keep his drinking problem a secret, he had acquired a reputation as a talented but inconsistent underachiever.

Continuing the Story

In 1980, Dennis had married his second wife, Nancy O'Neil, a model with a master's degree in communications from Boston College. Nancy pressed Dennis into confronting his alcoholism, and in early 1987 Dennis agreed to check into the Edgehill treatment center in Newport, Rhode Island. At Edgehill, Dennis kicked his drinking habit, and he approached the 1987 season in his best physical and mental shape in years.

To make things even better, that spring the Cubs traded Dennis to the Oakland Athletics, a talented team that was also among the best managed organizations in baseball. Oakland's manager, Tony La Russa, and pitching coach, Dave Duncan, convinced Dennis to move from his accustomed starting spot into a relievers' role, and the move was a terrific success. In 1988, Oakland dominated the American League, and Dennis was the best reliever in baseball, earning 45 saves to lead the majors and winning the most valuable

HONORS AND AWARDS	
1975	American League Rookie Pitcher of the Year
1977, 1982, 1988, 1990-91	American League All-Star Team
1988	American League Championship Series most valuable player *Sporting News* American League Fireman of the Year Major league record for the most saves in a league championship series (4)
1988, 1992	American League Rolaids Relief Award
1992	American League most valuable player American League Cy Young Award

player Award in the American League playoffs as the Athletics swept the Red Sox. The season ended in disappointment for the Athletics as they were trounced in the World Series by the underdog Los Angeles Dodgers, but Dennis had clearly found his baseball home at last.

In the first game of the 1988 Series, Dennis had a chance to show how he had matured since the days when he was a cocky youngster who infuriated opponents by dancing on the mound. With the Athletics leading 4-3 with two out in the bottom of the ninth inning, he faced Dodger pinch-hitter Kirk Gibson and threw two quick strikes. Gibson worked the count full and then hit a slider from Dennis into the right-field seats for a game winning home run. After the game, Dennis showed that he could be graceful under pressure, patiently answering reporters' questions for nearly an hour.

In 1989, Oakland breezed through the American League again, and Dennis was again terrific. His control, which had always been good, had become phenomenal; in 57 innings, he struck out 55 batters and walked only 3, one of the best ratios in history. He was so good that opposing managers often altered their strategy against Oakland, playing, in effect, seven- or eight-inning games; they knew that if the Athletics had the lead in the eighth inning or later, Dennis would pitch and the game was almost as good as over.

The Athletics avenged their World Series defeat that fall, sweeping the San Francisco Giants and earning recognition as the best team in more than a decade. Incredibly, Dennis was even better the next year, saving forty-eight games, striking out 73 and walking only 4 in 73 innings, and posting a microscopic 0.61 ERA as Oakland captured its third consecutive American League pennant. He had reached his potential at last.

Dennis had a stellar year in 1992, earning both the AL's Cy Young Award and the league's most valuable player award. He began the season with 36 consecutive saves and finished with a league-leading 51.

In his next three seasons, Dennis failed to keep his ERA below 4.00 and was traded in 1996 to St. Louis. He earned more than 30 saves in his two seasons with the Cardinals in spite of increasing injuries. For the 1998 season, Dennis returned to Boston, where he spent the first half of the season on the disabled list. He recorded only 1 save in 50 appearances and decided to retire after twenty-three seasons. He is the only pitcher in baseball history to record one hundred complete games and 200 saves.

Summary

Dennis Eckersley overcame arm troubles and alcoholism to regain his place among baseball's best. As the intimidating closer for the dominant team of the late 1980's, he made a strong argument for himself as the top reliever of all time.

Brook Wilson

Additional Sources:

Kirkjian, Tim. "An A-Plus." *Sports Illustrated* 82, no. 22 (1995).

Ratto, Ray. "Dennis Eckersley Helped Define A's Championship Era." *Baseball Digest* 55, no. 7 (1996).

Rolfe, John. "Eck! Dennis Eckersley of the Oakland A's Is the Best Relief Pitcher in Baseball." *Sports Illustrated for Kids* 5, no. 6 (1993).

Wulfe, Steve. "The Paintmaster." *Sports Illustrated* 77, no. 8 (1992).

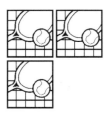

STEFAN EDBERG

Sport: Tennis

Born: January 19, 1966
Västervik, Sweden

Early Life

Stefan John Edberg's father, Bengt, was a policeman in Västervik, Sweden, where Stefan was born on January 19, 1966. Barbro Edberg, Bengt's wife, agreed with her husband that they should borrow money on their house to pay for their son's tennis lessons and travel to international tournaments.

In Sweden, the local tennis club charged about ten dollars a year for membership. It cost only fifty cents to play, but lessons became expensive as Stefan's skills advanced. Swedish youth attended school until four every afternoon and undertook their athletic pursuits outside school hours.

The taciturn temperament of Stefan's parents is reflected in their son. He is given neither to significant emotional swings nor to displays of temper on the courts. He was raised to believe that he must control his emotions. Only once, when he was fourteen, did Stefan yield to them. Disappointed by his play, he tried to break his aluminum racket by throwing it against a wall.

The Road to Excellence

In 1983, Stefan, quickly advancing beyond local play, became the first player ever to win a junior grand slam. He beat Boris Becker in the Wimbledon Junior Men's Singles. His early conviction to show few emotions on the court carried over into his professional career, which began in 1984, although sometimes his demeanor seemed to belie his frustration or discouragement when his game was going poorly.

Blond, boyish in appearance, Stefan projected an innocence and casualness in dealing with people. When he makes personal appearances, he directs his droll, good-natured humor at his fans.

Stefan Edberg after winning a match in the 1996 U.S. Open.

Having won the junior grand slam, Stefan knew he was good, but, modest and retiring as he is, he did not know how good. Only seventeen, in the back of his mind lurked the specters of countrymen Björn Borg, who had won the Italian Open by that age, and Mats Wilander, who had won the French. Therefore, the Milan Open in 1984 was important to Stefan. He was pitted against Wilander, a native of Smoland, the same small district in which Stefan's hometown lies. Defeating Wilander was a significant triumph. When Stefan played in the U.S. Open later in the year, however, John McEnroe defeated him soundly.

The Emerging Champion

After the U.S. Open, Stefan, never one to smoulder over defeats, teamed with Anders Jarryd and beat McEnroe and Peter Fleming in the 1984 men's doubles of the Davis Cup final between the United States and Sweden. At about this time, Tony Pickard became Edberg's coach, marking a turning point in Edberg's professional career. Pickard, a sales representative for products that Edberg endorses, was the sort of person Edberg needed to help him advance to his next level of professional excellence.

Realizing that, despite his obvious talent, Stefan had never really been pushed, Pickard, a close and dependable friend of the young player, put him under incredible pressure and taught him effective techniques with which to handle that pressure. Knowing that Stefan plays a strong serve-and-volley game and that his one-handed backhand delivers killing returns, Pickard helped Stefan capitalize on his strengths. He also kept him working on his forehand shots, not among his notable assets.

In 1985, the year after he turned professional, Stefan, largely through Pickard's effective training program, won the Australian Open and helped Sweden's Davis Cup team to prevail over West Germany. He also won the All-German Cham-

MAJOR CHAMPIONSHIP VICTORIES AND FINALS	
1985, 1987	Australian Open
1987	U.S. Open doubles (with Anders Jarryd)
1987, 1996	Australian Open doubles (with Jarryd; with Petr Korda)
1988, 1990	Wimbledon
1989	Wimbledon finalist French Open finalist
1990, 1992-93	Australian Open finalist
1991-92	U.S. Open

OTHER NOTABLE VICTORIES	
1984	Gold Medal, Olympic Men's Tennis Singles (demonstration sport) Milan Open
1984-85	On winning Swedish Davis Cup team
1985, 1987	U.S. Indoor Championship
1988	Swiss Indoor Championship Bronze Medal, Olympic Men's Tennis Singles
1989	The Masters
1990	ATP Championship

pionship over Becker in 1988. For the five years from 1985 to 1990, Stefan was consistently among the world's top five players, creeping up to second in 1987. Ivan Lendl was first.

Continuing the Story

In 1989, problems developed in Stefan's personal life, and it was not an easy year for him. He lost two Grand Slam finals and failed to prevail in five other major contests, presumably because his personal problems intruded on his playing. The situation came to a head when Stefan lost to Jimmy Connors in straight sets at the U.S. Open. Pickard realized the pressing need for Stefan to get back in stride, and Stefan, with his typical dedication and stoicism, devoted himself to intensive practice.

He began to emerge from his slump by defeating first Ivan Lendl and then Boris Becker in The Masters tournament. He continued to the Australian Open in 1990, but illness caused him to lose to Lendl by default. When they played the French Open some weeks later, both Stefan and Becker were poised to rob Lendl of his number one spot in world tennis. Both lost in the first round, however, and Pickard did not refrain

739

HONORS, AWARDS, AND MILESTONES

1984-96	Swedish Davis Cup team
1988-90	Adidas Sportsman of the Year
1990	Player of the Year
1990-91	Ranked number one by ATP

from telling his protégé in strident tones what was wrong with his game.

Stefan left France immediately for England to prepare for Wimbledon, determined to hone his game to the kind of perfection required for a win. He succeeded in defeating Becker in five sets, to become number one in world tennis. The Wimbledon contest was called for rain with Stefan in the lead. The twenty-four hour delay on Sunday apparently worked to Stefan's advantage; he remained calm and controlled during it and came back on Monday in full command of his game. His serves were impeccable, his volleys impressive. Even his forehand, on which he had been working hard, rose to new heights. Stefan lost in the semifinals of the 1991 Wimbledon to the unlikely eventual champion Michael Stich of Germany. A few months later, however, Stefan was back in top form during the U.S. Open, with a dazzling 3-set triumph over American Jim Courier that gave Stefan his fifth Grand Slam singles title (his seventh Grand Slam title overall). Afterward, he called the match the best one he had ever played.

Summary

As the foremost tennis player in the world in 1990, Stefan Edberg has won impressive cash prizes, making him one of the tennis world's highest earners. He has also been well rewarded for his endorsements. Despite the fame and wealth that have come to him, Stefan still flies tourist class and values the relative anonymity provided him in the London neighborhood of Kensington, where he lives quietly near his tennis coach.

He also owns a house in the south of France, where he can go when he needs more solitude than London offers. In many ways, this star without star quality is the Greta Garbo of tennis. His need for solitude and anonymity may well be the key to what he does with his athletic future.

R. Baird Shuman

Additional Sources:

Collins, Bud. "Stefan Edberg." In *Bud Collins' Tennis Encyclopedia,* edited by Bud Collins and Zander Hollander. 3d ed. Detroit: Visible Ink Press, 1997.

Higdon, David. "No More Mr. Nice Guy." *Tennis* 32 (October, 1996): 29-34.

Price, S. L. "A Man of Style, and Substance." *Sports Illustrated* 85 (September 9, 1996): 10-11.

Smith, Stan. "The Elegant Lessons of Edberg's Game." *Tennis* 32 (October, 1996): 37-40.

Trabert, Tony, and Mark Preston. "Edberg's Elegant Backhand Volley." *Tennis* 31 (January, 1996): 56-58.

GERTRUDE EDERLE

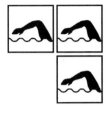

Sport: Swimming

Born: October 23, 1906
New York, New York

Early Life

Gertrude Caroline Ederle was born on October 23, 1906, in New York, New York. Gertrude was the third of six children. Her parents, Henry and Gertrude, were German immigrants. Her father was a successful butcher, and his store was next to the Ederle home where Gertrude was born. Gertrude was active in the Women's Swimming Association (WSA), but always found time to help her mother at home. She made her own clothes and sewed for her younger sisters.

She began to swim at the age of eight. Her father taught her to swim at the Ederles' summer cottage in Highlands, New Jersey. She joined the WSA at age twelve.

The Road to Excellence

Gertrude's coach was a swimming expert. Coach Louis de Brada Handley taught her the innovative eight-beat kick for the freestyle. She began showing signs of having great speed a year after joining the WSA. Gertrude won her first race at age twelve. She was an unknown swimmer until August 1, 1922, when she entered the 3½-mile international race for the Joseph P. Day Cup. The race drew more than fifty swimmers. Gertrude swam the race from Manhattan Beach to Brighton Beach in a record 1 hour 1 minute and 34.4 seconds. She won the race by a fifty-yard margin. She had never raced more than 220 yards.

By the end of the 1922 American Athletic Association Outdoor Championships, Gertrude had established herself as another great WSA swimmer. She consistently won short- as well as long-distance events. On September 4, 1922, she established six world records in a single 500-meter race. The records ranged from 150 yards to 500 meters. In the 1920's, it was a common practice for officials to time swimmers at multiple distances in the longer races.

Gertrude helped the WSA win national team titles in indoor and outdoor championships from 1922 through 1925. She had won 250 races by the end of 1924. In

Gertrude Ederle is greased up before a swim.

741

addition to races in the New York City area, she had competed in cities from Boston to Miami and in Bermuda and the Hawaiian Islands.

The Emerging Champion

Because of her strength and speed, Gertrude had established her reputation as a great swimmer soon after taking up the sport. She further distinguished herself, however, as an Olympian and an English Channel swimmer. She took her sport seriously soon after joining the WSA and was determined to succeed. An observer ridiculed her first attempts to learn the freestyle. She made up her mind to beat the girl who made fun of her swimming and established a personal goal to become a champion. She was fortunate to live in New York City and have access to the WSA.

In 1924, Gertrude won a place on the United States Olympic team, the second such team for American women. The 1924 Olympics were in Paris. Gertrude won a bronze medal in the 100-meter freestyle. She had been favored to win the event. She was also favored to win the 400-meter freestyle, but finished third and collected her second bronze medal.

She claimed her first gold medal in the 400-meter freestyle relay. She swam the first leg of the event and helped the United States team establish a new world record.

Gertrude never offered any excuses for not winning three gold medals in Paris. Some of the New York City newspapers indicated that she had muscle soreness and that may have been the reason she did not win the 100- and 400-meter freestyle races. After the Olympics, Gertrude turned professional.

Gertrude first tried to swim the English Channel on August 18, 1925. She had to quit after nearly nine hours. Some observers thought she swam too fast. On August 6, 1926, Gertrude succeeded in swimming the English Channel. In the 1920's, some people did not believe that a woman could swim the channel. She not only con-

quered the English Channel, but swam faster than any man had. She entered the water at Cape Gris-Nez, France, and walked out of the water at Kingsdown, England, 14 hours and 31 minutes later. The distance was 35 miles.

She was welcomed home by large crowds, who turned out for a ticker-tape parade in her honor. President Calvin Coolidge sent a congratulatory message.

Gertrude received many offers to perform in vaudeville shows and films. She toured in vaudeville for two years and received $2,000 a week. She appeared in one movie and swam in exhibitions. She canceled her vaudeville tour in June, 1928, because of illness. She later worked at an amusement park in Rye, New York.

In December 1933, she slipped on some broken tiles on stairs. She severely injured her back and spent four years in casts. She was told that she would never walk again. Gertrude's friend, Julia Lackwit, encouraged her and helped her to recover.

STATISTICS

Year	Competition	Event	Place	Time
1922	Manhattan Beach to Brighton Beach race	3.5 miles		1 hr. 1 mn. 34.4 sec.
	AAU Outdoor Championships	440-yard freestyle	1st	6:01.2
1923	AAU Outdoor Championships	440-yard freestyle	1st	6:35.4
		880-yard freestyle	1st	13:19.0
1924	Olympic Games	100-meter freestyle	Bronze	1:14.12
		400-meter freestyle	Bronze	6:04.8
		4×100-meter freestyle relay	Gold	4:58.8 WR
	AAU Outdoor Championships	880-yard freestyle	1st	13:59.0
1926	English Channel	35 miles		14 hrs. 31 mns. WR

Note: WR = World Record

Continuing the Story

In 1939, Billy Rose, the entertainer, invited Gertrude to participate in his swimming shows. The shows were also performed during the 1939 New York World's Fair. Billy's invitation provided another incentive for Gertrude to recover. She had to swim the whole length of a pool and stay in time with the music.

In the early 1950's, she went into semi-retirement. She spent some of her time teaching children to swim. She also officiated at New York

RECORDS AND MILESTONES
First woman to swim the English Channel (1926). She swam it faster than any man before her
Held 29 U.S. National and world records from 1921 to 1925
Broke 7 world records of various distances during one 500-meter swim at Brighton Beach (1922)
Was female counterpart to Johnny Weissmuller

HONORS AND AWARDS	
1965	Inducted into International Swimming Hall of Fame
1980	Inducted into Sudafed International Women's Sports Hall of Fame

City Parks Department swimming meets.

Gertrude had experienced a hearing loss when she was in her twenties. She helped others with hearing problems by teaching children at the Lexington School for the deaf. She also became an advisor to the aquatics team of the Flushing Young Men's Christian Association.

Gertrude's name was known by millions of Americans. Her swimming achievements helped to convince the public that strenuous physical activity was acceptable for women.

Summary

Gertrude Ederle won numerous national titles and broke nine world records. Her most widely recognized achievement occurred when she became the first woman to swim the English Channel.

Paula D. Welch

Additional Sources:

Adler, David A. *America's Champion Swimmer: Gertrude Ederle.* San Diego, Calif.: Harcourt, 2000.

Smith, Lissa, ed. *Nike is a Goddess: The History of Women in Sports.* New York: Atlantic Monthly Press, 1998.

Ware, Susan, ed. *Forgotten Heroes: Inspiring American Portraits from Our Leading Historians.* New York: Free Press, 1998.

Woolum, Janet. *Outstanding Women Athletes: Who They Are and How They Influenced Sports in America.* Phoenix, Ariz.: Oryx Press, 1998.

KRISZTINA EGERSZEGI

Sport: Swimming

Born: August 16, 1974
Budapest, Hungary

Early Life

Krisztina Egerszegi, the younger of two sisters, was born on August 16, 1974, in Budapest, Hungary, where her father worked for the local telephone company and her mother worked as a government planning manager. A petite child, Krisztina earned the nickname "Little Mouse," in part for her size and shy personality and in part because the first part of her surname, *egér,* means "mouse" in Hungarian.

The Road to Excellence

Krisztina began swimming at the age of four. Her athletic participation began in the sport of rhythmic gymnastics, but she soon followed in her older sister's footsteps and switched to competitive swimming.

As soon as she emerged as an elite swimmer, Krisztina enjoyed the opportunity to travel with the Hungarian team to train at swimming camps around the world—remarkable privileges in a small and poor country. Known as "sunshine chasers," Krisztina and her teammates traveled to where the weather was good to avoid the October-to-March flu epidemic in their homeland. Fortunately, the team had a sponsor, "Mr. Z," known as the godfather of Hungarian swimming, who provided the funds necessary for the team to train, travel, and compete.

The Emerging Champion

At the 1987 European Championships, Krisztina finished in fifth place in the 100-meter backstroke with a time of 1:02.92 and in fourth place in the 200-meter backstroke with a time of 2:13.46. She was only fourteen years old in September, 1988, when she placed second in the 100-meter backstroke (1:01.56) and won the 200-meter backstroke gold medal (2:09.29) at the Seoul Olympics. The stunning news of history's youngest Olympic swimming gold medalist swept through the swimming world. "Little Mouse" was, in fact, quite little; she weighed 42 pounds less than any of her opponents in the finals.

The 1989 European Championships saw Krisztina take second-place finishes in the 100-meter backstroke, the 200-meter backstroke, and the 400-meter individual medley. She continued to train around the world, singing while she swam during her practice sessions.

In 1991, Krisztina won the 200-meter backstroke (2:09.15) at the

Hungarian Krisztina Egerszegi swimming in a 1996 Olympic medley.

AP/Wide World Photos

STATISTICS

Year	Competition	Event	Place	Time
1988	Olympic Games	100-meter backstroke	Silver	1:01.56
		200-meter backstroke	Gold	2:09.29 OR
1991	World Championships	100-meter backstroke	1st	1:01.78
		200-meter backstroke	1st	2:09.15
	European Championships	100-meter backstroke	1st	1:00.31 WR
		200-meter backstroke	1st	2:06.62 WR
		400-meter individual medley	1st	4:39.78
1992	Olympic Games	100-meter backstroke	Gold	1:00.68 OR
		200-meter backstroke	Gold	2:07.06 OR
		400-meter individual medley	Gold	4:36.54
1993	European Championships	100-meter backstroke	1st	
		200-meter backstroke	1st	
		200-meter freestyle	1st	
		400-meter individual medley	1st	
1996	Olympic Games	200-meter backstroke	Gold	
		400-meter individual medley	Bronze	

Notes: OR = Olympic Record; WR = World Record

World Championships in Perth, Australia. Her 3-second margin over runner-up Dagmar Hase of Germany was viewed as impressive in the world of elite swimming, where winners are often decided by fractions of a second. Her performance in the 100-meter backstroke also earned her a gold medal and a personal-best time of 1:01.78.

The dedicated Hungarian swimmers trained for long hours, and their effort was rewarded. The Hungarian team, which consisted of only eleven swimmers, dominated the 1991 World Championships. The dynamite little team broke three records; in comparison, the forty-three swimmers on the U.S. team set only two records. With Krisztina as the leading force, the small Hungarian national team could not be taken lightly.

At the 1991 European Championships in Athens, Greece, Krisztina set world records in both her backstroke specialties. She took an amazing .28 second off the 100-meter backstroke record of 1:00.59, a record that had stood since 1984. The sub-minute backstroke time suddenly became the barrier for women to break. Then she dove back into the pool to lower the 200-meter backstroke record by almost 2 seconds to 2:06.62. She then continued to dominate the pool by winning a gold medal for the 400-meter individual medley with a time of 4:39.78.

Krisztina had become famous, and her performance at the European Championships was the cover story for the Hungarian sports weekly *Sport Plusz Foci*. She remained a typical teenage girl, carrying good-luck dolls to her meets and painting her fingernails to match her swimsuits. Although she was herself a celebrity, receiving fan mail that included many love letters, she continued to idolize her teammate Tamas Darnyi and former U.S. backstroker Betsy Mitchell.

Continuing the Story

For the 1992 Olympics, the young members of the Hungarian swim team, most of whom were of high school or college age, were granted time off from school in order to train. In exchange, they endured long hours in the pool and a strict daily routine. At the Hungarian championship meet at Budapest in July, Krisztina breezed through the 400-meter individual medley with an astonishing time of 4:38.30, .20 second better than the ten-year-old world record. At the awards ceremony, "Egér," as her teammates called her, shyly stepped up to receive her trophies. The Hungarian press began to refer to her as "Mighty Mouse."

During the 1992 Summer Olympics in Barcelona, Spain, Krisztina was in a class by herself. With capacity crowds of 10,700 spectators urging her on, she sailed through the backstroke events with long, smooth strokes. Her endurance allowed her to finish a full meter ahead of her challengers. She missed breaking both her record and the one-minute barrier in the 100-meter backstroke, but she established a new Olympic record at 1:00.68 and earned the gold medal. At one week shy of eighteen years, she was the only swimmer to improve her Olympic performance from four years before. She also maintained a hold on her Olympic record for the 200-meter backstroke and finished first in her other specialty, the 400-meter medley, becoming the only female athlete to leave Barcelona with three individual gold medals.

At the 1993 European Championships, Krisztina became the first swimmer to win four individual titles when she took first place in the 100-meter and 200-meter backstroke, the 200-meter butterfly, and the 400-meter individual medley events. She achieved another first at the 1996 Olympics, where she won the gold medal in the 200-meter backstroke. She became the first woman in any Olympic event to win five gold medals in individual events. Her margin of victory (4.15 seconds) was the largest in a women's 200-meter event in any sport.

In 2001 Krisztina received the ultimate honor when she was elected to the International Swimming Hall of Fame.

HONORS, AWARDS, AND MILESTONES

Youngest gold medalist in swimming in Olympic history, 1988

1991-92	Female World Swimmer of the Year
1993	First swimmer to win four individual titles in a single European championship
2001	Inducted into International Swimming Hall of Fame

Summary

Krisztina Egerszegi dominated the women's backstroke and individual medley while she was still in her teens. The tiny athlete set world and Olympic records while becoming a heroine to millions of Hungarians.

Her individual achievements as an Olympic athlete remain unparalleled, and her world records in the 100-meter and 200-meter backstrokes still stood in 2001.

Marcia J. Mackey

Additional Sources:

Cohen, Neil. "Krisztina Egerszegi." *Sports Illustrated for Kids* 5, no. 5 (1993).

Levinson, David, and Karen Christenson, eds. *Encyclopedia of World Sport: From Ancient Times to Present.* Santa Barbara, Calif.: ABC-CLIO, 1996.

Lord, Craig, and Sylvie Josse. "Queen Kristina: Hungary's Golden Girl." *Swimming World and Junior Swimmer* 37, no. 1 (1996).

Wallechinsky, David. *The Complete Book of the Olympics.* Boston: Little, Brown and Company, 1991.

HICHAM EL GUERROUJ

Sport: Track and field (middle-distance runs)

Born: September 14, 1974
Berkane, Morocco

Early Life

Hicham El Guerrouj (pronounced HISH-um el guh-ROOSH) was born in Berkane, Morocco, on September 14, 1974. He was the fourth child of seven born to Ayachi El Guerrouj, a local restaurant owner. Hicham's first sport, like that of many Moroccans, was soccer. His hero, however, was Said Aouita, the Moroccan distance champion, who in 1984 won the 5,000-meter gold medal at the Los Angeles Olympic Games. With encouragement from his mother and a schoolteacher, Hicham took up running at the age of fifteen. His first major success came in 1992, when the young runner placed third in the 5,000-meter final of the Junior World Championships in Seoul, Korea, running 13:46.79.

The Road to Excellence

At the Moroccan national training camp in Rabat, Hicham developed the disciplined lifestyle that led to his future success. He entered the world track and field scene in 1995 by winning the world indoor 1,500-meter title. However, he ran under the shadow of Algerian star Noureddine Morceli, arguably the world's best middle-distance runner and holder of six indoor and outdoor world records. Despite a second-place finish to Morceli at the Outdoor World Championships in Goteborg, Sweden, Hicham was outstanding in 1995. He set a personal best in the

1,500-meter in Cologne, Germany, clocking the world's third-fastest time, 3:31.16, and running the eighth-fastest mile in history in 3:48.69.

In preparation for the 1996 Olympic games in Atlanta, Georgia, Hicham ran another 1,500-meter personal record, 3:29.59. Less than one month later he lined up for the Olympic 1,500-meter final. The first three laps of the race were relatively slow. As the runners raced down the homestretch of the third lap, Hicham stepped up to make his move on Morceli. In a nightmarish sequence of events his spike caught on Morceli's heel, and he tumbled to the track. By the time Hicham recovered, it was too late. Morceli won the gold medal, and Hicham finished last. Devastated by the loss, he retreated under the sta-

Hicham El Guerrouj won the 1,500 meters in the World Track and Field Championships in 1999.

747

dium and wept inconsolably until receiving a phone call from King Hassan II of Morocco. The king encouraged Hicham, reminding him that there would be other chances. Moved, Hicham said that he became a new man that day.

For inspiration he carried a picture of himself after losing in Atlanta. One month after the Olympics, he had a rematch with Morceli at the Grand Prix Final in Milan, Italy, where he handed Morceli his first loss of the year.

The Emerging Champion

Over the next three years Hicham became the fastest middle-distance runner of all time. He began a streak of world-record performances on February 2, 1997, in Stuttgart, Germany, where he ran he ran 3:31.18, breaking Morceli's 1994 indoor 1,500-meter record by almost 3 seconds. Ten days later in Ghent, Belgium, Hicham lowered the indoor mile record to 3:48.45. To top off the season, he captured the 1,500-meter gold at the World Championships in Athens.

Hicham was undefeated in 1998, a season highlighted by his performance at the Golden Gala Meet in Rome. There, on July 14, he ran 1,500 meters in 3:26.00, more than a second faster than Morceli's world record. Hicham also captured all of the European Golden League Series 1,500-meter races, earning more than $500,000.

On July 7, 1999, Hicham broke Morceli's mile world record at the Golden Gala meet in Rome in a surprisingly competitive race. Middle-distance records are usually set by individuals finishing alone after following pacesetters through several laps. However, when Hicham glanced at the video monitor as he raced down the homestretch, he saw Noah Ngeny, a twenty-one-year-old Kenyan, at his shoulder. The two sprinted home, with Hicham finishing first in the world-record time of 3:43.13.

One month later Hicham defended his 1,500-meter crown at the World Championships in Seville, Spain, soundly defeating Ngeny in 3:28.57.

MAJOR CHAMPIONSHIPS				
Year	Competition	Event	Place	Time
1992	Junior World Championships	5,000 meters	3d	13:46.79
1995	World Indoor Championships	1,500 meters	1st	3:44.54
	World Outdoor Championships	1,500 meters	2d	3:35.28
1996	Olympic Games	1,500 meters	12th	3:40.75
1997	Sparkassan Cup	1,500 meters	1st	3:31.18 WR
	Indoor Competition	Mile	1st	3:48.45 WR
	World Indoor Championships	1,500 meters	1st	3:35.31
	World Outdoor Championships	1,500 meters	1st	3:35.83
1998	Golden Gala Meet	1,500 meters	1st	3:26.00 WR
1999	Golden Gala Meet	Mile	1st	3:43.13 WR
	World Outdoor Championships	1,500 meters	1st	3:27.57
	Golden League Meet	2,000 meters	1st	4:44.79 WR
2000	Olympic Games	1,500 meters	Silver	3:32.32

Note: WR = World Record

In September Hicham captured the 2,000-meter world record in Berlin, running 4:44.79 and breaking Morceli's record by over 3 seconds. By the end of 1999, Hicham held five world records, along with the second-fastest 3,000-meter time ever: 7:23.09.

Continuing the Story

Hicham was the clear favorite to win gold in the middle-distance events at the 2000 Olympic Games in Sydney, Australia. Since his bitter loss in Atlanta four years earlier, he had lost only one race at the 1,500-meter or mile distances and had won fifty-one consecutive races in a three-year streak. On the evening of September 29, in Sydney, Hicham lined up for the 1,500-meter Olympic final with the fastest preliminary time. After a blazing first lap, the race slowed and the runners packed in. With 600 meters (1,969 feet) to go, Hicham took the lead, while Ngeny followed close behind. With 50 meters (164 feet) left in the race Ngeny pulled up next to Hicham, and at 20 meters (65.6 feet) gained the few steps he needed to win. El Geurrouj finished second in 3:32.32 but was again devastated. He made no excuses, however, and congratulated Ngeny.

Prior to Sydney, Hicham declared that after the Olympics he would move up from the 1,500-meter run to race longer distances. Having established himself as the fastest middle-distance runner in history, similar success at longer distances seemed probable.

Summary

Hicham El Guerrouj is a devout Muslim who spends eleven months each year training at the Moroccan altitude camp in Ifrane in the Atlas Mountains. He generally trains five hours a day, including distance runs, speed workouts, and weightlifting. He also adheres to a strictly low-fat, high-carbohydrate diet. Hicham's discipline and good nature have made him the hero of Morocco and have earned him the patronage of the king. His phenomenal speed and efficient stride made him one of the greatest middle-distance runners of all time.

John G. Powell

Additional Sources:

Lindstrom, Sieg. "1,500 Meters: Ngeny Topples El Guerrouj." *Track and Field News*, December, 2000, 14.

Rushin, Steve. "Desert Star." *Sports Illustrated* 92 (May 8, 2000): 102-112.

Usher, Rod. "The Summer Olympics: The Ones to Beat—Hicham El Guerrouj." *Time* 156 (September 11, 2000): 87-88.

Wharton, David. "Fifteen Days to Olympics; Fall Guy, El Guerrouj, Probably the Best Middle-Distance Runner Ever, Remains Haunted by His 1996 Error." *Los Angeles Times*, July 2, 2000, p. D1.

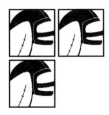

CARL ELLER

Sport: Football

Born: January 15, 1942
Winston-Salem, North Carolina

Early Life

Carl Lee Eller was born on January 15, 1942, in Winston-Salem, North Carolina, the son of Clarance McGee and Ernestine Eller. When Carl was in high school, his father died. Carl then worked construction jobs in the summer to help support the family. He went to Atkins High School, where he made All-State in football, lettered in track, served as class president, and acted the lead role in Sophocles' *Antigone.* Needless to say, Carl was a dedicated and well-rounded person.

The Road to Excellence

Carl did not get into organized football until his sophomore year in high school. Even then, most people in town knew about the 185-pound ninth-grader playing sandlot football. By the conclusion of his senior season, Carl was considered a prime collegiate prospect.

Carl graduated from high school in 1960 and accepted a football scholarship to the University of Minnesota. Carl joined fellow North Carolinian Bobby Bell to give Minnesota one of the finest pairs of defensive tackles ever to play college football together. In 1962, Carl and Bobby anchored the best college defense against the run in the nation. They held opponents to only 52.2 yards rushing per game. They also set a Big Ten Confer-

ence record by allowing opponents a total of only 58.2 yards per game. While Carl was a star on defense, he was also a fine blocker on offense. After his senior year, Carl was selected as an All-American tackle, and he played for the East in the East-West Shrine All-Star Game in 1963.

Carl was still in the shadow of the more outgoing Bobby Bell. They both started as sophomores and compiled similar statistics and awards, but Carl was not the colorful and witty team clown that Bobby was. Carl was described as being

HONORS AND AWARDS

1963	East-West Shrine All-Star Team
	College All-American
1968-71	NFL All-Pro Team
1969-72, 1974-75	NFL Pro Bowl Team
1971	Halas Trophy (co-recipient)
1980	NFL All-Pro Team of the 1970's

quiet, reflective, dignified, a nice guy, and a "gentlemanly giant." Carl was known to enjoy reading, theater, and jazz.

On the field for the Gophers, Carl was known for his quick, overwhelming pass-rush and jarring tackles. His coaches noticed that he was even better as an offensive blocker, however. Carl was willing to do whatever it took to help the team, even if it was not always noticeable to the fans.

At 6 feet 6 inches and 245 pounds, Carl had impressive speed. He could run the 40-yard dash in 4.5 seconds, a mark faster than many National Football League (NFL) running backs could achieve. The NFL's Minnesota Vikings selected Carl in the first round of the 1963 NFL draft. During training camp, he was switched to defensive end. Carl liked the change, because he had more freedom to use his speed to rush the passer, and he could use his size to knock down passes attempted over him.

The Emerging Champion

With all of his apparent success as an athlete, Carl had not quite found himself as a person. He was again considered quite shy during his early days with the Vikings. He felt awkward with newspaper reporters and had trouble answering their questions. Also, the Vikings were having difficulties between some of the blacks and whites on the team.

Along with Vikings teammate Jim Marshall, Carl helped ease and eventually eliminate these racial tensions. Carl's apartment in Minneapolis became a meeting place for players to discuss their problems. The responsibility helped Carl open up, and he became a leader on and off the field for the entire Vikings organization. He became a source of inspiration to his teammates,

and was known for his effective halftime speeches. Sometimes he would shout, and sometimes he would whisper, but always the effect was dramatic. His teammates knew that Carl would always try hard to win every time he played. Still, he knew the world would not come to an end if the team lost.

Carl became one of football's most respected defensive ends during his career (1964-1979). He was named All-Pro four times and played in six Pro Bowl games. He even occasionally joined the offensive line on short-yardage situations. He was once awarded a game ball for a block he threw that enabled a Viking back to score and win the game. He was a part of the "Purple People Eaters," a fearsome defensive line that included Alan Page, Jim Marshall, and Gary Larsen. Some of the modern rules governing passrushers, such as making the head slap technique illegal, were designed to control the dominance of the "Purple People Eaters." Marshall said that he and the other three players reached a point that they just knew what the others were doing and where they would be throughout the entire game. The four won numerous team and league awards. In 1971, Carl received the George Halas trophy as the NFL's best defensive player.

Carl became known off the field for his taste in clothes and his business ventures. He formed a business partnership with Marshall and a high school friend called Eller, Marshall and Blue Inc. He was even featured once in a *Life* magazine story about his stylish home and clothes.

Marshall and Carl were roommates on road games. They both were known to get very tense before games. Sometimes they would have water fights or pillow fights or even play chess to ease the tension. Even though Carl was fearsome on the field, he was always gracious to fans, often coming out of the locker room to chat with them after a tough game. He was often seen mingling with crowds at current Vikings games.

Carl played fifteen years with the Vikings before playing one final year with the Seattle Seahawks.

Continuing the Story

After his retirement from professional football in 1979, Carl encountered more problems of adjustment. He confronted his problems and

751

sought help. As a result, Carl started a counseling program for NFL drug rehabilitation. He also started his own career counseling company, called Triumph Life Center. He began working with athletes to deal with the pressures of being heroes and not being perfect. Carl has also been involved in the development of some of the principles of sport psychology. Before entering the counseling profession, Carl's imposing features landed him some acting roles and some television commercials. Performing would remain a side interest in light of Carl's business interests.

Carl later became a consultant to corporations and government programs. Trained as a specialist on behavioral and mental health provider networks, his client list includes Fortune 500 companies, sports organizations, colleges and universities, and professional and community groups from across the United States and abroad. At the state of Minnesota's department of human services, Carl developed and expanded health services for children and families, with an emphasis on children of color.

Summary

Carl Eller was an imposing, intense and dedicated lineman in the NFL. Before that, he was considered one of the best defensive tackles ever to have played in the Big Ten Conference. No matter what he has been involved in, he has overcome obstacles and has always striven to improve himself. A quiet man, Carl has let responsibility make him a leader as an athlete, businessman, and person.

Kevin R. Lasley

Additional Sources:

Zimmerman, Paul. "Gangs of Four, the Four-Man Defensive Lines Born in the 50's, Ruled the NFL Until Changes in the Game Spelled Their Doom." *Sports Illustrated* 83, no. 14 (October 6, 1995): 66-73.

HERB ELLIOTT

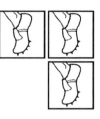

Sport: Track and field (middle-distance runs)

Born: February 25, 1938
       Perth, Western Australia, Australia

Early Life

The son of a furniture dealer, Herbert James Elliott was born in Perth, Western Australia, Australia, on February 25, 1938. He showed considerable promise as a middle-distance runner even in primary school. While in secondary school at

Australian Herb Elliott winning the 1,500-meter run in the 1960 Rome Olympics.

Aquinas College, Herb won the mile event in the Western Australia schoolboy competition with the credible time of 4 minutes 25.6 seconds, in the same year that England's Roger Bannister became the first to crack the 4-minute barrier for the mile run.

Herb's interest in running waned until sparked by a visit with his parents to the 1956 Olympic Games in Melbourne, where he was inspired by the running accomplishments of the Soviet Union's Vladimir Kuts, who won both the 5,000- and the 10,000-meter events. The running coach Percy Cerutty had visited Aquinas College in 1955, and after the Melbourne Games Herb's father arranged that his son would train with Cerutty at his running camp at Portsea, some sixty miles from Melbourne.

The Road to Excellence

At Portsea, Cerutty molded his runners through a challenging regimen which included lifting weights, running on the beaches and up and down 80-foot sandhills, and consumption of a diet that stressed dried fruit and nuts. In the evening they listened to poetry, philosophy, and music. It was a punishing and controversial training scheme, but Cerutty succeeded in turning out world-class runners, who included Australia's John Landy before Herb. The physical and mental sacrifices and preparations were successful, and in March, 1957, when he was just nineteen, Herb ran the mile in 4:00.4. He broke the 4-minute barrier in January, 1958, and that May, in the Coliseum in Los Angeles, California, he lowered his own best time to 3:57.8.

The Emerging Champion

Herb broke the world's record for the mile in Dublin, Ireland, on August 6, 1958, when he was twenty years old. Five runners finished under four minutes in that famous race, with Herb's time of 3:54.5 leading the way. Three weeks later, on August 28, 1958, he established a new world record for the metric mile, or the 1,500 meters, in Goteborg, Sweden, when he ran 3:36.0. Before the year ended he ran the mile in under 4 minutes on ten occasions, and he was chosen the Associated Press's male athlete of the year, only the second time a foreign athlete had been so honored.

In the aftermath of his record victories Herb was offered almost $250,000 by an American businessman to join a professional athletic tour. After debating for several weeks he declined, accepting instead a position with Australian Shell Chemical Company, which allowed him to work and also matriculate as a student at Melbourne University.

The year 1959 saw Herb run in only a few races and only once finish in under 4 minutes for the mile. There was some concern that he had lost his desire, but his reduced running schedule was a conscious decision to cut back his training so as to not burn himself out before the 1960 Olympic Games, which were to be held in Rome. Under Cerutty's direction, Herb resumed heavy training in early 1960, breaking 4 minutes for the twelfth time, in February in a race in Melbourne.

The 1,500 meters was one of the premier events of the 1960 Olympic Games. A number of prominent runners were among the participants, including East Germany's Siegfried Valentin, who had recently run the 1,500 meters in 3:36.5, the fastest time in almost two years, as well as America's Jim Burleson, France's Michael Jazy, and other world-class runners. Herb won his heat in 3:41.4, beating Burleson, with Valentin surprisingly not qualifying.

In the 1,500-meter final all the competitors had previously run under four minutes for the

MAJOR CHAMPIONSHIPS			
Year	Competition	Event	Place
1958	Commonwealth Games	880 yards	1st
		Mile	1st
1960	Olympics	1,500 meters	Gold

HONORS, AWARDS, AND RECORDS	
1958	World record for the mile (3:54.5)
	AP Male Athlete of the Year
	Made Member of the British Empire
1960	World record for 1,500 meters (3:35.6)

metric mile. Before the race Cerutty told Herb where he would be sitting, and he would wave a green and gold towel if a potential world record was in sight. At the end of the first lap Herb was fifth in the tightly packed field, and he took the lead with slightly more than a lap to go. Cerutty jumped out of the stands, waving his towel, but Herb could not remember under the pressure of the race what it signified. Keeping up his blistering pace, Herb finished in first place. Jazy was a distant second, a long 20 meters (65.6 feet) behind. It was one of the most decisive victories in Olympic 1,500-meter history, and the time of 3:35.6 was a new world record.

Continuing the Story

Never defeated in the mile or 1,500 meters, and with forty-four consecutive victories to his credit, Herb retired from running shortly after the Rome Olympic Games. He had married Anne Dudley in 1959 and had become a father. He soon published his autobiography and was made a Member of the British Empire in recognition of his contributions to Australian track and field. He subsequently pursued a successful career in business, eventually becoming the chief executive officer of the sporting goods company Puma in North America. He remained involved in Australia's athletics, serving as Australia's athlete liaison officer at both the 1992 Barcelona Games and the 1996 Atlanta Games. The 2000 Olympics were held in Sydney, and because of his running fame as well as his business experience, in 1997 Herb was appointed director of athlete services and corporate relations with the Australian Olympic Committee.

Summary

Herb Elliott's records have since been broken, but his races were often run on the slower cinder tracks rather than on the composition tracks of later decades, and only twice since 1960 have Olympic 1,500-meter runners registered faster times than his. Unbeaten when he retired at the young age of twenty-two, he is justly considered by many to be the best middle-distance runner of all time.

Eugene Larson

Additional Sources:

Clark, Ron, and Norman Harris. *Lonely Breed.* London: Pelham Books, 1968.

Elliott, Herb. *The Herb Elliott Story.* London: Cassell, 1961.

Johnson, William. "After the Golden Moment." *Sports Illustrated,* July 17, 1972, 28-31.

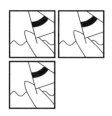

PAUL ELVSTRØM

Sport: Yachting

Born: February 25, 1928
Hellerup, Denmark

Early Life

Paul Elvstrøm was born on February 25, 1928, in Hellerup, Denmark, just a few miles north of the capital, Copenhagen. Hellerup is on the coast, and Paul's family had a history of seafaring. His father was a captain who had sailed around the notorious Cape Horn.

Paul was the youngest of four children, but the second was drowned while a toddler. One might have thought this would turn the family away from the sea, but Paul was rowing at the age of five, and sailing a small homemade boat soon after. He learned to sail largely by teaching himself, with great perseverance.

The Road to Excellence

Paul was racing at ten, and at twelve won his first race. With his older brother as his crew, Paul beat twenty adults by a wide margin. He joined the local Hellerup Sailing Club in 1940, and is still a member.

Just as Paul was getting serious about sailing, Germany occupied Denmark during World War II, and all sailing on the sea was forbidden. Paul did not give up sailing, however, because he bicycled to a nearby lake and continued to practice there. When he left school, he was apprenticed as a stone mason; later he became a building contractor. He did not enjoy these jobs, much preferring to be out sailing.

In 1948, at the age of nineteen, Paul was narrowly selected for the Danish Olympic sailing team. The Firefly dinghy, a 12-foot, two-sailed boat, was the class chosen for the single-handed racing series. The selectors were not sure of Paul because he had never even seen a Firefly dinghy, let alone sailed one. In his first Olympic race, the shy Paul retired from the race. An unsporting competitor bluffed Paul into thinking that he had broken a rule when he had not. In the races following, however, Paul finished sixth, third, twelfth, and fifth, and ended the series with two first places to give him the gold medal. Paul was always a sporting competitor, and while he took the rules to their limits, he always sailed fairly.

The Emerging Champion

For the 1952 Olympics, the Firefly class was replaced by the Finn class, a one-person, one-sailed boat of 14¾ feet. Finn boats require great strength to sail well, because they have a large sail area.

Hulton Getty/Archive Photos

Paul was one of the first sailors to realize that working out to build up muscle strength specifically for sailing would be a great advantage. He built a mockup boat in his basement so that he could practice hanging over the edge to keep the boat upright. In his second Olympics, Paul won his second gold medal in a fleet of twenty-eight competitors. In fact, his points lead was so great after the sixth race that he did not even need to compete in the seventh, but he did anyway, and won it, too.

The 1956 Olympics was held in very windy conditions, but Paul won his third consecutive gold medal, again in a Finn dinghy, with twenty competitors.

Between his third and fourth Olympics, Paul won five world championships in three different boat classes: 5-0-5's (16-foot dinghies), Finns, and Snipes (15½-foot dinghies). He was the top small-boat sailor in the world.

Over the years, Paul had suffered from painful headaches, and this problem was worsening. He was gripped by extreme nervous tension before and during races, and in 1959 he passed out in a race for the Snipe class world championship. He won the championship, but told the Danish Sports Federation that he would give up international competition because he found the pressure too great. He was talked into competing in the 1960 Olympics, but found himself barely able to sleep. He would arrive at the start almost at breaking point.

In addition to this pressure, in 1960 Paul was competing for a possible fourth consecutive gold medal. No one had ever achieved this feat in the Olympics in any sport. When a much larger fleet of thirty-five Finn boats took part in the 1960 Games, even more pressure was on Paul. Despite collapsing the night before the sixth race, he won it, and clinched his fourth gold medal. He was physically unable to compete in the seventh race because of his lack of sleep.

Continuing the Story

For five years, Paul gave up international competition. As an observer at the 1964 Olympics, he saw that sailing could be fun if one was not too in-

MAJOR CHAMPIONSHIP VICTORIES	
1948	Olympic gold medalist (Firefly class)
1952, 1956, 1960	Olympic gold medalist (Finn class)
1957-58	World Championship (5-0-5 class)
1958-59	World Championship (Finn class)
1959	World Championship (Snipe class)
1962	World Championship (Flying Dutchman class) (as crew)
1966	World Championship (5.5-meter class)
1966-67	World Championship (Star class)
1969, 1974	World Championship (Soling class)
1974, 1981	World Championship (½-ton class)

tensely involved. With new emphasis on enjoyment, Paul re-entered top-level sailing, and won three more world championships in the 5.5-meter (35-foot keelboat), Star (22-foot keelboat), and Soling (26¾-foot keelboat) classes.

In the 1968 Olympics, Paul was entered in the Star class, and finished a much happier fourth. In 1972, Paul also failed to win a medal, finishing thirteenth in the Soling class, and it looked as though his Olympic career was over. He concentrated more on his successful sailmaking and boat equipment businesses, and on writing sailing books. His most famous book is a simplified version of the sailing rules, together with little plastic boat models to recreate racing incidents.

In 1982, Paul was awarded the Olympic Order in Bronze for his extraordinary volunteer effort as an Olympic amateur athlete. By 1984, Paul was married, with four adult daughters, but amazingly, he was chosen for the Danish team again. His youngest daughter, Trine, crewed for him in the Tornado catamaran class, one of the world's fastest, most demanding boats to sail. Paul narrowly missed the bronze medal. Clearly having fun now, Paul qualified for the 1988 Olympics, his eighth Games, in the Tornado class, again with his daughter. He thus completed a forty-year span of Olympic competition in his sixtieth year.

In 1990, Paul was awarded the Beppe Croce Trophy of the International Yacht Racing Union, sailing's governing body, for lifetime dedication to yachting.

Summary

Paul Elvstrøm's ability to overcome physical and mental problems and return to top-level sailing, his long timespan of successful international competition, and his sportmanship have made

HONORS AND AWARDS	
1982	Olympic Order in Bronze
1990	International Yacht Racing Union Beppe Croce Trophy

him a legend in small-boat racing. He is absolutely devoted to his sport, and to helping newcomers find the same fulfillment he has. He is known worldwide through his sailmaking, racing equipment, and publications.

Shirley H. M. Reekie

Additional Sources:

Dear, Ian. *The America's Cup: An Informal History.* New York: Dodd, Mead, 1980.

Elvstrom, Paul. *Elvstrom Speaks on Yacht Racing.* Chicago: Quadrangle, 1969.

_____. *Expert Dinghy and Keelboat Racing.* Chicago: Quadrangle Books, 1968.

_____. *Paul Elvstrom Explains the Yacht Racing Rules.* Edited by Richard Creagh-Osborne. Clinton Corners, N.Y.: J. de Graff, 1977.

JOHN ELWAY

Sport: Football

Born: June 28, 1960
　　　Port Angeles, Washington

Early Life

One of the most gifted athletes to play quarterback in the National Football League was born on June 28, 1960, in Port Angeles, Washington. John Albert Elway, the son of Jack and Janet Elway, grew up in a very close, affectionate family. John had an especially warm relationship with his twin sister, Jana. Since John's father was a college football coach, the Elway family left Washington's rugged Olympic peninsula and moved

Denver Broncos quarterback John Elway about to pass the ball in the 1999 Super Bowl.

frequently while the children were growing up. But Jack Elway always found time to play various sports with his only son.

Although John's father never pressured him to excel at sports, he instructed him in football, basketball, and baseball. When John was three years old, he swung his first plastic baseball bat, holding it in a perfect righthander's stance. But his father taught him how to swing it from the left hand as well, so he would learn to bat from both sides of the plate. When the family moved to Los Angeles, John's father first searched for a school for John with a football team known for its passing attack. Having chosen the best school district for his boy, he then began the search for a home to buy in that district.

The Road to Excellence

At Granada Hills High School, John made straight A's and played football to his heart's content, throwing as many as 40 passes in a game. After John had passed for 3,000 yards in twelve games, his coach began to realize he was professional quarterback material. John's father had long known this, for even when John was young, he had exceptional vision: He was able to see everything happening on the basketball court or the football field. In football, he could see the whole field without being distracted by his focus on the primary receiver.

After high school, John accepted Stanford University's invitation to play for their team. At Stanford, he played starting quarterback in his sophomore year; after that season, his coach was already predicting that John would eventually win the Heisman Trophy. In fact, he was the first sophomore in eighteen years to make an All-America First Team, and was chosen as West Coast and PTC Player of the Year.

Meanwhile, Elway studied economics, maintaining a B average. He was awarded the National

759

Collegiate Athletic Association (NCAA) Today's Top Five Award for not only his athletic success and leadership qualities, but also for his academic prowess. He also participated in the Fiesta Bowl-NCAA drug education program. In the summers, John played baseball. As a senior, he was contracted to play baseball for the New York Yankees farm team for $140,000.

In 1982, John returned to Stanford for his last football season, and he led the NCAA Division I with 24 touchdown passes. He set NCAA Division I career records for completions, interception avoidance, passing attempts, and most games with 200 or more passing yards. He was a consensus All-American, but he came in second in votes for the Heisman Trophy.

The Emerging Champion

Not surprisingly, John was chosen first in the 1983 National Football League (NFL) draft, but he refused to play for the Baltimore Colts, the team that had selected him. He threatened to become a baseball player rather than play for the Colts' coach, who was known to be a brutal disciplinarian. A week later, the Colts traded the rights to John to the Denver Broncos, who soon signed him to a long-term contract.

Even before starting his professional football career, John was already the most well-known

rookie quarterback since Joe Namath. His arrival in Denver caused tremendous commotion, with fans and media around him at all times. He became known as the Duke of Denver. John, whose twin sister describes him as happiest behind a mask at a Halloween party, was never comfortable with too much attention. He would have to learn to get used to it, however, as he gained increasing national prominence.

John began his first season under the weight of high expectations. It was a tough season. He was not prepared for the speed at which professionals play the game, and he was inexperienced at figuring out the complex NFL defenses. As a result, John completed only 47.5 percent of his 259 passes for 1,663 yards. He thought about quitting football.

One of John's strengths, competitiveness, made him persevere. He studied films during the offseason and worked out with weights, building himself up. By his third NFL season it all paid off: He led the NFL in total offense and completed 54 percent of his 605 passes, throwing 22 touchdowns.

While John had matured as a player, there were still times when he threw too many interceptions. He believed stubbornly that his all-powerful arm and fast feet could do anything he wanted. His habit was to try to make great plays

STATISTICS

Season	GP	PA	PC	Pct.	Yds.	Avg.	TD	Int.
1983	11	259	123	47.5	1,663	6.4	7	14
1984	15	380	214	56.3	2,598	6.8	18	15
1985	16	605	327	54.0	3,891	6.4	22	23
1986	16	504	280	55.6	3,485	6.9	19	13
1987	12	410	224	54.6	3,198	7.8	19	12
1988	15	496	274	55.2	3,309	6.7	17	19
1989	15	416	223	53.6	3,051	7.3	18	18
1990	16	502	294	58.6	3,526	7.0	15	14
1991	16	451	242	53.7	3,253	7.2	13	12
1992	12	316	174	55.1	2,242	7.1	10	17
1993	16	551	348	63.2	4,030	7.3	25	10
1994	14	494	307	62.1	3,490	7.1	16	10
1995	16	542	316	58.3	3,970	7.3	26	14
1996	15	466	287	61.6	3,328	7.1	26	14
1997	16	502	280	55.8	3,635	7.2	27	11
1998	13	356	210	59.0	2,806	7.9	22	10
Totals	**234**	**7,250**	**4,123**	**56.9**	**51,475**	**7.1**	**300**	**226**

Notes: GP = games played; PA = passes attempted; PC = passes completed; Pct. = percent completed; Yds. = yards; Avg. = average yards per attempt; TD = touchdowns; Int. = interceptions

all the time—as his fans expected—relying on improvisation and instinct. He soon learned he was trying to do too much, and that he needed to play smart, read defenses better, and accept what the defenses gave him.

By the 1986 season, he posted numbers that showed he had achieved the greatness long predicted for him: 280 of 504 passes for 3,485 yards and 19 touchdowns. That year he posted only 13 interceptions. In 1986, 1987, and 1989, he led the Broncos to victories in the American Football Conference (AFC) championship games and on to the Super Bowl. Some said John was the one-man team who made it possible.

Continuing the Story

In 1990, when Denver reached Super Bowl XXIV, the experience was a fiasco—a loss of 55-10 to San Francisco. Instead of John, the 49ers' Joe Montana earned most valuable player honors. John and his father stayed up all that night playing ping-pong, both of them grudging losers unable to call it quits.

In 1993 John was named AFC most valuable player by the NFL Players Association and AFC Offensive Player of the Year by United Press International. He was the starting quarterback in the 1994 Pro Bowl after a regular season that saw him lead the AFC in all six major quarterback statistical categories. John's 1993 statistics and rankings included a 92.8 rating (first in the AFC, third in the NFL), 551 attempts (first in the NFL), 348 completions (first in the NFL), a 63.2 completion percentage (first in the AFC, third in the NFL), 25 touchdown passes (first in the AFC, second in the NFL), and 4,030 yards (first in the AFC).

In 1996 John earned his fifth Pro Bowl selection and was again a statistical leader. That year he moved into third place in all-time career passing yards and became one of only three NFL players to have thrown for 45,000 yards in a career. John also surpassed Hall of Famer Fran Tarkenton as the winningest starting quarterback in NFL history.

In 1997 and 1998 John continued to be a statistical leader and cement his place in NFL history as one of the top NFL quarterbacks of all time.

HONORS AND AWARDS	
1980, 1982	*Sporting News* College All-American
1982	Camp Award
1983	NCAA Today's Top Five Award Overall first choice in the NFL draft
1986, 1987, 1993, 1994, 1996	NFL Pro Bowl Team
1987	Associated Press NFL Player of the Year United Press International AFC Offensive Player of the Year *Sporting News* NFL All-Star Team
1993	AFC most valuable player United Press International AFC Offensive Player of the Year
1999	Super Bowl most valuable player

He finally capped his career in Super Bowl XXXII on January 25, 1998, by leading the Broncos to a 31-24 victory over the Green Bay Packers, and in Super Bowl XXXIII on January 31, 1999, by contributing to a 34-19 win against the Atlanta Falcons. With two Super Bowl victories to his credit, John announced his retirement from professional football in April, 1999.

Summary

John Elway is considered by some to be the most gifted athlete ever to play quarterback in the NFL. After he joined the Denver Broncos in 1984, the team became the American Football Conference's premier franchise. After a number of attempts, John and the Denver Broncos finally triumphed in the Super Bowl in 1998 and 1999.

Nan White

Additional Sources:

Christopher, Matt. *In the Huddle with . . . John Elway.* Boston: Little, Brown, 1999.

Dufresne, Jim. *Quarterbacks: McMahon, Eason, Elway, Fouts.* Worthington, Ohio: Willowisp, 1986.

Hirshberg, Dan. *John Elway.* Philadelphia: Chelsea House, 1997.

Latimer, Clay. *John Elway, Armed and Dangerous.* Lenexa, Kans.: Addax, 1998.

Silver, Michael. "Seven Up." *Sports Illustrated* 86, no. 5 (February 2, 1998): 50-63.

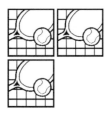

ROY EMERSON

Sport: Tennis

Born: November 3, 1936
Blackbutt, Queensland, Australia

Early Life

Roy Stanley Emerson was born on November 3, 1936, in Blackbutt, Queensland, Australia. He grew up on the family farm in the outback of Queensland. As a young boy, it was his duty to milk the cows every morning. The family dairy farm was about eight hundred acres in size. Roy learned early to be responsible and to work hard.

The family farm had a tennis court, and Roy began to play on it at the age of eight. The court was very popular with all members of the Emerson family, including Roy's sister Daphne, who became an excellent player in her own right. By the age of eleven, Roy had already started winning tennis trophies. He impressed his father so much that the family moved to Brisbane so that Roy could take advantage of the opportunities offered by a city the size of Brisbane.

The Road to Excellence

Before moving his family to Brisbane, Roy's father had consulted Norman Brimson, who, as Roy's coach in Blackbutt, saw great potential for young Roy. Because the Emersons were financially well off, Roy was able to attend private schools, where he could develop solid academic skills while continuing to improve his athletic prowess. Roy was a very talented athlete in many sports. He was able to run the 100-yard dash in 10.6 seconds when he was fourteen. Roy was always a hard worker. The family ethic that he had learned on the outback farm served him very well as he moved up in the Australian tennis ranks. He was selected for the Queensland senior team at the relatively young age of fifteen. Roy trained and practiced religiously. No one was in better shape than Roy on the tennis court.

Roy began his exposure to the international world of tennis at the age of seventeen under the legendary Australian tennis coach and Davis

Roy Emerson at the U. S. Tennis Championships in 1962.

Cup Captain Harry Hopman. For a boy from the outback of Australia, it was definitely a learning experience. His eyes were opened to the world around him, but he never lost sight of his tennis game and the sacrifice necessary to reach the top of his chosen sport. Roy had to rely on superior fitness to wear down his opponents. His quickness and agility were used to defeat adversaries who possessed greater technical skills. The culmination of all his efforts was when he won his first Australian Championship in 1961, at the age of twenty-four.

The Emerging Champion

Even though Roy did not win his first major singles title until 1961, he had already proven himself a solid doubles player. Roy and Neale Fraser had teamed in 1959 to win doubles titles at Wimbledon, the United States National Championship, and the Italian Championship. They also won the French Championship and the United States National Championship again in 1960. Roy was not only developing as a champion player, but he was also being recognized as a marvelous sportsman. His behavior was always impeccable, and he received a number of awards for his good sportsmanship.

Under the management of Hopman, the Australian tennis world was blossoming. A very talented group of players was rising to the top ranks and included some of the greats of the game. In the 1950's, Ken Rosewall and Lew Hoad were the big names of Australian tennis. The 1960's saw the rise of Rod Laver, Mal Anderson—who was to marry Roy's sister Daphne—and Roy himself, as well as Fred Stolle, Tony Roche, and John Newcombe. Each made a name for himself in the annals of tennis, and Roy was one of the stars who left his mark on the game. Besides winning the Australian singles title in 1961, Roy also won the United States National Championship singles

MAJOR CHAMPIONSHIP VICTORIES AND FINALS	
1959, 1961, 1971	Wimbledon doubles (with Neale Fraser; with Rod Laver)
1959-60, 1965-66	U.S. National Championship doubles (with Fraser; with Fred Stolle)
1960-61, 1964-65	Australian Championship doubles finalist (with Fraser; with Marty Mulligan; with Fletcher; with Stolle)
1960-65	French Championship doubles (with Fraser; with Laver; with Manual Santana; with Ken Fletcher; with Stolle)
1961, 1963-67	Australian Championship
1961, 1964	U.S. National Championship
1962	U.S. National Championship finalist Australian Championship finalist French Championship finalist
1962, 1966	Australian Championship doubles (with Fraser; with Stolle)
1963, 1967	French Championship
1964-65	Wimbledon
1967	French Championship doubles finalist (with Fletcher)
1968-69	French Open doubles finalist (with Laver)
1969	Australian Open doubles (with Laver)
1970	U.S. Open doubles finalist (with Laver)

OTHER NOTABLE VICTORIES	
1959, 1961, 1966	Italian Championship doubles (with Fraser)
1959-62, 1964-67	On winning Australian Davis Cup team
1964	Canadian Championship
1967	German Championship
1971	U.S. Pro Championship doubles (with Laver)
1986	Grand Masters Championship doubles (with Stolle)

title. In 1962, Roy was to be runner-up to Laver in the Australian, French, and U.S. singles finals. Laver also won the Wimbledon title that year and, therefore, won what is know in tennis as the Grand Slam. Laver was only the second man in the history of tennis to win all four Grand Slam singles titles in the same year. It was believed that Roy had a good chance of duplicating Laver's feat. With Laver joining the professional circuit in 1963—and therefore becoming ineligible to compete for the major titles—Roy had his best chance to win the Grand Slam. The closest Roy came, however, to winning all four Grand Slam titles in one year was in 1964. The only title that escaped him that year was the French Championship.

Continuing the Story

Roy may have never held all four Grand Slam titles in the same year, but he is one of only four

HONORS AND AWARDS
1982   Inducted into International Tennis Hall of Fame

MILESTONES
Australian Davis Cup team (1959-67) 28 Grand Slam titles

tennis players to win all four titles in their careers. The other three are Fred Perry, Don Budge, and Laver. Roy won his last major singles title in 1967. In that year, he won the Australian, French, and German singles titles. In his career, he won all the Grand Slam singles titles at least twice, for a total of twelve. Roy also totaled sixteen doubles titles in the four major tournaments. In 1968, he joined the professional ranks, and after professionals were finally allowed to compete for the major titles, he and Laver teamed to win the 1969 Australian Open doubles title and the 1971 Wimbledon doubles title. Always loyal to Australia, Roy competed on its Davis Cup team from 1957 to 1967. A devoted family man, Roy and his wife, Joy, and their children settled in Brisbane in the early 1960's near his parents. Roy has done public relations work and always presented himself as an upstanding individual. He has competed in the Legends tour. By the 1980's, Roy was considering Newport Beach, California, as home.

Summary

Roy Emerson has established himself as one of the greats of tennis. Between 1961 and 1967, he was never ranked lower than number four in the world and he was ranked number one twice. Never a boastful person, Roy is somewhat of an unknown champion. Yet he stands in elite company as one of only four men to win all four Grand Slam singles titles. He is an example of what hard work and determination can do for a tennis player who may not be the most naturally talented athlete. His position in tennis is secure and his versatility as a player almost unequaled.

Michael Jeffrys

Additional Sources:

Collins, Bud. "Roy Emerson." In *Bud Collins' Tennis Encyclopedia,* edited by Bud Collins and Zander Hollander. 3d ed. Detroit: Visible Ink Press, 1997.

LeCompte, Tom. "Legend for Hire." *Tennis* 36 (July, 2000): 20.

Lorge, Barry. "Roy Emerson: The Wildest, Craziest, Classiest Champion." *Tennis* 26 (March, 1985): 76-84.

"The Wisdom of Emmo." *Tennis* 32 (March, 1997): 42-44.

KORNELIA ENDER

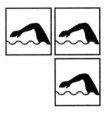

Sport: Swimming

Born: October 25, 1958
Plauen, East Germany

Early Life

Kornelia Ender was born on October 25, 1958, in Plauen in what was then East Germany. Like most of Germany, her birthplace still showed the effects of World War II, but her town was in the area controlled by the Soviet Union and had a Communist government. Kornelia's grandfather had been killed during the war, but her father and mother had escaped without injury. Her grandmother escaped to the United States when Kornelia was only a few weeks old.

Because of the limited opportunities for education and economic achievement under the East German Communist government, sports offered unusual opportunities for talented young people. While on vacation at the beach with her parents at age eight, Kornelia, nicknamed "Konny," was spotted swimming by a swim coach, who convinced her parents to place her in training as a competitive swimmer.

Swim training for East German girls, even at very young ages, was a very strict affair involving long-distance swims every day and lifting weights—a practice not then followed by swim coaches in any other country.

The Road to Excellence

Kornelia burst on the world-class swimming scene in 1972 as a thirteen-year-old member of the East German Olympic swim team. It is not unusual for athletes in their early teens to appear on Olympic gymnastics teams, but usually a competitive swimmer at age thirteen does not have the physical strength to compete against people eighteen years old or more. For Kornelia, all those months of training with weights had obviously made a difference.

The 1972 Olympics were held in the German city of Munich. Kornelia did extremely well for a thirteen-year-old, winning two silver medals. Her joy and excitement, like that of all the Olympians, was overshadowed by a terrorist attack made on the Israeli team in which several of the Israeli athletes were murdered. Kornelia's career was just beginning, however.

In 1973, Kornelia, now fourteen, set her first world record at the East German Championships by swimming the 100-meter freestyle in 58.25 sec-

onds. The next day, she set a world record in the physically demanding 100-meter butterfly event. Her time was 1 minute 2.31 seconds. Less than a month later, at a swim meet in The Netherlands, Kornelia broke her own freestyle record by swimming the event in 58.12 seconds. Then, a month later, at the World Swimming Championships in Belgrade, Yugoslavia, Kornelia again broke her own 100-meter freestyle record twice, once in a preliminary qualifying event and again in the finals of the race. Her new record was 57.54 seconds.

After this, it is not surprising that European sports fans in a public poll selected Kornelia as European Sports Figure of the Year in 1973.

The Emerging Champion

As a fifteen-year-old, Kornelia was hitting her peak. Her stamina and body strength were still increasing, and she had the necessary competitive experience to be a "smart" swimmer who could pace herself. She was still known more as a European sports star than a worldwide figure because the East German government did not permit its athletes to travel widely. Also, many people in the United States had heard rumors that East

German women athletes took strength and growth-enhancing drugs. It is true that Kornelia was large for her age at 5 feet 9 inches and 139 pounds, but her very large shoulder muscles seem to have come from lifting weights and not from drugs.

Shortly before her sixteenth birthday, at the European Swimming Championships in Vienna, Austria, Kornelia again lowered her world record in the 100-meter freestyle to 56.96 seconds, and three days later set a world record in the 200-meter freestyle of 2 minutes 3.22 seconds. Kornelia took a very reasonable view of her world records, describing herself as an easy-going person who enjoyed swimming, no matter how long it might be before someone broke her records. Following this meet, Kornelia made her first brief visit to the United States.

At the East German Swimming Championships in 1975, Kornelia broke the 100-meter butterfly record again. The next month, at the World Aquatics Championships in Colombia, she did the same thing again, with a time of 1 minute 1.33 seconds. At the same contest, Kornelia again set a 100-meter freestyle world record with a time of 56.22 seconds. At the end of that year, *Swimming World* magazine named Kornelia Swimmer of the Year.

Continuing the Story

It was clear that the 1976 Summer Olympic Games in Montreal, Canada, would be the high point of Kornelia Ender's career. She was, at that point, the most physically powerful female swimmer in Olympic history.

In her very first event of the Montreal Olympics, the 100-meter freestyle, Kornelia both took the gold medal and set a new world record of 55.65 seconds. Just three days later, Kornelia performed an astounding feat. First on the program was the 100-meter butterfly, and Kornelia won the gold medal while equaling her own world record time set just seven weeks earlier. By the

STATISTICS

Year	Competition	Event	Place	Time
1972	Olympic Games	200-meter individual medley	Silver	—
		200-meter medley relay	Silver	—
1973	World Championships	100-meter freestyle	1st	57.54
		100-meter butterfly	1st	1:02.53
		200-meter individual medley	2d	2:21.21
		4×100-meter freestyle relay	1st	3:52.45
		4×100-meter medley relay	1st	4:16.84
1974	European Championships	100-meter freestyle	1st	59.96 WR
		200-meter freestyle	1st	2:03.22 WR
		4×100-meter medley relay	1st	—
1975	World Championships	100-meter freestyle	1st	56.50 WR
		200-meter freestyle	2d	2:02.69
		100-meter butterfly	1st	1:01.24 WR
		4×100-meter freestyle relay	1st	3:49.37
		4×100-meter medley relay	1st	4:14.74
1976	Olympic Games	100-meter freestyle	Gold	55.65 WR, OR
		200-meter freestyle	Gold	1:59.26 WR, OR
		100-meter butterfly	Gold	1:00.13 WR, OR
		4×100-meter freestyle relay	Silver	3:45.50
		4×100 medley relay	Gold	4:07.95

Notes: OR = Olympic Record; WR = World Record

RECORDS

Set 23 world records
First woman under 2 mns. for the 200-meter freestyle

HONORS AND AWARDS

1973	European Sports Figure of the Year
1973, 1975-76	World Swimmer of the Year
1975	*Swimming World* magazine Swimmer of the Year
1981	Inducted into International Swimming Hall of Fame

time she had finished receiving her medal on the victory stand, she had only five minutes to change swimsuits, do some quick stretching exercises, and get on the starting block for the 200-meter freestyle. For the first 150 meters, the race was a dead heat with American swimmer Shirley Babashoff, but at 175 meters, Kornelia began to pull ahead and finished the race with a tremendous sprint, winning by 3 meters. In twenty-seven minutes, Kornelia had won two Olympic gold medals.

This busy day was followed by a special treat, as Kornelia was allowed by her government to meet her grandmother, whom she had not seen since Kornelia was only one month old.

By the end of the Montreal Olympics, Kornelia had four gold medals: three individual event medals and one team relay medal. That was the largest number of medals ever won by a female Olympic swimmer.

Summary

Shortly after the 1976 Olympics, Kornelia Ender announced her retirement from competitive swimming. She was engaged to another German swimmer, Roland Matthes, and planned to attend college to study medicine. She kept her easy-going attitude about swimming, proud of her accomplishments but ready to achieve other things in life.

Despite the many denials from East German athletes regarding the use of performance-enhancing drugs, former coaches have admitted to the widespread administration of such drugs. However, the program of growth- and performance-enhancing steroids was forced upon athletes against their will and perhaps without their knowledge. While controversy still remains regarding Kornelia's legacy as an Olympic champion, many believe that her success as an Olympic swimmer can be credited to her intense physical training that began at the age of six.

Michael R. Bradley

Additional Sources:

Besford, Pat. *Encyclopedia of Swimming*. New York: St. Martin's Press, 1976.

Levinson, David, and Karen Christenson, eds. *Encyclopedia of World Sport: From Ancient Times to Present*. Santa Barbara, Calif.: ABC-CLIO, 1996.

Moore, Kenny. "Babashoff and Ender." *Sports Illustrated* 77, no. 2 (1992).

Wallechinsky, David. *The Complete Book of the Olympics*. Boston: Little, Brown and Company, 1991.

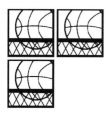

ALEX ENGLISH

Sport: Basketball

Born: January 5, 1954
Columbia, South Carolina

Early Life

Alexander English was born on January 5, 1954, in Columbia, South Carolina. Alex came from a very large family. With twelve hungry mouths to feed, his grandparents (who raised the children) had a continual struggle to make enough money to support the family.

Despite the hardships, Alex had a happy childhood in Columbia. His first contact with organized basketball came when he enrolled at Dunbar High School. Alex was an outstanding high school player, and became a recognized talent in the area.

Courtesy of Amateur Athletic Foundation of Los Angeles

Although basketball became a major part of Alex's high school experience, he was always an interested student in the classroom. Unlike many of his teammates, Alex was determined that basketball would not distract him from his schoolwork.

The Road to Excellence

Following his impressive high school basketball performances, Alex was recruited by many universities from all over the United States. In the end he chose to stay near home, and he committed to the University of South Carolina. Alex was a promising player in high school, but at the collegiate level he blossomed into an outstanding player who displayed the potential to go all the way to the National Basketball Association (NBA).

Alex made the transition to college basketball very smoothly. He started every game in his four-year college career at South Carolina. Playing under coach Frank McGuire, Alex produced scintillating performances that endeared him to the Gamecock fans. He became one of the first black sports stars on the South Carolina campus. In four years as a Gamecock forward, Alex pulled down over 1,000 rebounds and shot over 50 percent from the field. In all he amassed a school record of 1,972 points.

Alex realized that basketball had given him a great opportunity to become educated. While at South Carolina, Alex took the opportunity to further his academic development as much as possible. As a result he emerged as a gifted student. Alex was particularly interested in the humanities, especially creative writing. Indeed, as an undergraduate student, Alex developed an interest in poetry that has endured to this day. As a result of his hard work in the classroom, Alex graduated from the University of South Carolina in 1976 with a bachelor's degree in English.

768

STATISTICS

Season	GP	FGM	FG%	FTM	FT%	Reb.	Ast.	TP	PPG
1976-77	60	132	.477	46	.767	168	25	310	5.2
1977-78	82	343	.542	104	.727	395	129	790	9.6
1978-79	81	563	.511	173	.752	655	271	1,299	16.0
1979-80	78	553	.501	210	.789	605	224	1,318	16.9
1980-81	81	768	.494	390	.850	646	290	1,929	23.8
1981-82	82	855	.551	372	.840	558	433	2,082	25.4
1982-83	82	959	.516	406	.829	601	397	2,326	**28.4**
1983-84	82	907	.529	352	.824	464	406	2,167	26.4
1984-85	81	939	.518	383	.829	458	344	2,262	27.9
1985-86	81	951	.504	511	.862	405	320	2,414	29.8
1986-87	82	965	.503	411	.844	344	422	2,345	28.6
1987-88	80	843	.495	314	.828	373	377	2,000	25.0
1988-89	82	924	.491	325	.858	326	383	2,175	26.5
1989-90	80	635	.491	161	.880	286	225	1,433	17.9
1990-91	79	322	.439	118	.850	254	105	763	9.7
Totals	**1,193**	**10,659**	**.507**	**4,276**	**.832**	**6,538**	**4,351**	**25,613**	**21.5**

Notes: Boldface indicates statistical leader. GP = games played; FGM = field goals made; FG% = field goal percentage; FTM = free throws made; FT% = free throw percentage; Reb. = rebounds; Ast. = assists; TP = total points; PPG = points per game

The Emerging Champion

In the 1976 NBA draft, Alex was the second-round pick of the Milwaukee Bucks. Once again Alex was faced with the challenge of having to prove himself at a higher level of basketball, and it was by no means assured that he would succeed in the professional game. In his first two seasons, this shy and unassuming 6-foot 7-inch forward adjusted slowly to the rigors of the NBA. Without setting the world on fire he made steady progress, and in his second season shot an excellent 54.2 percent from the field.

Inexplicably, Don Nelson, the shrewd Bucks coach, released Alex following the 1978-1979 season. The Indiana Pacers signed him in June of the same year. With the Pacers, Alex developed into a highly competent NBA player. In what turned out to be his only campaign with the Indiana club, Alex was fourth on the team in scoring (16.0 points per game), third in assists (271), and second in rebounding (8.1 per game) and field goal percentage (51.1 percent).

Clearly, Indiana had acquired a prized asset in Alex. However, rather than hold on to their jewel in the making, the Pacer management decided to trade their up-and-coming star for an established superstar. In 1979 Indiana traded Alex and a first-round draft pick to Denver for George McGinnis, who had starred for the Pacers in their American Basketball Association (ABA) days.

The trade was a disaster for the Pacers. Whereas McGinnis failed to rediscover his glory days, Alex moved to the Nuggets and established himself as one of the NBA's best forwards.

Continuing the Story

By the time of his arrival in Denver, Alex was rapidly maturing into an outstanding NBA player. His first full season with the Nuggets gave a warning of what was to come in the next nine seasons: Alex scored 23.8 points per game and shot 49.4 percent from the field.

Alex became renowned throughout the NBA for his elegant and productive shooting. From 1982 to 1988 he consistently finished among the top scorers in the league. Averaging at least 23 points per game, Alex was a perennial NBA All-Star. In 1982-1983 he even topped the NBA scoring charts with an average of 28.4 points per game. However, it was the 1984-1985 season that best demonstrated Alex's qualities as an all-around basketball player. In that season, in addition to scoring 27.9 points per game, he led the Denver franchise in offensive rebounds, blocked shots, and minutes played.

For much of the 1980's, Alex was the key component in the Nuggets team. However, off the court Alex once again proved that he was much more than a mere basketball player. While with Denver Alex became well known for his poetry,

HONORS AND AWARDS

1982-89	NBA All-Star Team
1982-83, 1986	All-NBA Team
1988	J. Walter Kennedy Citizenship Award
1993	Uniform Number 2 retired by Denver Nuggets
1996	NBA 50 Greatest Players of All Time Team
1997	Inducted into Naismith Memorial Basketball Hall of Fame

and he even published a volume of his own work. During this period Alex also starred in the motion picture *Amazing Grace and Chuck* (1987). Ironically, playing the role of a member of the Boston Celtics, Alex tackled the thorny anti-nuclear question in what proved to be one of the most novel sports films ever made.

Alex finally left Denver at the end of the 1989-1990 season, and signed a one-year contract with the Dallas Mavericks. Although his career was drawing to a close, Alex still possessed the scoring skills with which he had made his mark in the NBA.

After having scored 25,613 points in his illustrious career, Alex retired from the NBA in 1991. At age thirty-seven, he played one year in Italy for Depi Napoli in 1991-1992, averaging 13.9 points in eighteen games. In 1992, he was named the director of player programs of the National Basketball Players Association. His duties included managing programs dealing with player orientation in the NBA, alcohol and drug abuse, education, career-planning programs, and improvement of the communities where NBA teams were located.

The Denver Nuggets retired Alex's number 2 uniform in 1993. As part of the celebration of the golden anniversary of the NBA, Alex was named to the NBA's 50 Greatest Players of All Time Team in 1996. In 1997, he received the ultimate basketball honor when he was inducted into the Basketball Hall of Fame.

In 1998, Alex was appointed as the first commissioner of the International Basketball Association (IBA), which has ten teams in the Midwestern United States and Canada. Alex oversaw league operations, resolved game disputes, and enhanced the league's profile, as he continued to develop a positive working relationship between the IBA and the NBA.

Summary

Alex English was one of the superstars of basketball during the 1980's, becoming one of the top NBA scorers of all time. The game of basketball gave Alex the opportunity to get an education and have a very comfortable lifestyle. Despite fame and fortune, Alex remained a level-headed individual and developed interests in other areas, all of which enabled him to become a thoughtful, sensitive, and well-rounded individual.

David L. Andrews

Additional Sources:

Bjarkman, Peter C. *The Biographical History of Basketball.* Chicago: Masters Press, 1998.

Dolin, Nick, Chris Dolin, and David Check. *Basketball Stars: The Greatest Players in the History of the Game.* New York: Black Dog and Leventhal, 1997.

Mallozzi, Vincent M. *Basketball: The Legends and the Game.* Willowdale, Ont.: Firefly Books, 1998.

Shouler, Kenneth A. *The Experts Pick Basketball's Best Fifty Players in the Last Fifty Years.* Lenexa, Kans.: Addax, 1998.

JULIUS ERVING

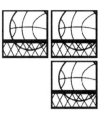

Sport: Basketball

Born: February 22, 1950
Hempstead, New York

Early Life

Julius Winfield Erving II was born on February 22, 1950, at Hempstead on Long Island, New York. Julius's early life was very hard. His father left home when he was only three, leaving his mother to support two sons and a daughter.

Money was scarce in the household, and Julius's mother had a variety of jobs to make ends meet. This meant Julius was often left on his own, and he usually ended up playing in the streets. It was on the streets that Julius discovered basketball, and as he got older Julius spent more and more of his time practicing.

The local Salvation Army Youth Center was the first organized team that Julius played for, and with them he traveled all over Long Island. Playing for the Salvation Army, Julius visited places that he would never have been able to, were it not for basketball. From a very early age, Julius was made aware that his beloved game could provide him with many opportunities in life.

The Road to Excellence

After years of struggling, Julius's family gained a bit of stability following his mother's remarriage in 1963. The family then moved to Roosevelt, Long Island. Here Julius's basketball game went from strength to strength, as he spent hours at the Roosevelt Park playground perfecting his game and developing the incredible moves for which he was to become famous.

By the time Julius entered Roosevelt High School, he was already

AP/Wide World Photos

Julius Erving (left) of the Philadelphia 76ers wards off Cleveland Cavalier John Williams in a 1987 game.

an accomplished player. He started on the fresh-man basketball team and was quickly promoted to the varsity. It was while at Roosevelt High that Julius picked up the nickname of "The Doctor." Throughout his high school career, Julius continued to improve. By his senior year, the 6-foot 3-inch, 165-pound wisp was the star of the team.

Julius's play brought him to the attention of college coaches, and he was recruited by more than a hundred universities. He thought long and hard about which college to attend, as he was determined to go to the institution that would give him the best education. In the end, Julius decided to go to the University of Massachusetts. He started there in the fall of 1968 and swiftly became a well-known figure on campus. Spectators would even get to games early in order to watch his spectacular warm-up drills.

Under the guidance of the Massachusetts coach, Jack Leaman, Julius developed into a complete basketball player. He was capable of dominating a game with his scoring, rebounding, passing, and defensive skills. As a sophomore, Julius averaged 25.7 points and 20.9 rebounds per game, and 26.9 points and 19.5 rebounds per game as a junior. Julius was destined to have an outstanding career in professional basketball, but as it would happen,

his entry into the pro game occurred slightly earlier than expected.

The Emerging Champion

The American Basketball Association (ABA) was set up in 1967 in competition against the National Basketball Association (NBA). The ABA was committed to stealing some of the NBA's popularity, and set about this by signing top college players before they had used up their four years of college eligibility.

As one of the premier college players in the nation, Julius was predictably offered pro contracts by numerous ABA teams. These offers put him in an extremely difficult position, for Julius valued his education and had a great deal of affection for and loyalty to the University of Massachusetts. In the end, however, Julius decided that a professional contract would give his family much needed financial support. In 1971, following his junior year, Julius signed a four-year contract with the Virginia Squires of the ABA. The contract was worth $500,000.

In 1971-1972, Julius had an outstanding rookie season in the ABA, averaging 27.3 points and 15.7 rebounds per game. Already he was one of the best players in the league. In his second season, Julius won the ABA scoring title, averaging 31.9 points per game. By this time he was the

STATISTICS

Season	GP	FGM	FG%	FTM	FT%	Reb.	Ast.	TP	PPG
1971-72	84	910	.498	467	.745	1,319	335	2,290	27.3
1972-73	71	894	.496	475	.776	867	298	2,268	**31.9**
1973-74	84	914	.512	454	.766	899	434	2,299	**27.4**
1974-75	84	914	.506	486	.799	914	462	2,343	27.9
1975-76	84	949	.507	530	.801	925	423	2,462	**29.3**
1976-77	82	685	.499	400	.777	695	306	1,770	21.6
1977-78	74	611	.502	306	.845	481	279	1,528	20.6
1978-79	78	715	.491	373	.745	564	357	1,803	23.1
1979-80	78	838	.519	420	.787	576	355	2,100	26.9
1980-81	82	794	.521	422	.787	657	364	2,014	24.6
1981-82	81	780	.546	411	.763	557	319	1,974	24.4
1982-83	72	605	.517	330	.759	491	263	1,542	21.4
1983-84	77	678	.512	364	.754	532	309	1,727	22.4
1984-85	78	610	.494	338	.765	414	233	1,561	20.0
1985-86	74	521	.480	289	.785	370	248	1,340	18.1
1986-87	60	400	.471	191	.813	264	191	1,005	16.8
Totals	1,243	11,818	.506	6,256	.777	10,525	5,176	30,026	24.2

Notes: Boldface indicates statistical leader. GP = games played; FGM = field goals made; FG% = field goal percentage; FTM = free throws made; FT% = free throw percentage; Reb. = rebounds; Ast. = assists; TP = total points; PPG = points per game

best player in the league. Julius's play—a mixture of power and finesse characterized by breathtaking dunks, delicate lay-ups, and athletic rebounding—made him very popular with the fans and ensured the Squires a large following.

Unfortunately for Julius, the Virginia Squires were having financial problems and found it increasingly harder to honor his contract. Julius had already made an unsuccessful attempt to sign with the Atlanta Hawks of the NBA, so when in 1973 the Squires could not pay Julius the money he was owed, they agreed to trade him. Subsequently, Julius signed a seven-year, $2 million contract with the ABA's New York Nets. In doing so, Julius made a triumphant return to his hometown as one of the finest players in professional basketball.

Continuing the Story

Julius continued his outstanding exploits with the Nets. In his three seasons with the team he led them to two ABA championships, garnering for himself three league and two playoff most valuable player awards. Julius was fast becoming a legendary figure in basketball. His awesome displays dominated both the play of his team and that of the whole league. In many respects Julius Erving had become the American Basketball Association.

All the time Julius was setting basketball alight in the ABA, there were always doubters and skeptics who said he could never survive in the more demanding setting of the NBA. In 1976, Julius was handed the opportunity to prove once and for all that he was one of the greatest players to have played the game. In 1976, after concerted financial pressure was put on the league, the ABA folded. Following an elongated contract dispute with the Nets (who were one of the four ABA teams to join the NBA), Julius found himself starting his NBA career with the Philadelphia 76ers.

The star of the ABA soon became the star of the NBA, as Julius steered the 76ers to the playoffs in each of his eleven seasons with the club. Julius was also an NBA All-Star in all eleven seasons, winning the All-Star Game most valuable player award in 1977 and 1983, and winning the NBA's most valuable player award in 1981. However, Julius's proudest achievement came in 1983, when he led the 76ers to a coveted NBA

HONORS AND AWARDS	
1972	ABA All-Rookie Team All-ABA Second Team
1972-76	ABA All-Star Team
1973-76	All-ABA First Team
1974-76	ABA most valuable player
1974, 1976	ABA Playoffs most valuable player
1976	ABA All-Defensive Team
1977-87	NBA All-Star Team
1977, 1983	NBA All-Star Game most valuable player
1977, 1984	All-NBA Second Team
1978, 1980-83	All-NBA First Team
1980	NBA 35th Anniversary All Time Team
1981	NBA most valuable player
1983	J. Walter Kennedy Citizenship Award
1993	Inducted into Naismith Memorial Basketball Hall of Fame
1996	NBA 50 Greatest Players of All Time Team
1999	Named one of the twenty best NBA players of all time Uniform number 32 retired by New Jersey Nets Uniform number 6 retired by Philadelphia 76ers

championship. In the last few years of his professional career, Julius helped the 76ers build for the future by guiding up-and-coming stars such as Charles Barkley.

Most basketball experts say that "Doctor J." saved the ABA and kept the NBA afloat with his exciting, free-form style of basketball. During his career in professional basketball, he came to represent the essence of citizenship and sportsmanship. In 1993, he was justly honored for his basketball heroics by being inducted into the Basketball Hall of Fame. In 1996, Julius was named to the NBA's 50 Greatest Players of All Time Team. In 1999, he was named one of the twenty best NBA players of all time.

After his retirement from the NBA, Julius forged a successful business and broadcasting career. He purchased a Coca-Cola bottling plant in Philadelphia and cable television stations in New York and New Jersey. Julius has served as the in-studio analyst for the National Broadcasting Corporation (NBC) during its coverage of NBA action. In 2000, Julius accepted a job as executive vice president of the Orlando Magic.

773

Summary

Julius Erving was arguably the most complete basketball player of all time. His skill, grace, and commitment dominated the professional game for over fifteen years. However, without his caring, supportive, and unselfish attitude, Julius would not have become the great champion that he was.

David L. Andrews

Additional Sources:

Dolin, Nick, Chris Dolin, and David Check. *Basketball Stars: The Greatest Players in the History of the Game.* New York: Black Dog and Leventhal, 1997.

Macht, Norman L., Mitchell Nauffts, and Sean Dolan. *Julius Erving.* Broomall, Pa.: Chelsea House, 1994.

Mallozzi, Vincent M. *Basketball: The Legends and the Game.* Willowdale, Ont.: Firefly Books, 1998.

Shouler, Kenneth A. *The Experts Pick Basketball's Best Fifty Players in the Last Fifty Years.* Lenexa, Kans.: Addax, 1998.

Wilker, Josh, and Richard S. Rennert. *Julius Erving.* Broomall, Pa.: Chelsea House, 1995.

PHIL ESPOSITO

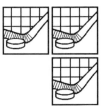

Sport: Ice hockey

Born: February 20, 1942
      Sault Ste. Marie, Ontario, Canada

Early Life

Philip Anthony Esposito was born on February 20, 1942, in Sault Ste. Marie, Ontario, Canada, a steel town of eighty thousand on the river linking Lakes Superior and Huron. Phil and his younger brother, Tony, were the only children of Patrick Esposito, a second-generation Italian-Canadian who worked on ore boats before becoming a welder and, later, foreman with a trucking firm.

Phil and Tony spent their earliest years in a tough neighborhood, but the family later moved. Patrick, a hockey enthusiast who encouraged his boys' interest in sports, turned their basement into a huge recreation room where they played indoor hockey using a rolled-up woolen sock for a puck.

School was difficult for Phil. Hockey became his major obsession, a National Hockey League (NHL) career, his dream. In the winter, the Esposito brothers would get up before 5:00 A.M., load equipment on a toboggan, and pull it across town to the rink for practice before school.

Phil Esposito controls the puck in a game against Montreal in 1970.

775

The Road to Excellence

Young Tony, a future graduate of Michigan Technological University and NHL star goalie with Chicago, played in the nets while Phil practiced shooting. Unlike many hockey greats, Phil's route to stardom was neither direct nor rapid via youth leagues, then amateur experience. His first attempts to make local Bantam and Midget teams, at ages twelve and fourteen, were unsuccessful.

Phil began a low, uncertain ascent through the Chicago Black Hawks farm system, quitting school in 1960, to his later regret. In that year, he failed to make the St. Catharines Junior A Teepees and played Junior B hockey at Sarnia. Moving up to Junior A at nineteen, with only one year of amateur eligibility left, Phil was advised to quit by friends who considered him too old, pudgy, and awkward.

Rudy Pilous, Black Hawks coach and Teepees team owner, told Phil he could make the professional ranks if he cut his weight to 200 pounds. After his successful Junior A season in 1961-1962, Phil played six professional games as a replacement with the Soo Thunderbirds. Skating with a cast over a recently broken wrist, the determined youngster made 3 assists. The Black Hawks now assigned him to their Syracuse minor league

club, which completed the 1962-1963 season in St. Louis. Phil finished the year with an impressive 90 points in seventy-one games. After he scored 80 points in 43 games for St. Louis in 1963-1964, Chicago finally brought Phil up to play at center position in mid-January.

The Emerging Champion

Phil had only 3 goals and 2 assists in twenty-seven games in 1964, but scored more than 20 goals in each of the next three seasons, playing center on a line with the legendary Bobby Hull. Hull praised Phil's playmaking. Nevertheless, in 1967 Chicago traded him to Boston, a perennial last-place club.

In Boston, Phil blossomed as a superstar. The inspired leadership of Phil and Boston's spectacular defenseman, Bobby Orr, transformed the lowly Bruins into an NHL power. Phil's jolly, boisterous humor was good for team morale. In 1968-1969, Phil became the first NHL player to breach the 100-point mark in a season when he won the scoring race over Hull with 126 points. In the 1970-1971 season, Phil's 76 goals and 152 points stood as towering league records until Wayne Gretzky shattered both in the early 1980's.

Phil's strongest assets were his superb stickhandling and puck control, even in heavy traffic. He hovered in the slot area near the goal, waiting to score on passes or rebounds. His wide stance and big frame made it difficult for defensemen to knock him off position. An enemy goalie described Phil as "all arms and legs" and "12 feet wide" when he approached with the puck. Although his shot was not the hardest, he could hit open corners with great accuracy.

At 6 feet 1 inch and 210 pounds, Phil looked anything but graceful on the ice. Because he took fewer strides than most skaters, he appeared slow. Phil once joked that he would not walk across the street to see himself play. Unlike Orr, he seldom made the big plays that brought crowds screaming to their feet, but he got the job done.

Continuing the Story

From 1968 through 1975, Phil made eight consecutive All-Star team selections and won two most valuable player awards and five scoring titles. In 1972, he blunted the arguments of

STATISTICS

Season	GP	G	Ast.	Pts.	PIM
1963-64	27	3	2	5	2
1964-65	70	23	32	55	44
1965-66	69	27	26	53	49
1966-67	69	21	40	61	40
1967-68	74	35	49	84	21
1968-69	74	49	77	126	79
1969-70	76	43	56	99	50
1970-71	78	76	76	152	71
1971-72	76	66	67	133	76
1972-73	78	55	75	130	87
1973-74	78	68	77	145	58
1974-75	79	61	66	127	62
1975-76	74	35	48	83	31
1976-77	80	34	46	80	52
1977-78	79	38	43	81	53
1978-79	80	42	36	78	14
1979-80	80	34	44	78	73
1980-81	41	7	13	20	20
Totals	1,282	717	873	1,590	887

Notes: GP = games played; G = goals; Ast. = assists; Pts. = points; PIM = penalties in minutes

HONORS AND AWARDS

1968, 1975	NHL Second Team All-Star
1969, 1974	Hart Memorial Trophy
1969-74	NHL First Team All-Star
1969, 1970-74	Art Ross Trophy
1970, 1973	Lester B. Pearson Award
1972	Team Canada Member Awarded Order of Canada
1978	Lester Patrick Trophy
1984	Inducted into Hockey Hall of Fame Uniform number 7 retired by Boston Bruins

critics who attributed his great scoring totals to the presence of teammate Bobby Orr and weaker competition in an expanded league. That year witnessed the first international showdown between the surprising Soviets and a collection of NHL stars called Team Canada. Phil almost singlehandedly staved off defeat for the stunned Canadians, who fell behind 3-1-1 after five games. Phil dominated play with 7 goals and 6 assists in the eight-game competition. The series was tied going into the last game in Moscow. Phil scored Canada's first goal, to tie the game, but the Soviets took a 5-3 lead into the final period. Despite double coverage, Phil scored, making it 5-4. In the closing minutes, Phil assisted the game-tying score, deflected with his extraordinary reach a Soviet shot that was heading into an open corner of the net, and then, in a wild finish, set up the winning goal with 34 seconds remaining. For saving the honor of the country, Phil received its highest decoration, the Order of Canada. He was also chosen Canada's top athlete.

In 1975, Boston sent their veteran superstar to the New York Rangers. After Phil's final career game in January, 1981, seventeen thousand appreciative Madison Square Garden fans stood chanting "Espo, Espo, Espo" and called him back on the ice for a thunderous tribute. Phil retired with 717 goals and 1,590 career points. Phil remained active in hockey following his retirement, first as the general manager for the New York Rangers and later as the founder and general manager of the expansion team Tampa Bay Thunder. Phil's success as a general manager, however, never matched his ability on the ice. Many of his administrative decisions while with the Rangers were highly criticized, and in 1998 he was fired as general manager of Tampa Bay.

Phil married his high school sweetheart, Linda Lavasseur, in 1963. He is the father of two daughters.

Summary
Phil Esposito showed admirable persistence in pursuing his boyhood career hopes. He retained confidence in his ability when lesser men might have given up. As a result, Phil persevered and became one of hockey's all-time great scorers. Phil thoroughly relished playing hockey. His upbeat, fun-loving attitude as a sportsman made him popular with teammates and fans.

David A. Crain

Additional Sources:
Burchard, Marshall, and Sue Burchard. *Sports Hero, Phil Esposito.* New York: Putnam, 1975

Esposito, Phil, with Gerald Eskenazi. *Hockey Is My Life.* New York: Dodd, Mead, 1972.

Libby, Bill. *Phil Esposito: Hockey's Greatest Scorer.* New York: G. P. Putnam's Sons, 1975.

EUSEBIO

Sport: Soccer

Born: January 25, 1942
Lourenço Marques, Portuguese East
Africa (now Mozambique)

Early Life

Eusebio da Silva Ferreira was born on January 25, 1942, in Lourenço Marques, Mozambique, which was then known as Portuguese East Africa. Eusebio was born in a squalid section of Lourenço Marques and lived his early life in shanty houses. His family was very poor.

School had little to offer the young Eusebio. He spent most of his time in the streets of his shantytown playing soccer barefoot with other poor boys. No one could have imagined that the little street urchin would one day become one of the most famous soccer players in the world.

The Road to Excellence

The young Eusebio did make a considerable impact as a soccer player, and he became well known in the area in which he lived. He was strong, fast, skillful, and courageous. People all around began talking about the young boy with such prodigious talent.

At fifteen, Eusebio was signed by the leading club in the city, Sporting Clube de Lourenço Marques. The club decided to take a gamble on the untried but talented youngster.

Becoming a professional soccer player transformed Eusebio's life. As a signing bonus he was given a new pair of soccer boots, and on receiving them he wept. They were the first boots he had ever owned.

Eusebio may have been inexperienced, but he took little time in making an impact as a professional. In his three years with Sporting Clube he scored 55 goals, and his dazzling exploits on the field came to the attention of the soccer-playing world.

In 1960 the Brazilian manager, José Bauer, came to Mozambique to see for himself just how good Eusebio was. He came away extremely impressed. Bauer was convinced that Eusebio could have an impact upon world soccer.

In the early 1960's Mozambique was still a part of Portuguese East Africa, and Bauer was convinced that Eusebio should go to Portugal to play. In 1960 Bauer contacted Bela Guttmann, the manager of Benfica, Portugal's leading club,

Eusebio in 1972.

Hulton Getty/Archive Photos

778

HONORS AND AWARDS

1962	European Cup champion
1963-65, 1967-69, 1971-73	Portuguese League Champion
1965	European Player of the Year
1966	World Cup high scorer (9 goals)

MILESTONES

77 international appearances for Portugal
46 international goals
Inducted into International Football Hall of Fame

and told him what great potential Eusebio had. Bauer recommended that Benfica sign the African prodigy.

Guttman took Bauer's advice and arranged for Eusebio to travel to Portugal. Amid great secrecy Eusebio arrived. However, he had to wait until 1961 before his registration was cleared and he could make his debut for Benfica.

The Emerging Champion

Eusebio played his first game for Benfica in a club tournament in Paris. In that competition he came up against Pelé, who was already established as one of the best players in the world. Eusebio rose to the challenge and proved himself to be Pelé's equal, and they both became the stars of the tournament. Eusebio even managed to score three goals against Santos, Pelé's team.

Even though Benfica had just won the European Cup, Eusebio settled into the team very quickly. Indeed, his dynamic displays at center forward led to his selection to the Portuguese national team within months of his debut for Benfica. Already Eusebio was dominating Portuguese football, and he continued to do so throughout his fourteen-year career with Benfica.

With Eusebio at the helm, Benfica went from strength to strength. The team dominated Portuguese league and cup competitions and performed heroically in Europe, retaining the European Cup in 1962 and finishing as runner-up in 1963, 1965, and 1968. In the 1962 final, Eusebio inspired his team to a 5-3 win against mighty Real Madrid. On that night, Eusebio could proudly lay claim to being the king of European soccer. In 1965, Eusebio's coronation was confirmed when he was noted European Player of the Year. He

certainly deserved his nickname of the "Black Pearl."

Continuing the Story

The 1966 World Cup tournament, played in England, provided Eusebio with the most memorable moments of his career. He was the highest goal scorer in the competition, with nine goals in six games. Almost single-handedly, he took Portugal to a third-place finish in the tournament.

In the quarterfinal game, Portugal was down 3-0 to North Korea, the surprise team of the tournament. Staring defeat in the face, Eusebio took over, scoring 4 goals and setting up the 5th for a grateful teammate. In Portugal's 5-3 win, Eusebio had engineered one of the most remarkable comebacks in soccer history.

The incredible victory against North Korea set up a semifinal meeting against England, the home nation. In front of a huge crowd that was willing England to victory, Eusebio played his heart out. Although he scored another goal, Eusebio could not prevent the eventual tournament winners from progressing into the final; England won the riveting game 2-1. Still, Eusebio's individual displays against North Korea and England demonstrated to everyone that he was one of the most exciting players in the world.

By 1966, nobody could doubt Eusebio's ability. The Brazilian team Vasco de Gama even offered Benfica $500,000 for Eusebio's services. They thought that Eusebio was the only player in the world who could provide a counter-attraction to the great Pelé. They were probably correct. The major part of Eusebio's career was spent at Benfica, where he led the club to ten league championships and five cup wins in his fourteen seasons. During this time, he was the leading scorer in Portugal on nine occasions, and he also managed to play a record seventy-seven games for Portugal's national team.

Like any outstanding goal scorer, Eusebio received some brutal treatment from opposing defenders. The battering finally took its toll, and at the end of the 1975 season, Eusebio left Benfica to play in the United States. In the less physical world of the North American Soccer League, he could again demonstrate the skills that had thrilled European crowds for a decade and a half.

Summary

Eusebio went from abject poverty to world fame and fortune. From the time he left Africa, Eusebio was constantly expected to prove himself, to see if he could make the grade. He hurdled every challenge that confronted him, and his fast, skillful, and determined play brought him the goals and the acclaim he richly deserved.

David L. Andrews

Additional Sources:

Henshaw, Richard. *The Encyclopedia of World Soccer.* Washington, D.C.: New Republic Books, 1979.

Hollander, Zander. *The American Encyclopedia of Soccer.* New York: Everett House, 1980.

JANET EVANS

Sport: Swimming

Born: August 28, 1971
Placentia, California

Early Life

Born on August 28, 1971, Janet Evans grew up in Placentia, California, where Southern California's desertlike environment made swimming a popular sport. When she was only a toddler, Janet learned how to swim the four strokes—butterfly, backstroke, breaststroke, and freestyle—while she swam for Placentia's local swim team. Janet's parents, Paul and Barbara Evans, never pressured their children to continue competitive swimming but were always supportive.

Janet began swimming almost before she could walk. As the youngest member of her family, Janet always wanted to do whatever her two older

U.S. Swimming

brothers did. When Janet's mother, Barbara Evans, took her sons to the local YMCA for swimming lessons, one-year-old Janet joined them.

The Road to Excellence

Janet and her brothers decided to join the Fullerton aquatic sports team when Janet was nine. The following year, ten-year-old Janet set a national age-group record in the 200-yard freestyle.

Until Janet proved otherwise, most people thought that a swimmer's speed depended on the swimmer's size. Bigger swimmers swam faster than smaller swimmers. Yet Janet, who was always one of the littlest people in her age group, never considered herself to be small. In fact, when Janet swam the 1,650-yard freestyle in her first national swim meet (the United States Junior Olympics), she was a whole year younger than her competitors. She swam faster than her older and larger competitors by taking more strokes per lap.

Her comparatively small size figured into her swimming style throughout her career—even at the 1988 Olympic Games. She first thought about swimming in the Olympics when she was fourteen, after she had narrowly missed the 800-meter and 1,500-meter freestyle qualifying times for the 1986 U.S. World Championship team. Janet was becoming an Olympic hopeful, however, and she went on to swim those events in the 1986 Goodwill Games in Moscow.

The Emerging Champion

By 1986, Janet's swimming played a major part in the Evanses' lives. She swam under the coaching of Bud McAllister and Don Wagner of the Fullerton aquatic sports team and Tom Milich of the El Dorado High School swim team. Her mother and father shared car-pool duties, taking her to morning and afternoon practices on school

781

days and on weekends. Her swimming and school schedules required dedication and an early-to-bed, early-to-rise attitude. Janet made more time to swim not only because she excelled but also because she enjoyed traveling, meeting people, and the camaraderie of belonging to a team.

Janet's coaches described her swimming style as unorthodox but unusually efficient. Rather than the usual bent-at-the-elbow arm in freestyle, Janet kept her arms straight—a "windmill" stroke that was technically correct under the water.

Although Janet had earlier developed a faster turnover in order to keep up with larger and taller competitors, her quicker stroke became a habit; Janet always swam as fast as she could at every swim practice. Doctors who studied Janet's stroke concluded that she was physiologically unique. More than one of them found that her lung capacity and her way of breathing allowed her to be extremely energy efficient. In addition to working out hard and swimming fast during each practice, Janet mentally prepared herself before every swim meet by visualizing herself swimming the race and by knowing what to expect from her opponents.

In 1987, all of Janet's hard work and dedication paid off. Not only did she earn three national titles, but she also set three world records. In July, Janet set her first world records at the United States Swimming Long Course National Championships in Clovis, California, for the 800-meter freestyle and the 1,500-meter freestyle. That December, she set the world record in the 400-meter freestyle at the United States Open in Orlando, Florida. For her efforts, she was honored with the United States Swimming Swimmer of the Year award. As the Olympics neared, Janet's times continued to improve. She was the first woman to swim faster than 16 minutes in the 1,500-meter freestyle and was faster in that event than the 1972 Olympic men's gold medalist.

Finally, at the 1988 Olympic Games in Seoul, Korea, Janet earned three gold medals for the 400-meter freestyle (a world record), the 800-meter freestyle (an Olympic record), and the 400-meter individual medley (an American record). Janet was the only American woman to win a gold medal in an individual swimming event in Seoul.

STATISTICS

Year	Competition	Event	Place	Time
1985	U.S. Nationals	400-meter individual medley	6th	4:57.29
1986	U.S. Nationals	800-meter freestyle	3d	8:39.04
		1,500-meter freestyle	2d	—
		400-meter freestyle	4th	4:54.98
		400-meter individual medley	4th	—
1987	U.S. Nationals	400-meter freestyle	1st	4:08.69
		800-meter freestyle	1st	8:22.44 WR
		1,500-meter freestyle	1st	16:00.73 WR
		400-meter individual medley	1st	4:41.74
1988	Olympic Games	400-meter freestyle	Gold	4:03.85 OR, WR, AR
		800-meter freestyle	Gold	8:20.20 OR
		400-meter individual medley	Gold	4:37.76 AR
1989	U.S. Nationals	400-meter freestyle	1st	—
		800-meter freestyle	1st	—
		200-meter individual medley	1st	—
		400-meter individual medley	1st	—
1990	NCAA Championships	500-yard freestyle	1st	4:34.39 AR
		1,650-yard freestyle	1st	15:39.14 AR
		400-yard individual medley	1st	4:07.59
		800-yard freestyle relay	1st	7:07.58
	U.S. Nationals	200-meter freestyle	1st	—
		400-meter freestyle	1st	—
		800-meter freestyle	1st	—
		200-meter backstroke	3d	—
		400-meter individual medley	2d	—
1991	NCAA Championships	500-yard freestyle	1st	4:38.71
		1,650-yard freestyle	1st	15:45.98
		400-yard individual medley	2d	4:11.25
		800-yard freestyle relay	1st	7:09.48
	U.S. Nationals	400-meter freestyle	1st	4:09.11
		800-meter freestyle	1st	8:30.75
		400-meter individual medley	1st	4:44.07
		1,500-meter freestyle	1st	16:11.22
		200-meter backstroke	6th	2:14.03
	World Championships	200-meter freestyle	2d	2:00.67
		400-meter freestyle	1st	4:08.63
		800-meter freestyle	1st	8:24.05
1992	Olympic Games	400-meter freestyle	Silver	4:07.37
		800-meter freestyle	Gold	8:25.52

Notes: OR = Olympic Record; WR = World Record; AR = American Record

Continuing the Story

As a high school senior, seventeen-year-old Janet had already earned three Olympic gold medals. She was the Fiesta Bowl Grand Marshal and was in the Macy's Thanksgiving Day Parade. She met the president of the United States and was called by the "Tonight Show." She signed many autographs and was covered by *Time, Newsweek, Sports Illustrated,* and *Life.* Yet despite all that, Janet preferred to be "just Janet"; she enjoyed spending time with friends and practicing the piano.

In 1989, Janet attended Stanford University. She lived in a dormitory and chose to major in communications. Not ready to throw in the towel, however, she also chose to continue her swimming career. That year, she broke her own world record in the 800-meter freestyle; she set her first American record in a short-course (25-yard) pool in the 1,650-yard freestyle, and she won the James E. Sullivan Memorial Award as the nation's top amateur athlete of 1989.

In 1990 Janet swept the NCAA Championships with first-place finishes in the 500-yard and 1,650-yard freestyle, the 400-yard individual medley, and the 800-yard freestyle relay. She repeated her victories the following year in three of the events and took second in the 400-yard individual medley.

Janet won the gold in the 800-meter freestyle at the 1992 Olympics as well as the silver in 400-meter freestyle. She continued to dominate the 400- and 800-meter freestyle events at the U.S. nationals and the World Championships in 1993. Her remarkable pace began to slow in 1995, however, when her best finish in the Summer Nationals was second place in the 400-meter freestyle.

Appearing in her third Olympics in 1996, Janet suffered her worst disappointment in international competition. After finishing ninth in qualifying heats for the 400-meter freestyle, she chose not to compete in the finals. She finished a distant sixth in the 800-meter freestyle.

HONORS AND AWARDS	
1986-88	Phillips Performance Award
1987	Performance of the Year Award U.S. Swimming Swimmer of the Year
1987-89	Robert J.H. Kiphuth Award
1989	Sullivan Award U.S. Olympic Committee Sportsman of the Year Women's Sports Foundation Amateur Sportswoman of the Year
2001	Inducted into International Swimming Hall of Fame

After eight years of gold medals and world records, Janet decided to retire from competition. In eight years, she had earned four Olympic gold medals, forty-five national titles, and seventeen international titles, and she had set three world records and six American records.

In 2001 Janet was elected to the International Swimming Hall of Fame.

Summary

Dubbed "America's Golden Girl," Janet Evans proved that a small-boned, 5-foot 7-inch-tall, 105-pound woman could swim as far and at a faster speed than larger competitors. Her remarkable success and charismatic personality won the hearts of fans and competitors alike. Above all, Janet showed that being a winner means being happy with one's best effort.

Sheril A Palermo

Additional Sources:

Hasday, Judy L. *Extraordinary Women Athletes.* New York: Children's Press, 2000.

Hickok, Ralph. *A Who's Who of Sports Champions.* Boston: Houghton Mifflin, 1995.

"Janet Evans." *Current Biography* 57, no. 7 (1996).

Skow, John. "One Last Splash." *Time* 148, no. 1 (1996).

Whitten, Phillip. "Janet Evans: The Queen Steps Down." *Swimming World and Junior Swimmer* 37, no. 12 (1996).

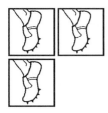

LEE EVANS

Sport: Track and field (middle-distance runs)

Born: February 25, 1947
Madera, California

Early Life

Lee Edward Evans grew up as a young boy picking cotton in California's Central Valley. He later called his work in the cotton fields a form of slavery because of how little he was paid. This early life experience with civil rights helped shape him into someone who has tried to improve the plight of African Americans, especially in athletics. Lee started his formal competitive career in track and field at the age of fourteen, when he ran a 62-second 400-meter dash in the eighth grade. In the ninth grade, Lee ran the 400 meters in 55 seconds and the 800 meters in 2 minutes 15 seconds.

The Road to Excellence

Lee became an outstanding quarter-miler as a junior at Overfelt High School in San Jose, California, in 1964. He ran the 400 meters in 48.2 seconds and placed fourth in the California state meet. As a senior, he improved to 46.9 seconds

American runner Lee Evans (center), Larry James (left), and Ronald Freeman wave black berets on the medal stands at the 1968 Mexico City Olympics.

784

STATISTICS

Year	Competition	Event	Place
1966	Amateur Athletic Union	400 yards	1st
1967	Amateur Athletic Union	400 meters	1st
	Pan-American Games	400 meters	1st
		1,600-meter relay	1st
1968	Amateur Athletic Union	400 meters	1st
	U.S. Olympic Trials	400 meters	1st
	Olympic Games	400 meters	Gold
	Olympic Games	1,600-meter relay	Gold
1969	Amateur Athletic Union	400 meters	1st
1972	Amateur Athletic Union	400 meters	1st

around one turn of the track in the 400 meters and 47.5 seconds for two turns. However, he pulled a muscle in a qualifying heat at the state meet and did not finish.

Lee enrolled at San Jose State Community College after high school and was undefeated in 1966. His freshman time of 45.2 seconds in the 400 meters was a new National Junior College record, and he tied the 400-meter record of 45.8 seconds. At the national Amateur Athletic Union (AAU) meet that same year Lee ran in 45.9 to win the 400 meters. Lee was developing into a disciplined, consistent runner with a powerful surging finish. Based on his outstanding progress, *Track and Field News* named Lee the junior college athlete of the year for 1966 and ranked him third in the world for 400 meters.

The Emerging Champion

In 1967, Lee joined teammate Tommie Smith, the 1968 Olympic gold medalist in the 200 meters, at San Jose State University. Together, under coach Bud Winter's leadership, they would lead San Jose State to numerous individual sprint and sprint relay victories during the late 1960's. In a highly publicized 400-meter duel in May of 1967, Lee and Smith, both undefeated, raced for the world record. Smith took the race and set a world record of 44.8 seconds, while Lee ran a personal best and the fastest non-winning 400 meters on record at that time at 45.3 seconds.

Lee rallied late that same year to win the national AAU Championship, and he won the 400 meters at the Pan-American Games in 44.9 seconds. He also ran a leg of the gold medal Pan-American Games 1,600-meter relay team. In 1968, Lee was defeated only once in the 400 meters leading up to the Olympic trials 400 meters, which he won in a world record time of 44 seconds.

At the 1968 Olympic Games in Mexico City, Lee was one of several militant black athletes who threatened to boycott the competition. His San Jose State teammates Tommie Smith and John Carlos (first and third respectively in the Olympic 200-meter final) were banned from the Olympics following their race for staging a Black Power protest during their medal ceremony. Lee wanted to join the protest and not compete in his final heat, but Carlos persuaded him to run. Lee responded by setting a world record of 43.86 seconds. He also ran the anchor leg of the winning 1,600-meter relay team, which set a world record of 2:56.1. Lee and his fellow African American teammates celebrated their win on the victory stand by wearing black berets. His record in the 400 meters lasted for twenty years, until Butch Reynolds broke it in 1988.

Continuing the Story

Following the Mexico City Olympics Lee continued to compete and won his fourth AAU 400-meter championship in 1969. He trained and raced much less consistently until 1972, when he won his fifth 400-meter AAU championship, but he failed to qualify for the 1972 Munich Olympic Games in the 400 meters when he finished fourth at the U.S. Olympic trials. However, he did earn a spot on the 1,600-meter relay team.

HONORS, AWARDS, AND RECORDS

1966	*Track and Field News* Junior College Athlete of the Year
1968	Set world record for 400 meters
	Ranked number one in the world in the 400 meters by *Track and Field News*
1969	*Track and Field News* 400 meters/440 yards Athlete of the Decade (1960-1970)
1989	Inducted into U.S. Olympic Hall of Fame
2000	*Track and Field News* 400 meters/440 yards Athlete of the 1950-1974 Era

Unfortunately, Lee did not get to compete at the Munich games because two of his fellow black teammates, Vince Matthews and Wayne Collett, were banned from further competition when they did not stand at attention during the medal ceremonies for the individual 400-meter event.

Lee became a professional in the short-lived International Track Association following the Munich Games. During the 1973 indoor track and field season he ran 600 meters in 1:16.7 and set an indoor world mark of 1:02.9 for the 500 meters. He was reinstated as an amateur in 1980 and ran a remarkable 46.5-second 400 meters at the age of thirty-three.

Following Lee's competitive days he spent his time as a teacher and coach in Africa. He was a Fulbright Scholar who has coached several Olympic track and field champions. He was named to the U.S. Olympic Hall of Fame in 1989. In the spring of 2000 he became an assistant track and field sprint coach at the University of Washington in Seattle.

Summary

Lee Evans was the most outstanding 400-meter runner in the United States during the 1960's and 1970's. He went from picking cotton as a youngster to become an Olympic champion and a leader for fellow African American athletes who stood up against societal prejudice. He will always be known for his longevity and competitive spirit in middle-distance runs.

Tinker D. Murray

Additional Sources:

Brennan, Christine. "Evans Staying Right on Track." *The Washington Post,* June 5, 1996, p. B2.

Hickok, Ralph. *A Who's Who of Sports Champions.* New York: Houghton Mifflin, 1995.

Lawson, Gerald. *World Record Breakers in Track and Field Athletics.* Champaign, Ill.: Human Kinetics, 1997.

Noverr, Douglas A. *Biographical Dictionary of American Sports.* Westport, Conn.: Greenwood Press, 1988.

JOHNNY EVERS

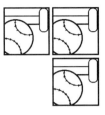

Sport: Baseball

Born: July 21, 1881
Troy, New York
Died: March 28, 1947
Albany, New York

Early Life

John Joseph Evers (pronounced "Eve-rrs") was born July 21, 1881, not far from New York's state capital at Albany on the Hudson River. A feisty Irish chatterbox, he had an unremarkable childhood notable mainly for his tendency to get into fistfights with stronger and older boys in his working-class neighborhood. He soon found that baseball was one pastime in which his small size did not work against him. Dropping out of high school, he became a professional ballplayer, working his way up through the minor leagues. A shortstop, he was an agile fielder and a lefthanded slap hitter whose tight-lipped intensity and perpetual scowl influenced his teammates to dub him "The Crab."

The Road to Excellence

At the age of twenty-one, Johnny received a summons to the big leagues. The Chicago Cubs, a team with a remarkable past but one that was completing its fourth consecutive losing season, needed an infielder. The scrawny Evers, who weighed scarcely 105 pounds when he reported to the Chicago West Side Park in September, 1902, did not impress the hefty regulars. Not until the veteran second baseman Bobby Lowe broke his knee early in the 1903 season did Johnny get a chance to become a

day-to-day player in the Cub lineup. In that rookie year, he hit .293, a high batting average for that era, and soon showed himself to be the best fielding second baseman in the National League, teaming with shortstop Joe Tinker and first baseman Frank Chance to form the legendary double-play combination, "Tinker to Evers to Chance."

The Emerging Champion

Finishing thirteen games behind John Mc-Graw's hated New York Giants in both 1904 and 1905, the Cubs gradually built a championship team around their sterling infielders, an All-Star catcher, and a growing group of hard-throwing young pitchers. In 1906, they set an all-time rec-

ord for single season victories, followed in 1907 and 1908 by world championships, and, after a second-place finish in 1909, another pennant in 1910. Hitting second in the lineup and snapping up almost everything hit to the right side of the infield, Johnny was one of the brightest stars in the Chicago galaxy. Over the five-year period from 1906 to 1910, he stole a total of 187 bases.

On September 23, 1908, the Giants and Cubs were deadlocked at 1-1 in the bottom half of the ninth inning when two New York singles put Giants on first and third with two outs. Shortstop Al Bridwell then lined a clean hit to center field, and the game appeared to be over. An alert Evers noticed that the runner on first base, Fred Merkle, had run for the clubhouse without ever touching second base. Johnny called for the ball and tagged the bag for the third out of the inning, thus canceling the winning run. The umpires declared a tie game, which the league president ordered to be played over at the end of the season. With the Cubs and Giants having identical won-lost records at that point, the October 8, playoff game, which the Cubs won, decided the pennant.

A "money" player, Johnny hit .350 in both the 1907 and 1908 World Series victories over the Detroit Tigers. When he was forced by a broken leg to watch the 1910 Series from the grandstand, the Cubs lost to Philadelphia.

Continuing the Story

As the Cub dynasty began to crumble in 1911, Johnny, as eager and high-strung as ever, pushed himself beyond his emotional limit. After forty-six games, he suffered a nervous breakdown and spent the rest of the season keeping an eye on his two men's shoe stores, which sold "Everswear," both in Chicago and in his hometown of Troy, New York.

In 1912, he made a resounding comeback, hitting .341, fourth in the National League. That winter, the Chicago owners broke up the Cubs, trading away several of the stars of the previous decade, including Manager Chance, and made Johnny the team's new manager. Although he hit .284 and scored 81 runs while leading the decimated club to a third-place finish, Johnny was traded to the Boston Braves at the end of the season.

After residing in the last place as late as July 4, the "miracle Braves" of 1914 won the National League pennant by 10½ games over John McGraw's Giants. They then accomplished a shocking four-game sweep of the formidable Philadelphia Athletics, winners of the fall classic three times during the previous four years. Team Captain Evers scored 81 runs and led all second basemen in fielding percentage, for which he received a Chalmers automobile for being the

STATISTICS

Season	GP	AB	Hits	2B	3B	HR	Runs	RBI	BA	SA
1902	26	89	20	0	0	0	7	2	.225	.225
1903	124	464	136	27	7	0	70	52	.293	.381
1904	152	532	141	14	7	0	49	47	.265	.318
1905	99	340	94	11	2	1	44	37	.276	.329
1906	154	533	136	17	6	1	65	51	.255	.315
1907	151	508	127	18	4	2	66	51	.250	.313
1908	126	416	125	19	6	0	83	37	.300	.375
1909	127	463	122	19	6	1	88	24	.263	.337
1910	125	433	114	11	7	0	87	28	.263	.321
1911	46	155	35	4	3	0	29	7	.226	.290
1912	143	478	163	23	11	1	73	63	.341	.441
1913	315	444	126	20	5	3	81	49	.284	.372
1914	139	491	137	20	3	1	81	40	.279	.338
1915	83	278	73	4	1	1	38	22	.263	.295
1916	71	241	52	4	1	0	33	15	.216	.241
1917	80	266	57	5	1	1	25	12	.214	.252
1922	1	3	0	0	0	0	0	1	.000	.000
1929	1	0	0	0	0	0	0	0	—	—
Totals	**1,783**	**6,134**	**1,658**	**216**	**70**	**12**	**919**	**538**	**.270**	**.334**

Notes: GP = games played; AB = at bats; 2B = doubles; 3B = triples; HR = home runs; RBI = runs batted in; BA = batting average; SA = slugging average

HONORS AND AWARDS

1914	National League most valuable player
1946	Inducted into National Baseball Hall of Fame

league's most valuable player. In the Series, he hit a resounding .438. It was his last great season.

A part-time player for the Braves for three more years, Johnny suffered an arm injury in 1917 that ended his playing career. In 1921, he managed the Cubs again but was dismissed in August with the team bogged down in seventh place. Then it was back to the retail shoe business, except for one season (1924) managing the hapless Chicago White Sox to a cellar finish in the American League. Johnny suffered a stroke in 1942 and lived thereafter as a lonely invalid until death claimed him five years later in Albany, New York, on March 28, 1947.

Summary

Johnny Evers hit only 12 home runs during his entire major league career. His lifetime batting average was only .270. Statistically, he never led in any offensive category, and, although he once led in fielding percentage, he twice had more errors than any other second baseman. Yet he was almost universally recognized as one of the leading players of his day. His spirit, his quick intelligence, and his ability to deliver when the game was on the line made him a respected leader on the field and a natural choice to coauthor (with sportswriter Hugh Fullerton) a best-selling volume on "inside baseball" entitled *Touching Second* (1910).

Norman B. Ferris

Additional Sources:

Hickok, Ralph. *A Who's Who of Sports Champions.* Boston: Houghton Mifflin, 1995.

Porter, David L., ed. *Biographical Dictionary of American Sports: Baseball.* Westport, Conn.: Greenwood Press, 1987.

Shatzkin, Mike, et al., eds. *The Ballplayers: Baseball's Ultimate Biographical Reference.* New York: William Morrow, 1990.

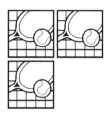

CHRIS EVERT

Sport: Tennis

Born: December 21, 1954
Fort Lauderdale, Florida

Early Life

Christine Marie Evert was born on December 21, 1954, in Fort Lauderdale, Florida. She is the daughter of tennis teaching professional Jimmy Evert and his wife, Colette. She is the second child in a family of five children and the oldest daughter. Chris was brought up in a strict, lower-middle-class Catholic family. She attended St. Anthony's Junior School and St. Thomas Aquinas High School in Fort Lauderdale, Florida.

Her father gave Chris her first tennis lessons in the summer before her sixth birthday. When she first started practicing, she was unable to return enough balls to hit with other children. Chris sacrificed many hours of summer fun to practice tennis. When school started, she practiced from the time school was out until time for dinner and on weekends. Her father sacrificed also by working overtime at the courts to pay for the cost of his children's tennis training.

The Road to Excellence

Chris learned to play on clay courts, and this surface was perfect for her style of play because she was not very aggressive or powerful. She was, however, accurate and hit the ball hard and with pace. She played with a two-handed backhand because she was small and lacked the strength to hold her racket in one hand.

Her father taught Chris that the player with the fewest errors is usually the winner and that players should never express their feelings on the court. Her style of play, which was based on this philosophy, enabled her to make very few errors and to defeat many opponents.

In 1962, during the week of her eighth birthday, Chris competed in her first tournament, the Orange Bowl Junior Tournament in Miami, Florida. She and her partner won the doubles championship. Chris won her first singles tournament at age ten. Her

Chris Evert during the semi-final round of Wimbledon in 1976.

MAJOR CHAMPIONSHIP VICTORIES AND FINALS

1973	French Open finalist
1973, 1978-80, 1982, 1984-85	Wimbledon finalist
1974, 1975	French Open doubles (with Olga Morozova; with Martina Navratilova)
1974-75, 1979-80, 1983, 1985-86	French Open
1974, 1976, 1981	Wimbledon
1974, 1988	Australian Open finalist
1975-78, 1980, 1982	U.S. Open
1976	Wimbledon doubles (with Navratilova)
1979, 1983-84	U.S. Open finalist
1982, 1984	Australian Open

OTHER NOTABLE VICTORIES

1971-73, 1976-77, 1979-85	On winning U.S. Wightman Cup team
1972-73, 1975, 1977	Virginia Slims Championship
1972-75, 1979-80	U.S. Clay Court Championship
1974, 1980, 1984-85	Canadian Open
1974, 1975	Italian Open doubles (with Morozova; with Navratilova)
1974-75, 1980-82	Italian Open
1977-82, 1986	On winning U.S. Federation Cup team
1978	U.S. Indoor Championship
1980	Player's International
1983, 1985	German Open

excellent baseline game was a result of many hours of practice, which helped her to perfect her strokes and to develop the mental toughness she needed to win matches. Because she was so controlled on the court, Chris was called such names as "Little Miss Cool" and the "Ice Maiden."

Chris continued to compete in junior tournaments in Florida in the 1960's. In 1968, she won the fourteen-and-under National Singles Tournament. In 1970, at age fifteen, Chris won her first major tournament. She defeated Margaret Court, who was ranked number one in the world, at a clay court tournament in North Carolina.

The Emerging Champion

After defeating Court, Chris competed on the United States team that won the 1971 Wightman Cup. She also competed in her first United States

Open at Forest Hills, New York, where she established herself as a player who would help to change women's tennis forever.

In 1972, Chris turned professional on her eighteenth birthday. She was ranked third in the world and reached the semifinals of her first Wimbledon and U.S. Open. In 1973, she reached the first two of her thirty-four Grand Slam finals. In 1974 at nineteen years of age, she won her first Wimbledon. Chris was ranked number one in the world from 1975 to 1977 and 1980 to 1981. From 1974 to 1981, Chris won twelve of her eighteen Grand Slam singles titles, Wimbledon three times, and the U.S. Open five times.

In the spring of 1980, she won the French and Italian opens, reached the finals of Wimbledon, won her fifth U.S. Open championship, and a Grand Slam title. Chris won her third Wimbledon crown in 1981. This was the seventh and last year she would be ranked number one in the world.

From 1982 to 1986, Chris was number two in the world behind Martina Navratilova and increased her Grand Slam titles to thirteen in thirteen years. Chris shared four Grand Slam titles with Navratilova in 1982 but defeated her to claim the 1982 Australian Open title. Chris defeated Navratilova in the French Open in 1985 and 1986, and in the 1985 Virginia Slims of Florida tournament. Chris lost to Navratilova at Wimbledon in 1978, 1982, 1985, and 1988. This intense rivalry between the two kept Chris competing in the 1980's when she might have quit professional tennis.

In 1987, Chris lost in the quarterfinals of the U.S. Open for the first time in seventeen U.S. Opens. She also lost in the first round of the Virginia Slims Championships. Chris, however, reached her last Grand Slam final at the 1988 Australian Open. She also made it to the semifinals of Wimbledon and the U.S. Open in 1988.

791

MILESTONES

Ranked number one by WTA (1975-78, 1980-82)
U.S. Wightman Cup team (1971-73, 1975-85)
56-match win streak in 1974
U.S. Federation Cup team (1977-82, 1986-87)
157 professional singles titles
21 Grand Slam titles
125-match win streak on clay from 1973 to 1979

HONORS AND AWARDS

1971	Lebair Sportsmanship Trophy
	Maureen Connolly Brinker Award
1974-75, 1977, 1980	Associated Press Female Athlete of the Year
1976	*Sports Illustrated* Sportswoman of the Year
1979	Karen Krantzcke Sportsmanship Award
1981	WTA Player of the Year
	Women's Sports Foundation Professional Athlete of the Year
	Inducted into Sudafed International Women's Sports Hall of Fame
1982	Service Bowl Award
1985	Women's Sports Foundation Greatest Woman Athlete of the Last 25 Years
1990	Flo Hyman Award
1995	Inducted into International Tennis Hall of Fame

Chris got to three finals in a row in the spring of 1989. She also made it to the semifinals of the 1989 Wimbledon championships and the quarterfinals of the U.S. Open. It appeared that 1989 would be the first year in her professional career that she had not won a tennis tournament. In October, however, she won five straight Federation Cup matches and helped the United States team win the competition in Tokyo.

Continuing the Story

After Chris Evert officially retired from professional tennis in October, 1989, she was remembered for her many accomplishments and contributions. Chris missed the game of tennis as well.

Tennis helped her to excel and gain the confidence she needed to overcome her shyness.

Chris's first marriage was to tennis player John Lloyd. After competing as Chris Evert Lloyd for several years, she was divorced from Lloyd in 1987. The following year she married ex-Olympic skier Andy Mill and later had two sons. Although retired, she remained on as the touring professional for the Polo Club in Boca Raton, Florida. Chris has also stayed active in tennis through her charity work and as a tennis commentator for network television.

Summary

Chris Evert became a world-class athlete because she was motivated and controlled and because she had excellent concentration and consistent strokes. No one in the history of tennis has played as skillfully and successfully for so many continuous years as has Chris. She won with humility and lost with dignity.

Jane Kirkpatrick

Additional Sources:

Collins, Bud. "Chris Evert." In *Bud Collins' Tennis Encyclopedia,* edited by Bud Collins and Zander Hollander. 3d ed. Detroit: Visible Ink Press, 1997.

Evert, Chris. *Chrissie, My Own Story.* New York: Simon and Schuster, 1982.

Lloyd, Chris, and John Lloyd, with Carol Thatcher. *Lloyd on Lloyd.* New York: Beaufort Books, 1986.

Phillips, Betty Lou. *Chris Evert, First Lady of Tennis.* New York: J. Messner, 1977.

Sabin, Francene. *Set Point: The Story of Chris Evert.* New York: Putnam, 1977.

Schwabacher, Martin. "Chris Evert." In *Superstars of Women's Tennis.* Philadelphia: Chelsea House, 1997.

PATRICK EWING

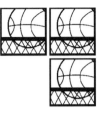

Sport: Basketball

Born: August 5, 1962
Kingston, Jamaica

Early Life

Patrick Ewing was born into a poor family in Kingston, Jamaica, on August 5, 1962, the fifth of seven children of Carl and Dorothy Ewing. As a boy, Patrick, who was always big for his age, enjoyed drawing and demonstrated a talent for soccer and cricket, Jamaica's most popular sports. When he was nine, his mother emigrated to the United States, and the other family members followed her over the next few years.

In 1975, thirteen-year-old Patrick joined his family in Cambridge, Massachusetts, where his parents had found work. He was already more than 6 feet tall, and it was not long before he was invited to try basketball—a sport he had never played before. At Cambridge's Rindge and Latin High School, he blossomed under the coaching of Mike Jarvis, leading the school to three consecutive state titles. He also continued to grow; by his senior year, he was more than 7 feet tall. In 1980, after his junior year, he became the first high-school player to be invited to try out for the U.S. Olympic basketball team. His height and obvious basketball talent made him one of the most sought-after college recruits in the country, and he received dozens of scholarship offers.

The Road to Excellence

Patrick chose to attend Georgetown University in Washington, D.C., in part because the school's coach, John Thompson, was himself nearly 7 feet tall. Patrick said that he thought another very tall man would be better able to relate to him, both as a player and as a person.

In his freshman season, Patrick, a huge yet agile center, led the Hoyas into the finals of the National Collegiate Athletic Association (NCAA) tournament. He had grown to almost 240

pounds, and he was enormously strong; he became known for his powerful dunks, and his exceptionally long arms made him an intimidating shot-blocker. Although the Hoyas lost the championship game to a University of North

Courtesy NBA

Carolina team that starred Michael Jordan and James Worthy, Patrick impressed fans around the country with his rebounding and ferocious defense.

In his junior year, Patrick led Georgetown back to the finals. This time the Hoyas emerged on top, beating the University of Houston Cougars and their star center Hakeem Olajuwon for the NCAA championship. That summer, too, Patrick helped the U.S. team to take the gold medal at the Los Angeles Olympics.

Despite the temptation of the enormous money he could make by turning professional, Patrick chose to stay in school and earn his degree in four years; he explained that he had made a promise to finish on time to his mother, who died shortly before his graduation. In his senior year, Georgetown made it to the NCAA finals again. Although the favored Hoyas were upset by Villanova, Patrick received the Naismith Award, the Rupp Trophy, and the Eastman Award as college Player of the Year.

The Emerging Champion

After Patrick's senior season, the New York Knicks of the National Basketball Association (NBA) chose him with the first pick of the 1985 NBA draft. The Knicks, a once-proud team that had fallen on hard times, looked to the huge

young center as a potential savior. He thus began the challenge of a professional career with the added burden of meeting the high expectations of the tough New York fans and media.

In his first NBA season, Patrick won the league's Rookie of the Year Award, averaging 20.0 points and 9.0 rebounds a game and playing impressive defense. The Knicks finished last in the NBA's Atlantic Division in his first two seasons with the team, however, and though Patrick had established himself as one of the game's top players, he was criticized for failing to lead the team out of its doldrums.

Continuing the Story

Patrick silenced his critics by continuing to improve. He led the Knicks back into the playoffs in the 1987-88 season, and by the 1990's New York was again one of the NBA's premier franchises. He became a perennial All-Star selection, pulling down more than 10 rebounds a game year after year and averaging as many as 28.6 points a game.

In 1992, Patrick's status among the game's greatest players was confirmed when he was named to the U.S. "Dream Team" at the Barcelona Olympics. He started at center on the U.S. team alongside such greats as Magic Johnson, Michael Jordan, Larry Bird, and Charles Barkley,

STATISTICS

Season	GP	FGM	FG%	FTM	FT%	Reb.	Ast.	TP	PPG
1985-86	50	386	.474	226	.739	451	102	998	20.0
1986-87	63	530	.503	296	.713	555	104	1,356	21.5
1987-88	82	656	.555	341	.716	676	125	1,653	20.2
1988-89	80	727	.567	361	.746	740	188	1,815	22.7
1989-90	82	922	.551	502	.775	893	182	2,347	28.6
1990-91	81	845	.514	464	.745	905	244	2,154	26.6
1991-92	82	796	.522	377	.738	921	156	1,970	24.0
1992-93	81	779	.503	400	.719	980	151	1,959	24.2
1993-94	79	745	.496	445	.765	885	179	1,939	24.5
1994-95	79	730	.503	420	.750	867	212	1,886	23.9
1995-96	76	678	.466	351	.761	806	160	1,711	22.5
1996-97	78	655	.488	439	.754	834	156	1,751	22.4
1997-98	26	203	.504	134	.720	265	28	540	20.8
1998-99	38	247	.435	163	.706	377	43	657	17.3
1999-00	62	361	.466	207	.731	604	58	929	15.0
2000-01	79	294	.430	172	.685	585	92	760	9.6
Totals	**1,118**	**9,554**	**.505**	**5,298**	**.740**	**11,344**	**2,180**	**24,425**	**21.0**

Notes: GP = games played; FGM = field goals made; FG% = field goal percentage; FTM = free throws made; FT% = free throw percentage; Reb. = rebounds; Ast. = assists; TP = total points; PPG = points per game

HONORS AND AWARDS

1983-85	College All-American
1984	NCAA Division I Tournament Most Outstanding Player
1984, 1992	Gold Medal, Olympic Basketball
1985	Eastman Award Naismith Award Rupp Trophy
1986	NBA All-Rookie Team NBA Rookie of the Year
1986, 1988-94	NBA All-Star Team
1988-89, 1990-93, 1996-97	All-NBA Second Team
1988-89, 1992	NBA All-Defensive Second Team
1990	All-NBA First Team
1996	NBA 50 Greatest Players of All Time Team
1997-2001	President of NBA Players Association

becoming one of the first players to win a second Olympic gold medal in men's basketball.

Patrick led the Knicks to the NBA finals in 1994, where they lost in seven games to the Houston Rockets. In 1996 Patrick received the prestigious honor of being named to the NBA's 50 Greatest Players of All Time Team. On November 19, 1996, he scored his twenty-thousandth point against the Orlando Magic. On an attempted dunk play in December, 1997, he tore ligaments and dislocated the lunate bone in his right wrist and spent the rest of the season in rehabilitation. After some rather rapid healing, Patrick returned to play against the Indiana Pacers in the Eastern Conference semifinals.

Patrick was elected the president of the NBA Players Association for a four-year term in 1997. He was the key man for the players during the NBA lockout in 1998 and eventually helped work out a settlement. Patrick took some criticism for the role he played in the negotiations, being accused of dragging the proceedings out longer than needed and frustrating fans by saying that the players were only fighting for their livelihoods.

On September 1, 2000, Patrick was traded to the Seattle Sonics in a complicated three-team deal. He left the Knicks as their all-time leading scorer and rebounder, as well as being first in a number of other major categories for the Knicks. After one disappointing season with the Sonics, Patrick became a free agent and signed with the Orlando Magic.

Summary

Patrick Ewing allied his tremendous talent with a ferocity that made him one of the most intimidating basketball players of all time. His natural skills and his will to win helped to make his amateur teams champions on every level and made him a top professional as well.

Patrick has displayed some talent in films, appearing in *Senseless* (1998), *Space Jam* (1996), and *Forget Paris* (1995), as well as making a number of cameo appearances on television programs.

Robert McClenaghan

Additional Sources:

Kalinsky, George, and Phil Berger. *The New York Knicks: The Official Fiftieth Anniversary Celebration.* New York: Macmillan, 1996.

Kavanagh, Jack. *Sports Great: Patrick Ewing.* Berkeley Heights, N.J.: Enslow Publishers, 1992.

Mallozzi, Vincent M. *Basketball: The Legends and the Game.* Willowdale, Ont.: Firefly Books, 1998.

Shouler, Kenneth A. *The Experts Pick Basketball's Best Fifty Players in the Last Fifty Years.* Lenexa, Kans.: Addax, 1998.

Wiener, Paul. *Patrick Ewing.* Broomall, Pa.: Chelsea House, 1995.

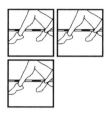

RAY EWRY

Sport: Track and field (standing jumps)

Born: October 14, 1873
Lafayette, Indiana
Died: September 29, 1937
Douglaston, New York

Early Life

Raymond Clarence Ewry, "The Rubber Man," was born on October 14, 1873, in Lafayette, Indiana, to George and Elizabeth Ewry. His grandfather had been a Lafayette pioneer and lived next to John Purdue, founder of Purdue University. Although Ray Ewry's name may not be familiar to many, he won more gold medals (ten) than any other athlete in modern Olympic history.

As a small boy growing up in midwestern America, Ray was a frail youth and his poor health worried his parents. Partially paralyzed by polio, he was confined to a wheelchair and had little opportunity to enjoy his childhood. His doctor recommended exercise to rebuild his legs, and Ray began an intensive program on his own. He began with simple calisthenics and, when he became strong enough, he started jumping. His therapy turned into his sport. As he matured, he grew tall (6 feet 3 inches) and stayed skinny (153 pounds), with incredibly long, thin legs. They had become so powerful by the time he attended local Purdue University that he was on the verge of becoming the greatest jumper of his day.

The Road to Excellence

While at Purdue (from 1890 to 1897), "Deac" Ewry studied mechanical engineering and earned a graduate degree. He also was a star receiver on the football team, until a shoulder in-

Ray Ewry competes in the now-defunct standing high jump at the 1908 Olympic games in London.

Hulton Getty/Archive Photos

jury ended his career, and captain of the track team. He specialized in the standing jumps. He participated in the first Purdue Field Day in 1891, and, in the same year, set a state record in the standing long jump at the Indiana Collegiate Meet at Terre Haute.

After graduation, Ray competed for the Chicago Athletic Association for a year, then took a job in New York as a city hydraulics engineer. While there, he joined the New York Athletic Club in 1898, which launched him on his incredible Olympic career when it included him in the group of athletes it sent to the second modern Olympic Games in Paris in 1900. He was to compete in what are today rather obscure events, the standing long jump, the standing high jump, and the standing triple jump. Ray would become the first Big Ten athlete to win an Olympic gold medal.

The Emerging Champion

On Monday, July 16, 1900, Ray Ewry, the man who could not walk as a child, became part of Olympic sports legend. His lifetime of exercise and hard work had made him a champion. He won gold medals in all the events in which he competed. His performance in the standing high jump established a world record. From a stationary start, he cleared a height of 5 feet 5 inches. His complete dominance of this event was indicated by the fact that the second place finisher jumped only 5 feet. Ray also set Olympic records in the standing long jump (10 feet 6½ inches) and standing triple jump (34 feet 8½ inches), in which he surpassed his nearest competitor by more than 2 feet. These were awesome achievements—yet for Ray Ewry, they were only the beginning of his all-time string of ten consecutive victories through the 1908 Olympics.

Continuing the Story

The Ray Ewry era continued at the next Olympic Games in St. Louis in 1904. There he won the same three events again, this time setting a world

record in the standing long jump at 11 feet 4⅞ inches. In 1906, the Greeks held an unofficial Olympic Games at Athens (Intercalated or Interim Games). Ray was a member of the American team and once more dominated his events. The standing triple jump had been discontinued, so Ewry had to settle for golds in his other two favorite events. His marks, however, did not equal his previous performances at Paris and St. Louis. On this occasion, Ray's wife, Nelle, who was the greatest influence on his career (and, it was said, the one who kept him in training), accompanied him to Athens as the United States team cook. She was at the jumping pits urging her husband on to his two gold medals.

Ray Ewry's final Olympic appearance was at the 1908 London Games. By this time, Ray was thirty-four years old, but his performance did not reflect this. On Monday, July 20, he again won the standing long jump. Three days later, he ended his Olympic career with a victory in the standing high jump, bringing his total gold medal count to ten, unrivaled by any other Olympic athlete. Adding to his illustrious record were fifteen American championships, and he also held the amateur record (9 feet 3 inches) in an even more obscure event, the backward standing long jump.

In later life, Ray was a track official. After 1912, he served on the New York Board of Water Sup-

STATISTICS

Year	Competition	Event	Place	Distance/Height
1898	National AAU Championships	Standing long jump	1st	10′ 11″
1900	Olympic Games	Standing high jump	Gold	5′ 5″ WR
		Standing long jump	Gold	10′ 6¼″ OR
		Standing triple jump	Gold	34′ 8½″ OR
1904	Olympic Games	Standing high jump	Gold	5′ 3″
		Standing long jump	Gold	11′ 4⅞″ WR
		Standing triple jump	Gold	34′ 7¼″
1906	Olympic Games (Interim)	Standing long jump	Gold	10′ 10″
		Standing high jump	Gold	5′ 1¼″
	National AAU Championships	Standing long jump	1st	11′ 1½″
1907	National AAU Championships	Standing long jump	1st	10′ 8″
1908	Olympic Games	Standing high jump	Gold	5′ 2″
		Standing long jump	Gold	10′ 11¼″
1909	National AAU Championships	Standing long jump	1st	11′ 0″
1910	National AAU Championships	Standing long jump	1st	10′ 10½″

Notes: OR = Olympic Record; WR = World Record

RECORDS

Won virtually every championship during his career

Won most gold medals in all events (standing high jump, standing long jump, standing triple jump)

HONORS AND AWARDS

1974	Inducted into National Track and Field Hall of Fame
1983	Inducted into U.S. Olympic Hall of Fame
1990	Honored on a U.S. postage stamp

---

ply and was supervising engineer on the Ashokan System. He died at his home in Douglaston, New York, at the age of sixty-three on September 29, 1937. His accomplishments were mostly forgotten until they were resurrected in the publicity surrounding the 1984 Los Angeles Olympics. In 1990, the United States Post Office issued a stamp commemorating Ray Ewry's Olympic victories.

Summary

Ray Ewry was a sports phenomenon. His career reads like a film script, an inspirational story that saw a crippled child overcome his maladies through hard work to become one of the world's greatest athletes. Over an eight-year period (1900 to 1908), Ray Ewry competed in three official Olympic Games and the Intercalated Games at Athens. He was never defeated in Olympic competition and won more gold medals than any other modern Olympic athlete. Ironically, if he had competed today, there would be no Ray Ewry story. The events in which he excelled had all been discontinued as Olympic events by 1912. Consequently, no one can ever surpass his particular achievements.

Robert B. Kebric

Additional Sources:

Brown, Gene, ed. *The New York Times Encyclopedia of Sports.* 15 vols. New York: Arno Press, 1979-1980.

Collins, Douglas. *Olympic Dreams: One Hundred Years of Excellence.* New York: Universe, 1996.

Findling, John E., and Kimberly D. Pelle, eds. *Historical Dictionary of the Modern Olympic Movement.* Westport, Conn.: Greenwood Press, 1996.

Porter, David L., ed. *Biographical Dictionary of American Sports: Outdoor Sports.* Westport, Conn.: Greenwood Press, 1988.

NICK FALDO

Sport: Golf

Born: July 18, 1957
Welwyn Garden City, Hertfordshire,
England

Early Life

Nicholas Alexander Faldo was born July 18, 1957, in Welwyn Garden City, Hertfordshire, England. His parents, Joyce and George Faldo, tried to instill in their only child the ambition to be the best at what he did. While instruction in dancing, speaking, music, and modeling did not hold his attention, individual sports such as swimming and cycling did. Nick's interest in golf was inspired in 1971 while he was viewing the telecast of the Masters Tournament from the United States. After watching Jack Nicklaus play on the fairways and greens of the Augusta National course, Nick told his mother that he wanted to try golf.

The Road to Excellence

Within a year, Nick was playing to a 7 handicap at the Welwyn Garden City golf club. Ian Connelly, the club professional, saw early signs of Nick's determination to master the game. One afternoon, Connelly taught Nick a drill for maintaining an easy tempo in his swing. That evening, as the teacher was leaving the parking lot, Nick called to him to show him how well he had learned the drill by practicing for several hours. Nick's determination and willingness to practice long hours showed remarkable results. Within four years of taking up golf, he became the dominant amateur player in Great Britain. At eighteen, he became the youngest player to win the English Amateur Championship.

Nick enrolled at the University of Houston in the United States with the intention of improving his play, but he found that golf coach Dave Williams's system did not mesh well with his own practice methods. He left Houston after one semester and joined the professional European golf tour at the age of nineteen.

The Emerging Champion

Nick's first full year as a professional was very successful. He finished eighth on the Order of Merit, the system used to rank European golfers. In his first Ryder Cup team competition against the United States in 1977, the twenty-year-old Nick won all three of his matches, including a victory over Tom Watson, one of the world's best players. His overall performance in 1977 earned

English golfer Nick Faldo chips a shot in the 2000 U.S. Open.

799

him recognition as Rookie of the Year on the European Tour.

His success continued in 1978 when he won the European Professional Golfers' Association (PGA) championship. By 1983, he had emerged as the leading player in Europe; that year, he won five tournaments on the European Tour, ranked first on the Order of Merit, and became the first player on the tour to exceed £100,000 in earnings. Following this success, Nick began to look for further ways to improve his golf swing with the help of teaching professional David Ledbetter. Nick's height (6 feet 3 inches) and long legs (35-inch inseam) posed problems of balance in his full swing. By widening his stance to the approximate width of his shoulders, adjusting the flex in his knees to get an athletic posture rather than a stooped one, and setting his club angle early in the swing, Nick was able to improve his leg action and get a flatter swing. The new approach resulted in lower ball flight, a definite asset in windy conditions.

During the transition period in which Nick rebuilt his swing through countless hours of practice, his tournament results suffered. He was willing to endure the slump, however, in order to develop techniques that would win major championships.

Continuing the Story

Nick Faldo's determination and persistence gained him recognition as a world-class player in 1987. He scored his first victory in three years at the Spanish Open in Madrid, then won the British Open at Muirfield. Setting his goals on major world championships, he won the French Open and the Volvo Masters in 1988. A loss to Curtis Strange in the 1988 U.S. Open only increased his desire. In 1989, he won the Masters Tournament in the United States and then defended his title in 1990 by defeating Raymond Floyd in a playoff. He followed his Masters triumph by winning the British Open later in 1990 at the famous Old Course at St. Andrews, Scotland, giving him two major championships in one year. He added a third British Open title to his record by winning at Muirfield again in 1992.

The 1993 Sony World Rankings showed Nick Faldo as the world's top professional golfer based on his three-year cumulative record, which included nine championships all over the globe. His wife Gill and his daughter Natalie provided the stability that enabled him to keep his life as a golf professional in perspective while maintaining his ambition to win major championships.

Nick continued to win throughout the 1990's, winning major tournament victories in every year between 1993 and 1998, including a dramatic third victory in the Masters in 1996. Down by six strokes to Greg Norman, Nick shot a final-round 71 and won by 5 strokes. Nick had two top-ten finishes in 1999 and one in 2000, placing seventh in the U.S. Open. He finished the year ranked ninth on the PGA tour in driving accuracy.

Summary

Nick Faldo's willingness to refine and improve his playing techniques, focus his energies on each tournament, and concentrate on the subtle

MAJOR CHAMPIONSHIP VICTORIES	
1987, 1990, 1992	British Open
1989-90, 1996	The Masters
OTHER NOTABLE VICTORIES	
1977	Skol Lager
1978	Colgate PGA Championship
1980-81	Sun Alliance PGA Championship
1983	Paco Rabanne French Open Ebel Swiss Open-European Masters
1984	Heritage Classic
1987	Peugeot Spanish Open
1988	Volvo Masters
1988-89	Peugeot French Open
1989	Dunhill British Masters Suntory World Match Play Championship
1990, 1993	Johnnie Walker Asian Classic
1991-93	Carrolls Irish Open
1992	GA European Open Scandinavian Masters Toyota World Match Play Championship
1994	Alfred Dunhill Open
1995	Doral-Ryder Open
1997	Nissan Open
1998	World Cup of Golf (Team)

HONORS AND AWARDS

1977-97	Ryder Cup team
1987	Member of the Order of the British Empire
1989-90, 1992	European Golfer of the Year
1990	PGA Player of the Year

details involved in playing each stroke during competition made him a serious contender in every tournament. His high goals reflect his ambition to be the best at what he does.

Ray Sobczak

Additional Sources:

Barrett, David. "Nick Faldo." *Golf Magazine* 40, no. 7 (1998).

Faldo, Nick. *Faldo: In Search of Perfection.* London: Weidenfeld and Nicholson, 1994.

Faldo, Nick, with Vivian Saunders. *Golf: The Winning Formula.* New York: Lyons & Burford, 1989.

Rubenstein, Lorne. "Simple Questions, Complicated Answers." *Golf Magazine* 42, no. 6 (2000).

Strange, Curtis. "Starting Over." *Golf Magazine* 41, no. 1 (1999).

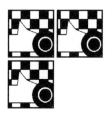

JUAN MANUEL FANGIO

Sport: Auto racing

Born: June 24, 1911
        Balcarce, Argentina
Died: July 17, 1995
        Buenos Aires, Argentina

Early Life

Juan Manuel Fangio was born on June 24, 1911, in Balcarce, Argentina. He was the youngest of four children, two boys and two girls. Juan's parents were Italian immigrants.

Because of the family's poverty, Juan went to work at the age of ten, when he became an apprentice mechanic at a local garage. This job in-spired his love of everything to do with automobiles. Many of the cars in which he first raced were built almost from scratch by Juan himself.

Juan's career as a driver had a late start, partly as a result of illness as a teenager. Success did not come overnight; he was in his late twenties before he began to win races regularly.

The Road to Excellence

In the years leading up to World War II, motor racing grew rapidly as a spectator sport. As a result, competition grew more intense, and the sport became highly organized. The number of

Juan Manuel Fangio before the 1953 Modena Grand Prix.

GRAND PRIX VICTORIES

1950,1954-55	Belgian Grand Prix
1950,1957	Monaco Grand Prix
1950-51,1954,1957	French Grand Prix
1951	Spanish Grand Prix
1951,1954	Swiss Grand Prix
1953-55	Italian Grand Prix
1954,1956-57	German Grand Prix
1954-57	Argentinean Grand Prix
1955	Dutch Grand Prix
1956	British Grand Prix

cars with different engine capacities and body types grew, so that competition had to be strictly regulated. Technical improvements also meant longer races, making endurance an additional feature of competition.

Juan's first important win came in 1940 in a race that placed almost impossible demands of endurance on both car and driver. This was the Gran Premio Internacional del Norte, a race from Buenos Aires to Lima, Peru, and back—a distance of some six thousand miles. Not even the rough roads on which Juan learned competitive driving could have prepared him for the race's forbidding terrain and challenging variations of climate. Juan repeated his success in this race in 1942; both times, he drove a Chevrolet.

The period between his two Gran Premio victories saw Juan win almost every Grand Prix race in Argentina, including four in 1942 alone, together with other endurance races. War interrupted motor sports in Argentina for five years beginning in 1942; when racing resumed, the dictator Juan Perón was in power. A reluctant Juan was recruited to be his country's representative in international Grand Prix racing. At the age of thirty-six, and lacking in experience of Formula One racing at the highest level, Juan began to prepare for his greatest professional challenge. In 1949, he raced his sponsors' Maserati for the first time against Europe's top drivers.

The Emerging Champion

The world of Formula One racing consisted at that time of a large number of races; of these, only a few awarded points toward the world championship. Largely centered on European tracks and drivers, the Formula One circuit was a test of Juan's character as well as of his skill. In ad-

dition, he was more than just a participant in the sport. He was also an ambassador for his country.

Juan's first season competing for the Formula One World Championship was a brilliant success, with six victories in races that counted for the championship. The next year, 1950, he was invited to drive for the official Alfa Romeo team, and he was equally impressive. In both years, and for the rest of his career, Juan was also phenomenally successful in nonchampionship Grand Prix races and endurance races, such as the Twenty-Four Hours of Le Mans, the Pan-American Road Race, and the Mille Miglia.

In 1951, Juan won his first world championship in an Alfa Romeo. A brilliant beginning to the next season came to nothing after he suffered a serious accident, but he returned to place second in the world championship in 1953. In 1954, his skill and nerve began to raise his performances to legendary status, when he won the first of his four consecutive world championships. The Mercedes automobiles in which he won the 1954 and 1955 championships were, he said, his favorites. When Mercedes withdrew from Grand Prix competition, Juan became the number-one driver for Ferrari.

In 1957, his final world championship year, he returned to the Maserati team. He clinched the championship that year by placing first in twelve of the fourteen points-awarding races, and second in the other two. The high point of Juan's 1957 season, and perhaps his most remarkable single achievement in Grand Prix racing, was in the German Grand Prix at the daunting Nürburg ring. His ability to make the most of his car and deal with pressure produced a come-from-behind win.

This race was the ultimate reward for all the hard work and long hours spent as a young mechanic and racing under adverse conditions. Those days of apprenticeship gave Juan a remarkable sensitivity to the power and potential of his car, enabling him to win races when the competition seemed to have superior vehicles. His early experience in endurance races also trained him to respond quickly and decisively to the unexpected. The combination of knowledge, temperament, and skill made Juan a model of consistency and smoothness in one of the most dangerous sports.

803

HONORS AND AWARDS

1951,1954-57	World Championship of Drivers
1990	International Motorsports Hall of Fame

Continuing the Story

Juan retired in 1958. He had won twenty-four Grand Prix races, at that time a remarkable achievement—particularly in view of the intense competition between manufacturers, the number of great young drivers in the early postwar period, and the promotion of Formula One racing as an international glamour sport. In terms of overall achievement, Juan's career is more impressive than any of his competitors'. His number of total victories exceeds anyone else's, as does his percentage of victories in races started.

Although his skill and reputation took Juan to some of the most fashionable and famous places in the world, his attachment to his native Balcarce, and to Argentina, remained strong. His achievements made him a national hero and brought international respect to his country. After his retirement, he returned home and established a racetrack at Balcarce. Later, he became president of the Argentina division of Mercedes-Benz.

When Juan first came to Europe to race, his short stature and unathletic appearance prevented him from being taken seriously. Like many other champions, Juan made his response at the proper time and place—in his car, taking the checkered flag.

Summary

Juan Manuel Fangio combined a finely tuned temperament with the courage and determination essential to effective competition at the highest level. His career provides a striking example of how a blend of personality and skill can make an athlete resemble an artist.

George O'Brien

Additional Sources:

Bergandi, Hector Luis. "Fangio at the Nurburgring: Twenty-six Years After His Most Memorable Race." *Road and Track* 34 (June, 1983): 86-95.

Fangio, Juan Manuel. *My Twenty Years of Racing: The Autobiography of the Five Times World Champion.* London: Temple Press, 1961.

Levine, Leo. "Juan Manuel Fangio 1911-1995: The Greatest Grand Prix Driver Ever." *Road and Track* 47, no. 2 (October, 1995): 142-146.

Ludvigsen, Karl. *Juan Manuel Fangio: Motor Racing's Grand Master.* Sparkford, England: Haynes, 1999.

Risz, Joe, and Hector Bergandi. "Juan Manuel Fangio: Time Hasn't Forgotten This World Champion." *Road and Track* 34 (December, 1982): 20-21.

Rodriguez, Arnol. "Fangio's Kidnappers: Interview with Arnol Rodriguez, Leader of the Group That Kidnapped Legendary Racing Driver Juan Manuel Fangio in 1958." Interview by Andy Wilman. *Road and Track* 49, no. 10 (June, 1998): 109-112.

GREAT ATHLETES

Sport Index

BASKETBALL

Country Index

This index lists athletes by the countries—including some dependencies—with which they are most closely associated by virtue of their citizenship, residence, or membership on national teams. Many names are listed under more than one country, but some athletes are not listed under the countries in which they were born because they have no other meaningful ties with those countries. The index is intended to serve only as a guide and not be a definitive list of nationalities or birthplaces.

Name Index